JOURNAL AND LETTERS

OF THE LATE

SAMUEL CURWEN

AMS PRESS

NEW YORK

B. Blythe Pinxit 1772.

Lith. of Endicott New York.

S. Purviance

AGED 57.

JOURNAL AND LETTERS

OF THE LATE

SAMUEL CURWEN,

JUDGE OF ADMIRALTY, ETC.,

AN ·AMERICAN REFUGEE IN ENGLAND,

FROM

1775 TO 1784,

COMPRISING REMARKS ON THE PROMINENT MEN AND MEASURES
OF THAT PERIOD.

TO WHICH ARE ADDED,

BIOGRAPHICAL NOTICES

OF MANY

AMERICAN LOYALISTS AND OTHER EMINENT PERSONS.

BY

GEORGE ATKINSON WARD,

MEMBER OF THE NEW-YORK HISTORICAL SOCIETY.

"For my native country I feel a filial fondness ; her follies I lament, her
misfortunes I pity ; her good I ardently wish, and to be restored to her embraces
is the warmest of my desires."   S. CURWEN, JAN. 10, 1780. PAGE 231.

NEW-YORK :

C. S. FRANCIS AND CO., 252 BROADWAY.

BOSTON :

J. H. FRANCIS, 128 WASHINGTON-STREET.

1842.

Library of Congress Cataloging in Publication Data

Curwen, Samuel, 1715-1802.
  Journal and letters of the late Sameul Curwen.

    1. Curwen, Samuel, 1715-1802.   2. American
loyalists.   3.   United States--History--Revolution--
Biography.   4. England--Description and travel--1701
-1800.   I.   Ward, George Atkinson, ed.   II.   Title.
E278.C9A4 1973   973.3'14   72-1002
ISBN 0-404-01889-0

973.31
C982f

73-7834
Reprinted from the edition of 1842, Boston
First AMS edition published in 1973
Manufactured in the United States of America

AMS PRESS INC.
NEW YORK, N. Y.   10003

PREFACE.

THE original manuscripts from which the body of the following work has been compiled, were sent in detached parts by the respected writer to his niece, a grand-parent of the editor, (in whose family they have remained for more than sixty years,) with the following injunction, viz. :

" These papers were written partly by way of pastime, and partly with a view to future amusement, should it please the Sovereign Disposer of life to lengthen mine beyond the period of banishment and restore me again to my native country; otherwise may they prove an entertainment to my friends, to whom I commend them, requesting their care to keep them from the inspection of all others, they being negligently written and but for the eye of candor and friendship, without method or order, as memory served, whereby many faults and anachronisms happened (if a technical expression applied to more important events may be used about such insignificant trifles); if they shall afford them the least amusement, my purpose will be answered."

The editor considers the present publication of these papers not only as in no. wise a violation of the injunction of his venerated relative, but as due to his memory, to exhibit to his countrymen the purity of his motives, and the ardent affection he bore towards his native land, even when constrained by a sense of duty to turn his back upon it. Another inducement for the publication is furnished by the incidental light thrown upon the character of his brethren in exile, of whom scarcely any now survive, but whose numerous descendants feel a deep sense of the injustice to which most of them, in a season of great popular excitement, were unfortunately subjected, who, under less adverse circumstances, had filled with honor civil posts of high trust, and led to victory our arms in the provincial wars. As the just fame of such as have distinguished themselves in important public concerns has ever been esteemed among the most valued treasures of civilized nations, that of these loyalists, banished for opinion's sake, seems to call for a proper vindication at the hands of an impartial posterity, while the contrast of their later with their earlier fortunes presents strong claims to the sympathy of mankind.

The success of recent publications in the department of historical writing having induced the belief that the period has arrived when a sealed book may be opened, and a dispassionate examination had of the circumstances connected with that portion of our history in which the character of this proscribed class of our countrymen is involved, this work is offered with the hope of removing to some extent, if not fully, whatever obloquy has been unjustly cast upon their names, and to show that they were, in many instances, not the less actuated by lofty principle than those who embraced the popular opinions of the day, and adopted measures which resulted in such transcendant success.

The editor has endeavored to present in the Supplement, if not a full, at least a brief account of every prominent loyalist, as well as of other persons of note, mentioned in the work; and he regrets that want of information, notwithstanding every effort to obtain it, has in some cases rendered his notices extremely imperfect, and in others left no alternative but to omit them altogether.

Before the publication was decided upon, the editor submitted the work to Dr. Sparks, the distinguished American historian, and to George Folsom, Esq., of the publishing committee of the New York Historical Society, and editor of the society's recent excellent volume of Collections; whose favorable opinion of the historical value of the journal and correspondence of Judge Curwen, expressed in their respective letters already laid before the public, confirmed him in the design of giving to the light these interesting relics of a former generation, to which he feared his private regard for the memory of the venerated author might have attached undue importance. He presents his sincere thanks to those gentlemen for their encouraging letters, and the kind interest they have taken in the matter.

The work is now submitted to the public by the Editor, without endorsing principles at variance with the spirit of the age; and should it prove successful and draw into this new field more competent laborers, the chief end of the publication will be attained.

G. A. WARD.

New-York, November, 1842.

CONTENTS.

INTRODUCTORY MEMOIR OF THE AUTHOR.

JOURNAL AND LETTERS.

1

SUPPLEMENT.

BIOGRAPHICAL NOTICES.

INTRODUCTORY MEMOIR.

THE paternal ancestry of SAMUEL CURWEN, the author of the Journal and Correspondence now submitted to the public, were for many centuries amongst the leading families in the county of Cumberland, in the north of England, where the family seat, named Workington Hall, still remains. George Curwin, his immediate ancestor, was an early emigrant to New England, having established his residence in 1638 at Salem, in the then recent colony of Massachusetts Bay, where he continued to reside during the residue of a long life. He was highly esteemed by his contemporaries, for his active and energetic character, and for several years represented his adopted town in the " General Court," or legislative assembly of the colony. He also commanded a squadron of horse in the Indian wars that spread desolation throughout the frontier settlements of New England, and assisted in checking the inroads of the savage foe. He died at Salem in 1685, at the age of seventy-four years, leaving a large estate. His son, Jonathan Corwin,* was of the provincial council named in the Massachusetts charter granted by William and Mary in 1691, and a judge of the superior court of the province; he married a daughter of Sir Henry Gibbs. George Curwin, a fruit of this connection, was the father of our author: he graduated at Harvard College, (then the only collegiate institution in British America,) in 1701, and was for a short period pastor of a church at Salem. He died in 1717, at the early age of thirty-five years.

* The orthography of this name, like that of many others, seems to have varied at different periods, both in England and America ; our author after his visit to England wrote it *Curwen.*

2

The subject of this memoir was born in 1715, and graduated at Harvard College in 1735; he subsequently pursued the usual course of preparatory studies for the church, but his health proving inadequate to the labours of the profession, he was obliged to relinquish the design. Disappointment in an affair of the heart induced him to travel in England and on the Continent, and the following letter to his only brother, then temporarily absent, shows the melancholy state of his mind at that time.

TO GEORGE CURWIN.

Salem, 16th July, 1738. *Sunday evening.*

DEAR GEORGE :

It will no doubt be somewhat surprising and unexpected to hear of my being gone, especially at such a time as this, the reason of which may not perhaps be so proper to tell you by letter; but if I could have had the happiness of informing you more fully in person, I should have done so. Besides the extreme hurry and other concurring circumstances forbid it. Had I not engaged too far to retreat, I know not whether the various rumours spread abroad had not stopped me. Yet extremities, you know, often dispose one to that which otherwise would not have been undertaken. To say no more, I am gone, and God alone, the sovereign disposer of all things, knows the issue; no human prudence is equal to the uncertainty of events.

I have to request you never to credit the least report or give ear to what people say concerning me, (censure now-a-days being the delight as well as the chiefest quality of the generality of mankind,) as my affairs are not understood by any one. Show Madam Lynde and Mr. Benjamin Lynde all imaginable respect; they have expressed much greater good will than any one else, therefore omit no opportunity of thanks to them and Mr. William Lynde, who has undertaken a great service for me. Let not any former misunderstandings hinder your freely conversing together; it will, I can assure you, be your fault alone if it doth ; the business he has undertaken will necessarily lead to it, and I hope I have not chosen a person disagreeable to you.

My will is in the hands of Mr. Benjamin Lynde, which I have

made to secure the honor of the family, and if possible to maintain them in some repute in case of your death;—may God long preserve you. My dealings with sundry persons have more fully than ever confirmed me in the maxim to treat all persons as if they were dishonest; I mean no more than not to rely too much on their faith and honor; too much good nature in common dealings is no profitable principle now-a-days. Nor do I know whether it be a breach of Christian charity to suppose our New Englanders such; there is most certainly a contracted selfish temper in most persons, which almost inclines one to think that justice and honor in their full latitude are little understood.

The time of my stay abroad, if there happens no war, is uncertain, (although I am not resolved at all hazards to gratify my curiosity by travelling;) it may in that case be eight months, perhaps much longer; otherwise I shall return in the same vessel.

I am, dear George, in all respects,

Your most affectionate brother,

S. Curwen.

On his return, Mr. Curwen engaged in commercial pursuits with uprightness and success. His business was subsequently interrupted by the depredations of French cruisers, fitted out from Louisburg in the island of Cape Breton. New England suffered immensely in her commerce from the same cause, and her enterprising people resolved upon the reduction of that stronghold of the enemy at all hazards. Accordingly, we find what was generally considered a romantic expedition set on foot for this purpose in the winter of 1744–5; and Mr. Curwen as a captain, and his brother as a commissary, joined it. The command of this expedition, comprising some four thousand New England militia, was given to General Pepperell,* who having suffered largely from the depredations of French cruisers, advanced several thousand pounds towards the outfit.

The result of the expedition was completely successful, and reflected great credit on the participators in it. The General was

* See Supplement for biographical notices of Sir William Pepperell and other conspicuous persons whose names occur in this work.

created a baronet of Great Britain, an honor never before conferred on a native of the North American provinces.

The following are extracts from Mr. Curwen's journal kept during the campaign.

" *Boston, March* 23, 1745.   The General is embarking, and we shall sail this afternoon.—Commodore Warren is coming to our assistance, which with the blessing of God will be of great advantage.—There will go down in the first embarkation at least twenty-five hundred soldiers.

Sheepscot, March 27.   We have in our mess Mr. Walter,* our chaplain, who is a very pleasant companion.—I dined to-day on board of Capt. Grant, who to-morrow with Capt. King will breakfast with me.—Our troops were landed at Chapeaurouge on the 29th March.

Canso, April 17.   Wrote home for provisions and stores to be sent in case the goods I expect shall arrive safe from England.—We are almost reduced to pork and pease.

Our men-of-war and privateers are stationed all round the Island to prevent vessels going in or coming out. This evening another prize arrived, taken by Capt. Donahue, in the Swan of Marblehead, who behaved very bravely.   The prize had captured the packet sent from Boston to Canso† to notify us that Commodore Warren was coming to our assistance, which heightens our spirits.

Canso, April 22.   Capt. Durell is come in this afternoon to our assistance ; as yet we have no news of Commodore Warren ; hope it will not be long before he arrives with an account of the French men-of-war expected.   Our last transport arrived this afternoon ; we had almost given her up.

I believe our campaign will be short, and expect the place will surrender without bloodshed.

Last night our chaplain and doctor went with two companies

* Son of Rev. Nath. Walter of Roxbury ; his son Rev. Dr. William Walter, a proscribed refugee, became Dean of Shelburne, Nova Scotia, returned to Boston in 1792 as rector of Christ Church, and died 1800, Æ. 64. He married a daughter of Ch. Justice Lynde.

† Canso or Canseau was taken by the French and Indians, the houses were burnt and fisheries destroyed, the garrison and inhabitants made prisoners, and sent to Louisburg.

to attack St. Peter's, and we are momently looking for their return.
I long to be once within the walls of Louisburg.   This is the
strangest country I ever knew ; not two fair days together.
'*Canso, April* 27.   The Connecticut fleet arrived, and Col.
Lathrop handed me my letter.   The scheme of attacking Louis-
burg is altered every day.

Commodore Warren has arrived.   I trust the expedition will
prove successful, and that our friends will remember we are going
against our common enemy.   May 1st, a small party went to the
harbour and burned a small quantity of wine, brandy, and naval stores.

Camp before Louisburg, May 6.   We have got possession of
the Grand Battery; the French departed from it three days ago;
they spiked all the guns, but we have got seven of them clear, and
five of them are continually playing upon the town.   Our soldiers
are all in good heart, and I doubt not in a few days we shall have
the town.   We have taken a great number of prisoners.

Commodore Warren this day came ashore to visit the General;
he and all our officers have a good understanding among themselves.

Yesterday a gun at the Grand Battery split and wounded five
of our men.   They now and then throw a bomb, but do no damage.

This morning came in Col. Moulton with his detachment from
St. Peter's, which they have demolished with the loss of but one
man.   Providence has signally smiled, and I doubt not the campaign will be crowned with success.   I am willing to undergo
any thing for the good of our cause.

Camp before Louisburg, May 12, 1745.   Commodore Warren has had two hundred marines and sailors ashore for three days
past in order to attack the Island battery, but something or other
has always prevented its accomplishment, so the Commodore has
ordered them all aboard and gone on board himself not a little dis-
satisfied.

Camp before Louisburg, May 26.   Commodore Warren has
taken the Vigilante, a 64 gun ship from France, coming with ammunition for this garrison.   She was manned with five hundred
men, had five hundred barrels gunpowder on board: she lost
thirty men before she struck.   The command of her is given to
Captain Douglass, who before had the Mermaid, and Capt Mon-

tague is to have the Mermaid. This has given new life to all our officers and soldiers.

Capt. Gayton is safely arrived at last, which affords great joy, for we almost despaired of him, being out so long after all· the transports had arrived that left under his convoy.

Capt. Fletcher has had the misfortune to lose ten men by the Indians; seven killed, and three taken prisoners. They went ashore ten miles above where we lay to get wood, and keeping no guard, were beset by the Indians and cut off.

Camp before Louisburg, June 2d. We have made an attempt upon the Island battery, and failed. Abbot, a townsman of mine, was wounded in the leg, and I fear he will lose his life.—An hundred men are missing, and we are in hopes they are taken, as two boats laden with men were seen going into the town after the attack, when the French gave three hurrahs. Young Gray is dead, and three of Capt. Grant's men are missing, all of Salem. Our scouts have had an engagement with a number of French and Indians which we routed; killed thirty and wounded forty; we lost but six killed; among them is the brave Capt. Dimmock, of Barnstable, and twenty wounded, some very dangerously. Our men got under the very walls before the French fired a gun.

Louisburg, June 17th, 1745. The Governor, aware of our preparations for a general assault, thought it best to capitulate, and has just surrendered the city to our arms.

Louisburg, July 25th, 1745. An East India ship, worth at least £200,000 sterling, came off the harbour, and fired a gun for a pilot. The Commodore sent out two sixty gun ships, which came up with, and took her in three hours; we had the pleasure from the walls to see her strike to them. Two others, sent out three weeks before her, bound hither, are hourly expected to heave in sight. Col. Graham goes to-morrow in a sloop as a flag of truce for Canada, with about thirty French prisoners; he is the only Englishman that goes in her.

I am going on board Capt. Lovett to St. Peter's, with a number of my soldiers, to guard the wood-vessels going there : our affairs will soon be settled, and I shall, to my great joy, return home."

FROM WILLIAM LYNDE.

Salem, July 27, **1745.**

CAPT. CURWEN:

I have had the pleasure of but one letter from you since you left us.—If no more East Indiamen, &c. drop in, yet a line on any occasion will be very agreeable. I should be glad to hear of the event of these ships being at Louisburg, and what effect their coming will have on the fleet, army, New England, the nation, or any particulars of them, or concerning Louisburg ; the French fishery, settlements on the island, &c., if not too troublesome to you.

I hope New England will be the happier for the event of the expedition, which is known to have been too bold a stroke for your enemy—how it will turn out is doubtful, since many are competitors for the honor. We here assure ourselves of the Governor's good designs and influence on our part. I could *say* more than write on this article, and cannot but be sanguine for the honor of our country and friends, whose all was involved in the happy issue of the expedition. We hope daily to hear of the Governor's arrival and good measures for the general advantage. The fleet assume their full share, from all accounts, and have much popularity ashore ; doubt not of the influence of omnipotent gold, which perhaps they have a greater share of, than of honor or jurisdiction on land. How you stand inclined yourself, I know not, though don't doubt your zeal for our country and friends.

As to occurrences at Salem ; trade has been successful, and no losses ;—if the Dutch break this year, you know how it will affect. We hear from New-York and *viâ* Lisbon of some five French men-of-war, designing for Cape Breton ; perhaps to convoy the Indiamen. Undoubtedly you may expect some *viâ* Lisbon advices ; they say Genoa has declared for the French and Spaniards. From New-York they say the Duke of Tuscany is Emperor, but it is doubted here. I believe there is matter enough in Europe for a long war ; but perhaps you have later news than we. Our government has declared war against the Penobscot Indians, who have broke in on our new settlements ; so that we are at war with all eastern Indians ; they are doubtless put on by the French of Canada. New England has enough on her hands, though the season is hopeful and trade brisk. Some particulars I could give verbatim,

which I cannot write ; hope to see you soon here, and spend some
pleasant hours with you, as we have spent many past.   Give my
hearty service to your brother and Capt. Grant.   My brother* desires you would excuse his not writing by this opportunity.   Capt.
Hillyer is now going to sail, having given but short notice.

Believe me, dear Sir, your real friend,   WILLIAM LYNDE.

A late writer thus describes this expedition, which is among the
most remarkable in our history—" The French had built a city and
fortress on the island of Cape Breton, at immense cost, and of
immense strength, which in honor of the King was called " Louisburg." Their fisheries in the seas in its vicinity (as was ascertained by Mr. Kilby, as agent of Governor Shirley, of Massachusetts), produced *one million and four hundred thousand* quintals
annually, and they annoyed the colonial fishermen so much, that
the fishing interest of Massachusetts and New Hampshire resolved on
the destruction of Louisburg, and the expulsion of the French from
the fishing grounds.   Application was made to Gov. Shirley accordingly, by Vaughan, a son of the Lt. Governor of New Hampshire, who was largely interested in the fisheries, and whose fishermen had imparted to him valuable information as to the weak
parts of its defences.   The subject was considered in secret session,
the first ever held in the Colonies.   After much difficulty, and after
having been negatived once, it was resolved to undertake the destruction of this wonderful city.   But the Colonies south of New
England declined to aid in so mad an enterprise, though urged to
do so ; and Dr. Franklin, as if forgetting that he ' was Boston born,'
ridiculed the project, in one of the wittiest letters that he ever
wrote.   The spirit of New England was up.   A feeling something
like that which caused the Crusades, prevailed among her people,
high and low.   Religion shouted " Popery"—and even Whitefield made a recruiting house of the sanctuary ; and he not only
preached *delenda est Carthago*, but one of his followers actually
joined the troop as chaplain, and carried an axe at the shoulder,
with which to hew down the Catholic images in the churches of
the fated city.   On sailing, the troops were furnished with line
and other gear to catch fish on the passage.   The original plan of

* Benjamin Lynde, afterwards Chief Justice Sup. Court.

attack was not observed, but to the surprise of all, the city fell, and Pepperell was rewarded most magnificently, while Vaughan, who claimed to have conceived its destruction, and who certainly did much to effect it, and was second in command and performed extraordinary feats of valor before it, was suffered to die neglected, though he went to London in person to press his claims. At the peace of 1749, Louisburg was restored to France, much to the displeasure of New England. In the war with France, which preceded the Revolution by about twenty years, it was captured a second time, and miners were sent from England to reduce its walls to rubbish. In its second capture, Wolfe distinguished himself much. He sailed from this doomed city for Quebec, at the head of 8000 men, to rise from a sick bed, and ' die satisfied' on the plains which his name has made immortal. Louisburg is now desolate. Its walls were built of bricks brought from France. Twenty-five years and thirty millions of livres were spent in building it. It had nunneries, and palaces, and two hundred and six cannon were mounted to perpetuate French dominion over it. Six thousand troops garrisoned its fortress, and a fleet of ships of the line and frigates were moored in its waters. But yet, though all called it the "Dunkirk" of America, because of its exceeding strength, it fell—and now it is almost unknown that such a place existed. Its captors, by keeping the flag of France in its place, after they became its masters, decoyed and captured ships and cargoes worth some millions of dollars, but now, none but fishermen visit it, and they for shelter and not for traffick.—That such a city existed at so early a period in our history, is a marvel ; that such a city yielded to the farmers and fishermen of New England, is almost incredible. The lovers of the wonderful may read the works which contain accounts of its rise and ruin, and be satisfied that ' truth *is* sometimes stranger than fiction.'

" The influence of the expedition to Louisburg has been felt ever since. When, thirty years after it, the northern colonies became embroiled with the mother country, many of those who belonged to it were still alive. The confidence which their skill and success inspired was incalculable.—When Gen. Gage was fortifying Boston neck, the American people, whose curiosity led them to watch the progress of the works, used to say that ' Gage's mud

walls are nothing to old Louisburg's.' 'The drum that beat
along the road to Lexington,' said Edward Everett, ' had been at
Louisburg.' This is literally true. Gridley, who had laid out the
works on Breed's or Bunker Hill, on the night previous to the
memorable 17th of June, was the engineer of the colonial forces
at the siege of Louisburg,—and many who rose to distinction in the
Revolution, were associated with him in the same perilous enterprise. In truth, the biographers and letters of the men of the
Revolution, teem with incidents and allusions to this,—the great
event of colonial history."

Soon after Mr. Curwen's return from the reduction of Louisburg
he resumed his mercantile pursuits, which were continued for many
years with various success, yet he never failed in meeting all his
engagements.—In 1759 he was appointed Impost Officer for Essex
county, which office he filled for fifteen years, his commission being
renewed at intervals of three years during that period.

He was a member of a club instituted for improvement in philosophy and literature in his native town, in which originated the
Social Library in 1760, and the Philosophical Library, which were
afterwards united, and became the foundation of the Athenæum, in
1810. The meetings of this club were interrupted by the Revolution,
but were resumed and continued many years afterwards. Among
the members were Dr. Holyoke, who was president of several literary and scientific societies, and died at the age of a hundred years
and six months, in 1829; and who with the Hon. Samson S. Blowers,
Chief Justice of Nova Scotia, now living, are the only alumni
of Harvard University out of thirty-six hundred graduates, that
have arrived at that great age; Hon. Benjamin Lynde and Hon.
Nathaniel Ropes, judges of the superior court; Hon. Andrew
Oliver, Judge of the Common Pleas; William Pynchon, Esq.,
an eminent lawyer; Rev. Wm. McGilchrist and Rev. Thomas
Barnard; Stephen Higginson, Esq., an eminent merchant, who afterwards removed to Boston; Hon. Wm. Browne, judge of the
superior court, afterwards Governor of Bermuda; Col. Benjamin
Pickman, Col. Peter Frye, and Thomas Robie, Esq. These gentlemen possessed literary attainments of a high order, and though ardently attached to their country, took different views of its interests.

The four last, together with Mr. Curwen, in consequence of the spirit of persecution which succeeded the battle of Lexington, fearing that the high-toned conduct of the people would bring ruin on their country, became loyalist refugees, and retreated to England. A brief account of the state of affairs in the colony of Massachusetts at the period immediately preceding the Revolution, may serve as an appropriate introduction to the parties and events referred to in the following pages.

We find at the commencement of Governor Bernard's administration in Massachusetts, in 1760, the final reduction of the Canadas causing a general jubilee throughout the continent; for the colonists had only suffered from their French and Indian neighbors, and these being at length completely subdued, they felt that they could now sit under their own vines and fig-trees, having none to molest or to make them afraid. They had felt the burden of government less than any people who had received such benefits from it ; and it was a common aspiration in the public prayers of the day, that the civil and religious privileges they enjoyed might be transmitted to their posterity forever. In 1763, Mr. James Otis, (afterwards the great leader of opposition to Gov. Bernard's measures,) in his address, as moderator of the first town-meeting at Boston after the peace, remarked, that " no other constitution of civil government had yet appeared in the world so admirably adapted to the preservation of the great purposes of liberty and knowledge as that of Great Britain. Every person in America is of common right, by acts of Parliament, and the laws of God, entitled to all the essential privileges of Britons. The true interests of Great Britain and her colonies are mutual, and what God in his providence has united, let no man dare attempt to pull asunder."

There does not appear to have been any cause for dissatisfaction in the colonies at that period, and there was no complaint of the invasion of the rights of the people by any of the governments. Soon, however, the disturbances in England reached America, and the cry of " *Wilkes and liberty*" in London was echoed in Boston, and resounded through the colonies.

Accounts were received before the session of the legislature of Massachusetts in 1764, that a bill had passed the House of Commons, imposing duties on articles heretofore exempted, which af-

forded a good opportunity to bring the officers of the crown into
disrepute, should they attempt to carry the law into effect. All
who were desirous of keeping up the authority of law, were branded
with the name of tories; their characters were assailed in the newspapers, and they were charged with promoting measures to restrict
the natural and chartered rights and liberties of the people. The
law was attacked by Mr. Otis in a pamphlet, in which he asks this
question: " If taxes are laid in any shape without our having a
legal representative where they are made, are we not reduced from
the character of subjects to the miserable state of tributary slaves ?"
He allows the right of parliament to tax the colonies, provided they
are represented; and had not the colonists soon after declared
against it, this privilege would probably have been conceded ; for
Mr. Grenville and many influential members of the government,
acknowledged themselves in favor of the measure. On the passage
of the stamp-act, there appeared a general determination to oppose
it throughout the colonies, and Mr. Andrew Oliver, afterwards
Lieutenant Governor, having been appointed distributor of the
stamps for Massachusetts, a mob attacked and destroyed a building
lately erected by him, as was supposed for a stamp-office ; on which
he gave notice of his intention to resign, and never to act in that
capacity. Lieut. Governor Hutchinson's house was the next evening attacked, with little damage ; but on the 26th August, 1765,
his windows and doors were burst in, and every article of furniture
and property that it contained, destroyed, to the amount of twenty-
four hundred pounds sterling, besides a great mass of public and
private papers of inestimable value. From this time governmental
power ceased in Boston. Smuggling had been extensively carried
on at that port for years. In 1766 exertions were made on
the part of government to prevent this illegal traffick by prose-
cuting the parties concerned, which induced the most abusive
and licentious attacks on the governor and all the officers of the
crown. False and groundless as these charges were, they gained
too ready a credence with the people, as they were directed against
their rulers. At length, however, Mr. Sewall (afterwards attorney-
general), in a series of papers signed *Philanthropos*, refuted the
charges, and silenced the calumniators.

The stamp-act was repealed, and the duty on molasses reduced from 3d. to one penny per gallon; and for a short time, at the close of the year 1766, the colonies reposed in tranquillity. This calm was, however, interrupted the next year by the refusal of the Assembly of New York to submit to parliamentary authority, by making provision for quartering the king's troops. In 1768, the Governor laid before the assembly of Massachusetts a letter from Lord Hillsborough, secretary of state, directing him to dissolve the same unless an obnoxious vote, passed in February, should be rescinded; and this being refused by a vote of 92 to 17, the minority were ever after reproachfully termed "*rescinders.*" In April, 1769, Governor Bernard received orders to embark for England; and on his arrival, his conduct having met the approbation of the administration, he was created a baronet. He had been treated with great bitterness here, which however was owing in part to certain of his letters to England, in which he infers the necessity of the king's appointing a royal council instead of that elected by the people, and recommends an act to authorize the king to supersede all commissions which had been issued to improper (i. e. disaffected) persons. The destruction of the East India Company's tea at Boston in 1773, only was wanting by their leaders to involve the body of the people in the same circumstances in which their course of opposition measures had placed them.

The leading principles of the Revolution, viz., a denial of the right of taxation by Parliament, a claim of the privilege of juries in admiralty courts, and the right of trial only in places where offences are committed, should have been allowed to rest upon the broad basis of their respective merits. Private letters, surreptitiously obtained in England, written by Governor Hutchinson and Lieut. Governor Oliver, (whose spotless lives, devoted, as they believed, to the best interests of their fellow men, had acquired for them an almost unbounded influence,) were announced with great pomp and circumstance by legislative resolves; and garbled extracts were circulated, and unjust inferences drawn, before the letters themselves were permitted to be printed, which would have proved a sufficient antidote to the poison so invidiously diffused.—The distemper, however, was much arrested by a series of papers under the signature Philolethes, from the pen of Mr. Sewall, developing the disguised craft and fallacies which pervaded this deep contrivance, and written with such moderation and candour that the calumniators thought it best to leave these pieces unanswered, and suffer the flame to die away, intending to keep the embers in reserve for raising a new flame at a more propitious time for their purposes.—Governor Hutchinson* had represented the transaction of the 5th of March 1770 (commonly called the Boston massacre), in his letters to the secretary of state, far more favourably for the town than the evidence at the trial afterwards warranted, yet the Assembly considered him as inimical to the province for conforming to his instructions, and withstanding their attempts to compel him to yield the prerogative of the crown; and the council instead of supporting him sided with the House. The designs of particular persons to bring about a revolution and attain independency, were apparent to the Governor, but he did not think it possible that the people would be induced to declare for it.

Under the discouragements of the times Governor Hutchinson determined to visit England, and have at least a temporary relief; but before he received an answer to his request, his able and estimable coadjutor, Lieut. Governor Oliver,* succumbed to the unwarranted attacks upon him, and fell a victim to wounded sensibility on the 3d of March, 1774.

In a letter from the Earl of Dartmouth, granting Gov. Hutchinson's wished-for permission to visit England, dated April 9, 1774, he says: " It is impossible you can have any doubt of the light in which your conduct on the late trying occasion is seen by the king and his servants. I cannot however content myself without repeating to you what cannot fail to give you the strongest consolation and satisfaction, that it is his majesty's intention to testify his approbation of your services to all mankind by an early mark of his favor.† This expectation will contribute much to alleviate the anxiety of your mind, and to support you under any difficulties you may yet have to encounter; but you will allow me to say, that to a mind like yours there are secret sources of tranquillity that are superior to such great and encouraging considerations. The conscious sense which you possess of an upright and uniform regard to

* See Supplement.

† A baronetcy was offered Gov. Hutchinson and declined, which ought to satisfy his countrymen of the uprightness of his political motives.

the duty of your situation, joined to a dispassionate and real concern for the welfare of the people over whom you preside, which equally appear throughout the correspondence that I have had with you, do at this moment, if I am not deceived in my opinion of you, supply you with that steadiness and fortitude which discover themselves in your firm and temperate conduct, and which under such support it is not in the power of the most unreasonable prejudice, or even of the most inveterate malice to shake or intimidate."

General Gage having arrived with power to administer the government, Governor Hutchinson sailed on the 1st of June, 1774, for England. Before his departure he had received addresses from a hundred and twenty merchants of Boston; from all the gentlemen of the law, with few exceptions; from the magistrates of Middlesex and Plymouth, and the principal gentlemen of Salem and Marblehead, all expressing entire approbation of his public conduct and their affectionate wishes for his prosperity. These addresses gave great offence to the disaffected portion of the community, and many of those who signed them, afterwards stigmatized as " *Addressers*," were compelled by the people to make public recantations in the newspapers. Mr. Curwen, who had subscribed the Salem address, declined to obey the popular voice, saying that the prescribed recantation contained more than in conscience he could own; and that as to live under the character of reproach which the fury of party might throw upon him, was too painful a reflection to suffer for a moment, he therefore resolved to withdraw from the impending storm. He accordingly embarked for Philadelphia, on the 23d of April, 1775, and thence for London on the 13th of the following month.

Mr. Curwen had been in the commission of the peace for thirty years, and at the time of his departure was a Judge of Admiralty, in which office he was immediately succeeded by Timothy Pickering, the patriot, who afterwards so ably filled distinguished offices in the army, in the cabinet of Washington, and the councils of our country. Judge Curwen returned in the autumn of 1784, much to the satisfaction of his friends, and was never molested for his political course.

Mr. Curwen was in early life married to a daughter of Hon.

Daniel Russell, of Charlestown, and a sister of Hon. Chambers Russell, whom he survived many years.

He died in his native town, in April, 1802, at the advanced age of eighty-six years. He possessed a fine literary taste, was a scholar and a Christian. He left no lineal descendants; but in order that the name might not become extinct in New England, at his request just·before his death, a collateral relative since deceased assumed it, who has left three sons residing at Salem, who bear the name.

Of the families of the exiled loyalists, scattered as they have been over the world, it is no small matter to obtain information; while some grace the peerage and baronetage of England, of many of the exiled Refugees scarce a descendant, even in a collateral branch, is to be found. Of the loyalists that remained to run the risk of the spirit of the people, the task has been less difficult.

Of nearly two hundred that were banished by the government of Massachusetts, upwards of sixty were graduates of Harvard College. And of the five judges of the supreme court of that province at the commencement of the difficulties, the Hon. William Cushing alone was of patriot principles, who was afterwards on the bench of the supreme court of the United States.

JOURNAL AND LETTERS.

CHAPTER I.

Philadelphia, May 4, 1775. Since the late unhappy affairs at Concord and Lexington, finding the spirit of the people to rise on every fresh alarm, (which has been almost hourly,) and their tempers to get more and more soured and malevolent against all moderate men, whom they see fit to reproach as enemies of their country by the name of tories, among whom I am unhappily (although unjustly) ranked; and unable longer to bear their undeserved reproaches and menaces hourly denounced against myself and others, I think it a duty I owe myself to withdraw for a while from the storm which to my foreboding mind is approaching. Having in vain endeavoured to persuade my wife to accompany me, her apprehensions of danger from an incensed soldiery, a people licentious and enthusiastically mad and broken loose from all the restraints of law or religion, being less terrible to her than a short passage on the ocean; and being moreover encouraged by her, I left my late peaceful home (in my sixtieth year) in search of personal security and those rights which by the laws of God I ought to have enjoyed undisturbed there, and embarked at Beverly on board the schooner Lively, Captain Johnson, bound hither, on Sunday the 23d ultimo, and have just arrived. Hoping to find an asylum amongst quakers and Dutchmen, who I presume from former experience have too great a regard for ease and property to sacrifice either at this time of doubtful disputation on the altar of an unknown goddess, or rather doubtful divinity.

My fellow-passengers were Andrew Cabot,* his wife and child, and Andrew Dodge.* My townsman, Benjamin Goodhue,† was

---

* Merchants of Beverly.   † See Supplement.

4

kind enough to come on board, and having made my kinsman and correspondent, Samuel Smith, acquainted with my arrival, he was pleased to come on board also, and his first salutation, " *We will protect you though a tory*," embarrassed me not a little ; but soon recovering my surprise, we fell into a friendly conversation, and he taking me to his house, I dined with his family and their minister, Mr. Sproat, suffering some mortification in the cause of truth. After an invitation to make his house my home during my stay here, which I did not accept, I took leave, and went in pursuit of lodgings, and on enquiring at several houses, ascertained they were full, or for particular reasons would not take me ; and so many refused as made it fearful whether, like Cain, I had not a discouraging mark upon me, or a strong feature of toryism.   The whole city appears to be deep in congressional principles, and inveterate against " *Hutchinsonian Addressers.*" Happily we at length arrived at one Mrs. Swords', a widow lady, in Chestnut-street, with whom I found quarters, rendered more agreeable by S. Waterhouse's company, who also lodges here.

May 5, 1775.   I find the drums beating, colours flying, and detachments of newly raised militia parading the streets ;—the whole country appears determined to assume a military character, and this city, throwing off her pacific aspect, is forming military companies, a plan being laid for thirty-three ; composed of all ranks and nations, uniting shoulder to shoulder, they form so many patriotic bands to oppose like the invincible Macedonian phalanx, the progress and increase of parliamentary authority.   The Quakers, not to be behind in manifesting their aversion, have obtained permission of the city committee to make up two companies of *Friends* exclusively, and they are to be commanded by Samuel Marshall and Thomas Mifflin,* both of that persuasion.

So powerful is the love of liberty, and so great the dread of ministerial designs, that the strongest prejudices and habits have given way and are controlled by the former.

The House this day having received a message from the governor with Lord North's conciliatory plan, has on a full debate rejected it, being resolved to adhere to the union.

---

* See Supplement.

Joseph Lee* hearing I was in the city, came to see me, and advised my going to London.

May 6, 1775. Saw Pelatiah Webster,† who at the instance of Mr Goodhue treats me civilly. Having had several intimations that my residence here would be unpleasant, if allowed at all, when it shall be known that I am what is called "*an addresser;*" besides, solicited to sign "*a recantation,*" which may contain more than in conscience I can subscribe; and after all with the uncertainty whether it will answer the purpose, or should it barely, to live and die under the character of reproach and ignominy, which the outrageous fury of party may throw upon me, is a reflection too painful for a moment to support. I have, therefore, consulted the few friends I think it worth while to advise with, and on the result, am determined to proceed to London in the vessel in which I came here.

On the credit of Samuel Smith and Sons, I have with their assistance procured flour to freight a vessel.

May 7, 1775.—*Sunday.* Went with Mr. Smith to Archstreet meeting house; Mr. Sproat entertained us with a truly American patriotic sermon, pathetically lamenting the evils we are suffering from wicked and tyrannical ministers; exhorting us manfully to oppose them.

At 2 o'clock at the wharf, a large collection of people were waiting news from London, Capt. Robinson having just anchored. The only news was, that the restraining bill respecting New-England, and the other respecting the southern colonies, were passed.

Dr. Franklin arrived last night, which was announced by ringing of bells to the great joy of the city. I cannot but promise myself some good, as his knowledge and experience must have influence in the approaching Congress, which will I doubt not listen to his judgment. He is, it is said, to return to England again soon, at Lord Chatham's instance, who tells him he must be on the spot at the opening of Parliament.

May 9, 1775. Dined with Stephen Collins; passed the evening at Joseph Reed's,* in company with Col. WASHINGTON, (a

---

* See Supplement.

† In July, 1774, this gentleman directed his correspondent at Boston, to pay £10 to the commitee for the relief of sufferers by the Boston Port Bill.

fine figure and of a most easy and agreeable address,) Richard
Henry Lee, and Col. Harrison, three of the Virginia delegates.—
Besides Mr. and Mrs. Reed, were Mrs. Deberdt,* Dr. Shippen,
and Thomas Smith. I staid till twelve o'clock, the conversation
being chiefly on the most feasible and prudent method of stopping
up the channel of the Delaware to prevent the coming up of any
large ships to the city; I could not perceive the least disposition to
accommodate matters.

Col. Caswell and Mr. Hewes, the North Carolina delegates,
arrived this day, and are at our lodgings.

May 10, 1775. Early in the morning a great number of persons rode out several miles, hearing that the eastern delegates
were approaching, when about 11 o'clock the cavalcade appeared,
(I being near the upper end of Fore street;) first two or three
hundred gentlemen on horseback, preceded, however, by the newly-
chosen city military officers, two and two, with drawn swords,
followed by John Hancock and Samuel Adams in a phaeton and
pair, the former looking as if his journey and high living, or solicitude to support the dignity of the first man in Massachusetts,
had impaired his health. Next came John Adams and Thomas
Cushing in a single horse chaise; behind followed Robert Treat
Paine, and after him the New York delegation, and some from the
province of Connecticut, etc., etc. The rear was brought up by
a hundred carriages, the streets crowded with people of all ages,
sexes and ranks. The procession marched with a slow, solemn
pace; on its entrance into the city all the bells were set to ringing
and chiming, and every mark of respect that could be, was expressed:—not much I presume to the secret liking of their fellow
delegates from the other colonies, who doubtless had to digest the
distinction as easily as they could.

May 11, 1775. Col. Caswell was innoculated for the small
pox. Mr. Lee again repeated his advice of my going to London.
Dined with J. B. Smith; rode with him to his farm six miles
out. Drank tea with Mr. Lee and Startin.

May 12, 1775. Sent my baggage on board the Lively—re-

---

* The mother of Mrs. Reed and widow of the Massachusetts Assembly
agent to the British government.

ceived a letter from Stephen Collins to Mr. Neat of London—paid
my respects to Mrs. Deberdt, and received a letter to her son. Received my invoice of flour from Samuel Smith and Sons. Mr.
Startin presented me with an open letter on Wilkinson and Co.
Birmingham, and Mr. Reed and lady gave me letters to their brother,
Dennis Deberdt, London. From post office took Rivington's two
last newspapers, and received from the publishers all the present
week's Philadelphia papers. Messrs. Lee and Webster took leave,
and with my fellow passenger, Mr. Webster's son Pelatiah, I went
on board the Lively.

May 16, 1775. Spoke Capt. Waterman in a schooner from
Nantucket, who brought me a letter from Nathan Goodale, stating
that his family, Mr. Pynchon's, and Mr. Orne's, had arrived there,
to which I replied.

TO NATHAN GOODALE, ESQ.

In the Delaware, May 16, 1775.

DEAR SIR :

You can scarce conceive my joy at hearing that my neighbours,
suffering in the same cause as myself, and for whom I sincerely
profess a friendship, were in a secure retreat. Continue there by
all means, safe from the alarms and dangers you have fled from.

Philadelphia is wholly American, strong friends to congressional measures; at least, no man is hardy enough to express a
doubt of the feasibility of their projects. Mr. Joseph Lee leads a
recluse life there. The inhabitants are displeased that the New
Englanders make it their city of refuge. The new established
post (instead of the old eastern one which is stopped,) admits no
letters to pass but those franked; the contents of which must be
known to one of the committee to be entitled to that benefit.

Yours truly,

SAML. CURWEN.

June 1, 1775. At Sea. The Otter sloop-of-war, from Boston,
brought us to at 9 o'clock, and informed us all was quiet when
she left. The provincial forces, amounting to fifteen thousand
men, were waiting the determination of the Congress; that forty-five

transports with the three generals, had arrived there eight days ago ; and that a great fire happened there, beginning at the barrack stores on the docks, and consuming all from thence to King-street. She detained us two hours in order to send letters to England.

July 3, 1775. Arrived at Dover, England, at 11 o'clock, A. M. Mr. Webster and myself concluded to take coach for London after visiting the Castle. We first ascended to one of the square towers, in height 134 steps, from which in a clear day the French shore is to be seen, and a most agreeable view into the country. The town of Dover seems under foot, and even the steeples scarce as high as the foot of the hill. We next visited Julius Cæsar's tower, (said to have been built by him,) old and in ruins ; on the plains of it is a battery of twenty four pounders,—one of brass, 24 feet long, called Queen Elizabeth's pocket-piece, given her by Holland at the time of its emancipation from Spain. It is curiously ornamented with the arms of England and Holland ; was cast in 1544 ; weighs six tons, and carries a twelve pound shot seven miles. The well is 375 feet deep. The original key supposed to be eighteen hundred years old, is 21 inches long, and weighs three or four pounds. We also saw a sword of state five feet long, the handle twelve inches. At the coffee-house met James Teal, a son of the widow of the late Gov. Belcher of Massachusetts by her first husband. He wished to convey intelligence of his residence here to his mother in New England ; his letters have miscarried for some time past.

London, July 4. Arrived at the New England coffee-house, Threadneedle-street, at 7 o'clock P. M.—July 5. Met my townsman and friend Benjamin Pickman, which rejoiced me ; we walked to Westminster Hall,—in Chancery saw Sir Thomas Sewell, master of the rolls, sitting with his hat on,—at Common Pleas saw Judge Blackstone and Sergeant Glynn; and the King's Bench, Lord Mansfield and Mr. Sergeant Wedderburne. Lord Mansfield's manner is like the late Judge Dudley's of Massachusetts. His peering eyes denote a penetration and comprehension peculiarly his own. Mr. Wedderburne spoke, but at no great length.

July 9, 1775. Went to old Jewry meeting-house, where I met Gov. Hutchinson, his son and daughter,—a cordial reception and invitation to visit him.   Mr. Isaac Smith and Mr. Deberdt sat in the pew next me.

TO WILLIAM PYNCHON, ESQ., SALEM.

London, July 7, 1775.

DEAR SIR :

I am glad for the calm season at Salem ;—could I have been safe on the same conditions I find my friends permitted to reside at home, I would joyfully have accepted them.   However, this calm I fear cannot last long ; for if Congress does not offer terms that administration think they can in honour accept, I have good grounds for saying the most vigorous measures will be pursued, which I fear will cause the destruction of my country.   There is an army of New Englanders here.   My old friend Mr. Sayre, a city banker, married to a lady of fortune, invited me to dine with him in company with my friend Mr. Deberdt.

Let Mr. and Mrs. Cabot know that her niece Mrs. Copley,* with whom I dined yesterday at Mr. Bromfield's, Islington, is well, and expects her husband on his passage from Italy.

Yours truly,
S. CURWEN.

July 11, 1775.   Waited upon Governor Hutchinson, (in company with B. Pickman,) for the first time ; were well received, and invited to dinner for Saturday.

July 18, 1775.   Evening to Vauxhall Gardens ; fine gravelled walks, shrubbery, and covered alcoves lighted by lamps, and rendered a most enchanting spot.   Tables spread under the trees for entertainment.   In one of the open retreats is a most finished piece of statuary of Handel, sitting on a harp in a loose dress.

July 20, 1775.   To J. Lane's house with B. Pickman, passed the evening there in company with Samuel Quincy, Jonathan Sewall, and David Green.

July 21, 1775.   By boat from Temple stairs to Ranelagh ; a numerous company of well dressed people there, among them the Duke of Gloucester and French ambassador.

---

* Lady of the great artist.

July 22, 1775. Spent the day at Hempsted, in company with Isaac Smith, Samuel Quincy, David Green, and P. Webster.

TO REV. THOMAS BARNARD, SALEM.

London, 22d July, 1775.

Dear Sir :

The dissipation, self-forgetfulness, and vicious indulgences of every kind, which characterize this metropolis, are not to be wondered at. The temptations are too great for that degree of philosophy and religion ordinarily possessed by the bulk of mankind. The unbounded riches of many afford the means of every species of luxury, which, (thank God,) our part of America is ignorant of, and the example of the wealthy and great is contagious. Ten miles round is filled with pleasant villas, and Sunday is allotted to visiting them. The congregation at old Jewry meeting-house, respectable for its appearance, did not exceed a hundred. The preacher is called a Presbyterian, and all of that denomination here are on a broader and more liberal plan of divinity than those who go by the name of Independents, such as the " Pinner's Hall Divines" and their associates. The style of the preachers in London (of our way) is more just and correct than ours in New England. To my surprise I saw an auditor taking notes. Notes for prayer or thanksgivings are never read, and the mention of such cases is deferred to the last prayer. Admission to the pews is by a female, who unlocks the doors, (all having locks ;) strangers are conducted to the table pew in the centre, where the sacrament is administered.

*   *   *   *   *

TO WILLIAM PYNCHON, ESQ., SALEM.

London, 25th July, 1775.

Dear Sir :

I dropped in at Guild-hall, where Judge Nares was sitting at the City Common Pleas ; on his cushion were worked the city arms,— and also on the Recorder's, I presume to remind them of the city rights. I was fortunate in procuring a seat just behind Sergeant Davy, and heard as far as my imperfect organs (and the noise and confusion) would admit. While he was opening the case, he was obliged to rise out of his seat, step forward and lean down to hear, in a manner unbecoming the dignity of a judge. Every fact of importance delivered by a witness was noted down by the judge as well as counsel. The noise was much greater than would be allowed in our American courts. I have seen the Lord Mayor in his court ; but this court seems more like a reference business than any thing else. Through uncommon good fortune, I have, without the customary delay of two or three weeks, been admitted into the British Museum, Montague House, a truly royal institution for the preservation of the productions of nature and art. Saw the first Bible printed by authority, on vellum, and turning to the 91st Psalm, 5th verse, instead of " *Thou shalt not be afraid of the terrors by night*," etc., I saw the following : " *Thou shalt not fear the bugs and vermin by night*," etc. There are many other as remarkable differences, but had not time to examine many texts.

I am just informed of a most melancholy event, the destruction of Charlestown in Massachusetts by the king's troops, which all agree in ; the other parts of the story are told differently. Mr. Brecknock says the king's troops would not fight, but laid down their arms, which is the reason of the great carnage among the officers. My distress and anxiety for my friends and countrymen embitter every hour. May it please God to inspire men of influence on either side the Atlantic, with juster sentiments of the real interest of Great Britain and the colonies than they seem to have possessed hitherto.   Yours truly,

S. CURWEN.

July 27. Dined at Mr. Sayre's, in company with four gentlemen and Lady Francis Sherard, only daughter of the late Earl of Harborough ; returned home in Mr. Sayre's coach.

July 28. By invitation dined at Grocers' Company feast at their hall in the Poultry. A procession was formed after dinner (band playing,) and halted behind the chair of the new elected master, when the secretary put a tiara on his head ; while another officer held a large golden cup filled with wine, drank to him, and delivered it ; and the master on taking it drank to the prosperity of the company. The ceremony was also had towards the newly made wardens.

July 29. Dined with Governor Hutchinson, in company with Mr. Joseph Green, Mr. Mauduit, and Mr. Ward Nicholas Boylston; the latter gave us an entertaining narrative of his travels through Syria, Palestine, and Egypt.

July 30. Sunday attended worship at Dr. Fordyce's meeting-house, Monkwell-street. He discoursed with great energy and pathos, abounding with flowers of rhetoric, metaphor, and with uncommon theatric gesture, equal if not beyond Mr. Whitefield.

In the vestry room is hanging the original license from Charles II. to Mr. Doolittle for this present house of worship. Took tea with Dr. Fordyce, at Mr. Kennedy's, and passed an agreeable hour in conversation.

August 3. Walked along Hyde Park wall till arrived at the turnpike between that and the Green Park; at the gate of the former stands a noble house, built by the present Lord Chancellor Apsley,* on ground taken out of the park, and given him by the king for that purpose. Saw their majesties returning from the drawing room, the king in a sedan chair surmounted by a crown, dressed in very light cloth with silver buttons; the queen carried by two porters in a chair, dressed in lemon-colored flowered silk, on a light cream-colored ground. They passed between two lines, observed, smiled, and bowed as they passed.

TO DR. JOHN PRINCE, HALIFAX.

London, August 4, 1775.

DEAR SIR:

I presume you little expected to hear from a fellow sufferer in the cause of loyalty, a whole army of whom are here lamenting their own and their country's unhappy fate. I heard of your escape, and a circumstance connected with it that must render your existence more tolerable, viz., that you were accompanied by your wife and children, and I cordially rejoice in your and their deliverance from the evils which attend our common friends in Salem, and elsewhere in New England. What melancholy scenes they and we are to go through before this unnatural controversy is ended, God only knows!—May you and I be prepared for the worst events. If any of our common friends are in Halifax, be

* Afterwards Earl Bathurst.

pleased to remember me to them in the kindest manner. Our old friend Ben. Pickman desires to be remembered to you.

With much regard, etc.,

S. CURWEN.

August 4. At Mr. Boylston's saw many curiosities he brought from Egypt, the Holy Land, etc. Amongst others the locust in pods, the supposed food of John the Baptist.

August 5. Dined at Gov. Hutchinson's, in company with Joseph Hooper, Benjamin Pickman, Joseph Taylor, Isaac Smith, Mr. Silsbee, and the governor's family.

August 6. At Old Jewry meeting-house—communion day— in which service Governor Hutchinson, his son Elisha, Mr. Pickman, and myself participated. The minister brought the elements, and repeated to each communicant some pertinent expression of Scripture, waiting till each had received.

TO NATHAN GOODALE, ESQ., NANTUCKET.

London, August 8, 1775.

DEAR SIR :

It really appears to me that administration will proceed to such extremities as will terminate in the ruin of England and the colonies. It is a capital mistake of our American friends to expect insurrections here ; there is not a shadow of hope for such an event. The manufactories are in full employ, and one of the warmest of the friends of America told me that letters from Manchester expressed joy that no American orders had been sent, otherwise there must have been disappointment somewhere. What effects may follow in the spring if orders from Russia and Spain are not received, I cannot foresee :—some foretell discontent in the country which will affect the stocks ; whether these will happen depends on contingencies of which I am not a judge. There appears to be a tenderness in the minds of many here for America, even of those who disapprove of the principles of an entire independence of the British legislature, and ardently wish an effort may be taken to accommodate. It is said most vigorous measures will take place in the spring if no offer be made on the part of the colonists.

With much regard, etc. S. CURWEN.

August 23, 1775. Went to Sir John Fielding's office, Bow-street — examination of prisoners for robberies, assaults, etc. He is a venerable gentleman and blind (as justice is represented); his queries manifested a mild deportment, ready apprehension and great penetration. Visited Hampton Court and gardens, which are exceedingly beautiful, although deserted by the royal family. Here are chairs of state with rich canopies, tapestry in gold and silver grounds, containing Scripture and ancient stories of Greece and Rome—adorned also with reigning beauties of the court of Charles II.—of the founders of the different orders of monks, friars, nuns, etc., of former kings, queens, etc. ; Madonnas, the Supper, etc. The ceilings in high colouring and fine preservation, by Verrio, were as pleasing to me as any part of the ornaments, as they referred to incidents in Charles II.d's story. This palace consists of several squares mostly old, and in same state (decay of time excepted) as in Henry VIII th's time, when by the envy of the courtiers Cardinal Wolsey (who built it for his own use) was obliged to present it to the king. The front on the garden facing the river is magnificent and in good repair.

Thence to Windsor—St. George's chapel in excellent repair. Here are deposited the bodies of Henry VIII. and one of his queens, and Charles I. in the midst of the choir. In the side aisles are funeral monuments of former kings, of which I recollect Edward IV. and VI. ; some ancient nobility, and many canons of the Roman church, with their images in sacerdotal garments cut in brass, let into flat grave-stones on the floor; stalls for the knights of the garter; the choir decorated with carvings, and the windows filled with oil paintings of Scripture stories. We then ascended the royal apartments in the castle, consisting as at Hampton Court of an armory, the walls being covered with pikes, halberds, matchlocks, small arms, etc., disposed in a variety of figures. Over the mantel-piece a fine full length of George Prince of Denmark (husband of Queen Anne) on horseback ; the horse seemed alive. The other rooms hung in rich tapestry on gold and other grounds, with paintings, originals and copies of the best masters. In Queen Anne's china-closet were wooden sconces gilt, on which are set china porcelain jars of various shapes up to the ceiling. In a small apartment is to be seen a table fastened to the wall, whereon is a little flag of white satin, with the banner of France worked into it, fastened by silver clasps to a slender reed of black ebony capped with silver, which the Duke of Marlborough is obliged to present, and lay on that spot on the 2d of August annually, before twelve o'clock at midday, on forfeiture of his palace of Blenheim and the manor belonging to it ; this being the tenure by which he holds them, agreeably to act of parliament. From the terrace we saw almost under feet Eton college, another noble monument of Gothic architecture. In a square stands a brazen statue of Henry VI., the founder in royāl robes.

Visited Welbore Ellis's seat at Twickenham, formerly Pope's ; the *grotto*, being arches under the house about a man's height, (admitting a prospect into the longest shady contemplative walk, five feet wide, in the garden,) filled with small flint-stones, Bristol and other kinds in mortar, a few pieces of glass on the top and sides : two or three niches filled with the busts of Pope and others ;—there is also in a cross alley a statue of Terence, and in an addition (made by Mr. Stanhope, late owner,) over the centre of an arch, is a niche filled with a bust of Pope, and underneath are the following lines :

> " The humble roof ; the garden's scanty line,
> Ill spoke the genius of a bard divine ;
> But fancy now displays a fairer scope,
> And *Stanhope's* plans unfold the soul of *Pope.*"

Mr. Stanhope's addition is by far the most elegant part, wherein are many foreign trees, such as the cedar of Lebanon, weeping willows, etc. ; also a green-house filled with flowers, plants and fruits. In a retired part of the grounds stands a plain obelisk, eighteen feet high, dedicated by Pope to his mother, with the following inscription :—

" Ah EDITHA !

MATRUM OPTIMA,

MULIERUM AMANTISSIMA,

VALE !"*

---

* " Alas ! Editha, best of Mothers, most affectionate of Women, Farewell !"

TO HON. WILLIAM BROWNE, BOSTON.

London, 31*st Aug.* 1775.

DEAR SIR:

As far as my experience reaches, I have observed that the upper ranks, most of the capital stockholders, and I am told the principal nobility, are for forcing supremacy of parliament over the colonies; and from the middle ranks down are opposed to it. America furnishes matter for disputes in coffee-houses, sometimes warm, but without abuse or ill nature, and there it ends. It is unfashionable and even disreputable to look askew on one another for difference of opinion in political matters; the doctrine of toleration, if not better understood, is, thank God, better practised here than in America; otherwise there would not be such numbers of unhappy exiles suffering every disadvantage.

Incredible quantities of ammunition and stores shipped and shipping from Tower-wharf for America, manifests the intention of administration to prosecute the plan of subjection of the colonies to the authority of parliament; for that is the only dispute, as it is understood here. Administration would gladly have met the colonies half way or more, had there appeared any inclination to accept terms in any degree consistent with the honor and dignity of the mother country. Now, no alternative; an absolute independence of the colonies on Great Britain, or an explicit acknowledgment of the British legislature over all the dominions of the empire. The proclamation which you will receive by this conveyance was published the day before yesterday at the Royal Exchange, with all the circumstances of indignity the lord mayor could throw on it.

Instead of the languid measures hitherto pursued, more active ones will succeed, and then wo to poor Massachusetts, which, like the scape-goat, must bear the sins of many. Do urge our remaining friends to flee from the destruction that will speedily overtake that devoted colony.

You will not wonder at the luxury, dissipation and profligacy of manners said to reign in this capital, when you consider that the temptation to indulgence, from the lowest haunts to the most elegant and expensive rendezvous of the noble and polished world, are almost beyond the power of numbers to reckon up.

Please make my compliments to Judge Sewall and all other friends and acquaintances with you; and in the kindest manner remember me to Mrs. Browne.

Very truly your friend,

S. CURWEN.

Sept. 17. Attended public worship at the "Reformed Liturgy Assembly," Essex House, Essex-street, Strand; heard Rev. Theophilus Lindsey, the Unitarian reformist, who gave up a living in Yorkshire, (worth three hundred a year,) on the rejection of the petition to parliament for a revisal and amendment of the common prayer. Preacher serious, style good, discourse useful.

Sept. 20. At the Charter House, a foundation by Thomas Sutton, Esq., at a cost of £12,000 sterling, for classically educating forty boys, and supporting eighty old bachelors and widowers, who are to receive yearly a black cloak, without which never to appear at meals, nor with it without the walks;—besides ten pounds in cash, house-rent, food, and firing. They have about forty acres (enclosed by a brick wall twenty feet high,) laid out in gardens; at the entrance are the arms of the donor, formed by small pebbles of the size of acorns.

Sept. 21. At the Disputation-club, Queen's arms; question debated, " *Is it not injustice in the administration to pursue measures at the cost of the price of blood, without any benefit to the nation?*"—which was voted in the affirmative, but not without a few dissentients.

Oct. 11. Governor Hutchinson came in his coach with Mr. Copley from Mr. Bromfield's, and took Mr. Pickman and myself to his house, where we dined in company with Mr. Bliss, Mr. W. N. Boylston, Mrs. Copley, and the family.

Nov. 18. News by a packet from New-York, that Gov. Tryon and Gov. Campbell are obliged to retreat from their respective governments on shipboard; and that Dr. Franklin had arrived at the provincial camp at Cambridge to advise Gen. Washington to attempt the lines on the neck;—and that Samuel Adams and Mr. Dickinson were at odds.

Nov. 29. Saw Mr. Garrick in Hamlet at Drury Lane; in my eye more perfect in the expression of his face than in the accent and pronunciation of his voice, which, however, was much beyond the standard of his fellow actors.

Dec. 1.   At great St. Helen's, Bishopgate-street, where I saw a monument to Sir Thomas Bancroft, a lord mayor's officer, and an oppressive knave, who had heaped up much wealth, which he left with trustees to be improved till his rising from the dead ; which he imagined would take place after a certain period, when his wealth was to be returned to him.   In the meantime, he ordered that his corpse should be laid and kept in a coffin, (with a lock which he could draw back,) and deposited in a tomb with a glass window and a glass door, to be opened once a year on a given day, to be shown to any spectator ; all which has been complied with hitherto.   But his trustees have with these ill-gotten gains erected an alms-house at Mile-end, for the support of poor women and children.

Made another unsuccessful attempt to enter the gallery of the House of Commons, to hear the third and last reading of the bill prohibiting all commerce with America ; learned at the door that it is to remain shut to strangers, for the pretended reason that the floor of the house is too small and the gallery necessary for the use of members ; confirmed by Mr. George Hayley, a city member, whom I met in the Strand.

Thence to Herald's office, where Parson Peters, with his friend Mr. Punderson, lodges ; the latter has lately arrived from Boston, having escaped by rowing himself in a cockboat eighteen miles into the sound from his native place, Norwich, Connecticut, and being taken up by a vessel and put on board the Rose man-of-war, Capt. Wallace, and conveyed to Boston.   It seems he was harshly dealt with by the " *sons of liberty*," being obliged to make two confessions to save his life ; notwithstanding which he was hunted, pursued, and threatened, and narrowly escaped death, (or the Simsbury mines, to which he was finally adjudged, and he thinks with the loss of his eyes,) which would have been his fate but for his seasonable and providential retreat.

TO HON. WILLIAM BROWNE, BOSTON.

London, Dec. 4th, 1775.

DEAR SIR :

Yours of 7th Oct. affords me a pleasingly sensible proof of the truth of King Solomon's observation; " News from a far country is as refreshing as cold water to a thirsty soul."

Uncertain what may be the fate of this, I am restrained from writing what might prove amusing, perhaps informing; should it fall short of its intended destination, and get into the hands of the provincials, though containing nothing prejudicial to the interests of America, even in their own view, nor reflecting on the character of any individual, the most innocent expressions, by the force of party prejudice, might be construed into a sense entirely foreign to one's intention, and render one obnoxious or ridiculous. Were I ever so much of a mind to write on politics, I profess not to have such connections as to justify any positive declarations concerning the determination of the cabinet council, and whoever does, you may be assured, if he writes more than the court pleases to publish in the Gazette, arrogates pretensions, to which he has no claim.

I will just hint what appears to be a matter of notoriety here : the opposition in parliament is too inconsiderable in numbers, weight and measures to hinder the progress of administration in their plans respecting America. Both houses repose entire confidence in the king and his ministers' resolution not to relinquish the idea of compelling the submission of all subjects within the limits of the British Empire to the authority of the supreme legislature : preparations for which are making for increasing the number of troops, to be sent over time enough for a vigorous push next season. The events of war are uncertain, and victory is by many thought doubtful,—yet it is more than whispered by some that America had better be dispeopled than remain in its present state of anarchy,—much more independent. Should this idea regulate future measures, and should government despair of subduing them, one may, without the spirit of prophecy, see beforehand what terrible destructive evils will then befall our poor, devoted, once happy country. " O fortunatus," etc.   Very truly yours,

                                                S. CURWEN.

Dec. 12. To Newington to view the house and grounds of Dr. Watts' friend Gunston, celebrated in his poem " *Sacred to Virtue*," now owned by a daughter of Lady Abney, a niece of Gunston.

6

In the hall is a half length of Caryl, the commentator on Job, and by his side his wife, mother of Mr. Gunston and Lady Abney; also Sir Thomas Abney and his lady. To Dr. Watts' study, being occupied by the lady, we could not gain admittance. From the balcony we had extensive views of the town and country, and through and over the whole, as well as the house, are spread a neatness and arrangement superior to any spot I ever beheld.

Dec. 15.   At Covent Garden, to see Mrs. Barry as Constance in king John—a fine person, and esteemed the best actress now on the stage.

Dec. 17.   At Foundling Hospital chapel; Mr. Bromley preached. Compared the example of Jesus with that of the most perfect of heathen antiquity, Zeno, founder of the Stoic sect, in whose honor Athens declared by public edict, that he had exemplified in his life the precepts he taught, but of whose inconsistency the preacher enumerated several gross instances, not much to the credit of mere human reason, in comparison with the most eminent and brightest of mere men recorded in the Scriptures, in whom great infirmities and even follies are to be perceived; his example only, pure and spotless, being fit to be proposed to mankind for their practice and imitation.

Dec. 18.   At New England coffee-house, where I read in the New-York paper that forts St. John and Chamblé had surrendered to the provincials commanded by Col. Montgomery, formerly a captain in the regular service, and well esteemed. The garrison was commanded by Major Preston, with six hundred regulars and Canadians. The provincials immediately investing the fort were only two hundred in number. The officers are to be sent home or down to General Gage, the commander-in-chief in America, in order to be transported. The provincials are supposed to be designed for Montreal, Gen. Carleton retiring there after a defeat.— News of a contrary kind is, that Falmouth* in Casco Bay, consisting of 139 dwelling houses and 278 stores, warehouses, etc., together with many vessels, was burnt by Captain Mowatt of the Canseau sloop-of-war, after two hours notice to remove, for joining, as the captain was pleased in his letter to the inhabitants to term it, with the rebels; the particular crime or crimes not mentioned.

* Now Portland, Maine.

Dec. 22. Walked to Brompton-Row with B. Pickman, to dine with Judge Sewall, who meeting us in the Strand two days ago, appointed this day. The family, besides Samuel Quincy, who attended Mrs. Sewall and Mrs. Green home, having been to see the king robe and assent to the American prohibitory bill from the throne. After dinner Governor Hutchinson entered and invited Judge Sewall, B. Pickman and myself to dine with him to-morrow.

Dec. 23. At Temple Bar took coach to Governor Hutchinson's, where dined in company with Mr. Joseph Green, Mr. Copley, the limner and lady with family, and his children. In our way through Clerkenwell Green we saw five couple of young persons chained together, going under care of tip-staves to Bridewell prison. The news of the taking of St. John and Chamblé on Sorel-river confirmed by an arrival from Quebec which left 14th November.

Dec. 25. At Chapel Royal, St. James's ; saw the king and queen, who joined in the services with becoming devotion. Bishop of London preached.

Mr. R. Clarke arrived from Boston yesterday, only twenty-one days passage. All safe at Salem. The provincials have seized a ship with five hundred casks gunpowder, cannon, mortars, and stores de guerre et de bouche ; their activity and success is astonishing.

TO REV. ISAAC SMITH, IN LONDON.

Islington, December 27, 1775.

MY DEAR SIR :

I last evening received your favor of the 24th inst., and it afforded me great pleasure to observe that a weekly New England club was likely to be made up; and I am mortified that the extreme coldness of the weather, and the indisposition I have labored under for several weeks, prevent my being in town this day. Be pleased to make my compliments to my brother exiles. Yesterday I received letters from Salem of 18th and 20th November ; all was well and quiet there, except a small fracas on account of an expression said to have been uttered by Mr. Timothy Orne, which gave offence to the ruling powers of the town, who assembled and by force took him out of his house into School-street in the evening, designing to inflict the modern punishment of tarring and feathering on him; but by the influence of the Committee of Safety and his promise to appear before the Committee next morning, he was suffered to depart; accordingly, the next morning he appeared in person; and he to whom it was reported he had used the expression appearing and denying it, promising to submit to the present government, pay the taxes required for support of it, and demean himself quietly and submissively, and take care to avoid for the future making use of unadvised expressions, his present offence should be forgiven.

Mr. Lowell of Newburyport is an acting justice, the only one of the "*addressers*" commissioned. The inferior court bench in Essex is filled by Caleb Cushing, B. Greenleaf, Timothy Pickering, Jr., and Dr. Samuel Holton; the last but one is the only acting justice in our part of the county. Joshua Ward and John Gardner are in commission of the peace. On the supreme bench, John Adams, William Cushing, William Reed and Peasely Sargent, all of whom 'tis said accept. Major Hawley refuses all employment, saying what he did was purely to serve his country.

Very truly yours,

S. Curwen.

Dec. 31. Went to Holloway mount, passing through King John's palace-spot; nothing standing but the original front gateway, under an arch and two pieces of old stone wall, man-height, making part of the wall of stable. Evening at Silver-street meeting-house lecture; Mr. Smith pathetically addressed the young, middle-aged and old on the close of the year:

May the afflictions I have suffered the past year, in an unhappy banishment from my family, friends and country, be the means of increasing my reliance on, and submission to the all-disposing hand of the wise and righteous Governor of the universe.

January 1, 1776. May the events of the following year, however unfavorable to the pride of my heart, be productive of more moral improvement than the last.

Jan. 5. Visited Joseph Green—afterwards to Samuel Quincy's, where I met Mr. Flucker, Judge Sewall and lady, Samuel Sewall, and Harrison Gray, who are bound to the theatre to see the Jubilee, which is to be exquisitely decorated in the scenery.

Jan. 20. Accompanied by B. Pickman and Wm. Cabot, went to Panton-street, Haymarket, to see Mr. Fisher, lately arrived from America ; he had gone out as well as Mr. Flucker. From thence we went to Gov. Hutchinson's, and after a short stay departed through the park to Samuel Quincy's and David Green's lodgings, Parliament-street, where we met Judge Sewall, Mr. Samuel Sewall, Mr. Flucker, Mr. Harrison Gray, and Mr. Oxnard ; R. Clark and Jonathan Clark going out of the door, whom I saw for the first time since their arrival.

Jan. 26. Received a line from Mr. Isaac Smith, inviting me to a dinner at the Adelphi tavern, designed as an introduction to a New England club, which I have been long desirous of establishing.

Jan. 28. Almost as cold as ever I felt in New England.

Jan. 29. Cold without abatement from yesterday, which will ever be known as the cold Sunday, $8\frac{1}{2}$ by Farenheit. The Thames passed over on the ice : generous collections for the suffering poor. The gains of the laborer are almost always spent on Sunday at furthest; foresight and provision for a future day, is not a virtue known among them. The fires here not to be compared to our large American ones of oak and walnut, nor near so comfortable ; would that I was away!

February 1. To the Adelphi, Strand, where by appointment met twenty-one of my countrymen, who have agreed on a weekly dinner here, viz. :

Messrs. Richard Clark, Joseph Green, Jonathan Bliss, Jonathan Sewall, Joseph Waldo, S. S. Blowers, Elisha Hutchinson, William Hutchinson, Samuel Sewall, Samuel Quincy, Isaac Smith, Harrison Gray, David Greene, Jonathan Clark, Thomas Flucker, Joseph Taylor, Daniel Silsbee, Thomas Brinley, William Cabot, John S. Copley, and Nathaniel Coffin. Samuel Porter, Edward Oxnard, Benj. Pickman, Jno. Amory, Judge Robert Auchmuty and Major Urquhart, absent, are members of this New England club, as is also Gov. Hutchinson.

London, Feb. 9. Passing through Westminster Hall, I stopped for a small space at the courts of common pleas and king's bench ; at the former were sitting the Chief Justice De Grey and his associates, one of whom was the famous Sir William Blackstone, author of the well known commentaries on the laws of England ; but no cause of importance, or lawyer of note speaking, I proceeded to the latter, where was sitting that excellent useful judge, but mischievous politician, Lord Mansfield. For the same reason as the former I quitted my stand here, and retreated to the House of Commons' committee-chamber, where for an hour or two I was entertained at the examination of witnesses in the Worcester contested election. The committee sat on an elevated bench, and looked like a court of sessions ; the causes managed by advocates with regularity and decency. One of the committee was Sir George Saville, the chairman Ferguson—all took minutes as is usual in all the courts. Thence to Judge Sewall's, Brompton-row, where met a few New England friends at dinner ; among them Mr. Thomas Robie, whom I was very glad to see, he having arrived in England from Halifax but three days since. By him I received a letter from Dr. John Prince in answer to mine dated in August.

FROM HON. WILLIAM BROWNE.

Boston, Jan. 8, 1776.

*   *   *   *   *   *   *

George Dodge, in a schooner from Dominica, and Ingersol in a schooner of Hasket Derby's from Jamaica, were lately sent in. The property of both vessels was transferred to merchants in the West Indies to cover their interest.

James Grant is here from Halifax ; he has the promise of a commission in the army, and to keep his rank. About two months ago Mr. Marston of Marblehead, came by night from Col. Fowles' farm. He knows nothing about Salem. His wife died last summer.

The other day Gen. Robinson showed me the devices upon the denominations of the continental bills. On one is represented a heavy shower of rain falling on a new settled country, motto around it " *Serenabit ;*" on another, a hand plucking the branches from a tea-plant, with the motto, " *Sustine vel abstine ;*" on a third a hawk contending with a stork, motto "*Exitus in dubio est ;*" on a fourth, an ancient crown on a pedestal, motto " *Si recte facias ;*" on a fifth a beaver gnawing down a full grown oak, motto "*Perseverando ;*" on a sixth an Irish harp, motto "*Majora majoribus consonant.*" They are the inventions of Dr. Franklin.

When I wrote to you in October I forgot to send you the following list of officers in part of the rebel army, found in the pocket

of one of their sergeants, who was killed on the 17th June, on the
heights of Charlestown, viz. :

Col. Gerrish, Newbury.
Lt. Col. Parker, Chelmsford.
Major Bigelow, Worcester.
Lt. Col. Henshaw, Leicester.
Maj. Brooks.
Lt. Col. Holden.
Adjt. Green.
Col. Whitney.
Col. Woodbridge.
Major Buttrick.
Col. Porter.
Major Miller.
Col. Doolittle, Petersham.
Adjt. B. Moore.
Col. Frye.
Gen. Whitcomb, Bolton.
Col. William Prescott.
Gen. Ward, Shrewsbury.
Col. Peirce.
Gen. Pomeroy, Northampton.
Col. Patterson, Richmond.
Adjt. Guager.
Col. Nixon, Framingham.
Col. Ward, Southborough.
Maj. Sawyer.
Adjt. Warner.
Maj. Wm. Moore, Paxton.
Maj. Cady.
Adjt. Hunt.
Adjt. Holman.
Adjt. Hart.
Col. Mansfield.
Adjt. Putnam.
Maj. Jackson.
Lt. Col. Hudson or Hutchins.
Adjt. Hardy.

Col. Gardner, Cambridge.
Col. Bridge, Chelmsford.
Lt. Col. Brickett, Haverhill.
Lt. Col. Clark.
Major Stacey.
Major Wood, Pepperell.
Lt. Col. Powell.
Adjt. Holden.
Adjt. Gen. Js. Keith, Easton.
Col. Green.
Maj. Baldwin.
Adjt. Woodbridge.
Secretary J. Ward.
Adjt. Montague.
Adjt. Fox.
Lt. Col. Robinson, Dorchester.
Adjt. Febiger.
Adj. Stevens.
Col. Bond, Watertown.
Col. Simmons.
Lt. Col. Whitney, Harvard.
Lt. Col. J. Reid, near Manad-
nock.
Adjt. Marston.
Maj. Brigade, Samuel Osgood.
Lt. Col Moulton.
Maj. Putnam.
Lt. Col. Putnam.
Maj. Poor.
Maj. Durkee, Norwich.
Capt. Butler, Peterborough.
Joseph Trumbull, Judge Advo-
cate, Norwich.
Adjt. Handy.
Lt. Col. Storer.

Those who have obtained leave to exchange the town for a country residence the last two months, are taken on board an armed ship at Hancock's wharf and are landed at Point Shirley, where they are cleansed and aired for the benefit of their brethren who have not had the small pox.

I sent a verbal message to Mrs. Curwen by Bella McLeroy, informing her of your safe arrival and health; but was discouraged by Mrs. Gardiner from trusting her with your letter, which I still have in my desk with those lately received, and know not if I can ever send them until you will suffer them to be inspected at headquarters on both sides the lines. Mrs. Browne and William desire their best regards. Pray present mine to all friends with you, and if you ever desire to hear from me again, give me reason to think so by sending me a circumstantial account of yourself and of what what passes on your side of the water.

I am your affectionate friend,

WM. BROWNE.

London, Feb. 15. Dined with New England Club at Adelphi Tavern; was introduced to Sir Francis Bernard, and saw there, for the first time since his arrival, Mr. Fisher, who promises to spend a day with me soon. Received a letter from Col. Browne, at Boston, acquainting me of the sad destruction of wooden houses for want of fuel, till of late thirteen vessels arrived with coals, &c., raising the despondency of the people.

Feb. 27. The city polled for a chamberlain; candidates, aldermen Wilkes and Hopkins. The latter succeeded, to the no small mortification of the Wilkites, who exceed in numbers, among the lower classes, the friends of Hopkins. Mr. Wilkes must look upon himself as one of the people, and lost henceforth to all importance.

Feb. 29. Dined with Mr. Gilbert Harrison, and delivered my letter of credit from Mr. Timmins to Messrs. Harrison and Ansley.

March 2. At Parson Peters' saw Mr. Troutbeck, lately arrived from Halifax, and Mr. Wiswall; mutually invited each other to visit, and gave cards.

March 4. James Russell and his friend Mr. Newman dined with me; received a card from Messrs. Clarke excusing themselves, being pre-engaged.

March 10. To Tichfield-street to pay my respects to Gov. Oliver's lady; thence to Judge Sewall's, Brompton-Row, where dined.

March 13. At Covent Garden, obtained a very convenient place in the first front seat lower gallery, when the oratorio called the Messiah was performed—the whole stage an orchestra; in the centre a spacious organ embellished by a portrait of Handel surrounded with a glory, or such rays as are placed round the heads of the saints of the Romish calendar—our musical saint's performances being as much read and studied here as their manuals of devotion are by their admirers. The form of the orchestra amphitheatrical and the seats concentric, except of the vocal performers, who sat in chairs in front. The leading singers were Mrs. Wrighton, Mrs. Weischell, Mr. Leoni, etc.—nearly eighty performers in all. The first violin, professor La Motte; the first flute, Mr. Florio. The music was noble, grand, full, sonorous, and awfully majestic; the whole assembly as one, rising, added a solemnity which swelled and filled my soul with an—I know not what, that exalted it beyond itself, bringing to my raised imagination a full view of that sacred assembly of blessed spirits which surround the throne of God.

March 14. Surveyed the New River works at Spafields—thence to see the ravages of the late fire at the Savoy, and through to the gardens belonging to Somerset House, now about to be pulled down, and the ground between it and the river filled up. I cannot but think with regret on so many noble and royal apartments in good repair, to be destroyed to build offices for the army, that bridle of the nation, its scourge, and will be its future ruin.

March 19. Attended lecture at Salters' Hall. Dr. Price gave an excellent sermon from " *Forgive us our debts as we forgive our debtors.*" He observed that this was the only original part of the Lord's prayer, (the rest being found in the Jewish liturgy,) and was designed to inculcate the distinguishing characteristic of his religion, universal love and good will to all mankind, making it the very condition on which our hopes of forgiveness are suspended. As forgiveness of injuries and love of all mankind are the most amiable of all virtues, so are they the most difficult to be practised, and ought therefore to be the more endeavored after; and nothing can recommend us better to divine favor and acceptance.

7

March 21. Mr. Heard, Norroy king-of-arms, having given me
a letter to A. Farley, Esq., Chapter House, I went, accompanied
by William Cabot, Samuel Porter, Judge Sewall and his kinsman
Samuel Sewall, and I. Bliss, and presenting my letter, we were admitted to a sight of Doomsday Books. One, in the fold of a folio,
contained a valuation or estimate made for an equal tax of all the
counties of England in the time of William the Conqueror, except
the three northern counties of Cumberland, Westmoreland, and
Durham, and the three counties of Essex, Sussex, and Kent, which
are contained in a smaller fold or large octavo. Sussex contained
but nine landholders *in capite ;* all tenures being then from the
crown, all the rest being mesne lords or tenants under them. The
writing is fair and well preserved, but difficult to be read from its
abbreviations in a multitude of places. The initial letters stand for
words. The spelling of that age is very different from ours ; many
terms not known now being then in common use. The chapter
house is of a peculiar construction, and was formerly the parliament house in the time of the Edwards, etc., and contains rolls of
court of King's Bench, Exchequer, etc., for many ages back.
Evening, at a show called *Les Ombres Chinoises,* at which saw
Earl Temple [supposed author of Junius] and lady, with several
well-dressed people of fashion—about forty spectators in all. The
" *Ombres*" were awkward and unnatural except the puppet dancing
—an insipid show.

March 24. Heard Dr. Fleming preach at Pinners' Hall; his
ideas clear, and his delivery moderate and devout. He complained
of those mystics who denied the use of reason in matters of religion ; said it was subversive of it, and contrary to the whole tenor
of the canon of Scripture, and rendered as useless and unmeaning
the motives and threatenings proposed to us therein for our obedience,
and progress in virtue and holiness ; declared mankind free agents,
endowed with the power of volition and choice, which was the
foundation of all religious obedience, and without which we were
not accountable. He denied the merit of Christ's sacrifice to render
us objects of divine acceptance, which, he said, by the divine promise was to be obtained by man's own serious and diligent performances.

March 25. Drank tea at Mr. Green's in company with Gov.

Hutchinson, whom I had not seen for some weeks, and who expressed an uneasiness at my neglect to call, which I accounted for as arising from concurrent disappointments.

March 31. At Joseph Green's in the evening, where I met Samuel Quincy.

April 1, A. M. At Gov. Hutchinson's; he was alone, reading a new pamphlet entitled "*An Inquiry whether Great Britain or America is most in fault.*" I accepted an invitation to return to dinner: taking leave for the present, I departed, walking through the palace and park to Mr. Bliss's lodgings, where I met Judge Sewall, Mr. Oxnard and Mr. Smith; returned to the governor's, with whom only young Oliver and myself dined. From thence, in passing through Leicester-square, I called in at Mr. Copley's to see Mr. Clarke and the family, who kindly pressed my staying to tea; and in the mean time amused myself by seeing his performances in painting. He was then at work on a family piece containing himself, Mr. Clarke, his wife and four children, of all of whom I observed a very striking likeness. At tea was present Mr. West, a Philadelphian, a most masterly hand in historic painting; author of the well-known and applauded piece, now in print, called "*West's Death of Wolfe*," and taken from his painting. He is now at work on a piece called the "*Death of Stephen*," for the king, and for which he is to have one thousand pounds. Mr. West is the king's history-painter, and was kind enough to put me into a way of obtaining a sight of the queen's palace, which he tells me contains, except Houghton Hall, the finest collection of capital paintings of any house in England. Returned with Mr. Clarke, who was going to see his son Jonathan, sick.

April 3. Breakfasted with Smith and Oxnard, where I found Samuel Quincy and David Green, Judge Sewall and a Lieutenant Merrick. Bought Dr. Price on "*Civil Liberty and the American War.*"

Went with Mr. Clarke to procure more convenient lodgings for his sick son, which we found as recommended by Dr. Pitcairn in Cross-street, in what is called the Queen's house, said to be a palace of Elizabeth's, on a small scale, low and in the taste of the sixteenth century. The remains of the porter's lodge at the bottom of the garden, in a peculiar style, are yet seen. In one of the lower rooms is a painting on the windows with the date of 1588.

April 4.   At our New England club dinner, twenty-five members present.

April 6.   At Portuguese synagogue; a master informed me that the common people cannot read the Pentateuch without points, although it contains only alphabetic characters; that the points were invented about the time of Christ in the reign of Tiberius, and that they are necessary to ascertain the sense, which in many places would be wholly unintelligible without them, and that it would cost six months study to understand the language so as to follow them in their prayers.

April 7.   Dined with Gov. Hutchinson, and we took tea at Mr. Joseph Green's.

April 10.   Took a view of West's pictures : amongst others which filled two rooms, were the original of the death of Wolfe, sold to Lord Grosvenor for six hundred guineas, about seven by five feet, in high estimation, although censured by an anonymous writer in yesterday's " *Advertiser ;*" Lord Clive's receiving the Dewannah from the nabob, figures about twelve inches high and likenesses well preserved,—fifteen feet by eight ; and many other groups of modern persons in ancient characters.   Likewise the death of Stephen, the proto-martyr, and at the period of his being received after his death by his friends; the figures seven feet, the size of the picture about sixteen feet by seven ; designed for the altar of St. Stephen, Walbrook—six hundred guineas to be received for it, which Mr. West esteems so small a price that he considers it a gift to the church.

April 11.   Visited Tylney House, Epping forest, in company with Messrs. Flucker and Hutchinson.   The walls of the ball-room covered with tapestry of the most lively tints, being the story of Telemaque—the ceiling covered with paintings by Mr. Kent.   The state dining-room is adorned with copies of capital paintings, three of Titian.   The state bedchamber hung with crimson damask, lined with deckered silk, which I am told is India work and cost two thousand pounds.   Two other rooms hung in figured velvet on satin ground, and crimson velvet with broad gold lace.

Dined at Mr. K's with five of my countrymen, among them

a Mr. Bourne, lately arrived from Halifax; he appears a grave, solid man, whose acquaintance I think I shall esteem.

April 14. Attended public worship at Dr. Price's in the afternoon, and in company with Benjamin Pickman took tea with him. Mr. Pickman had a long conversation with Dr. Price on American affairs, but their sentiments were widely different.

April 15. Mr. Boylston called, and we went to Parliament-street to see the procession of the Peers to Westminster Hall to attend the trial of the Duchess of Kingston; the lords wore their robes. The queen, two princes and two princesses, and the peeresses and ladies in great multitudes attended, and made a most brilliant appearance.

April 17. Went with B. Pickman to Highgate, where dined with Mr. Boylston, and after dinner to Caen Wood, the seat of Lord Mansfield. The house elegant, not large:—the centre is a noble portico, the walls of the hall, saloon, chambers, etc. covered with paper of India or Chinese figures—the library a beautiful room, (having a fine prospect of St. Paul's, distant about seven miles, through a wood, over a lawn, and ending in a fine piece of water,) contains the largest mirrors I ever saw, being seven and a half feet high by three and a half in breadth. In the hall are two tables of jet-black marble. The walls hung with portraits of Lord Mansfield and lady, who was a daughter of Finch, Earl of Nottingham.

April 22. Visited Mr. Hughes seventeen miles out, at Hoddesdon, Herts; the grounds laid out with great taste.

April 23. Walked to Ware, which contains five hundred houses, besides a great curiosity called "the great bed of Ware," which is twelve feet square—the posts, which are of uncommon size, are carved with white and red roses, built, it is said, at the union of the houses of York and Lancaster; the date, 1463, is painted on the centre of the headboard, which with the tester is of wood in the same style, laid out in compartments and surrounded with roses. The whole weighs half a ton : twenty persons can repose comfortably on it.

April 24. Walked through the Rye-field to the Rye House, famous as the rendezvous of those who concerted the plot of that name :—the room in which they met was once a chapel ; indeed, the whole appears as the remains of a famous seat. The walls brick, and moulded round, forming two high round towers, joined together by a line of defence; holes in the walls for arrows, etc.

On returning home, passed a farm called Nether Hall, belonging to a Mr. Archer; here are the remains of a palace, said to have been King Harold's before the conquest. The house, which was very large, has been pulled down; two lofty brick towers remain, with a wall of equal height, crowned with battlements, and within a moat surrounding an acre of land covered with ruins. In one of the angles is a watch-tower, now converted into a hen-roost. Arriving at home, found John Inman, brother of Ralph, our countryman, who dined with us; he is of a blunt humor, easy and jolly; with him and a Mr. Musgrave we set off to Mr. Dauteville's, at Brocksburn, by invitation; passed an agreeable evening at Mr. Hughes'.

May 1. The young chimney-sweepers with their sooty and chalked faces are dressed out with ribbons and gilt paper, a grotesque and merry-andrew appearance. With their brushes and scrapers they made a kind of musical sound, raising contributions on their employers and others. The milk-maids appeared in fine and fantastic attire, and carried on their heads pyramids of three or four feet in height, finely decorated. In Ave-Mary lane saw the milkmen and maids again with a *garland* so called; being a pyramid consisting of seven or eight stories, in the four angles of which stood a silver tankard, and on the sides, between each, lessening in height as the stories rose, stood a silver salver, the top crowned with a chased silver tea-kettle, round which were placed sundry small pieces of plate; the whole adorned with wreaths and festoons of flowers, gilt paper, etc., carried on a bier and hand-barrow, it being a custom amongst them to collect of the customers a yearly contribution. The wrought silver appeared worth many hundreds of pounds, and is borrowed for the occasion.

May 3. Dined with H——— H———, Esq., Capt. T———, and B. Pickman, at Jerusalem tavern; on my way meeting Mr. Elisha Hutchinson, who informed me of Col. Browne and son's arrival.

May 4. Called on my friend Browne, who had sent a message last evening by Mr. Pickman to invite his three countrymen to his lodgings. Col. Browne acquainted me with some facts relative to the unfortunate abandonment of Boston by the king's troops; which after all has the appearance of being forced. Would to God this ill-judged, unnatural quarrel was ended, but I fear thousands of useful innocents must be sacrificed to the wickedness, pride and folly of unprincipled men. Many of our countrymen called during our stay.

May 5. To Magdalen Hospital; heard the Rev. Dr. *Dodd* preach from John xv. 17, " *These things I command you, that ye love one another.*"—A most elegant, sensible, serious and pathetic discourse, enough to have warmed a heart not callous to the impressions of pity. I own my eyes flowed with tears of compassion.

May 7. Attempted to get into Drury Lane theatre, to see Mr. Garrick in the character of Archer, but the crowd so great, that after suffering thumps, squeezes, and almost suffocation for two hours, I was obliged to retire without effecting it. Went to Mr. Silsbee's lodgings to tea.

May 8. Visited Mr. Fisher, who very politely received me, and appeared glad to see me; from thence to Gov. Hutchinson's, who was alone—having before called at Col. Browne's (my towns-man and friend) lodgings, whom I did not see, being gone abroad. Thence to Judge Sewall's in Brompton-Row, but meeting Mr. Harrison Gray near the house, was told that neither he nor Mr. Porter were at home. Called again at Col. Browne's, where I found Col. Saltonstall; they both agreed to dine with me.

May 9. With Col. Browne went to St. Paul's to hear the music for the benefit of the sons of clergy. Dr. Porteus* preached to a crowded assembly. The archbishop of Canterbury, the bishop of London, the lord mayor and sheriffs, in their formalities present.

May 10. Met at Col. Browne's Gov. Hutchinson, Judge Sewall and Col. Saltonstall; proceeded to Westminster Hall, heard opinions from Judges De Grey, Gould, Blackstone and Nares respecting a verdict.

May 11. Advices of the arrival of a vessel which left Philadelphia by consent of Congress, on the owner's paying them as duty one third the cost of vessel and cargo; and that Arnold is appointed a major general, and still remained before Quebec, five thousand men having been sent from Philadelphia. Took tea with Mr. Copley and Mr. Clark.

---

* Afterwards bishop of Chester.

May 13. Walked to Walworth, the gardens of a Mr. Maddocks, a noted florist, wherein I saw the greatest variety of finely variegated tulips I believe in England.

May 14. Went to the exhibition-room in the Strand, where were more than fifty people viewing the pictures, models, etc., as contained in a book delivered to each at entering. There were many performances and some very excellent in their kind, of which the view of the eruption of Vesuvius and a few night pieces struck me most.

May 15. Visited Pinchbeck's to view stained glass ; most elegant figures, finest tints, in the new revived art, by a Mr. Jervais; among which were two full lengths of Christ and Moses, bought at seventy guineas by a clergyman, and presented to Westminster Abbey. From thence to the exhibition-room of the Royal Academy, in Pall-mall, where were to be seen a most curious colection of elegant and capital performances in oil, crayons, enamel, sculpture, etc., a great number present. Meeting Colonels Browne and Saltonstall at the door of their lodgings, agreed to meet them at the Exchange and dine together at three o'clock.

May 17. Took tea at Mr. J. Green's; Harrison Gray and other company there ; having dined with eleven New Englanders at St. Clement's coffee-house.

May 20. Took lodgings with a Mr. Palmer at the Herald's office.

May 21. Visited the Boar's-head tavern, Cannon-street, to view the very room or rather spot in which Prince Harry with Falstaff used to assemble with their friends Nym, Bardolph, etc., to hold their nocturnal frolicks. Agreed to make a company, (if feasible,) to dine next Thursday. Returned home, where found Richard Routh, who came with B. Pickman.

June 2. Called at Mr. Copley's, Leicester-square; afterwards at No. 11 Haymarket, the lodgings of Col. Browne and Col. Saltonstall.

June 5. Walked to Mr. Green's ; Major Brattle entered, and we three took coach to Drury Lane, to see for the last time Garrick in Richard III. by command of their majesties, but were too late—house filled.

June 6. To Westminster Hall to hear the sentence of Gen.

Smith and Mr, Hollis for bribing a borough, who are to be imprisoned six months, and pay one thousand marks.

TO REV. ISAAC SMITH, EXETER.

London, June 6, 1776.

DEAR SIR :

We have received advices from America, though not authenticated enough to find a place in the Court Gazette, still generally believed ; there are some who doubt the whole.

Gov. Tryon in his letters by the packet from New-York, which left 2d May, writes that " Arnold having received a reinforcement, made a second attack on Quebec, but finding it impracticable to take it by storm, he, on the 19th April, after five days' attempt, retreated ; in the meantime, the Isis, with eight hundred men on board two transports which arrived with her, having landed, immediately joined the garrison and issued out, disturbing them on their march, and destroying seven hundred and fifty men." It is reported that eighty men taken last February on Montgomery's defeat from the New England regiments, incorporated with the garrison and behaved bravely ; on the contrary, seventy of the regulars entered among the provincials, and turning against them when hard pushed, occasioned the carnage stated above. Gen. Lee is said to be taken with seventy men by a party of Gen. Clinton's, as he was reconnoitering, without firing a gun ; the story is told in three different ways, but finds credit. A vessel from Halifax has arrived, bringing their Governor Legge to answer complaints. Gen. Washington has issued a proclamation, forbidding all rapine and plunder in Boston, a source of comfort to our friends here. There is a long list of military stores in the papers, said to have been left at Boston by Gen. Howe, but it is thought to be a false account.

London, my favorite place of abode, is, as the peasant said, " *a sad lickpenny*," and truly one cannot breathe the vital air without great expense. The numerous applications to the treasury by Americans whose pretensions are so much beyond mine, exclude the most distant hope of relief for me, should inadvertence or more unjustifiable principles of conduct reduce me to the necessity of asking a favor, which I am determined at all events to defer to the

8

longest period, if it please the great Disposer of events to prolong
my uneasy abode in this country of aliens for many days yet to
come.

To communicate with a friend is almost the only relief from distracting thoughts; for the harmless amusements in which I was
engaged last summer and fall, and which served to dissipate
uneasy reflections, now having lost their novelty, delight no
more.

Yours truly,

S. CURWEN.

June 8. Dined with Judge Sewall at Brompton-Row; and
with him, his wife and sister, Mr. Blowers and wife, Samuel Sewall
and William Browne, was admitted to the queen's palace in St.
James's Park. The rooms are large, lofty, and extremely well
filled with pictures; many of them said to be originals of the best
masters; amongst them are seven Cartoons of Raphael, and a
large collection of miniatures in gilt frames and under glass. From
thence to tea at Col. Browne's, afterwards to the opera house;
entertained with the opera of Antigono, the Signors Rousini and
Gabrieli, principal performers, interludes of exquisitely fine dancing.

June 10. Read "*Common Sense*," published in America, and
republished here, in favor of American independence; and also
"*Plain Truth*," an answer to it; and Provost Smith's oration on
the Quebec heroes, Montgomery, etc.

TO DR. CHARLES RUSSELL, ANTIGUA.

London, June 10, 1776.

DEAR SIR :

I congratulate you on your retreat from the land of oppression
and tyranny; for surely, greater never appeared since the days of
Nimrod. I sincerely wish well to my native country, and am of
opinion that the happiness of it depends on restraining the violences
and outrages of profligate and unprincipled men, who run riot
against all the laws of justice, truth and religion. Sad and deplorable is the condition of those few that like Abdiel, amidst hostile
bands of fallen spirits, retain their primitive loyalty. So strangely
unprosperous hitherto have been the measures of administration in

America, that the active provincials have taken courage, and accomplished what in contemplation would have appeared morally impossible. Gen. Burgoyne sailed from hence ten weeks ago for Canada with four thousand Brunswickers and seven or eight regiments; Lord Howe in the Eagle about a month, and the first division of Hessians, consisting of eight or ten thousand, about a fortnight before him. Gen. Howe, his brother, with nine thousand was at Halifax the beginning of April. The second division, ('tis said,) will sail this week, consisting of four thousand, which completes the whole number of foreign troops. The whole of the regular army on the continent will not be short of forty thousand men. It is surprising what little seeming effect the loss of American orders has on the manufactories; they have been in full employ ever since the dispute arose; stocks are not one jot lessened, the people in general little moved by it; business and amusements so totally engross all ranks and orders here that administration finds no difficulty on that score to pursue their plans. The general disapprobation of that folly of independence which America now evidently aims at, makes it a difficult part for her friends to act.

By letters from Salem to the 16th April I find they were in a quiet state there, and hugging themselves in the fatal error that government had abandoned the design of reducing them to obedience. Six vessels laden with refugees are arrived from Halifax, amongst whom are R. Lechmere, I. Vassal, Col. Oliver, Treasurer Gray, etc. Those who bring property here may do well enough, but for those who expect reimbursement for losses, or a supply for present support, will find to their cost the hand of charity very cold; the latter may be kept from starving, and beyond that their hopes are vain. " *Blessed is he* (saith Pope) *that expecteth nothing, for he shall never be disappointed ;*" nor a more interesting truth was ever uttered.

I find my finances so visibly lessening, that I wish I could remove from this expensive country, (being heartily tired of it,) and old as I am, would gladly enter into a business connection anywhere consistently with decency and integrity, which I would fain preserve. The use of the property I left behind me I fear I shall never be the better for; little did I expect from affluence to be reduced to such rigid economy as prudence now exacts. To beg is a meanness I wish never to be reduced to, and to starve is stupid; one comfort, as I am fast declining into the vale of life, my miseries cannot probably be of long continuance.

With great esteem, etc.

S. CURWEN.

June 13. Went early to call on my townsmen Messrs. Dalglish and Hastie;* met Capt. Poynton; Mr. Hastie delivered me a letter from Mr. Pynchon. Mr. Thomas Danforth, late from Boston by the way of Halifax, and Mr. R. Russell, called and staid with me till eleven o'clock at night.

June 15. Accompanied Mr. Danforth to Gov. Hutchinson's and Judge Sewall's.

June 18. Called on Mr. Hughes, who invited me to a second visit to his seat at Hoddesdon; showed me a Massachusetts libel for a transport from London, signed by the new judge of admiralty, Timothy Pickering, jun. Dr. Sylvester Gardner bitterly laments his unhappy situation at Halifax, with a deplorable account of his losses at leaving Boston, etc.

June 19. To the British Museum, accompanied by Mr. Danforth. In the library I saw King John's original charter called Magna Charta; a book of prayers of Queen Elizabeth, executed finely by herself, the writing very plain, letters fair and well preserved, the covering of red velvet worked in flowers by her own hand. The Alexandrian manuscript copy of the Bible, said to have been written in the fourth century, containing the gospel of Nicodemus, a forgery composed in that age; all written on parchment, in capitals, without distinction of words, or verse, or sentences. Also many of the letters of Charles I., amongst which the original of his to Glamorgan, a papist, in Ireland, promising to make good his engagement to him in establishing the Roman Catholic religion there, and toleration of it in England.

Thursday, June 20. Accompanied Mr. Danforth to Judge Oliver's lodgings, in Jermyn-street, and with him and his son proceeded through the Park to Westminster Hall, expecting to hear Lord Rochfort and Mr. Sayre's case, but it did not come on. Just

* Importers of Salem.

looking into Chancery, I observed the judges as they were going
out of King's Bench turned about and saluted with a bow. Chief
Justice Lord Mansfield's train borne up by a gentleman. Chief
Justice of Common Pleas, Sir William De Grey, made a speech on
a trial between a Mr. Popham, etc., on an election affair.

Met my townsman, Samuel Grant; the first time I have seen
him since his arrival from Mississippi.

June 21. Called at Messrs. Browne and Saltonstall's lodgings,
where I saw Col. Morrow and Mr. Johonnot, of Boston, refugees,
for the first time since their arrival.

Mr. Bourne, one of my countrymen, brought me a letter which
came by a Cape Ann schooner, dated Salem, 21st April—when all
was well. My friend's advices concerning the discipline and
number of the provincial troops, and the number and strength of
the American navy, will prove, when put to the test, to be a delusive fancy: civil wars in time make good generals and soldiers, but
the immense inequality will, I suppose, put an end to this war before they will have time to qualify ; in any case, America must be
ruined, perhaps desolated. I pray God inspire all with a spirit of
moderation and wishes for a reconcilement and oblivion of past
confusions; and may the righteous flourish as the palm-tree, and
the wicked wither and their root consume away.

June 23. At Rolls' Chapel. Dr. Hurd, bishop of Litchfield
and Coventry, preached an ingenious discourse. Mr. Browne, R.
Clark, E. Hutchinson, Mr. Lloyd, Mr. Johonnot, Judge Oliver and
son, accompanied me.

TO MR. ISAAC SMITH, EXETER.

London, June 26, 1776.

DEAR SIR :

I have received a letter from Rev. Thomas Barnard, of Salem,
filled with American fancies; their power, strength, grandeur, and
prowess, by land and sea ; their policy, patriotism, industry, progress in the useful arts, and their fixed determination to withstand
the attacks of tyranny, etc., etc. All these fanciful notions will,
(too soon, alas! to their sorrow,) like Ephraim's goodness, " van-
ish as the morning cloud and early dew," and prove to be fatal
delusions.

Two or three companies of Bostonians are lately arrived from
Halifax. I am determined to take a journey westward, and shall
stop as near you as possible. I shall, however, depart hence as
Abraham did from the land of the Chaldees, not knowing whither
I go; fain would I trust in the same kind protecting hand that
guided that good old patriarch; would to God I had his faith, but
fear my future allotments will be poverty and pilgrimage.

Your friend, etc.

S. CURWEN.

London, June 27. At Westminster Hall to hear Lord Rochfort, secretary of state, and Mr. Sayre's case, for false imprisonment
and seizing the latter's papers. Verdict, one thousand pounds for
the latter. Tried before Chief Justice De Grey.

July 1. Breakfasted with Col. Saltonstall; afterwards to
Judge Oliver's to have a sight of Dr. Elliott's letters, conceived in
the whig strain.

July 3. With Mr. Browne visited Bunhill Fields burying-
ground to view Judge Chambers Russell's grave—passed John
Bunyan's tomb, 1688.

July 5. At Croydon, where the Duke of Bedford has a hunting seat. In this place he and the Marquis of Blandford,* youths
of twelve and thirteen, are at a boarding-school. I arrived at
Mrs. Grosvenor's, the lodgings of the two Ingersolls, D. and J.,
and to the latter I had a letter from D. Deberdt, recommending me
to the house, which I found full, and am therefore disappointed.
Thence to the church; the vicar is Dr. Apthorp, my countryman;
it is in excellent repair; in a separate corner are the tombs of six
archbishops, viz. Grindall, Whitgift, and Sheldon, with statues over
them and placed against the wall, and in decumbent postures, in
episcopal habits and crowns, the latter of white marble polished,
and on the entablature the emblems of mortality in middle relief,
executed in a masterly manner in Italy; the three others are Wake,
Potter, and Herring, in flat tombs, and their names, &c. inscribed.
Dined with the Ingersolls at Mrs. Grosvenor's.

July 8. Paid visits to Mr. Fisher and Col. Saltonstall; left a

---

* Afterwards duke of Marlborough.

card at Gov. Hutchinson's, who is in the country. Took tea at
Mr. Blowers' in company with Judge Sewall and family.

July 10.   At Guildhall—Court Common Pleas, in which sat
Chief Justice De Grey—King's Bench, Lord Chief Justice Mansfield—the former addressed the jury in a case of slander in a most
agreeable manner.

Speaking of the Standard in Cornhill sometimes referred to in
books relative to distances, I called on an inhabitant there, but
could get no satisfaction, he telling me he had himself inquired
about it to no purpose. But very few are acquainted with the
curiosities, etc., the knowledge being confined to those skilled in
city history.

July 13.   Breakfasted with Mr. Oxnard and Mr. Silsbee.
Asked a man how far it was to Chelsea, and was answered, in the
true New-England style, "*I don't know—about half a mile.*"
This I note as the first instance, to my remembrance, of the like I
have met with on this side the water.

Had a free conversation with a couple of conversible gentlemen,
not commonly to be met with; the better sort or gentry being too
proud or reserved to mix with those they don't know, or to indulge
a promiscuous chat.

July 14.   Worshipped at Allhallows, Lombard-street; the officiating priest was Mr. Peters, the refugee from Hebron, Connecticut;* his text 2 Peter chap. iii. verses 1 and 2, "*But grow in
grace,*" etc.   Mr. Peters dined with me.

---

* Author of a travestied history of Connecticut.

CHAPTER II.

London, July 15. Walked out with the intention of paying my respects to Gov. Hutchinson before leaving London—met him in the Park with Mr. Flucker, and took leave; receiving copies of two letters with leave to show them to Mr. Isaac Smith, one being to himself and the other to Mr. Hollis, both from Dr. Elliott, and intercepted by Gen. Howe.

Tuesday, July 16. Left home at an early hour in the Salisbury coach. On Hounslow heath, through which we passed, three monuments of human folly and divine justice—as many gibbets with the remains of so many wretches, hanging in chains; a little beyond, a high obelisk crowned with a large gilt ball, erected by the late duke of Cumberland at his lodge in Windsor Park. On the other hand, at a distance of twenty rods from the road, another obelisk, ending in a blunt point; two miles further stands a more lofty one, scarcely finished, of four stories, illuminated by square windows, the design of the present duke. The road from Wallop to Salisbury is delightfully pleasant, and hard as a garden gravel-walk; at four miles' distance is to be seen the spire of the cathedral, supposed to be the highest in England. The land rising gradually from the plain till the sight is bounded by a ridge of high hills, from the rising filled with enclosures, rows and clumps of trees, and many farm-houses; alighted at Salisbury at seven o'clock in the evening.

Salisbury, July 17. Started for Stonehenge, a distance of eleven miles, the first five through highly cultivated grounds. At the distance of three miles from the city, on the right, is to be seen an eminence apparently of an oval figure, lying beyond the improved grounds, enclosed with hedges, etc., which seems to be raised by art, or formed into its present shape or figure, at least, by the hands and industry of man; the ascent to the plain on which its base stands is above the level of the improvements on the hither side ; it is an easy slope at an angle of 45°, and measures round one mile ; on the rim of the first slope are cornfields ; within is a slope of the same figure as the lower, rising nearly to the same height; in a plain on one side is planted a small group of trees; this spot in former days was the site of *Old Sarum*, containing about sixty acres, unless I am misinformed, without one house on it, now entitled to send two members to parliament. On the lower plain, and bordering on the slope, stands one house, where dwells a family supplying the curious who visit there with punch, wine, and tea. The view under this long range of hills presents a most pleasing and variegated prospect.

Turning out of the road over the lawn, void of trees, bushes, stones, and as even as a bowling green, we soon arrived in sight of the object of our pursuit, STONEHENGE : its first appearance resembled a company of men ; in different views it assumed very different shapes. About a mile from this place, encompassing it in a circular line, stand many of those bodies of earth called barrows or tumuli, supposed burial places of the Druids ; their form is globular, from nine to twelve feet in height, and from thirty-five to forty in diameter :—their surfaces smooth, all of the same shape, and not very different in size. I viewed them well, and remembering that they never could be counted, I nevertheless set about the task with confidence of success ;—my first enumeration was eighty, second eighty-two, third and fourth different, so that I was convinced of the difficulty of the task and gave it up—almost imagining that the Druid presiding over these sacred ruins puzzles and confounds the minds of all who make the iniquitous attempt.— The outside row of stones is an imperfect oval, eighteen in number ; those upright are about seventeen feet high and about four feet wide. Eight very large, but not of so great length, lying flatwise on the tops of the outside row—nine on the tops of those within ; fourteen small uprights stand within, in different directions or lines ; twenty-eight, perhaps more, lying out of the ground—two lying in the ground, that look as if in their natural bed. Two columns of the largest size and of an uneven surface stand upright; in one of these near the end, is a small hollow, the size and shape of what Don Quixote took for Mambrino's helmet. In the other near the ground, is a small hollow of the size

9

of a pint basin, said to have been impressed when the devil threw
the rock at the friar and struck him on the heel. Many other tra-
ditions, tales and follies are related by the credulous and superstitious vulgar about this wonderful pile. There is no appearance of
the chisel or hammer, but in two of the rocks, one very large has
on each end an excavation about fourteen inches long and about
seven deep, designed to be placed on the upright ones. The upright one, of which the former lies at its foot, has on top a circular
rising just the size of those below, and seems as if intended to be
let into the hollows to keep the arch stones and those lying on the
tops of the uprights steady and secure. And I doubt not the cross
stones lying still on the tops of the uprights are secured the same
way. This pile stands on a lofty eminence of great extent and has
on it neither tree, bush, shrub or stone within many miles on either
side, and is called " the plain of Salisbury." Thence at a distance
of seven miles, I was admitted to Lord Pembroke's seat. In the
court are fine busts and statues. The house is a noble building,
round a square; the front is a plan of Inigo Jones, looks over a
lawn, through which is a natural river improved by art; through
the lawn are interspersed clumps of trees, statues and bustos, vases
and obelisks, rendering the spot delightful beyond description.
The rooms are filled with antique statues, busts, vases, urns, sarco-
phagi without number. Among other things a *curalis sella* made
of iron and brass—the stone coffin that Terence's remains were
deposited in, and the urn that contained the ashes of Horace;—
also an exact model of the Venus of Medicis and the Apollo Belvidere;—was it not for the complaisance due the fair sex, I should
prefer the latter to the former, and believe it is to that principle
alone that antiquarians are so lavish in their praises of the goddess. On returning to Salisbury, three miles, after dinner I strolled
to the cathedral; the pulpit of stone is in the body of the church,
the reading desk is in the choir; the ceiling curious and finely
painted and gilded, laid out in compartments of many figures, with
roses, &c. in the centre. The windows filled with paintings; the
buttresses, pillars and decorations are similar to Westminster
Abbey. This cathedral is supposed to be five or six centuries old;
it stands in a place called Salisbury Close, surrounded by walls,
having three gates that are shut every night. It has privileges

distinct from the town, and is the residence of the bishop and his clergy, besides private families.

Took coach for Exeter.

July 27.   Two despatches from America on their way to London, with advices that an engagement had happened between Gen. Howe and the Americans, with a loss of 18,000 men on both sides, and so great was the carnage that one regiment had but five men left.   On inquiry I believe the account cannot be true to the extent of loss.

July 28.—*Exeter.*   It is remarkable that in many of the churches of this city are placed in compartments, or tablets against the walls in many places, collections of texts of Scripture.   It is believed that the cathedral has been standing nine hundred years, and its ancient appearance justifies it; the military garb some of the statues are dressed in is of the period of the ninth and tenth centuries.

July 30.   Attended divine service in the cathedral, to hear, as is the custom, the assize sermon preached before the judges, who were Barons Eyre and Hotham ; the preacher, a Mr. Simmons ; a sensible and serious discourse from Proverbs 14: 34, " *Righteousness exalteth a nation.*"

TO THOMAS DANFORTH, ESQ., BROMPTON-ROW, LONDON.

Exeter, July 30, 1776.

DEAR SIR :

* * * * * * * * * *

Dined at Whitchurch ; we were joined at table by five gentlemen of the turf, going to the Andover races in this vicinity : the jokes flew freely, and excited laughter among themselves and afforded me some amusement, although conceived in terms to which I was unaccustomed ;—their boisterous mirth and manners brought to my mind the descriptions to be met with in books, of gentlemen of that character, and is a proof that they have justly copied the originals.   Again we took fresh horses, and in an hour measured eight miles, passing the Earl of Portsmouth's seat, remarkable for nothing that I could see, (but yet it covers more ground than the neighboring farm houses,) lying just before we entered the Andover race grounds, an extent of two or three miles under a range of naked hills on one side, and on the other by enclosures beyond which the road runs, and on which we met and overtook multitudes of each sex, every rank and condition, dressed in their best attire, to partake of the diversions of the race; being too early, we missed a sight I would gladly have enjoyed. At a distance of three miles we descended into the town of Andover, which like the situations of most towns in England, is in a bottom, containing two hundred houses, a church and town hall, with open market under it, and adorned with a spire on the top, and a modern structure, as many of the houses are.

*   *   *   *   *   *   *   *   *   *

At the distance of eight miles from Salisbury, we passed through five or six villages of houses with mud walls and thatched roofs, such only being seen for many miles in the west. Alighted at last at the Red Lion in Salisbury, having rode eighty-three miles in fifteen hours. The houses in Salisbury are in ancient style of building, and contain five thousand inhabitants. I peeped into the cathedral during service; the worshippers were the dean, five or six ecclesiastics, eight singing boys, and eight as miserable looking wretches as ever entered the doors of a hospital; they were literally, as the gospel says of those who are called, " the blind, the halt," &c., and are hired to attend : and without this expedient I fancy the lay hearers would be as few as Dr. Swift's congregation. The ceiling is as gaudy as gold and paint can make it, and in the taste of Henry VIIth's chapel, but not open work, and by its appearance has been neglected for some centuries. In short, it looks like an old neglected military officer out of service, with his regimentals worn threadbare and soiled. Indeed the whole church is so slovenly and dirtily kept, that a stranger would judge that these stewards of the Lord's inheritance regarded the revenues more than the repairs of the mansion house. The pews or seats are in a declining, and if not soon propped up, will be in a decumbent state ;—the pulpit of stone, perhaps to denote the blockish quality of its possessors. A curious statue of St. Osmond is here, said to have been brought from old Sarum, and supposed of the eleventh or twelfth century ; but where he lived or died is not within the compass of my reading.*

* Chancellor of England and Bishop of Salisbury under William the Conqueror.

Having performed a ride of ninety miles in seventeen hours, alighted in this city of Exeter, my distance from London being one hundred and seventy-two miles. The number of inhabitants is scarcely seven-eighths as numerous as at Boston in New England ; standing on much less ground, and on an eminence in the centre of a bottom encompassed by distant high hills; on one side runs the river Exe, over it a bridge some centuries old. The streets narrow and dirty—houses of ancient style. The city is encompassed with a wall, in some places almost entire, very high, and crowned with battlements ;—perhaps more gates, gateways and arches here than in any other place in England. I was told that forty years ago there was not a coach to be seen in the city. Here are nineteen parish churches, not one with a spire, but having large towers and battlements ; and eleven meeting-houses for Presbyterians, Quakers, Methodists, Catholics, and Jews. The castle lately demolished to make room for a court-house. The cathedral front is *adorned* with sixty mutilated statues, having the appearance of a thousand years. Among the various monuments within, is one erected many ages since, to perpetuate the remembrance of an enthusiast, who died a martyr to his folly in presuming to fast in imitation of our Saviour ; being a just resemblance of a body wasted by hunger to a skeleton.

I am, with great regard,
S. CURWEN.

Exeter, August 1. Attended the assizes at the castle ; the cause before Baron Eyre was a suit of Lord Clifford, a Roman Catholic peer, against a Mr. Prode, for encroaching on the rights of his manor of Ringmoor, within which is part of the town of Teignmouth, lying on the river Tyne. Lord Clifford claimed up to high water mark, below which for 178 feet he had built and enclosed ; but on the trial Lord Clifford made an offer to compromise the claim, allowing Mr. Prode to enjoy one half his encroachment for three lives or ninety-nine years, paying yearly ten shillings, and surrendering the other half, which terms were acceded to, and the trial was quashed.

August 5. Removed to Sidmouth, a watering place, where I propose to reside some time with my friend, Rev. Isaac Smith, who officiates as minister to the dissenting congregation, partly made up of the company resorting hither for the benefit of sea-bathing and drinking the waters. I am now at Mr. Follet's.

August 12. Sidmouth consists of about a hundred houses, built of mud walls and thatched roofs, except a very few with Cornish tile and with shingles, very low, situated in a bottom or vale; the lands about are under good improvement. On each side stand two ridges of hills, ending in cliffs, the foot washed by the tide. In the town is an old church with a clock and a meeting house. The inhabitants chiefly hired out to the Newfoundland traders, and for the most part in low circumstances. The town is within the manor of Sir Wilmot Prideaux, whose ancestor having mortgaged the estate to the ancestor of a person now insane, the leases cannot be renewed, and therefore the houses are going to decay, none inclining to repair more than necessary at an uncertainty.

TO DR. CHARLES RUSSELL, ANTIGUA.

Sidmouth, August 14, 1776.

DEAR SIR :

Your letter has given me great pain ; people in similar circumstances of distress must be brutal not to feel for one another. Let us endeavor to fortify our minds against despondency ; perhaps our prospects will brighten ; if not, reason and a submissive disposition may greatly alleviate, though they cannot wholly remove the weight of trouble. I sincerely wish you and your connections a removal of the sufferings you are at present under.

You are candid enough to place my demand to the right account. I would sooner have endured hunger than needlessly add to any one's distresses, much less those for whom I am bound by many ties to promote their happiness and interest. Do not remember the demand, consult your convenience ; I have not wanted, although am reduced to a rigid economy, which you know was not my case in New England. This watering place, the resort of much genteel company for sea bathing, is the most frugal place in England ; it is in Devonshire, in the neighborhood of Exeter, and about two hundred miles from London.

Your favors, ever esteemed, I ask a continuance of, and remain, etc.   S. CURWEN.

FROM THOMAS DANFORTH.

Knightsbridge, August 18, 1776.

MY DEAR SIR :

Since the fathers fell asleep, all things continue as they were. I have received your two epistles, though the last but two or three days ago, it having lain some time at Palmer's, from whence I removed a fortnight this day to Mr. Pemberthy's in Queen's Row, six or eight houses north of Judge Sewall's, where I have very agreeable lodgings. I neglected answering particularly your first letter, expecting every day a second, and having nothing particular by way of news. I have now determined to write, news or no news, and as you know it is not against my conscience to affirm that I saw the same velvet in the loom, for the same reason I think it very innocent to make a small budget of news. You will therefore be pleased to understand and be informed, that a few days ago the Commissioners with Nathaniel Coffin, Mr. Porter, the Comptroller, the Inspector General, Col. Leonard, Mr. Barack, Mr. Mather, Mr. Faneuil, etc., etc., arrived from Halifax ; what reception they will meet with, is uncertain. You see without doubt in the papers the news from the army at Staten Island. Sheriff Loring writes Col. Hatch, that he expects to spend the winter in Roxbury, and shall clean up his house there for his place of residence.

Col. Tyng writes to Judge Sewall, that when he is settled in his house, which he proposes to take at Amboy, he shall be more particular. It seems that the accounts they have from the deserters are very encouraging ; that they are much divided upon the matter of independency. I think that the enemies of opposition to Parliament may regard the matter in that light, and appear openly ; that this will be a lucky handle, and will finally be the means of oversetting the combination. It is said that there is a large party in South Carolina, Maryland, Connecticut, and New Hampshire, in opposition ; these will assist the king's troops when they are well warmed in dispute with their brethren. It would not be strange if the rebel interest should melt like snow in a hot sun, when once it begins to fail. All but the congress have an excuse for revolting, and think that they save their honor. Thousands will revolt from them upon a specious pretence, who never would if such could not be found.   You have seen in the papers an account of the Yankee privateer brought into the river; one Johnston of Boston, is master, and Downer of Roxbury, surgeon.   The prisoners are now on board of a 74 gun ship at Sheerness.   They give a more favorable account of the situation of the friends of government than we have before had, but some allowances must be made.   Daniel Bliss writes from Quebec, that they have reason to think that above a thousand men about Albany are ready to join Gen. Burgoyne; he makes the loss of the rebels in that expedition to be 2000 men, killed, prisoners, and by sickness, upon a moderate computation. The 400 men, inhabitants of Staten Island, with others as they come in, are put under command of Gen. Ruggles, who is to keep possession of the island.   I am much obliged by your agreeable account of your journey, but an account of your journey to London again will be more agreeable, which I hope will be soon.   Our friend Bourne is gone into the country, so that I am at some loss to give you so particular an account of the lottery as I could wish.   There is much about Molesworth's Plan in the Ledger of this day.   I shall examine it, and if it does not contain the whole matter, will insert the remainder before I close this letter.   Bourne said that he discouraged him from purchasing chances.   Brattle, Boylston, etc., have returned from France.   I have heard nothing farther of Porter.   Treasurer Gray, Abel Willard of Lancaster, and I, have just come from Salters' Hall meeting-house, where we heard a Mr. Pickard of Carter-street, near St. Paul's.   Being down in the city, I took up Molesworth's publication, and found it to be the same with what is contained in the Ledger.   I see that there is an order in the papers for all the militia of New-York to be in readiness to march.   There will probably be warm work.   I find that you give no account of your situation in your letter.   I suppose you have found the diamond mine, and choose to engross the whole profits.   I have paid Col. Pickman as you desired,—he made no observations.   Mrs. Bray did not know how to direct me to pay for the wine and ale, so that remains as it was.   I should copy all your excuses for your letter, were it not that I suppose they are fresh in your memory.   I hate both writing fairly and copying my own letters particularly.   I think I have covered the

same quantity of paper, and have therefore a right to close. To
conclude therefore, please remember me to the Doctor. Salute
Priscilla and Aquila, and all the pretty girls who are in Exon.
Your very humble servant,
THOS. DANFORTH.

TO REV. ISAAC SMITH, SIDMOUTH.

Bristol, August 24, 1776.

DEAR SIR:

The regret with which I left Sidmouth was in some measure
balanced by the agreeableness of the day. To pass by our first
stage, the least amusing, our second to moisten our driver and
horses, for both often want watering, was on the borders of Blackdown at a place called Southhast, and at " *the sine of George Inn,
heer all sorts of leckers are sold ;*" besides the peculiar taste of the
painter in spelling, the letters were of so doubtful a form that my
fellow traveller, Mr. Davis, chose to read " *leckys,*" which word,
(if to be found in the Devonshire nomenclature I am ignorant of
its meaning,) he, being skilled in provincial dialects, may be acquainted with. Our third stage was at the Castle inn, Taunton ;
on our way hither we saw a hill called *Quantook*, so like our
Indian names I could not help remarking it. After a small
delay we proceeded to Hillbishop, and dined at the hospitable table
of Mr. Jirrald ;* his good husbandry is fully repaid by a plentiful
harvest of apricots, nectarines and apples ; nor is his table without
the best cider England affords, which is scarcely equalled by the
most sparkling champagne. Our next stage was at Bridgewater ;
from the inn we walked to Miss Sealy's garden, planned to promote the wise purposes of thought and meditation. Here we re-
galed ourselves with green gages and gooseberries, the boughs
being loaded. At the bottom of the garden is a small piece of
water, filled with large carp, brought to the surface by pieces of
bread thrown in, which they rose to catch, a pleasing sight I never
before had. Our next stage was eighteen miles to Cross, where
we were told the beds were full, and they had no horses ; so we

---

* A dissenting minister.

could not pass the night nor be carried further :—however, we met
a friendly stranger in Mr. Cornelius Frye, of Bristol, who gave up
his room.   Here we supped all together and passed our time so-
ciably, talking treason and justifying American independence.
Next morning we left at seven, and passing Clifton on the left
covered with excellent improvements, arrived at Bristol, the Bush
inn opposite the Exchange.

Yours truly,

S. CURWEN.

Bristol, August 24.   Called at Mr. Waldo's; he being absent,
I left a card.   Soon after he came and carried me to his house to
dinner, in company with John Boylston and Mr. Browne;—after
dinner walked over Kingsdown Hill to the Hot Wells on the
banks of the Avon, where I took a glass of the water and returned
to the inn.   Soon after left for Birmingham, through Newport,
Gloucester, and Upton, which latter reminded me of the incident of
the amiable Sophia Western's muff, which Tom Jones picked up in
his own bed.   There are many originals of Squire Western, but I
am told Mr. Allen, late of Bath, was the character from which
Mr. Allworthy was drawn.   Hence to Worcester, a handsome town,
wide streets, a fine cathedral in good repair, but not abounding in
funeral monuments.   At last we arrived at Birmingham, which, in
its general appearance, looks more like Boston than any place in
England.

Birmingham, August 26.   Hearing that Judge Oliver and Mr.
Lloyd were in town, I repaired to the inn, but they had departed.
I met them soon after as they were leaving town for London *via*
Woodstock, and gave a letter to Mr. Danforth.

August 28.   Walked out and met a Quaker at the door of his
house, near the outskirts of the town, on the Litchfield road, commanding an agreeable prospect bounded by distant hills in an am-
phitheatric line; engaged him in conversation, and by invitation
went in for half an hour; found him a sensible man and a *warm
American*, as most of the middling classes are through the kingdom, as far as my experience reaches.   Beyond the Tweed, I know
not; however, the Scotch within, to my knowledge are antiministe-
rialists.   Passed an agreeable day at Mr. Russell's, two miles out of

town; he is of the house of Smith, Son & Russell, who ship largely to New-York and Boston. He has been in America, and is her steady and ardent advocate.

August 31. Stepped to a gun-maker's to see a rifle, (the first I ever saw,) and many other pieces of peculiar construction I was a stranger to; the master is to make six hundred rifles for government, but is in principle an antiministerialist, as is the whole town.

Sept. 6. Sir William Meredith the other day declared at Matlock, that he looked on the violent measures against America to be very impolitic, and that Lord North was of the same mind, and only joined out of respect for the king, who was warm and determined to pursue such at all events, even though with the loss of a hundred thousand men. It will be well if a pertinacious adherence to a certain plan of conduct respecting that unhappy country be not productive of evil fruits to the interests of the king and empire. May it please God to infuse wisdom, prudence, and moderation into the breasts of those on whose counsels the fate of both depend.

Sept. 9. A letter in the London Chronicle, said to have been brought by the Isabella, an advice-boat from Quebec, relates a defeat of the provincials before Crown Point, with the loss of eight hundred killed, eight hundred wounded, and four hundred taken prisoners; and that the garrison is in Gen. Carleton's hands, said to have been obtained July 23d; a story well told, but which wants proof.

Sept. 10. Was told as we passed Castle inn, that Lord North was momently expected there from Sandwell, the Earl of Dartmouth's seat.

Sept. 11. Took coach for Bristol by the way of Tewksbury; met an officer who gave himself great liberties respecting America, to which I took the freedom of giving several severe checks, and my companion spared not till he was thoroughly silenced and humbled; he said many ungenerous, foolish and false things, and I did not forbear telling him so.

Sept. 16. At 11 o'clock P. M. departed from Birmingham for Bristol; at Worcester took a relay of horses, and arrived at Tewksbury at breakfast; went to the church, almost the magnitude of a cathedral, which contains many curiosities; in a flat grave just before the choir is buried Prince Henry, son of Margaret of

Anjou, widow of the unfortunate King Henry VI., who was slain by Richard, Duke of Gloucester, after the defeat of the Queen at " the battle of the bloody meadow," so called from the tradition that it overflowed with the blood of the slain on that occasion. Here is, also, in a kneeling posture, a statue of George, Duke of Clarence, who is said to have been drowned in a butt of malmsey : —Richard, Earl of Warwick, the king-maker :—Osrick, a king of Northumberland, who founded a church on the spot where this church stands. In two hours after leaving this place we arrived at Gloucester, and in the cathedral saw among many monuments that of the unfortunate King Edward II., who was murdered at Berkeley Castle. Here also lies another unfortunate prince, Robert, Duke of Normandy, whose younger brother, William Rufus, seized the crown of England during his absence on a visit to the Holy Land ; he was imprisoned many years in the Castle of Cardiff.— Over his grave is a statue in a decumbent posture, made of Irish oak, which, when struck, sounds as if of metal. This cathedral is kept in fine order ; has a vaulted choir, and the most elegant cloisters of any in England. Arrived at Bristol at 8 o'clock evening.

Bristol, Sept. 18. To Ratcliff church, supposed to be the first in point of elegance and magnitude of all the parish churches in England. It has not in its construction one nail or piece of iron, being built and supported by stone and marble only. It consists of three aisles, besides two projections which give it the form of a cross ;—in one stands a great font, and in the other several funeral monuments. Over the altar are placed three masterly paintings by Hogarth, on the subject of the burial, resurrection, and ascension ; for which he received a thousand pounds.

In this church lies buried Admiral Penn, with an inscription recounting his exploits on a pillar ; and suspended on the same pillar below are his military garb, sword, cuirass, helmet, gloves, etc. This gentleman's services were rewarded by the royal grant of Pennsylvania to his son William Penn, the founder of that province.

Took tea and passed the evening with Mr. Eveleigh, a native of Charleston, South Carolina; educated at Harvard College, three or four years after me, who on hearing my name recollected it, having been schooled at Cambridge under Master Coolidge and

boarded at the President's house.   He and his family are hearty in
the cause of America.

Sept. 19.   Accompanied Mr. Bourne, one of my countrymen,
to the crown-glass manufactory, where the whole process was
shown.—On 'change met my countryman Mr. Joseph Waldo,
who procured tickets for our admission to Mr. Gouldney's grotto at
Clifton, with whom, Francis Waldo, and Capt. Aldredge, (brother
of the late Col. Bradstreet's lady, and born in Nova Scotia,) we
proceeded over Brandon hill, the summit whereof yields the most
ravishing view that imagination can form, having a large portion
of the city under foot; and a finely cultivated country for an
amazing extent has the appearance of a continued village, interspersed with towns and seats; the prospect enlivened with live
hedges, lofty trees, Dumday tower, Kingwood, and the river Avon,
running through the city and joined with another called the Frome,
over both which are bridges; on the latter are the larger ships,
and on the former only smaller craft.   Just as we arrived at the
gates, there passed by in his solitary walk, whom accident threw
in our way, a countryman, Mr. Harrison Gray, son of our late
(Massachusetts) treasurer, who, with his wife, had for a season left
London and retired to this place, and whom I was glad to see.
Parting at the gate, we were soon admitted, and, attended by the
gardener, were conducted through the gravel-walks, kept in the
nicest order, the whole bearing the appearance of care and industry; it is on a moderate scale, but well filled with orange and
lemon trees, etc., and a small piece of water abounding in gold and
silver fish, supplied from a natural fountain so lofty that a fire-
engine is erected at one end of the terrace; the stream runs under
ground for a distance and discharges itself through an urn, on which
a Neptune rests with his trident.   The ground between it and the
engine is made rough, scraggy, and woody, to resemble a wilderness, which I passed going through the main walk.   We arrived
at the door of the grotto, situated under the terrace; the object
that presented itself to our view was a lion in a sitting posture,
and behind, in a dark cave, a lioness, the latter so like life that I
could hardly persuade myself to the contrary.   The form of the
grotto is octangular, its roof a semicircle, having a dome with a
round window in the centre; the diameter about twenty feet on each

side, from the door in front to the mouth of the cave in which the
lioness is sitting ; to the right and left of the entrance the roof is
supported by pillars ; covered as its roof and sides are with a variety of shells, stones, spars, petrifactions, etc., the mountains, even
the bowels of the earth and the bottom of the sea, seem to have
been pillaged to furnish materials to adorn this curious subterraneous recess.　On the left hand, beyond the dome and under a rough,
cragged stone arch, is a small quadrangular stone basin of water
supplied by small streams, issuing through almost imperceptible
channels, over which, in a lying posture, is a female deity.　On
the other hand stands a door, the light and shade of which is so
artfully painted that it deceived the company, who thought it a
passage into the garden on a flight of stairs ; the most perfect de-
ception I ever saw.　On the door was a miniature of a female face
with a seemingly broken glass covering it, in the same style and
manner, and producing the like effect.　From hence we ascended
the terrace-walk four hundred feet in length, the front of the garden raised forty feet supported by a brick wall ; the rear bounded
by a border of flowers, and behind a shrubbery of lofty trees.　On
the right is an octangular structure ending in a dome eighteen feet
in diameter, with seats all round, and having as many windows as
it has sides, which affords as many prospects, except on the side of
the garden, where they are darkened, yielding three delightful
perspectives.

Leaving this charming spot and Clifton, I bade adieu to my
companions, and after dinner I departed for Shepton-Mallet, and
on my arrival met my friend and countryman Mr. Isaac Smith ;
thus ends my ramble for a few weeks.

Shepton Mallet, Sept. 20.　Walked to the market-cross, an open
structure supported by Gothic arches and pillars, and ornamented
in front by a few mutilated statues, but whether of saints or heroes
of antiquity, I know not.　A few gentlemen of fortune live here,
but many worthy clothiers ; there are two places of worship, an
Episcopal and a Presbyterian, and the number of inhabitants is said
to be seven thousand.　A Mr. Ames with whom I am acquainted
lives here on his six hundred a year.

Sept. 23.　Rode through Lord Ilchester's park, passing by
the late Lord Berkeley's estate, and through a vale to Lord Arun-

dle's. One passes on a flight of noble steps to the centre door letting into the hall;—the walls are adorned with paintings of the most celebrated artists. There is a cabinet of Pope Sixtus Quintus, which stands on a mahogany frame;—the front is of ebony; and amber pillars, set with sapphires, emeralds and other precious stones, and miniatures of all the Perotti family from which he sprang, and elegantly executed in white alabaster. In the drawers are prints of the principal royal and noble families of Europe in metal frames.

In these grounds is an airy cross, bought of the city of Bristol and transported here; in the Gothic style, four stories; in each are four niches filled with kings in their regalia, supposed to have been benefactors to the city; the names in part are, Henry VI., Edward IV., John, Charles I. and II. and Queen Elizabeth. It is finely decorated, and in the highest preservation.

Procured a guide to attend us to Alfred's Tower, which we intended to visit before taking leave of Stourton. We soon arrived at Inson Hill on whose summit stands the tower, and which is said to be the spot on which Alfred erected his standard against the Danes; mostly a terraced walk. The tower an open triangular structure, the angles covered by round towers; in one is a flight of 221 steps making 155 in height; on this is a sound balcony of 20 feet high, on the top a kind of cross standing on a globe. The entrance into it is through a Gothic arched door—ten feet above is a stone niche under a finely ornamented arch. In the centre is a Saxon crown supported by double Gothic pillars; on each side stands the statue of Alfred in military habiliments and larger than life, holding a sceptre in his right hand, his left resting on a sword.— Below is a tablet, on which is the following :

IN MEMORY OF

ALFRED THE GREAT,

WHO ON THIS SUMMIT ERECTED HIS STANDARD AGAINST DANISH INVADERS.

HE INSTITUTED JURIES, ESTABLISHED A MILITIA,

CREATED AND EXERTED A NAVAL FORCE;

A PHILOSOPHER AND A CHRISTIAN ;

THE FATHER OF HIS PEOPLE,

THE FOUNDER OF THE ENGLISH MONARCHY AND

LIBERTY.

Leaving this grateful monument, dedicated to the memory of the most deserving monarch England ever saw, I returned home.

Sept. 25.   To the Poor House to see the *spinning-jennies*, which of late through the folly and madness of the spinners and weavers have been the occasion of a riot in this town, which a party of dragoons were called in to quell, who are yet continued to prevent future ones; three were killed and a number wounded, and but for the government orders to avoid bloodshed, more would have been.   These machines are to twist the threads after the first course run from the common wheels, which despatch about three or four times as fast as by hand in the customary way.   They have been in use some years in the north, and a premium obtained for them from the Society of Arts and Sciences.   They contain thirty-six spindles turned by a common axis, communicating with a wheel placed horizontally.

Sept. 28.   Walked with Mr. Morgan over the hills to the remains of a Roman-way ; the ditch continues, although in an imperfect state, and carried over Mendip hill, running from north to south, and from shore to shore.

CHAPTER III.

Shepton Mallet, Oct. 1. Rode to Bath ;—large meeting of clothiers from neighboring towns in Somerset and Wiltshire, to concert
measures to establish, if practicable, the use of the spinning-jenny in
these parts, which the weavers raised a mob to prevent. Two companies of dragoons are posted in this town for security of the
manufacturers, against the infatuated multitude. Met Col. Saltonstall, who with Mr. Boylston has taken lodgings here for some
time past. Departed for Lord Weymouth's seat, called Longleat ;
his grounds contain the whole parish of Horningsham. Over the
entrance in front is the date as follows : —" *Erected by Sir John
Thynne,* 1569." The front is an addition to the old structure, the
remains of a Carthusian monastery standing round a large square
court. Within are pictures of Henry VIII., Sir Thomas Overbury,
Lord Strafford, beheaded in the time of Charles I.,—Henry IV. of
France,—Charles I. when Prince of Wales, and his brother James
II. when Duke of York, General Monck,—Charles II. and his
Queen, Archbishop Juxton,—Mary Queen of Scotts, Robert Dudley
Earl of Leicester, Lady Nottingham,—Archbishop Laud, Cardinal
Richelieu,—Sir Thomas Graham,—Count Tekeli and lady.

Oct. 11. Visited Glastonbury Abbey ruins, attended by a guide
named Thomas, who is as great a curiosity as the ruins ; for we
had no sooner entered on the holy ground than he doffed his beaver and hugged it under his arm, while with a solemn tone and
manner indicative of unshaken faith in the legendary tales which
the folly of credulity and superstition have handed down, by oral
tradition as well as books, through a long succession of ages, he
began by informing us of some circumstances relative to a chapel
standing entire, which I had no wish to enter, nor do I remember
the tale. Proceeding on we approached the walls of the chapel
in ruins, but not to prevent a perfect idea of the size ;—making a
sudden stop, our guide told us with a solemn voice that the ground

11

we stood on was twenty-two feet above the natural surface, raised by the rubbish from the monastery; which, if true, is a proof of the immensity of the building, and the uncommon thickness of its walls, the site of which covers fifteen to twenty acres. Descending to the lower chapel, at present filled with dirt to the capitals of the pillars, eight feet, this he told us was the spot where Joseph of Arimathea built a chapel of hurdles and boughs of trees, twenty-three years after the crucifixion. In the upper chapel remain the niches and pedestals on which stood the images of saints of solid gold.

After hearing many tedious stories and incredibilities, we proceeded to survey the outside, dormitory, chapter-house, etc. In the centre of the east end stood the chapel of the first Saxon Christian king of this island;—from whence through the ruins, at a considerable distance, is to be seen the further or western end of the double chapel we first entered; both side walls are standing up to the roof, and part of the eastern wall, under an arch of eighty feet in height, and fifty in width, entire all but the crown. The sight of this brought to my mind the magnificent ruins of Palmyra, although its ornaments were not of such exquisite workmanship; these being Gothic, but highly finished. Near an angle at the eastern end stands a small room; lately this was turned into a cow-house, but not one of the brutal intruders survived a year, as the guide informed us of his own certain knowledge.

Within this holy ground is the holy thorn-tree. I had liberty to pluck a branch, proposing to preserve it till my arrival in America, (if it shall please God to grant me that favor.) The three trees now standing blossom yearly within the Christian holy-days, which it is the peculiar quality of this species to do, without supposing a miracle; but the craft of these reverend impostors knew very well how to turn a natural event into something miraculous, and the superstitious folly and ignorance of the multitude for a long course of ages has confirmed them in the same groundless notions.

We arrived soon at a pleasant road, having in view extensive prospects of waste lands, called moors; ascending a lofty ridge on the left, lay that called King's Sedgemoor, remarkable for the defeat of the Duke of Monmouth by his uncle, King James the Second.

From hence, on one of these hills, is to be seen the obelisk erected to the memory of the late Sir William Pynsent by the Earl of Chatham; a cheap purchase of an estate of eighty thousand pounds, besides ten thousand in money, left to a man the testator never saw. The stage from Glastonbury to Bridgewater throughout extremely pleasant; the distance of fifteen miles we passed in an hour and a half; thence to Enmore Castle about four miles, a seat of the Earl of Egmont, which is built in the form of the ancient baronial castles. Leaving this imitation of old English architecture, we rode to Castle inn, Taunton, where we lodged: next day to Sidmouth.

Sidmouth, Oct. 13. Attended worship at my friend Mr. Isaac Smith's, who preached from these words, " *The Lord is my portion,*" which was the last sermon he preached in America: the congregation the largest I had known since my residence here.

Oct. 17. Rode to Slade, the seat of a Mr. Lee, one of Mr. Smith's hearers, who purchased of the father of the famous Dr. Shebbeare, one of the writers for the court against America. Took a stroll to the cliffs on the seaside, yielding a delightful prospect.

Oct. 18. Rode out to view an ancient encampment, supposed Danish, and is called Hembury, about fourteen miles. Fording the gentle stream of Syd, we pursued our course over Cove Hill, so called, being a lofty range, affording on each side very pleasant views of a finely improved country; here we met a number of huntsmen on foot, with their long poles and a great number of dogs, at default, unable to recover the track of the hare, which had found means to elude the dogs' scent. A little beyond the village of Burcherton is the seat of the well-known Admiral Graves, whose base, unworthy conduct in America has justly brought the curses of the people on his head, displeased his sovereign and the ministry, and rendered himself deservedly the contempt of all. His house is at the foot of the hill on which Hembury fort stands. This fort is situated on the extremity of a lofty ridge of hills, in a parish of the same name, four miles north of Honiton, and is supposed to have been a Danish encampment, (formed in one of their incursions, about a thousand years ago,) from its roundish form, the Roman being all angular; there are many such in these parts, though few so entire. Its form is a very long oval; and measures, from the low parapet or line of raised earth on the northeasterly quarter at its further end, to the edge or brow of the ditch at the southwesterly, (in which direction it runs exclusive of the ditches athwart the hill, to defend or secure the centre enclosure,) about a thousand feet; and the width of the hill on its summit on which the encampment stands, with the middle included, is about a hundred feet. It stands very high, and commands a view of the vales on each side to a great extent. From the foot of the hill in front, for a considerable distance on either side, it is of a quick ascent; but from the foot of the hill in front there is an easy slope, as regular as a glacis, although of ten times its length and breadth; the rest of this long range, in a circular form, rises from the plains below as far as the eye can discern, regularly and sudden, rendering the approach difficult, except from the summit, which is continued to a great extent. There are three fosses carried nine feet round the encampment, the last deeper and wider than the rest; the slope is about sixty feet. The earth wall, if it may be so called, contains fifteen to twenty acres. Here may be traced the foundations of one or two buildings, which spot I presume was the officers' tents, the place of arms and magazine. The avenue on the south side, for there is but one, communicates with a walk running the whole width of the hill, and is bounded by a parapet of raised earth, at twenty feet from the entrance into the middle inclosure; between this and the brow of the hill at the southwest, is, I suppose, the encampment of the army, and here may be seen the effects of labor; but what were the works, enough does not remain to enable us to judge. Having surveyed these remains of ancient military defence, we descended by the common road, and arrived at home in about three hours.

Oct. 20. Mr. Samuel Follett drank tea with us; he is an old Newfoundland trader, was in New England in 1726, and built a ship at Charlestown.

Exeter, Oct. 26. In the Bristol Gazette is the following: "Gen. Howe had landed the British army on the island of New-York on the 15th September; the provincials had fled from the city, with great precipitation and much loss, towards Kingsbridge, where they were entrenched to the number of twenty thousand. Gen. Howe, having taken possession of New-York, was encamped with his army of twenty-two thousand within cannon-shot of the

Americans, and it was hourly expected he would make a grand attack upon them." This intelligence came by the Hanover Planter to Bristol, who spoke with the Galatea, Capt. Jordan, who left New-York the 17th of September. The unaccountable story of abandoning New-York, without a formal attack made on it, needs explanation; no doubt there were justifiable reasons for it.

Oct. 29. A busy week here, many persons daily arriving from all quarters, at the instance and charge of the competitors Baring and Cholwich, who are up for the representation of this city in parliament in room of Mr. Waters. The hands of the city officers are fully occupied in making out freedoms to those who have a right to it. The dispute runs high, " *Cholwich forever*" momently bawled; " *Baring*" not so often, though many think he may carry his election; papers are printed and public houses kept open by both, at great expense. The joke would be complete should an unthought-of rival step in and succeed.

Oct. 30. Rode out to Lord Courtnay's Belvidere, (about seven miles,) a triangular structure of Portland stone; from the top is an extensive prospect, having on one side Exeter, Topsham, and several seats; on the other, Lympstone, Exmouth, Star Cross, Lord Courtnay's seat, Gov. Pawke's, a nabob late of Madras, the river Exe from near its mouth, and vessels in the channel, and, what is more curious, the house wherein the great Sir Francis Drake was born and lived, situated on the other side of the river, opposite the Belvidere.

Oct. 31. Mr. Shepard tells me there is great danger of a French war; may the nation be preserved from this dreadful calamity.

TO THE HON. JUDGE SEWALL, BROMPTON-ROW, LONDON.

Exeter, Oct. 31, 1776.

DEAR SIR :

By a letter from Mr. Danforth I was informed some of my countrymen were about to apply to the administration for relief.— As my residence has been much longer than the most, and the suddenness of my departure from home rendering it morally impossible for me to become possessed of much money, and my pretensions, for aught I know, being as good as any and better than many, I presume I shall not be the only exile left in a forlorn condition if any provision be made ; and if never made, forlorn I shall truly be, my finances every day very sensibly lessening. Had I received Mr. Deberdt's letter in time I should have returned to London, but it was otherwise ; and if my presence now can be dispensed with, it will be more agreeable, as I live pleasantly enough among a few acquaintances, at the rate of twenty guineas a year, in a state of rigid economy that I never before was reduced to the necessity of putting in practice.

In my answer to Mr. Deberdt, I referred him to you, whose friendship on this occasion I doubted not, nor need I now repeat my request of your assistance if that shall be necessary.

With great regard, etc.

S. Curwen.

Nov. 1.   I was informed that a messenger from General Howe had just passed through the city, with advice that the provincial entrenchments, containing nine thousand men from New-York, were forced, General Washington wounded and taken, and ten thousand men on both sides killed ; some other circumstances are brought, but not to be divulged till six hours after the messenger's departure from Exeter.   Should this news prove true, I wish it may not puff the British general with pride, and fill him with false notions of the unequalled prowess and invincibility of the British troops, nor indispose him to offer moderate terms ; and I trust congress may be willing to prevent further effusion of blood and destruction of property by hearkening to reasonable proposals, which 1 hope the House have authority to make.

Nov. 2.   It is obvious the government is apprehensive of a rupture, saying, " it is expedient we should be in a respectable state of defence."   The truth is there have been some discouraging accounts from France for this week past, respecting the intentions of that court to assist the colonies, and advices from Spain say their ports are declared open to the English colonists ; upon these events press-warrants are dispersed through this kingdom, and eight hundred were taken on the Thames in one day into the service, and five pounds per man are offered for able-bodied sailors.   The report of yesterday is contradicted in part ; Gen. Washington is not taken, but six thousand Americans, and but two thousand

British. This wants confirmation. It is also added that part of the provincials only were engaged—a lame account. The fears of some and the hopes of others dispose the people to the belief of any improbabilities, nay, self-evident falsehoods.

Nov. 6.   The important day has at length arrived, the election of a member to parliament; the city alive, except myself, who am dead to curiosity.   Interest and the hope of victory have inspired all here with ardor.   It is amusing to see how warmly their passions are engaged.

Read Sharp's Travels in Italy; entertaining enough; his style not above mediocrity; his picture of the country, if just, must render his own more dear to those who know how to make a just estimate of all the valuable enjoyments of life.   In reading the above I learn that in the state of Florence are nearly twenty-seven thousand of the holy order, or if you please, the ecclesiastical troops are under a solemn vow of obedience to a foreign potentate; these with their connections, relations and dependencies, render the authority of the civil power extremely precarious in case they unite with a discontented party.

Amongst other instances of management in electioneering, is the practice of closeting and locking up, beds being provided in secure apartments to prevent the voters being spirited away to the other side, of which there have been some instances, after the expense of fetching them in from distant parts.—To prevent confusion and injustice, in the present election it is agreed to vote by tallies, that is, each candidate to present by turns a certain number, say ten or twenty.   The majority of the city chamber is for Cholwich; the church for Baring, whose managers are the most opulent, active and knowing : the contest fierce, some wounds and broken heads, but no deaths ; enough to convince me of the deplorable venality of the nation, and the high expectations derivable from a seat in that assembly of untutored, inexperienced youths, (for half, I believe, have not seen thirty,) called the Parliament of Great Britain, or the great council of the nation.   The number of voters in this city is about fourteen hundred ; and I am told two hundred of the most solid, judicious and prudent, thinking neither of the candidates suitable, decline any concern, it being immaterial to them whether Baring or Cholwich be the tool of administration.

The charge on each side, five thousand pounds, is doubtless intend-ed to be reimbursed from the national fund, for (not their services but) their votes! Would to God this great source of ministerial power and influence, and the increasing cause of our public evils, the national debt, was reduced to a moderate sum: a sponge is dreadful in thought, and would be the ruin of some millions of in-nocent widows and orphans; may that be prevented by a wise and prudent expedient, if within the compass of human knowledge and power. May a public and disinterested spirit spring up and yet be the stability of our times.

Nov. 8. By the Gazette the wonderful account brought from America is, as usual, greatly diminished respecting the valor and bravery of one side, number of slain, etc. on the other; 6000 provincials and 2000 regulars are reduced to 400 provincials and 15 regulars!! However, by the same intelligence, it seems one quarter of New-York is burnt, and some lurkers menace the de-struction of the whole city, to prevent which Gen. Howe is using assiduous endeavors to discover these incendiaries and prevent the intended conflagration.

Nov. 9. Walked out to the Guildhall to see the conclusion of the poll ended by the sheriff's declaring Mr. Baring duly elected, the excess being one hundred and one votes. The unsuccessful candidate, Mr. Cholwich, supported by the city chamber, went home to put as good a face on their disappointment as they could, amidst loud huzzas, flags displayed, having various devices, of which two were as follows:—the one divided into four compart-ments, between each half the word "*Cholwich*," and in the com-partments "*no bribery;*" the other was the coat armor of his father-in-law, (that is to be,) Sir John Duntze, properly embla-zoned, and in a scroll underneath these words, "*free and indepen-dent.*" Mr. Baring, as is usual, was accompanied by a numerous crowd, said to be ten thousand, huzzaing, clapping hands, etc. The house he adjourned to was in the yard next to ours, and to honor him variegated lamps were suspended in front, forming these words, "*Baring forever*," surmounted by a crown. The evening closed with a grand display of fireworks.

Nov. 11. Mr. Baring's friends wear favors of blue and purple ribbons, and some ladies wear an emblematical device in allusion to the successful candidate's name, *being a bear with a ring in his nose*, enamelled pendant on a blue ribbon. The day was ushered in by music and a procession, with flags inscribed " *Baring and Trade.*" The inhabitants of this city appear proud, unsocial and solitary, neither conversible nor hospitable ; but a few unceremonious, hearty friends will render any place tolerable, and such for that reason is this city for the present.

Nov. 26. A report prevails that Gen. Burgoyne has destroyed all the provincial forces on the lake.

The later advice is, that Gen. Burgoyne became master of the lake by taking, burning and destroying the naval force on the 12th ult.

Dec. 3. This day is published a single sheet letter from a master of a transport, giving account of the defeat of provincials at Kingsbridge by Gen. Howe, having forced the entrenchments, killing, wounding and taking eight thousand with a loss of two thousand only, on the 17th October ; the remainder supposed to be fled to Philadelphia.

Sunday, Dec. 8. Mr. Towgood preached an excellent discourse, from Isaiah lvii. 15. In his prayer the most just and proper expression for the king and royal family, and all in authority, both as ministers of state and executive officers ; and although a warm and hearty advocate for America, and her claims of exemption from British legislation, right of taxation, yet moderate and dutiful enough for me, who am far removed from wishing its entire independence ; for it is my firm belief it would sooner bring on oppression and tyranny there than the former right allowed in its full extent. May it please God to prevent both ; may the unreasonable and baneful wishes and attempts of all violent men be disappointed.

Dec. 13. The state fast, appointed by the king's proclamation, on account of the American war ; Bishop Keppel preached from Deut. xxxiii. 27, " The eternal God is thy refuge," etc., a seasonable and candid discourse ; he calls this " *a civil war*," and the Americans " *our unhappy fellow-subjects :*" attempted no justification of the measures of government. I was pleased with his candor and judgment.

Dec. 18. By a Mr. Lloyd of the 20th regiment, just arrived in

12

the *Lord Howe* frigate from Quebec, and who was on the lake with Burgoyne and Carleton, a report is brought that a merchant-man met the *Active* frigate at sea, and learned that Gen. Wash-ington had abandoned the lines at Kingsbridge, left his cannon and stores, and that his army is mouldered away; that New-York, New-Jersey, Pennsylvania and Maryland have deserted the union, and declared for government; speaks of the Yankees, as he is pleased to call them, in the most contemptuous terms, as cowards, poltroons, cruel, and possessing every bad quality the depraved heart can be cursed with; and says the regulars at Trois-Rivieres took five hundred prisoners, killed one hundred, and lost only three men, who were killed by Yankees, who had got upon trees and fired down on them.

It is my earnest wish the despised Americans may convince these conceited islanders, that without regular standing armies our conti-nent can furnish brave soldiers and judicious and expert command-ers, by some knock-down, irrefragable argument; for then, and not till then, may we expect generous or fair treatment. It piques my pride, I confess, to hear us called "*our colonies, our plantations,*" in such terms and with such airs as if our property and persons were absolutely theirs, like the "villains" and their cottages in the old feudal system, so long since abolished, though the spirit or leaven is not totally gone, it seems.

TO MR. GEORGE RUSSELL, AT MOSELEY WAKE GREEN,
NEAR BIRMINGHAM.

Exeter, December, 20, 1776.

DEAR SIR:

I have delayed answering you till this time from an hourly ex-pectation of hearing some important advices from New-York; but in this I have been hitherto mistaken, the season having too far advanced to expect any military achievements by the British forces, and the Americans you know have formed no active plan of opera-tion by land; confining their views of activity to the depredatory naval department. As to a treaty, I am without the smallest hopes of its taking place at present; the Americans do not despair of maintaining their independence, and the court, I am told, has not given up its view of laying America at its feet, for such is and has

been the court language, and the intention to force her to submit
to the unconditional authority of parliament ;—however, should
Gen. Washington be beaten out of his entrenchments, it would be
but one advantage out of a score that must be gained to make
them "lower their topsails." The Americans are not without
resources, whatever may be thought on that subject in England.

Among others France and Spain are no idle lookers on ; resentment as well as political reasons influence them to keep the tram-
mels on the neck of our court till a favorable opportunity may
offer to strike a blow which shall effectually humble the pride of
Great Britain, perhaps destroy her independence, or at best reduce
her to a state of as little importance in the grand political balance
of Europe as Portugal or Genoa now holds ; and that is the general
opinion here whatever may be the opinion elsewhere. As to the
objects of the impolicy of our court, we know from history that
statesmen to gain a present purpose sometimes disregard the true
interests and honor of the nation and all distant consequences.
The King of Spain is England's avowed enemy ; the court owes
this country a grudge for her success against her commerce and
garrisons last war ; nor does France love her better ; and ever since
her open opposition to the ambitious views of that court in the
beginning of Louis XIVth's reign, who aimed at universal empire,
has looked on her rising greatness with a jealous, not to say
envious eye. It is no proof of want of bravery in the Americans
not to face the regulars ; many good reasons may be assigned to
justify their conduct, and though it be the ground of much reproach
here, I see in it the effect of sound judgment—that little dependence can be placed on newly raised troops is well known the world
over. On account of the amazing expense with which Great
Britain carries on a land war in America, unless she can command
the troops of Europe and the wealth of the Indies, men and money
must in a few campaigns be wanting ; with regard to the insidious
offers made to America, as the warm partisans against the court
call them, I pretend not to such acquaintance with court measures
to determine about it ; if they be so, the greater is the pity. They
may however, if that should be the case, be taken in the snares
laid for others, and if good be derived from evil, thanks to an overruling Providence, who sometimes makes itself subservient to the

happiness of society. That more treasure must be consumed and more blood spilled before this impolitic, destructive and fatal war is ended, will, I trust, not prove a melancholy truth.

The accounts of the burning of the city of New-York in the Gazette, are full, explicit and intelligible; more than one fourth is destroyed, beginning at the fort and all along the Broadway, taking in the college, etc.; and that it was fired by some northern man, is undoubted. A Mr. Smith, son of a clergyman of Weymouth in Massachusetts Bay, whom and whose family I knew very well, was concerned, taken, and I believe executed on due proof.

I remain, truly yours,

S. CURWEN.

Exeter, Dec. 21. I am informed that by a letter from an officer of character, Arnold and the provincials are represented as behaving with great intrepidity and good conduct; and their defeat was owing to the superior weight of metal on the side of their enemies. I am rejoiced to find justice done my countrymen, and that there are those who can look through the vista of party, see truth and speak it. The news of the defeat of General Washington at Kingsbridge is confirmed.

Dec. 22. The above defeat is not very important, save the loss of cannon; few prisoners taken, fewer killed, the retreat not deficient in military skill on the side of the provincials, nor much to the reputation of the British general; a rencounter not badly nor unsuccessfully conducted on the American side.

Dec. 23. The unimportant, insignificant, fribbling governor of Virginia is come back to England.

Dec. 26. Lord Barrington in his private judgment condemns the present war as unjust, and will prove ineffectual, but votes with government, as a minister of state.

TO THE HON. JUDGE SEWALL.

Exeter, Dec. 31, 1776.

DEAR SIR:

My little bark is in imminent hazard of being stranded unless the wind shifts quickly, or some friendly boat appears for its relief. In plain English, my purse is nearly empty;—which circumstance has of late frequently reminded me of an emblematical device in the beginning of Fuller's History of the Holy Wars, wherein on the right is a purse distended with gold and standing upright, on the left the same turned upside down, in a lank condition, emptied wholly of its contents, with these words under the former, "*we went out full*," and under the latter, "*we returned empty*." I do not know but I am departed from my country, family and friends, on as foolish and fantastic grounds as the misguided devotees of that time did to rescue the Holy Land from infidels, though on opposite principles, I confess; they to fight, I to avoid fighting. I now begin to tremble lest the same fate awaits me that befell them. I dislike the motives of the chief agents in America, and their whole system from its first small beginnings to its full monstrous growth of independency; and I trust from a very just motive, *love of my country;* which this place I am convinced has no tendency to promote the welfare of. But what of that? It is my duty, and sure the state is not to reward the loyalty of every subject; the court in this case would have more than enough to do to satisfy the demands of all claimants.

I cannot foresee what I may hereafter do, but easily that I must suffer hunger and nakedness in the comfortless mansions of the wretched. These ideas I have not been accustomed to associate. Seneca and many moral writers, heathen as well as Christian, with all the fathers of the church, luxuriating in the midst of plenty, have furnished the world with elaborate, entertaining, and edifying treatises on contentment, and the duty of submission and resignation under pain, sickness, and poverty with her long train of horrors, and really they are amusing to a mind at ease and free from the apprehensions of suffering, and make a pretty figure on paper; but book philosophy and practical philosophy differ from each other widely. Let Seneca and the long list of moralists be brought to the mouth of the cave of poverty; let hunger, thirst and nakedness, in all their grisly terrifying shapes stare them in the face, then let them, if they can, exemplify these ideal doctrines; let a man pricked, torn, goaded, and surrounded by the briers and thorns sown thick in the path of poverty, take out his table-book and write a treatise on contentment and submission to these severities of his lot, and with a face of composure be able to recommend the pleasing doctrines by his own example, I will believe the existence of such a singular phenomenon ; but till I can see such an instance in real life, which I never yet have seen, I must doubt the existence of it anywhere but in books and systems.   Human practice knows no such airy notions.   History tells of savages singing amid tortures, but the instances of unfeeling savages are the instances of unfeeling savages only ; civilized societies furnished with the means and comforts and elegancies of life, afford no instances of such barbarous insensibilities.   Job, indeed, is recommended as a pattern to be imitated for patience under the grievous sufferings of loss of property, and pain ; but he, as was natural to expect in his wretchedness, cursed the day of his birth, and who can express himself with more impatience ?   Poverty with all her attendant evils, to one unaccustomed to her presence till old age, is too formidable to be vanquished by philosophy and religion ; nor is there a mind in such a situation, in its own natural forces, capable of supporting itself, and not bending under the weight of grief and despair.   My doctrine perhaps you may refuse your assent to, but I have said nothing my reason doth not dictate in the coolest hours of reflection.   On the present occasion I feel the force of these truths in a much more striking manner.   With respect to my circumstances, I will just add that several of my letters containing orders for remittances were intercepted, by order I suppose of the Amphyctionic states of America, or the lesser *logan mogans* of some particular colony, by which manœuvre my friends knew no more of my circumstances than if I was in the region of the moon.

The melancholy event in your family drew from my eyes the tears of sympathy, well knowing the grief of a tender parent for the loss of a beloved offspring ; and if you will not apply to me Augustus' answer to the Trojan ambassador, I will add, you may believe with sincerity, my real and unfeigned grief at the loss, which I pray God to support you under.

Yours, etc.

S. CURWEN.

CHAPTER IV.

Exeter, Jan. 1, 1777.—This day is very near the commencement of my sixty-second year, being three days later; my birthday was the 28th ult.; may this year be more productive of moral improvement than my last was, and if it shall please the righteous Disposer of human events to continue the dark cloud now hanging over me another year, may he support me under the dispensation, and enable me to discharge my duty, if not with alacrity, with composure and an unreluctant temper.

June 5. Attended worship at Bow-church. Mr. Manning preached a pleasing discourse on *"friendship,"* which, like all fine pictures, was too highly colored and above life.

TO THOMAS DANFORTH, ESQ., LONDON.

Exeter, Jan. 11, 1777.

DEAR SIR :

The success of the British arms does not raise my hopes; the political states of America have resources much greater than you and I may be acquainted with. The courts of France and Spain are too vigilant to let slip so fair an occasion of revenging themselves for the losses and disgraces of their fleets and armies, sustained from British troops last war, not to avail themselves of this conjuncture. The advices from both countries but too justly afford shrewd suspicions of their unfriendly designs towards Great Britain, and God only knows the consequences; the colonies may be lost, and Great Britain, perhaps, in the event, may be very well off if she can maintain her own independence. These are suggestions of a mind in quite a different state from your "head-quarter" folks, who, in our country language, count their chickens before they are hatched; if they would deign to take me into their counsels, I should advise them to be more sure of a victory before they celebrate the triumph. The continuance of our evils is to my sickly

imagination much longer than the court conceives; but what is to become of me in the mean time? I need not take a peep into futurity to know.   *   *   *   *   *   *   *   *
I want to know a thousand things, and ask a thousand questions, which you at the source of intelligence are acquainted with, relative to America and American exiles, but of which I am as ignorant as if in New Zealand. If I continue here much longer, I shall be fitter for a hermit's cell; indeed I have thought, nay, often wished for one, which at my time of life, and with my prospects, would be a most welcome retreat.

I remain yours,   S. CURWEN.

TO HON. JUDGE SEWALL, LONDON.

Exeter, Jan. 19, 1777.

     *   *   *   *   *   *   *

DEAR SIR:

So little did I know myself, so ignorant of consequences I might have foreseen and avoided, had I possessed common discernment, that, for what now appears to me a chimera, I abandoned my dwelling, friends and means of life, which you know I possessed in no small degree, and might, as the event proves, have retained on the comparative trifling condition of insults, reproaches, and perhaps a dress of tar and feathers;—an alternative I now see much to be preferred to the distresses of mind I am daily suffering. The licentiousness of an unruly rabble, saving personal outrages, with a plentiful purse, is an envied state to liberty, in the mildest government on earth, attached to poverty with its horrid train of evils; this you may regard as a paradox, and so will all who are at ease.

I think it is Lucan who says, a good man struggling under the storms of fate in adverse fortune, is a noble sight, and well pleasing to the gods. It may be so—may it be his condition on whom the gods have bestowed fortitude enough to oppose the storms; for myself I had rather sail on a pacific ocean, and would willingly dispense with some degree of honorable exaltation hereafter for a more favorable state of trial here. But enough of this;—to come to matter of fact.

     *   *   *   *   *   *   *

With great esteem,

S. CURWEN.

Jan. 31. Lord Chesterfield being asked what he thought of the three Georges, answered, " 1, George the wise, 2, George the prudent, 3, George the unfortunate."—I am afraid his inflexible temper, and the falling off of one of the richest jewels from his crown on the day of his coronation, forebodes a dismemberment of the most rich and valuable of the English dominions ;—whether Ireland, America, or the East Indies, I pretend not to foretell, but fear one or the other, perhaps all. France and Spain will not fail to avail themselves of our national folly to revenge their former losses and disgraces. The English, though brave, are not discerning ; they every day increase the relative strength of the enemy by lessening their own real power. The end may possibly be, instead of securing the dependence of the American colonies, the loss of their own independence. May God in his mercy prevent this mortifying event, if it shall be for the general good.

TO HON. JUDGE SEWALL.

Exeter, Feb. 5, 1777.

DEAR SIR :

Accept my sincere thanks for your last kind and friendly favor, and for the prospect it afforded me of hearing again soon. * * * * I presume the * * * * are too full of more important concerns to attend to these lesser matters; however if it be * * * * and we may rely on a * * * * I can cheerfully dispense with a few weeks' delay ; * * * * but such is the whirl and impotence of human affairs, that while we are on this stage we are often obliged to play different parts ; I wish never to act an unworthy one ; my only solicitude now is to pass off with decency, and escape without a hiss,—but enough of this.

On the possession of Rhode Island without loss of blood, may it be attended with better consequences than my gloomy, foreboding mind suggests. I fear France and Spain too closely watch the motions of this nation to suffer us to avail ourselves of the advantages gained over the foolish, deluded countrymen of ours, which, but for the duplicity of those courts, would yield me a pleasing prospect.   *   *   *   *   *   *

I often think of our common progenitor, Father Adam, on

13

his being driven out of Paradise by an angel with his flaming sword :

> " The world was all before him, where to choose
> His place of rest, and Providence his guide."

With this difference between us, his banishment was by an angel, and for a transgression ; mine by men almost as bad as devils, and for none :—I am afraid our lot is also different in a third respect, he had Providence for his guide, and I seem to be left to an ill-judging, foolish mind !   *   *   *   *   *   *
*   *   As you are at the source of intelligence, shall be glad to be favored with an answer to the following queries: viz.—Is there a probability of a French or Spanish war ? And in that case, will Great Britain send more troops to America ? Will General Clinton be reinforced ?   Will any Americans be allowed to depart for America, and in what character ?   And if so, will it be prudent for me to embrace the opportunity and depart ?   Have you seen the Articles of Confederation ?   Are they real, or fictitious and made here ?   Is there any late news from Generals Howe or Clinton ?   And if so, what is it ?

*   *   *   *   *   *   *

Very truly yours,
S. CURWEN.

Feb. 13.   A reverend, known by the name of the *Maccaroni Doctor*, is in Poultry Compter for forgery, and has confessed to the sum of £4200 sterling ;· his real name Dodd ; he figures in the *tete-a-tetes* in the magazines, and unless defamed, is a worthless character, though noted for some serious publications in the common routine.   He has two chapels and the Magdalen under his care.

It is reported that six hundred Hessians in an engagement with the provincials are slain, and many wounded.

Feb. 20.   The American high treason bill having passed through two readings and to be printed, giving the king power to imprison any person suspected of favoring, aiding or abetting the Americans, without liberty of bail or mainprize, has raised an alarm in people's minds universally, as it suspends the habeas corpus act, that great bulwark of English liberty, as it is called; and it is supposed to aim at some characters obnoxious to administration.   Such is the language of those who do not affect the present ministerial measures respecting America, while the advocates on the other hand plead the necessity of such a bill to render government secure, as without it those who are and shall be hereafter taken, cannot be kept in custody and brought to trial for what they call piracy and treason.   May the remains of English liberty and the constitution not be overlooked and lost in this fatal quarrel.   Charles James Fox said on this occasion, that four acts were over, and this was the first scene in the fifth act, (alluding to the enormous power given the crown,) and shows the precarious tenure on which the liberty of England is held.

TO REV. ISAAC SMITH, SIDMOUTH.

Exeter, Feb. 20, 1777.

DEAR SIR:

I have received a long letter from Judge Sewall, in consequence of which I am going to London, and shall depart from hence next week.   God bless you and succeed your pious endeavors to reform a very wicked world.   May we preserve ourselves unpolluted from the defilements thereof ; pray don't neglect to write to your old friend and companion.

S. CURWEN.

TO THOMAS DANFORTH, ESQ., LONDON.

Exeter, Feb. 20 , 1777.

DEAR SIR :

Your information of *   *   *   *   *   puts into my memory many proverbs, of which, if it did not look too like Sancho Panza, I could string near a dozen *apropos.*   You tell me it is owing to my being considered a merchant simply ; truly I think I have proved myself a very simple merchant, and brought my wares to a wretched poor market—thanks to the kind misadvisers of *   *   *   * but they forgot or perhaps never knew that I had been in the commission of the peace more than thirty years ; nearly the same period was impost officer for the county of Essex, and a captain in the first Cape Breton regiment, for which I have never received any gratuity or recompense ; but no matter, past services are easily forgotten, and the *novi homines* are like to reap all the emoluments.

Please put the inclosed into a bag for Bilboa at New Lloyd's Coffee-house, Exchange ; be assured it contains no love or treason ; the times admit of writing on neither.

As to my return to London, I must not think of it, for the operation of this new law, like the fifth act in the reign of Charles II., banishes me effectually, and of course from every corporation in England, and will oblige me to take up my residence from henceforth in some village.

I remain, etc.

S. Curwen.

Exeter, Feb. 27. Set off at six o'clock in the diligence for Plymouth ; at ten alighted at Ashburton, nineteen miles, for breakfast ; at three arrived at Plymouth.

Feb. 28. Having taken a view of Catwater harbor, Plym river, etc., I proceeded to the citadel, standing on an eminence, being the eastern extremity of a range of bluff highlands commanding a fair prospect of the entrance from the sound, in the middle whereof is an island, fortified ; the town appearing almost under foot. Procuring a coach, rode to the Dock, lying at the distance of two miles, passing through a settlement of a hundred houses on the hither side of a stream dividing Lord Edgecombe's estate from Sir John St. Aubin, on whose land the dock is built, and of whom the ground is rented, paying him yearly as lord of the manor. There are many ships in the yard, chiefly on the Tamar river, (to the east of which the dock-yard lies,) amongst others the Royal Sovereign, the Queen, the Augusta, the Invincible ; and at the quay lay the Blenheim of ninety guns, on board of which I was ; and on the stocks three large ones, and the Royal George of one hundred guns. Passed from thence to the dock, compassed by hewn stone, into which the water flows to the height of twenty-six feet in some and less in others ; the water is measured by pillars, whereon figures are marked, and is admitted by great gates, open and shut as needed. The rope-walks are of stone, of a thousand feet in length ; the work is wrought under cover, the pitch and tar

being in vaulted cellars run athwart the building, having no communication with each other.   Each particular department has its
place detached from the other, and each store distant from another.
The stores are immense, and nothing less than the riches of the
whole earth seem capable of supporting such an expense.   The
numbers daily employed in the various branches are, I am told, ten
thousand in the yard, and regularly called over three times a day.
The great regularity with which business is conducted is very observable, and, indeed, considering the incredible variety of branches,
and immense quantities of stores, the most perplexing confusions
would otherwise ensue.   I did not hear an oath, nor see any rude-
ness during my stay in the yard.   Within the walls are the officers'
houses, and many very genteel, particularly the row in which
the commander lives, with a handsome avenue and a decent chapel.
At twelve o'clock the workmen regularly go out in order, two and
two, to their dinner, and the axmen suffered to take as many chips
as they can carry, furnishing families with fuel, and the unmarried
with pocket-money.   A little beyond the yard, containing fifty or
sixty acres, inclosed with a high wall, is the gun-dock, a square
where the artillery apparatus is lodged, and a small commodious
armory, but very much inferior to that of the same size in the
Tower of London.   On our return took the route through the quarter
called the Storehouse, detached from the dock by a river, over
which is a bridge, and belongs to Lord Edgecombe, consisting of
a hundred houses, and additions are daily making; in this is a building
called the long-room, appropriated to tea, punch, wine, etc., for private companies and public assemblies, and there is an elegant room
with drawing-rooms adjoining, nearly fifty feet long, about thirty
wide, and twenty-five high, with two handsome glass chandeliers
and a music-gallery; not far from this is a building with large
areas encompassed by high stone fences, called the Old Mill Prison,
now fitting up to receive American prisoners.   From this we ascended a high bluff-head reaching to the citadel; whilst here, was
not a little mortified to see an American privateer prize coming
into the harbor from Dartmouth, nor were my ears a little
wounded to hear another sold by auction.

   Plymouth, March 1.   Being called at six o'clock, I arose and
entered the vehicle alone, taking up a country couple at Squire

Parker's lodge; first stage at Ivy bridge, eleven miles, where breakfasted, and from thence alighted at 12 o'clock at Totness, from whence I departed to Mrs. Wingate's, late Sophia Reed, who kindly received me; from thence, after an hour's rest, set off for Newton Abbott and Newton Bushel, separated only by a bridge, the former being the name the whole goes by: passing by Mr. Coxe's seat called Penmore Park, and at six o'clock alighted in the churchyard, Exeter.

Exeter, March 7.   I received a letter from London informing me of my wife's health and welfare in November last, and that she had been obliged to pay ten pounds sterling to find a man for the American army in my stead.   This intelligence I received by a letter from Doctor John Prince, at Halifax.   Left for Bristol in the diligence, and arrived at the Bush tavern, opposite the Exchange, at eight o'clock evening.

Bristol, March 8.   Entered the diligence for London at one o'clock at night—the frost was so intense that our breaths formed a hard cake of ice on the glass, scarce to be taken off by the nails. At the city of Bath we arrived, a distance of twelve miles, almost stiffened with cold; here I attempted to thaw myself, but this expedient I fancy only rendered my body and feet more susceptible of the cold; suffering, till the sun arose and chased away the frost, inconceivable pain.   At Calne we changed horses again, and attempted a second thaw with better success than the first, being aided by the sun then beginning to bless the upper hemisphere, shining in a cloudless sky.   From hence to Marlborough the road lies over a place called the Down; at the entrance is a hill, insulated in the form of a half egg, with the summit cut down to a plain, and is called Silbury, supposed to be made by art or the hand of man, on which are some of the bodies of earth like those surrounding Stonehenge, called *tumuli ;* conjectured to be burying places of the ancient Druids.   Hence to Froxfield, on the borders of which is an almshouse for the reception of forty-five tradesmen's widows; it has two fronts, each one hundred and fifty feet long, of brick.   The next town is Hungerford; hence to Newbury, a town larger in extent and more numerous in inhabitants than Marlborough.   Near this town are many single houses, which have the appearance of wealthy persons' residences; and on a pleasant plain, commanding also a view of Newbury, lying to the right as one comes from Bath, is a parish called Speen ; at the entrance is a lofty building to be seen about half a mile distant, on a ridge of hills, having a round tower called Dunnington Castle ; the road lies through a street built on what is called Speen lands, belonging to the parish of that name, but is connected by buildings continued to Newbury town, spreading a great extent on a low plain in a bottom.   Here we took fresh horses, passing through two or three villages to Reading, the distance of which from London is thirty-nine miles ; this, the chief town of Berkshire, contains between two and three thousand houses; from a little beyond Marlborough to Reading, the land is a continued flat, much of it improved, the roads like garden gravel-walks, and very pleasant.   At Bayswater we again shifted horses, and again at Hounslow ; between those two places lies the noted heath called by the name of the latter, which we passed over with a slow, solemn pace in the dark, being more than an hour in crossing it.   We arrived safe at eight o'clock, evening, at the Swan-with-two-Necks Inn, Doctors' Commons.

London, March 9.   Set forward for Judge Sewall's, where I dined and passed the evening, Colonels Saltonstall and Phipps being of the company : from thence I proceeded to Brompton-Row, where Thomas Danforth, Edward Oxnard, and Jonathan Clarke lodged, and here I engaged lodgings.

March 10.   Walked out to Judge Sewall's, he having the day before engaged to accompany me to the Treasury, where after a compliment I received information of a hundred pounds down, and a hundred per annum during the troubles in America, which I esteem as a providential provision procured by the friendship of my respected friend Judge Sewall. 1 received an order on the bank ; accompanied by him and Mr. Thomas Danforth, I took a note at the cashier's office for seventy pounds payable to myself on demand, and thirty pounds in cash, departing very joyous and I hope grateful to that Being who has, by friends, been pleased in the midst of gloomy prospects to set my feet on firm ground and establish my goings: may I wisely improve this gracious indulgence.

Brompton-Row, Kensington, March 11.   Took an early walk to London, and meeting Governor Hutchinson, was invited to dinner, which I accepted, and receiving his address (147 New Bond-street) arrived at it; company beside myself, his son Elisha and daughter, was Mr. B. Hallowell. After dinner repaired to Haymarket theatre, where was entertained in a very full house by the humorous George Alexander Stevens' lecture on heads.

March 12. Spent the evening with the Club, consisting of twelve American exiles, at the Treasurer's house, Mr. Harrison Gray's.

March 31. Rode to Hackney with Judge Sewall to see his son Jonathan at school; returned to his house to dinner, where I passed the evening.

TO REV. ISAAC SMITH, SIDMOUTH.

No. 23 *Brompton-Row, March* 19, 1777.

DEAR SIR:

I am at length at my moorings in this port, not much to my content except in this one circumstance, the early receipt of the *unum necessarium ;* this, though it chases away all apprehensions of future want, does not in every situation yield positive happiness; perhaps I am enigmatical,—the solution must be deferred to a personal interview hereafter.

The only article of political news is that Gen. Washington was, about the beginning of the present year, declared Lord Protector of the thirteen United States of America. Mr. Timmins is arrived from Boston *via* Cork; he left Plymouth about the first of February; says the affair of the Hessians was brought to Boston in four days and put them in high spirits; that the harbor of Boston is strongly fortified from the lighthouse and Point Alderton to Fort Nell; the people sanguine in their expectations of a French war, encouraged in their errors by the Danish, French and Spanish traders, who are numerous in the port. King-street (Boston) almost as much thronged with people of all nations, etc., as the Strand or Cornhill; two hundred and eighty-three prizes carried in by the 23d December; four vessels with goods from France, with powder, small arms, clothing and other articles ; one with twenty thousand suits of military clothing, an article not a little wanted among them. Young R * * * S * * * has made twenty thousand pounds sterling by privateering, and S. A. Otis the most important, busy man, as well as one of the richest there, etc.

I fancy I shall take my flight northward, as birds of passage you know do, on the approach of spring. There are twenty Americans going out with goods to New-York and Rhode Island in the spring; I think the adventures rash. Mr. Amory is delayed by his wife's illness, which it is judged will soon end in mortality· I have received a letter from Thomas Russell* of Boston, and Russell Wyer of Salem, written in the beginning of February, all well.

Yours truly,

S. Curwen.

Kensington, March 20. Evening at club at Mr. Harrison Gray's.

Sunday, March 23. To Christ Church Hospital to see the children, to the number of eight hundred, sup; admitted by a ticket signed John Lane, one of the governors. The hall is a hundred feet in length, and twenty feet in height,—on one side of which are three pictures, the middle one sixty feet long and fifteen high; in the centre King William; on the same range courtiers, life-guardsmen, etc. In the foreground on one hand, hospital children of the males, and on the other females, and all in their proper garbs :—on the left, or the first from the door, of the same length is a painting of King Edward surrounded by his court with a roll, by me supposed to represent the first charter of this institution, he being the founder thereof; and on the other, a piece of the same size as the last, with a full length of Charles II., with astronomical and mathematical apparatus, perhaps to denote him to be the founder of the mathematical school here.—Three tables were spread, on each side of which benches; on a raised platform are circular seats for the spectators, in the centre front a two armed chair for the governor, or treasurer, whose name is Burford. Prayers are read by one of the upper boys in a pulpit erected against the wall; then singing by the boys accompanied by an organ; afterwards supper, consisting only of bread and butter; grace before and after, by one of the boys in the pulpit, and service concludes with an anthem. The boys

---

* An opulent and distinguished merchant of Boston, whose widow married Sir Grenville, son of Sir John Temple, first Consul General from Great Britain to the United States.

come up in pairs to the platform to make their bow, and retire, some with large pitchers, others with small wooden bowls, others with table-cloths folded up under their arms, others with large baskets in which the bread was brought, and others with lighted candles.

March 27.   Walked out with Judge Sewall and Mr. A. Willard to Cromwell's garden, which is in ill repair; drank tea at the house of the former, and passed the evening with the New England Club, say " *Brompton-Row Tory Club,*" at Mr. Blowers'.

March 31.   Evening with the club at H. Gray's.

April 3.   Dined at Treasurer Gray's with Col. Browne and John Sargent.

TO REV. ISAAC SMITH, SIDMOUTH.

23 *Brompton-Row, Kensington, April* 6, 1777.

DEAR SIR :

I have nothing to communicate worth a minute's attention. The various news that each morning produces, the following day contradicts; however, in general, perhaps it may be new to you to know that the tories here believe the American game of independency is nearly up; not so your doubting friend.   Nay, so very sure are some, that there is no small talk of going off in August. You will scarce meet one that entertains the least shadow of a doubt that government must succeed in the utmost extent of its views before the fall; the reasons and probability of which I have not discernment enough to see.   I wish the old Latin proverb may not with too much propriety be applied to these implicit believers, " *Canunt triumphum ante victoriam.*"*

I wrote you in my last that several, to the number of twenty, were going off to New-York.   I now add that another cargo of twelve or fifteen, among whom is young Chipman, is to depart in a vessel of 250 tons, laden with goods to the amount of £80,000 sterling, defended by a force of 17 guns and 17 men, in ten days.   It is reported that the new levies, British and German, going to General Howe, are in number eight thousand, and that General Burgoyne is already gone, and is to take with him from

---

* " They celebrate the triumph before the victory is gained."

Canada by way of St. Lawrence river, the greater part of the troops at present stationed there ; no further attempts being to be made on the lakes this season.   Our head-quarter folks say that Lord George Germaine declared to Col. Phips, who is going this day to Halifax with Admiral Montague *viâ* Newfoundland, that the first advices from America, he doubts not, will be joyful.   All here are expecting to hear that General Howe is in possession of Philadelphia.   On the contrary, the Philadelphia papers are full of the great exploits of the American troops against the royal army, and the promising appearances of affairs on their side ; and if Gen. Washington and Gen. Gates' letters are genuine, Gen. Howe and his forces are not in so fair a way to possess themselves of that capital as our folks seem to fancy.   Mr. Dickinson's defection has proved a false alarm, he being only retired to his estate seventy miles from Philadelphia, for what reasons politicians disagree.   His brother Dickinson and his brother-in-law Cadwallader, are both commanders in the American army.   Last night I heard read the following, from a letter dated Portsmouth, April 10, viz., "Two thousand Anspachers sailed for New-York under convoy of the Somerset and Mercury : three thousand more Germans are expected here to sail directly, under the St. Albans."

Yesterday morn the late right reverend the Bishop of London's corpse was carried by our door on a hearse to its place of interment at Fulham—successor unknown ; probably the bench of bishops will take care that the see of London do not stand long vacant, under the modest pretence of *Nolo Episcopari.*

Yours truly,

S. Curwen.

April 11.   Drank tea and passed the evening at Mr. and Mrs. Savage's, in company with Mr. and Mrs. Carpenter* and Judge Sewall.

* Of Salem.

CHAPTER V.

April 17, 1777. At seven A. M. departed in company with
Judge Sewall and Mr. A. Willard, on our intended journey to Ipswich; our first stage at Rumford, a distance of sixteen miles; this
town consists of about two hundred houses, some few modern.
The next stage at a town called Ingatestone, not unlike the former
for size and style, distance twelve miles; Witham was our third
stage, our fourth Colchester, famous for the manufacture of baizes,
and here oysters are taken from the sea and put into pits, in order
to give them that coppery taste so grateful to an Englishman's
palate, and so disgustful to a New Englander's. The streets are
ill paved with smallish pebbles, to my feet so harsh and hurtful as
to occasion frequent complaints. In our progress came to the castle, built in form of one of the old barons, not improbable to have
been one; it is a square; the angles defended by round towers,
pierced like the body of the castle with narrow and long holes,
through which the inmates were wont to defend themselves by
arrows; the whole crowned with battlements formerly, the remains
being still to be seen. The parade contains a quarter of an acre,
and is now cleared of the barracks it was once encumbered with;
in a room up one flight of stairs, is the library, belonging to a Mr.
Grey, minister for the town, consisting of about two thousand old
books. Here a weekly society meet; its institution, orders and
purposes, my curiosity did not prompt me to make any inquiry
into :—hence to the chapel so called, an empty room, containing
only a reading desk, with a large folio Bible and a large wooden
chair. This castle was in the time of the civil wars defended by
Sir Charles Lucas and Sir George Lisle for the royal cause, who
were, after its surrender, shot on the parade and buried under a
small church in the road; the precise spot on which they stood is
carefully preserved in memory, and told the curious visitant. The
only inhabitants are a family in one of the round towers, and the
rooks who occupy the holes on the outside in great numbers. The

site of the castle is somewhat high, has pleasant walks round, planted with trees, and commands the neighboring grounds that lie below it, except on the town side. On the same plain from this spot we passed through the streets to another quarter of the town, in which lie the St. John's Abbey gardens, now known by the name of the pinnacle gardens, for reasons unknown to us, and are surrounded by a lofty brick wall, and strengthened by buttresses in good repair. These I suppose are the walls of the ancient monastery grounds, embracing twenty acres. Hence we proceeded home, and attended by our complaisant landlord, were admitted to a sight of a tesselated Roman pavement lately discovered in a gentleman's garden, supposed by antiquarians to have been the pretorium of an old Roman encampment, it being a known fact that Julius Cesar landed in his second invasion of Britain in the neighborhood of this place. It is probable hereabouts was a Roman station, and the discovery of this piece of Roman work renders the conjecture not improbable.

From hence we proceeded over to a Mr. Great's, to see the portraits of Sir John Jacquey and his lady, some of the first establishers of the baize manufactories here. These pieces are executed on wood, by Vandyke, in 1623; we were told they are judged to be capital paintings, and it is highly probable they are, if our information be true that the possessors' descendants of this couple have been offered a thousand guineas for them.

Colchester, April 18. Departed at nine o'clock hence for Mistley, a village in the lands of Richard Rigby, Esq., who is lord of this manor. In two hours we alighted at his gardens, in extent four acres within the walls; his hot and green-houses are in fine order, and supplied with common trees and shrubs, plants and vines, but no exotics that are not fructiferous and of the useful kinds. Thence through the pleasure grounds to the house, where, being conducted through a more than Cretan labyrinth, at length arrived; it is new and elegant, but its extent does not rise above mediocrity; its ornaments are silk hangings of cream color, with faint shades of blue, red, etc.; chairs the same with three very large looking-glasses, a beautiful chimney-piece, of polished marble; other chimney furniture, and a pyrometer I had never seen before.

We arrived at Ipswich, distant from Colchester twenty-two

miles, where we dined. From the inn, accompanied by the master, we walked along the old wall of the town to Mr. John Fonnerau's park; the house wherein he dwells belonging to it is called Christ Church, and was formerly a monastery of friars. The town consists of old-built, ill-fashioned structures, and contains about ten thousand souls. Its only trade is coals, imported from the north; but few people stirring in the streets, a visible decay. It lies on the river Orwell, and is the chief county town. The corn market has a small octagonal building, about twenty feet in diameter; in the centre on top stands a female statue as large as life, with a fillet round her eyes; in her right hand a sword, and in her left a pair of scales, loose hung, moving up and down with every puff of wind, perhaps to denote the instability of modern justice, or how apt it is to swerve from the right line when urged by force or interest, or moved by flattery.

Ipswich, April 19. After breakfast departed from this solitary unpleasing town, very like its namesake in New England in its general complexion, and in two hours arrived at Stowmarket; and soon after at St. Edmundsbury at two o'clock. Accompanied by the landlord we went to view the ruins of the Abbey of St. Edmund of Saxon time, scattered over near twenty acres now owned by Sir Charles Dacres and his maiden sister. The remains of this stupendous building are astonishing, many foundations of walls and pillars being yet to be seen; the casings almost entirely taken away, scarce any part of the front or sides being left except here and there a stone which serve to show the materials. Some of the walls were thirty feet thick. The pillars appear to have been from eight to twelve feet; and an arch, of which the foundation yet remains, was said to have been seventy feet high, and is near forty in width. The foundation also of the Abbot's hall remains; its area forty-five feet each side. In a spot, perhaps the dormitory, a few years since was digged up the body of the Duke of Beaufort, brother to the Duke of Bedford, Regent of France during the minority of Henry VI., and was entire; a hand taken from it is preserved in spirits, and in the keeping of a physician here. The grand entrance is preserved entire, and is a square lofty tower; its angles, like all the ancient fortified structures, covered with round towers rising up to the top. The passage way through is under a lofty arch defended by great gates that are kept shut. Many particulars were told us respecting the various parts of the house, appurtenances and avenues, but not being noted at the time, are forgotten. Among the notitia of this place by desire I insert, that the steeple of St. James's church stands at fifty feet distance from the body of the church. A house containing four windows in front being between; and on the steeple on the same side are two hour plates of clocks, to answer what purpose was beyond my reach.

At three o'clock we departed from this pleasant, handsome and agreeable town. On the right, about ten miles distant, Ely Minster or Cathedral appeared in view. At twelve miles from last stage is Newmarket, an indifferent inn, however frequented by dukes and lords. We passed through the race grounds;—the races were instituted to keep and preserve a race of good horses in honor of the nation; but as the institution is debased, it is not the best horse that wins the race, but that which is destined for it by combination; indeed, some descend so low as to circumvent one another. The diversion becoming a public nuisance by spreading itself, the legislature took cognizance of it, and by the 13th George II. a law was passed in relation to it. Departed for Cambridge over a plain champaign uninclosed country, which all this quarter of the country seems to consist of; at this place we arrived at seven o'clock, at the White Bear inn, where we were indifferently treated at our first alighting, through the driver's foolish neglect or mistake in not denoting that dignity and importance each gentleman should assume on the road in order to be respectfully treated; however, he seemed afterwards to be sensible of his own false judgment, and partly made amends.

Cambridge, April 20. At ten o'clock, taking a servant of the inn along with us, we walked out in order to have a sight of the inside of King's College chapel, that, by delay at Trinity College, we lost. This latter is by far the most magnificent in the University; has two spacious quadrangles, the front and one of the squares are of Portland freestone, having a beautiful reservoir of water in the midst; the chambers occupy two sides, the hall and * * * * room another side, and the fourth by the chapel, which contained nothing remarkable but a full length statue of Sir Isaac

Newton in the porch. The other square contains chambers on all sides except the north or west, and is wholly improved by the college library, a noble room of two hundred feet in length by about seventy wide, filled with forty thousand volumes; the alcoves having on top the busts of the most famous ancient philosophers on one side, and the most famous of the modern English authors, etc. on the other. Here we were shown a perfect Egyptian mummy, the flesh like a smoked tongue. In the same apartment was a curious inscription in Greek capitals, without distinction of sentences or words, on a marble about eighteen inches square, having a plain pediment on the top; it is called *Marmor Sandavicensis*, being presented by Lord Sandwich. There are also to be seen some mutilated antique pillars and capitals with inscriptions in Greek characters, placed on the grand staircases leading to the library, given by Mr. Wortley Montague or his sister Lady Bute, since her death, but which I forget; and among them his bust in marble.

From hence we departed through the college walks on the banks of the river Cam, running on the back of King's College, Trinity College, Caius, Trinity Hall, Clare Hall and St. John's College; over the river are three handsome stone bridges for foot walking, and between them a wooden bridge called the bridleway, for horses and carriages; the banks of the river within the college grounds are faced with stone, the lawn carried down to its very edge, with many slips for the advantage of the company who shall please to divert themselves in boats on the water, flowing in a very gentle stream about two rods wide. The pleasure grounds are laid out in most agreeable gravel-walks kept in the nicest order, shaded with lofty trees; they are extensive, all on a level, and agreeable. Leaving these delightful walks we proceeded to the chapel; it being shut, we turned our walk to take a view of the other buildings. A Mr. Pearce, a fellow of St. John's College, whom I met in the walks, invited us to his chamber, where we abode a few minutes to look in a book for an answer to a question I put them concerning the age of an ancient manuscript in the University library, and for the key of the library, to which he conducted us. It is not a handsome room, nor contains a large collection of books; it was scarcely larger than our old Harvard

College library, and like it consisting of old books chiefly.   Mr. Prior was of this college, and left it a noble folio volume of all his works, bound in morocco, finely gilt.   Here we also saw a most elegant folio edition of Dr. Samuel Clarke's Julius Cæsar's Commentaries.

Having returned to our inn, we dined, and soon departed in a post-chaise through a very level road to our designed stage, Barkway, distant sixteen miles, where we lodged and breakfasted. This very indifferent collection of old fashioned buildings we soon left, and entered on the fine improvements of Herts. The agreeable unevenness of the earth, the verdure of the fields and corn grounds, and excellent improvements for which this county is noted, rendered our travelling for many miles delightfully pleasant.   At Ware alighted in two hours from our departure from the last stage, stopping at the Saracen's Head, to gratify my companions, whose curiosity urged them to take a view of the great bed, which I before described, and made, as our informant told us, for the use of King Edward IV. in 1463.   From hence we took the course to Hartford, lying three miles out of our direct road to London, and in two hours from hence were set down at Judge Sewall's door, after a ramble of one hundred and eighty miles ; and so good-by, Essex, Suffolk, and Cambridgeshire.

Passed the afternoon and evening at Judge Sewall's.

April 25.   With Mr. Savage attended Longford's sales under Covent Garden piazza—viewed and examined his medals and coins; Roman, Grecian, Egyptian, Saxon, and English.   Saw a brass farthing of the time of the Commonwealth that sold for three pounds four.

April 29.   Attended the exhibition in Piccadilly of Society of Artists of Great Britain ; was really surprised at the meanness of the portraits; nothing appeared to my eye well executed but some fruit-pieces and a few miniatures in crayons and water colors. From hence Mr. Silsbee and myself adjourned to Mr. Joseph Green's ; we drank tea and passed a pleasant hour.   Stopped by the way at Ely Palace, so called, on Holborn hill, now sold and pulling down to build two rows of houses.   There are yet standing the chapel and hall in the old Gothic taste.

15

TO REV. ISAAC SMITH, SIDMOUTH, DEVON.

Brompton-Row, April 30, 1777.

DEAR SIR :

Your favor of the 25th I received last night, and am obliged to you for the intelligence it contains; all of which respecting our own country was new to me, having not heard a syllable of it before ; the daily news inserted in the public papers proves for the most part to be manufactured here, and what is not, in event turns out to be premature and void of truth.   Nothing can be depended on but what comes to us prepared by court cookery in the Gazette, nor do I think administration to blame for withholding part, the whole truth not being fit to be divulged in these captious, licentious times.   I have wholly laid aside all regard to what is said to be brought by expresses from America, but what comes immediately from General or Lord Howe, or is contained in the American news-papers, of which we have now and then a sight in the New England Coffee-house.   Nothing very important has of late come from that quarter, except the death of General Washington and the taking of Ticonderoga, both of these yet being matters of doubt and dispute, as people wish, fear, or hope.   Since my last I have rambled through Essex, Suffolk, Cambridgeshire and Hertford for five days, in company with Judge Sewall and Mr. Abel Willard, and am now about departing, say next Monday, for Oxford, and from thence *quô fata trahant ;* designing never to make London or its environs my future abode ;—the inhabitants, however, I hold in much higher estimation than those of almost every other place.

*   *   *   *   *   *   *   *

God bless your reverence, and succeed your pious endeavors to reform your flock, and I hope for and depend on your prayers, and remain,

Very truly your friend,

S. CURWEN.

Brompton-Row, Kensington, May 1, 1777.   Dined at Gilbert Harrison's with my friend John Timmins, the two Debloises,* Benjamin Faneuil, and two ladies.

* Late of Salem.

May 3. Dined at Judge Sewall's; from thence walked to London to engage a seat in the diligence to Oxford, designing to take that city in my way to the country, where for some months I propose to abide, but in what quarter chance must determine. I go hence like Abraham of old; may the same kind and almighty Protector be my guide and defence.

May 5. Departed in the diligence, in which we found a late Oxford scholar, who proved a pleasant, chatty, well-bred companion; the road for the first eight miles as far as Acton, clear, level and pleasant as a garden gravel-walk: from thence it assumed a different face, and from Uxbridge to Oxford, especially through Buckinghamshire, generally a rich soil and well improved lands. The other towns lying in the road were Beaconsfield and High Wycombe; in the latter lies Lord Shelburne's seat, pleasure grounds and park all in view; a little beyond is Lord Despenser's, much more cultivated and in better order. On the right and on an eminence, stands an edifice styled " the Mausoleum," of a peculiar construction; but the inclination of my fellow travellers permitted me not to take a nearer view than the transient sight as we passed the road. From hence through a parish called Stoken-Church, and on bad roads, we arrived at the Star inn, Oxford, not having stopped to refresh; here we called for dinner and engaged lodgings.

Oxford, May 6. After breakfast walked out to deliver Dr. Chandler's letter to a fellow of Queen's College, named Monkhouse, who received us respectfully enough, detained us in his room an hour, and from thence conducted us through the hall, chapel, library of his own college, and after settling the route went to the theatre, Radcliffe library, Clarendon press, and the schools. After repeated invitations to dine in their hall, we declined for the purpose of examining the Oxford Guide in our retirement. In the hall of Jesus College were admitted to a sight of the plate; among others is a bowl and ladle of silver double gilt, and holding ten gallons, the gift of Sir Watkins William Wynne; here is also a book of the college statutes written on vellum, and kept in a glass case, having the characters as perfect and just as if struck on copperplate. From hence to our lodgings; soon after our companion Mr. Monkhouse came and conducted us through the Radcliffe Infirmary, open to all the nation, and filled with every conceivable

accommodation and supply, and kept in the neatest order. From
thence to the observatory, and from thence to the park, being a
long circular laid gravel walk round the improved fields, part of
which is bordered by lofty elms ; its high situation affords a fine
extended prospect of the country under high cultivation ; part of
the city on the other side adds to the pleasure of the walk.

The grounds belong to Merton College, but the walks are
maintained at the University expense and common to it ; on our return back we met two gownsmen both of our college, (Harvard,)
one of whom was Dr. Nicholson mentioned in the superscription of
our letter, with whom and a Mr. Hamilton, (a partner in the print-
ing of the Oxford Bibles and Prayer Book, the sole liberty of which
is confined to the two Universities and the king's press,) and a few
gentlemen besides in the common room which all the colleges are
furnished with.   7th. Breakfasted at Mr. Deblois's by invitation, and
after returned to our lodgings, to which Mr. Monkhouse soon came
and conducted us to the Divinity school, having a curious roof of
stone, and in as bold a style as King's College Chapel, Cambridge ;
from thence returned back into the convocation room ; and here
we spent some time in looking into the statute book and *libro nigro ;*
in the anteroom I saw the vice chancellor in his robes and the two
proctors, waiting for the completing a convocation, (consisting of
twelve at least.)   We were in hopes to see a baccalaureate degree
given to one of the students of Queen's College, but the difficulty
of making a convocation delayed the ceremony too long for our
leisure ; by this delay was deprived of a sight I should have been
greatly pleased with.   Hence we ascended to the picture gallery,
and from thence to the Bodleian library, which did not come up
to my idea ; 'tis an old room, its form an H ; there are many recesses surrounded with lattice work in which the students retire
to read, transcribe, etc.; saw but few employed in that business.
From hence we passed over to the Ashmolean museum ; here we
were entertained but indifferently.   In the staircase are a dead
Christ of Carrachi, and the Tradescant family, by what hands I
know not ; in the room a small miniature of St. Cuthbert in a gold
gorget, said to have been worn by Alfred the Great ; some very
nice frivolous carvings in peach and cherry stones ; the hat Brad-
shaw is said to have had on when he sat in judgment and condemn-

ed king Charles; the skull of Cromwell, said to be known by a small excrescence on the bone just above the eye, etc.

Retreated to the inn, dined, and being attended by G. Deblois's father, I walked to Christ Church College, the most noble of any in the University; entered the picture rooms, crowded by paintings of the most celebrated masters, being the gift of the late General Guise, for the reception of which these rooms were fitted. Above is the library of very fine bound books, placed in a room of about two hundred feet long, sixty wide, and twenty-five high; the ceiling finely stuccoed as well as the walls in each kind of relief, in oval and other figured compartments. The books are in cases of oak, handsomely carved, and many seats in the same style. The hall into which I entered whilst some of the students were at dinner, is a noble room of the length apparently of the library, and wider; the ceiling is of oak, supported from above, and in the centre of each square compartment into which it is laid, is a gilt rose; the walls in a line on each side filled with portraits, on the ends with full lengths. I remember none of them but Lord Mansfield's, over the door in his judicial robes. Here I was accosted by a well bred sensible young student, with whom I held conversation. Leaving him I departed, passing through the walk belonging to this college, of a mile in length, bordered on each side for part of the way by lofty trees, rendering it most delightful. Our next delay was at Corpus Christi, into the chapel of which I just peeped, and from thence into Oriel; both of these are small foundations. Arriving at the inn, dismissed my attendant, and soon after being called upon according to promise by Mr. Monkhouse, with whom I went to the schools. In two apartments the Arundelian marbles (and collection of statues presented to the University by the Countess of Pembroke) are kept; the statues are larger and smaller than the life.

From hence we adjourned to Allsouls College; the house for the reception of the books was built by Col. Codrington, formerly a member of this house, whose statue in white marble stands in the centre of the room, a noble one indeed;—the ceiling and walls elegantly stuccoed, the books, very numerous, stand in beautiful cases; a fund producing two thousand pounds a year is allotted for the increasing of it; by this provision it will in time become the largest and best in the University. From thence we adjourned to the chapel, a beautiful room ; over the altar stands a masterly performance of a Mr. Minkes, the Spanish king's painter, of Christ making himself known to Mary Magdalene in the garden, just at the point of time when she having said to him, "If thou be the gardener, and have borne him hence, tell me where thou hast laid him ;" he replied, "Mary," and she turning about discovered it was the Lord ; this filling her with surprise, admiration, love, a mixture of all these various passions is finely expressed in her countenance ; and in his, self-composure, dignity, meekness. Over this, in a semi-circular compartment, are many full lengths, being the assumption of the founder Henry Chichely ; he is dressed in rich robes, his eyes raised upwards, attended by angels.

From this pleasing spot we proceeded to Christ Church College, in Peckwater-square ; meeting Sir Francis Bernard* with a son now educating here, was introduced to Doctor Leigh of Baliol College, who was elected in 1727, and is now a sprightly and active little old gentleman of eighty-six. We reached the church, said to be almost the only remains of a public building in the Norman style, supposed to have been standing eight or nine hundred years. It was anciently an Abbey church, dedicated to St. Frideswide, whose tomb is yet standing ; here we were shown several pieces of richly embossed double gilt plate, some of which were dug from the ruins of Oshey Abbey, where it had been lying for ages. The old abbey, distant from hence about eight miles, has been removed to this spot. Passed this evening as the last, in the same common room, and with the same company, with the addition of one or two more, hearing many sarcastic speeches concerning our New England follies and absurdities ; but every country has its characteristic ones, and that comforts me under the but too just ridicule we are loaded with.

May 8. Took our farewell of G. Deblois's father and family— walking out in order to take our last leave of Mr. Monkhouse, whom we met, and were conducted by him through New College and its pleasant grounds, and back to the inn ; making our acknowledgments, we took leave, and soon entering the post-chaise,

* Governor of Massachusetts from 1760 to 1769.

departed for Woodstock, distant six miles, through dirty roads; were set down at the Bear inn. We loitered through the town, and at three o'clock, the hour appointed for viewing Blenheim House, we proceeded to the park gate, an enormous portal, in the triumphal style, with an inscription cut in the list, importing by whom and when it was erected; from this we have an oblique view of that enormous load of building called Blenheim House, the first sight of which reminded me of that sarcastic couplet on the architect:

> " Lie heavy on him, earth, for he
> Hath laid a cumbrous pile on thee."

The near approach did not fail to add to the disgust I first received:—the huge piles that sustain the arcades, the almost unspannible pillars, and the inordinate size and clumsiness of its outside appearance, were fully recompensed by the elegance and grandeur of the rooms, the beauty of the tapestry, and the capital paintings with which the apartments are filled. The saloon is a noble room; the library possesses a grandeur and elegance inexpressible. From this famed edifice we returned the same way by which we entered, took a post-chaise and rode across the country to Bicester, through fields and private grounds, passing gates, etc., the soil light and barren; few fields of grain, but chiefly uninclosed heaths for sheep walks. This town has no manufactures, wood scarce and coals dear: it abounds in houses for the sale of spirituous liquors; we met in our ramble not less than a score. Lodged at the King's Arms, the most magnificent edifice of the whole.

Bicester, May 9. Departed early for Buckingham, and alighting at Lord Temple's Arms, we breakfasted, and soon after left for Stow Gardens, passing for a mile over a straight, level road through Lord George Germaine's grounds, adjoining to the gardens on the borders of which, and facing the road, stands a light, lofty triumphal arch; leaving this on our left, we proceeded to the inn, and from thence to the gate; being admitted, we remained two hours in going through the gardens and house, the front of which is built in a more pleasing style by far than Blenheim, not, however, to be compared to it in extent and compass. These gardens are not to be matched for grandeur, variety and taste in England, perhaps the

world. They are capable of amusing for a much longer time than
I could allot, being viewed by me *currente pede.*—Having trav-
ersed the pleasure grounds half through, we arrived at the house,
the front of which has a very noble and airy appearance; ascending a lofty flight of steps, we saw an elderly person sitting on a
settee in half mourning, by the front door under the portico supported by lofty pillars of the Corinthian order; approaching nearer
I espied a star on his right breast, by which I recognized Earl
Temple. Pulling off my hat, I was going to retire, when he put
his hand to his hat, and beckoned with the other to approach,
which we did, and entered the great hall yet unfinished, the whole
front having been lately taken down; the outside is finished, but
within is yet in hand; many of the rooms are in disorder, though
enough to manifest the elegance and grandeur of the owner's taste
and riches. From hence we set forward, passing through my
lord's grounds five miles, and Whittlebury Forest, belonging to the
estate of the Duke of Grafton, called Easton; which, with the
other grounds we passed, till our arrival at the turnpike road, were
insufferably bad, besides being delayed by a multitude of gates, for
which purpose we brought a young lad to open them. The appearance of the earth in this stage was greatly altered for the better, being diversified with hills and dales under better cultivation,
and the nature of the soil more fertile. The fences for many miles
of rails, such as are frequent in our own country, intended to defend
the young live hedges just set out, inclosures here just beginning to
take place. At 4 o'clock alighted at the Saracen's Head, Worcester; here we abode no longer than to dine, and taking another
post-chaise, departed for Daventry, passing through a village
called Whadon, where we supped and lodged.

Daventry, May 10. A. M. Took coach for Coventry, passing
through a finely improved, fertile country, and in three hours
alighted at an inn just without the city; a regiment of horse
called the Inniskilliners, were reviewing; a body of stout, likely
men, dressed in red turned up with buff, and exceedingly well
mounted.

Coventry is an old built city, noted for the ribbon weaving business; here we were delayed some time; took fresh horses; our
road lay over a new canal between Oxford and the last mentioned

city, designed for the cheaper and more expeditious conveyance of
coals that these parts abound in, by which the former will be supplied at less than half the present price. In our road lay a village,
called Dunchurch ; a little beyond is a long terrace road raised
above the level nearly three feet, and continued for more than
three miles almost in a straight line, and bordered on each side by
evergreens and elms, planted by the lord of the royalty, through
whose lands it runs, rendering it inexpressibly pleasing to the eye
of the traveller.

From Coventry to Birmingham we were delayed by scores of
wagons bound from thence, laden with goods, coals, etc., and at
four o'clock alighted at the Dolphin inn, Birmingham, in the street
called the Bullring, where we intend to remain ten days, (after a
circuit of a hundred and fifty miles,) if agreeable.

Birmingham, May 13.   Being called upon by Mr. G. Russell,
we set off on foot for his house at Moseley Wake Green, having
been invited the Sunday before to dine on this day ; our company
consisted of his brother and lady and sister.

May 17.   Waited on Mr. Wilkinson at his house, but he was
absent ; afterwards went with my companion to the locks on the
canal, and saw several boats go through, an amusing sight to him
which he had never seen before.

May 19.   Having engaged horses the night before at eight
o'clock, booted and spurred we mounted our Rosinantes, and departed for the Leasowes, late pleasure grounds of the famed Shen-
stone, and Hagley, the estate of Lord Littleton ; the former distant
six miles, the latter eleven, on the same road.   Here we arrived
at eleven o'clock, passing through a town called Hales Owen, of
considerable extent, and by its appearance in the same way of
business as Birmingham.   Attended by the gardener in the absence
of the park keeper, we walked over my lord's grounds, almost in
the centre of which stands Hagley parish church, a small building
in a shady recess ; passing this we ascended an eminence.   On a
plain surrounded on all sides but in front with lofty trees, stands a
pillar with a statue of the late Prince of Wales, (father of his
present majesty,) dedicated to his memory by the late Lord Littleton, who was one of the prince's household and favorites.   This
spot commanded a sloping view of a pleasant lawn, bounded by

the mansion house, a large oblong edifice of two stories and an attic, with a low four-square tower on each angle, and a flat roof. The exterior of the house is plain and void of ornament; over the lawns are planted clumps of trees by which the views are diversified. From the heights in narrow channels run many small streams, one discharging itself into a pool filled with trout, etc.; over this is thrown a bridge with an alcove. The grounds contain in extent four hundred acres; and trees are planted so artificially as to yield an appearance hardly to be distinguished from nature a little improved; here are to be seen pillars, urns, rotundas, alcoves and field seats judiciously disposed: amongst them an urn dedicated to the memory of Alexander Pope, on which is an inscription savoring of flattery.

Returning by the way we went, we alighted at the Golden Cross, Hales Owen, where we were furnished with a room by ourselves and dinner. On this day was held a fair in this town; seeing a large multitude collected I would fain have mixed with the people, but the curiosity of my companion not prompting him, and my fatigue by an execrable hard trotter rendering me indisposed to needless exercise, prevented our seeing the humors of this part of the country. In passing the road a few furlongs before, we arrived at this town; about an inn were collected two companies of tradesmen with black rods tipped with brass. They assemble at certain times and are under certain rules; have a public box, supplying a fund to be employed in maintaining the sick, blind, wounded and disabled, and finally burying members and their wives. Their regulations have a happy tendency to promote among the laboring handicraftsmen cleanliness, good manners, order and sociability.

The road to Hagley in general is though level but tolerably good; the views pleasing; at two o'clock we arrived at the Leasowes, now in possession of a Squire Horne. Attended by the gardener we entered through what is called the priory gate, a gateway and arch formed by old stumps and moss, communicating with a serpentine walk on a shady bank of a stream running through a craggy wild bottom to the pool now emptied of its waters. It is supplied also by another meandering stream, on the banks of which are judiciously placed statues, urns, and resting seats, from each of which appear most agreeable and diverting objects, varied from each other in every remove, consisting of hills, dales, streams, houses, and clumps, rows, and forests of trees on lands in high culti- vation. The closing scene was a natural perspective view of a charming cascade running in various directions, the whole, almost, the eye could trace through bending oaks and osiers, from a spot whereon is placed an urn inscribed to Virgil and called his grotto or recess. Hence to the mossy bower or grotto, where after resting I reluctantly mounted my horse, and arrived at my new lodgings No. 20 Moor-street, at eight o'clock, much fatigued.

CHAPTER VI.

Birmingham, May 20, 1777.　Breakfasted with Mr. G. Russell, and with him proceeded to a Mr. Onion's, in order to have a sight of his auriculas and polyanthuses, of which he has a great variety, and of the finest hues and stripes.　Mr. Russell having invited company to meet us, we returned to his house to dinner, and passed the day agreeably.　Arrived at our lodgings before nine o'clock.

May 22.　A fair begins here to day, proclaimed by the bailiffs, constables, wardens, etc., in procession, beginning at eleven o'clock. Streets crowded, many people coming in from the country; a day of jollity rather than business, and the evening ends in riot, drunkenness, etc.　The low bailiff is the first officer in dignity, and by custom is chosen from the dissenters.　He nominates the jury, who appoints the constables; he also presides in the courts leet, gives a yearly feast, and has no further concern in town affairs.　His service continues a year.　The high constable inspects the markets, and is appointed for life by the lord lieutenant of the county.

May 24.　Walked to Soho Gardens; the grounds naturally capable of improvements in a high degree; they already consist of gravel walks in the serpentine form, shrubbery, flower borders, an occasional cascade running down a narrow pebbled canal, and emerging into a pond below, containing two islands.　Took an afternoon ramble with my companion to Ashton Park, now in possession of Lady Holt, about two miles distant; the richness of the soil and high cultivation they are in, almost ravished my companion. It is almost surrounded with a lofty brick wall, and is agreeably diversified by rows of trees, clumps and single trees, with many large spots of clean lands.　The house is of brick in the old Gothic style, very large, having battlements on its top and round turrets. The church standing on the lands and adjoining the avenues of the mansion house of the estate of Sir Charles Holt, is remarkable for the smallness of the building, and the loftiness of the tower and spire. Returned home not a little fatigued.

May 26. Left Birmingham for Sheffield, our first intended stage being the city of Litchfield, sixteen miles; roads level and sandy, the lands in sight barren and uninclosed. Just without the city, and in a field adjoining, we saw for the first time the English militia; the men were as likely and well accoutred as the king's troops, and as clean and well dressed. Arrived at the George inn, where we bespoke dinner, and while it was preparing, walked forth to view the city and cathedral; the former of about eight thousand inhabitants, houses mostly in the old style, few shops and little appearance of business. The cathedral is a venerable pile; round the western part of the building stand in mutilated condition many statues, being defaced, as some of its inside ornaments were by the zealots of Cromwell's party in the unhappy times of Charles I. There is nothing remarkable within except a curiously wrought screen of stone, separating the altar from the chapel of the Ten Virgins, to whom it was dedicated, and where prayers at six in the morning are daily said. The niches in which the Virgins stood have remained unfilled ever since the pious purgators of those times of confusion before mentioned; and as another instance of their enthusiastic madness, they broke to pieces all the stained glass belonging to this church. Over the western door is an inscription, stating that this church was erected in the 657th year of the Christian era, was endowed by Offa in the Saxon times, and by Henry II. and Richard I. since. In a flat tomb against the fourth wall lies a Dean Haywood, who, many years since, fantastically attempting to imitate our Saviour in fasting forty days, died in fourteen, a martyr to his folly; two statues, one resembling him in his full bulk, and the other in his emaciated state, remain as monuments to perpetuate his impious folly.

From this survey we returned to dinner. Arrived at Burton at four o'clock, over roads almost an entire level, as soft as a carpet, and in a straight direction as far as the eye could reach. At the distance of eight miles from our last stage we passed the Trent, near to where the great Staffordshire canal (joining the Trent and Severn) begins; crossing and recrossing it, and travelling on its banks and within sight for many miles. This canal is carried over the small river Dove and many streams. Took our departure for Derby; the roads as pleasing as last stage till near the town, when the face of the country became hilly and uneven, yielding a new picture to the eye. Stopped at the George-and-Dragon inn, Derby; took tea, and accompanied by my fellow traveller, rambled through the town, which appears to be of considerable extent, having four Episcopal churches. The streets are paved with small pebbles; some of them of a convenient width, the rest narrow, having a gutter in the middle, common to most of the paved towns. Here is a square, paved, serving as a parade for the military, parties of which are posted in every great town. One side is built on arches, forming a shelter for the inhabitants from inclement weather. There is great appearance of trade, and, indeed, the silk mills, flatting and rolling mills, and lead works, employ many hands. Here are also many shops, which for size and arrangement resemble those of London.

Derby, May 27. We visited the famous silk mills, and were told by the master workman that ninety-seven thousand movements were set to work by a single large water wheel. The house is two hundred feet long and thirty-six feet wide, and has five floors, each filled by machines.

From thence made a visit to the porcelain manufactory;—the principal ingredient is common flint stones reduced to an impalpable powder after being broken in a water mill. All the images are cast in very small parts at first, joined together by hand, as the head, the hands, etc.; the moulds are made of plaster of Paris, and not bigger than the outside shell of a large walnut, which they resemble, and like them consist of four parts. The fancy pieces, as flowers, images, etc., are formed a clear liquor poured into the moulds; in less than two minutes, by absorbing the liquor, leaves a solid figure, which after it is dried is painted, gilded, etc., and passes the fire four several times, and if gilt undergoes polishing to bring it to its lustre.

From this cursory survey we returned to our inn, and departed for Lord Scarsdale's seat, called Kiddlestone, four miles distant. Arrived at the portal and lodge in the form of a triumphal arch built of stone; through this we were admitted into the park, observable for the greatest quantity of large white oaks and elms.

About a mile from the entrance over a straight, clean carpet road, we came to the lawn terminated by the house, making a noble appearance ; passing a large handsome stone bridge thrown over a fine stream made by art. On the lawn, on every side of the house, are large single oaks, also many clumps and rows, which with the great herds of horned cattle make a most picturesque view. The entrance to the house is by a double flight of steps under a grand portico, being formed of noble columns supporting a pediment, having in front my lord's arms, and crowned on the top with three female figures, erect, representing plenty, peace, and wisdom. The centre contains the great hall, and on the back front the saloon ; the ceiling of the former is supported by fourteen red veined alabaster fluted pillars of the Corinthian order on each side ; its height 40 feet, length 67, and width 42 ; the pannels of the doors light airy *papier maché* manufacture ; the designs are from Greek and Roman mythology ; the flooring the most beautiful clear oak, taken from my lord's forests, as the pillars are from his own quarry, and bear an excellent polish. The wings are connected by circular corridors, and in each wing twenty-one rooms on a floor elegantly finished and furnished. The state bed has very curiously carved posts, its furniture and hangings blue damask ; my lady's dressing plate the greatest in quantity of any I have seen except the queen's, and is silver embossed double gilt. My lady was at home, and remained to indulge us with a sight of every part of the house. The living of my lord and lady when in the country is quite in the family way. Their eldest daughter, going in a loose country dress to take a ramble over the lawn, on discovering us retreated back and disappeared. This house for situation, elegance and grandeur united, need not yield to any.

From this pleasing spot we departed for Ashburn, the first town on the peak ; 'tis a country town, has a market and an Episcopal church, but is remarkable for nothing that I could learn except its being a station for those whose curiosity brings them rather to view Dovedale and Islam gardens, the residence of old Chaucer, where strangers are shown the very spot in which he wrote many of his pieces.

May 28. Rising early we departed in a post-chaise for Castleton, situated near the mouth of the Devil's Peak ; the road is over bare and dreary hills ; the whole country that is inclosed is by stone walls, being extremely barren of trees, shrubs, and bushes, many hundred acres together not having the appearance of either. The divisions of land much larger than to be met with elsewhere, and scarce a house to be seen, being situated, I presume, in bottoms laid from the road; the sheep are small, and distinguished from all others by a kind of ruff or ridge of long hair round the neck; from the plain we descended into the town, lying in the bottom, in a road encompassing half the ridge of mountains, extending to a great length from hence; this road in many places is very steep, and at almost every step hazardous, and the accident of the horses stumbling, the reins breaking, or wheels coming off, would throw one down a precipice, when nothing short of a miracle could preserve him from destruction. The tower of the church, of an ordinary height, when first discovered seemed to be many hundred feet beneath us. Arrived at the George inn, and took the guide, who seasonably arrived with some gentlemen whom he had just attended through the cavern.

Set off from the inn to visit this remarkable subterraneous frightful pit, etc., distance from hence about five hundred yards; the entrance is between two lofty eminences, almost perpendicular, or rather overhanging, of a height eighty-seven yards; its appearance awfully great and terrifying; part is craggy and clothed in trees and shrubs. The passage into this natural cave is under an arch fourteen yards high and forty wide, rising somewhat higher; within the first cave resides a woman of thirty-seven years of age, who was born in a hut here, and has inhabited it ever since;—besides her, here are dwelling two more families, and several of the town's people who daily resort here to labor in the twine spinning, in which business more than a score are daily employed. Light enough is admitted to do that and any common work; from the mouth to the further end of post cavern is eighty yards, and from thence to the first water is seventy yards, making in all one hundred and fifty yards. Over this water, fourteen yards in length, I was conveyed in a small boat, for the greater part of the distance lying on my back; the arch being too low to sit upright. The depth of the water is two and a half feet, which the guide, Robert Dakin, waded through, pushing the boat before him. My companion choosing me to explore the unknown regions, I first entered, and he took the second passage, and I waited for him before I pro-

ceeded. At the further end of the first cave, a good woman with
a dozen candles attended to furnish each of us with one, which,
having lighted, each took in his hand and proceeded from the
first water, one by one, in a narrow path to another cavern distant
ninety yards, the width of which was seventy yards, and height
forty; from hence at a small distance is the second water, over
which I was carried first on our guide's back ten yards; its depth
is perhaps a foot. My companion next followed at the right of
the attendants, and forded it on foot. Our next stage was in a
cave called Roger Rains, from a continual dropping through the
rocks and earth. The entrance to the grand cavern is under an
arch fifteen rods high; this forms a kind of hanging gallery, on
the top of which stood seven singers, each holding a lighted candle
in his hand. They entertained us with " *Fill, fill the glasses ;*"
the splendor of the lights reflected from the vaulted roof, and the
grand echo, pleased us beyond expression. On our return we were
saluted by this same company with " *God save the king.*" From
hence we went forward to the Devil's cellar; of the origin of this
name we could not be informed; there is nothing in its appearance hideous, nor from whence we could conjecture its name.
Here we descended fifty yards on a road of firm sand, and from
hence the path leads to the cascade, which is heard at considerable distance; the discharge is by a stream dividing itself into
two channels, crossing the cavern and continued under the hill, at
the bottom of which, at its opposite foot, it forms a small river.
From hence to a place called " the top," and thence to the
four regular arches, as regular as if formed by design; and from
hence to Tom of Lincoln, (so called from its resemblance to the top
of a bell and its enormous magnitude,) and from thence to the extremity of the cavern, distant from its mouth seven hundred and
fifty yards. The level at the further end of the cavern was taken
by Doctor Solander and Mr. Banks, and is two hundred and fifty
yards;—the charming appearance of the external light on our approach towards the first cave, on our return back, excited a most
pleasing sensation. Over the cavern is an ancient fortification in
the Roman manner. After discharging the customary dues for
candles, singers, etc., through a crowd of beggars who always
attend strangers at the mouth on their return, which we were cau-

17

tioned to neglect, passed on to our inn, where we dined, and soon
departed for Sheffield, where we arrived about six o'clock, and
alighted at the George inn.

Sheffield, May 29. Presented an introductory letter from Mr.
George Russell of Birmingham to his correspondent, a Mr. Broomhead, whose reception of us at first was cool, but his after de-
meanor and hospitality much more than counterbalanced the
former; I rather imputed it to an honest bluntness and ignorance
of forms. He is a wealthy cutler, whose principal business lay in
the American line. Attended by him we walked round the town
to several branches, as rolling mills, grinding cutlery, white lead
mill, etc. After dinner strolled amongst the multitude to the race
ground called " Crooke's Moor;" the number supposed to be full
twenty thousand. From a lofty stand opposite the ground I had a
full view of the race; four heats were run, the first by seven horses;
the plate, a silver gilt cup, worth seventy pounds, was gained
by a horse called " Why not," who, on the two first heats was
almost distanced. The humors of the race I had an opportunity
of seeing in perfection; the different passions wherewith they were
agitated afforded me no small diversion. The horses were called
by the names of their riders, who were differently clothed, as pink,
orange, scarlet, striped, etc. etc. The plate procured by subscription of the town, was carried by the constable attended by the town
officers in their habits, preceded by a flag. On the ground were
erected many stands, and all filled; the last heat was scarcely
over till nine o'clock in the evening.

May 30. Called on Mr. J. Broomhead, and with him walked
through the town to the colliery, so called, being a road-way
from the Duke of Norfolk's pits to the yard, in which the coal
is taken up into carts and conveyed to town; the descent easy,
and by means of a spring, the carts, without horses, under the guidance of a man, being conveyed by a sort of self-motion for more
than a mile. At the end of the way the carts are run on stages,
through which, by tilting them, the contents are discharged. After
a view of this curious contrivance, we retired homewards, but
meeting Mr. Aspden of Philadelphia, a gentleman with whom we
dined at Mr. Smith's in Birmingham a few days before, agreed to
join company, and immediately departed in a stage coach from

Sheffield, and arrived at Black Barnsley through a delightful though uneven road; distance fourteen miles. Here we took post-chaises, and in two hours alighted at Wakefield, a clothing town, wherein appear evident tokens of taste in building and of wealth; the avenues to it delightful, the roads like a carpet walk, on one side a raised terrace walk for foot passengers, flagged for more than two miles; the lands hereabouts excellent, and under the most improved cultivation. The Westgate-street has the noblest appearance of any I ever saw, out of London; its pavements in the best order; its length near half a mile, and width ten rods. Were it not for some old, low buildings, London could not boast a more magnificent street. It has a very large Episcopal church, with a remarkably lofty tower and spire. The principal character in the novel called "*The Vicar of Wakefield*" was taken from the late vicar of this church, named Johnson, whose peculiarly odd and singular humor has exposed his memory to the ridicule of that satire. W soon after departed for Leeds in a post-chaise, through good roads and fertile lands: from Sheffield to Leeds the face of the country is more pleasing, the lands in better improvement and more peopled, than in more than twenty counties I have passed through in England; alighted at the "Old King's Arms" at nine o'clock, where we supped and lodged.

Leeds, May 31. Sent our names to S. Elam and waited breakfast; he soon came, but having taken his, declined partaking with us. We walked forth under his guidance, and took dinner with him afterwards; rambled to a village called Armley, to see a scribbling mill, by which more wool is discharged than ten hands can do in the same time. It is performed by a horse, but its construction cannot be described, not being exposed to open view, it being a favor shown to Mr. Elam, on whose account we were favored with a sight of it. Too nice an inspection would have excited suspicion, which we wished to avoid. The manufacturers of every kind through England are not pleased to admit strangers to a sight of the machines and process of their business. From thence we returned back on the sides of the canal, which for the first time is to be opened with ceremony next Wednesday; no part of it has hitherto been used.

June 2. This town is said to contain ten thousand people,

many well-filled shops, and various trades; its principal business in
narrow and coarse woollen cloths, consigned to foreign orders, but
little to London or inland trade; many of its merchants are
wealthy. It has a large cloth market of brick, of three ranges,
each range having two walks, and the walks are called King-street,
Queen-street, Cheapside, etc. Set off for Huddersfield, distant sixteen miles, and is the town to which the merchants of Leeds, Halifax and Wakefield resort to buy cloths from the clothiers abounding
in this neighborhood. The town of Huddersfield is very old-built,
and has a wretched appearance. The butchery was built by Sir
John Ramsey, proprietor of the land, whose rent is seventy pounds.
After dinner we entered a post-chaise for Halifax, where we arrived
at six o'clock.

This town is supposed to be larger than Leeds; its streets, if it
can be said to have any, are excellently paved, and have a convenient flagged walk on each side raised; lying uneven they are
always clean; but in general they are narrow and short, each end
bounded by a triangular house; many large and well-built ones
in, but more just without the town. The situation of the town is
on an uneven, low eminence, surrounded by lofty hills on all sides
in the most improved condition, laid out in lots bounded by live
hedges, rows of trees, and stone walls, almost as even as the walls
of a house. The whole country for many miles within view
abounds in manufactories and farm houses; the people here are
numerous and industrious, their houses very cleanly. Amongst
other kinds of good conduct, we in our rambles saw fifteen children employed in bending wires and preparing them in the various
branches of card making, and were told their earnings were from
two and sixpence to five shillings a week; which employment
not only keeps their little minds from vice, but renders them early
capable of providing for their own support, and takes a heavy burden from their poor parents. We entered a nap-raising mill; the
process is performed by laying a cloth under an instrument divided
into little squares of the diameter of the nap designed to be raised,
or rather larger, carried by water. This instrument is about eight
feet long and two feet wide, and is jostled backwards and forwards by means of a little gage filled with teeth suited to a cog-
wheel, which receives its motion from another communicating

with the great wheel. By Mr. Aspden's desire, we accompanied him immediately on our arrival to a Mr. Rawson's seat, a little out of Halifax, called "*Stony-ride*," meaning *Stony-road*, the road to it being stony, (the Yorkshire people often using an *i* for an *o*.) This was a friend to whom he had a letter; neither Mr. Rawson nor his sons were at home; but soon after our return to the inn one of his sons came, and would have engaged us to accompany him back, but it being late, we declined it for this evening, which he passed and supped with us.

Halifax, June 3. Rambled with my companions to the lofty surrounding hills, from whence we had an ample view of the town; only one parish church, the mother of twelve of the neighboring ones; sectaries of various kinds abound here. By the manufacturers living hereabouts there is building of stone, a large and commodious market house, containing a square of one hundred and ten yards by ninety; its lower story is fronted by short square pillars, forming arcades, on the back part of which are rooms for each separate manufacturer, of twelve feet by eight, and before the rooms a covered walk of four feet wide; the second story is supported by square pillars cut into rustic, with a walk before as below, but more open and spacious, the pillars not being so large. The floor of the third story is surrounded by Doric pillars supporting the roof, containing the same accommodations as below; the height of each story twelve feet. The town is all built of stone, very irregular, but its streets the best paved of any town in England, London not excepted, and from the unevenness of the ground always clean. By the hospitality of Mr. Rawson we were delayed here for two days, whose importunity would not suffer us to depart till Thursday the fifth. We passed our time pleasantly enough in visiting among other things his copperas works; the copperas made from that part of common pit coal called slate, charged with sulphur; its process easy and short, being collected and thrown into a large heap, perhaps of two or three hundred tons;—water poured on it, which, filtering through, passes by pipes into an underground cistern or large receiver, is boiled, and from thence carried into a smaller cistern like the distillers'; there remaining until it cools and crystallizes.

Thursday, June 5. Departed from Halifax in a post-chaise,

taking leave of our late companion Aspden, who left us at the inn for Preston, on horseback. Pursuing the road we ascended a long hill of more than a mile, and soon arrived at a very lofty ridge of the most desolate and forlorn appearance, called Blackstone Edge, continuing for several miles. The road level, hard and straight, and on that score pleasant ; the land waste and of a russet hue, covered with furze ; not a tree, shrub, bush or plant, hedge or wall to be seen. From hence we descended into low grounds, well inhabited and improved ; in one respect this part of England is more pleasing than the others ; the grounds are covered with houses, each manufacturer having a small farm or parcel of land besides his trade to depend on, there being more freeholders or owners of small farms and plantations here than in any county of the kingdom. We arrived at Rochdale about two o'clock, engaged dinner, and took a ramble. The church stands on a hill, to which the ascent is by a hundred stone steps. This town is remarkable for many wealthy merchants ; it has a large woollen market, the merchants from Halifax, etc., repairing hither weekly ; the neighborhood abounds in clothiers. From hence the road to Manchester, distant about thirteen miles, is level and sandy, the soil light, the general nature of the land in this county, where the people speak an uncouth, peculiar dialect, unintelligible to the ears of strangers. About six o'clock we alighted at the " Spread-eagle inn," and procured private lodgings at Mrs. Barlow's, next door to the inn.

Manchester, June 6. Walked out to the Duke of Bridgewater's canal, and on its banks met Mr. Nelson, who for some time lodged at Mrs. Leavitt's in Salem, New England ; he is from Ireland, passing through the manufacturing towns to London. We stepped into St. John's church, a small but elegant edifice in Gothic style ; over the altar is a fine stained-glass window, executed at York ; three erect images of St. Peter, Christ, and St. James, the colors quite lively, which the meridian lustre of the sun's rays not a little assisted. In the vestry is another window by the same hand ; on this is stained the founder's name, a Squire Byrom. This church was finished in 1769 ; its tower is crowned with battlements and high pinnacles ; the body of the church having such also all around its roof. From hence we adjourned to the Castlefield, to see the exercise of the militia, making as good appearance as the king's troops in discipline and dress. This field is an eminence of oval form, and here are supposed to be the remains of an old Roman encampment, the outside wall and cement yet to be seen. From this place we adjourned to the " Royal Oak" ordinary.

June 7. With Mr. Nelson set off for the canal, intending to take a passage to Worsley to visit the Duke of Bridgewater's coal mines. After some delay we entered the passage boat, drawn by a horse in the manner of the Trek-schuits in Holland. Arrived at Worsley in two hours, passing athwart the river Irwell, over which the canal runs, being raised on arches not less than fifty feet in height above that stream. In many places the bottom of the canal is considerably higher than the level of the neighboring grounds. Sent compliments to Mr. Gilbert, the steward, asking the favor of seeing the duke's under-ground works, which was granted, and we stepped into the boat, passing into an archway partly of brick and partly cut through the stone, of about three and a half feet high; we received at entering six lighted candles. This arch-way, called a funnel, runs into the body of the mountain almost in a direct line three thousand feet, its medium depth beneath the surface about eighty feet; we were half an hour passing that distance. Here begins the first under-ground road to the pits, ascending into the wagon road, so called, about four feet above the water, being a highway for the wagons, containing about a ton weight of the form of a mill-hopper, running on wheels, to convey the coals to the barges or boats. Under the guidance of a miner, with each a lighted candle in his hand, we proceeded through an arched-way about five feet high, walking with our bodies at an angle of less than sixty degrees, through a road of three feet in width, a length of eight hundred yards, arrived at the coal mine, which appearing about five feet through the roof, was supported by many posts, the area being about twenty feet square and height scarce four. From this dismal abode, which my companion, whose name was Chandler, would fain have dissuaded me from proceeding to visit, after remaining a few minutes, I hastened back to our boat. One may go six miles by water in various directions, the wagon ways to the pits lying below the level of the water; it is said the distance from the mouth is six miles in the funnel. A hundred men are daily employed, and each turns out a ton a day; the miners' wages two shillings, and the laborers' about one shilling. Price of coal at the pit twopence per hundred weight; at the key threepence halfpenny, and at the door fourpence halfpenny. The boat having left, we returned to town on foot, five miles through fields and vacant lands.

The centre of this town of Manchester consists principally of old buildings; its streets narrow, irregularly built, with many capital houses interspersed. By act of parliament old buildings are taken down to enlarge the streets. It has a few good ones; King-street is the best built, is long and sufficiently wide; most of its houses noble. Great additions of buildings and streets are daily making, and of a larger size than at Birmingham, nor have all the new ones so dusky a face as in that town, and in that respect are fairer and better; for extent of ground whereon it stands, nor number of inhabitants, does the latter exceed or in my opinion come up to it. The disposition and manners of this people, as given by themselves, are inhospitable and boorish. I have seen nothing to contradict this assertion, though my slender acquaintance will not justify me in giving that character. In all the manufacturing towns there is a jealousy and suspicion of strangers; an acquaintance with one manufacturer effectually debars one from connection with a second in the same business. It is with difficulty one is admitted to see their works, and in many cases it is impracticable, express prohibitions being given by the masters. The dissenters are some of the most wealthy merchants and manufacturers here, but mortally abhorred by the Jacobites. The dress of the people here savors not much of the London mode in general; the people are remarkable for coarseness of feature, and the language is unintelligible.

Manchester, June 8. Attended public worship at a dissenters' meeting house, both services. Walked to the end of Danesgate, and drank tea at our companion Nelson's lodgings; and were amused by the free and unrestrained chat of his landlady, named Hudson, a quaker in religion, and jacobite in political principle. The number of the latter description since the English prince mounted the throne is somewhat lessened here, as I am told by our landlady, who is in the abdicated family's interest, which is here openly professed; all of that party putting up large oak boughs over their doors on the 29th May to express joy at the glorious event of the restoration of the Stuart family to the English throne; many such I saw. The ladies, who, if they take a part, are ever violent, scruple not openly and without restraint to drink Prince Charles's health, and express their wishes for his restoration to his paternal kingdoms. I saw the house wherein the prince, as he is called, dwelt whilst here, (at the time of his invasion;) the gentleman and his family still remain in it, and steady to their principles, which, however, did not hurry them into lengths that exposed them to the resentment of government. His name is Dixon, and his house is in Market-street lane, on the left as one goes from the market; and our host, a Mr. Bower, with whom we passed a very social evening at his house in Leigh-street, told us Lord John Murray and his secretary lodged at his house at that time. One of those executed here in the last rebellion was a son of a woman who had borne twenty-nine children.

June 9. Passed the day in rambling about town with our new-found companion, Nelson.

June 11. Having agreed to join Mr. Nelson in a post-chaise to York, in the neighborhood of which we propose to cease from our labors, and hoping the rewards of a cheap plentiful country to reside in for some time, for this purpose we went to engage a chaise at the old "White Swan Inn," where we saw three young countrymen, a Capt. Gore, Mr. Joy and son, at the end of their ramble northward from London, designing to return to Bristol by way of Wolverhampton. My fellow traveller on this discovery, tired of his expensive ramble, immediately took fire and determined to abandon me, and accompany them on their intended route; loth to part in this quarter and in the situation I was then in, for certain prudential reasons, agreed to his fantastic plan, though entirely contrary to my wish and views; and having disengaged ourselves from Mr. Nelson, to his mortification, engaged a post-chaise to Macclesfield. On the 12th June we proceeded on through a road of seven miles paved with pebbles to Stockport, a considerable town, having some reputable buildings; its streets are narrow and paved. From hence to Macclesfield lying in Cheshire about twelve miles, being our first stage from Manchester. At five miles from

18

this is the seat of Sir George Warren, surrounded by finely improved lands and pleasure grounds, lying on my left. A little beyond on the right is the seat of Charles Leigh, Esq., possessed of four thousand a year, and of a considerable tract adjoining to Manchester, which he has laid out in streets to be let on building leases. At Macclesfield we alighted, breakfasted, etc., departed for Leek, a distance of thirteen miles; the former town has a silk mill or mills, and a manufactory which appears not to have much business. The town in general is ill built, the houses, as in most manufacturing places, of most credit in its environs. From the George inn we departed not greatly pleased with the host's attendance, nor I with my companion's behavior here.

Leek, at which I now am, has a manufactory of silk and ribbons, and one for hair-buttons; the former chiefly for the great dealers at Coventry, though very largely for foreign orders and the London supply, as well as the inland towns. From hence to Sandon, called in this country language Sand, is a distance of eighteen miles, which we were four hours in passing. Here we alighted at " the Dog and Duck," supped and lodged; the former as quietly served up, and as genteelly, as could be in London ; the town is small, houses scattering, and of an indifferent aspect.

June 13. Departed without breakfast for Stafford, the county town; the roads in general are sandy, but on our approaching the town, the lands assumed a better face. The main street through which we passed is paved, the houses well built, full shops, and an appearance of business and of wealth. On our right, at the distance of a mile, stands on the summit of an insulated hill, cut, as should seem, by art into a cone about one third down, a stone edifice, like a lofty tower, which is the only remains of Stafford Castle, making an agreeable object to a traveller. From hence the lands and roads are greatly altered for the better ; fine pastures, excellent live hedge fences, and rows of trees in great abundance. Our next stage was a distance of ten miles, at a place called Penkridge ; here again we took another driver, carriage and horses, and through a most excellent turnpike road and a delightfully improved country, arrived at the old " Angel Inn," Wolverhampton, where we dined, and having despatched a messenger for my old friend Timmins, he soon arrived; by his invitation accompanied him and our companion to see the great manufactory of Taylor and Jones, (who are also exporting merchants,) for japanning tin, paper snuff boxes, iron tools, etc. This town is large, has a capital manufactory in the lock and hinge way, and most other branches of the iron business, and is supposed to contain twenty thousand inhabitants. Like all the old towns it is ill built, and like Birmingham has a dusky look. Once for all, its numbers I judge are overrated; every town and borough is so. After repeated invitations to remain we departed before six o'clock for Stourbridge, distant ten miles, to which we arrived at half past seven, being driven Jehu like through roads as level, hard and pleasant as a garden gravel walk ; the country yielding a pleasant view from good husbandry, fruitful soil, lofty trees and live hedges. We were agreeably disappointed, for instead of a pitiful, mean town, as its avenues seemed to threaten, we found a well built, large, lively and rich town, having a noble, wide and convenient street a mile long, with cross streets well paved. It is famous for glass, nails, heavy iron work, as anvils, etc., and some cloth manufactories. After rambling for an hour over the town, we supped and retired to rest.

Stourbridge, June 14. Set off at eight o'clock and arrived at the " Crown" inn, Bromesgrove, twelve miles, at ten ; a respectable town, but it contains no large manufactories ; the only one of any consideration is for linen cloth. The lands about here in an excellent state of husbandry and fertile ; farm-houses and gentlemen's seats more numerous in this and the following stage than on any road we had passed in this route, except the west riding of Yorkshire, to which it bears a comparison. Were set down at the Bell inn, Broad-street, Worcester, at twelve o'clock ; a very handsome, well built city, having spacious, airy streets, a noble cathedral and elegant modern houses ; its shops large and well filled, the town lively and full of business ; its inhabitants have the character of being polite and genteel, and indeed they have more the air of Londoners than at any place I have seen. The Severn runs on one side of the city, by which conveyance is easy to Gloucester, the distance being twenty-eight miles, performed in seven hours in small vessels. Here is a manufacture of porcelain, said to be the best made in England. While rambling through the streets we fell by accident into the cathedral green, and meeting a boy with

a prayer book in one hand and the church key in the other, he
accosted us with, " Gentlemen, are ye a mind to go into the church?"
and on our answering in the affirmative, the doorkeeper admitted
us. It has many old monuments, (as well as modern,) particularly
that of King John, whose body by his desire was buried in the choir
just before the high altar, over which spot is a flat statue of him.
Here also lies in a little chapel the body of Prince Arthur, eldest
son of Henry VII., and likewise an Oswald, a bishop of this
see before the Norman conquest; the only modern I thought worthy
to remember, is the worthy Dr. Hough, about forty years since a
bishop of this see. The chapter house, also used as a library, is of
an oval form, and its walls to a considerable height covered with
cases faced with glass, and very well filled with books. In this
city is a magnificent town hall, having below many full length
portraits. This being market day the streets were so thronged that
our chaise could scarce make its way through to the inn. Having
spent four hours in this beautiful and pleasant place, we departed
for Tewksbury, a considerable town; here the apple orchards
began to appear of uncommon height and bigness. From the
western quarter of Staffordshire to the very houses of Bristol,
through the delightful counties of Worcester and Gloucester, the
fields, pastures and enclosures have an uncommon richness and
verdure; fruit and forest trees in greater abundance and larger
girth and greater height than are to be seen elsewhere in England.
Tewksbury has no capital manufacture except for white cotton
stockings, for which it is noted. It is remarkable, however, for a
parish church one hundred and seven yards long, and more than
twenty-five broad; its roof supported by round shafted pillars seven
yards in girth, contains several old monuments. The first I observed
was Richard Nevil, the great Earl of Warwick, called the king-
maker, raised on a lofty monument scarce as big as the life, in a
kneeling posture with uplifted closed hands; in a chapel are
decumbent his daughter and her husband George, Duke of Clarence;
and in a flat grave just before the door of the choir, is the tomb of
Henry, son of the unfortunate Henry VI.

June 15. From the Sun inn, Tewksbury, we departad before
breakfast, and through rough and dirty roads arrived at the " Bell"
inn, Gloucester, at nine o'clock; notwithstanding the fine plenti-

ful harvests of corn, cider, and pasturage, for which this county is noted, for miles around the city the houses are small, dirty, and in ill repair, the avenues slovenly, fences and walls in a ruinous state, the barns generally of wood, all tottering to their fall; the bridges the meanest and in the worst condition anywhere to be passed. After breakfast and dressing, we all attended worship in the cathedral, being decently and respectfully provided with seats in the choir; the service was chanted. The dean and sub-dean performed the communion service. From church I repaired to our inn, leaving my fellow travellers to pursue their ramble till dinner time. Dirty narrow streets, and mean, ill repaired houses, constitute too great a part of this city to render it an agreeable residence. After dinner, young Joy and I rambled into the cathedral; the cloisters are reckoned the finest in England; after viewing them we retreated into the church, and meeting one of the vergers, were conducted by him to the old monuments. Thence back to the inn, when we took coach and left the city, part of our company being already gone. The next stage was at Newport, consisting only of four inns and a dissenting meeting house, distant from our last stage fifteen miles, and from Bristol eighteen; the roads are dirty and rough, the slovenliness of the farmers' houses and the richness of soil, were as before; here we lodged.

Newport, June 16. After breakfast departed alone, our fellow travellers being already gone, and at twelve o'clock alighted at the " White Lion" inn, Broad-street, Bristol; dined and afterwards visited Radcliffe church: drank tea at Mr. Waldo's.

Bristol, June 17. Breakfasted at Mr. Waldo's; walked to Hot Wells, and Mr. Gouldney's grotto; after dinner accompanied my fellow travellers to Taylor's glass works; in our way through " Long-row," were attacked by the virulent tongue of a vixen, who saluted us by the names of " damned American rebels," etc. In our return from Hot Wells, we passed a person dressed in green, with a small round hat flapped before, very like an English country gentleman, who is the supposed Count Falkenstein, under which character the Emperor of Germany travels incog. Removed our trunks to a Mr. Sladen's in Queen's square.

CHAPTER VII.

Bristol, June 18, 1777. This being the day in which Mr. Chester, the county member elect, is to make his triumphal entry into the city, it was ushered in by ringing of bells and discharging of cannon, the noise of which early disturbed my rest. On the towers of all the churches were displayed colors and jacks; ensigns and pendants on most of the vessels at the quays. On Brandon hill were placed twenty-two cannon, discharging several rounds in the day, answered by the vessels. After dinner I strolled through the streets that were lined with people, reaching from the extent of the city on the farther side quite through and up to the rising grounds on the Down, beyond Park-street, the windows on each side filled to behold the great man. My stand was on the open space on the hither side of the bridge over the Frome; the procession began at seven o'clock; footmen two and two, then followed others on horseback, two and two in the centre. Mr. Chester preceded, and was followed by more than a thousand persons, of whom one hundred and fifty were mounted and clad in new blue coats and breeches, with buff waistcoats, the Duke of Beaufort's hunting garb. These were headed by the champion dressed in blue silk, armed cap-a-pie, and at all points, bearing in his hand a mace that he waved every hundred steps; stopping his horse at the same time, on which arose three loud huzzas. The rear was brought up by nearly a hundred carriages; the day was devoted to mirth and festivity, nor was the following night without its share. The Duke of Beaufort, whose man Mr. Chester was, privately left the procession just before its arrival in town, and took a stand in a friend's house with his duchess to see the parade through the town, and enjoy the triumph over his rival without observation.

TO REV. ISAAC SMITH, SIDMOUTH, DEVON.

Bristol, June 19, 1777.

DEAR SIR:

After a long, expensive, and not very pleasing tour, I am at length set down, for some weeks' abode at least, in this city. My experience, dearly enough bought, teaches me that manufacturing towns are not proper places of residence for idle people, either on account of pleasure or profit;—the expenses of living being as high almost as at St. James's in every such town, how far distant soever from the capital. The spirit of bargaining and taking advantage runs through every line of life there, but in the north it is cruelly predominant. I know not but I may ramble before cold weather again to the west, for Exeter with all its faults is paradise itself to Manchester or any town in the north I have seen.

Having by accident met Mr. John Boylston in the American Coffee-house, who informs me he is going off to-morrow for Exeter, I would not fail to embrace so fair an opportunity to let you hear from me, though I had nothing but that simple article to acquaint you with. Nothing will yield me more satisfaction than to hear of your and my other friends' welfare in the west. I had the pleasure to see Counsellor White, now on a tour through North Wales, &c.; be pleased to make my compliments to his family and my acquaintance in your neighborhood. God bless your reverence, and succeed your pious endeavors to reform your flock. You have mine, and I hope for your prayers, and remain,

Your assured friend,
S. Curwen.

June 22. Walked to the cathedral, entering just as service was about to be begun. Mr. Haynes, a canon, preached; a likely figure, but a dull heavy writer and speaker:—the church is kept in nice order. One half of this building was demolished by Cromwell when he bombarded it, and forced Prince Rupert to retire, who for some time kept him out, but was at last forced to abandon it. From hence adjourned to the mayor's chapel, in which I saw several monuments erected A. D. 1268–9, it having been I presume the chapel of a knight templar's house. Here we heard the conclusion of an excellent sermon by the chaplain, Mr. Ireland. In the afternoon, attended worship at St. Stephen's. Evening, at Mr. J. Waldo's, in Brunswick square.

June 25. Passed the afternoon and evening at Mr. Barnes' at quadrille with Mr. Waldo and Mr. Oxnard; also met S. Porter there, on his return from Wales.

June 26. In the evening stopped in our rambles at Lady Huntingdon's chapel, where heard a sensible preacher on the doctrine of love.

June 27. Walked out with Mr. Sewall and Mr. Oxnard through Stapleton to the late Lord Bottetourt's seat and pleasure grounds, now the duchess dowager of Beaufort's; the house is situated on the brow of a hill, standing on a lofty foundation of stone; its front, as approached from Stapleton, has each angle covered with six square towers, and between an open piazza below; the whole house crowned with battlements. It is built of white stone, and possesses an extensive view of the pleasure grounds, and a finely improved country all before it. After tea took a second ramble to Bedminster church-yard.

June 29. Attended worship at the mayor's chapel, met Mr. Boutineau, with whom we took a few rounds in the college green amidst genteel company, and received invitations to tea. In the afternoon, meeting Mr. Barnes and F. Waldo, we joined them going to St. Nicholas' church; a Dr. Buck preached an excellent sermon, and delivered it with great propriety and fervency.

TO WILLIAM BROWNE, ESQ., LONDON.

Queen's Square, Bristol, July 8, 1777.

DEAR SIR:

After a long and expensive ramble to no good purpose, I am at length in this city, proposing to make it my abode for a month or longer;—to what place I shall retreat from hence I am undetermined, though somewhere to the west, as that is a quarter of great plenty and of the least expense. The report of the cheapness of living in Yorkshire is a mere fable, especially in or near the neighborhood of the manufacturing towns, in the west riding, or even in Lancashire as far as Manchester, which last place nothing but interest or superior motives could confine me to.

The distance I am from London, (and probably shall be for many months,) will deprive me of hearing or reading the current news, but few papers falling into my hands; and coffee-houses, the resort of newsmongers and political dabblers, I rarely enter; so if you will now and then employ a few of your leisure moments to let me hear from you, I shall esteem it a favor.

I am, dear sir, very truly yours,

S. Curwen.

July 9. Walked five miles out to see Dundry tower, the steeple so called of a church situated on a lofty ridge commanding an extensive prospect over the Severn into Wales, far into the St. George's Channel, into Somerset, Gloucestershire, and far beyond. Strolling along the quay, met a Swansea coaster, and partly agreed to make a tour through the southern and western parts of Wales.

July 11. Went to the theatre; saw the West Indian and the Misers, the former entertaining; Major O'Flaherty well taken off by Mr. Moody, the best imitation of an Irishman I ever saw; — the latter an unnatural plot, and but illy performed to a very full house.

July 17. Set off on horseback for Bath; fine roads, sun excessively hot and scorching, almost choked by the dust which arose in clouds by the carriages and horses we overtook in great numbers. Alighted at the ;Shakspeare inn, High-street; visited the public places of resort; rambled about the city, dined, and at four o'clock departed by the way of Keynsham for Bristol.

July 18. Drank tea with Mr. Francis Waldo at his lodgings; afterwards adjourned to the theatre, where I was agreeably entertained.

July 23. This day news arrived of the capture of the Fox, man-of-war, of twenty-eight guns, by some American privateers. Unless more spirited measures take place, or others are employed to plan or execute, I know not whether this island itself will not be surrounded by ships from the western continent and their allies. Two ships, just sailed from Bristol, were taken in St. George's channel; and several to and from Ireland, etc., within a month. The nation is in a lethargy, and for aught that appears is like to continue so; treachery, venality, or inability, will, it is to be feared, destroy this devoted people.

July 24. News *via* Liverpool; Gen. Howe burnt Brunswick about 20th June, broke up his camp, going to abandon the Jerseys,

19

to strengthen his lines at Kingsbridge, apprehending an attack there; and with the remainder of his forces and the ships to go up the North river on a secret expedition. The Boston fleet of eighteen privateers sailed with orders to keep together for twenty-five days, and afterwards each to repair to their several destinations. The Newfoundland fishery disturbed, the ships on Grand Bank scattered; some sunk, the whole almost dispersed and ruined. London and the trading parts, even those attached to the government, I am told, begin to grow very uneasy and talk loud. If it should continue, a change in administration must succeed. Alas! to what a low ebb is this nation fallen, that lately gave law to the potent states of France and Spain, in a contest confessedly unequal on the side of its own subjects; but such is the state of human affairs. Goliath was humbled and slain by little David, and those provinces that lately sued to Great Britain for protection and aid, now boldly defy and enter the lists against that very power.

July 26. Took passage to Swansea with Capt. Hawkins, and at eleven o'clock, with two pilot boats ahead, cast off from the quay. In four hours discharged our pilot boat in King Road, five miles from Bristol; we soon grounded, and there remained all night. The return of the ebb served instead of a favorable wind, to carry us to our port of destination. Indeed, it was, as the sailors say, right in our teeth; the strength however of the current is such as to overpower a light gale, in which case vessels coming in or going out drop anchor during the ebb or flood, when unfavorable. This night proved dark and misty; just after midnight we dropped anchor; daylight discovered the master's judgment in selecting his ground to anchor on. We arrived without harm to a stony beach called the ferry place, below the quay about a quarter of a mile.

Swansea, July 29. Attended a court-baron, instituted for determining pecuniary cases under forty shillings, and is equivalent to our justice's court in New England; it is, I presume, appendant to every manor, the lords of which have the nominating, if not the appointing of the officers to this trust. The manor in which this town lies is called Gower, and belongs to the Duke of Beaufort, who chooses its chief magistrate, called Portreve; the present is Mr. Gabriel Powel, justice also in the former court, and whom I saw on the bench.   This town is the first in Glamorganshire for commerce and manufactures, twelve hundred vessels being yearly employed; its staples are coals, copper-plates, and white iron.   The ore for the former, and blocks for the latter, are brought hither in their own vessels from Cornwall, and when manufactured, transported to Bristol chiefly.   The town consists of twenty-five hundred inhabitants, who occupy about three hundred and fifty houses, few elegant or large ; a market-house, erected at Cromwell's expense, the inhabitants being in his interest.   Here are several Episcopal and Dissenting churches, a synagogue and Quaker meeting-house. Service is said and sermons preached in the Welsh tongue once in three weeks.   A custom prevails here of raising the earth on the summit of the grave in the form and size of the coffin beneath, and sticking in herbs and flowers, and during the season of roses, of spreading the leaves thereon.   The country inhabitants almost universally use the Welsh as their mother tongue, scarcely understanding a word of the English, which they call Sasnic, meaning Saxon, to distinguish it from the true British, which was on the invasion narrowed to the small districts of Wales and Cornwall ; English in this principality is taught as the dead languages by the grammar. In a place called Gower the inhabitants speak no Welsh, but beyond they talk in no other tongue ; in the midland counties scarce any thing but Welsh is spoken or known.   Pembrokeshire was settled some ages since by Yorkshire and west country folks, whose descendants retain their native tongue, and are ignorant of the country speech.   In general the inhabitants affect to speak of England as a foreign country, and as we on the west of the Atlantic, saying from England, to England, etc.   The Welsh appear a hardy race, short, clumsy, and strongly built.   The extensive white iron or tin plate works, and copper also, which abound, I fancy is prejudicial to the products of the earth ; and the appearance of the land justifies the opinion.   I am told the land is good, but I confess it has a dreary look ; the lofty hills are, however, enlivened, though bare of trees, (their natural vesture,) by the great number of small huts, so prettily and agreeably scattered over the sides of the hills, being painted white, with the fences or stone walls encompassing them, or forming the courts or yards.

July 30.   A stranger sent in his name, Calvert, desiring an introduction to me; he had married a niece of the late Mr. Gwynn, of Newburyport, Massachusetts, who was one of the co-heiresses, and he wished to inquire about his late uncle's affairs; but I could give only an imperfect account; when I last saw his uncle he had a wife and effects, supposed about two thousand pounds. I took breakfast with Mr. Calvert, and one of the company was the Dr. Collins to whom I had a letter from Mr. Barnes; but he not choosing to make himself known, we took no notice of each other, though we were both apprised of our meeting together, which I thought on his part an impropriety. My companion's capricious resolution to return back, and the ill reception of my letter, were considerations that prevailed with me to accompany him, and we immediately set about preparing for a departure; and thus was my design of remaining some months in this principality frustrated by an injudicious connection which might have been foreseen and avoided. It is with no little reluctance I abandon my only intention of coming to these parts, which was to possess myself of the knowledge of the peculiar manners, customs, and language of these genuine descendants of the old Celts, that had long been the object of my wishes, and I greatly regret my facility in giving it up. But an unseasonable, ill-placed compliance, or perhaps want of proper resolution to undertake a solitary residence in a district of an unknown people, of a strange language, might have co-operated to produce my determination. In passing the road I reckoned one hundred and thirty chimneys in the great copper works lying on the banks of the Swansea, a river just above the town. Dined and took leave, and bent my course to the ferry; was soon wafted over the river Tawy in a boat guided by a rope, the rapidity of the tide rendering such an expedient necessary; having landed, we jumped into a carriage standing on the shore ready to receive us.

The next town is Neath, which consists of about one hundred and fifty houses, and is situated on the Bristol Channel, or about the embouchure of the Severn; it is a place of some trade in the same way as the former, though not to so great an extent.

On the farther side of the river are the remains of a magnificent monastery, but under what denomination its former occupants were, I did not learn, having only a passing view. Just beyond the town on the same side of the river, are the seat and grounds of Sir

Herbert Mackworth, under excellent improvement. Standing in the court of the inn, I heard one tell another that the lad then passing by, was the male descendant of him whose name was Pendrell, by whom King Charles II. was concealed on the oak at Boscobel, (now standing,) after Cromwell's defeat of the Scotch army at Worcester.

Neath, July 31. Left the inn at eight o'clock, and alighted at the Bear inn, Cowbridge, twelve miles; a long, straggling town, of better built houses, and to appearance larger than Neath, though of less trade. Changed horses and started for Cardiff, where we alighted in two hours, distance twelve miles. It is a small but neat and clean town, the shire town of the county of Glamorgan; streets well paved; has one Episcopal church, houses modern, but none lofty or much decorated. The inhabitants here and farther on towards Monmouth, begin to anglicize and lose the Welsh language and manners, few or none speaking it in town, though the mountaineers all over the principality make it their mother tongue, and politically, and I think prudently, continue it. The villages and towns that have the least connection with trade, retain their original tongue in greater use. North Wales, more particularly than South, has less mixture of foreigners. After an hour's rest, we set off in a post-chaise for the mountain country, to obtain a sight of a singular bridge over the river Taaffe, consisting of only one arch, spreading one hundred and forty-two feet, in height thirty-four above the water. This surprising undertaking was planned, and after two disappointments, executed by a mason named Thomas Edwards, still living :—it is said to be the greatest work of the kind in the world, exceeding the Rialto at Venice. Visitors say it would do honor to Roman magnificence in the most flourishing times of the empire. Asking a question of a passenger, he replied, " *Dim Saesneg,*" which was as much as if he had said, " *I do not understand English.*"

Cardiff, August 1. After breakfast walked through the town to the castle, remarkable for its being the prison of the unfortunate Robert, eldest son of the first William, and Duke of Normandy, who was not only deprived of his right to that dukedom, and the kingdom of England, the government of which last was his by right of primogeniture; but being made a prisoner by his younger brother Henry, he languished here twenty-six years, till death kindly released him, at once, from captivity and suffering. This castle is almost entire, and seems less ruined than any of the ancient ones not in possession of the crown. The dungeon where the prince was kept is shown; it lies under the outward tower, the descent by six steps, secured by two doors, one within another; the apartment about eighteen feet high and the same in diameter; of an octagon form, having an arched roof, admitting no light but through a wicket just under the covering, jutting out from the body of the tower. The extent of the castle within the walls is about twelve acres.

From hence repaired to the inn, and took carriage for Newport. After my departure learned that a daughter of the late Parson Pigot of Marblehead, was an inhabitant of this place. Arrived at Newport at twelve, and remained an hour, rambling through the town, which, like Cowbridge, is long and straggling, and the houses of a mean appearance. On the bank of the river Uske, near the foot of the bridge on the town side, are the remains of an old castle in ruins, reduced by Cromwell to its present state, as, I am told, were all the castles in this country, where they abounded, scarce a town being without one; passed by several in sight of the road, and all in a like decaying condition. At the inn we dined, and loitered till five o'clock, waiting for the flow of the tide, and then with a fair but faint breeze, entered the boat and loosed from the Welsh shore. In forty minutes arrived at the Gloucester side, and waited no longer than while the horses were putting to; and taking our seats, were conveyed across a pleasant, extensive country, filled with herds of black cattle and large flocks of sheep, bordered by a circular range of finely improved hills. In an hour arrived at the city end of Durdhamdown, and soon alighted at our late lodgings in Queen's square, having finished a tour of two hundred miles in seven days. From henceforth determined to consult the genius, turn, and temper of my future companions; my late fellow traveller's want of curiosity, etc. etc., renders him a very unfit companion, and frustrates every purpose of rambling.

Bristol, August 3. Attended worship at St. Stephen's; Dean Tucker preached. Returned home *viâ* Hot Wells.

TO REV. ISAAC SMITH, SIDMOUTH, DEVON.

Bristol, August 4, 1777.

DEAR SIR :

The dark aspect of affairs in America on the side of government, renders it likely that England or some foreign country will, for many months to come, be the residence of the wretched American fugitives. Our head-quarter folks have, I learn, lowered their topsails, and talk in a less positive strain ; fear and apprehensions seem to have succeeded assurance.

Of late I made a short ramble into Wales, and over many eminences, to which the hills in Devon are not to be compared ; the middling and poor inhabitants are not unlike our Indians, though inferior in size ; their manners as coarse and language as uncouth, differing from the English as much as their customs, many of which are peculiar. The outside of all their houses and walls is kept white-washed, at a distance giving them a lively and pleasant look ; the inside is filthy enough. The women, like our Indian squaws, carry their young slung round them, some before and some behind their backs. Cardiff, the chief town of the county, is near the bank of the river Taaffe, and in a pleasant vale of fine improvements, surrounded by high mountains, cultivated to their summits. Within two miles, and in sight, is the town of Llandaff, having a cathedral of a respectable appearance :—the churches in this country, however, make but an indifferent appearance, being of diminutive size. About twelve miles from this toward the mountains, my curiosity carried me to view a most astonishing piece of architecture in a bridge, called *bont-y-pridd*, consisting of one arch, in span one hundred and forty-two feet, and rising from the spring of the arch thirty-four ; planned and executed by a common mason, who is now employed at a similar work in Radnor. This natural architect is also to execute another bridge at Swansea, over the river Tawy, the middle arch of it to rise one hundred and eight feet above the surface of the water at full sea, and of a width sufficient for a large vessel to pass through.

Yours,

S. CURWEN.

August 7. Attended worship at the college ; Bishop Newton, well known in the learned world by his writings, confirmed about nine score persons, chiefly females, from fourteen to thirty years of age.

August 10. Attended worship at Mayor's Chapel, Baron Hotham, the nisi prius judge, present, accompanied by the mayor, in their formalities.

TO REV. ISAAC SMITH, DEVON.

Bristol, August 1 5, 1777.

DEAR SIR :

A late rumor from the south that had exhilarated our sinking spirits, is now momently abating of its credibility, though it was told in a way and with circumstances that induced a universal belief. The report I refer to you must undoubtedly have heard. My faith in a speedy return to our native country is, as it ever has been, faint; those, on the contrary, with whom it is my fate to bear company, have cherished, and still please themselves with the fond, delusive hope that the disturbances on the western continent will subside upon the least success of the British arms, and hourly expect to hear of Gen. Burgoyne's arrival at Albany ; from whence they date the end of troubles there. But supposing that to take place, I foresee a great deal to be done before the fierce spirits of the people in America will settle down into a submission to a power they dread, and have been taught to detest. Besides, I cannot help thinking France will interpose and prevent a future connection between Great Britain and the colonies ; perhaps, not thinking it prudent to declare whilst the recovery of them remains doubtful. This you may call a suggestion of fear, and it may be the effect of a sickly disturbed imagination ; I presume, however, I am not a singular instance.

With real regard, yours, etc.

S. CURWEN.

August 19. By the ship Lady Gage, from New-York, July 15th, advices that General Heister is returning to Europe ; that the troops are withdrawn from the Jerseys ; that Lord Howe and General Howe are embarking, destination unknown ;—

discouraging news for government, and is a convincing proof I should think that an insurrection excited by an enthusiastic ardor for liberty, rightly or wrongly understood, and in such distant provinces, is not to be easily quelled. A contemptuous idea of the weakness of the colonies, and their inability to withstand the power of this opulent state, is the chief if not the only source of the present discouraging condition of their affairs in North America.

August 20. Advices from New-York are that General Prescott was surprised and carried off at midnight from a detached house a little beyond his line, by a few daring sailors who landed on the island. This was done in revenge for General Prescott's setting a price on General Arnold's head, dead or alive, to be brought in. General Pigot succeeds the former in command. That Lord Howe and General Howe were soon to leave New-York with seventeen thousand troops, destination not known, supposed northward, to act in concert with General St. Leger, who is coming down through the Mohawk country. That General Burgoyne has taken Ticonderoga, and a confirmation of the capture of the " *Fox*" man-of-war by the Hancock and Boston privateers. 'Tis also stated that the Massachusetts people begin to be discontented, and accuse each other of folly in engaging in an opposition that seems to promise such bitter fruits. Should Great Britain be able to establish a line of communication between Canada and New-York, and thereby separate the northern colonies from the southern, wo to the promoters and abettors of these disputes, and good-by to Congressional authority. The Indians will naturally fall into the heaviest scale, especially when enforced by such powerful motives as Great Britain can offer. Should that event take place, God preserve my poor country from the desolating judgments—from a merciless savage war.

August 26. Intending for a long walk, took my course for Rownham passage, proceeding over Leighdown through a Mrs. Gordon's grounds, late Lady Trenchard, which she exchanged for a husband. This house sheltered King Charles II. after his defeat and flight from Worcester ; he was in the kitchen when his pursuers entered, in the character of a scullion, and the cook maid struck him with a ladle, calling him a careless dog, and ordering him to wind up the jack, which he obeyed, getting on a stool for the purpose.

The house is a large, noble, old-fashioned structure. In the court yard is a piece of water filled with carp. Dined at King's Weston, and returned to lodgings much fatigued. King's Weston is an estate belonging to Lord Clifford, family name Southwell. At the inn I heard that Lord and Lady Clifford had that morning set off for France, on account of the ill health of the latter, leaving a dead child in the house to be buried when convenient.

August 28. The annual Gloucestershire feast this day; the procession, headed by the Duke of Beaufort, walked from Concert Hall to the inn.

Sept. 2. Had a passing view of the half yearly fair held in St. James's church-yard. Saw exposed in huts, sheds, etc., along the street called Horse-fair, cloths, linen, hose, and every article in the grocery and bauble way;—besides the buyers, there were numerous flocks of such characters as compose our Cambridge Common gentry on commencement days, and for the like purposes, festivity and fuddling.

Sept. 3. Evening at Judge Sewall's, who introduced me to Dean Tucker, a famous political divine and anti-colonist, who judges them a burden to Great Britain, and presses administration to cast them off.

Sept. 6. Had an hour's conversation with a stranger on 'change; a rare event, people in England being greatly indisposed to join with unknown persons. The Bristolians are, however, remarkable for early inquiries into the character of all strangers, from commercial motives, and soon fasten on all worth making a property of, if practicable; all others, of how great estimation soever, are in general neglected. This city is remarkable for sharp dealings; there runs a proverb, " *one Jew is equal to two Genoese, one Bristolian to two Jews.*"

Sept. 7. At the college, the cathedral so called, Dr. Stonehouse preached; he was a practitioner of medicine, and has now turned his attention to spiritual maladies. His discourse serious and sensible, and his delivery with becoming energy, very unlike the insipid coldness prevalent among the preferment-seeking, amusement-hunting, "macaroni parsons," who, to the shame and dishonor of this age and nation, constitute the bulk of those of the established clergy that possess valuable livings.

In the afternoon, walked to a street adjoining King's square to attend John Wesley's preachment; he being seated on a decent scaffold, addressed about two thousand people, consisting of the middle and lower ranks. The preacher's language was plain and intelligible, without descending to vulgarisms.

Sept. 14. In the afternoon I attended once more John Wesley, having the heavens for his canopy; he began with an extempore prayer, followed by a hymn of his own composing, and adapted to the subject of his discourse. He wears his own gray hair, or a wig so very like that my eye could not distinguish. He is not a graceful speaker, his voice being weak and harsh; he is attended by great numbers of the middling and lower classes; is said to have humanized the almost savage colliers of Kingswood, who, before his time, were almost as fierce and unmanageable as the wild beasts of the wilderness. He wears an Oxford master's gown; his attention seemingly not directed to manner and behavior,—not rude, but negligent, dress cleanly, not neat. He is always visiting the numerous societies of his own forming in England, Scotland, Wales, and Ireland; though near eighty years old, he reads without spectacles the smallest print. He rises at four, preaches every day at five, and once besides; an uncommon instance of physical ability.

Sept. 26. It is reported that General Howe is gone to Boston, and if he makes a successful landing, and is powerful enough to penetrate into the country, wo betide my poor native land. A few days will undeceive us with regard to the object of Gen. Howe's expedition.

Sept. 29. Mr. Timmins and Judge Sewall visited me. Evening at Mr. Barnes's, where took tea with thirteen Americans. The Temple church is so denominated from its having belonged to the knights templars, which powerful and dangerous body of men was dissolved about A. D. 1270.

TO REV. ISAAC SMITH, SIDMOUTH.

Bristol, October 6, 1777.

DEAR SIR:

It is my intention to pass a fortnight with you, and could wish, if convenient, to meet you at Exeter. I long expected the pleasure of seeing you here, but now despair of it, having seen Mr. John

Waldo, who informs me you have laid aside all thoughts of a journey northward. The number of our country folks here is eighteen, viz.: Mr. Boutineau and lady, Mr. Benjamin Faneuil and lady, Judge Sewall and lady, Mr. Barnes and lady and niece, Mr. Fenton and daughter and son, Mr. Fr. Waldo, Mr. Timmins, Colonel Hatch's two daughters at school, and myself.

Gov. Hutchinson, in a letter to Judge Sewall, writes that the news respecting the defeat of the Americans at Saratoga is corroborated by other circumstances concurring to establish the credibility of the lieutenant's letter; the remainder of the story stands on its own bottom, or in other words is doubtful; it is, however, believed by some that two hundred of the royal army fell in the attack, and of the Americans fifteen hundred are killed, wounded, and prisoners, with artillery and stores. He also writes that he has it from high authority, that Lord George Germaine believes Lord Howe gone to Chesapeake bay, but the King to the northward; my belief is that this is a stroke of court policy, to keep down discontent in the minds of people who begin to grow impatient.

Your real friend,

S. CURWEN.

Oct. 4. Before the " Lexington " privateer was taken, she had burnt, sunk, and destroyed fifty-two British vessels, on the coast of Great Britain and Ireland, as appears by her log-book, as well as by papers and letters found on board.

Oct. 21. Rose at six o'clock, and went a coursing with two grayhounds and a spaniel for hares. Started one, and left her in a turnip-field; returned about two o'clock, not greatly fatigued, after a ramble of fifteen miles over hedge fences, ditches, etc.

Oct. 28. Had a sight of the Pennsylvania test, which manifests a confidence in their ability to support their lately acquired authority. It is a triumph to a few; misery to many, I fear.

Oct. 31. Departed at four o'clock from Bristol, in the diligence, with two other passengers, brothers; the one a parson of cheerful humor, and of the learned tribe; the other, late from the East Indies with a few thousand pounds, which he was early retiring to enjoy whilst he had a relish for the pleasures of sense. Breakfasted at White Heart Cross, dined at Bridgewater, and at half past eight alighted at Exeter, eighty-two miles in sixteen hours.

Exeter, November 1. Departed on horseback, attended by a servant with my portmanteau, and in three hours alighted at my friend Isaac Smith's lodgings at Sidmouth.

Sidmouth, Nov. 7. Rode to Beer, a fishing town, containing perhaps a hundred houses, mud walls and thatched roofs; the inhabitants in looks and dress resembling Marblehead folks. Stopped on our return at a farm called Baldash; met here Mr. Cornish, dissenting minister of Collyton, who is a cordial advocate for America and its independence; he is for retiring to woods and caves to avoid religious persecution.

Nov. 10. Started on horseback for Axminster, through Kilmington; from an eminence on the road is a delightful prospect of the vale through which the Axe flows in a serpentine direction, under fine improvement, bordered by hills of a moderate height; pastures and fields to the summit, from which saw Seaton at the mouth of the river, supposed to have been a Roman port, no trace of which remains. In this road lies a stately old house, called Ashe, wherein John Churchill, the great Duke of Marlborough, was born; a village of no account called Musbury, and at the extremity Axminster, where we dined at the Green Dragon, and were introduced to the carpet manufactory, named from the town; invented and still carried on by an ingenious and obliging person of the dissenting profession. Here is also wrought, besides his own, of a peculiar construction, Turkey carpet, so very like in figure, color, and thickness, as not to be distinguished from the genuine article. They are wrought in perpendicular looms, by females, whose fingers move with a velocity beyond the power of the eye to follow. The shute, consisting of as many colors as the shades of the figures, is placed aloft on a bar, through rings running thereon, each ring passing a distinct color through. There was making a beautiful one of thirty-six feet square, (amounting to ninety-six pounds,) for the Countess of Salisbury. The knowledge of this manufacture he obtained thus: an old ragged fellow, in military garb, called and said he had wrought all over Europe in the Turkey carpet way; he was engaged immediately, and complete success has resulted, not only in this kind but also in the Wilton and Axminster.

We passed a dirty road in the dark and alighted at Thorncombe. The late vicar was father of Commodore Samuel Hood, who lately commanded a squadron at Boston. Supped and passed the night here, next morning left early; at eleven o'clock arrived at Lyme Regis, lying in south channel in an exposed situation : it is a place of little trade, supplying the neighborhood with coals imported here from the north. It is also a watering place, being accommodated with a few bathing machines, a terrace facing the beach, and near adjoining for walking; a long room for tea and cards, of a southern aspect, and a neat assembly room. About twelve hundred inhabitants, (chiefly dissenters,) and about two hundred houses. Here is now standing, the George inn, wherein the Duke of Monmouth first slept on his invasion. For the security of vessels coming in here, there is a circular pier of several hundred running feet, built by the ever famous Sir John Oldcastle, Lord Cobham, and from him denominated the Cob. The next stage, Culliford, at Mr. John Carsluck's seat of Wishcombe, where we were kindly entertained and lodged. This place is called from its situation; " wish," in Devonshire dialect means *weary*, and " combe" *vale*,—which well describes it.

Nov. 12. At meridian took leave and departed through the country to Slade, seat of Mr. Lee, one of Mr. Smith's parishioners; called and notified him of our intention to dine, and passed forward to Brunscombe, consisting of five clusters of small huts of mud walls and thatched roofs. This parish, formerly an estate of the Brunscombe family, was given to a monastery at Caen, in Normandy, and remained appended to it till the downfall of popery in England. Dined and took tea with Mr. Lee, and resuming our saddles, took leave, and crossing Salcombe hills, alighted at our lodgings, after a circuitous ramble of forty-seven miles in four days; the roads for the greater part more dirty, stony, and disagreeable than are generally to be passed in our own country.

Sidmouth, Nov. 17. Took an airing over Peak hill,—evening in a large company at Mr. William Carsluck's; Coddington house his seat; took tea and a generous and elegant supper.

Nov. 18. Rode out, passing a farm called Thorn, from a thorn bush or tree standing on a road near by, said to be more than three hundred years old.

Nov. 19.   Rode to St. Mary, Ottery, about eight miles out ; it is a parish, a hundred, and a manor ; the lords, Sir George Young and Sir John Duntze.   It is situated in a vale, the river Otter running through the midst, from which the town takes its name.   The centre is modern, built of brick, covered with pantile, a fire some years ago having destroyed the old buildings, it has a market, an Episcopal church in the cathedral style of building ; by tradition erected in 1060, a few years before the Norman invasion ; it has a look of antiquity, and is marked with decay within and without.

Nov. 20.   At ten o'clock departed from Ottery, and at one alighted in Exeter at my intended lodgings in Fore-street.

Exeter, Nov. 22.   Walked abroad, had a conversation with young Reed, just returned from Salem, having been carried in there in a prize ; from whom I learnt there was no business scarcely but privateering, which he represents as surprisingly successful.

By the papers, I learn the king in his speech takes notice of " *the obstinacy of his rebellious subjects in America,*" and promises himself " *all needful assistance from his faithful Commons.*"   It will be well if additional supplies, and an increase of foreign troops, do not prove a source of intolerable evil.   Would to God an expedient could be devised to terminate this unnatural quarrel, consistent with the honor of both parties ; but this I fear is a vain wish.   The Dutch, from a sordid thirst of gain, the French, from their dread of the rising power of Great Britain united with the colonies, and Spain, from an attachment to the court of Versailles, are too deeply concerned to permit a re-union.   Lord Chatham, on motion for an address in the king's speech, says, " Without an immediate restoration of tranquillity, this nation is ruined and undone. What has been the conduct of ministers ?   Have they endeavored to conciliate the affection and obedience of their ancient brethren ? They have gone to Germany, sought the alliance of every pitiful, paltry prince, to cut the throats of their loyal, brave, and injured brethren in America.   They have entered into mercenary treaties with those human butchers for the purchase and sale of human blood.   But, my lords, this is not all ; they have let the savages of America loose upon their innocent and unoffending brethren, upon the aged, weak, and defenceless ; on old men, women, and children ; upon babes at the breast, to be cut, mangled, sacrificed, burnt, roasted; nay, to be eaten.   These are the allies Great Britain now has; carnage, desolation and destruction, wherever her arms are carried, is her new adopted mode of making war.   Our ministers have made alliances at German shambles, and with the barbarians of America, with merciless torturers of their species. Whom they will next apply to, I cannot tell." Such is Lord Chatham's fire, such his oratory, such his indignation against ministerial measures.

Dec. 14.   This day General Burgoyne's mortifying capitulation arrived in town.   Nothing could be more disgraceful and humiliating, unless a submission to the victor's power without terms.   The loss of the military chest estimated at seventy-five thousand pounds, the finest train of artillery ever sent out of this kingdom before; all the boasted acquisitions of the year's campaign gone at a blow, and Canada on the point of joining the grand American alliance.

In the House of Commons, on the 12th inst., after Lord Barrington's report of army estimates, Col. Barré rose and called on Lord George Germaine to inform the house whether the report of the surrender of General Burgoyne with his army and artillery was true or false; which Lord George did in a short narrative, and said intelligence had been received of the capture by the way of Quebec, which struck the house with astonishment; and after a short pause Col. Barré rose, and with an averted look, said : " Great God! who can refrain from rage and indignation when the planner of so much misery relates with the utmost composure, the horrid tale of a British army destroyed ?   We all know the General's bravery and skill ; he did not surrender whilst there was a possibility of defence ; but while justice demands a just eulogium, what must we say of the man who reduced so gallant an officer to so sad an alternative without the smallest advantage to his country ?"

Dec. 18.   From a correspondent at the west of the town, I learn that the language about the court is nowise lowered by the last news from America ; " *delenda est Carthago.*" The old politicians, neither biassed by hatred to Americans, nor interested in the destruction of the colonies, shake their heads at this language.

Dec. 25, *Christmas.*   Service at cathedral.   No shops opened entirely, nor business publicly or generally carried on :—though

the day is otherwise negligently enough observed, nor indeed can
more be expected, considering the low ebb of religion here.

Soon after the surrender of Burgoyne was announced by
Lord George Germaine in parliament, an adjournment took place
till after the holidays, whereupon Sir George Young, Mr. Baring,
the Exeter member, and Mr. Barré, hurried down, and it was suspected that this foreboded a new parliament, a new ministry, new
measures, and that the most active opposition is coming into play;
a few days will undeceive the public, however. On confirmation
of the American news, Manchester offered to raise a thousand men
at their own expense, to be ready for service in America in two
months, and was followed soon after by Liverpool. It is said there
are to be proposals for raising two thousand men out of each
parish through the kingdom; that the American secretary will
resign, and Lord Hillsborough succeed him.

Dec. 31.   The lenity shown to General Burgoyne and his army
is allowed on all hands to do more honor to America, than the lau-
rels, reaped by the Howes, can bring to this distracted country. God
knows what is for the best, but I fear our perpetual banishment
from America is written in the book of fate; nothing but the
hopes of once more revisiting my native soil, enjoying my old
friends within my own little domain, has hitherto supported my
drooping courage; but that prop taken away leaves me in a condition too distressing to think of; however, amidst the increasing
evils of old age I have this consolation, that, mortifying as my lot
is, severe as my sufferings may be, their continuance cannot be
lasting.

Accompanied by Mr. Smith, drank tea with Mr. Towgood, and
they passed the evening and supped with me; and thus ends the
old year.   Mr. Pope observes:

> " With added years, if life bring nothing new,
>   But like a sieve let every blessing through,
>   Some joys still lost, as each vain year runs o'er,
>   And all we gain some sad reflection more :
>   Is that a birth-day ? 'tis, alas ! too clear,
>   'Tis but the funeral of the former year."

21

CHAPTER VIII.

TO DR. DAUBENY, LONDON.

Exeter, Jan. 3, 1778.

DEAR SIR :

By my friend Col. Browne's letter, received yesterday, I am informed of Col. Frye's arrival at Halifax, and of your quitting Salem
and arrival in London.   Pray inform me whether his and your departure from your settled abode arose from the requirements of the
new established governments; if there be any in our province of
sufficient authority to restrain the lower classes from their insolence
and outrageous behavior, who, when the bands of society are unhappily loosened and the laws are forced into silence, do not neglect to avail themselves of those times to run riot against peace,
order and security, the most valuable blessings of social civil
life ;—whether there be any civil government established in our
province—what it is—who the administrators—who are our Salem
magistrates—its condition with respect to order, trade, religion—
the state of our society and the situation of our friends ?   I could
fill a sheet with questions, but, loth to tax your good nature too
heavily, forbear.   With congratulations on your safe arrival in a
land of plenty, and freedom from persecution, either on the score
of religion or politics,

I remain your friend,

S. CURWEN.

Jan. 6.   Evening at Mr. N.'s, with Mrs. N. and Mrs. Tremlet,
sisters, of excellent understanding, great reading and refined taste.

Jan. 12.   Bishop Ross installed arch-deacon in the chapter
house, as on Saturday he was prebend, and on the following days
this week is to be successively canon, treasurer, and bishop ; each
ceremony being ushered, accompanied, or announced by tolling the

great bell, and afterwards the chimes play. On the demise of a
bishop, the king in effect chooses under the fallacious compliment
of recommendation to the chapter, consisting of dean, prebends,
canons, etc., with a *congé d'elire*, or liberty to choose for that purpose ; the choice falls of course on the person recommended, and
is so understood. He is then presented, kisses the king's hand on
his preferment, and is installed by proxy in the distant see. He is
personally enthroned when his new lordship pleases ; how long it
may be before we are to be favored with his personal presence, it
is not said.

TO REV. ISAAC SMITH, SIDMOUTH.

Exeter, Jan. 17, 1778.

DEAR SIR :

The account of General Burgoyne's surrender is confirmed, and
what think you of the Congress now ? Of American independence ? Of laying the colonies at the ministers' feet ? Of Lord
S.'s boast of passing through the continent from one end to the
other with five thousand British troops ; and with a handful of men
keeping that extensive continent in subjection ? Of the invincibility of the said troops ? Of the raw, undisciplined, beggarly
rabble of the northern colonies ? Of the humiliating surrender of
a British general, five thousand troops, seven thousand small arms,
and thirty-six pieces of brass artillery, to the aforesaid rabble ?
What think you of the pompous proclamation of the said general ?
Of the figure he is now making in the streets of Boston, compared
to his late parading there, accompanied by his vainly fancied invincible cohorts, now, alas ! rendered as harmless and inoffensive
animals as you and I ? Of the condition General Howe is now or
soon may be in, should the combined army of Washington and
Gates, numerous as it may be, perhaps exceeding his own in the
proportion of two to one, elated with success, inflamed with an enthusiastic ardor, invest Philadelphia, defended by an army almost
worn out by incessant labor, having, as the papers say, the shovel
and firelock always in their hands, and greatly weakened by losses ?
What think you of the twenty thousand men voted in parliament a
few days since, in addition to the army now in America ? Where
are they to be raised ? Is not Russia on the verge of a war with

the Turks ?   Have not the two great potentates of Germany re- fused to suffer their country to be further drained of its inhabitants ? Is not Denmark too feeble, thinly peopled, and jealous of its potent neighbors, to furnish men ?   Have we any alliance with Sweden ? Is not Holland in the same predicament with the former, and does not its commercial system forbid lending us aid ?   Is not Portugal too poor, dependent, and unable if disposed ?   Is not Spain unwil- ling and unable, and too much inclined to follow French politics ? Nay, does not the impolicy of hiring troops from her, if willing and able, appear too glaring even in the most desperate case ?   And is not France too insidious and insincere, too much interested both in regard to politics and commerce, to apply to her for assistance ; nay, would it not be too dangerous, considering her former state and connections there ?   Have not the Switzers too strong a sense of liberty themselves to engage against a cause wherein civil liberty is pretended to be invaded ?

Pray what resources, then, has Great Britain, without allies able or willing to afford the needed help ?   Can her own country furnish the requisite numbers ?   Can the manufacturers spare, with- out essential injury to its commerce, a supply from thence ?   Does she abound in laborers ?   Are there not, rather, complaints that men of the lower classes are wanting ?   Have not the recruiting parties found great difficulty in raising men ?   And is it not well known that business goes on slowly and heavily at this day ?   Would not an act of parliament to press men for the American service, (and without it, it cannot be done,) raise disturbances and insurrections think you ?   Would not raising new regiments from among the Catholics of Ireland disaffect the bulk of the nation ?   In this sad dilemma, which way can administration turn to extricate them- selves ? How can they escape out of this labyrinth wherein they are intricated ?   What measures can be adopted consistent with the honor and dignity of this late mighty empire—alas, how fallen !—that gave law but a few years ago to two of the most powerful, politic, and wealthy states in Europe, and thereby peace to almost all the world ?   Common sense and prudence, in the case of a private person, suggests, that when convinced his measures of conduct are inadequate and incompetent to answer his wishes and designs, to retrace his mistaken steps, pursue other measures, and undo what has been done wrong; for it most surely is less dishonorable to correct errors than pertinaciously continue in a track confessedly wrong and fatal. Does not the American secretary, Lord George Germaine, seem to be of this mind, when he announced General Burgoyne's surrender in the house, declaring, at the same time, the impracticability of carrying on this war any longer? Has this an appearance of a pacific intention, or does it seem designed, as has been suggested, to lull the opposition? (which, however, I don't consider but as the effect of party misrepresentation; for you know party views every thing in false lights.) Think you this an individual opinion, uncommunicated to his brethren in administration, and unknown in the privy council, delivered without their privity, connivance or consent? Is it probable he will long hold a post in which he must take so active a part as his duty requires, in promoting measures, in his judgment ineffectual, and which cannot long be supported? If a difference in the higher departments begins, and a derangement in administration should take place, where will it end? I shall tremble for the consequences at this period, as it will weaken government when most it stands in need of support from a general concurrence. Did not Lord North seem to yield to the idea of conciliatory measures? The designs of a court are deep and hidden; who, by searching, can find them out, till time, the great revealer of secret things, exposes to view the wisdom or folly, the policy or impolicy of cabinet councils? The language of the court, the papers say, is, as it ever has been, " *delenda est Carthago ;* if this be not slander, wo betide my poor country. I confess I feel too strongly the *amor patriæ* not to wish it may be slander; its enemies will never, I hope, exult over its ruins; but its inhabitants be timely brought to a just sense and sight of their real interest and security, which in my view consists only in a close connection with this country.

Vigorous measures are talked of there; but in parliament the language held by the ministers seems mild, leaning toward an adjustment of matters otherwise than by the *ultima ratio regum;* the out-door talk is just the reverse : unhappy the state of society and government that renders such conduct in any regard expedient. Should government seriously wish and intend to settle this quarrel amicably, what can be the first step? The present situation of

administration puts me in mind of a story relative to Sir Christopher
Wren, who went yearly to visit King's College Chapel, Cambridge,
remarkable for its roof; on being asked whether he could construct
such another, replied, " Tell me where to place the first stone, and
I will engage to execute it." Are not our state architects as much
perplexed and embarrassed where to lay the first foundation stone
whereon to erect a temple to peace and concord? Could they ever
devise a plan of accommodation dictated by wisdom itself short of
American independence? Would the United States condescend to
enter into a treaty with this kingdom after so many proofs of their
ability to defeat their designs and resist their most vigorous efforts,
and from whom they have received so many supposed indignities,
severities, and oppressions? I quit my theme and lay down my
pen to read the news just brought in; but before I record it, let me
premise that not a syllable of it finds credit with me; it is as follows:—" General Vaughan, who burnt Esopus and made such cruel
havoc up Hudson river, is defeated by General Putnam; he and his
army prisoners; that the former has got between General Clinton and
New-York with a separate army; that General Washington had
forced General Howe's lines, destroyed and taken seven thousand
men." Should this, or half of it be true, I warrant (without gift
of prophecy) the game is up. I forgot to add, Arnold is not killed,
only wounded in the leg, and with General Green gone forward
to Quebec; the American works on the Delaware not yet forced,
so that the two brothers Howe can as yet have communication
together till that event takes place. General Howe's situation
must be very disagreeable, not to say dangerous. I will add a few
lines to fill the sheet. Newspapers are crowded with articles of
the offers of towns and counties to enable his majesty's government
to carry on the war against America, which by some means is now
become to be considered as less a ministerial affair than some time
ago; should the proposed numbers, however, be taken out of the
manufactories, I dare engage trade will sensibly feel it. Would to
God, that moderate and just views of the real interests of both
countries might possess the minds of those who direct the public
measures here and there. That peace may again take place, and
trade and agriculture and commerce be established on a lasting
basis, is the most ardent wish of your friend,   S. CURWEN.

Jan. 26. I am told the officers lately arrived from America, generally declare the conquest of it is a vain expectation, even with a very great additional force. Notwithstanding this, the ardor of the nation for subduing what is called the " *American Rebellion*," seems to spread like a flame from north to south ; the new troops talked of as proposed to be raised immediately, are as follows :—Battalion of Highlanders under Lord M'Leod, 1000 ; Manchester volunteers, 1000 ; Duke of Argyle's Highlanders, 2000 ; Duke of Athol's Highlanders, 1000 ; Colonel Gordon's do., 1000 ; Duke of Hamilton's regiment of Arran, 1000 ; Colonel Dalrymple's loyal Lowlanders, 1000 ; midland Highlanders, 1000 ; Sutherland's and Mackay's Highlanders, 1000 ; Earl of Seaforth's Highlanders, 1000 ; Dutch brigades to be augmented, 5000 ; Irish Roman Catholics, 5000 ; ten English battalions, 10,000 :—31,000.

Lord Abington's motion to be considered in parliament, against the constitutionality of persons, corporations, towns, cities or counties to raise men, and arm and equip them ; and if he defends his position, it will put a stop to the loyalty of Manchester, Liverpool, Norfolk county, and some Scotch lords, who have made offers of money and men for carrying on the American war. Lord Abington's motion was for summoning the judges to attend the house, that their opinions on this matter may be known ; he considered it not only repugnant to the principles of the constitution, but expressly against the letter of the law. The attempt to raise men in Warwickshire and Norfolk has failed, from the opposition of the gentry and others.

Dr. Robertson, in his history of Scotland, says : " When men have been accustomed to break through the common boundaries of subjects, and their minds are influenced with the passions which civil war inspires, it is mere pedantry and ignorance to measure their conduct by those rules which can be applied only when government is in a state of order and tranquillity. A nation, when obliged to employ such extraordinary efforts in defence of its liberties, avails itself of every thing to promote its great end, and the necessity of the case and importance of the object, justify a departure from the common and established forms of the constitution." This is precisely what a sensible American, whose mind is strongly impressed with the right of resistance to the authority and arms of the mother country, would offer in defence of the many hardships and violences imposed on his fellow-countrymen at the present momentous crisis.

Jan. 30.   This being in Church of England language, " *King Charles's martyrdom*," it is farcically observed as a fast day ; churches open and service suitable to the solemn occasion read. To complete the absurdity here, the pulpit of the cathedral was covered with black cloth ; the tip-staves, sword, and mace, carried before the mayor in the same grim garb.

TO WILLIAM BROWNE, ESQ., LONDON.

Exeter, January 30, 1778.

DEAR SIR :

General Burgoyne's defeat will, I think, prove a prelude to a succession of fatal events.   The rapid increase of military skill and courage that enthusiasm produces, and the great numbers of European commanders and engineers of experience now incorporated amongst the Americans, are considerations that extinguish my expectation of the success of the following campaign, even should Great Britain send over in season the number of troops ordered by parliament, (and which do not amount to what all who have lately arrived from America agree to be necessary to insure success, or rather, in any good degree, render it probable.)   May those evils my gloomy mind forebodes, exist only in imagination ; but I must confess I see, perhaps through a false vista, the expedition already ended in the disgrace of this powerful and wealthy kingdom, and in the ruin of that once singularly happy, but now, alas ! deluded, wretched America ; for, disconnected from this country, wretched it must necessarily be, if anarchy and the most grievous oppressions and taxes can make a people so.   How weak, inconsistent, and dangerous is human conduct, when guided by lawless ambition, or any false or wrong motives !   Into what dreadful evils are communities often plunged by hearkening to the declamations of pretended patriots, of crafty, selfish, unprincipled demagogues of this and many other countries ; history furnishes us a present mortifying proof and example.

You may console yourself in the late disgrace of the British arms, with the hope that it may revive the ardor and bravery hitherto so peculiarly characteristic of British troops, but similar causes do not always produce similar effects. At the time you refer to, Rome was in the meridian of her glory, war the profession of her citizens; her inhabitants, through all her ranks, were at that period actuated by the *amor patriæ*, a principle publicly derided in this age. Do not think me a cynic, when I say, I fear this nation has sunk into too selfish, degenerate, luxurious a sloth, to rise into such manly, noble exertions as her critical situation seems to demand : for which this people have in times past been famed, as the disaster you mention formerly produced among the Romans, and as heretofore within my own memory, has been the case with this very people. But the breast of every Roman was warmed with the *amor patriæ* at that period, and with this principle he could brave dangers, and even death, to bring honor to his country ;—when riches poured in upon them from all quarters of the world, when manners degenerated, and selfish regards succeeded to the love of country; when luxurious tables and effeminacy among the higher ranks took the place of frugal meals, and manly fortitude, with the sense of honor sunk into venality and court dependence, they then became abject, desponding, cowardly, and were exposed to every invader, and instead of bravely defending, abandoned even their lands and wealth to be possessed by their courageous army; and such will always be the condition of every people in similar periods of its state. But away with politics.

You ask when I intend to come to London ; to take a long, expensive journey that road, I have not at present in contemplation. Abstract Col. Browne, and a few acquaintances, and London, in the present state of my finances, has not charms strong enough to attract me thither. With no relish for the amusements and dissipations of that unavoidably chargeable residence, I should ill exchange my frugal and comfortable board, in a decent family, at eight shillings, for twenty, and a long train of *et ceteras*, amounting to thirty-five more under strictest economy. It would add much to my enjoyment, to have the company of my friend Col. Browne, with or without a friend or two ; but to encourage his taking so long and tedious a journey, I dare not, having nothing to offer him by way of equivalent for his trouble, ignorant as I am of his taste and views of living : however, should a plan of frugality, inclination to

22

ramble, or curiosity, push you out of the metropolis, as the season grows milder, and chance or design direct your steps to this plentiful and cheap quarter, take the following short imperfect sketch.

Exeter, for its numbers, is somewhat less than Boston ; in buildings as unlike as the wrinkled age of fourscore differs from the healthy, florid complexion of thirty. To your or any eye familiar to modern structures, this place will appear as uncouth as a female tricked out in a ruff and fardingale, or in the court dress of old Queen Bess. I am led to this comparison, from having often heard that the houses, especially in Fore-street, are of her age, and indeed they no more resemble the modern than the dress of that day does the present. The streets are narrow, ill-paved, and (I wonder why not to a proverb) dirty. There is a row of buildings in the form of the crescent at Bath, in the so called modern style ; but it is crowded in a corner, out of sight ; built on land belonging to the Duke of Bedford, and goes by the name of his title, on the site of a late noble palace, wherein Henrietta, the youngest daughter of Charles I., was born during his troubles. Within the walls are three walks for taking the air ; on the north, a circular one, lying back of the castle, encompassed with trees, through which, on the outer side, over a vale filled with houses and improved fields, are cut vistas ; much frequented here is also the church-yard, or the inclosure within walls and gates ; round St. Peter's, the cathedral, another hard gravel walk called the Friars, commanding a fine field view, besides many others without the city. And for in-door amusements, a theatre, concerts, a coffee-house, called Moll's, and a hotel, both in the church-yard, where the London papers are brought four days in the week.

Having filled my sheet, I conclude abruptly, like Hudibras breaking off in the middle.

Very sincerely yours,

S. Curwen.

Feb. 3. This was the day appointed for the enthronization or installation of Bishop Ross in the episcopal seat. The ceremony was performed by Archdeacon Hull of Barnstaple, the proxy, and one of the canons of St. Peter's. The chapter, consisting of the dean, canons, prebendaries, &c. &c., a set of well-fed priests, all of the largest dimensions, (except the first, who was in London,) walked in procession to the cathedral, preceded by the officers properly habited, and whose coming was announced by the sound of the great bell. Having arrived into the church, the chapter proceeded to the throne, where they all sat down; after being seated a short space, the proxy arose, and advancing to the front, read an oration in praise of the late bishop; concluding with an encomium on the present one, in which he declared he took *real*, *actual*, *and corporal* possession of the episcopal chair; these words being the same he used, and I fancy an essential part of the form. The seat, or throne, as it is called, is of a singular construction, and the most magnificent of any; it is a square of sixteen feet, lined with crimson silk, the cushions velvet of the same color, edged with a broad gold fringe; the canopy thirty feet high, supported by four wrought posts, carved up to the ceiling in Gothic open work, decreasing till it ends in pinnacles; opposite stands the pulpit; both at the upper end of the choir.

Henry Grove, a dissenting minister of Taunton, well known by his writings among those of the same profession, wrote Nos. 588, 601, 626 and 635, in the 8th volume of the Spectator; and Mr. Parr, lately deceased in this city of Exeter, in his eighty-eighth year, wrote those signed A. B. in the 6th and 7th volumes, and some others, the signature of which his son, Surgeon Parr, told me he had forgotten.

Feb. 10. Received a letter from William Cabot, London, informing me that by a letter from Nathan Goodale, Salem, all friends are well.

Feb. 14. Received a friendly letter from Mr. Timmins. His wife at Boston, seeing no end to the disturbances, is going to pluck up stakes, and remove with flocks, herds, and children.

Lord Camden said the other day in the house of peers, on the Duke of Richmond's motion to consider the state of the nation, with liberty to refer to such papers as were before them, " the origin of the mistake of our ministers in commencing the American war, was this: they ignorantly supposed the Americans to be cowards, and foolishly imagined the French to be idiots."

Mr. Woodbridge's answer to the Duke of Richmond (on the 9th inst.) was, that by Lloyd's coffee-house books, the number of

British vessels taken from May, 1776, to the present time by American privateers, was seven hundred and thirty-three, containing upwards of thirteen thousand men. That the aggregate value of the ships and cargoes, after deducting one hundred and seventy-four retaken and restored, amounted to £4,823,000 sterling. The number of American privateers one hundred and seventy-three. That American products had greatly advanced in price; tobacco from sevenpence to two-and-tenpence,—pitch, from eight shillings to thirty-six; tar, turpentine, oil, and pig iron, in the same proportion.

Feb. 15. At the George dissenting meeting-house Sir Henry Trelawney, of fifteen hundred a year, an Oxford-bred scholar, preached from " *O worship the Lord in the beauty of holiness.*" Taking a religious turn, he had fallen into Methodism, and set out a flaming preacher of their notions, to episcopal orders superadding dissenting admonition of the lowest kind. He has charge of a small flock in the neighborhood of his own estate ; his natural good sense has cooled his first heat, and he now addresses with fervor, but candor and affection, a crowded assembly. Just as he entered, before service began, an elderly lady in the pew adjoining to the one I sat in, sunk down in a fainting fit, and breathed her last without a groan or struggle.

TO WILLIAM BROWNE, ESQ., LONDON.

Exeter, February 17, 1778.

DEAR SIR :

I would fain persuade myself my good friend does not entertain unfavorable sentiments of the rectitude of my principles, whatever doubts he may have of the justness of my opinion respecting the appearance of things at this juncture, and the probable issue of this destructive quarrel between Great Britain and the colonies. I presume it needs no proof to convince him of my leaving America under a strong conviction of the almost physical impossibility of her waging a successful war with this powerful state, and therefore of the unjustifiableness, imprudence, impolicy, and even madness of the undertaking. Nothing short of such a state of mind could absolve me from the imputation of the extremest folly to abandon my country, friends, and estate, and all my hopes in this world, at my time of life, with but little money, few connections here, and no expectations.

      *   *   *   *   *   *   *   *   *   *

The pernicious system of politics adopted by France, ever since she raised her views to universal empire under Louis XIV., has justly brought on her the detested character of unfaithful, false, crafty, and perfidious; so that French faith now, like Punic of old, you are sensible, goes current in Europe for the four preceding characters; nor has the late behavior of the court of Versailles failed to verify the disgraceful imputation: even at the very time the ministers of France, upon some spirited remonstrances from our court, were pouring forth a profusion of seemingly fair promises and specious declarations of amity into the lap of Lord Stormont, ordering a few vessels with, and a few without cargoes, to be restored to their right owners, and even shutting up their ports, on paper, against American privateers; even at that very time, they were not only conniving at, but carrying on a contraband trade to the revolted colonies. In the port of Nantz there lay, ready to sail for America, three or four large ships, laden with all kinds of merchandise, cannon, and artillery stores, and waiting for a fair wind. Is it not a well known fact that the most successful depredations on the trade of this island, that have ever taken place in Europe or the West Indies, are now making on the latter by French pirates, under congressional colors, and that prizes are daily selling at open market, and all pretences to reclaim denied; now and then, indeed, to save appearances, in imitation of ministers on this side the water, a few feeble, unregarded prohibitions are issued, but none executed to effect.

Spain, whose political and commercial interests so naturally ally it to England, that it is even a proverb, " *Paz con Inglaterra y guerra con todo el mundo,*"* celebrated from time immemorial for honor, true magnanimity, and fidelity to its promises, has ever since the Bourbon idiot that now fills its throne, * * * and ever since the days of his pusillanimous father, adopted French manners, frivolity, levity, dress, politics, and faith, to the expulsion of true Castilian gravity, dress, honor, and regard to the real interest of the

---

     * " Peace with England, if war with the rest of the world."

country. Witness the shuffling and chicanery of the court of Madrid just before the ill-judged declaration of the last war ; review the authentic accounts of the friendly reception of the American and French privateers, and the open trade of the colonies at Bilboa, Cadiz, and all the ports of Spain during these troubles, though royal orders, edicts, and mandates, tagged with an " *Y el Rey*," have been successively transmitted down to the seaports. So well are the court purposes understood, that within four weeks, two or three English prizes were publicly sold in one of the southern ports, in open day, and the privateers refreshed and furnished with all needed stores, and unmolested suffered to depart, laden with the substance and property of the subjects of England. King Solomon says, " where the word of a king is, there is power ;" this he said from his own experience. Who in his wits can believe that the Spaniards, or that abject Turkey-race of pirates inhabiting on the opposite shore, durst have acted thus in defiance of their sovereign, if they had not well known the artful distinction between his secret and revealed will ? With regard to the article of Nantz and a Spanish port, they are facts that stand, for aught I know, on the same footing of credibility with the other articles of foreign intelligence that pass uncontradicted ; and if these be facts, and facts are of a stubborn nature, and bend not to our wishes, they carry conviction, what must we not infer, loth as we may be ? The natural inference is, that both these two courts do invariably adhere to the line of conduct marked out by them from the commencement of this trouble, to distress the government as much as it is in their power, and to steal away our trade. The officers that throughout the winter arrived at the western ports, passing through this city in their journey to London, have one and all declared, as some reports are, that thirty thousand men, at least, in addition to those already in America, are necessary to effectuate the reduction of the continent. Probably these persons speak the sentiments of the army ; there is not, that I know, reason to think them disaffected to the service, nor partial to America. The foregoing convictions are the grounds of my fears, apprehensions, and as you ask me whence I fetch my facts, my reply is, from the common spring-head of popular intelligence. My practice is not to hunt after newspapers, as I seldom go to the coffee-houses ; but when they fall by accident into my hands, I indiscriminately read all, from the Court Gazette, published by authority, to the Sherburne Mercury. The public papers, I well know, are justly stigmatized vehicles of falsehood and sedition : I rarely attend to political essays or remarks, scarce ever give them even a cursory glance; articles of foreign intelligence I credit as far as they are free from self-evident inconsistencies, in respect of time and other circumstances. As to country, my principal view in the choice has ever been the instructive and entertaining; nor am I unhappy in my few acquaintances here; my chief companion is a philosopher of my old friend the Rev. Mr. Gilchrist's stamp, and too deeply engaged in moral and philosophical researches to trouble one with politics, for that is rarely a topic of conversation.

My friend, in reading this tedious letter, will see the high value set upon his good opinion, and trust his candor will make due allowance for our difference in small matters, while in essentials we keep " the *faith whole and undefiled*."

Wishing you increasing felicity, I remain

Your affectionate friend,

S. CURWEN.

Feb. 25. The ministry on the 23d inst. received advices from Lord Stormont that five ships of the line and three frigates had sailed from Brest to Nantz, in order to convey eighteen transports to America, laden with all kinds of military stores, agreeably to the commercial treaty subsisting between the French and Americans; the transports to return laden with tobacco from Virginia.

TO REV. ISAAC SMITH, SIDMOUTH.

Exeter, Feb. 25, 1778.

DEAR SIR :

I presume you have seen Lord North's answer to Charles James Fox and Mr. Grenville in the house ;* *'tis possible, nay, too probable, but 'tis not authenticated by the ambassador.*" This fatal treaty is at length executed; the *coup de grace* is given to British glory

---

* To the inquiry whether it was true that a treaty had been made between France and America.

—its sun is set—alas, how fallen! How short-sighted is human wisdom, how weak is human power at best! The roar of the British lion will no more be heard; the French cock may now crow and strut undisturbed.

Americans that lately were humble supplicants to Great Britain for aid against a few French troops and Indian savages, disturbing her frontier settlements, have dared—what have they dared?—to renounce her authority; have set her power at defiance; reduced her commerce; defeated her armies; sunk her national credit, nay, insulted her coasts, established their independence in spite of all efforts, and, tell it not in Gath, allied itself to her natural, professed, and most dangerous enemy.

*   *   *   *   *   *   *

Your friend,   S. CURWEN.

Feb. 28.   Received Lord North's two acts respecting the right of taxation confined to commerce, and appointing commissioners to adjust all matters in dispute. These offers are, I fear, too late; the fatal treaty with France is already signed.

March 2.   By the mayor's zeal for a strict observance of the fast, an order to prohibit hair-dressers and bakers exercising their callings was published. In Canon Barlow's sermon in St. Peter's were these remarkable expressions, which for a dignitary of the established church wishing to rise, are singularly and dangerously bold. He said, " the war with America was unjust; that they are a religious people and may expect a blessing, and we the reverse."

March 6.   The court hurried away the Andromeda with Lord North's conciliatory propositions to the Howes in America.

March 8.   Yesterday the French ambassador declared to Lord Weymouth, that France had signed a treaty of amity and alliance, or of friendship and commerce, with the United States of America, who, said he, are in full possession of independence, as pronounced by them on the fourth of July, 1776, without stipulating any exclusive advantages in favor of the French nation, and that the United States have reserved to themselves liberty of treating with every nation whatever, upon the same footing of especiality and reciprocity.

Being in the country, our advices from London are that a war with France is dreaded; there is fear of a general bankruptcy.— It is further said the present administration is almost universally reprobated—'tis in my mind a doubt whether in the dregs of the state less interested ministers can be found, though perhaps of more salutary politics, but the problem time only can solve. All men here love money and power too ardently to sacrifice either to interest or peace of state. 'Tis therefore, I fancy, equally indifferent who are or shall be our political cooks; the pottage, I fear, will be spoiled. Stocks have fallen to 59 1-2, which has produced an almost universal panic.

March 15. Despatches for the Howes passed through this city; contents a secret.

TO DR. JOHN PRINCE, HALIFAX.

Exeter, March 15, 1778.

Dear Sir :

Your favor of the 20th Jan. came to my hands a few days since from London; the advice of your retreat to Halifax I received in a letter from my friend ˙Col. Browne. The spirit of intolerance among our New England brethren I vainly wished might have abated, they having, at the period of your departure, nothing to dread from the few individuals who could not, *toto corde*, embrace the political orthodoxy of the multitude and their directors. I doubt not that prudence would have screened and secured you from the rage and insult of the lower classes, and rendered life tolerable, if prudence could have had its due influence; but, such is the popular violence when once it unhappily takes place, and may be exercised without restraint and fear of punishment, that like an irresistible torrent it bears down all before it; laws, justice, truth, religion, the rights of humanity, civility, conscience, are made to rush impetuous down the mighty stream.

I ardently wish once more to visit my *natale solum*, and impatiently wait for the day of my redemption; would I could say it draweth nigh, but I see no end of the baneful ill-omened war, for news has arrived of a declaration by France against us. Should it prove true, Great Britain has the worst to fear; even her inde-

23

pendency is at stake ; for aught I can see, France has drawn down from the interior almost all her troops to the English channel. She has forty-four capital ships ready for sea; not a vessel is allowed to go to Newfoundland from France, in order to man the fleet. La Motte Piquet with five capital ships and eighteen large transports sailed about a fortnight since, avowedly bound to America, laden with military stores. Spain has forty capital ships ready for sea, which are waiting only for the arrival of the Vera Cruz fleet ; should then these united fleets of more than fourscore ships attempt invasion, Great Britain has only thirty-seven ships of the line and eleven frigates to oppose them.

Lord North has proposed terms of reconciliation, but nothing short of independency will go down with the colonies. France will support them ; all thoughts of conquest, of unconditional submission, be assured, are given up ; and I fear much more, that the colonies have, contrary to their real interest and safety, entered into a league offensive and defensive against the parent state.— But it is a melancholy truth, which almost every day's experience verifies, that passion and resentment often urge men and states to actions and courses destructive of their manifest interest and safety, and such will America find in the end this alliance will prove, should Great Britain in the event become thereby oppressed. I could wish (but wishes, alas, are vain) America had seen her interest in another point of light; far, very far am I from wishing her oppressed, or her liberties restrained; I am fully convinced the colonies will never find any good purpose answered by independence. God only knows what is before us, and may we be prepared for his allotments with submissive resignation.

I find myself fast declining into the vale of life, therefore less able to struggle with the unavoidable evils of this inconstant state, than in the days of more strength and vigor.

Believe me, with real regard, yours,

S. CURWEN.

TO GEORGE RUSSELL, ESQ., BIRMINGHAM.

Exeter, March 16, 1778.

DEAR SIR :

The dark and threatening cloud hanging over this island calls aloud for a more serious turn of mind than seems to characterize the present period; but how sadly true is the reverse of such a state of mind amongst us at this day; thoughtlessness, levity, frivolous manners, mirth and music, seem to have seized, and engross the upper ranks; attention to business and a supine disregard to national danger and honor, do they not too justly characterize the middle ranks? As for the *canaille*, they are here, as they ever have been, and will be in all states and times, stupidly indifferent and unconcerned in the midst of impending destruction. If the features of this ill-favored portrait are in your opinion too harsh, believe me, it was not drawn by a pencil dipped in gall, nor dictated by envious misanthropy; I am no cynic, nor cursed with the spirit of a cloistered monk. The warmest regards to the country which by long residence has become an *altera patria*, and holds the second place in my affection, few and faint as my connections with individuals are,—the most earnest wishes of my heart for its safety, and foreboding apprehensions of its danger and dishonor, occasion the painful reflections that cease not hourly to distress my mind.

When I contemplate the decline and final period of states great and powerful, and their causes, which in the history of the world are found to be uniformly the same; that often in the midst of thoughtless security and apparent safety they are on the brink of ruin, and often suddenly and unexpectedly plunged irretrievably therein; that as divines say with regard to men, and experience confirms its truth in both respects, " *in the midst of life we are in death ;*"—I cannot review the state of Great Britain four years since, and regard the present alarming crisis without horror, without trembling. Perhaps to a mind by nature formed and turned as mine unhappily is, to doubt and despondency, danger may present a more ghastly, terrifying aspect than is natural; be it so, may my apprehensions exist only in imagination. I had much rather have weakness of judgment, ignorance and error justly imputed to me, than that the event should verify my predictive fears:—I had rather be a mistaken man than a true prophet.

France and Spain, to compare great things with small, like the heroes in romance, are armed *cap-a-pie*, at all points, ready to sally forth, not like those redoubted sons of Mars and Venus to relieve distress, but to cause it.　　　　　　　Your friend, &c.

　　　　　　　　　　　　　　　　　　　S. Curwen.

March 17.　This being assize week, Judges Perryn and Hotham were waited on by the sheriff and his officers, about two dozen in livery.　Commission sat in Guildhall :—Baron Perryn on the bench; great celerity in despatching business, and great interruption by talking, which the court authorities could not remove.

March 20.　Heard the dreaded sound, war declared against France !　It is reported the house of lords is almost in a tumult, and that they implore the king to drive from his service his ministers, and take Lords Chatham, Camden, and Shelburne.

March 21.　The judges left the city, escorted out by the sheriff and his train,—trumpets preceding, etc.

CHAPTER IX.

TO JUDGE SEWALL, LONDON.

Exeter, March 23, 1778.

DEAR SIR:

I was meditating an answer to your favor, when the alarming intelligence of the French court's perfidious dealings, and the hourly expectation of war against her, arrived here. The *dénouement* of the plot, by the French ambassador's declaring in form to Lord Weymouth his court's interference and engagement to support the claims of Congress, seems at present to render all speculation on the subject of Great Britain's further attempts to reduce her late deluded subjects in America needless: presuming all thoughts in regard to vigorous efforts being to be laid aside, superseded, at least for the present, as the papers inform us no more troops are to be sent out.

These events my fears have been long predictive of; not that I pretend to the spirit of prophecy, or the gift of second sight. States, like individuals, are liable to so many sudden and unlooked for vicissitudes, disappointments, untoward accidents, and evils that neither wisdom can foresee, nor power nor prudence prevent; he whose mind, not however to the increase of his enjoyment, leans towards doubts, fears, and apprehensions of evils, generally finds more events corresponding to his forebodings, than he whose attention is turned to the brighter and more pleasing views that hope presents.

The plan Lord North has offered, is, it seems to me, founded in wisdom and sound policy, as you observe it contains nearly all that America can reasonably wish for, and as it is, thence she can derive more real happiness and safety than is fondly and vainly expected from their favorite, long wished for, and perhaps short-lived independence:—for should Great Britain in this expected war be oppressed, what will save some of the colonies from falling a prey to the insatiable ambition of those powerful crowns united, I know not ; it would be well if they should be satisfied with the recovery of their late possessions there.   The consideration of the burden necessary to maintain an independent state with dignity has never yet, I presume, during the feverish paroxysm of our new legislators and government-modellers, been a subject of calculation ; for however fertile their brains have been of expedients, they are, I fear, but indifferently skilled in political arithmetic.

Your sentiments on the operation of the two conciliatory acts, and answers to objectors, appear to me to be perfectly just, and I am happy to say mine are so completely coincident, that had I taken as many hours, as probably were employed in writing them down, I could not have expressed them in terms so clear, concise, and satisfactory to myself as in the letter I am now considering ; I can therefore subscribe to them *toto ex animo*. The improbability of their acceptance of the terms offered on the other side of the water, and of Great Britain's ability to force them into a compliance at present, seems to be a matter out of dispute.   I am not vain enough to wish myself in the king's councils, but I ardently wish that imaginary principle of national honor, the king's honor, might in this critical and dangerous condition the nation seems to be in, be dispensed with and given up to infinitely more important considerations, notwithstanding the clamors and reproaches to be expected from discontented, interested party men.   That the war, should it unfortunately soon commence, to vindicate the king's honor or nation's, must produce disgrace and irreparable losses to the nation, a review of the present force Great Britain has, her foreign dominions, etc., and the force requisite to secure her right, may perhaps convince :—nor less so, Great Britain's inability at present to force a compliance or convince them by military exertions, that it is their interest to accept her reasonable offers.   The lucky minute for such an offer is past, irretrievably past, and a series of surprising events, owing to ill concerted plans, interested views, a total disregard to the public weal, or, if you please, a certain fatality, has taken place, by which colonies of inestimable value are lost to this country ; and I wish the loss may end there.

The subject that at present most employs and oppresses my mind is the critical and dangerous situation that the kingdom seems to be in.   The tottering condition of national credit, the weak state of the navy, the great power of the enemy, and the low price of stocks, as low as at the end of the last eight years' war, when the nation was almost drained of its specie, are the considerations on which I form my opinion.   Lord North, on presenting the king's rescript to the house, uttered what was sufficiently alarming, that the *reluctance* to the present loan arose not so much from the prospect of war, as *the largeness of the national debt ;* it is of little importance what is the cause, should a national bankruptcy happen. Should another panic like that of last Saturday again seize the monied men, and continue, and the loan be stopped, no one but may foresee the most dreadful consequences ; should the present loan be completed, a new war would require another of equal amount, and the low price of stocks continuing, it will be well, if instead of £450,000 premium paid more than in 1765, £900,000 would tempt the lenders to advance, unless new resources can be found, which my ignorance on this point makes me incompetent to judge.   It is a fact of too much notoriety to be denied, if the contractors avail themselves of the immense debt by this artful, selfish management, the public is supplied at an extravagant, unreasonable profit to the lenders, founded I suppose on this principle, that a sponge, sooner or later, must wipe all out at a stroke.   It is certain the more government has occasion to borrow, proportionably are its disadvantages in procuring supplies ; and unless a new and reformed system of economy be adopted, the premiums may not unlikely rise to cent per cent, especially if Mr. Burke's assertions in the House of Commons be true, that the contractors made a profit of 57 1-2 per cent.   Should America be lost to this country, with her will be lost a considerable revenue, and what can be substituted in its room, financiers can best tell us.   Should a war with the Bourbon family be attended with any possessions in the East or West Indies, and thereby other valuable branches of the revenue be cut off, I leave you to judge the distresses that must unavoidably befall this nation.   The wealth of all nations is exhaustible. All things are called greater or less, stronger or weaker, by comparison.   The fleet of Great Britain is, in itself considered, great and formidable, but when compared to the united fleet of the two Bourbons, whether it does in its present condition deserve that character, no Englishman will, I presume, affirm :—fifty-one English line of battle ships, no one in his senses will say are a match for eighty-six French and Spanish ships of equal force. Confident as we may be of the superiority of our English sailors to all other nations in vigor, bravery and skill, we should be loth to put our liberties or independency on the success of a battle fought under such confessedly disadvantageous and unequal circumstances; and the ability of Great Britain to build and fit for the sea such an additional number as will put us on an equal or superior footing, before some fatal blow be struck, is a question on which the well-being if not existence of this kingdom as an independent state may depend. In my view I could wish national as well as royal honor might in this case be yielded up to the infinitely more important consideration of our self-preservation, and the gross affronts offered by France pocketed till they can be resented with a fair chance of coming off victors in the quarrel. Should a war speedily be entered into before we are better prepared for offence and defence, I can't help fearing this late powerful and flourishing empire to be hastening by large strides to irrevocable ruin and indelible disgrace, and but too likely to furnish a second instance in this period of a once great, rich and powerful state reduced to insignificancy in the political scale of Europe, by a dismemberment of some of its most valuable appendages, consigned over to its ambitious and more powerful neighbors. I wish posterity may not quote Poland and Great Britain as states in the same predicament from the future annals of Europe.

This ill-favored picture probably you may laugh at, but it is to be remembered you are supported by hopes, I oppressed by fears; you in the train of Heraclitus, I of the weeping philosopher; but nature has formed us of different materials in our original contexture, and on my part habit and accident have confirmed the unhappy bias. Whatever your sentiments may be of this reverie, dream, rhapsody, or whatever indignant epithet you may perhaps justly enough think it deserving of; I know you will believe me when I tell you they are the real sentiments of a mind oppressed with concern for the safety, welfare and honor of a country, which by long residence has become my *altera patriæ*, and for aught I know will continue to be so till I take my flight to the upper regions, or time shall cease to be no more with me here. Continue to think favorably, and believe me what is my highest ambition to be, an honest man, and your affectionate friend,

S. CURWEN.

Exeter, March 31.   Witnessed a long dispute on American affairs between Mr. Bretland and Mr. Erving.   I did not interfere; the opponents neither convinced nor conquered, as is usual in such cases.

April 8.   Heard of Rebecca Tyng's marriage to John Lowell of Newburyport.   Visited Mr. Tremlet's on David's hill with company as follows: the parson of the parish and lady, Mr. Pearce, Mrs. Abbot and Miss Hicks; after tea passed half an hour in his delightful garden; he presented me with a beautiful bouquet of a great variety of odoriferous flowers, now adorning my room.

April 9.   Mr. Erving called me out to walk; our course Cowley bridge.   He seems of a sensible, grave turn, not unacquainted with moral science, and exceedingly communicative. Afterwards rode to Topsham on horseback; passed by an estate kept in the male branch of a family, without addition or diminution ever since the conquest.

April 11.   With Mr. and Miss Bretland rambled through Winiford lane to Heavitree; in one of the buttresses of the church grows out a yew-tree, three feet high, cut into a fanciful form, and supposed to receive its nourishment from cement moistened by rain and dew.   The church has marks of age and decay.

April 13.   Mr. Smith from Sidmouth breakfasted with me; visited Mr. Morgan confined by illness; there met Mr. Berry of Crediton.   The land tax at four shillings in the pound produces two millions; the real tax on a medium is two shillings nearly, which, being a tenth part of income, makes that to be twenty millions.   Should an expensive war or some unforeseen accident throw the nation into a convulsion, and discourage lending and lessen supplies, it would, of course, reduce the value of lands, perhaps to twenty-five years purchase; their real value then would be five hundred millions.   Court value of the kingdom supposed to be eighteen millions, for the following reasons, viz.: fifteen millions were brought into the mint to be new coined on proclamation; the remainder, coin of George II. and III., full weight, still con--

tinuing current, amount to three millions. Amount of fabrics, plate, etc. etc., on a modest computation, is worth one hundred millions ; making in all six hundred millions.

A nation possessing more than twice as much as it owes, need not fear bankruptcy ;—England's debt being one hundred and sixty millions. I pretend not to judge what would be the full issue of a shock to national credit, much less dare I determine ; but I confess, I fear it would be followed by dreadful convulsions, and produce cruel ravages and carnage among the lower classes, who, being deprived of daily subsistence for want of daily employ, on stoppage of trade and manufactures, would not contentedly sit down and suffer themselves with their wives and little ones to perish with hunger ; nor even those whose large incomes, derived from national funds, being now stopped, are reduced to a level with the most indigent, and whose wants being supplied from their charity, are now their equal fellow-sufferers.

List of men by last returns, for America 19,381 ; prisoners 5,336 ; sick 4,639 ; loss in navy 4,314 ; army in New-York, Philadelphia, Rhode Island and Canada 36,731 ; to recruit army to what it was last year 11,885 ; captures made by Americans amount to £2,600,000.

April 20. On horseback to Spencecomb, the seat of Mr. Rowe, near Crediton, in company with Mr. and Miss Bretland ; passed an agreeable day, with a numerous company ; this is a week of festivity following Easter Sunday—hospitably lodged and entertained ; our host is of the rank called gentlemen-farmers, or landholders in fee of estates from £100 to £800 sterling per annum. A medal has lately been struck at Paris, by order of Monsieur Voltaire, in honor of General Washington ; on one side is the bust of the general, with this inscription : " G. Washington, Esq., commander of the continental army in America." The reverse is decorated with the emblems of war, and the following : " Washington reunit par une rare assemblage les talens du Guerrier et les vertus du Sage."

April 26. Commissioners appointed to go over to America to settle the dispute, if practicable, Earl of Carlisle, Lord Howe, Sir Wm. Howe, Wm. Eden, Esq., and Governor Johnston, sailed from Spithead on the 22d, and I fear it will prove a *re infectâ* business.

TO HON. WILLIAM BROWNE, LONDON.

Exeter, April 26, 1778.

DEAR SIR:

By our common friend, Mr. Smith, just returned by way of Bristol, I am informed Mrs. Browne is with you; 'tis with great sincerity I congratulate her and you on her safe arrival; would to God it had been under more favorable circumstances; such as they are, your religion and philosophy, I am well assured, can improve them to the best purposes. I presume London will not long continue the place of your abode; if you have no predilection for a particular quarter, and are deliberating what course to take, nothing shall be wanting on my part to afford you all the information respecting these parts you may wish to have. It would yield me inexpressible satisfaction, could Exeter, or its neighborhood, be your choice; I can assure you, that for cheapness, plenty and good provisions, especially fish, poultry, game, and garden stuff, no place excels and few equal it. Late conversations with Col. Erving, from whom I had intimations of your desire to him last January to be informed relative to these parts, (who owns himself to blame in not attending to it,) induce the foregoing. If your views are fixed, I wish the pleasure of your abode may be equal to your highest wishes. A line from my worthy friend will never fail to be a most acceptable present. With the warmest wishes for your felicity, I am

Yours and Mrs. Browne's affectionate friend,

S. CURWEN.

TO JOHN TIMMINS, ESQ., LONDON.

Exeter, April 30, 1778.

DEAR SIR:

I have this day received a letter from Eben. West, now on board the Medway, lying in the Downs, who is in want of necessaries. He was with me in my business at the commencement of the troubles in New England, and by consent, left me to go to sea in his father's employ, till taken by the Enterprise frigate, on the 20th of last July, carried to Gibraltar, and from thence brought to England, where he has been ever since. I think it but charity to

advance a little for him, and therefore wish you to convey two
guineas to him for me. I presume Mr. William Cabot would not
refuse an old neighbor's son some small assistance, nor Col. Browne
a young suffering townsman, to whom, as occasion may serve, you
will do me a favor by mentioning his name, with the situation he
is in; nor would it be improper if they could procure a small supply of money from his countrymen, who must have a fellow-feeling
of others' sufferings, at the same time themselves experiencing the
evil of banishment from their country and the means of subsistence.

I am your obliged friend and humble servant,

S. Curwen.

May 1. Walked with Col. Erving to Mr. John Tremlet's
house, David's hill, (the supposed site of an old Roman temple,)
to see a lamp having Diana's emblem, a crescent; the points
crowned each with a ball, and thought to belong to a temple of
the goddess there, judged of more than two thousand years' antiquity. This being May-day, the milk maids walk in procession
with their pyramid of plate, as usual on this day.

May 5. Mr. Smith brought me a Massachusetts exclusion bill,
whereby all who left New England after 19th April, 1775, are forever banished, and their estates forfeited.

May 7. Took tea at Col. Erving's, with Mr. Smith; agreed
on a journey to Tiverton with them.

May 8. At nine o'clock set out in a post-chaise with Mr. and
Mrs. Erving, and my friend Mr. Smith on horseback, to Tiverton.
Alighted at Three Tuns inn, at twelve o'clock, passing on a pleasant turnpike fourteen miles. This town is supported by serge-
making, for which it was formerly noted, now believed to be on
the decline. Some houses in good taste; it has two dissenting
congregations and one Anabaptist; the Episcopal church is a
venerable pile, low, outside greatly ornamented; tower lofty, the
inside contains many funereal monuments, some of ancient date.

Here is a noted school, called Blandell's, famous in the west;
sends off yearly some students to Oxford and Cambridge; its numbers about fourscore. Besides here is an academy for dissenters'
children, kept by a Mr. Kiddle, the minister, and one for young
ladies. Has abundance of shops. Adjoining the church is a lofty

situation, commanding an extensive and pleasing view of the neigh-boring vale, through which the Exe runs, bounded by a long range of moderately high hills improved and inclosed to summit; returned home by eight o'clock.

May 9.   Rode with Mr. Cross to Star Cross, at the mouth of the river Exe, opposite Exmouth.

May 11.   Removed my lodgings to Sidmouth, and for which purpose I mounted my Rosinante, and departed in company with Mr. Smith, after dinner, having ordered the messenger on with my baggage.   Taking the road through Topsham, we staged it at Ebford, the seat of the widow Lee, a wealthy, hospitable, dissent-ing lady ; here we alighted and took tea.   The family having with-drawn to the house in the neighborhood, called the "Hermitage," to divert themselves at a game of quadrille, that our coming inter-rupted, notwithstanding repeated desires to the contrary.   The family consists of an elderly lady, daughter and her husband, a Mr. Yates and young parson Jarvis, the dissenting ministers of Lime-stone.   From thence we departed, passing through Woodbury, Ot-terton, and across Peak hill, and arrived at my former lodgings at Robert Follet's.

Sidmouth, May 13.   Rode to Wishcombe in company with William Carsluck and two young ladies named Upjohn of Exeter; dined, drank tea, and returned before eight o'clock.

May 21.   Rode to Taunton ; passing through Honiton and Blackdown, I arrived at Whiteheart, visited Mr. Welman and Parson Ward; drank tea with the latter.   Evening and supper at Mr. Toulmin's, the Baptist minister ; lodged at the inn.   Next morning departed for Poundisford, the seat of a Mr. Hawker, a dissenting worthy gentleman of fortune ; passed an agreeable day, and lodged there.

Poundisford, May 23.   At eleven o'clock, in company with Mr. Hawker we departed, shaping our course for Chard, where we arrived at two o'clock.   Between our two stages, on a lofty ridge, are the remains of an old castle, in the country dialect *Laratch;* supposed, but I know not for what reason, to have been of Roman construction.   Chard, where we arrived about two o'clock, is a manufacturing town ; its lifeless appearance but too justly confirms the general opinion that its trade is in a consumptive state; its buildings hardly above the village style, one wide commodious street, paved, having several reputable houses in it. One Episcopal church, and two or three dissenting meeting-houses; the manufacturing towns generally abound in people of the latter persuasion. At five o'clock left, and passing over an excellent turnpike road, entered Axminster, distant seven miles, without alighting, and proceeded on to Seaton, where we in vain attempted to find the remains, if any, of the old Roman port said to have been established here, but it was *hic labor, hoc opus*. Turning our backs to the English channel, we proceeded to Mr. Slade's at Colyton, here taking up our rest for two nights; the doctor supplying this pulpit in exchange with Mr. Cornish, the minister, who did his duty at Sidmouth.

Colyton, May 24. Entertained by the conversation of Mr. Slade's youngest daughter, excelling the common standard in point of understanding, knowledge, and good breeding. Took a field walk with all the family, and to the top of a hill commanding a view of a finely improved country all around, including the whole vale from the mouth of the Axe to Axminster.

May 25. We set off at meridian, proceeding to Baldash, the seat of a Mr. Hook, where we abode till I had bargained for a horse to be sent me at an agreed time; from hence departed for Wishcombe; dined and passed the evening at cards with Mr. John Carsluck, his sister Miss C., and a Miss Snell, very agreeably; pressed to lodge, but Mr. Smith withstood their entreaties, and carried me off reluctantly enough at nine o'clock.

May 28. Walked on the beach and up Salcomb hill with Messrs. Erving and Smith; an extensive prospect from Portland to the Start; within these two headlands fifteen leagues; the bay is called Carnarvon.

TO HON. JUDGE SEWALL, BRISTOL.

Sidmouth, May 31, 1778.

DEAR SIR:

Your favors of the 1st ult. and 8th inst. were delivered to me yesterday afternoon, by the hands of a fair young lady in the alcove on the beach, in this place, being the second day of my removal hither from Exeter, which makes since my arrival in England just

the number of mother Rowlandson's " removes." Having taken
minutes of them, I fancy they cannot fail under the correct hand of
a judicious friend to form a sensible appendix in the next edition of
that curious performance, unless you prefer the following title :—
" The perils and peregrinations of a tory or refugee, in quest of
civil liberty, which the author fondly imagined was to be enjoyed
in higher perfection in the land he travelled through, than in that
he precipitately abandoned, without money to support, friends to
advise, or wisdom to guide him."

Having made a short ramble the other day to Taunton and its
neighborhood, it came into my mind to point out to you the most
agreeable route, should you continue of the mind to take a journey
to these parts during the bathing season. As you will doubtless
prefer a post-chaise, you may command your own time, and choose
your road ; in this case you will find the Wells road as pleasant as
any. On your arrival there, you will not fail to take a view of the
cathedral, which presents perhaps as fine, if not the finest front of
any old Gothic church in England. Within, it is renowned that I
know of, for nothing ; its size is one of the smallest, and its bishop's
palace one of the largest, and has the appearance from the moat
and battlements to have been the residence rather of a warlike
baron, than of a peaceable minister of religion. From hence, at
about four miles distant, is a natural cavern in the Mendip hills,
called Okey or Wolkey Hole ; it is well worth visiting, and is of
the same kind, although not so deep, as that of the Peak of Derby.
From hence to Bridgewater, the famous Glastonbury monastery lies
right on your road, where you will probably stop at the inn. Your
curiosity when there cannot fail of being highly gratified by a view
of its remains, of which it is, however, almost pillaged. Between
this last place and Bridgewater, the turnpike is delightful, and if
your driver should be as complaisant as mine, he will run you a
distance of fifteen miles in an hour and a half. In this stage you
will pass over a ridge dividing the great Somerset moor, extending
beyond the reach of the eye, and filled with innumerable herds of
black cattle, from that called King's Sedgemore, lying on the left,
celebrated you know in history for the defeat of the unfortunate
Duke of Monmouth, in 1685. Far beyond, on that side, is seen
the obelisk raised by the late Lord Chatham to the memory of his

benefactor, Sir William Pynsent. From Bridgewater, at four or
five miles distant, lying two miles out of the road to Taunton, lies
Enmore Castle, a seat of Lord Egmont, built on the plan and in
the style of the old baronial castles.

Your next stage is the pretty town of Taunton, situated in a
vale or bottom called Taunton-Deanvale, remarkable for length,
breadth, and fertility; of the former thirty miles, second ten or
twelve, and for the latter exceeded by none. In this stands the
tower of its principal church, called Mary Magdalen, which will attract your attention, being more crowded with Gothic decorations
than any edifice of that size that has fallen under your view.

Should you think it proper to take the road over Blackdown,
and so through Honiton, rather than through Wellington and Col-
lumpton road, you will on the ascent of Blackdon hill, about
five miles this side of Taunton, before you have reached the summit, on a retrospection of the whole length and breadth of the vale,
see cultivation in its highest state of improvement, and a luxuri-
ancy, verdure and fruitage, no other region can boast of. You will,
I doubt not, join with me in saying so pleasing a rural view is not
to be seen but from this spot. From Taunton to Honiton is seventeen miles, and from thence to this place is nine, or to Exeter sixteen. You will, I know, take this intimation in good part.

Very affectionately your friend,

S. CURWEN.

June 1. Dr. Price, in his fast sermon on Feb. 10, speaking of
the dependence of a nation's safety on righteous men, has the following : " There is a distant country, once united to this, where every
inhabitant has in his house, as a part of his furniture, a book on
law and government, to enable him to understand his colonial
rights ; a musket to enable him to defend those rights ; and a Bible
to understand and practise religion. What can hurt such a country ? Is it any wonder we have not succeeded ? How secure
must it be while it preserves its virtue against all attacks."

June 12. Between five and six o'clock rode with my two fellow boarders to Ottery beacon, commanding a prospect of Ottery
vale as far as Sir George Young's seat, in the neighborhood of
Honiton. Continued ride over the ridge till Honiton appeared in

view; returned in a mist through Sidbury, Sidford, etc., and in a moist plight at eight o'clock dismounted.

June 13. A large fleet appeared in the offing; near thirty capital ships, judged to be Keppel's. Invited by Mr. Skaddon to a sight of the cane King Charles I. had in his hand at his trial, from whence the gold head dropped off in court; interpreted by the credulous as an ill omen.—It is a beautiful stick, and finely shaded, and I suppose as much revered by his infatuated admirers, as Aaron's rod that budded was by the devout Israelites. He also possesses the Duke of Northumberland's golden key as Lord Chamberlain, which, when he acts in that capacity, is fastened to his pocket flaps. Also King Charles II.'s cabinet, and some fine old royal porcelain, as precious relics of infinite value.

June 15. An early ride to Peak hill; a distant sight of Portland and about Abbotsbury.

June 22. Rode with Mr. Ogburn to Woodbury Castle, so called, the remains of a Danish fort, standing on the edge of a lofty range of hills; the ramparts of earth and ditches still remain. The place of arms contains about five acres: on the highest point is a house built for hunting parties, etc., the roof projects in front, supported by four pillars in rustic order, the bark remaining unstripped. From hence to Exmouth to dinner; a famous bathing town; nearly four hundred strangers have been here at a time. More handsome houses than Sidmouth; returned home before eight o'clock.

June 24. This day my friend Mr. Isaac Smith was ordained to the pastoral office over the little congregation of dissenters here. A minister of the Episcopal church, whose curiosity prompted him to attend, continued through the whole service, expressed great delight at, and approbation of the performances, and a high opinion of the solemnity and propriety of the whole. Pity that the narrowness of party keeps asunder and divides in affection men engaged in the same worthy design, and servants of the same kind and benevolent master, whose chief command is mutual love and good-will.

June 28. Mr. Berguyn, a North Carolina gentleman, called on his way to Falmouth to take passage in a packet for America; encouraged by their assembly having voted to admit all refugees who apply.

25

June 30.   Admiral Keppel's fleet has taken three French frigates.

TO HON. WILLIAM BROWNE, CARDIFF, SOUTH WALES.

Sidmouth, June 30, 1778.
DEAR SIR:

I hope this will not be as long on the road as your favor of the 12th of May, that came to hand only a month after date. I delayed an answer that I might be more explicit to your question about the houses I mentioned to you; they are not furnished, but furniture is to be obtained at fifteen per cent., beds and such articles at twelve. This I have from Col. Erving, who is now at Exeter, but does not propose to abide there longer than the 25th of September, when his lease will expire. Where to retreat he seems undetermined; he wishes to reside among people hospitable, social, unceremonious and not dressy; if such can be found. He requests you to inform him through me, whether you have received any information respecting Abergavenny in Monmouth. Is it pleasant, and has it a plentiful and cheap market? Are furnished houses to be had cheap? Are the people hospitable, social, and disposed to form an unceremonious acquaintance, and are they expensive in dress and dinners? The same is requested respecting Cowbridge and Cardiff. Do you intend remaining at your present abode for a long time, and who is with you in your neighborhood, and do they propose to remain?

My present companions are Dr. Smith, just ordained over his little flock here, and our countryman Mr. Ogburn, in the same house; to which number I expect in ten days will be added Mr. and Mrs. Sewall from Bristol. This place is a watering place, resorted to by the neighboring gentry. Having bought a pony, I make frequent excursions into the country hereabouts, passing my time as agreeably as the untoward circumstances of my affairs allow. Should I not be happy enough to enlarge my party, I intend to make a ten days' ramble through Cornwall with my friend Dr. Smith, who has become an inhabitant, and may continue to be for some years.

Should that report induce Mr. Erving's retreating to your

quarters, and you continue where you are, I may pass a month with you before winter.

Yours truly,

S. CURWEN.

July 1. With Messrs. Smith and Ogburn rode to Honiton, to see the annual procession of lace-makers; alighted at the Golden Lion, and was soon called over and invited to dine at a Mrs. Youat's, whose daughter is presidentess of this society, in number exceeding a hundred. They have an afternoon sermon, and afterwards walk in procession, in the following order :—the presidentess with a wand adorned with flowers; then four maidens, eight years old, with each a basket of flowers and large boquets, walking between two arches adorned with flowers; then follow the patronesses, each with a white wand ; then the standard-bearer, followed by two dozen couple, with a standard-bearer attending them. In this order they paraded through the principal streets, and then adjourned to the Golden Lion inn to take tea and pass the evening in dancing and festivity. To this we were invited, but my occasions calling me to Exeter, and a want of relish for such mirth, concurred to send me off the ground before the street parade was over, leaving my companions to return home by moonlight. Lodged at the " Valiant Soldier," Exeter.

Sidmouth, July 8. Rode to Hull-down to see the Exeter races. The cup with two hundred guineas won by Mr. Wildman's horse Lubin; sport indifferent. The dust and heat were insufferable, the numbers present supposed to be ten thousand.

July 10. Judge Sewall visited us ; in the afternoon walked with him to Peak hill.

July 14. Received a letter from Peter Frye, Esq., without mention of time or place.

TO MR. JOHN TIMMINS, LONDON.

Sidmouth, July 12, 1778.

DEAR SIR :

I should be glad to see you at this bathing town of mud walls and thatched roofs. Judge Sewall and lady, Samuel Sewall, Mr. Smith, and Mr. Ogburn are here; and at Exeter, fourteen miles off, are Col. Erving's family, Col. Vassall, Mr. Lechmere; and late Lieut. Governor Oliver is soon to be there. The advices from Boston discover a disposition I could scarce expect to hear. I presumed in this flourishing state of their affairs, none durst whisper a doubt of the omnipotency of the Congress, allied as they are to France.   Very truly,

S. CURWEN.

TO MR. GEORGE RUSSELL, B'RMINGHAM.

Sidmouth, July 13, 1778.

DEAR SIR :

Accept my warmest thanks for your kind solicitude about my health, which is but in an ill state; having a few days since received a shock of the kind which confined me last winter, and nearly translated me to another, or rather no state of existence. Don't let this expression hurt you; I mean not a doubt of a future state, but whether the soul does not remain inactive during its separation from the body, and until roused by the last trumpet to life and activity, is a doctrine I cannot entirely disprove; but no more of principles. My mind is as easy, submissive and resigned, as a conviction that the divine conduct is right can make it; to aid which, I muster up all my religion and philosophy, sometimes with success; sometimes nature oppressed sinks under the burden.

Having proposed in my answer to follow the order of your letter, I come to a tender point, the condition of the amiable and worthy partner of your soul, for whom I feel more than a common friend's affection and regard; you have my earnest prayers that her life may be continued till it shall cease to be a blessing; nor can our fondest wishes, guided by reason, extend further. The vicissitudes daily taking place should be daily lessons to teach us the vanity of too fondly expecting felicity from flattering, transitory circumstances here below. Should it please the sovereign disposer of life to deprive you of your dearest friend, may you experience all the advantages that religion and true philosophy afford; as I doubt not you view the evils of life with too religious an eye not to consider every event, however irksome at present, as capable of yielding the most solid, pure, and lasting comfort in the final issue.

This day I received a letter from an old friend, now in banishment with his wife and children at Halifax, conceived in the common plaintive strain with all letters from that quarter ; complaining of the spiritless measures of administration and their military servants. In truth, vigor and activity seem not the characteristic of this nation at this period ; the continued series of untoward events on the side of Great Britain, in this unnatural contest between her and the colonies, has, I fear, given the *coup de grace* to her glory. The sun of Britain is past the meridian and declining fast to the west, and America is for ever emancipated from the legislative authority of this once potent empire ; alas ! no more so. The prophetic falling off of the best jewel from our king's crown when on his head at coronation, is now accomplished by the loss of America, which I consider irrevocably gone ; whether to their advantage, is a point, I fancy, the Congress and I should not join issue in :— the burden of supporting an independency with dignity is too heavy for America to bear, especially the northern colonies, unless the patriots there will discharge the troublesome public trusts and offices without pecuniary emoluments ; requiring a much greater degree of virtue, self-denial, and public spirit, than I think now does or indeed ever did exist there, unless in profession.

I fancy by this time I have tired my friend in reading, as I confess I have myself in writing, and conclude by wishing he may live long, and see many prosperous days.

Your affectionate friend,

S. CURWEN.

July 15.   Went off with Mr. Withers in his phaeton, accompanied by Messrs. Smith, Jarvis and Meservale, to Beer ; dined at King's Head ; afternoon, were rowed a league out, and remained out two hours.

CHAPTER X.

Sidmouth, July 17. Set off alone on an excursion to the west;
at nine o'clock passing over Peak hill, through Otterton, and over
Welbry common; my first stage at Mr. Withers', Lympston, intentionally to persuade him to accompany me to Teignmouth, agreeably
to a vague promise from him the preceding day. He was gone to
Exeter. I then proceeded through Star Cross and Dawlish Sands;
on the other side of the beach is an extensive sea and land view;
from hence is about four miles to Teignmouth, where arrived at
six o'clock at Globe inn, facing the sands and beach. This is a
bathing town, and resorted to by more, and company of higher rank
than Sidmouth can boast. It is irregularly built, but the houses
more in number and of incomparably better appearance. The
beach for bathing lies at some distance from the town. Lodged
here.

July 18. Rose early, took the road to Newton Bushel, distant
six miles, through Bishop Stanton, passing also through King's
Stanton. Newton has three hundred houses, decently built; shops
of almost every kind of goods, streets paved, two Episcopal and
one Presbyterian church. Breakfasted and soon set off, passing at
half a mile distant an old fashioned seat called Ford, belonging to
Lord Courtenay, in whose manor this town lies. From hence to
Dartmouth, lying sixteen miles distant; the land in the approaches
thereto hilly and uneven, but all improved; at three alighted at
a Mrs. Quick's, in a place called Kingsware; this is a cluster of
houses on the hither side of the river Dart, where the harbor pilots
dwell, and has an Episcopal church. Ferried over much the
width of Charlestown ferry, about half a mile within the extreme
points of the harbor.

Dartmouth, July 20. At twelve A. M. departed for Torbay,
five miles distant; an ugly town, houses low, and for the greater
part slovenly in appearance; among them, however, a few decent
ones. The lower point adjoining the quay occupied by those who

depend on the hook and line; here being no fewer than fourscore boats daily employed in that service, all with a mast and sail, and four to two tons burthen. They supply Exeter, Bath, Bristol, etc., quite across the country nearly a hundred miles north from them. Dined at George inn, and took leave of Brixholm. Thence to Barry Pomeroy, an estate of the Duke of Somerset, the house large, but avenues in a neglected state; magnificent edifices and expansive pleasure grounds seem not to be this duke's taste, or a scanty purse restrains it. Hence to Bridgtown, contained in the parish of Barry Pomeroy and part of the manor of the same name, within which I was told Totness stands. The duke derives from his estate here two thousand pounds yearly. Totness is a corporation and a parliamentary borough; is remarkable for the singularity of its address to the first George of the Brunswick line at his accession to the throne of these kingdoms; after the usual flattery, such as is always paid to a new race of princes, they offered his majesty sixteen shillings in the pound of their estates, and the other four if he should want it, as a proof of their loyalty.

July 21. Arose at seven o'clock, mounted my horse, rode to Newton, before mentioned; stopped there for a night.

July 22. After breakfast departed for Chudleigh, but missing the road, passed over Hull-down, leading to Dawlish, and arrived at one o'clock at Exeter; Mr. Erving happening in sight, urged my driving with him.

Exeter, July 24. After visiting my old acquaintances, returned to Sidmourh by eight o'clock, evening.

Sidmouth, July 26. Met Mr. George Eveleigh, a gentleman of South Carolina, educated both at school and college at Cambridge, New England, whom I remember a school-boy when I was in college; now the father of five grown up children.

TO MR. JOHN TIMMINS, LONDON.

Sidmouth, July 28, 1778.

DEAR SIR:

Please let me know whether you have received any late advices from Boston or New England, by which you are informed of the situation of the country, respecting its political, civil, or religious condition; the temper and disposition of its inhabitants respecting those who have left the country ; their inclinations or ability to continue the war. Would that the execrable spirit of persecution might abate, they be restored to reason, and I to my native country ; an event I ardently long for : indeed, I sometimes feel resolution enough to attempt to go and throw myself on the mercy of those whom party rage has rendered almost insensible to the tender feelings of humanity ; but fear, and a settled aversion to their levelling principles and persecuting practices, disarms me.

With truth, your friend,

S. CURWEN.

August 16. News received that Congress has rejected any treaty with the British commissioners ; as might easily have been, and was, I believe, fully imagined by all the world would be the case at this late period, without an express specific acknowledgment of their independency.

Axminster, August 18. Walked to beach ; seven bathing machines standing there, dragged into the water by a horse each. The alcove and ball room larger and more respectable than at Sidmouth.

TO MR. JOHN TIMMINS, LONDON.

Sidmouth, August 31, 1778.

DEAR SIR :

The dangerous, distrustful situation the nation is in, makes me tremble for the next news from abroad, lest it shake the government to its centre. In the annals of this country, I know of no period in which England stood on a narrower point ; not in 1688, nor even when the Scotch rebels had penetrated as far as Derby, in 1745. The designs of Providence are inscrutable, not to be controlled by human policy, nor defeated by human strength.

Although I have, all along, doubted that Congress would accept terms short of independence, I confess myself not a little deranged at the confirmation of it. That Congress should be loth to quit their authority, is not to be wondered at, for it is the nature of power to endeavor to preserve itself ; but I cannot help flattering myself with hopes that America will soon see her interest in a different point of light from Congress, and disappoint the ambitious views of men, however well qualified they may be to govern, evidently disposed to sacrifice that country's happiness to their lust of power. God only knows what will be the issue of the troubles; may it please him to save her from ruin, and accomplish a happy re-union with this, and on a lasting basis.

Your assured friend,

S. CURWEN.

Sept. 11. Keppel's and Byron's fleets are sources of incredible reports from street and tavern politicians; should both these sea commanders be defeated, none knows the consequences—fatal ones may be justly apprehended; this country was never in a more perilous situation.

Sept. 21. The day of our half-yearly fair; great numbers came in, passing on the beach to view the sea, going off in boats, eating, drinking and buying, in the sheds and booths erected on the lower parts of the streets, and filled with confectionary, toys, hardware, ribbons, etc. Rode to Exeter in the evening.

Sept. 28. Departed on horseback, accompanied by Mr. Smith, on an intended ramble to Weymouth and Portland. First stage to Colyton, nine miles, where we dined. Hence to Charmouth, a straggling town that extends from the top to the bottom of a long hill, and contains one street of perhaps a hundred houses; passing through, we arrived at a villa, two miles distant, part of the manor of the Earl of Arundel, a Roman Catholic peer, of which persuasion most of the inhabitants on his lordship's estate here are. The next cluster of houses on the road was Morkam's lake, which with the former scarce make up a hundred houses. Our next and last stage for this day Bridport, at the Bull inn, where we supped and lodged.

Sept. 29. Left for Abbotsbury, ten miles distant; the land along the sea-shore a desert, not so much as a tree, shrub or bush was to be seen. Passed through Weymouth to Melcomb Regis, over bridge laid across the Wey, so called, being a small arm of the sea, dividing these two towns. The latter lying on the land side, is a neck formed by the bend, almost at right angles with the river Wey, and is the place whereon the beach lies and visitors reside. The market is large and better supplied than in the former.

There is a range of brick buildings, twelve in number, tasty and commodious, facing the beach, and but a small distance above it; at the end is an elegant assembly-room, and at a small distance are shops of all kinds of articles, millinery, toys, etc. Coffee-houses, circulating libraries, etc. The beach is furnished with twenty-two machines for bathing, in finer taste than any I have seen. This town, like Weymouth, is concerned in shipping; its quay is long enough for sixty vessels; not half that number then in port. It has two Episcopal churches and a Presbyterian meeting-house. Weymouth is on the outer or south side of the river, consisting principally of one street, well paved, but narrow. In front of the town is a quay, facing Melcomb, filled with vessels. After dining, we sallied forth; finding nothing further to entertain us, soon returned, and ordering forth our horses, took our departure towards Portland, the last stage. The passage to it is over a water called the *Fleet*, between a beach seven miles in length and the main land; by this beach Portland is joined to the main, but the way is scarce ever attempted, consisting of small loose stones or deep sand, so that a horse would sink down half-leg deep; this approach, therefore, must be too tedious to be used. The road from Melcomb to the island or peninsula is over a lofty plain of a mile in length; from hence is a hard gravel beach of over a mile: and opposite the road stands an edifice in ruins, styled a castle, having however more the look of a mansion house deserted by its owner, its solitary black site rendering it an uncomfortable residence. We soon measured the beach, and were wafted over the Fleet by a rope-ferry, as it is called in New England dialect. But the beach on the Portland side, of a mile and a half, required a more leisurely pace. The first village on the island of Portland is called Chesilton, of about a hundred houses of reputable aspect;—situation low, on the plain of a beach; from hence, being an easy ascent of half a mile, we came to two villages.

In the morning (30th), climbed up the lofty plain to the spot the flag-staff is erected on, being the northernmost summit, having the castle situate at the northern exetremity, from which may be seen at one view as far into the English channel as eye can reach; to Isle of Wight in the east, and to the north a vast extent of country. Portland island is about five miles in length, breadth two; on the land side it is defended by a castle before mentioned. On the southern cliffs are two light-houses. Mounted our horses, and in our course lay, in the middle road, the first village, called Reffon, which contains the only church on the island, encompassed by stone wall, inclosing an acre of yard. Passed through *Ishwell, Wikeham, Eison, Weston*, and returned to the rope-ferry by which we came to the island, and at one o'clock arrived at Crown inn, Melcomb. Thence through *Upway*, situated in a fertile vale, abounding in trees and hedges. The next village, lying a little out of our way, is Winterborne Monkton; the latter epithet I suppose denotes for what it was remarkable. Through this village we passed to *Maiden Castle*, a famous encampment of Roman construction, supposed to have been built by them soon after their first invasion. In their times Dorchester, two miles distant, was their winter, as this spot was their summer residence. It is said to be the only remains of the kind in Great Britain—form oval; contains within the inner intrenchment many acres, enough to hold three legions or eighteen thousand men. The intrenchments entire, four without the other at each end—two on each side or flank, encompassing the whole—depth thirty feet. It has a stupendous appearance, and looks like a work of a people capable of any undertaking, however difficult. Thence we jogged on to Dorchester.

Dorchester, Oct. 1. Rambled over the town: here are assize and session-house, prison and bridewell; about 2500 inhabitants; houses decent, and streets paved. Avenues to the town pleasant at all quarters, being lined with a row of trees on each side for two miles; from hence at ten o'clock we departed, shaping our course towards the remains of Roman antiquity, the occasion of our coming hither; and in half an hour arrived at the amphitheatre, which is entirely of earth; the forms whereon the benches were laid for spectators are yet entire. The outer line an oval, the earth thrown up in the manner of an encampment, and about twenty feet high, encompassing the whole; the area or space wherein spectacles were exhibited, measures forty or fifty yards longest diameter; two rows of benches, judged spacious enough to hold two thousand spectators. Having satisfied curiosity, proceeded through fields for the castle, lying on a lofty ridge at about a mile and a half further. Having finished our survey, and amused ourselves with fine prospects, we ascended by another quarter to the fields and inclosures adjoining hereto ; crossing which, at length reached turnpike at a village called Martinston, from hence to Winterburn-Stepleton and Clenston ; here we met the great London road to Plymouth and the west ; glad once again to salute it and forsake the cross-roads that are but indifferent at best, and some execrable ; in this we kept till arrival at first and last stage of this day, alighting in about two hours at Bull inn, Bridport, distant from Dorchester seventeen miles. The business for which this town is famed, and carried on to great extent, is in sail-cloth and white cordage ; in size little inferior to Dorset.

Bridport, Oct. 2. To Axminster, Honiton, and Wishcombe, where lodged.

Oct. 3. Alighted at Mrs. Godfrey's, my new lodging-house in Sidmouth.

Sidmouth, Oct. 10. Spirit of privateering against France surprisingly raised ; success incredible : three East India ships homeward bound taken, and thirty-six St. Domingo and Martinico ships, and a multitude of others.

Oct. 26. Accompanied Mr. Smith to Mr. William Lloyd's, at Otterton, a substantial farmer. In conversation on different ranks of mankind, and different consequent mode of living, my companion told us the following tale from an Irish lady. A young countrywoman of hers wished she might be queen for a month, for then, said she, I would have bacon with my broth. To which our hostess added one of the like kind : a young lad of Cornwall wished he might be king, for then, said he, I would ride on gates and eat fat bacon with my broth. The demands of nature are few and easily satisfied ; it is education and use that increase our appetites and render them troublesome.

Oct. 27. Evening Mr. Smith visited me. Our sentiments on toleration differ ; he holds that every subject in a state has an absolute right to unlimited toleration, be his principles what they may. I think no man should be persecuted for opinion's sake, yet he has no right to complain of any disabilities he may be under, whose avowed persuasion is, that faith is not to be kept with those whose religious tenets differ from his own, whose religion absolves him from most solemn engagements, nay, who thinks himself in con-

science bound to violate promises, vows and oaths; nay, further,
thinks it highly meritorious to disturb the peace and overthrow the
very government he has sworn to support, when his priest directs
and opportunity presents. Opinions, merely such, the magistrate
ought by no means to concern himself with, nor be subject to his
control; and therefore every peaceable man has an equal claim to
his protection in his person and property.

By letters from Lord Cornwallis at New-York, it appears Count
D'Estaing had been obliged hastily to retreat with his squadron
from Rhode Island by the arrival of Lord Howe, with twenty line-
of-battle ships and twenty frigates; that a severe storm parted
the fleets; that the Americans by a bridge of boats had landed
twelve thousand men on the island, and that General Clinton had
strengthened his garrison by several detachments he himself had
brought from New-York; that Gen. Lee, being accused of cow-
ardice and bad conduct, was suspended by a court martial.

Oct. 28. Lord Howe has arrived from Rhode Island in the
Eagle. Four of our frigates have been sunk at Rhode Island, when
invested by D'Estaing and the Provincials; also twenty-three ships
destroyed.

The Bostonians are said to be out of humor with their new
friends and allies, and no wonder; French government, laws,
religion, manners, and policy, are totally alien and unnatural to
Americans, and will sit uneasy till custom and long use have fa-
miliarized them.

Nov. 17. Rode to Beer with Mr. Smith; visited the vicar of
Seaton and Beer, a character truly original; a great humorist and
punster, not unlike Rev. Mather Byles of Boston in that line. He
is of enormous bulk, confined by gout, which he told us was his
third attack, resembling, in his own language, a furnace heated
seven times hotter than the former; compared himself, in the midst
of excruciating pains, to his holiness seated to receive adoration in
his sanctified chair; treated us hospitably, and was very facetious.

Nov. 23. Took my leave of Sidmouth, my residence for approaching winter being to be at Exeter; passed the road in two
hours and a half, and sat down at new lodgings in Fore-street, near
East-gate.

Exeter, Nov. 26. With Mr. Smith road to Newton Abbot to

visit a Capt. Hendley, returned from Newfoundland, taken by Capt. Babson and carried into Boston, where and at Cape Ann he resided six weeks. He reports that the country is in a distressed condition, wanting almost every comfort; no trade but privateering, by which some have been raised from nothing to affluence : says the inhabitants are embittered against the French, who have engrossed all the trade, from whom they do not in return receive any advantage of labor or supplies, but their own goods at exorbitant prices. Wretched effects of civil discord ! How deplorable is the situation, how wretched the prospects of that once happy region, which security, peace and plenty have of late abandoned.

December 4. Visited my venerable and reverend friend, Mr. Towgood; he is one of very few to whose respectful and undissembled welcome I am not a little indebted ; to whom my grateful acknowledgments are due. The river Exe, by late rains swelled beyond the memory of forty years, has caused great damage. The two islands lying within the banks of the river over against this city, overflown; on them are tucks for drying woollen cloths that are dyed and pressed in the city.

December 16. Attended for the first time Arden's course of lectures on experimental philosophy, being the second of the course, held in a chamber in the castle ; more than threescore present, and continued two hours: subject, electricity.

December 21. Received a letter from Judge Sewall, full as usual of humor and hopes.

FROM HON. J. SEWALL.

Bristol, December 18, 1778.

Dear Sir :

Till I had the pleasure of receiving your favor of the 1st inst., I was as much at a loss from what part of this or any other globe I should hear of you, as I was with respect to a certain commander-in-chief, when, to use the words of a friend in a late letter from New-York, " after having proceeded up the Delaware within twenty miles of Philadelphia, his place of destination, when a looker-on would say they must (from the reason and nature of things) land at Wilmington, instead of which he sees them tack about

—away they come—down the river again—huzza—make a circle
round Asspeak, up Chesapeake, and after travelling in the heat of
the season, in a hell of a climate, over a monstrous extent of country, they arrive at Philadelphia—'*the army in high spirits.*'"
Don't you think my friend's description is truly Shandean? However, matters I hope are mending; the account you give me from
America, seems to be confirmed from all quarters. Judge Howard
is lately arrived here from New-York; he tells me that a number
of gentlemen of influence and property, who have been lying on
their oars to see which way the game would finally go, as I suppose, have lately come in, among whom is the famous Mr. Smith,
the lawyer;* that they, together with Mr. Galloway, are unani-'
mously of opinion, that from the unexpected tyranny of the Congress
and their sub-devils, the almost universal poverty and distress of
the people, and the general aversion to French connections, the
quondam union of the thirteen states is upon the point of dissolution,
and that nothing is wanting but a single effort to crush the rebellion, root and branch. Judge Howard says he heard Smith say,
"if Great Britain don't conquer the colonies, it can only be because
she *wont;*" that these gentlemen have been much with the commissioners, by whom they have been greatly attended to. With
these favorable accounts from America, I can't help connecting
the union that appears in parliament, respecting the grand point,
the reduction of the colonies; for though the opposition to ministry
is still faintly kept up for form's sake, yet the language is so different from that held in former sessions, that I can't help thinking a
sense of public danger, and a regard to national interest and honor,
begin to prevail over private resentments. From all these appearances, I augur well; and I am happy in finding the general opinion
among my friends and acquaintances is, that the prospect of a
speedy and happy suppression of the rebellion is fairer now than it
ever has been. Come, my dear friend, cheer up; don't think of
going to that "country from whose bourne no traveller returns,"
though there be no sin or sorrow, before you have seen a happy
end to the sorrows and sins of your country. It will be such glo-

* The historian of New-York, and chief justice during the war . subsequently of Canada.

rious news to carry with you, that it is well worth waiting patiently
for many years; but I hope you will have it in one year; and then,
I doubt not, you will find yourself more *able to combat the unavoidable evils of this state militant,* and be less in a hurry to set out for
that unknown country, which must be your next stage.

The situation of American loyalists, I confess, is enough to have
provoked Job's wife, if not Job himself; but still we must be men,
philosophers, and Christians ; and bearing up with patience, resignation and fortitude, against unavoidable sufferings, is our duty in
each of these characters.

There, sir, is a Roland for your Oliver, in the serious way.
My friends and family here are all well, and wish your health and
happiness. If you see my good friend the doctor before he receives a
letter from me, present him my best respects.

Adieu,

J. Sewall.

TO HON. WILLIAM BROWNE, COWBRIDGE, WALES.

Exeter, Dec. 26, 1778.

Dear Sir :

I have often in fancy, whilst reading a letter from a friend,
transported myself into his presence, and considered myself as attending to his personal conversation, thereby increasing my own
enjoyment. This curious effect may perhaps be peculiar to me;
however, I am pleasing myself that my friend Col. Browne,
although not apt to be carried into the regions of fancy, may on
occasion be capable of an innocent delusion of this kind.

Without further preface, my chief intention in this scrawl is to
amuse this dark gloomy season with the recital of a few circumstances relative to our own country that were told me by Capt.
Hendley, who was taken into Boston by an American privateer,
and passed six weeks there and at Cape Ann. The inhabitants,
he said, seemed discontented, and would gladly exchange their unhappy condition for peace and a connection with their old friends,
could a constitutional line be drawn, and America be thereby freed
from the future attacks of administration. That they are dissatis-
fied with their new allies, against whom there are great heart-
burnings; that all commerce is in the hands of the French, and

commodities held at an unreasonable height; not a store belonging to the inhabitants contains any European goods, all being in the hands of the French, for which they will receive nothing but money, taking in return no supplies from the Anglo-Americans, nor employing a laborer; in short, that the French are not of the least advantage to them in any respect; that privateering, the only resource of the merchants, is almost annihilated by the great shock the adventurers that way have received;—that the European articles of import are extremely wanted, and at an enormous price; that the French are hated, and in turn they despise and oppress the inhabitants, between whom and themselves there are frequent quarrels; and one that lately made a noise in our papers here, which happened at Boston a few months since, was occasioned solely by the opposition of the natives to the French, no English soldier or sailor being then in town; that those who now rule the roast there are like a certain class of men mentioned in Scripture, taken from the lowest of the people, and too tenacious of their ill-acquired power and honors to part with them, or to suffer the least intimation of reconcilement with Great Britain: honors did I say?—for a moment I forgot Addison's incontrovertible adage,

> " When vice prevails,
> The post of honor is a private station."

I fear the measure of these men's folly is not yet quite full, but I am egregiously mistaken if they are not making hasty strides to their utter undoing.   On advice of an order of the Congress for a valuation of estates, real and personal, through their extended domains, the Massachusetts Bay assembly incontestably, unanimously and promptly refused compliance, and despatched Mr. Hancock to Philadelphia with their determination and remonstrance.   Their bills of credit, which at first emission passed at the rate of four and sixpence the dollar, had sunk to one and threepence, and passed current only by permission at one and sixpence.   The houses in Boston and all along the coast are stripped of every article of furniture and valuable effects, save what is absolutely necessary for constant use, the inhabitants being in continued dread of a descent on the coast, which, indeed, they have but too probable grounds to apprehend.   A passenger, lately fled from America on the score of sufferings there, declares the late menace in the commissioners' proclamation will assuredly effect what neither persuasions nor threats have yet had force enough to bring about, a solid and firm union of all ranks and classes, for want of which alone in the middle colonies, he says, the British army has not, long since, been driven into the sea. The manifesto, which I presume you have seen, issued by the Congress in consequence of that proclamation, renders it more than probable that should the dreadful expedient threatened take place, history will hardly furnish a parallel to the cruelty and carnage of the following campaign, which God in his infinite mercy prevent. I presume, before receipt of this, you will have seen the account of Lords Cornwallis and Carlisle's return to Great Britain, and the shattered condition of Byron's fleet, on which was placed such confidence and dependence, having sustained a loss, it is to be feared, of several capital ships. The almost uninterrupted series of untoward events and curious accidents which have befallen this people since the commencement of these mutual confusions and strifes, has not seldom reminded me of a passage in the song of Deborah and Barak; I wish for form's sake I could recollect our New England version; "They fought from heaven, the stars in their courses fought against Sisera." This text is not quoted by way of comparison; I would not have you suppose that I mean to compare the hosts of Sisera to the British army, for in truth I do not think the Americans to be the chosen people of God, or their armies the armies of the living God, though they have only and simply *Deo auspice* for their motto on their bills and standards. I should have finished the above by adding somewhat of a more cheerful strain, but having finished my sheet must conclude with affectionate regards to Mrs. Browne, your son and self.

S. Curwen.

Dec. 25. There have been twenty-eight king's ships, privateers and letters of marque carried into Brest, from 20th ult. to 10th inst.; a very respectable number, truly, considering the English are lords of the ocean! Of the twenty-eight bishops only four voted to adopt the new mode of carrying on the war by spreading carnage and desolation through America, as decreed in the commissioners' proclamation. Whatever excuses or reasons politicians may assign for extending or securing temporal dominion by such cut-throat measures, these four servants of the meek and lowly Jesus have exhibited a spirit that should through the duration of time render them infamous, and their names and memory proverbially detestable. In the papers received to-day appears a manifesto of Congress in answer to the commissioners' proclamation, announcing a retaliation of like measures.

Dec. 28. This day I am arrived at my grand climacteric, having just completed my sixty-third year: with more propriety than old Jacob may I say, "*few and evil have been the days of the years of my life.*" For what I am reserved, is known to God only; many have been my deliverances, many the deaths I have been rescued from. May my remaining days be employed to more valuable purposes, and to my own real honor and advantage, temporal and eternal. Visited by Mr. George Eveleigh, with whom and family I have an agreeable acquaintance. He was one of the first couple my old friend Mr. McGilchrist married in South Carolina, the ceremony performed at Wands in Christ Church parish. He was educated at Harvard College, and boarded with President Wadsworth; at first sight of me at Bristol two years ago, he recognized my name and person; having been at school in Cambridge while I was a student in college.

CHAPTER XI.

Exeter, Jan. 1, 1779. A delightful day; visited Mr. Eveleigh, and by invitation passed the afternoon and evening there. Why should presents be made upon the first day of January more than at any other time? The original of this custom is attributed to the reign of Romulus, and Tatius king of the Sabines, who governed jointly in Rome in the seventh year of the city. It is said that Tatius, having been presented on the first of January with some boughs out of the forest of the goddess Strenia in token of good luck, began this custom, and called the present *strena*. The Romans made this a holiday, and consecrated it to the honor of Janus, offering sacrifices to him; and the people went in throngs to Mount Tarpeia, where Janus had an altar clothed anew, and chose to begin their respective employments on this day. They wished one another good luck, and were very careful not to speak any thing ill-natured or quarrelsome. The common presents among the meaner sort were dates, figs and honey, which were usually covered with leaf gold: and those who were under the protection of great men used to add a piece of money. In the reign of Augustus, the populace, gentry and senators used to send him new-year's gifts, and if he was not in town, they carried them to the capitol. From the Romans this custom went to the Greeks, and from the heathens to the Christians, who early came into the practice of making presents to the magistrates. Some of the fathers write strenuously against this practice on account of the immoralities committed under the cover of protection:—but since the governments of the several nations of Europe have become Christianized, the custom is still retained as a token of friendship, love and respect.

TO MR. JOHN TIMMINS, LONDON.

Exeter, Jan. 17, 1779.

Dear Sir:

Inability to provide for one's own support is a mortifying consideration that embitters almost every circumstance of life. Once

I thought health with virtue and a competency a happy condition; now I think otherwise; experience has taught me that more is necessary to human happiness. Without something in pursuit, rightly or wrongly estimated worthy, life is insipid;—a connection with my fellow men, constant employment, and a much less sum would render me more pleased with the world and myself, than the supplies I receive whilst I dream the blank of life along, unknowing and unknown. Did I know how to emancipate myself from this tediously uniform state of little more than mere animal life, not an hour should pass before I would fly to any quarter of the habitable earth to accomplish it. My past inactive state often reminds me of a Latin adage, "*fruges consumere natus,*" a reproach I can but ill brook. Man by the kind intention of his Creator was formed for useful action; selfish ease, indulgence and repose injures both body and mind; the former without exercise cannot maintain its health and strength, nor will the latter, if unemployed on laudable, worthy objects, refuse to stoop to base ones, or destroy its vigor for want of exertion, or by sensual indulgence.

Your mention of the proscription act in your letter I fancy I did not understand, never having seen any names inserted in any act; if you mean that lately in our newspapers wherein the refugees are forbidden under penalty of transportation to return, and threatened with death in case of a second entrance within the United States, that I have seen, but none other of the kind.

Yours,

S. CURWEN.

Jan. 23. The last "Remembrancer" contains a list of refugees banished by act of the Massachusetts government, specifying only four out of the thirteen from Salem, viz., William Browne, Benjamin Pickman, John Prince, and John Sargent. The omission of my name affords no comfort, fearing it may operate disadvantageously here, being dependent on the bounty of the court.

Jan. 30. This day is, in Church of England language, "*Charles's martyrdom.*" Attended service; Archdeacon Hull of Barnstaple, preached a furious, high-tory address to a thin audience.

TO REV. ISAAC SMITH, SIDMOUTH.

Exeter, Feb. 1, 1779.

DEAR SIR :

I hope your New England toryism will not end in English ja-
cobinism, as your letter seems to indicate. Curiosity led me last
night to the cathedral, where, if you are a real believer that those
sufferings of the pretended martyr were undeserved, your ears
would have been charmed with Archdeacon Hull's encomium on
him, and your liberal breast fired with indignant rage at his cruel
persecutors. But really, when I see the solemn mockery of a pulpit clothed in black, the staves of the city officers covered with the
same grim color, no music in the service of the day, which generally constitutes so essential a part of Christian worship ; God most
earnestly entreated not to lay this miscalled murder to the charge
of the nation, or to require his blood at their hands, who, to compass his own tyrannous purposes, would have involved (and really
did as far as in him lay) this island and Ireland in confusion, carnage and desolation ; and further that nothing less than the blood
of the Son of God can expiate this (in the Church language) inhu-
man and execrable (but I durst affirm justly deserved) murder, I
cannot fail to wish government would lay aside a service which
insults common sense, is a mere religious grimace, and which all
liberal minds justly despise. Were you to have seen the pitiful and
thin company, you would have wagered odds that they were hardened wretches, and went merely to save appearances.

I thank you for the mention of my name to your father, which,
if I judge from former experience, will be productive of no very
comfortable effects to me ; my friends having, I fear, adhered to the
notion that my departure was an intentional and full adieu. The
omission of my name in the banishment act I fear will prove injurious to me here. That your father makes no mention of government or the temper of the people, I presume arises from his prudence
and the surveillance of the rulers there, which is, I fancy, strict
enough.

Very affectionately,

S. CURWEN.

Feb. 15. Evening walked with Mr. Eveleigh's family through

Fore-street to see illumination on occasion of Admiral Keppel's acquittal by court martial on a charge of Sir Hugh Palliser ; the result is the highest approbation of his conduct.   London has voted thanks for his bravery and the freedom of the city, and all large cities and towns are following the example.

Feb. 20.   James Russell on his way to Dartmouth, came here to inform me that it was debated in Massachusetts Assembly whether my name should be inserted in the exclusion bill, and carried by a small majority in my favor after a warm debate.

TO REV. ISAAC SMITH, SIDMOUTH.

Exeter, Feb. 19, 1779.

DEAR SIR :

I presume I am to expect all that is worth hearing from Judge Sewall's letter to you.   All well in Salem the last of December, so Mr. Russell informs me.   Two or three persons, I am told, who had not money enough for shoes for their feet, are now riding in coaches of their own in Boston.   Solomon says, " I have seen servants on horseback and princes walking on foot ;" I really think the royal preacher was a prophet, and pointed at the events of our day ; at least the present state of English America verifies the remark.

Though the general election be not for these two years, a canvass for votes has begun already.   Rolle against Baring and Cholwich, who have combined with the church and chambers.   I have seen one instance and heard of another of such gross condescension, that it has given me a thorough dislike to parliamentary canvassing, and manifests the pitiful notions of a nation's honor, virtue and regard to public interest, which no man of common sense and real integrity, and not poisoned by corrupt principles and practices of the times, can stoop to, and which nothing but sinister, selfish views can digest and submit to.   Men of recluse lives only, such as monks and speculative system makers, vent their spleen on the manners, customs, principles and practices of their day, and call their times the dregs and refuse.   I will therefore suppose it always was, and ever will be the case, with ambitious men, to use the same low arts and base flattering compliances to gain their selfish ends ; be it so, it is still unworthy conduct.   God forbid that

wealth, power and influence achieved by such means as reason
condemns and honor despises, shall ever be in my possession. The
nearer I approach the verge of life, the juster I fancy my notions
are, and if indeed they shall prove so, I hope to be finally rid of all
essential errors before I put off this mortal coil and become an associate of pure, refined, unembodied intelligences.

Yours, etc.,

S. Curwen.

TO JONATHAN SEWALL, ESQ., BRISTOL.

Exeter, March 6, 1779.

Dear Sir :

I delayed answering your last favor, in hopes to transmit you
some little intelligence about our own country by means of a Salem
captain, who was taken on his passage to Cadiz, and carried into
Bristol, from whence he set off for London, and after a short abode
passed over to France. His sudden flight from this land of toryism
and tyranny has deprived me of wished and expected information
respecting my family and friends, but instead of granting my request signified in a letter I wrote, he did not think it consistent
with the purity of his principles to correspond with a refugee, as
he told Mr. Timmins.

The banishment act, which party resentment dictated, will, like
all overstrained penal measures, be its own destroyer, and the malicious designs of its promoters be frustrated by the very means employed to manifest their venom and spite against the friends of law-
ful government and the constitutional rights of their country ; nay,
it was soon clamored against, and a noted brother counsellor of
your honor's, whom you well know, of the doubtful or rather
double gender, has publicly declared it to be a mad act, to which
one may add, as ever disgraced tyranny itself. How unlike is the
conduct of our countrymen, who, whilst contending or pretending
to contend for civil liberty, are contriving and exciting, with the
most rigorous severity, plans of oppression against many of their innocent fellow subjects, feeble and unarmed, merely for speculative
opinions, to the disgrace of their pretensions—I say how unlike is
this conduct to those generous Athenians who undertook the expulsion of the thirty tyrants that had usurped the government of that

city : themselves reinstated in the rank of citizens, their desires were gratified; they did not persecute with everlasting hatred their enemies, but, determined not to yield to that slavery to which those had basely submitted, they invited them to share the freedom which themselves had so gloriously acquired. The above quotation, my worthy friend will candidly suppose is only applied by way of illustration, not comparison, which, however, does not run on all fours, as the saying is. I was going to set down a few remarks on the present state of the nation as it appears to my view; for the good of the nation, you know, in which each individual's happiness is involved, is of too much importance to be neglected by any who wish well to their country; but having made so many false judgments, and remembering the substance in a former favor, my courage fails, and I think it more prudent to keep my ideas in my own breast. There have been circulating, among some, curious and amusing enough inconsistencies relating to General Campbell in Georgia, from whose successful invasion multitudes augur the quick reduction of America, and have taken anticipatory possession of the remains of D'Estaing's fleet that the flames and sea have not devoured, with Martinique and Guadaloupe. Unluckily the truth of one report dispels, in the minds of judicious people, the succeeding one, consigning it to forgetfulness, which I presume is pretty much the case with you, unless the privateering business engrosses the attention of your Bristol traders, which is not the case with us; but little concern that way and a declining trade leave our commercial gentry time enough on their hands, now employed in the laudable purpose of talking and disputing for the honor of Keppel and the good of the nation. These political dabblers, together with clergy and attornies, rendezvous at Mills' coffee-house, the mart of politics and scandal, and, I assure you, figure away as notably as Fielding's coffee-house politicians, and are not altogether unequal to them.

Having taken some pains, I hope you will be able to read the foregoing, notwithstanding the abbreviations, which, for despatch, I have used.

I am your affectionate friend,

S. Curwen.

Exeter, March 17.   Attended a trial at Common Pleas in the castle, Judges Hotham and Perryn ; evening, returning home met a large crowd hallooing, having blue cockades in their hats, with an old man at their head, and streamers flying at the end of long sticks ; it proved a triumph for victory gained over the parish priest in a tithe case :—I am told it is a customary practice.

April 2.   Good Friday.   Canon Moore preached at cathedral an excellent sermon, as his always are ; he is called Bishop Keppel's sermon-writer, as the latter is not considered a good writer.

April 12.   Went to deliver a letter to Mr. and Mrs. Erving, for Judge Sewall at Bristol, they being about to depart.

TO DR. CHARLES RUSSELL, ANTIGUA.

Exeter, April 2, 1779

DEAR SIR :

You are now very near the intended seat of war ; may your little island be protected from the ravages of the enemy.   As the events of war are doubtful, I promise myself no certain advantages from the junction of Admirals Byron and Barrington ;—shall think it no unfavorable campaign if we can retain our present possessions, expecting no conquests besides St. Lucia, the surrender of which, in sight of a superior French army and navy to British troops, does immortal honor to the victors' bravery and skill.   The newspapers that are the mints of falsehood, are daily deceiving us with relations of great distress in the French islands, great dissatisfaction and heart-burnings between Daville, the governor of Martinico, and D'Estaing ; that the latter has, with a disabled fleet and a scanty stock of provisions, been blocked up in Port Royal harbor, Martinico ; but our newspaper fabricators have so many purposes to serve quite distinct from truth and the good of society, that I rarely put into my list of facts what for amusement only I read there.

Five or six thousand new levies are designed for America; our privateers have been successful against the East and West Indian French fleets, and the French have nearly balanced accounts by taking and destroying near twenty of our frigates, besides prizes, of which Lloyd's list presents us weekly with no contemptible numbers.

The king's troops are in possession of Georgia, from which some augur the reduction of all America, but from what reason I cannot perceive ; one, two, or three colonies are but part of the confederacy, and there must be some capital defeat, I presume, to cool the ardor of minds so united as the Americans are at present.

I remain your friend, etc.,

S. CURWEN.

(The above inclosed to William Cabot, London, to be delivered into Samuel Quincy's hands, who is soon going off to Antigua as comptroller at Parkenbay.)

May 10. Walked to Poltimore, the seat of the late Sir Richard Bampfield, five miles out :—this miser for his penuriousness was called *Tenpenny Dick,* endeavoring to reduce laborers' day wages to that sum. It is an irregular old edifice, and its office, deserted by its owner, foreshows approaching ruin. The heir, whose name is Sir Charles Warwick Bampfield, is of so different a humor from the late miser, that, in the space of eighteen months he has puffed off sixty thousand pounds in cash, and an income from lands of eight thousand a year, so far as to require many years' mortgages, which the estate is now under, with an allowance of three hundred a year only. It is said his expenses during his paroxysms of folly was thirty pounds an hour ; a sad instance of folly, thoughtlessness, extravagance, and compliance with the luxurious taste and dissipation of the present age.

May 13, *Ascension Day.* The limits of each parish surveyed by committees, a great number of boys attendant, carrying long slender white rods in their hands ; at certain intervals stopping and making loud huzzas.

A British fleet of nearly five hundred sail remains wind-bound in Torbay under Admiral Arbuthnot, commanding over forty men-of-war.

May 18. Byron's fleet, left in the West Indies, worsted by D'Estaing. By Lord Gower's (president of the council) own acknowledgment in the House of Lords, the nation is in a woful plight, and justly alarmed lest Spain should take part against us, as Count Almadava, their ambassador, intimated when he should leave :—in which case it is my belief we have every thing to fear, the combined fleets greatly exceeding ours. Ireland discontented and seemingly ready to join an invader; Scotland uneasy; mutinies and discontent in the fleet,—distraction, etc., in councils.

May 19.   Col. Erving and family removing to Exmouth, by which I have lost one source of much enjoyment;—repeatedly pressed to reside in summer with them, which I have hitherto withstood from a dislike to watering places. A fleet of sixteen ships of the line and ninety transports, it is reported, were seen steering towards Ireland; should they land a general defection is to be feared.

June 5.   This day informed by Lord Clifford's priest, that I may have admittance to see his curiously wrought bed, presented by the old Duchess of Norfolk, said to be the richest in Europe, for which the queen has offered ten thousand pounds, and been refused. It is said there are four thousand Romish priests and fifteen hundred dissenting ministers of all persuasions in England and Wales. The former succeed in making converts.

June 20.   Yesterday Lord North announced in the House of Commons that the Spanish minister had left.

June 23.   It is said favorable news has arrived to government;—what a pity that views and passions of mankind were not coincident with their real interest, enjoyment and felicity; but, alas! they are at odds too frequently,—in the future world all wrongs will be rectified.

June 28.   Mr. John Sargent, my townsman, brought a letter from Col. Browne, at Cowbridge; he proposes to abide with me five or six days.

July 8.   At Lympston, ordination of Mr. Jarvis's brother; met my friends Mr. Smith and John Sargent from Sidmouth. The actors were Sir H. Trelawney, Dr. Kippis, of London, and Dr. Priestley, who preached, and exhibited a picture of his own principles, denying in express terms need of particular aids in all cases since Christ's appearance, being only necessary for the establishment of a religion;—declaring man to be in a similar state respecting moral means as earth is in regard to seed put into it; if it had been in a previous state of fitness for bringing forth, its product would be in proportion; if otherwise, small or none at all.

July 14.   Spectators on cliffs amazed with the sight of the grand fleet sailing out of Torbay.

Exmouth, July 18. Attended worship at Lady Glenorchy's chapel; principles inculcated not unlike those at Lady Huntington's chapel. The preacher a Scotchman, (with a master of arts gown,) a missionary of Lady G., who, with Mr. Holmes of Exeter, fitted this chapel for the propagation of Scotch orthodoxy. Afternoon, at Withycomb-Raleigh parish, lying at the mouth of the river Exe ; the houses are chiefly low, with mud walls and thatched roofs; though there are a considerable number of brick, covered with slate, reputable and handsome, owned chiefly by Exeter people, who come down in shoals on Saturday afternoons for the purpose of pastime and festivity among themselves on Sundays ;— this being almost the only resort on that day, when the town is full of them, not, as I am told, to the emolument or wish of the inhabitants.

July 22. Received a letter from Mr. Bretland, Exeter, inclosing a card left for me by Governor Hutchinson on his way to London from the west, whither he had been with C. Russell.

Aug. 17. Visited by Mr. Smith and Samuel Sewall from Sidmouth; reported that the combined fleet of France and Spain are off Plymouth; people along the coast and through the country alarmed.

Aug. 23. A levelling spirit has unhappily taken place among the lower classes; menacing expressions ; they more than whisper their wishes that the French may land, adding they had as lief have a Louis as a George to reign over them.

Exeter, Sept. 6. Am informed that I am suspected to be an American spy, disaffected to government; this was reported by one Calhier, a violent hater of the inhabitants of the American continent and of all its friends and well-wishers : his malice I despise, and his power to injure me with government I defy. Exeter has become the seat of scandal, pride, inhospitality, foppery; an awkward imitation of London manners, to their folly, prevails.

Sept. 23. Left in the coach for Bristol, passing through Wellington, Taunton, Bridgewater, and Cross, and arrived at White Hart inn, Bristol, where lodged.

Sept. 24. Took lodgings at Mrs. Froade's, York-street, Brunswick-square.

TO MR. GEORGE RUSSELL, BIRMINGHAM.

Bristol, Sept. 28, 1779.

Dear Sir :

The alarming condition of public affairs of late has, I presume, engaged your attention, and that of every thoughtful man ; what remains for Great Britain to hope, I know not ; the causes of fear are too many and too obvious to escape the observation of the most thoughtless and inconsiderate. It is to be wished she may save at least a part of her foreign dominions ; which, if not secured by treaty before the following campaign, will, I fear, fall a sacrifice to the ambition of France and Spain, and the resentment of America ; notwithstanding the late successes of Sir George Collier, who has wounded the latter in the naval way, though not I believe essentially. To counterweigh this, I fear Sir James Wright, the late governor, despatched from hence to reassume the government of Georgia, whose sudden departure from thence to New-York, and General Provost's abandoning his troops at Beaufort, prove beyond a doubt the pitiful condition they were in, and the great probability of their falling a prey to Hopkins' squadron by sea, and the provincial arms by land. What a wretched conclusion of so hopeful a beginning, as it seems the royal army had at least in expectation when they first set forward in their expedition against Charleston ; which seems as if destined by Providence to bring disgrace on the British arms.

I have just returned to this place with Colonel Erving's family, to whom I am indebted for most of my happiness for more than a year at Sidmouth, Exeter, and last at Exmouth. The latter disagreeable by too great a mixture of Exeter folks, " who view with eye malign and looks askance," as Milton describes Satan to have done ; all strangers seeming to them as intruders on their property, as they consider Exmouth, and appropriated only to their pleasure : thither many families resort on Sundays, their day of festivity and amusement.   Yours truly,   S. Curwen.

TO WILLIAM BROWNE, ESQ., COWBRIDGE, WALES.

Bristol, Sept. 28, 1779.

Dear Sir :

I presume you cannot in your distant retreat form an idea of

the great distress the southern coast of this island was in during
the continuance of the combined fleets in our channel, especially
on the lower coasts of Devon and Cornwall. The flight of the
inhabitants from Plymouth to Exeter and inland parts during the
panic there, spread terror and dismay wherever they came; except to a few, who wished Sir Charles Hardy would, with his
thirty-seven ships and fourteen frigates, meet the Hectors of France
and Spain, having sixty-seven ships and fifty frigates; and give
them, as they phrased it, a sound drubbing : for they were sure of
victory in case of an engagement. But thanks to the favorable stars
of Great Britain, at that moment in the ascendant, wiser heads
governed public councils; he slipped by them and got safely up
to Spithead.

This day we have heard that Paul Jones, in the French king's
service, has taken a forty-four gun frigate, and entered the harbor
of Hull, and destroyed sixteen ships.

What think you of Sir George Collier's Penobscot expedition ?
The loss of so many ships must be insupportably heavy on our province, and perhaps irreparable ; however, it is a great relief to the
English trade, they being all large ships of war, and our sailors
expert and adroit in privateering business.

Very truly yours,   S. CURWEN.

Sept. 28. Visited Colonel Erving and family; afterwards
dined and took tea with my worthy friend, Judge Sewall; his
company, Mr. and Mrs. Faneuil. From thence I went to see Mrs.
Gardiner, her husband the doctor, and their daughter, Love Eppes.
Meeting Colonel Oliver, late lieutenant-governor of Massachusetts,
he informed me of his residence.

Sept. 29. Invited personally by Colonel Oliver to a family
dinner, meeting only his daughters and his brother-in-law, John
Vassal.

Sept. 30. By the Ladies' Magazine for August, I perceive that
the Massachusett's Bay government limits the return of the refugees,
or even absentees, to July, 1780.

Oct. 9. Took tea at Mr. Erving's; his daughter handed me
an ancient manuscript copy of Goldsmith's Hermit, and Mr. Russell's lines on his wife, both excellent.

Oct. 15. Dined with Mr. Vassal in Queen's-square, in company with Dr. Gardiner and Robert Hallowell, the elder of the Simpsons, Mr. Vassal's lady, and Miss Davis. At dinner, informed by Dr. Gardiner, of many circumstances relating to my countrymen's behavior during the siege of Boston, with which I was not before acquainted; and which, if true, proves that that people, like all mankind, when civil commotions take place, are maddened into party rage. I dare say, nothing peculiarly bad, cruel, wrong, or unjust, characterizes that people at this unhappy period.

Oct. 17. Papers filled with unauthenticated reports of France having swept the coast of Africa, and taken all our forts.

TO REV. ISAAC SMITH, SIDMOUTH.

Bristol, Oct. 28, 1779.

DEAR SIR :

I should not have delayed acknowledging the receipt of your last favor until this day, had I not undertaken by my friend Eveleigh's request to furnish your reverence with an authentic and minute detail of the progress of the British army to Charleston, their retreat, and late (for it seems to be shrewdly suspected here, that at present they are in the hands and keeping of the French and Congress,) dangerous and suffering condition at Beaufort. I am afraid there are too strong reasons for apprehending that event, it being rumored here, and generally believed, that administration has received undoubted intelligence of D'Estaing's destination to Georgia and the southern coast, with six thousand troops, and a much larger naval armament than Great Britain has in those seas to oppose them, with any probability of success, under Arbuthnot.

Should General Clinton, as the papers have lately intimated, drain New York of five or six thousand troops, and proceed to Georgia, and with a slender convoy (comparatively I mean) meet D'Estaing, it is not difficult to foretell the fate of the American war; but this is mere supposition and chance, you will say; the former may arrive on the coast time enough to land himself and troops, and send off his transports. It will be well for England if he should, for the fate of their claims and pretensions on that continent depends on that single circumstance; should the two fleets meet in open sea, the odds will be so unfavorable on our side, as to approach the worst consequences. The Penobscot affair does Sir George Collier's conduct and bravery great credit, leaves an indelible stain on our countrymen and our province, at present in a defenceless condition; to balance this account the British cause has suffered a disgrace and loss of equal magnitude at Stony Point. Perhaps you have not heard, that but for a misunderstanding between the American generals, Verplanck's Point on the opposite shore had suffered the same fate. Mr. * * * * * read me a letter from Mr. * * * * *, of Falmouth, [now Portland, Maine,] wherein he describes the sufferings of people late in comfortable circumstances, and many in a condition truly pitiable. It raised a sympathy in my breast; I could not restrain the tear of pity, the only part of humanity in my power; nor was I a little hurt by the manner in which it was told; political zeal, like religious, can steel the heart against the feelings of nature. The succedaneum or substitute for bread, of which some have not tasted for months, was dried plaice, powdered. Zeal, for aught I know, is sharpened rather than blunted by sufferings, though that and some other letters suggest that the people are almost worried out by the hardships and evils of war; many no doubt are those, I presume, who gain nothing by it; of which there are but few except the persecuted. I pray God shorten the time of their tribulation; may all soon experience the blessings of peace, and unite in thanksgiving with one heart and one mouth.

Very truly your friend,
S. CURWEN.

Nov. 3. Dined with Messrs. Simpson and Waldo, in company with Peter Frye, Benjamin Pickman and Richard Routh.

Nov. 16. Visited Mr. Lechmere; drank tea with Judge Sewall.

Nov. 26. Visited Mr. Barnes and Col. Oliver with Peter Frye; dined with them and Benjamin Pickman at Mr. Lechmere's; conversing on American politics and Salem affairs.

Nov. 28. Dined with Col. Oliver in company with Peter Frye and Benjamin Pickman.

Dec. 14. Dined at Judge Sewall's, and played quadrille with Mrs. Faneuil, Mrs. Sewall and Mr. Francis Waldo.

Dec. 21.   Visited Col. Erving; drank tea by Mrs. Sewall's invitation, and passed the evening in company with Mr. J. Vassal and lady, and niece Davis, and Mr. R. Hallowell and lady.

Dec. 23.   Received two letters from Richard Ward and wife, (my niece,) the first since my absence; and one from William Pynchon.

TO DR. CHARLES RUSSELL, ANTIGUA.

Bristol, Dec. 23, 1779.

DEAR CHARLES :

The numerous papers that will go with the fleet, renders it needless for me to send such intelligence as I can at best but imperfectly furnish you with.   There is little, however, of newspaper *news,* besides what is contained in the Gazette, (which does not always give in full, but perhaps as much information as is prudent,) little, I mean, of what relates to the public.   The old proverb justly says, truth lies in a well, and difficult it is to draw it up.   I believe that of fifty reports five only will be founded in fact.   It is the distemperature of the times, not peculiar to this period, however, (as the jaundiced eye gives its hue to every object,) to present only the party complexion of the relator; for all the world here is divided into American and anti-American, ministerial and anti-ministerial. One fact I will venture to relate, to which I was an eye and ear witness : residing at Exmouth while the combined fleets of France and Spain rode masters of the English channel, in sight for many days together of Plymouth, it is hardly credible how the brave, magnanimous hearts of the English forsook them ; a panic seized the country.   The town of Plymouth was, as quick as thought, drained of its inhabitants and property, and all the neighborhood ; the people flying spread terror as they fled ; even the plague, or an earthquake, could hardly have produced more terrific apprehensions.   Strange and unaccountable organization and state of the human mind and body, that sudden fear should produce effects more distressing than a deliberate, sensible view of danger !   It is equally unaccountable that the enemy did not land ; for had they at Cawsand bay, then without any defence or works to annoy, and a safe shore, with three or four thousand men, (unprovided as we then were with munitions of war,) Plymouth, with the docks, works, and shipping, would have fallen a prey to the invaders. There was not wadding enough for one round in the garrison. That the enemy did not land and attack Sir Charles Hardy, then lying off Scilly Islands with a very inferior fleet, viz., thirty-seven of the line and twelve frigates, with his sixty-seven capital ships and thrice that number of frigates, is to be accounted for only on the same principle that Ahitophel's wise counsel was rejected; for nothing could save our fleet from defeat, and the kingdom from ravage and desolation in consequence; but by an overruling power, whose wisdom appoints and limits empires and their duration, this kingdom is preserved; the wisdom of the wise we see sometimes turned to foolishness, and weakness made to triumph over strength and courage.

Since those alarms of two months back, another has succeeded of perhaps equal magnitude: Ireland, availing herself of the distresses of her imperious, domineering sister kingdom, has raised forty thousand men with arms in their hands, independent of government, and a majority of 143 to 42 in their House of Commons; and loudly and peremptorily demands a free trade, which this country has, however bitter the dose, with seeming complacency and readiness, granted. It is said the Irish are satisfied, and have besides offered to raise twenty thousand men; but where men think themselves abridged of their natural rights, and have, or think they have power to recover them, it will be lucky for Old England if the Irish do not proceed to require other concessions. The former is not in a condition to reject her demands, or to force her obedience. I will not say Ireland can maintain her independence, but there are powers willing and ready to support her resistance, and England cannot go to war with all Europe. In truth, she receives ungrateful returns for her generosity, unequalled by any state since government obtained amongst mankind—but enough of this.

I have received a second letter from my friend, William Pynchon, Esq., and his relation in answer to my complaint of my banishment is truly pitiable; what he says will serve instead of a hundred instances to exhibit to your view a picture of the distressful situation of some of our friends, viz.: "If you knew half the inconveniences your continuance here would have occasioned, it would surely lessen your discontent; had you lost your business, all your debts, the fruits of many years' labor; been driven to sell your house and lands for payment of your debts and expenses; and thus reduced, you still would not freely nor safely walk the streets, by reason of party rage and malevolence and the uncontrolled rancor of some men."

This comforts me, and ought to console you and every other sufferer.   I remain, dear Charles,

Your affectionate friend,

S. CURWEN.

Dec. 26.   Capt. Carpenter called in my absence; he is master of the cartel ship from Boston, lately arrived; friends well at Salem a month ago, when he left.   Went to dock and saw Capt. Carpenter, who handed me letters from Mr. Nathan Goodale, containing gentle hints relating to surprising revolutions in property, which in such times of civil commotions ever take place.

Dec. 29.   Capt. Carpenter dined with me, and passed the evening; he gave me a more circumstantial relation of Salem, its inhabitants, and concerns, its present commercial and civil state, than I had received from any one before, though I fancy it is somewhat too highly colored.

Dec. 30.   Visited Mrs. Erving and presented her a Massachusetts Bay apple, which she said she should taste with a high relish, adding, " to that country I feel as great partiality and love as to my native land."

Dec. 31.   My young townsman, William Cabot, came down from London to visit me, by invitation, in order to confer with Capt. Carpenter.   Evening at Judge Sewall's, in company with Mr. and Mrs. Hartford.   Thus ends another revolution of the sun.

CHAPTER XII.

Jan. 1, 1780.   Went with William Cabot through Clifton and Hot Wells; turned into merchants' dock to view the large Manilla ship unloading; her length 172 feet, a prize, estimated variously from £50,000 to £300,000.   Took tea at Mr. Wraxall's, passed an agreeable hour, conversation turning on history, fulfilment of prophecy, and convenience of *ladies' pattens.*   Mrs. Wraxall has been represented as a stiff religionist; the contrary this evening has afforded a proof of: perhaps devotion and a conversible humor have alternately the ascendant; at best we are but a very changing, uncertain, unsteady compound.

Jan. 5.   Left for Bath at ten, and arrived there in less than three hours; patrolled the streets, viewing the Crescent, Queens-square and Parade, Paragon-row, Pump-room; saw there a numerous company, walking, standing; playing whist the only *fashionable* game.   This city in gratitude to Beau Nash, master of ceremonies, had his picture taken at full length, and put up in the pump-room; and unluckily between small busts of the great Newton and Mr. Pope, which Lord Chesterfield seeing, uttered these stanzas, viz.:

> " Immortal Newton never spoke
>   More truth than here you'll find ;
> Nor Pope himself e'er penned a joke
>   Severer on mankind :
> The picture placed the busts between,
>   Adds to the satire's strength ;
> Wisdom and wit are little seen,
>   But folly at full length."

TO NATHAN GOODALE, ESQ., SALEM, N. E.

Bristol, Jan. 10, 1780.

DEAR SIR :

I am obliged for the information contained in your letter brought me by Capt. Carpenter, relative to my friends and acquaintances.

I am glad to hear that the members of the Monday night club are permitted to assemble without interruption. I wish the continuance of it, and an increase to each member of every valuable enjoyment, and thank them for their kind remembrance of me.

You may, if you please, acquaint Mrs. Sargent, with my compliments, that being about to write Col. Browne, I shall inform him of what you mention concerning her. You write me that as I am a friend to America, I shall always find friends there; that I acknowledge is a most desirable circumstance, but there are other considerations necessary to make any spot on earth an object worthy of any one's wish to reside in. My compliments to Mrs. Goodale and Miss Higginson, and your next neighbors, Mr. and Mrs. Cabot.

Yours, etc.,

S. Curwen.

TO WILLIAM PYNCHON, ESQ , SALEM, N. E.

Bristol, Jan. 10, 1780.

Dear Sir:

I commence writing, my worthy friend, without knowing on what subject or subjects, as there is scarce any that party prejudice may not wrongly interpret and draw unfavorable inferences from ; besides the governing powers in times of war, tumult and confusion assume a liberty to dispense with the settled regulations of the state in peaceable times, and among other precautions open letters from foreign parts. I fear you are in the same predicament ; perhaps it may be right, but it is a sad and mortifying restraint on distant friends, and prevents that agreeable intercourse, which supports friendship and adds to the enjoyments of life.

With regard to my peculiar situation, connection and sentiments, I must be reserved ; in general my condition is comfortable, although in England it requires as many hundreds as I can realize scores of pounds. Some people who came from your side of the Atlantic affect to prefer this country to their own, whether it be from affectation or a real preference, I pretend not to determine ; *pour moi,* I wish for nothing more than peace and to return thither ; no approaches to the former I can as yet perceive.

A few weeks since we heard of John Adams and Francis Dana's arrival at Paris from the Congress : little good fruit, however, is to be expected unless one or other of the parties are disposed to recede from their pretensions, which Great Britain seems not at all inclined to at present. For my native country I feel a filial fondness ; her follies I lament, her misfortunes I pity ; her good I ardently wish, and to be restored to her embraces is the warmest of my desires. This country is, or might be, a paradise of delights to those who enjoy a full purse, and are by education and habit formed to relish its delights, amusements and pursuits ; but for me America is good enough.

I was going on, having forgot to tell you that this is designed to acknowledge receipt of your two last agreeable favors, for which I acknowledge myself indebted to you in no less a sum than ten thousand thanks ; great as this sum is, I am rich in them, sincere ones too ; but I am not likely to lessen my capital from the demands of my American friends, you being one of the very few, to whom in the epistolary way I owe any debts. Ten letters from Salem are all I can boast in the course of almost five years, when scarce a countryman of ours but can count as many yearly. My complaints on this head have proved fruitless and vain, and have more than half determined me to suffer myself to be forgotten abroad, with a very few exceptions ; and render measure for measure, and repay silence by contempt. But the tender feelings of the heart are not to be wholly overcome ; what was anger and resentment, is by age, the endurance of evils ; and, perhaps, a better way of thinking, changed into grief : can you then wonder, situated as I am, at my anxiety and distress ? I do assure you the silence and neglect on the part of my friends and acquaintances, has, more than banishment, oppressed my mind ; the latter is not a light burden, and when added to the former, exceeds my religion and philosophy to support. The heart of old age, if not rendered callous by vicious indulgences, is tender as in infancy ; but, to quit the plaintive strain, —You tell me I forget *de Repub.*, &c. : I confess I am like poor Faithful in Pilgrim's Progress, ever almost in the slough of despair ; would it were in your power to dart a ray of hope into my gloomy mind. I thank my countrymen for the less unfavorable opinion conceived of me than some others. For my part, I would cheerfully promote to the extent of my power the good of individuals, and that of the public; but with regard to the latter, I cannot give my approbation to their whole system of politics. The present circumstances of affairs do not allow me to indulge one wish to return, till they are a little better settled; and can easily imagine the evils you suggest, which, at my time of life, would quickly overwhelm my poor crazy bark; hardly able to keep above water even where the waves are not rough. Please remember my kindest regards to all my acquaintance; particularly the members of the Monday night club, which I learn still subsists; I wish its continuance and increase of worthy members. I fear my worthy old friend, Mr. McGilchrist, has forgotten me; apropos, it has been my good fortune for a course of three winters passed in Exeter, to find a worthy and intimate friend, who, in his moral, religious, and philosophical character, bears the nearest resemblance to my said Salem friend. To him I am indebted for much useful information and entertainment; for his and the sake of a very few, I left that quarter with reluctance. It has been frequently in my thoughts to make a collection of the best pieces that the press affords, for the benefit of my friends and myself; but that depends on contingencies. The execution of that, and some other designs I have had in my mind and view, must be deferred, I fear, to a distant day.

Our friends are scattered all over the face of the land, and if soon to be summoned to appear before the last tribunal, they might truly be said to be brought from the east, west, north, and south. Present my kindest regards to Mrs. Pynchon and all your family. Sincerely wishing you a healthy body, quiet mind, and a full purse, which I think comprehends all earthly blessings,

I am, with perfect esteem, your friend,

S. CURWEN.

Jan. 13. Capt. Carpenter, young Jonathan Gardner, both of Salem, and a Mr. Leavitt, having arrived in a cartel ship from Boston, dined with me, and passed the afternoon and evening.

Jan. 20. Took tea with Mrs. Gardner, in company with Mr. Randolph, brother of the Congress member, though of contrary political principles.

Jan. 30. Charles's martyrdom; attended service in cathedral;

young Camplin preached a serious discourse from " Blessed are the dead that die in the Lord." He modestly and laudably avoided any reference to the day. I could not fail to notice the difference between this mock solemnity here and at Exeter :—here, no mayor nor corporation attended in a procession of city officers, with their staves covered with black, nor was the pulpit in the same grim color. The service was read, with singing, as on other church holidays; assembly of an indifferent appearance, far from numerous.

TO WILLIAM BROWNE, ESQ., COWBRIDGE, WALES.

Bristol, Feb. 10, 1780.

DEAR SIR :

Perhaps it may amuse you to be made acquainted with a few particulars relating to our own country and town, that may not have come to your knowledge. About six weeks ago a prize ship from Boston arrived here with thirty-six passengers, who were suffered to depart, under verbal promise to return back again to captivity if this government should not acknowledge the ship to be a cartel, and send back an equal number of Americans to Boston or to France. In the event, no notice is taken of them, as might be expected ; the ship is claimed, and as yet *sub judice*, though it is thought it will be determined in favor of the claimants. The American owner is a Mr. Mitchell, Irish by birth, American in principle and alliance, being married to a daughter of George Bethune. The master, a Mr. Carpenter, who you know married the youngest of the Gerrishes, and tried to be a loyalist (applying, unsuccessfully, however, for a pension) about two years since, whilst he resided with his wife at Brompton-row ; on his rejection he took wit in his anger and returned to Salem. From him and young Gardner, only son of Jonathan Gardner, Jr., I have obtained the annexed list of prices, which, instead of a score of arguments, may prove the low condition of Congressional credit, and show the exorbitant rate of the useful articles of life, and perhaps their scarcity. It is a melancholy truth, that whilst some are wallowing in undeserved wealth that plunder and rapine have thrown into their hands, the wisest, most peaceable, and most deserving, such as you and I know, are now suffering want, accompanied by many indignities that a licentious, lawless people can pour forth upon them.

Those who five years ago were the "*meaner people*," are now, by a strange revolution, become almost the only men of power, riches and influence; those who, on the contrary, were leaders and in the highest line of life, are glad at this time to be unknown and unnoticed to escape insult and plunder, the wretched condition of all who are not violent, and adopters of republican principles. The Cabots of Beverly, who, you know, had but five years ago a very moderate share of property, are now said to be by far the most wealthy in New England; Hasket Derby claims the second place in the list, and * * * * * * puts in for a place amongst the first three; Mr. Goodale, by agency concerns in privateers and buying shares, counts almost as many pounds as most of his neighbors. The following are persons of the most eminence for business in Salem, as far as my memory serves, viz.: Hasket Derby, William Pickman, George Crowninshield, William Vans, Capt. Harraden, a brave and notable privateer captain, Joseph Henfield, Capt. Silsbee, Samuel Gardner, Joseph and Joshua Grafton's sons, Francis Clarke, Capt. George Dodge's youngest sons, Jos. Orne. E. H. Derby's province tax is £11,000, and his neighbors complain he is not half taxed. The immensely large nominal sums which some are said to be worth, shrink into diminutive bulk when measured by the European standard of gold and silver. In New England a dollar bill is worth only 2 ⅔ of an English halfpenny. Pins at 1s. a piece, needles at 2s., beef 2s. 6d., veal 2s., mutton and lamb 1s. 6d., butter 6s. per lb., rum eight dollars per gallon, molasses two dollars, brown sugar 10s. per lb., loaf sugar 15s., Bohea tea seven dollars per lb., coffee five dollars, Irish pork sixty dollars per barrel, lemons 3s. apiece, wood twenty dollars a cord, ordinary French cloth twenty-two dollars a yard, hose nine dollars a pair. A suit of clothes which cost five guineas here, would cost five hundred dollars in Boston.   Yours, &c.

S. CURWEN.

Feb. 13. To the Moravian chapel; Mr. Washington, the settled minister, preached from, " *And being fashioned as a man*," etc. The great point insisted on, as usual, was, that the supreme Deity, the God and Father of all, or to use their own language, "*the eternal Jehovah, suffered death actually, truly and properly, in the person of Christ, or was the real suffering, dying being, who expired on the cross.*" In the course of these extemporaneous or memoriter effusions, such terms and expressions were used that made my blood more than once almost forsake its channels; in truth, I was astonished and hurt to an extreme degree, and it has caused me to resolve on forsaking this and all assemblies of like over-zealous orthodox tenets.

Feb. 16. To the "Wells" over St. Vincent's through Clifton, by Sir William Draper's; from thence across Brandon hill to Judge Sewall's, where drank tea in company with Mr. and Mrs. Barnes, Miss Arbuthnot, their niece, and Miss Russell.

Feb. 29. Took a walk and went on 'change with Mr. Erving; then a passage in the Bath coach at four o'clock, and at half past six alighted at the "*Three Tuns inn;*" from thence on foot to the coffee-house in Orange-grove, where I remained for two hours reading papers, drinking coffee, etc., and received information from John Boylston, my countryman, that my friend Isaac Smith, for whose sake I took this ramble, was to leave at nine to-morrow for Bristol; so I bespoke a seat in the same stage. Passed two hours in the streets and Abbey-square among the crowd—ears entertained by musketry discharged from the abbey leads and ringing of bells, to celebrate Sir G. Rodney's victory over Don Langara;—retired to the inn, supped and lodged. Gov. Hutchinson's son William died on the 20th instant.

Bath, March 1. After breakfast I entered the carriage and departed with my friend Smith, and at twelve o'clock alighted at the White Hart, Bristol. Mr. Smith dined with me; he having engaged himself to Mr. Wright and lady, who were this afternoon to pay a visit at Mr. Erving's, my friend and I joined company to tea; at eight o'clock with the family took a turn in Queen's-square, to view the illuminations, which were brilliant, in honor of Sir G. Rodney's victory of 16th January.

March 4. By invitation dined at Judge Sewall's with Mr. Smith, R. and N. Lechmere, Col. Oliver, Mr. Simpson, Mr. Francis Waldo and Mr. Vassal.

March 5. Engaged at tea to partake of Mrs. Bearpacker's

"mothering cake." It is a custom here on mid-lent Sunday for a cake to be brought to mothers, in conformity to which custom some females make a large one and present it to their acquaintance. This custom continues in Gloucestershire, and is said to be derived from Joseph's making himself known to his brethren.

March 6. Dined at Mr. F. Waldo's with Mr. Simpson, his nephew, and young Borland.

TO MR. LAKIN, BIRMINGHAM.

Bristol, March 6, 1780.

DEAR SIR:

You are pleased to compliment me on my knowledge of the state of affairs in America, but really, should I attempt a narrative of its present political and commercial condition, I fear it would be too imperfect to afford you much useful information. So great a revolution in both respects has taken place since my departure, so different is the channel of business, so little the concerns that I have amongst the commercial people here, and so slender my advices about them, being chiefly newspaper intelligence, which you know is not always the word of Apollo, that it would be rashness to commit to paper my undigested thoughts on those subjects. I strongly suspect the independency of America, or a system of political and civil government, will sooner or later be established there, to the utter overthrow of the navigation act of Charles II., and the commerce of Great Britain with the American colonies and her other foreign dominions, if she will be powerful enough to retain any, which I fear; in this case it may be easily discerned that by opening new channels, trade will assume a new face, and be conducted by very different people, and on quite different principles.

You propose undertaking a journey here, and I assure you of a cordial welcome to my lodgings, to pass your time while here; and as conversation admits of less restraint than writing, I shall with the greatest cheerfulness communicate as much as lies within the compass of my knowledge relating to the subject of your inquiry. I wish the benefit you might derive from my information would bear any proportion to the pleasure I shall receive in communicating; for you can scarce be more obliging than to afford me an occasion of paying in person my respects to him for whose former civilities I am indebted more than is in my power at present to discharge. To your kind inquiry I am happy to answer, my friends, far removed from the seat of war, escape descents on their coasts and inroads on their frontiers, which their brethren in the southern colonies unhappily do not. A more particular relation I must defer to a personal interview.

Yours truly,
S. Curwen.

March 11. Dined at Mr. Erving's with two daughters of a Mr. Ewen, who had been residents on Rhode Island, but driven off by civil storm; and being told that Capt. and Mrs. Fenton with myself, intended to dine with them at Brislington, expressed their pleasure to see us next Monday.

March 14. Took tea at Judge Sewall's; company Mr. Simpson, Mr. F. Waldo, Mr. Faneuil and lady, and Miss Russell.

April 14. Visited by Nathaniel Coffin and R. Hallowell; meeting widow Borland's eldest son John, recognized each other, made mutual compliments and invitations.

TO WILLIAM PYNCHON, ESQ., SALEM, N. E.

Bristol, April 19, 1780.

DEAR SIR :

The bearer, being acquainted with the state of our political affairs, will communicate more than would be prudent for me to commit to paper, should I be disposed to dabble in that dangerous business, politics. A tedious, uniformly insipid inactivity soon renders every place displeasing; but my removal from hence depends on contingencies not to be foreseen. If I leave, I shall engage in a week's ramble, and like the father of the faithful, go, not knowing whither; the world is all before me where to choose my place of rest, hitherto unfound, and with no land of promise before me.

*   *   *   *   *   *   *

Perhaps it may be amusing to you to be informed of the number of Americans in Bristol, who are comprised in· the following list :—

Col. Oliver and six daughters; Mr. R. Lechmere, his brother Nicholas, wife and two daughters; Mr. John Vassal, wife and niece, Miss Davis; Mr. Barnes, wife and niece; Miss Arbuthnot; Mr. Nathaniel Coffin, wife and family; Mr. Robert Hallowell, wife and children; Judge Sewall, wife, sister, and two sons; Samuel Sewall with his kinsman, Mr. Faneuil, and wife; Mr. Francis Waldo and Mr. Simpson, together with Mrs. Borland, a son and three daughters. I send this by young Gardner, who with Mr. Leavitt and Capt. Carpenter leaves us to-morrow, and will shift for their passage to America as they can.

Very truly,
S. Curwen.

TO MR. RICHARD WARD, SALEM, N. E.

Bristol, April 19, 1780.

Dear Sir:

Your two favors of the 5th and 12th of November are at hand. You say, that " to the many we have written you, we have received no answer ;" it is not a little unaccountable, that of many not one should have arrived to me before these two; for that in truth is the case. That neither you nor my niece should in the course of five years take the least notice of her only uncle, was in my judgment a singular instance of forgetfulness; that you was a partisan I well knew, though not in the rankest degree I hope; and it is natural that she should be biassed to the side you took, and I thus accounted for the dead silence through the long interval between my departure and the receipt of yours; but your declaration has explained the difficulty, and I find, greatly to my satisfaction, that other causes than those I suggested to myself have prevented my receiving those instances of notice and regard which your relation to me demanded. That I find no acknowledgment in yours of the receipt of even one of the many sent to my niece and you, is to be accounted for in the same way.

The Irish, availing themselves of the embarrassment of Great Britain, have got an enlargement of privileges, and talk of making further demands. That the war is at a distance from your own doors, the melancholy reports from the southward afford you the strongest reasons for daily thanks; may it not be your misfortune in the Massachusetts Bay to experience the sufferings, ravages, carnage and devastation of her sister southern colonies.

Absence from all I hold dear on earth is an evil, and the peculiar condition I am in, increases its severity; but I endeavor to muster my whole stock of religion and philosophy, and with the united aid of both, and a few amusements, life is tolerable. I cannot prevail with myself to quit a peaceful region, and attempt a passage across the Atlantic during this state of turmoil; should I choose a place to reside in on the western side of the globe, Halifax would not be the spot; nothing but the prospect of great gains, which reconciles all climates and people, would make that place in any degree tolerable; besides, the expense of living is as extravagant as in England, without any of its advantages to counterbalance their many inconveniences and evils. I thank you for the expressions of kindness and good-will from you both respecting my peace of mind. Tell your son, my namesake, I shall answer his letter soon.   With unfeigned regard, your uncle,

S. CURWEN.

April 24. This day, five years are complete since I abandoned my house, estate, effects and friends. God only knows whether I shall ever be restored to them, or they to me. Party rage, like jealousy and superstition, is cruel as the grave;—that moderation is a crime in times of civil confusions, many good, virtuous and peaceable persons, now suffering banishment from America, are the wretched proofs and instances.—May it please God to inspire with wisdom and true policy the principal conductors in this truly lamentable war on both sides the Atlantic, and give peace in our time. Did I know how to emancipate myself from this constrained, useless, uniform blank of life, and enter on an active course, I would joyfully seize the occasion.

Evening at theatre to see " Belle's Stratagem;" entertainment " Waterman." I would not indulge a cynical, surly disposition, but cannot help acknowledging that I find great disappointment at the theatrical performances. Actors fall below my idea of just imitation; to my seeming they overact, underact, or contradict nature;—a hero is a bully, a gentleman is a coxcomb, a coxcomb a fool, a lady affected, pert or insipid; but gamesters, chambermaids, footmen, indeed, the whole series of under-characters, not illy played.

April 28. A lethargy respecting the public interest has seized the people of this country; which the selfish principles, supremely governing, or rather tyrannizing over all ranks and orders, ages, sexes and conditions, has brought on them; they are devoted victims, and so I leave them to their impending fate. I really think that neither administration nor opposition is composed of uncommon characters; for if other men in each line were to succeed these that now figure on the political stage, the same, or nearly the same parts would be played; for in the corrupt state of this people, ministerial conduct, such as it is, is necessary; I do not say expedient, for the wheels of government cannot move an inch without money to grease them. Did the circumstances of things admit, I verily believe my favorite Lord North, who I take to be one of the best characters in the whole British empire, would shine one of the brightest luminaries that ever enlightened the political hemisphere.

Walked abroad, and met one of my countrymen; who informed me that, by a packet twenty-five days from New-York, advices had been received that General Clinton, after two months from thence, had arrived at Georgia; and had proceeded to within a mile and a half of Charleston, S. C., before which he was to have opened his batteries of forty cannon on the 11th of March; that the town had from four to six thousand troops within, and a great plenty of military and other stores; that it was divided into four parts by deep trenches or canals filled with water, intersecting each other at right angles; that the Americans were resolved to dispute the ground inch by inch; but party representation adds, however, that they had no great relish for a patriotic death.

Afternoon and evening at Judge Sewall's;—company, Mrs. Long of Ireland, Mr. and Mrs. Faneuil, Mr. Oxnard, with young Inman and his wife, a son of Ralph's, in the military line, and Miss Inman.

May 14. Evening at Lady Huntingdon's chapel; Mr. Wills preached; who took an affectionate leave, being about to depart on a converting progress through South Wales. He warmly contended against the damnable doctrine of Arianism; the professors of which, at one blow, he condemned to eternal perdition. Pity it is that orthodoxy, meaning thereby not right, just thinking, but the belief of established notions, under the sanction of civil authority, should always, in all cases, and at all times, be accompanied with uncharitableness; the understood characteristic of the false church.

May 17.   Public expectations are at the highest pitch respecting the success of General Clinton, and the great advantages government will derive from it; if it shall be the occasion, supposing he shall become possessed of Charleston, of producing a reconciliation on generous and safe terms, my joy will accompany the general acclamation.

May 19.   Nathaniel Coffin is going to Bath for his health. Meeting R. Hallowell in the street, he read some paragraphs in a letter from his father Gardiner at Poole, informing of the distresses of our country, discontent of people at the continuance of the troubles, and intimating wishes to return to former connections with this country, wherein I cordially join;—would that that happy event might soon take place, with honor and safety to all parties!

May 29.   This being Restoration-day, some houses are distinguished by oak branches in front, which is a mark of attachment to monarchy; and by many of regard to the excluded family, at least in some places, as Manchester, Exeter, &c.

June 5.   This being the appointed day for setting out on a tour of pleasure to the north by Judge Sewall, Samuel Sewall and myself, I was early notified by a thundering at the door; being awake, I soon descended, and found my friend's eldest son with a message, desiring my immediate presence at breakfast before departure.   Complying with the summons, on going over, I found the family up, and all things in readiness, but the owner of the carriage delayed us for an hour; at length it arrived, and taking leave of our friends, we set forward in an unpromising air; the morning being cloudy, with the appearance of rain, which through the day came down in the form of a drizzle.   At nine, we alighted at the Bell inn, Newport, distant eighteen miles; hence to Gloucester; roads for the greater part dirty and bad; grounds fertile; farm-houses, barns, and avenues slovenly; fences in ill repair and low.   At twelve alighted at King's Head inn, at the last mentioned place; here took a collation; taking a relay, departed for Newton.   Here it came into my head to inquire of our host, who seemed to be lazy man, whether his was the house referred to in Tom Jones, where Sophia Western's muff was picked up by her paramour; to which he replied in the affirmative, and offered to show the bed where it lay; had his invitation been to see the charming young lady herself, I doubt whether my answer would have been what I gave him.   Here we stopped no longer than to have fresh horses put to.   Hence to Worcester is twelve miles, and over excellent roads; pleasant hedges and well cultivated lands in view.

Worcester, June 6.   Strolled for two hours, viewing the cathedral and new bridge, which latter is now finishing, and a beautiful structure.   The new street leading to the centre of the city on one end, and to the bridge on the other, will, when completed, be a fine avenue, and among its greatest ornaments.   At ten departed hence to Horbrook, eleven miles; here took a new relay, and choosing the road through Kidderminster, alighted at Bridgenorth, distance from former stage sixteen miles.   This town lies in Salop, and for situation is most singular, part being on a lofty plain, faced with a rock in some spots nearly perpendicular, the ascent to which is by slopes and steps in a kind of serpentine line; on the front is a terrace, affording a view of the lower town.   The town is situated on both sides of the river Severn, communicating by a bridge; a well cultivated country is in prospect from the upper part, bounded by hills in a circular line, rising gradually one beyond another; the lands interspersed with rows, clumps and forests of trees, and scattered habitations of farm houses and gentlemen's seats.   In the upper town are the remains of an ancient castle, destroyed when Cromwell took the town, that before was in the king's interest; one side or line of the wall to the height of forty feet projects fifteen or eighteen feet, occasioned either by the settling of the ground, or by force of many cannon balls striking on it at once.   The effects on the front yet appear in the very many excavations in the stone of the size of eighteen and twenty-four pound balls; it is separated by a chasm or breach of twelve to fifteen feet wide, and as many long from the standing part; thickness six feet.   Cement, not of hard consistency, has retained its present state much beyond the memory of man.   Be it as it may, the inhabitants are well satisfied it will continue till a great convulsion of nature shall overturn the great fabric of the globe itself.   The town on the hill has two churches exempt from the bishop, and called "*peculiars*," under jurisdiction of the Whitmores, who have right of visitation ; also right of advowson, and can exercise all right of ecclesiastical jurisdiction except sacerdotal.

After an *en passant* survey, we took fresh horses and conveyance, and set off for Brosely, distant from hence eight miles; to this place arrived in an hour, took a look at the iron bridge. Next stage Much-Wenlock, distance hence twelve miles ; a pitiful inn and town, where we lodged ; Shrewsbury, our last stage, lying at twelve miles distance. Here we visited the residence of Samuel Porter, late of my native place, Salem ; but the *prima facie* view of my townsman's lodgings convinced us that it was not a fit place for us to remain at. After hearty congratulations, bid him adieu for the present, and returned back to the Talbot inn, leaving our other companions, Samuel Sewall and Samuel Porter, to measure the distance through the fields on foot, where they soon arrived after us. Here we proposed to fix our tent for two or three days; having bespoke dinner, we had a social *tête-a-tête*, and after a hearty meal, and a few glasses of port, took myself off to find out my other townsman, Capt. Poynton, who was also become a resident here, and whom I found at a namesake's, living on Pride hill, so called, within the town. After tea I took him to our companions, and all joining issued forth to see the town and ascertain the expense of living, which we found higher than at Bristol. Shrewsbury is populous, having several churches ; there is a most agreeable walk of a circular form on the banks of the Severn, half a mile in extent, and surrounded by lofty trees. There are still ruins of an old castle, now become private property and the seat of the owner, standing on a lofty eminence and commanding the town. There is also a large building intended for a foundling hospital, but not succeeding, is now fitted up for Spanish prisoners, when they catch them.

Shrewsbury, June 9. We reassumed our post-chaise seats and departed from " proud Salop," as it is called, for having refused the offer of the crown to make it a city, saying " it is better to be a large town than a small city"—leaving our two townsmen to their respective enjoyments. However, before leaving this place, I must observe, Mr. Samuel Sewall and myself, with Capt. Poynton, dined

at Samuel Porter's lodgings, which we found well provided; and
the next night, being the night preceding the one to our departure,
passed at the " Gullet" inn, the resort of all better sort to hear and
tell news. During my stay within, I heard read several letters
from lords, sirs, etc., from London, with relations of the mob that
was raging there. From hence to Ellesmere, sixteen miles, we ran
in two and a half hours, being accommodated with fresh horses;
thence to Wrexham, eleven miles; respectable in buildings, some
fine streets, a market and well built church, erected about the time
of the reformation; its tower superbly decorated in Gothic style.
Next stage was Chester, at eleven miles distance; stopped at the
Golden Talbot in Eastgate-street, house of best repute, large, with
a handsome coffee-room, ball and drawing rooms, it being the assembly house. This small city is singularly circumstanced, having
a delightful terrace walk on top of walls encompassing it round, in
length near two miles, defended with a breastwork or parapet
about three feet high; has no guns nor embrasures, nor platforms
for unevenness of surface within the walls and adjoining grass; the
walk in some places is but a'few feet above the level within, and
others as high as tops of chimneys. On the quarter bounded by
the river Dee it is sixty or eighty feet above the surface of the water;
on one or two streets is a covered way or walk raised one story
above the street called the rows; the ascent is by many flights of
steps from the streets, rendering it very convenient to foot passengers, especially in foul weather; these are filled with shops and
stores above and below; the passage ways are paved with flags,
the breadth twelve to fifteen feet. This city has the appearance
of antiquity, though there are many very genteel, tasty, and noble
houses; I should judge the number between two and three thousand, inhabitants about seventeen thousand. Just within the walls
is a most beautiful race-ground. I forgot to mention the cathedral,
of no great extent and rather indifferent appearance; it was however in decent repair, but contained nothing remarkable.

Having taken a view of the whole place, we took leave of Chester, designing for Manchester by way of Duke of Bridgewater's
canal from Warrington; on that route our first stage was Fords-
ham, an indifferent small village, distance ten miles. The keeper
of the inn an Irishman, not wanting in the characteristic mark of

that country, a bold unblushing face ; after a plausible commendation of his carriages and horses, he gave us a sorry post-chaise and a pair of miserable cattle; he yet had the impudence to apply to us to procure the land from Warrington to this paltry village to be made a turnpike, saying it would be pounds in his pocket, which I really doubt. He mistook us for *parliament-men*. From hence to Warrington ten miles ; the inn, the " *Red Lion*," tolerable. Streets narrow, dirty, and ill paved ; like many other towns, with a gutter running through the middle, rendering it inconvenient passing streets. This town abounds in dissenters, and has an academy for young preachers of that persuasion. Governor Hutchinson was to have been buried at Brompton yesterday.

Warrington, June 11. Set off on foot for London bridge, so called from its lying in the great London road across the canal, at two miles' distance herefrom. This spot is a common rendezvous whither flock all passengers whom curiosity prompts, or business urges, to sail up to Manchester, at twenty miles' distance ; or down to the locks at Runcorn, on the other hand, ten miles distant ; or across the Mersey to Liverpool, this being the common route. Two boats daily carry passengers up and down. Diverted from our intended route, Manchester, we turned our course to a contrary direction, sailing down to Runcorn to view the celebrated locks ; passed in our passage under sixteen bridges laid across the canal, consisting of one brick arch of eighteen to twenty-two feet span, and twelve feet high. Of these we were told there are sixty-four ; probable enough, including the branches and marine cut, for Judge Oliver counted on the grand canal forty-eight. The boats for passengers are fifty feet long and fifteen wide, and will hold a hundred persons. Arrived at Runcorn in two hours, and supped at " White Hart" inn. Samuel Sewall and myself having amused ourselves for two hours in seeing a barge enter from the river Mersey into the first lock and through to the canal, we returned back and met our companion the judge, whose curiosity did not stimulate him to stay so long in the cold as ours did ; and found the inn crowded with great numbers of jolly lads and lasses, met to congratulate our landlady's daughter, lately married and just returned home, after a week's absence. The concluding scene of Sunday, being considered in England as a relief from labor, is generally spent in ale-houses by the middling and lower sorts, in merry-making.

Runcorn, June 12.   Walked abroad, shaping my course to church-yard, where I saw the curate and his clerk; name of former was Sewell.   I returned by the way I went, acquainting my companions, who had arrived before me, of the adventures.   They regretted my neglect in making no inquiry, nor informing the curate of their name; but I was loth to incur the imputation of impertinence which he justly might have made, in instituting inquiries about such matters as people of this country are shy about communicating to strangers.   At eleven o'clock reshipped ourselves on board same barge, and returned back to whence we came, where, finding a chaise ready for Liverpool, we again diverged from our right-line course, Manchester, and struck off for that town, twenty miles distant; returning back to Warrington, proceeded to Prescott, at ten miles' distance, where took a relay. This town is noted for coal-pits and watch movements; from the former Liverpool is principally supplied by wagons.

Entered the city of Liverpool, so celebrated for its commercial character; houses by a great majority in middling and lower style, few rising above that mark ; streets long, narrow, crooked, and dirty in an eminent degree.   During our short abode here, we scarcely saw a well-dressed person, nor half a dozen gentlemen's carriages; few of the shops appear so well as in other great towns; dress and looks more like the inhabitants of Wapping, Shadwell, and Rotherhithe, than in the neighborhood of the Exchange, or any part of London above the Tower.   The whole complexion nautical, and so infinitely below all our expectations, that nought but the thoughts of the few hours we had to pass here rendered it tolerable.   The docks however are stupendously grand; the inner one, called Town Dock, lying in the centre of it, and filled with vessels exhibiting a forest of masts; besides this, are three very large ones lying in front of the city, communicating with each other by flood-gates, intermixed with dry ones for repairing.   The lower or new one has a fine wide quay on its outer side, an agreeable walk being lined with trees on either hand ; below this, on the river, is now building, nearly finished, a circular battery with embrasures for thirty cannon.   Parade and barracks are in hand,

and when completed will afford a charming walk and prospect if allowed to the inhabitants.

Liverpool, June 12.   Taking a circuitous ramble through this, to us, disgustful place, returned to inn, paid our bill, and entered the carriage we came in, which the driver and owner would fain, but for Judge and Samuel Sewall's resolution, have jockeyed us out of, designing craftily to shift us off to the common stage; but his plan being disappointed, we were replaced in our own carriage, with no company but ourselves.   Bidding adieu to Liverpool, we set forward to Prescott, where we took a relay and proceeded to Warrington; here we were detained two hours, waiting the arrival of boats.   At two o'clock we re-entered our apartment, filled with fresh passengers, among them Mrs. Dawson, wife of the governor of the Isle of Man, returning from an excursion; she was a native of Nova Scotia, and daughter of a Colonel Hamilton, and had resided in Boston.   Mr. Corbet, an attorney of Brosely, also added no inconsiderable pleasure by his social turn while sailing on an unruffled surface through a finely improved country, over hills and dales, rivers and bridges; in five hours we arrived safely at Manchester.   Examined the ingenious machinery and operations of calico-printing.   Took carriage for Castleton at the peak of Derby, passing through Stockport and Disley.   The country, as we approached the peak, hilly.   By persuasion the judge reluctantly walked out to the cave at Castleton, being desirous to defer it till following morning, accompanied by Samuel Sewall.   After breakfast, taking leave of the vale, we ascended the hill overlooking the town; the road extends to the further end in a circular line, affording a pleasing view of the lofty surrounding hills and a charming vale beneath, diversified with trees, live hedges, scattered farmhouses, villages, and towers; the descent on the side of the vale is quick, and in case of accident hazardous.   In ascending Mr. Sewall and myself chose the safest and most expeditious way on foot, not indeed the most comfortable, being surrounded by a gang of children who constantly accompany carriages, that necessarily move at a slow pace, soliciting charity with piteous looks and accents, which from earliest childhood they have been taught to frame.   At length we arrived at Bakewell, fourteen miles, and whilst changing horses I visited the church-yard on an eminence, whence is a pleasing view of the vale, rendered more so by its contrast with the naked, barren hills wherewith it is encompassed on all sides. This plain, with scarce a rising to intercept the sight for miles, abounds in pastures, grass and corn lands inclosed by live hedges, and trees in rows and clumps; of the latter there are many inclosures of considerable extent, and of great height and bulk. Most of the best improvements are on the Duke of Rutland's estate, who has a large and noble old mansion-house, called Haddon Hall, within sight of the traveller.

The road to Matlock is an excellent turnpike, through this delightful vale, distance twelve miles; the eye is refreshed a good part of the way with a sight of the river Dee, a gentle stream which continued to and beyond the last mentioned place, where we arrived at twelve o'clock. Dismissing the coach, we took up our abode in this indescribably pleasing, romantic spot for a few hours—sadly regretting after leaving it that we had not dedicated longer time to it. This cluster of half a dozen houses, including tradesmen's and the large inn for servants and short visitants, as our company, are filled with apartments for the'reception and accommodation of those who resort hither for sake of bathing, to which it is confined. Its remote situation, (its nearest neighbor on one hand Bakewell at ten miles, and on the other Derby at sixteen,) separates it, in a manner, from all society. It is situated on the banks of the Dee, which by the approach of the craggy hills contract to little more than the bed of the river, which flows even to the foot of them. This spot lies under a circular range of hills conforming to the course of the river; the side of this range is in spots clothed with bushes, shrubs, and trees of various dimensions, interspersed with bare spots and shelving rocks, overhanging and threatening instant fall. In some the ascent is quick, in other parts easy, and in the midst of this unpromising barren wild are levels that nature or industry have made, now improved as habitations for the poor but perhaps contented few, whose lot has cast them into this dreary spot; each hut being accommodated with a small plat for garden and yard. To the spectator on the other side, a view of these singularly situated habitations is picturesque and pleasing. Just below the houses for company's residence, on a plain lying but little above the level of the river, are covered baths, supplied by streams from hills, issuing under the foundation of houses, but they have no distinguishing character.

Crossing the ferry, of a hundred feet, we found a serpentine walk, cut and levelled for a quarter of a mile, then limited by a lead mine, now working. This walk is a delicious retreat in a sultry day, the trees on either hand forming an embowering shade; it is accommodated with field seats, from whence are vistas, two terminating in natural cascades, rendered, however, more perfect by art. Returning back from hence to end of walk, we began our ascent over slopes and steps to the summit of this very craggy hill, which is extremely tedious, and puts the lungs as well as muscles to no small exercise. About three fourths the way up stands an alcove to rest the weary traveller, where we were glad to avail ourselves of a seat for awhile. Having at length gained the summit, we thought ourselves fully repaid for fatigue by the charming prospect, both in respect to its extensiveness and variety. Though we were so exalted, the Fox, as it is called, being the extreme end of the range of mountains on other side, almost insulated, lifted its aspiring head nearly as much above us as we were above the surface of the river that we beheld flowing just under our feet. The manner in which visitors live together is social and harmonious; the meals taken in a common room, none having a precedence; their mixture promiscuous; attendance at a certain hour notified by a bell. Hither also they repair to form parties, as chance or inclination points, some to cross the water to serpentine walk, to climb the craggy cliff; others to ride on horseback, or in carriages; others again for cards.—Generally after supper cards or dancing fill up the space to time of repose. Their lonely situation contributes not a little to inspire all with a desire to promote mutual enjoyment, which is supposed to be met with here in this retired solitary retreat in a more extensive degree than in any other place of public resort through England. Here are manufactured neatly polished pieces, in the fancy way, of Derbyshire spar, stone, etc. Judge Sewall and myself bought each a sugar-basin and cream-bucket, edged with gilt pinchbeck, and ladles with metal handles of the same, having bought an egg-cup and pair of salts before at the Peak.

After dinner, departed over a fine turnpike, reaching to the town of Derby, distant sixteen miles, which we measured in two hours, and alighted at the "King's Head" inn. Here we met a singular phenomenon in the person of John Tompson, a waiter at this inn for forty-three years; the fifteen years immediately preceding the present service porter to Sir Robert Sutton, and the eleven years before that to the Earl of Ferrars. He is now eighty-seven, and although somewhat decrepit and stooping, carries no mark of age in his face, that still retains a rubicund complexion without a single wrinkle. His memory, and indeed all his faculties appear in full vigor. The Ferrars family show a respect for their former servant by sending a carriage for him now and then, especially at Christmas and holiday times, when he is made welcome; and "so late as last Christmas," said he, "I danced from eleven to four o'clock there, and good music inspires me with vigor to acquit myself to the satisfaction of my partners, and makes me, for the while, return to youth."

Derby, June 16. After breakfast we all repaired with a conductor to the silk mills, for which this town is famed, these being the originals of this kind of manufactures in England, having been introduced from Italy in a surreptitious manner by Sir Thomas Lambe. At twelve we departed for Burton on Trent, thence to "George" inn, Lichfield, and from thence to Birmingham, where stopped at the "Hen and Chickens," High-street. Soon after our arrival, S. Sewall and myself sallied forth, leaving the judge, reluctant to exercise, to entertain himself. It seems that sitting by the window, he espied a countryman of ours, resident here, passing by; on opening the casement, the other seeing him, came over and remained with him till our return. He called again, accompanied by Mr. Elisha Hutchinson, son of our late governor, who together passed an hour and then departed; the former inviting us to dine next day, promising to accompany us to the manufactories.

June 17. Soon after breakfast, Judge Oliver, being the other countryman before mentioned, agreeably to last evening's promise, came and in a post-chaise accompanied us to Bolton and Fothergill's manufactory, called Soho, about two miles out of town, for gun-barrel boring by a fire engine. From thence to a ramble *modo pedestri,* and afterwards to Judge Oliver's to dinner, and at tea Mr. Hutchinson joined us; in the evening went over to Mr. Lakin's.

June 18.   Soon after breakfast, Judge Sewall's impatience to be gone hurried us into a post-chaise, taking the road to Wolverhampton, distant from hence fourteen miles, passing through Wednesbury, where the coal-pits are that supply Birmingham with coals; we arrived at Wolverhampton in three hours.   The town contains one church, the parish is fifteen miles in length, reaching near Lichfield.   It is a deanery, and has a vicar or curate, salary from only £20 to £50, notwithstanding the pomposity of the churches;—this is annexed to Windsor.   From hence to Shiffnal, our next stage, is twelve miles; thence to Bronckton, a village, three miles from last inn, and to Brosely three miles, where we supped and lodged.

June 19.   Mr. Corbit, surgeon, coming to our inn in order to fulfil a promise of last night, accompanied us in a post-chaise, procured and ready against his arrival; entering the vehicle, our first visit was to the porcelain manufactory, noted for its fine Nankin blue color, no other colors attempted here ;—lately was sent off, as we were told by one of the burners, a complete set or table service for the royal table, a sample whereof we saw ; from hence directed our course to the iron bridge.   For a more perfect view of this curious and singular piece of pontal architecture, we returned back as many miles as the day's journey consisted of; and the world affords not its like : a bridge perfect in all its parts, composed entirely of cast iron.   It is laid over the Severn, from a town in Shropshire, called Brosely, to Colebrook-dale side, and adjoining a truly romantic spot noted for coal mines and iron stone, wherewith it abounds.   Dined at the inn, company same as last evening ; afterwards we all together walked to Surgeon Corbit's, our guide and attendant ; S. Sewall and myself drank coffee with his spouse. Leaving this house, Judge Sewall and myself returned to the inn, where I passed a heavy, sleepy evening ; S. Sewall was engaged in loyally celebrating General Clinton's success at Charleston, by discharging a two-pounder half loaded several times in a private garden !   The town of Brosely, where we now are, is long and straggling ; the houses seem to owe their present situation to mere chance ; in general it has a dark, sooty, dirty look, few only of the houses in decent style.

June 20.   Having accomplished the object of our return, and being accommodated with a post-chaise, took our departure, and in an hour were set down at Bridgenorth, having determined to take passage on the Severn to Worcester at thirty miles from this; this variety in mode of travelling an agreeable one, especially as the fare is but one shilling and sixpence, which consideration has weight with those whose bank begins to ebb fast, having already measured, of turnpike chiefly, almost five hundred miles. Adjusted all with the master for passage next day, the interval between the present hour and time of rest was chequered by eating, drinking, walking, and playing at backgammon.

June 21. Entered our conveyance, which we found common and for commodities instead of a passage boat; filled with wool and bulky articles some feet above the gunwale, leaving us and one fellow passenger but scanty room in stern sheets. First delay was at Brindley; here we refreshed with a collation; next at Stourport at junction of the great Staffordshire canal with Severn; at six o'clock landed at Worcester, just below old bridge. Jumped on shore, leaving companions and baggage, who, before they left the banks of the river, engaged to-morrow's passage to Gloucester, nearly same distance. From boat adjourned to the "Hop-pole" inn; soon after Mr. J. Vassal entered, we being seen by his servant; he is on his return from Birmingham, having been there on a reconnoitering plan, and speaks of it with the greatest dislike as a dirty, ill-built hole. So different are men's tastes that my companions make it daily a subject of their praises. For my own part I think it deserves neither extravagant praises, much less execrations. It is of an amazing extent, all its new streets spacious and straight, and not ill-built; here are many excellent buildings, and London itself does not exhibit a more spacious and well-built one than Newhall-street, though its paving is not of best quality. Bespoke beds and supper, and left the inn for a ramble; directed course to new bridge and then to Castle Mount, seeming a work of art, of a regular form, agreeable walk to the top or flat about eighteen feet over, having evergreens around its border. Hence returned back to inn. We partook of a splendid supper, which, with other acts of a different complexion from the late adopted plan of economy, shows that inconsistency is a common fault among frail men.

June 22. At twelve departed, our boat more lumbered and dirty than before, and passengers of still meaner sort; and it having taken three hours to arrive at a landing within three miles of Upton, to which we walked by land, distance passed by water being just seven miles from Gloucester. Under such ill-omened circumstances were discouraged from proceeding further by water, and therefore on arrival of boat, ordering out our baggage, and taking, as the sailors phrase it, London tack on board, proceeded to next stage of fifteen miles, called Newport, where changed horses. Our home is distant from this place eighteen miles; at three or four hundred yards without turnpike-gate at the head of Stokes, we crossed a short thick foot-pad, who, running out from under hedges, seized the reins of our horses, threatening instant death to the driver if he did not stop ; whereupon he stopped, and giving up the reins, ran to chaise door and was going to demand our money, when S. Sewall supposing him only a rude fellow, raising himself forward, made a push at him with his cane ; at which the pad retreated back a few paces, discharging his pistol at same instant, and ran off, presuming he had executed his threat, which was, "damn you, I'll do for you." Judge Sewall thought he perceived the wind of the bullet as it passed ; be that as it may, it was found next morning. It grazed the moulding, which diverted it from a course that otherwise must have entered S. Sewall's body, but how his head escaped is inconceivable ; it pierced through the lining and lodged between it and leather top, proving a slug near three quarters of an inch long, and was picked up next morning. Thursday evening, June 22, concluded a journey of five hundred miles in eighteen days.

TO MR. JOHN TIMMINS, LONDON.

Bristol, June 24, 1780.

DEAR SIR :

I take the earliest opportunity after my excursion of eighteen days to acknowledge the receipt of yours. I hope the execrable mob in London is thoroughly quelled, and the promoters of it in safe custody, ready for the execution of deserved justice; I wish government may arrive at the bottom of this infernal plot, for that there was one, no man in his senses can doubt. Through the great extent of country we passed during its rage, there appeared an universal detestation against them ; though should the flame catch at some populous places, there are villains enough to be found ready to join in plunder, rapine, murder and burning.

Very truly yours,

S. CURWEN.

June 30.   Walked to the quay to find a vessel bound to White-haven, intending, if practicable, a water conveyance to Workington, in Cumberland.

July 6.   Foot-pad taken in Bath-road ; Judge Sewall seeing him thinks he is the one that attacked us.

July 8.   Met Mr. R. Hallowell, who informed me of his going to London.   Received a letter from J. R., inclosing one from R. Ward, Salem, by Isa. White, via Amsterdam.

TO WILLIAM BROWNE, ESQ., COWBRIDGE, WALES.

Bristol, July 13, 1780.

DEAR SIR :

By two letters from Salem, one from our friend William Pynchon, of May 3, via Amsterdam, I am informed of the death of Mr. McGilchrist on the 20th of the former month ; a man of un-dissembled virtue and singular integrity, and the most friendly heart ; to whose memory I cannot fail to pay the tribute of a tear. Besides whom, the late ranting patriot J. W. is also gone to the former generations.   As for the rest, all our friends are well and longing, but as almost without hope, for the good old times, as is the common saying now, except among those, as he expresses it, whose enormous heaps have made them easy and insolent, and to wish for a continuance of those confusions by which they grow rich.   Our friend wishes to hear from you and other of our towns-men and friends here.   If you are disposed to oblige in this way, a letter inclosed to my care, left at the New England Coffee-House, London, soon to be my residence, shall be forwarded.   I am far from being sanguine of essential good effects from Clinton's success.

Truly yours,

S. CURWEN.

TO WILLIAM PYNCHON, ESQ.

Bristol, July 15, 1780.

DEAR SIR :

This may serve to inform you of the receipt of your favor of May 3, and to convey my acknowledgments therefor; nor do I know any favors more deserving of thanks than letters from distant friends and acquaintance ; in truth, I think, Solomon never uttered more truth, or discovered more knowledge of mankind, than in the following proverb : " Good news from a far country is as cold water to a thirsty soul." To be made acquainted with the welfare of my friends is among the first and warmest wishes of my heart, nor doth it feel more pleasurable sensations than are derived from that source. Since my last, the political state of affairs seems in many people's opinion to have taken a more favorable turn for this country, but good and ill often succeed each other in the whirl of human affairs in quick succession ; for amidst a deal of good news daily pouring in from abroad, a most tremendous cloud suddenly and unlooked for arose and covered our horizon, threatening instant destruction even to the very being of government itself. For some days it was feared the city of London would be laid in ashes, during which the most abandoned and profligate miscreants that were ever nourished by, or have proved the curse of society, were to have availed themselves of the conflagration and terror occasioned thereby, and plundered what the less cruel felons might have spared, perhaps murdering those against whom their spite might have been levelled. On the day that the petition of the Protestant associators, as they denominated themselves, was to be presented to the house, the subscribers were by an advertisement of Lord George Gordon, their president, desired to meet in St. George's Fields ; the reason alleged was, that no building in London was large enough to hold the expected numbers, and from thence to accompany him with the petition to the house—meaning by so numerous an appearance to give weight to it, or enforce it more effectually. The rabble, many of whom were signers, likely enough for the most villainous purposes, for with such the more mischief the better sport, joined, making no less a number, it is credibly said, than forty thousand ; a number of such characters, and under such circumstances, truly alarming ;

from hence they paraded through the borough of Southwark and along London streets, at first it is said orderly, but no sooner had they reached palace yard than they filled that and all the avenues leading to the house. Throwing off the mask, they bawled aloud for liberty and the Protestant religion; and now their insolence began, for many members of both houses undistinguishingly received marks of their indignant rage; some were stopped and threatened, otherwise abused and assaulted, pulled out of their carriages, and glad to get off without hats, wigs, with lacerated garments and flesh-wounds; whilst many were happy to retreat unhurt and absent themselves from the house for that day at least. The distinguishing badge they wore was a blue cockade, which the president, Lord George, had the boldness to wear in his hat to the house, but being espied, he was desired, nay, even menaced, and with reluctance suffered it to be taken out. The most sober, and many such, doubtless, there were among them, retired peaceably and in good order; but the rabble, by far the greater number, having raised themselves into a frenzy, for fire you know is kindled by collision, adjourned, resolving to plunder and destroy the houses of those who from liberal principles had promoted a relaxation of the supposed too great rigor of the act of William and Mary against papists, that had been for many months the occasion of a paper war on the subject, and excited a real or pretended terror in the minds of many who were, or affected to be, afraid of the increase and prevalence of popery. The houses of these and some unoffending Roman Catholics fell a sacrifice the first day to their rapine and malice; what became not plunder, was destroyed, or devoted to the flames. In the number were Sir George Saville's, a most worthy character, a steady whig, and an anti-ministerialist, but being a friend to taxation, and a man of property, was a suitable subject, and worthy of these sons of liberty and supporters of the Protestant cause to exercise their patriotism upon.

The second day, Lord Mansfield's house employed their patriotic labor; his valuable library, pictures, and household goods, to the amount of near thirty thousand pounds, were plundered, broken, destroyed and devoted to the flames;—among other things, was a large collection of manuscripts on various subjects, of immense loss to the world, it is said. In short, as Lord Loughborough, late Mr.

Wedderburne, says, seventy-two houses and four prisons are now lying in ruins; of the latter, the fine new building of Newgate-street prison, King's Bench, Clerkenwell, and Surry Bridewell; from whence were let loose all the debtors and felons who assisted in promoting those atrocious crimes, for which they were soon to have suffered the justice of the laws.   Had they directed their aim at the Bank the first or second day of their rage, it is to be feared they might have annihilated the books, papers, and records :—a blow that might have shaken government to its centre, and involved the nation in evils too horrid to mention.   The third day it was attacked; providentially, the fate of a score or two, and a strong party of dragoons and light-horse surrounding the palladium, saved it from the merciless claws of these ravening wolves. For three or four days, ten to fifteen houses were seen at one time in the centre of the metropolis lighted up by design ; and to complete this most abhorred plan of destruction, a design was formed to cut off the new river pipes, but, in the moment of execution, it was most happily prevented.

Thus this great city and the government are still preserved, monuments of divine forbearance :—it hath pleased Him who saith to the boisterous waves of the sea, " hitherto shalt thou come, and no further," to put a stop to the rage and madness of the people, and for the present to control the malicious designs of our inveterate enemies ; for, that the ravages of the late banditti took their rise from abroad, has a face of probability.   Though I cannot take upon me to warrant the following or any paragraph in the newspapers to be the word of Apollo, it is yet confidently asserted in them, that " a gentleman lately arrived from Holland has affirmed that he heard the French ambassador there declare openly, that London would be laid in ashes within a month."   So deep was the plan, and so seriously in earnest to ensure complete destruction, that such situations and kinds of business were pitched upon, as afforded the most combustible materials for supplying a fierce flame, as oil-dealers, distillers, warehouses, &c. ; but a kind interposing Providence stopped the devouring fire, and all is now once again settled, quiet, and, it is to be hoped, safe.   To secure which, and overawe the profligate and daring, enough of whom all great cities abound in, a large encampment is still continued in Hyde Park of light-horse, dragoons and foot, and are to be kept up during the summer; besides a party (notwithstanding the city mayor and patriotic gentry's remonstrance about city rights,) patrolling and keeping guard in London, to the great annoyance and terror of the turbulent and dangerous.

Bath and Bristol were intended to have been theatres whereon to have exhibited the future acts of the same tragedy. At the former, the Roman Catholic chapel and the priest's house were purged of all their effects that fell within the claws of these destructive harpies, and the combustibles they committed to the unrelenting flames: but a party of the Hereford militia, and a troop of dragoons, being at callable distance, seasonably arrived to prevent further mischief. The latter city, by a vigorous internal police taking early precautions, dispersed a threatening storm; three or four hundred banditti, collected in St. James's parish in this city for the patriotic purpose of rapine and burning, were, by a well timed early association, scattered and driven back to their dens; all the well disposed arming and patrolling through the streets for several nights. During this miscreantic insurrection, Judge Sewall, Samuel Sewall, and myself, were on an excursion in the country, wherein we dropped on the abode of our townsfolks, Samuel Porter and Captain Poynton; the former carrying indelible marks of personal identity, the latter of an amazingly increased bulk and gouty habit; their present abode is Shrewsbury. I rather envy than lament our worthy friend, Mr. McGilchrist, who is now in a more peaceable neighborhood, I dare say, than that he has quitted, and I fancy without regret; would that you and I were with him, resting, perhaps, in undisturbed quiet till the last grand tribunal scene shall open, and restore the sleeping dust to life and activity; or, perhaps, roving in the unbounded fields of immensity, exploring and admiring the astonishing operations of omnipotence.

Know you that the two great objects of American odium are now no more:—Governor Bernard died some time since, and lately Governor Hutchinson; suddenly, as he was stepping into his carriage.

Mr. Timmins has recovered from a very severe fit of sickness, and has taken up his residence with his family at Chelsea, for the benefit of the air. My future abode will be at London, or its neighborhood.   Letters will reach me there addressed to be left at the New England Coffee-House, Threadneedle-street.

With great esteem, your assured friend,

S. CURWEN.

July 16.   Attended worship at College; Mr. Porvis, one of the prebends, preached a very ingenious discourse; afterwards I was told it was not of his own composing; as it is not an unusual custom among the Episcopal clergy to read others' performances in the pulpit.   Afternoon saw Mr. Coates, who repeated his son's invitation to tea, and on returning home, finding no one waiting for me there, directed my footsteps to Bank-terrace, meeting a multitude, as is ever the custom on pleasant Sundays.

July 18.   From this day we have an addition to our family of my countryman Nicholas Lechmere; supped with him and a friend of his named Maddocks.

July 19.   Just finished a long letter to my friend Mr. Pynchon, inclosing Lord Loughborough's speech to grand jury on St. Margaret's hill at the trial of some of the London rioters.

July 23.   Afternoon walked with N. Lechmere over Durdham Down to Ostrick; crossed over to Cooke's Folly, a tower on the banks of the Avon.

July 30.   Drank tea at Mr. R. Lechmere's and after a social tete-a-tete walked with him, and lady and daughter and brother to College Green, where joined four Americans.   Wrote to advise my friend Timmins of my intention to bid adieu to Bristol, and make London my residence till I shall be no more, for I despair of ever leaving this island.

August 2.   By invitation dined at Mr. R. Lechmere's with Admiral Graves' lady, etc.

August 3.   Mr. N. Lechmere accompanied me to the stage for Bath, where took leave.   Found a female of fourteen only passenger.   At Temple-gate were joined by the well known Mr. Heathin, late of Honiton in Devonshire, with his maiden sister ; the former very loquacious, who without partiality seems a compound of strong sense, knowledge, vivacity and vanity. * * * * * * My attention was drawn to his reading the quack doctor's speech to the gaping mob, his attendants, in Launcelot Greaves, written by the late Dr.

Smollet; he solicited my interest with Mr. Nathaniel White, whose preaching I had attended, and proposed still to attend at old Jewry, in order to procure for him the use of his meeting-house on Sunday evenings for lecture. At six o'clock alighted at Castle inn, Market-street, Bath. After tea, taking a ramble met my said loquacious fellow-traveller; joining me, proceeded to a long walk in a lonely road, of which he seemed glad to avail himself to recount his own adventures.

Bath, August 4. Arose at seven o'clock, and joined by a Mr. Graves, a young clergyman of Suffolk, whose obliging, social behavior rendered him an agreeable companion. On the road, about half way to our first stage, a parson named Goddard overtaking us, alighted from his own horse, delivered it to a servant, and entered our carriage, adding a third to our company. For the first half hour, our two Oxonians kept to themselves the whole conversation, wherein were disclosed many clerical and academic tales, stories, and anecdotes; among others I recollect the following :—Dr. Barton, dean of Bristol and rector of St. Andrews, Holborn, who was, according to British mode of expression, dark, meaning stone-blind, being of a humorous disposition and great self-command, having a mind to entertain himself, invited four eminent persons in the same desolate condition as he was, to a dinner, none other being present but the servants. These were Sir John Fielding, of as eminent a character in the juridical line as perhaps any man in the civilized world; Mr. Stanley, the well known musician, and others whose names I forget. After partaking of a joyous feast, they took a humorous leave and departed. At eleven o'clock we alighted at the Black Lion in Devizes, where, after taking refreshment, I walked forth to ramble, and espied a sign, for quaintness of its device here noted. On the sign were painted five men, well known by the name of the "*five alls ;*" the first in order, according to present mode of arrangement of church before king, stands the parson in his sacerdotalibus; *he prays for all :* second, the lawyer, in his gown, band, and tie-wig; *he pleads for all :* third, the soldier in uniform, with a fierce countenance; *he fights for all :* fourth is a physician, with great wig and solemn phiz, and boluses and julips in his hand; *he kills or cures all :* the fifth and last is the farmer, with his settled, thoughtful countenance; *he pays for all.*

Leaving this place, with fresh horses, arrived at " *Great Castle*" inn, Marlborough, at two o'clock; distant thirty-two miles from Bath. This inn is famous through England for grandeur of structure, it having been a nobleman's mansion-house ; the excellence and expensiveness of its accommodations, provisions, etc., are of the highest style. Passed grounds wherein is a mount made by art, the ascent to the summit in a spiral line of so gentle a rising as to be imperceptible, in length half a mile, though encompassing it but four times. The mount does not exceed a hundred feet diameter, nor more in height ; the top is a plain, planted with trees, from which is to be seen a distant view of the town, consisting of one long street and a few short ones at right angles.

Newbury, our next stage, is a long town, consisting of buildings in middle and lower style, decent and in good repair; has one Episcopal church and four dissenting meeting-houses. Its inhabitants are avowed friends of American liberty, and disavowers of the war. Departed hence at seven o'clock, slept at the " George inn," Reading, a large, handsome, well-built town, principal of this fine county (Berkshire); from hence to Colebrook, where I stayed again and dined; then travelled my last stage, London, being set down at the Swan inn, Holborn bridge, at the end of Fleet-market, at six o'clock. After a short rest, daylight still remaining, as it did some hours after, I walked forth to view the ruins of Mr. Langdale's house, etc., almost adjoining the inn; proceeding forward to Newgate, but little distance, which was lying in a deplorable state of ruin, destroyed by the mob. I returned back to my inn, filled with honest but fervid indignation, which ought to warm the breast of every peaceable well wisher to order, laws, safety, and the rights of individuals : sleep put an end to my mortifying reflections.

CHAPTER XIII.

London, Aug. 8.   Engaged lodgings at Mrs. Councel's, No. 22 Castle-street, Falcon-square.

TO HON. JONATHAN SEWALL, BRISTOL.

London, Aug. 14, 1780.

DEAR SIR :

I have been told by Mr. Jos. Green and his wife, and with such an air of serious earnestness as to lead me almost into a belief of it, that advice had last Saturday been brought to town by a vessel said to have arrived from America, that on the 19th of May, the moon being just then beyond the full, the sky clear and unclouded at sunrise, and to all appearance promising a fine bright day, continuing some time in this state, when all at once a sudden darkness overspread the face of the heavens, and so palpably thick was it, that candles were lighted in the houses during its continuance till three o'clock in the afternoon, to conduct the common concerns and intercourse of life.   A short interval of light or twilight ensued, but was succeeded by a tenfold darker night than was ever known. Perhaps I am misinformed; if you have not heard of this extraordinary and uncommon phenomenon, suspend your belief till better or no information follows, or in the former case a fuller and more particular relation shall be made.   Time, the great revealer of secret things, will soon convince you of its truth or falsehood.   I am not myself determined in my opinion ; the belief of uncommon events requires strong evidence ; should this be true, you have astrologers, soothsayers, magicians, and wise men enough among you to explain its meaning.

Very truly, your friend,

S. CURWEN.

TO COL. WILLIAM BROWNE, COWBRIDGE.

London, August 16, 1780.

DEAR SIR :

The contents of my last were chiefly to acquaint you of the receipt of a letter from our common friend, Mr. Pynchon, dated
Salem, May 3. I shall now give you a part in his own words :
" I am pleased at having so safe a conveyance, but should be more
so could I write with freedom ; as I cannot, you will make allowances for my scrawl. I may, however, acquaint you that your
family and friends are in health, and bear with cheerfulness and
fortitude the rubs, jostlings and vexations of turbulent times ; they
are wishing to see you, to tell you a hundred things which might
make you laugh, admire, and sometimes stare. During the winter
we have been blocked up with snow ; the oldest inhabitant re-
members not such quantities of it on the earth at any one time.
But we are now thawed out, and begin to rejoice that the price of
wood is fallen from \$4,50 to \$3,00 a cord. Had other necessaries been proportionably dear, some of us might well wish for a
return of the good old times, as they are now called ; and those
whose enormous heaps have made them easy and insolent, might
wish for a continuance of the confusions by which they grew in
the Frenchman's style, " *horriblement riches.*" Our worthy friend
Mr. M'Gilchrist foretold that he should not live to see an end of it,
and feared that few of his old friends would ; he has gone into the
vale, a true prophet—he left us on the 20th April. His patience
and fortitude continued to the last ; his sickness and death were of
a piece with his life, and that you know was a lesson of virtue.
He delayed making his will a little too long ; some of his prejudices and resentments appeared on that occasion. He gave to
" the Society for propagation of the gospel in foreign parts" all
arrears coming to him, being three years' salary, and his part of
the donation made for missionaries who had suffered in these times.
I often wish to hear of Col. Browne and others of our town -
men and friends there."

In answer to a letter of mine some time ago, mentioning the
evils of exile at my time of life, he says, " What would your feelings have been, my good friend, if while here you had lost your
business, all your debts, the fruits of many years' labor ; had been

driven to sell your house and land for the payment of debts and expenses, and the remainder had sunk in your hands fifty per cent ; and that though thus reduced, you could not freely nor safely walk the streets by reason of party rage and malevolence, and the uncontrolled 'rancor of some men.'' A wretched and truly pitiable condition this ! a just picture, I fear, of American popular liberty. Dr. Charles Russell died at Antigua last June, and his brother James, who by lucky captures by a letter of marque has realized fifteen thousand pounds sterling, is soon to be settled a Bristol merchant, and bound in the matrimonial chain to Mr. R. Lechmere's second daughter, Mary, whom I think a fine, well accomplished lady. Mr. Jo. Green and wife told me the story of a dark day having occurred in New England, on the 19th of May, such as was never before known ;—in order to maintain the common intercourse of life, candles were lighted and kept burning. For my own part, though I am no believer in omens, I cannot but take this to be a most extraordinary and terrifying event. Darkness, in the oneirocritic art, denotes distress, anguish, trouble, loss, sickness, death, and the whole train of evils, physical and moral. Perhaps the fearful among our country folks may find in themselves a disposition to be reconciled to the thoughts of a reconnection with this country, which seems more likely to force terms on them than since this foolish, needless, baneful quarrel commenced.

Here, or in this neighborhood, I propose to continue till I shall take my flight to the upper regions, or descend to the shades below ; for I am quite unsettled in my own mind whether a state of activity or insensibility shall fill up the interval between death and the future state of endless existence.

My respectful compliments wait on Mrs. Browne and son ; and ardently wishing you and them the highest felicity, I remain,

With great esteem,
Your faithful friend,
S. Curwen.

P. S. Mr. Francis Waldo, who will soon be with you, will inform you of the troop of New Englanders resident in Bristol.

August 18. Took a long, solitary ramble through Charterhouse-square, thence through Gray's-Inn-lane to Clerkenwell-green, wherein is a building not before seen or heard about, called New Hicks Hall, or Middlesex Sessions House, a large and handsome structure; thence through Smithfield and Long-lane, a narrow, dismal, dirty street, to Aldersgate-street.

August 19.   Called at Francis Waldo's lodgings in Pall Mall, and at Arthur Savage's in Brompton-row, and left a card for the absentees; not a little jaded by the circumambulation.

August 20.   At Westminster Abbey ; the vergers not thinking proper to offer me a seat, I left the choir, and, like the multitude, passed the hour of devotion in gazing at the monuments and reading inscriptions.   From thence passing through cloisters, proceeded to Dean's court, inclosed in part by Westminster school buildings ; returning back, stayed in choir during part of prayer and sermon, and passed half an hour in poet's corner.   Thence to St. Margaret's church, the preacher having just then ascended the pulpit ; I was minded to stay, but these church-servants neglecting to open a pew door for me, I soon departed homewards.

August 23.   To artillery-ground to view manœuvres of the military association, who performed manual exercises, firings, and evolutions commendably.   My curiosity, though still active, is soon satisfied ; nor do I find a more convincing proof of its increasing imbecility, if the expression be not improper, than in this particular.

FROM HON. JONATHAN SEWALL.

Bristol, August 22, 1780.

DEAR SIR :

By a letter from Mr. Waldo to Mr. Simpson, the account of the miraculous darkness at Boston had reached Bristol before I was favored with yours.   The story I firmly believe to be true, but like many Jewish stories in the Old Testament, I take it not in a *literal*, but in a metaphorical or *allegorical* sense.   Take it as an allegory, and it is easily to be credited ; but as this kind of writing is now become rather obsolete, it is necessary to premise, that under the present tyranny in America, no man there dares write upon political subjects in *plain English ;* if he writes at all, it must be in *dark enigmas*, and in this scriptural style I presume the letter from

34

which you derive your intelligence is written. Interpret it thus
The writer wished to let his friend here know what effect the news
of the reduction of Charleston had upon the minds of the Boston
rebels, (or saints, if you like that word better,) but he dared not
communicate his intelligence in a language intelligible to all, and
therefore chose to give it in an allegory, trusting to the sagacity of
his friend, who, being a New England *saint*, as I presume, he
doubted not was well enough versed in Old Testament allegories,
to translate it into literal English, and thus it is :—On the 19th of
May, by a private hand, the news arrived of the surrender of
Charleston, and though at sunrise the sky was clear, and promised
a fine day, i. e., they were till that morning assured Clinton would
be defeated, yet this fatal news at once darkened their bright prospect and induced a gloomy horror, so that candles were lighted in
their houses,—i. e., Adams, Hancock, Dr. Cooper, and other rebel
leaders went from house to house to assure the people the news
could not be true. This was the short interval of light, or twilight,
that ensued; but soon after, on the same day, or perhaps the next,
(for allegories, you know, do not and need not go on all fours,)
an express arrived with an official account confirming the dark
tale, and then the twilight was succeeded by a tenfold darkness—
a dark horror and blackness of despair fell on all. This is my in-
terpretation. *Si quid novisti rectius istis, candidus imperti ; si non,
his utere mecum.** It is consoling, *pro tempore*, at least. In my
sense of the story, you are not *hummed* nor misinformed, but you
only, like many other commentators, misinterpret.

I cannot *devise* the meaning of your quaint *device* at the *devizes*,
unless *the five alls* intend five *shoemakers*, but this seems too
far-fetched to deserve even the epithet of " quaint ;" perhaps were
I to see the figures in their characteristic attitudes, I might make a
better guess ; but with my present data, I give it up, and wish you
would explain it, or if you choose to try my genius at expounding
enigmatical paintings, which, I assure you, is but a sorry one, give
me the characteristic attitudes; paint it to me as it is, and I'll try
again.

I am mightily pleased with the news of the day : La Nymphe

---

* " Pray adopt it ; unless you can suggest a better one."

taken by the Flora, which must be true, and the French seventy-four gun ship by the Bienfaisant, which, as I always hope the best, I hope is true; besides a frigate taken and carried into Halifax, which I likewise hope is true. I rejoice also that Admiral Geary is arrived in the Channel. I hope the eighteen Russian men-of-war will be taken into safe custody, and held till we are sure they can do no mischief. Were I his Majesty's premier, I would not for a moment trust a b—— of a queen, who could'murder her husband and mount his throne—there's no trusting such a jade ; if she means fair, her ships are safe in our hands ; if, on the other hand, as is most probable, she means, in conjunction with France and Spain, to play the devil, *obsta principiis* ought to be our motto. Nip her in the bud, secure these eighteen ships, and her marine power is annihilated—and considering the brimstone, besides murdering her husband which I would never forgive, has been the instigatrix of the northern association, why the deuce should we stand upon ceremony with her ? Why should England regard the laws of nations, while every power in Europe is setting them at defiance ? No, no. Providence, or their evil genius, has put them into our hands, and all nature will ridicule us if we let them escape. I hope his Majesty, God bless him, Lord North, Lord Sandwich, and all the lords of the council, God bless them all, see the thing in the light I do ; if they do, I am sure the Czarina's eighteen ships will soon be manned by British seamen, and added to the British fleet. Her consummate impudence in sending her fleet into our harbors, after the infamous step she has taken, and our own security, the first of all laws, will amply justify us. Tell Lord North what I say when you see him next.

I should not have troubled you with my scolding at the Empress of Russia, (against whom I have no personal enmity, except a little for the murder of her husband, which I think concerns all husbands,) had I not learned when I got half down the other side, that Danforth goes for London on Thursday, by whom I can send this, so that a cover will cost you nothing.

With very little malice against the Czarina, and none against any other of God's creation, I am your sincere friend and humble servant,   J. SEWALL.

MR. CURWEN.

FROM HON. WILLIAM BROWNE.

Cowbridge, Wales, August 22, 1780.

Dear Sir :

I give you many thanks for your kind favor just received, and gladly avail myself of your kindness to forward the inclosed, as addressed. I have also to acknowledge the receipt of two former letters, which have long lain before me, waiting for spirits to support the *ennui* of writing a single line. In short, to tell you a truth, our prospects with regard to America were till lately so unpromising, my finances were so small, my family and expenses so increased, that, added to the common catalogue of vexations which attach themselves to us all, more or less, every exertion became a burden, and I had nothing to do to be easy but to do nothing and care for nobody. Better expectations have produced better spirits, and brought with them better dispositions. It is with pleasure then that I wish to revive a correspondence with an old and much esteemed friend. It has puzzled all the wise men of Cowbridge to divine from what part of London you have dated your letter; various are the conjectures, some humorous and some plausible, but none satisfactory; so we have agreed to suspend our speculations until we could consult the inhabitant of this unknown region.

I thank you for the extract from Mr. Pynchon's letter. A detail of their sufferings would give us pain if they were all strangers; how much more then when we have so many friends among them? It brings, however, this pleasing reflection, that we made a wise choice in leaving them. When you have collected an authentic and satisfactory account of the phenomenon you mention to have happened at Boston,* I wish you would communicate it, with its circumstances, consequences, and impressions, unless it should first appear in some public print.

I think you do perfectly right to make choice of London for your residence the coming winter. It is the only place in which a single man can spend the gloomy months with any satisfaction. I wonder as much that more of our countrymen do not resort there at that season, as that so many of them continue there when they

---

* Dark day.

ought to be sporting in green fields and by the side of purling streams. *Sed trahit sua quemque voluptas.*[*]

I lately received a line from Mr. Porter, describing, in the most gaudy colors imaginable, the happiness to which his situation has introduced him, encouraging all the world to come to Shrewsbury, and promising every felicity that the golden age could ever boast of. What strange mortals we are! Some men are always happy where they are, some where they have been, and some where they shall be; and yet we are none of us satisfied with either past, present, or to come. I wish I could remove your doubts about the interval you mention, for then I could also administer some satisfaction to myself. At present I have only that of subscribing myself, dear sir,   Your affectionate friend,

WM. BROWNE.

MR. CURWEN.

August 25. Visited the ruins of King's Bench prison and Surrey bridewell, sad proofs of popular folly and violence; the former repairing.

TO THOMAS RUSSELL, ESQ., BOSTON.

London, August 25, 1780.

DEAR SIR :

I am ignorant in what light my silence to you may appear; indeed, I am not satisfied of the propriety of it myself; however, I doubt not your candor, when I declare upon honor, that want of real esteem and regard was not in the remotest view a cause. Your obliging favor demanded an answer and thanks; do not say it is too late now, for I now offer them with equal warmth and sincerity. I presume Lane and Fraser have long since informed you that I availed myself of your friendly offer, that did me an essential service; but having determined not to mention any circumstances relative to business in letters, for very obvious reasons, to which I have steadily adhered, you will therefore please to excuse any thing further on this head. Would that the safety of intercourse between the two countries by letter was greater, but God only

---

[*] " Every one follows the bent of his own inclinations."

knows when a period will be put to this execrably baneful war.
I fear it is hardly arrived to half its length, unless this country
gives up the chase, for the obstinacy of the Americans supplies the
want of resources.   Yesterday news arrived of the most melancholy
complexion.   Our western-bound fleet, the convoy and one ship
only excepted, fell into the hands of the French and Spaniards,
consisting of forty-nine merchant ships, transports and victuallers,
including five outward-bound East Indiamen.   This is the most
capital blow England ever felt by an enemy at sea ; particulars in
papers that accompany this.

*   *   *   *   *   *   *

Of the penchant of noble and wealthy ladies to vie with their
partners of the other sex in the laudable pursuit of gaming, etc.,
take the following instance: At the time of my first arrival in
London, a house opposite Governor Hutchinson's, in St. James'-
street, was then finishing, called " *Sçavoir vivre*," being a gaming-
house of the highest modern taste, perhaps much more magnificent
in architecture and furniture than English America can boast, and
designed for gentlemen exclusively.   The ladies' pride being piqued,
they bought up that which the governor lived in, and the two on
either side of it, and though in excellent repair, demolished them,
erecting in their room one in the same taste as its opposite neighbor ; and to this day these two temples are devoted to the worship
of the blind deity, *Fortune*, on whose altars are nightly sacrificed
thousands, besides the peace and support of many of her foolish
and equally blind devotees.   These, among a multitude of other
instances, are proofs and memorials of the expensive taste and diversions of this age and country.

Messrs. Byles and Brattle having been refused a residence in
their own country, renders my return (who I presume stand not so
fair as either of them) more doubtful, or rather more impracticable ;
and though it has ever been the first and the last wish of my heart
to return, and you know that very well, I presume you think a permission not obtainable, having received no encouragement on that
head.

Most ardently and sincerely wishing you every blessing, I am,
with love to Mrs. R. and little family,

Your obliged friend,   S. Curwen.

FROM HON. JONATHAN SEWALL.

Bristol, Aug. 24, 1780.

DEAR SIR :

Since I wrote you by Mr. Danforth, Mr. R. Temple and family have arrived here in thirty-two days from Boston, from whom I learn that the story of the dark day is literally true; but, as they relate it, the phenomenon was truly wonderful, far beyond my comprehension. They say the morning was not as you state, fine and clear, but rather lowering and drizzly, though far from dark ; that at nine o'clock an uncommon darkness came on, without any appearance of a thick cloud. Mr. Temple said it seemed as if a veil was drawn over them, which he seemed to look through, and see the heaven beyond it. The darkness increased till they were obliged to light candles, and this continued till three o'clock, when it lightened up a little ; but before sunset the darkness returned, and the night resembled the darkness of Egypt, which might be felt. It was so intense that many persons in Boston and the country were bewildered in going from house to house where they were intimately acquainted. They say that during the darkness in the day, the green grass appeared of a dark blue color ; and on the next morning, both the water and land were covered with a dark greasy or oily substance ; that the darkness extended northward, as far as Hudson river; and westward, as far as they had heard from—I say as far as Lake Champlain ; and that it was the devil spreading his wings over the northern rebellious colonies, and if they do not repent, the next time he will certainly fly off with them all. I give you this account to atone for my infidelity in my last, and with all the allowance I can make for the subtle workings of the imagination. I confess, I am puzzled to account for the appearance ; the young ladies, the Misses Temple, who were in Boston, say candles were lighted all the day in the shops and houses ; but in the evening, they were at a wedding-ball with a brilliant company ; which, if they don't exaggerate, would put me in mind of the inhabitants of the old world, who were eating and drinking, feasting and frolicking, till the flood came, &c. &c. They add another circumstance which increaseth the wonder ; namely, that during the darkness there was not the least appear-

ance of fog, smoke or haziness. I wish you would consult that
learned body, the Royal Society, upon this *lusus naturæ*, and let
me know the result; for I do not believe all the wise men of
Boston will be able to explain it.

I have seen Boston papers to the 17th of July; but they contain nothing new, except the arrival of the Chevalier de Ternay
at Rhode Island, with seven ships of the line and troops; upon
this occasion, all their pens are at work to rekindle the dying
patriotic fire. Washington, it seems, in expectation of de Ternay's
arrival, had made a requisition upon all the states, of men, horses,
provisions, &c.; but, by the complaints in the papers, the levies
went on heavily. The plan seems to be to muster their utmost force,
and in conjunction with the French, to attack New-York, and
drive the British forces from the continent. I wish they may have
courage to attempt it. General Kniphausen has burnt the little
village of Springfield in the Jerseys. A paper of July 6th, says,
General Clinton was returned to New-York; but that of the 17th
leaves him up North river, near forming a junction with General
Kniphausen. The ladies of Philadelphia have opened a subscription
for supplying the army with comforts and conveniences; they have
appointed a treasuress to receive, and a committee to distribute the
donations; and all the ladies upon the continent are earnestly and
pathetically exhorted to follow this laudable and patriotic example.
If the zeal and spirit of the peasants can again be raised, I think
this will prove a decisive campaign. Admirals Graves and Arbuthnot, it is said, are at New-York; so that if the Chevalier De
Ternay did not get away with ships very soon, they probably, ere
this, are added to the British navy; which would console for the
loss of the East and West Indiamen.

I must mention an advertisement I read in one of the papers,
which shows the value of the paper money there :—" *Forty dollars*
is offered a pound for horsehair, or *three shillings* in hard money."
Or which is better, " the advertiser will work it up at the halves !"

Yours very truly,

JONATHAN SEWALL.

August 26. Visited Mr. Jo. Scott :—dined at Mrs. Hay's,
with James Harwood and S. Conant, (two young Americans,

strangers to me,) and was after joined by Mr. Thomas Danforth, the first time of seeing him since my return, he having been absent on a three months' excursion to the westward; he brought me a humorous letter from Judge Sewall.

August 27.   Met S. Walsh and Peter Johonnot.

TO HON. WILLIAM BROWNE, COWBRIDGE, WALES.

London, August 29, 1780.

Dear Sir :

Mr. Francis Waldo's intended journey to Cowbridge on a visit to his sister, Mrs. Flucker, affords me opportunity of acknowledging receipt of your favor of the 27th inst. Yours endorsed to Mrs. Sargent will go off to-morrow for Holland under cover of mine; having ordered the bearer in case of capture, (though my letters contain neither treason, love, nor politics,) to throw them into the sea; yours will follow their fate. My present residence is not that of the gay and fashionable, and therefore unknown, suiting me in this state of degradation not a whit the less on that score. The different views and appearances that are daily arising in and about London, are as great and almost as frequent as the different phases of the moon in one of its revolutions, and render many spots and places a mere *terra incognita*, that to those who have been absent a few years were well known. For having about ten days since wandered to the further end of Mary le Bone, being designed to a distant quarter, on finding myself there, I inquired for the gardens which you remember to have been resorted to by company, and where fireworks were exhibited ; to my surprise the whole ground is laid out in streets and covered with grand and elegant houses, and even beyond it. In this ramble accident revealed a secret that has puzzled you and the wise men of Cowbridge, that probably I should otherwise never have possessed. Some months since a letter was addressed to me by James Russell, dated Manchester-square—the location of which was beyond the reach of my knowledge or any of those I had consulted, having never before heard of it; chance, however, in this ramble directing my steps among rows of new buildings, and directing also my eye to a corner house in an unfinished square of noble structures, inscribed Manchester-square, this unimportant secret was thereby revealed.

I am afraid your sunshine of happiness is a little overclouded by the mortifying advices in respect of our eastern and western fleets; the most capital blow England ever received by an enemy at sea since King William's reign, fourscore years ago, when nearly four hundred sail were lost at one time. The loss is estimated at a million, I hope it will not be more. To this another stroke has succeeded in the capture of twelve Quebec ships, supposed next in value to the East-Indiamen outward. I observe that Samuel Porter, our townsman, has presented to your view a picture in gaudy colors, as you expressed it, of the felicity of his situation; that he is pleased and contented, none has a right to doubt, for he affirms it, and he is a very honest fellow and knows his own feelings; but our tastes, however, are various as our faces, and he doubtless has not made an improper choice for himself, though I dare say Judge and Samuel Sewall could tell you it would not be a proper one for you or themselves; and were either to paint it, not in high, but modest colors, you would find a difficulty in restraining the exercise of the risible muscles. Diogenes was delighted to take his abode in a tub, and although one may disapprove his taste, who has a right to condemn his choice?

Pardon the dress of this letter; for ever since my arrival in town I find myself incapable of application; the present hurry and confusion, to which I have for several years been unused, dissipates and overwhelms the small share of spirits left me, and which old age is daily lessening. I am often reminded of "Taunton, dear Ned," as the song has it:

> " My head is astunned with the naise and the cries
>   Of their cruds and their creams, and their whot puden pies ;
>   And they keep zitch a naise all over the town,
>   Ich think that the world wor a turn'd up-zide-down."

With the kindest love and regards to Mrs. Browne and family, I remain your affectionate friend,

S. Curwen.

August 31. To Mr. Francis Waldo's, at " Gentlemen's Hotel," Pall Mall; met Mr. Jo. Greene on Holborn Hill, and walked to Brompton to call on Mr. and Mrs. Arthur Savage; both absent.

At a bookseller's in St. Paul's Church-yard, met my Scotch townsman Andrew Dalglish, from Glasgow, and he wishes me to recommend him private lodgings.   In the Strand met Mr. Frs. Waldo,
and accompanied him to Canon coffee-house, Spring Gardens, and
took tea, where were joined by Jo. Scott, and remained till
eleven o'clock in talking politics.   In the "Courant" of this day,
find a summary of form of government to be established in Massachusetts Bay, to commence next October.   It will be well if it be
productive of as much security as the old.   There are not wanting
those, I fancy, many on both sides the great water, who do with
me fear the dire consequences of an estrangement from governmental power and protection, and a pernicious alliance with a
faithless people; many there are as well affected to the real
interest of that country as the most ardent republicans.   If French
troops in the English colonies in North America be not pregnant
with direful evils, and destructive of American independence, my
foreboding fears are imaginary — may they prove so.   I wish, however, the hot-brained politicians there may in time foresee the
baneful consequences early enough to prevent them,—if not, wo
betide the inhabitants!   I heartily wish they never may experience
the cruelty and oppression that befell Flanders during the Duke of
Alva's sanguinary tyranny, and may its oppressions be of less duration, should they ever experience them from their present allies.
The politics of the court of Versailles are not in their nature formed
to promote the liberty of English subjects; nothing but party rage
intercepts between the mental eye and a truth visible as the sun at
meridian in a cloudless day.

    Sept. 2.   Circuited to Smithfield, in order to see the ceremony
of opening Bartholomew Fair by the Lord Mayor—just finished.
The whole is a mere rabble rout, relishable only by "mene peuple;" conducted by men, women, and children, in painted masks
and merry-andrew tawdry dresses.   The amusements consist in
jumping, dancing, riding on roundabout horses with legs, speech-
making, etc., performed on scaffolds; together with sleight-of-hand
tricks, in front rooms hired for that purpose; the ascent whereto
is by a kind of rough ladder-stairs, actors and performers inviting
in by a thousand antic postures and gestures.   Passages round lined

with booths and tents, crammed with gingerbread, pastry, and all kinds and varieties of baubles.

Sept. 3. To Richmond Gardens; they fall short of my expectations—a dead level, laid out in long, straight gravel walks, not in the best order—lined with trees and stumps, great numbers, we were told, cut down to serve the king's kitchen for fuel. A little beyond is a fine lawn. interspersed with trees, and accommodated with field seats, commanding a delightful view of the river Thames, here a smooth gentle stream, gliding along the side of a delightful raised terrace, eight feet high, between gardens or lawns, for a mile and a half, reaching to Kew *house*—for the pompous appellation of *palace* it merits not. This walk reminds me of Sir John Dunham's beautiful couplet:

> " Though deep yet clear, though gentle yet not dull ;
> Strong without rage, without o'erflowing full."

From this only pleasing spot departed, taking a final leave of these (I know not why) celebrated gardens, and directed our steps to the Queen's Terrace, so called, on Richmond Hill, commanding, though not a very extensive, yet a distinct and pleasing prospect, having many fine objects in command of the eye besides the river, which is almost under foot. Ascending to the top, passed the well known inn of Star and Garter, remarkable for its elegant accommodations, and consequent high charges, and entered park, celebrated for its natural beauties.

Sept. 9. Met Mr. J. Waldo, of Bristol, and a Capt. Fletcher, both violent Americans in principle ; the latter commander of a letter of truce, (falsely so called,) who brought over Mr. R. Temple and family.

Sept. 12. At Guildhall, to see the polling for city members for new parliament; conducted with regularity, the avenues crowded with distributers of party papers, bawling aloud for their employers' favorites, friends of the respective candidates bringing on voters, single and in shoals.

Sept. 15. Charles J. Fox shot ahead of Lord Lincoln greatly yesterday (candidates for Westminster) ; the latter, it is said, proposes to keep the election going on till after some borough elections are over, in order to have a numerous host of friends, but he must rally great numbers.

Sept. 16.   To Mr. Timmins's, and after an hour's abode, walked together ; encountered Van Coulster ; his shabby dress gave me uneasiness, indicating want ; he seemed in good spirits, however, and inquired my lodgings—gave him a card.

Sept. 17.   Attended worship at Lincoln's Inn chapel.   Samuel Peters preached—he is an indifferent speaker and composer—how he got there is as hard to conceive as straws in amber.   After, at Essex chapel, Mr. Lindsay preached to a very respectable looking assembly ; church is not crowded at this season—a most excellent discourse, delivered with suitable gravity, and, I am disposed to believe, sincerity.

Sept. 19.   Market crowded with mob huzzaing for Fox.

Sept. 21.   Election for sheriffs ; all but livery excluded from the hall on election of city officers.

Sept. 23.   Walking through Old Bailey, and seeing a great crowd, learnt that two pickpockets were to be whipped.   Jack Ketch, a short sturdy man, soon appeared with the culprits, one after the other ; the first seemed like an old offender, and was moderately lashed ; the mob said he had bought off the minister of justice ; he writhed but little.   The other was young, distress painted strongly on his countenance ; he cried loudly ; his back seemed unused to stripes ; from this time it will carry the marks of legal vengeance, and proofs of his folly and wickedness.   Going forward, passed through the Strand ; and returned by way of Covent Garden to see election, which had been ended and poll closed for two hours ; and the elected members, returning from the procession, were just entering James'-street, mounted on two arm chairs, placed on a board that was carried on eight men's shoulders, accompanied by thousands with tokens of victory : red and blue ribbons in their hats.

Sept. 25.   At Covent Garden theatre ; performance, Beggar's Opera ; parts well played, but great impropriety, not to say indecency, in Mrs. Kennedy's personating McHeath.   Bravery, gallantry, and a fearless disregard of death, the characteristics of that notorious highwayman ; which female softness awkwardly imitates. Following *entertainment*, falsely so called ; execrably foolish and childish. I am sorry to arraign even the shilling gallery for want of judgment, in suffering such unmeaning stuff to pass for a farce.

TO WILLIAM CABOT, ESQ., NO. 7, LAMBETH-TERRACE.

No. 22, Castle-street, Falcon-square, Sept. 28, 1780.

DEAR SIR :

Recollecting a request you made of me some months since by letter, I now acquaint you that by reason of absence of mind at that time, it was not in my memory that Mr. Lindsay, the minister of the Unitarian society meeting at Essex House in the Strand, had published a liturgy reformed agreeably to Dr. Samuel Clarke's plan, free from the errors and peculiarities of any and every particular sect among Christians; making the supreme God and Father of all, in contradistinction to every other being, *the sole object of religious worship ;* but in the name and as the disciples of Jesus Christ, whose Lord, head and master, all true Christians acknowledge him to be. If you have not bought one, they are to be had of Mr. Johnson, bookseller, 72 St. Paul's Church-yard. His mode of worship, I profess to think agreeable to the genuine spirit of the gospel, and myself to be one of his worshipping congregation. His plan, in my view, is scriptural ; his worship plain, simple, unmixed with superstitious, unmeaning ceremonies, as all establishments are more or less burdened with. His preaching is instructive; his delivery serious, pathetic, and intelligible ; his language energetic and clear ; the assembly, the most respectable for its numbers I ever saw.   Yours truly,

S. CURWEN.

Sept. 29. As I was walking in Holborn, observed a throng of ordinary people crowding round a chaise filled with young children of about seven years of age ; inquiring the reason, was informed they were young sinners who were accustomed to go about in the evening, purloining whatever they could lay their hands on, and were going to be consigned into the hands of justice. Great pity that so many children, capable of being trained to useful employments and become blessings to society, should be thus early initiated, by the wicked unthinking parents of the lower classes in this huge overgrown metropolis, in those pernicious practices of every species of vice the human heart can be tainted with, which renders them common pests, and most commonly brings them to the halter.

Oct. 6.   At Treasury, Mr. Rowe out of town ; no orders till the 20th—the delay a hardship ; every expedient is used that craft can devise and power execute to squeeze dependents.—Evening at Saddler's Wells ; a variety of exhibitions, tumbling in great variety ; among others was the following : a lad about six years old, standing on a man's hands, with arms outstretched, in an erect posture, turned his body backwards so as to bring his face in a line with his legs, and between them.   After continuing in this seemingly strained condition for a half minute, he gradually returned back to his natural shape, keeping his poise without any aid.   In rope-dancing were the two following instances : a young person, habited and in appearance a female to the waist, and like a boy downwards, on the curtain being drawn up, was first seen lying on her back, and swinging to and fro three feet above the floor of the stage ; rising without any assistance, she walked backwards and forwards on it ; whilst in motion, a whalebone hoop of greater diameter than her height was placed on the wire, into which she stepped and walked backwards and forwards as before, and whilst in it received in her hand a smaller hoop, whereon were placed two tumblers, about two thirds full of red liquor, and whilst she was swinging whirled the smaller hoop round many times without spilling a drop.   The same afterwards mounted a tight-rope, having baskets of the size of a half bushel fastened to her feet ; with these she walked backwards and forwards, displaying various motions.   After divesting herself of these incumbrances, she first walked as before backwards and forwards, leaping, vaulting, and throwing herself down.   Her performances on the tight-rope were accompanied by a balance-pole in her hand, and by two men who slightly touched the pole when it descended below the horizontal lines.   Whilst on the slack-rope, she went through the whole exercise of flourishing colors, consisting of a great variety of motions—holding a standard in each hand.

TO ARTHUR SAVAGE, ESQ., NO. 7, BROMPTON-ROW.

No. 22, Castle-street, Falcon-square, Oct. 14, 1780.

DEAR SIR :

Your agreeable and obliging favor of the 11th instant came to hand the day after its date; but a severe cold, yet confining me, prevented the attention your politeness demanded.

I thank you for the kind information it contained respecting the Roman denarii and English coins; a few of which, if not above the reach of my purse, I would gladly procure.

If my indisposition goes off and the weather permits, I will wait on you next Monday afternoon. With compliments to Mrs. and Miss Savage,   I remain, etc., etc.

S. CURWEN.

Oct. 15. Sunday afternoon, at the Temple. Stood for a time to take another stare at old Plowden's funeral monument; the figure in a decumbent posture, near the altar—a most expressive face; he died in 1585. This church is a noble old large structure, containing many funeral monuments and inscriptions. Just without the church, and under arches, lie in a decumbent posture ten Templars, in their military garb and appurtenances, contained within two separate inclosures. From church retreated with the company into the gardens, always open on Sundays between and after services.

Oct. 16. Visited Mr. A. Savage, and abode there till late in the evening.

Oct. 17. To Oxford-street, to examine some silver Roman denarii and Greek and English coins—for which they require far more than I think them worth—a Cromwell half-crown at thirty-six shillings! But I am not medal mad.

Oct. 18. Received an order from the treasury for my quarterly allowance. Bought ten silver Roman denarii. Mr. Samuel Hirst Sparhawk and Andrew Dalglish drank tea with me.

Oct. 19. Went with Mr. Sparhawk to Disputing Club, at King's Arms, Cornhill—Question : " Is it for the advantage of mankind, that at the institution of government, rewards should have been given to virtue, as well as punishments inflicted for vice ?" The proposer varied the question, or rather dispute, by repeatedly declaring the impossibility of establishing it, from the unsuccessful attempts of ancient nations, as Egyptians, Chinese, former and modern. This point was however contested, as in the instance of the Romans, who made some faint attempts in *corona civica* and *muralis*—allowing valor to be a virtue, and by exempting from taxes the father of four children, placing the increase in society in that predicament; and in modern times the French, in bestowing the order of St. Louis, and even the English in some instances, particularly the order of the Bath—the late honor and pension to Capt. Farmer's eldest son and widow; all of which had and have a tendency to raise an emulation in the breasts of gentlemen in that line. The whole of which and many other fine things on this side the question, were smartly and pointedly ridiculed by a Dr. Dodd, whose brilliancy of expression, liveliness of wit, and keenness of satire, kept the assembly in almost one continued roar of laughter and applause. Some of the speakers acquitted themselves to very general approbation, and none failed to receive marks of applause. However low public virtue and public spirit is thought to be, and unfortunately really is, I could not but remark, with great satisfaction and delight of soul, the loud and very general shouts of applause to every lively, just sentiment and expression in favor or in support of the virtues, public spirit, regard to the constitution, and the rights of mankind.

The room was large and handsomely furnished with glass chandeliers; and the entertainment so highly pleasing, amusing, and instructive, that I am determined to attend hereafter every Thursday evening, when circumstances shall permit. The president enters at eight o'clock, and continues till ten. When the question has been debated, and no one, after a silence of two minutes, offers to rise, he puts the question, or rather reads it very deliberately; the vote is then taken and declared; in the present question, in the negative.

Oct. 25. It being Accession-day, park guns fired—saw a great collection of people.

Oct. 26. Walked with Mr. Dalglish to Hempsted, passing Caen Wood, Lord Mansfield's seat; from thence to Highgate; at Gate-house we dined—from thence to Bagnigge-wells to tea—passing home, we abode there two hours, and departed to King's

Arms, Cornhill Disputing Club ;—question proposed was, " *Would it be proper at this crisis, considering our successes in South Carolina, to offer the Americans independence?*" After much warmth of expression on both sides, though without scurrility or abuse, the question was put; though the first time declared by the president uncertain on which side the majority lay, to me it appeared in the affirmative; none denied the president's declaration. The second time it was plainly in the negative.

Oct. 28. Had an agreeable tête-a-tête with Mr. T. Danforth, on his Holland tour. Dined at Mr. Sparhawk's; company J. Scott, B. Cutler, and a young Mr. Perkins, late from New-York. Heard many novel stories about America and the Americans.

TO REV. JOSEPH BRETLAND, EXETER.

London, Oct. 31, 1780.

DEAR SIR :

I should not have failed to have answered your obliging favor of the 30th ult. before this time, but the daily expectation of giving a satisfactory reply to your inquiry, (concerning the state of the air previous to the darkness on which your conjecture was founded,) has been the only cause of this delay. The young person who brought the relation first to London from Boston, being gone to Holland, has not yet returned ; nor has it been in my power to obtain sight of any one from that country since ; despairing of it for some length of time, I cannot prevail on myself to delay any longer.

Your ingenious accounting for the appearances during and after the darkness is natural, pleasing and intelligible. The trouble you have taken to commit your thoughts on the subject to writing, demands my thanks. The late performance of Dr. Priestley, which you wished me to read, I have bought and read with great delight ; for when the very existence of the Deity, as well as his moral government, is denied and made the scorn and subject of light mirth among the young, thoughtless and profligate, in conversation as well as in the writings of philosophers and pretenders to cool, dispassionate, unprejudiced reasoning, I am pleased to find one of Dr. Priestley's known abilities stand up in support of this most important of all the articles of belief. Two or three difficulties having occurred to me in reading, (which was done in a kind of *currente pede*,) I shall give it a second or third examination, and hope by the friendly aid of my worthy friend, to arrive at a more comprehensive knowledge of the subject. I am glad Mr. H.'s arrogance and malevolence, if you will allow the expression, against moral obligation, is corrected by so masterly a hand; but could wish the doctor had not rated his philosophical abilities so low; for should his defenders find the least mistake, misrepresentation or misquotation, his warmth will be construed to have proceeded from envy and a bitterness of spirit against an author of established fame; nor will the friends to that side of the question fail to magnify it and trumpet it forth to the doctor's disadvantage.

I am sorry I cannot give an answer of a contrary kind to my friend's wish, so flattering to my pride, of my return to Exeter; but the increasing infirmities of old age, the advanced season of the year, and, above all, the approaching period to the American dispute, forbid my leaving the city. I fancy you will wonder at the last reason assigned, but in truth that event, it is my real opinion, is much nearer than is generally expected. I acknowledge I am not acquainted with one courtier or court lounger, nor informed of the deliberations or opinions prevailing in the cabinet. It is from the appearances of affairs only I form my judgment. In a chequered state of things, as is the case in common wars, the sentiments, opinions and judgments of all men vary with the vicissitudinary, changing state of events; but in this baneful, woful quarrel, such a continued, unbroken series of disappointments, disasters and mortifying events have taken place, that it seems to me to be morally impossible but the eyes of all thoughtful, prudent, knowing men must open and discern the impolicy and impracticability of accomplishing the great end for which this war was undertaken—the reduction of the colonies to the obedience of the British parliament. It may be objected that our prospects are brightened, and we are in a course of conquering;—that I deny, for one swallow makes no summer. We have beaten the rebel army, and expelled that army out of Carolina with half their numbers; have rivetted the inhabitants to our interests; they are become loyalists and have sworn allegiance, and that they will always do whilst you can command their estates and persons. This reminds me of the lines in Hudibras:

> " 'Tis he that breaks an oath who makes it ;
> Not he who for convenience takes it."

That the Americans practise this rule is true, but how far they believe it to be just, I won't say. For proof I refer you to Rhode Island, Philadelphia, and those parts of Long Island and the Jerseys, relinquished; there are besides many other instances; while under British power they are loyal, that power removed, they as naturally return to their former condition as any elastic body returns to its natural form when the force is removed. That the reduction of South Carolina with the defeat of Gates will draw North Carolina and Virginia, I no more believe, than that Rodney will overpower either of the fleets of the combined powers, and of course take possession of some of their islands in the West Indies, which nobody dreams of.

The situation of this country respecting neutral powers, is alarming; should Portugal declare against us, we shall not have a port on the sea coast of this terrestrial globe to carry our prisoners into out of our own dominions, whilst all the nations far and near shelter and protect our enemies; and that she is on the point of forsaking our alliance is but too probable. If Great Britain shall retain her rank among the great nations of Europe, and a respectable part of her foreign possessions, the miracle of her salvation will be as great and auspicious as the deliverance of the children of Israel from the oppressive power of Pharaoh and his hosts when they stood trembling on the banks of the Red Sea, just before it opened by divine command to let them pass through, and thereby escape his power. Could my prayers and tears prevail, a plenty should not be wanting to save our country from utter ruin, to which I fear this once happy, favored isle is hastening by large strides.

Please make my compliments to such acquaintances as you know I did and ought to esteem, and believe me very truly,

Your friend,

S. CURWEN.

CHAPTER XIV.

London, Nov. 1, 1780. Went to Parliament House, through Court of Requests to lobby of House of Commons ; thence to passage to the House of Lords ; the crowd in both great. I could gain no admittance. I saw Lord George Germaine for the first time ; a large, stout, raw-boned man. Met Mr. R. Temple and family in the passage to the lords, waiting to see Mr. Querme of the black rod ; questioned him about the state of the air in New England previous to the mid-day darkness in May last year ; he remembered but little about that event, or declined to say much about it. In clearing the house to go to the lords to attend the king's acceptance of their speaker, and hear his speech from the throne, I was drawn away, when otherwise I might have seen Lord North, that for the space of five years, my residence in England, I have not hitherto been favored with.

Nov. 4. Accompanied Mr. Dalglish to La Belle Assemblée, or Ladies' Disputing Society. The question proposed was : " Would it not be prudent and proper, considering the great demand for public supplies, and the difficulty of raising them, to lay a tax on old bachelors ?" The lady who first spoke, moved to alter the question and include old maids, which was objected to by a fine young lady, who answered in a lively, pleasing manner ; her objection was, however, overruled by a vote put by the president. Question then stood as including old maids. Twelve female speakers stood forth in succession, and the question was carried in the affirmative. There were many excellent thoughts expressed and some witty ones ; some acquitted themselves to the approbation of the company. A few, through diffidence or forgetfulness, stopped short in mid-race, and sat down, unable to proceed ; these met with polite and kind indulgence, and were clapped by way of encouragement.

Nov. 8. Towards Guildhall meeting ; great crowds to view the preparations for to-morrow, when the mayor is to be sworn in and invested with the regalia of the chief magistracy. The floor of the hall is raised, half of the lower part partitioned off and inclosed for the entertainment of the lord mayor, aldermen, and common council, with their guests. In the central line, through the whole length, are hung three noble chandeliers, and round the walls, in festoons, are placed small lamps of different colors. The lady mayoress' drawing room is also adorned in the same manner, and a music gallery built up for the present occasion.

Nov. 9. Lord Mayor's day. My lord goes attended in a pompous procession from Guildhall to Queenhithe stairs, and thence in the city barge, gaudily decorated, by water to Whitehall stairs, from whence he rides in a coach to Westminster Hall, to be sworn into his new office by one of the barons of the exchequer. He returns by water to Blackfriars Bridge stairs, where he lands and goes in city stage coach to Guildhall, to partake of the banquet there provided, and pass the remainder of the day in festivity, accompanied by city councils, sheriffs, and other officers. Streets lined with crowds, besides company stands or tents erected in Cheapside, on both sides as far as King-street, leading to Guildhall. A man in complete armor attends the armorer's company on horseback, with such a weight of iron as renders his duty a heavy and fatiguing one. Called on by Samuel Sparhawk, to accompany me to a friend's house on Ludgate hill, for an advantageous sight of the procession, but being too early, continued our walk to the park, where we met Mr. Clark (father-in-law of Mr. Copley) for the first time since my return to London ; he kindly welcomed me back, and invited me to renew my visits at his house.

TO HON. JONATHAN SEWALL, BRISTOL.

London, Nov. 19, 1780.

DEAR SIR :

The delay to answer your favor of August 24, arose solely from successive diappointments in my endeavors to obtain a true and intelligible relation of the state of the air immediately preceding the darkness that covered the face of the heavens on the 19th of last May ; the knowledge of this circumstance seems necessary in order to assign a strictly philosophical reason for it. As the fact at present stands, all reasoning about it depends on the truth of hy-

potheses ; my philosophical friend, Mr. Bretland, of Exeter, has
sent the following conjectural account of its cause, which I shall
transcribe for your amusement, and doubt not you will think it both
ingenious and probable.

" The uncommon phenomenon of which you have favored me
with an account, is deserving the attention of philosophers : the
previous circumstances of the atmosphere where it happened, seem
necessary to enable me to give a satisfactory explication of its
causes. If I may be allowed to conjecture, I suppose that before
it came on, there had been much dry and warm weather, and an
extensive stagnation in the air. If these were the previous circumstances, it may, I think, be accounted for by supposing that the
air having been very much dried, and the putrefaction of lakes and
vegetable substances having become very great and extensive,
there was a copious ascent of vapors, which are well known to
have frequently a blue or purple tinge, and at the same time not
to form themselves into clouds sufficiently dense to obstruct the passage of the rays of light, or wholly interrupt the view of objects
between which and the observer's eye they may chance to be situated, though dense enough to reflect a very large proportion of the
rays of light from the upper surface, and sufficiently colored to
tinge the rays that pass through them, and so communicate their
own color to the objects on which these rays fell. Perhaps you
may more clearly apprehend my meaning by an example. Take
a spectacle-glass, of deep purple color, and look through it at an object, and you will find that you can see the object distinctly ; and
let the light shine through it upon an object, and you will observe
the object but faintly illuminated, and to receive in some degree the
color of the glass. Now the greasy substance that fell in the night,
seems to have formed during part of the day a vast spectacle-glass,
as I may call it, through which the heavens were visible, and from
the rays passing through which, the glass received a blue or purple tinge. The light that came through that immensely large glass
was so little that a great darkness was occasioned by the want of
those inconceivably more numerous rays that were reflected by the
upper surface of the great spectacle-glass, and had no object interposed, would have fallen as usual on the earth's surface. If the
boundaries of the vast spectacle-glass had been discoverable, the

people of Boston would have perceived that there was a vast cloud hanging over them; but as they looked through a medium, the limits of which they could not perceive, they were not able to discover any cloud, but as Mr. Temple justly remarked, the heavens seemed to be covered only with a large transparent veil."

So far my friend.—I could wish it were possible to procure a just account of this necessary circumstance in order to ascertain the true cause of so singular a phenomenon, but this I fear is not obtainable. How great was my disappointment at meeting your informant a few days since in the lobby of the House of Lords, where I had some conversation with him on the subject, but to no purpose, he I fancy not having examined it with a philosopher's attention, or even puzzled his head to investigate natural causes.

Much greater effects might have been expected from the almost miraculous success of Lord Cornwallis, than we have now reason to expect; but knowing my views of things are very different from yours, I will not trouble you with my foreboding fears, and shall bid adieu to the subject, which I never consider without reluctance.

Yours, truly,

S. CURWEN.

Nov. 11. Entered Chancery court, the chancellor sitting as he, or the master of the rolls when he presides, always does, with hat on, taking minutes of the case, as is customary in all the courts for judges to do.

Nov. 12. Attended worship at Essex House chapel; Mr. Lindsay preached. In mid-service, a well dressed Scotch lady entered the pew wherein a gentleman and myself were sitting. After service, she inquired of me if the preacher did not deny the divinity of Christ, or rather, she affirmed that he did; adding, she never heard it so plainly declared in public before; to which I assented, telling her this congregation was set up professedly on Unitarian principles; disavowing all other objects of religious worship and adoration, but the supreme, everlasting God, the Father and Lord of the universe, the God and Father of our Lord Jesus Christ; who, in the text, is declared to be the Son of the everlasting God. The settled members hold themselves the disciples of Christ, and members of that body of which he is head. She

further added, that Mr. L. was a Socinian; which I neither was
disposed nor could I deny, referring her to himself for a justification of his principles, as far as he could make it satisfactory to her,
if her curiosity or wishes led her to make further inquiries; giving
her a short relation of his conduct with respect to his forsaking the
Church of England, whereof he was a settled minister seven years
ago; but his scruples in relation to the divinity of Christ had
forced him to relinquish a valuable living, and lucrative, honorable
prospects in that establishment, for an uncertain support among
those of his own more liberal sentiments; and his integrity had
been rewarded here by this society. She seemed disposed to
lengthen our conversation, but having said all I had proposed to
impart at present, took a sudden leave.

After tea, called on Mr. Dalglish; whom, with his friend, I
accompanied in a coach to " Carlisle House," at a Sunday evening
entertainment, called the promenade, instituted in lieu of public
amusement; and to compensate for twelve tedious hours interval
laid under an interdict by the laws of the country, yet unrepealed
formally by the legislature, though effectually so in the houses of
the great and wealthy, from whence religion and charity are but
too generally banished.   The employment of the company is
simply walking through the rooms; being allowed tea, coffee, cho-
colate, lemonade, orgeat, negus, milk, &c.; admission by ticket,
cost, three shillings; dress, decent, full not required; some in
boots; one carelessly in spurs happening to catch a lady's flounce,
he was obliged to apologize and take them off.   The ladies were
rigged out in gaudy attire, attended by bucks, bloods, and macca-
ronies, though it is also resorted to by persons of irreproachable
character : among the wheat will be tares.   The arrangement of
the house is as follows :—From the vestibule where the tickets are
received, the entrance is through a short passage into the first room,
of a moderate size, covered with carpets, and furnished with wooden
chairs and seats in Chinese taste ; through this the company
passes to another of a larger size, furnished and accommodated as
the former ; passing this, you enter the long-room, about eighty
feet by forty ; this is the largest, and lighted with glass chandeliers
and branches fixed to side walls, against which stand sofas covered
with silk,—floors carpeted. Hence tending to the left, you cross

the hall, and enter the wilderness or grotto, having natural evergreens planted round the walls; the centre an oblong square, about twenty-five feet long and fifteen broad, fenced with an open railing, a few shrubs interspersed, flowering moss and grass; in one of the angles is a natural well, with a living spring, which the attendant told me was mineral. Fronting the entrance, in the centre, at the further end is a cave cased with petrifactions, stones artificially cut into resemblance of the former, and spars, with here and there a dim lamp so placed as to afford but an imperfect sight of surrounding objects. To the top of the arch leading to the cave, is an ascent of two flights of steps on each hand, and over it a room not unlike in form the cave below, painted in modern style in oval compartments, containing hieroglyphics and ancient stories; on the same elevation is a narrow gallery, continued on either side to about half the length of room, fronted near three feet high with an open Chinese fence or railing:—this room is about fifty feet deep by thirty wide, lighted as the others with variegated lamps, but rather dim; next enter into two tea rooms, each with tables for forty sets or parties.

So far for my imperfect description of this house, wherein the well known Mrs. Cornelly used to accommodate the nobility, etc. with masquerades and coteries. Dress of the ladies differed widely; one part swept their track by long trails, the other by an enormous size of hoops and petticoats. The company usually resorting there about seven hundred, as the ticket receiver told me;—this evening the house was thronged with a good thousand. The rooms were filled, so that we could scarce pass without jostling, interfering and elbowing; for my own part, being old, small and infirm, I received more than a score of full butt rencounters with females;—whether provision was not made for so large a company, or whatever the cause may be, it was full two hours before I could procure a dish of tea, after fifteen vain attempts, nor was I singular; and when served, it was in a slovenly manner on a dirty tea-stand. I never saw a place of public resort where the company was treated with so little respect by servants; even common tea-houses, whose character is far humbler, as " Bagnigge Wells," " White Conduit House," " Dog and Duck," etc., are in this respect preferable. It would be treating " Ranelagh" with great indignity to bring it into comparison with this which is designed to supply its place during the long vacation of that fashionable resort; nor are Vauxhall Gardens less than a thousand times beyond this in every eligible circumstance, unless I saw it under peculiar disadvantages.

Met Peter Frye and young William Eppes there; also saw the Duke of Queensbury, who I was told is a never failing attendant on places of dissipation, which his seeming age should, one might think, restrain him from such juvenile amusements; but old habits are strong, and too powerful to be resisted when long indulged. Tired of this scene I took myself off at the early hour of twelve, and bidding adieu to Carlisle House, after a few *égaremens* arrived with no small content at my own lodgings.

Nov. 14. While rambling, Montague House came in view; it occurred to me to take another view of the Museum; I entered and applied to Dr. Harper, the under-librarian, who referred me to the ticket porter for admission the following day at eleven o'clock. Arriving at home, Wm. Cabot drank tea with me; S. Sparhawk came in afterwards, and abode two hours; from whom I heard the first account of Arnold's intentional withdrawing himself and four or five thousand troops under his command from congressional service to the royal standard at New-York; the failure of this scheme of treachery, and his lucky escape from his enemies' hands. From him also the relation of the seizure of Mr. Laurens' papers, late president of the Congress, and now a state prisoner in the tower; giving an account of the desperate situation of their affairs, with complaints of failure of their resources, and their inability to support the war any longer without loans from Holland, France or Spain. The above comes from Benjamin Thompson,* a native of Massachusetts, (formerly an apprentice to my next door neighbor in Salem, Mr. John Appleton, an importer of British goods,) now under-secretary in the American department.

Nov. 15. Mr. Snelson calling at my lodgings by accident, I told him of my intention of visiting the British Museum, and took him with me. Dr. Gifford, the librarian, indulged me with the admittance of my companions without a ticket. The company numerous, of both sexes; several inquisitive and chatty ladies not a little heightening the entertainment. In the Harleian collection

---

* Afterwards Count Rumford.

was an ancient manuscript, near twelve hundred years old, most curiously illuminated; a copy of Genesis in Greek capitals, written by Origen's own hand in a quarto size, inclosed in a beautiful tin-gilt box resembling that fold, containing only its remains, being unfortunately almost wholly destroyed in the Cotton library conflagration many years ago. On the same shelves were also many others of distant antiquity in the same wretched plight with this. Here also is the remains of the original Magna Charta, granted by King John at Runnymead, part of which is scorched and illegible by the same catastrophe. An exact but not perfectly fac simile copy stands by its parent's side, with the arms of those noble barons who extorted it from that unworthy prince, emblazoned and surrounding it. Also that most valuable manuscript, the Alexandrian copy of the Bible, in Greek capitals, of fourteen hundred years' duration.

Among the shell-fish kind is one of the smallest size, which looks like the vertebræ of a small animal, for which an Italian curioso paid three thousand sequins. Sir Hans Sloane at length became possessed of it for thirty pounds sterling! Among pearls is one of the size of a pea, of a light purplish water, valued at five hundred pounds. So liberal of money are men of curiosity, that the last mentioned sum has been offered for it. The innumerable curiosities in the natural as well as artificial way, coming fast upon me, confounded my memory; the latter destroying the traces of the former by the quickness of their transition. Dr. Gifford's respectful and cheerful attention is very pleasing; he is eighty-one years old, lively and sprightly to an uncommon degree. I observed against the wall of the Cotton library a bust of Pope Benedict XIV., called from the liberality of his sentiments " the Protestant pope." In the room of antiquities received from Sir William Hamilton, and brought from Italy, is a vase having an inscription of Etruscan original, in the ancient mode of writing in Greece, soon after the importation of the sixteen letters from Phenicia by Cadmus.

Nov. 16. State lottery being to be drawn, curiosity led me to Guildhall, where a gallery for spectators is erected with seats, one of which I obtained for sixpence. The first object that struck me was a great number of clerks writing down the numbers of tickets and quality as they were proclaimed. The wheels were placed

on either hand upon a stage raised about six feet from the floor, at
the bottom of the hall under Beckford's statue; between were
seated the commissioners at a long table, and a boy at each wheel.
After delivering the ticket the boy raises his hand above his head
with fingers displayed open, and after two flourishes thrusts it into
the wheel, delivering the tickets severally to the man on either
side, who on cutting the tickets open, being tied and sealed, declares the number. To prevent future pranks from boys employed
to draw out the ñumbers, a commissioner sits in a box directly
opposite each boy and near him; who besides is obliged on taking
out each number to raise up his hand, holding the ticket between
his fore finger and thumb, delivering it to the man, who after
cutting it open announces its fate or fortune.

Walked to New England Coffee-house to inquire after new
lodgings; from thence to the Disputing Club at King's Arms
Tavern, Cornhill; the question to be spoken, for properly it was
not debated, was, " *Can the doctrine of polygamy, endeavored to be
established by a well known divine in a late publication, be defended
on the principles of reason, religion, or sound policy ?*" After many
humorous and some solid arguments against it, in defence however
of which no one stood up on Dr. Maddam the author's grounds,
it was voted in the negative, one hand only in affirmative, producing a hiss or laugh of contempt and indignation. A gentleman
whom I took to be in the law line, stood up and modestly said the
argument had not had a fair discussion, as no one appeared but to
condemn and reprobate; and after an apology, presumed to suppose it might under certain regulations and restrictions by the
legislature, in certain supposable cases, be allowed, whereby some
evils, the too common attendants of matrimony, might be avoided
without incurring greater evils. This met with not the least countenance, yet the speaker, who was a well behaved man of knowledge and ability, was treated with respect. It was moved that the
company should publicly reprobate the doctrine, but prudential
considerations prevailed to negative the motion.

Nov. 21. Left cards and compliments at Mr. Clarke's for
himself and Mr. and Mrs. Copley, who are abroad.

Nov. 22. Mrs. Cowley, a celebrated playwright, dined with
us; she is a small, sprightly body. Evening at a new play called
" *Generous Impostor.*"

Nov. 23.   Went to Crown Coffee-house to meet Mr. Arthur Savage, disappointed;—proceeded to Westminster Hall—courts sitting.   Saw Lord Loughborough for the first time since his title and presidency of the common pleas; he was single on the bench, being on trials after term.   Saw Judge Buller on king's bench; he appears shrewd, quick, ready, and promises for an active judge—this being my first sight of him since his advancement.

Nov. 24.   Taking out Mr. Dalglish, proceeded to Adelphi Hotel to visit, *en passant*, Col. Peter Frye and his daughter, Mrs. Oliver;* after a short stay departed for Westminster Hall, the doors of neither Lords nor Commons being open; returning passed through the Park, and met Samuel Sparhawk, who joined us to Spring Garden Coffee-house.

Nov. 28.   At Westminster Hall; courts sitting.   Mr. Justice Skinner, lately advanced to chief baronship on exchequer bench. Saw Mr. Justice Heath on common pleas bench, whom I knew and frequently saw a sergeant at Exeter, his birth place.

Nov. 29.   Six provinces out of seven of the Dutch union have acceded to the armed neutrality of the north, to prevent British search of neutral ships suspected of carrying naval and military stores to the enemy.

Sunday, December 3.   Walked up the Strand, when to my surprise I found myself all alone, not a person within sight, not a coach to be seen or heard; which, considering the hour, (five P. M.) was singular.   In this predicament I walked on a hundred yards or more; arrived at Spring Garden Coffee-house, and over a dish of tea read the Morning Post, containing letters of Generals Washington, Clinton, Arnold, and Major André.   The latter, though pitied here, perhaps justly, is doubtless to be ranked in the class of spies, and his punishment, however censured here, was in my mind not undeservedly inflicted, and to be justified by the universal practice of all nations, civilized and uncivilized, on persons of that character.

Dec. 4.   At New England Coffee-house, where conversed for the first time with William Jackson, from whom learnt particular circumstances of harsh treatment he received from fierce partisans in Boston, Newburyport, etc.

Dec. 5.   Evening at Patagonian Theatre, Exeter 'Change; a

* Afterwards the wife of Sir John Knight.

bauble of a thing. The show a burlesque farce, but I know not of what; performance in puppetry, speakers below the stage and invisible; machinery awkward, scenery pretty. Among the auditors was Lord Molesworth.

Dec. 12. Samuel H. Sparhawk called; accompanied him to Ladies' Disputing Club, at King's Arms, Cornhill. A lady presided and acquitted herself very commendably. *Question: " Was Adam or Eve most culpable in paradise?"* Mrs. President addressed the assembly with great propriety, just accent and pleasing voice; explaining the nature of the meeting; justifying ladies appearing to speak in a public promiscuous assembly. She was frequently applauded; on ascending the chair, she turned round and gracefully saluted the company, discovering perfect self-possession, void of all embarrassment. The other speakers also acquitted themselves laudably, and were frequently clapped. Some spoke, I won't say argued, on one side, some on the other; very little serious argument, unless declamation, quotations from Hudibras, etc. can be so denominated. The subject afforded matter for mirth, but the most serious speeches turned against the mother of us all.

The concluding speech was foreign to the question; the subject was the term " congress." The speakers were lively, and their wit and humor produced shouts of laughter. The principal speaker introduced her speech by observing that the word being understood here as implying rebellion, she at first apprehended American ladies were coming over in shoals to seduce the young gentlemen from our island ladies; but after considering the subject, and being informed by a clergyman, to whom she applied for its meaning, had found that the word has a harmless signification, and had been used on this side the water in treaties of peace, as the congress of ambassadors of belligerent powers at Nimeguen, Aix-la-Chapelle, etc., that it is derived from a Latin word signifying a meeting together to compose or reunite discordant parties. She was pleased to hear it was not likely to give disgust to our state physicians, who were laudably employing their skill and labor in administering harsh medicines to the disordered members of our consumptive empire. After a series of lively observations, she closed by wishing success to the institution, and that it may do honor to female eloquence. Question being put, whether Adam was most in fault, vote by three hands only, negatived by one. Thus Eve stands acquitted in this female school of oratory of being the most guilty, though I fancy the major part considered as females are not so clear in the affirmative.

Mrs. Hayley, the great frequenter of all public city assemblies, was there. A small interruption happened by a dirty boy's mixing with the company; the president declared her surprise at it. In all large public collections of people of mixed character, persons of unruly disposition are to be found, who will indulge themselves in undue freedoms, if it can be done with impunity.

Dec. 14. Col. Browne called on me twice to-day in my absence.

Dec. 15. Called on Col. Browne and also on Arthur Savage; both out, the latter gone to Bristol with William Cabot. In my way, met Thomas Hutchinson, whom I had not seen for four years.

Dec. 17. Afternoon, accompanied by John Parkhouse, I attended the famous Herries' chapel of ease, St. John square; he preached in an animated style, with oratorical delivery, to an audience crowded and respectable.

Dec. 19. Called on Mr. R. Clarke, in company with Col. Browne; we were invited to Mr. Copley's picture-room, wherein were two exhibition pieces, viz., Brooke Watson's wonderful deliverance from a great shark that had twice seized him, and had bitten off one leg. The other piece, Copley's own family, comprising himself, wife, and three children, and his father-in-law, Mr. Clark. Here is also a large piece representing the House of Lords, when Lord Chatham, in the height of his patriotic zeal, was seized with a fit which proved fatal; the piece represents the moment of his being raised from the floor on which he had fallen, and was lying in the arms and lap of the Duke of Cumberland, his son-in-law; number of lords sixty, in their dresses, attitudes, etc., either as they then stood, or as the painter fancied they might, faces taken from life as they successively sat for this purpose. It is to be engraved for a print, deliverable next August twelvemonth, at three guineas each. Mrs. Hay appeared in view so very like, that the first glance announced for whom it was intended. After amusing ourselves for some time, took leave and separated at door. This day removed my lodgings to No. 10 Furnival's Inn court. Appear ances are for enjoyment here; experience manifold has taught me not to rely on them, nor shall I draw up a verdict till supported by issue at departure.

Dec. 20.   William Jackson called, (he lodges at No. 5 this court,) and passed the evening till tea.

Dec. 21.   More snow has fallen than has been known to be on ground at once, or in same space of time, for many years.

Dec. 23.   Samuel H. Sparhawk called to let me know he had received letters from New England so late as October 19.   Mr. Jos. Green died about three weeks ago.

Dec. 26.   Called on Mr. Peters; he was absent, being officially engaged at church, this being St. Andrew's day.

Dec. 28.   This is my birth-day, allowing for difference occasioned by altering the style. This day I have completed a circle of sixty-four years; but to how little moral advantage, it humiliates me to think. May the short remainder of my probationary state be marked with brighter lines, and the review of the interval, the present and last hour of my rational life, when that awful and important hour shall arrive, yield me a comfort that the retrospect of the past cannot afford.

Being at Furnival's Inn Coffee-house, Mr. Peters and a Methodist parson entered, joining company and conversation for a short time.

Dec. 29.   Paid my first mourning visit to Mr. Joseph Green's widow; she seems greatly oppressed with grief.

Dec. 31.   Attended public worship at Essex-street chapel.

CHAPTER XV.

London, January 1, 1781. The first day of the new year; may it please God to crown the endeavors of good men to bring about that desirable event, peace and quietness among the contending powers, before another annual revolution, to the honor and safety of all concerned.

Jan. 2. Dined at Barley-mow, Salisbury court. Meeting Harrison Gray, learnt the capture of the vessel in which S. Conant sailed from Holland ; she was carried into Cork. By this means, several letters I addressed to different friends are thrown into the abyss.

Jan. 3. I know not whether the mercantile portion of the nation consider aught but present objects—view of gain by privateering—always successful at commencement of war. Ships of the enemy being generally unprepared for defence, fall an easy prey; they therefore seem pleased with the spirited declaration of the sovereign, if it may be called, of war. Letters of marque and reprisal offered. By Lloyd's books three hundred Dutch merchant ships are taken and safely moored in our ports, and more than three thousand sailors. But this additional weight, added to that of France, Spain and America, already on our hands, the successful issue of which we seem to have but too much cause to despair of, calls for united bravery, intrepidity, and efforts that this nation has in times of like imminent danger exerted, and by divine favor, with unexpected success. May we still experience the same kind and favorable interposition, and make more grateful returns. Dined in Salisbury court. Samuel Sparhawk drank tea with me, and told me of my townsman Col. Browne's advancement to the governorship of Bermuda ; an unexpected elevation, and I doubt not acceptable to himself, encumbered, as he is, with a wife and three children.

Jan. 6. Mr. Peters and Mr. Erving called; the latter's lodgings, Charlotte-street, Islington.

Jan. 9. Accompanied Mr. Dalglish to Covent Garden Theatre; comedy, Busy-body,—entertainment, the tasty performance of *Freemason procession,*—scenery pompous, former part to my taste unpleasing—Harlequin in dumb show ; why he is said to be a freemason, I cannot divine, unless investing him with a square, one of their badges, suspended by a ribbon and hung round his neck, so constitutes him. The skipping about of an antic dressed out in a merry-andrew's coat, his face covered with black crape, and a wooden sword by his side, put on for the purpose of showing how ready he is at drawing it forth to slap his brother antics on face, shoulders, etc. ; displaying the wonders of his transforming power in converting trunks, dogs, and chests, into watch-boxes, arbors, chimney-pieces, etc. ; his principal aim being to make grimaces and wry faces at his favorite Columbine, who, by the way, is a fine-looking girl, and made to be deeply in love with a fantastic ape, without one probable reason for it. These species of pantomime seem at present greatly in vogue ; to arraign the taste is perhaps conceited ; but this remark will never come to light, if ever, till, 1 dare say, it will be as despised as it is now relished, especially by the more enlightened class ; as to the lower, they ever were and ever will be too gross for any entertainment above the lowest humor. I am, I confess, so totally void of all relish for such diversions, that I forbear condemning them, although I consider them as a proof among many others of the depravity of the present day. I would fain call it vulgar, but too many box spectators seem to enjoy it and join the galleries. I can't, however, but believe that all sensible persons do disapprove of these shows as unworthy, but dare not openly avow their opinion. The comedy was excellent, and well performed ; and much exceeds in point of wit, plot, etc., the, to me, flattish sentimental compositions of the present day, with a few exceptions. After the silly harlequin had skipped behind scenes, a most grand procession began, preceded by a standard of light red color, the ground of all the following ones : the first contained a scroll whereon was painted in large golden letters, ENOCH, the first grand-master ; his representative following, accompanied by two attendants ; at a little interval appeared, NIMROD, second grand-master, with his representative and four attendants ; next was brought the front of the temple of the Sun at Thebes; afterwards, the great pyramid of Egypt and the sphynx; then, front of the temple of Jerusalem, built by King Solomon; Pharaoh's two daughters next followed, attended by their Egyptian and Jewish female and male servants, the high-priest properly habited, holding a pot of incense in his hand,—breast-plate, and other insignia on,—closing with a long stream of attendants and servants in rear; next, front of Pantheon at Rome, the founder or repairer, for it is uncertain which, M. Agrippa's name in a list under the capital; then, temple of Jerusalem, built by Herod, destroyed by Vespasian, represented as in flames; next, William the Conqueror, and behind him was carried a prospective view of the tower of London, as if built by him; then, Edward the Third, accompanied by his son clad in black armor, from thence denominated the Black Prince,—giving liberty to, and taking the chains off the legs of two captive kings, John of France, and James II. of Scotland, at the instance of his son, followed by a train of attendants; the front of St. Peter's at Rome then succeeded, Julius II. having in his hand a crosier, and on his head a triple crown,—alluding to his regal authority: he was attended by a train of ecclesiastic officers and servants, and had the keys hanging to his girdle, as lord chamberlain of the state-rooms in the upper regions, and jailer in the lower dungeons;—and like Jack Ketch, who sometimes has a practice of his own office tried on himself, it will be a wonder if some of the pontifical jailers, when others succeed, have not the keys of lower apartments turned upon them.

Next in order came Queen Elizabeth, dressed in royal robes, and attended by her servants, both state and domestic; then followed King James, surrounded by court sycophants; front of banqueting-house as it now stands, undefiled and undilapidated; next, Guy Fawkes, in dress of his day, holding a dark lantern,—alluding to the gunpowder-plot,—he was forcibly seized and carried off; next followed Inigo Jones, the restorer of Greek and Roman taste in architecture, preceded by an ensign, having his name in a scroll, with the masonic letters D. G. W.; then came Charles II. and attendants, followed by the front of St. Paul's, the present noble structure, founded in his reign; at length appeared William and Mary, the former holding a sheet of paper with this inscription, *Bill of Rights,*—words that I wish could be indelibly impressed on the minds of kings, lords, commons, courtiers, and people of this island; for, on the practical remembrance of this short sentence, depends the security of this unparalleled constitution, which I verily fear is near its dissolution. Then followed the grand-master, seated in a magnificent alcove; then an arch, having an inscription, *Ancient Masonry ;* then two pillars, on the top of each a globe,—on one the celestial, the other a terrestrial,—and on a list, by which they were kept steady, was inscribed *Modern Masonry.* The last in the procession were Solomon and Pharaoh's daughter, seated on a throne of state, and over it a rich canopy raised by six steps; on the bottom steps, on each side, stood two lions guardant, between them two young Egyptian damsels, dressed in white,—and on each side of the throne, all the principal personages of the procession ranged, with standards displayed, made a grand and glittering appearance. A fine chorus was sung, and when ended, a universal shout of applause rang through the house, and the curtain dropped.

Jan. 10. An extremely cold day, scarcely ever exceeded in New England; abode within all day, glad to have a shelter, which many a poor wretch wants. I never felt stronger reasons for gratitude; may the sense of it ever remain on my mind, for sure I am it is a most pleasing sensation or feeling.

Jan. 12. Mr. Timmins brought me a packet from Salem, by way of St. Kitt's, containing a long letter from Dr. Holyoke, and one from Richard Ward.

Jan. 15. Colonel Erving and Mr. Arthur Savage called.

Jan. 16. Visited Mr. Wiswall; accompanied Mr. Dalglish, at his desire, to a visit at Samuel H. Sparhawk's. A second unsuccessful one to Mr. Hughes, who was keeping his birth-day at his sister Hutchin's.

Jan. 17. Drank tea with Mr. Barnes, his lodgings, No. 5 our court; in conversation till eleven.

Jan. 19. Visited Treasurer Gray,—he absent; his son John at home. S. H. Sparhawk and Mr. Barnes took tea with me, and passed evening; former says a Mrs. Thompson, arrived from New England, informs that people in Massachusetts utter complaints and discontents at Congress and the French without restraint;—when common sense resumes its reign, as it usually does, sooner or later, the scales which party zeal had clapped over the eyes of the deluded people will fall off, and they will discover the errors their own madness and ill-judged submission to leaders of selfish wicked schemes have seduced them into.   She adds, continental dollar bills have, notwithstanding congressional authority, sunk to sixteen for one since their emission, though sent abroad for the express purpose of restoring their credit ; so ineffectual is human power to create something out of nothing ; also reports, that taxes are risen to such a height as to exceed the produce of the land. Those who have left America since the rupture, have brought accounts so exaggerated that renders it prudent to receive them with caution, and not give too hasty credit.   However, that the people are oppressed with taxes, is notorious ; that they are in want of money, of the common essential articles, is also well known ; and personal safety is very precarious, etc.   Nothing, I presume, but despair, under the power of an American and French army, can reduce this once happy people. May these destructive locusts soon be expelled from the face of the country, and selfish purposes be abandoned ; for the true interest of the English government consists in a friendly and indissoluble union of all its members.

Jan. 21. To No. 8 Haymarket, to see Lieut. William Browne, (my friend Col. Browne's son,) of the 38th regiment ; he had departed for Portsmouth in order to take shipping for Gibraltar.

TO JONATHAN SEWALL, ESQ., BRISTOL.

London, Jan. 23, 1781.

DEAR SIR :

A few days since, I received a long letter from our common friend, Doctor Holyoke, who informs me that the winter of '79— 80, exceeded any since 1740. It began before the middle of December, and it should seem, lasted till June nearly ; no vegetation taking place till the last week in May ; that the snow continued to fall till the 11th of January, when it was between two and three feet deep.   Not a day in all January, nor till 10th of February, was it warmer at eight o'clock A. M. than twenty-eight degrees of Farenheit's scale,—which I fancy pretty thoroughly cooled them ; and, on the 29th of January, the mercury stood at six degrees below zero within doors, and abroad sunk two degrees lower. Under all our distresses, we here enjoy, he says, one prospect promising public happiness in future :—four or five years since, less than half a pint of Siberian wheat was sown among them, producing so incredibly, that, in the northern counties of New England especially, there is reason to believe the harvest this year will yield seed enough for the whole state another year.

Notwithstanding the evil doings of our countrymen, are not you pleased to think they are likely to become independent of the southern colonies, and eat, like the inhabitants of the other improved countries on the face of the earth, Christian's food, and be no longer confined to that which everywhere else is raised only for the nourishment of horses and poultry ? I am glad at heart, but fear that even this blessing, like food taken into a disordered stomach abounding in acrimonious juices, but the more increases its morbid state—for this unexpected supply, and at this juncture, will afford the crafty, political, and spiritual misguides among them but too plausible an occasion to trumpet forth this seemingly seasonable interposition of divine Providence in their favor, and confirm and harden them, amidst all their sufferings, in their infatuated destructive resistance to a power as necessary in my mind to their safety and honor as a parent to his children in an infant state. Nor do I fancy it would be a difficult matter for the aforementioned gentry to persuade them that Moses and Joshua's prophetical declarations to the children of Israel, that they should possess a land flowing with milk and honey, and be filled with the finest of the wheat— the two former of which you know they had plenty enough before, —did ultimately refer to themselves, was typical of them, and was now accomplishing—so entirely do they seem to have surrendered up their understandings to the insinuations and influence of their guides. The last year's taxes in Massachusetts were more than commensurate to the produce of their lands, under the best improvement ; if the force that keeps them under such deplorable circumstances is not insurmountable, their political folly exceeds any recorded in history.

With perfect esteem, your friend,
S. Curwen.

TO REV. ISAAC SMITH, SIDMOUTH.

London, Jan. 24, 1781.

DEAR SIR :

Were I to write a theme, as you know was customary in the last years at our schools, and should choose Tully's celebrated line for the subject, " *cedant arma togæ, concedat laurea linguæ,*" our Massachusetts might be quoted as an example. For amidst the din and clash of arms, the hurry, tumult, and confusion of war, as though they were enjoying the sweetest blessings of a well established, secure peace, the rulers of the present government there have instituted and incorporated a society for promoting literature and the liberal arts, etc., by the name of the " *American Academy of Arts and Sciences* ;" of which the following is a short relation, received lately from my friend Dr. Holyoke : " Our legislature has lately incorporated sundry gentlemen in the several counties, to the number of sixty, enabling them to hold real and personal estate, and has granted them other ample powers and privileges, for the purpose of promoting those arts and sciences which may be either useful or ornamental to society." To which he adds, " I doubt not, you will wish the society may flourish ; the cause of science being the cause of humanity." I do fervently wish its encouragement and increase ; glad at heart that they have been disposed to promote any plan to soften that ferocity and hardness of heart which war, rapine, and plunder have lately spread among them, and which the wisest and most prudent among them have viewed with horror. I have never read this paragraph in my friend's letter, but it reminded me of a line in Horace, unless I mistake the author, *Emollit mores nec sinit esse feros.** I was, for a time, at a loss to account for their choice of this particular period for such a purpose, considering the great and important business upon their hands of forming a new state, etc., but am now fully satisfied the foregoing hint was the true and pressing cause.

Dr. Langdon has quitted the chair of the presidency of Harvard College, but for what reason I am not acquainted.

The late emission of paper by Congress cannot find credit enough to obtain a currency—the old bills are eighty for one.

I remain truly yours,   S. CURWEN.

* Letters soften and refine the character.

TO ROWLAND SAVAGE, ESQ., HALIFAX.

London, Jan. 25, 1781.

DEAR SIR:

By mere accident, going to the " *Blue Post*," almost opposite my lodgings, I saw Mrs. Savage, which gave me great pleasure; by her I was informed of your appointment at Halifax, being the first intelligence concerning you since my ill-omened departure from America. Hope your post affords a genteel subsistence; in these times, no unfavorable circumstance to refugees, in which case I most heartily congratulate you. Wishing you a supply and continuance of all needful blessings,   I am your friend,

                                        S. CURWEN.

Jan. 27. Mr. Barnes called on me to inquire about Colonel Erving's lodgings, Islington.

Jan. 28. At St. Paul's—Dr. Whitfield preached; company, as usual, small but respectable. Passed an hour at Gray's Inn Coffee-house; received a list of the seized and forfeited estates in Massachusetts.

Feb. 1. Dined at White Heart inn, Bishopgate-street, at Mr. Dalglish's invitation, in company with Messrs. H. Hughes, Hutchins, John Inman, and Whitlock.

Feb. 5. At Westminster Hall, being the important day of Lord George Gordon's trial; floor stowed as bale goods in a ship, and as closely packed. Soon took myself off, rather than hazard death by suffocation:—the collection was miscellaneous. Trial lasted till four o'clock next morning, when he was acquitted on the score of insanity.

Feb. 6. Accompanied Mr. Arthur Savage to Clerkenwell, by his desire, to view an old secularized religious house, called Priory, now belonging to the Duke of Portland, tenanted by a carpenter and undertaker, who civilly accompanied us through; there is now nothing remaining of old buildings but a small portion of cloisters, at the end whereof is cut, " *Jordan Bridget, Murrell Bridget, founders*, 1100." In a distant part are small remains of a wall, supposed to be in a state of decay, and the two arches, a larger and a smaller, the former ornamented, and both portions of a circle, which form prevailed before the introduction of the Gothic or Norman styles. Returning from thence, turned into a court of several narrow alleys, filled with small huttish kind of houses, the habitations of filth and vice, named *Blueberry Alley,* notorious for its constant supply of Tyburn. Ten have been dragged out from thence in one session, for thievery and other enormities, and graced the halter. Met our late Mr. Fisher; I turned in with him to Mr. Hutchins' auction room, who was then employed in disposing of natural and artificial curiosities, from the South Sea, just imported in the "Resolution."

Feb. 7. Visited Col. Browne and lady; meeting Mr. Dalglish, took him with me, and after a short stay departed to Mr. Timmins's; thence to Mr. Arthur Savage's, Brompton-row.

Feb. 9. Mr. Dalglish called for me to accompany him to Greenwich Hospital; walking to Gracechurch-street, after half an hour's delay, entered stage and soon arrived there, and thoroughly examined it within and without. Dined in a detached room belonging to a tavern in the town, built and projecting over the river Thames, from whence is a view of the Isle of Dogs, Blackwall and Long Reach. Returned in stage; in our passage was told the following : — an inhabitant of this town walks every day and has done so for some years back, from seven to eight miles, having measured within the period from whence the computation began to some months since, forty-five thousand miles. Evening at Crown Tavern Lodge; Quick, the celebrated comedian, was raised to masonry— a humorous, funny companion, who I fancy intends to entertain the public with the secrets of this society.

Feb. 10. Accompanied Mr. Barnes to St. Nicholas College Abbey, Old Fish-street. Dr. Porteus, Bishop of Chester, preached an excellent and elegant sermon, in style and composition, and pleasingly delivered.

Feb. 13. Visited by Parson Peters, and Parson Clarke, late a townsman; from a cold taken on board a prison ship in Boston harbor, to which he was consigned by the patriots in punishment of toryism, he has lost his voice, and is scarce able to articulate. This, added to his deafness, renders him a lonely, pitiable object; he has received twenty pounds per annum from the society for propagating the gospel—government declining to give him a settled stipend, though it has once and again presented him with a scanty gratuity.

Feb. 15.   At Col. Browne's.   Mrs. Browne informed me of her treatment at Salem and Boston, after her husband's departure to England.

Feb. 16.   At Bow church to hear an annual sermon to society for propagating the gospel in *partibus transmarinis;* Dr. Hurd, bishop of Lichfield and Coventry preached ; present the lord mayor, two sheriffs, two archbishops, Butler of Oxford, Thomas of Rochester, and Markham of York.

Feb. 19.   Evening, at an address on heads, exhibited in transparency, as follows : Sterne, a pathetic apostrophe ; Capt. Cook, the celebrated circumnavigator, an encomium, etc.   Breslau's surprising tricks on cards followed, interluded with music, and an imitation of the thrush, blackbird, sky-lark, nightingale, wood-lark and quail.

Feb. 24.   To theatre to see Mrs. Cowley's new play ; unfortunately it was hissed off the stage just before the conclusion of the last act ; being in its progress of acting alternately and frequently hissed by its foes and cheered by its friends ; the latter proved the minority, and therefore unsuccessful, as all in minorities are in state and church, as well as theatres.   Many came for the express purpose of supporting or damning it ; her husband, a writer in one of the daily papers, employs his pen in criticising works of all other stage writers, and has by the severity of his remarks raised up a host of determined foes, to crush whatever proceeds from his quarter ; though no foreign considerations were needed to banish this piece from the stage, its own intrinsic unworthiness was more than enough ; being a low performance, and unworthy the pen of the author of " *Belle's Stratagem*" and " *Who's the Dupe.*" Knowing the writer and her connections, I feel severely for them, especially, too, as her brother is a fellow lodger, whose exquisite delicacy of feeling must be cruelly wounded on this occasion.   The prologue and epilogue were excellent, and did great credit to the performers, Mr. Lewis and Miss Young, who were rewarded with universal applause.

Feb. 26.   Drank tea at the widow Greene's in company with two Misses Joye of Boston, by whom I was informed of the follow-

ing : viz., a younger son of Francis Greene from Boston, who was
born deaf and dumb, who was under the tuition of a person in
Scotland, in the course of one year arrived to the power of forming
articulate sounds, and can now converse on any subject so intelli-
gibly as to be understood without difficulty by those acquainted
with him; music only excepted; he writes letters with propriety
and even elegance.   This person engages to instruct dumb pupils
in all languages, and has examples of his success to prove his art;
he has more than a hundred now under his management.   A proposal is about to be presented to the king by the Duke of Montague for establishing academies in several parts of England, to
instruct children of the poorer sort in this unhappy predicament, on
a public foundation ;—may it succeed, and thereby be brought into
usefulness many of promising parts.   This plan is suggested by Dr.
Hunter, whose avocations render it impracticable to himself.

March 8.   Met three of my countrymen at three different
times, Dr. Perkins, Mr. R. Clarke, and Mr. Elisha Hutchinson.

March 10.   Col. now Governor Browne, called on me with
complaints of my neglect, which sundry avocations caused.

March 11.   At Charing Cross just as there was passing a most
pompous procession of funeral coaches, attended on each side by
numerous flambeaux-men holding in their hands lighted torches in
branches of four.

March 12.   Passed eight hours at Col. Browne's in a friendly
tête-a-tête.

March 22.   To Westminster Hall, and passing through, came
to foot of steps leading to the lobby of the House of Commons,
where, seeing an officer standing unemployed, I inquired about the
disposition and arrangement of rooms belonging to, and under and
adjoining the pile called St. Stephen's Chapel, lords' house, star
chamber, painted and Jerusalem chamber; and from him received
a more particular and satisfactory account than I had ever before
had.   Proceeding thence to the lobby of the commons house, I
found it filled with gentry in livery; just peeping in, I went directly to the hatch leading to the antechamber of the gallery, which
the old enfeebled keeper opened to me.   After the delay of a
quarter of an hour, I obtained entrance, and found many persons
there before me.   The house was very full below; among others

Lord North, whom I discovered on the treasury bench by his blue ribbon.   The members sit with their hats on, but always uncover when they rise to speak, and on departure salute the chair by a bow.   The speaker is always covered, and with the clerks habited in black gowns; after some time he commanded to order, and some members to their seats; then directing his looks to a Mr. Minchin with a motion of his head, the member arose, when a profound silence ensued, and continued to be strictly observed through the whole of the speech.   He began by informing the house of a motion he had to make and the subject of it, viz.: That a regular and intelligible account should be rendered of the money granted by parliament for the navy, for which inquiry and motion he assigned three reasons; one being the waste in expenditure.   The proof of this article arose from thirteen ships, of which he mentioned one instance only as a specimen; the others were in the same predicament.   The Narcissus, in 1772, was estimated at £3,000, to complete with guns and stores; on estimate of 1778 she was put in at £5,000; in 1779 £5,500; and in 1780 at £3,600; in the total £17,100.   At the end of that period she lay in dock untouched, without a farthing's worth of stores or one gun on board, and in the same unfit, unrepaired condition as at first. During the course of his speech he was now and then interrupted by a murmur on the other side the house, which was at times succeeded by " hear him, hear him," and very generally attended to.

Sir George Young followed, but was less minded.   Sir Charles Bunbury spoke next, who made a long and more formal oration on same side, pretty well listened to, and frequently complimented with " hear him, hear him ;" which expression was also used to two men who followed, viz. Admiral Keppel, who spoke well, and with some warmth, and Sir Hugh Palliser, who was called by name by his party.   He arose and began by justifying the admiralty, attributing the present state of the navy, though respectable, to malignant influence of party, which has, he said, diffused itself effectually into the king's dock-yards, teaching the inmates to form associations, whereby wise measures of the admiralty had in some degree been defeated.   He having finished and set down, the house resounded with " Burke, Burke ;" hereupon the Irish orator arose, and in a loud and manly voice, with singular energy and compass of expression, and a torrent of eloquence, reprobated Sir Hugh's account, exposed the futility of his arguments, excited universal attention, and frequently raised more than a smile in the features of his listening hearers.   I should have mentioned Mr. Penton, one of the navy board, who rose next to the motion maker, and justified the accounts rendered, as a mode adopted and by experience found the best for more than a century past; to which the reply was that he had mistaken the meaning of the objections in three particulars.

March 23.   With Mr. Danforth fetched a long walk to Session Green in Paddington Road.

TO DR. EDWARD A. HOLYOKE, SALEM.

London, March 23, 1781.

DEAR SIR :

Meeting the bearer this afternoon, he informed me of his intended departure to-morrow for New-York.   The shortness of the warning puts it out of my power to be so particular in my answer to your agreeable favor as it was my determination to be.   In my next, if I can procure a conveyance not exposed to state inquisition, I shall fulfil my first purpose.   I am now to acknowledge the pleasing and interesting relations yours conveyed, and am glad that at any rate our native country is and has been free from those oppressions, sufferings, and distressing evils that intestine commotions and rage of civil war have subjected our unhappy fellow-subjects in the southern colonies to.   Whether you have had real enjoyments compared to its confessedly happy days within our remembrance, I pretend not to affirm or deny ; the accounts from those who have for these two or three years since escaped from thence and took refuge here, are such as do not excite the most fervent wishes in the breasts of our countrymen here, who enjoy peace and the comforts of life, to return back again soon.   One would think from the establishment of an academy of arts and sciences at a time when the country is oppressed by a destructive war, yet uncertain of the event, that the rulers of your state labored under *l'étourdie des hommes du bois,* or possessed the magnanimity of the old Roman senators; be that as it may, I wish its continuance and success.

I am now going to relate a fact you would perhaps have thought incredible; the day on which I completed two hundred and ninety-six weeks' residence on this island, favored me with a sight I had never before had, of that extraordinary person, Lord North; though I confess curiosity had more than a score of times led me to the lobby of the commons house and the gallery, but accident procured me what my wishes and endeavors had failed in hitherto:—for carelessly strolling without design into Westminster Hall, I obtained admission to the gallery, where I had an opportunity of seeing him with a full treasury bench and house. The great Irish born orator, Mr. Burke, spoke, and his thundering elocution fixed the attention of the house, and his wit and satire diverted them, and produced peals of laughter. More it is needless and would not be prudent to mention. There are some appearances that the Empress of Russia's mediation may be attended with salutary effects. May a stop be put to the further effusion of English blood; too much has been spilt already in this destructive quarrel for independence.

Very truly your friend,
S. CURWEN.

April 2. Went to Leicester-square to pay Mr. R. Clarke a visit, but seeing a nobleman's carriage at the door, presumed he was sitting to Mr. Copley, and that therefore my company may be inconvenient.

April 3. Abel Willard and young Borland called to-day in my absence, and left their address. Called on Mr. Dalglish, and invited him to accompany me to Woolwich; he readily complying, we walked to Charing Cross and took coach to Greenwich; the stage being gone from thence, we walked to Woolwich, about three miles. Passing through the town, we went on towards artillery-park, wherein is an immense quantity of brass and iron ordnance, mortars and shot of all dimensions; passing through we arrived at the place where the convicts were employed in labor, each having a chain on both legs just long enough for him to walk conveniently, with a string tied thereto reaching to the waist to keep the chain from falling down to the ankles. I am told there are about five hundred employed, bringing dirt, sand and gravel from barges on small carts, some in wheeling barrows, others in various ways as they are qualified.   The effects of their labor is visible in a sea wall of earth, six hundred yards long, and having a broad convenient footpath on top ; they are now employed in making and sodding a new artillery parade.   1 could not refrain from many mortifying reflections on the sad necessity human governments are under to treat with such severity so many of our fellow-creatures, furnished with the noble powers of reason and understanding, and capable of employing them to the most useful purposes.   Dined at Crown and Anchor, and returned by eight o'clock.

April 5.   Mr. Arthur Savage and Mr. F. calling, we went to St. Lawrence Jewry, to hear a sermon to the governors of the London Hospital, from the excellent and worthy Bishop of Chester, Dr. Porteus.   He possesses a good enunciation and pleasant voice, somewhat earnest, style elegant, periods happy and finely turned, without any appearance of art or affectation.   On the whole he is a delightful speaker, never failing to instruct and charm a serious and attentive hearer.

Received a letter from Rev. Thomas Barnard, inclosed in one from Benjamin Pickman at Warwick.

April 6.   Drank tea at Mr. Copley's, with whom his father-in-law, Mr. R. Clark, resides ; all the family present.

April 8.   Accompanied Col. Browne to hear the famed pulpit orator, Mr. Duchée, late of Philadelphia, at Tavistock chapel, Broad-court, Longacre, who figures even in London.   His performance, in point of language and delivery, greatly pleased us. Dined and passed the evening at Col. Browne's.

April 11.   Mr. Sparhawk, Rev. Mr. Peters, and Rev. Mr. Clark took tea with me.

April 13.   Good-Friday.   To Westminster Abbey ; entering, I found the choir shut ; no service, or over, but could not learn which ; so totally ignorant or unconcerned are people here in general of every thing not their immediate business or pursuit.   Returning, I stepped in at Whitehall chapel, the Dean of Rochester was preaching.   Lord North and Judge Oliver attended at same place, though I knew it not till informed by the latter, at whose house I drank tea, and there met Mr. and Mrs. Elisha Hutchinson.   Since my last visit to Westminster Abbey, to my surprise I find a white marble monument erected to the honor of Dr. Isaac Watts; he is represented as clad in a loose dress, sitting in a thoughtful posture, his head covered with lank hairs resting on his left hand; his right leaning on a table, holding a pen, denoting his having just finished a sentence; his arm seized and grasped by a female figure, in loose attire, which I suppose to represent one of the virtues.

April 14. Visited Mr. Maddocks the florist's garden at Camberwell; a fine show of auriculas and hyacinths.

April 17. Accompanied Thomas Goldthwait to Wiswall's lodgings by his desire, he having called on me for that purpose, in order to offer him the living at Dunmore in Essex, which the rector gave Mr. Goldthwait leave to offer to any American clergyman out of employ. The terms offered were fifty pounds salary, and considerable emoluments; for life, or as long as Mr. Wiswall shall please; the neighborhood is represented as agreeable. Met Samuel Porter and sundry others of my countrymen in the Park.

April 18. Evening at Covent Garden, to see "*A new way to pay old debts;*" entertainment, "*Barnaby Brittle;*" this part by Quick, who also acted Justice Greedy. In the whole were some humorous strokes,—many low ones,—all applauded.

April 19. Went to Mr. Benjamin Thompson's lodgings, Pall Mall.

April 21. Went to see a model of ancient Rome; scale, one inch to ninety feet, making a square of twelve feet: but the topographical or ground scale does not hold with respect to height of buildings, pillars, etc., appearing on a larger scale. Meeting Mr. Timmins, received an invitation to dine; and at two o'clock set off for his house on foot; in the meantime, Mr. Wiswall coming to my door, instead of entering pursued his design of walking. Directed our way through the fields to Islington Spa, Saddler's Wells, Bagnigge Wells, places he had never before seen. Returned by the way of Hatton Garden or street; at Mr. Timmins's met Gilbert Harrison; returned home *modo pedestri.*

April 25. Rambled with Col. Browne round Mary-le-Bone; in the neighborhood of a spot, late gardens, I saw for first time an old brick building called Queen Mary's country seat, in pretty nearly the same condition she left it more than two centuries since; being in a villa some miles from the city of London, in its then circumscribed limits, three-fourths of the way to it now built being then country. It is low studded and lofty roof, small windows, many juttings and projections; is now in private hands, the Duke of Portland's, and is used as a boarding-school. The grounds remain unaltered.

April 26. Mr. Goldthwait and Mr. Danforth dined with me; at five we departed by assignment to Mrs. Hay's; Col. Browne and lady were to have been of the party, which accident prevented. We had Mr. and Mrs. Atkinson, late of Boston, and Mr. Greene, who in dress equalled a nobleman of the highest rank and quality, girded with a military side weapon.

April 27. Colonel Erving and Mr. Dalglish called; the latter for me to accompany him to the commons' house. The subject of debate was the East India officers,—the motion by Lord North; his opponents were Burke, Charles J. Fox, etc.

April 28. Visited my friend Governor Browne; confined by an ill turn which seized him violently. I called to acquaint Mrs. Browne, that " *Belle's Stratagem* " was to be acted to-night, having engaged to accompany her to see it.

April 29, *Sunday.* At Essex House chapel, Dr. Priestley preached an excellent discourse; proving beyond contradiction that religion and virtue are the only just sources of true delight and joy, or as he modified the language, of settled, calm serenity of mind. It was a discourse worthy a Christian divine, and happy would those be on whose minds those blessed truths were impressed in indelible characters. Rev. Mr. Wiswall was by my invitation my fellow-worshipper at Essex House. Afternoon service, Mr. Lindsay preached. My companion drank tea with me, expressing in conversation his professional dislike of Mr. Lindsay's attempt to reform the liturgy. Religious prejudice is the unhappy leaven of a narrow education, and manifests a fettered mind. I hope I have sufficient reasons to rejoice that mine is free from those manacles. I plainly see it may be politically useful to state managers and hierarchists, whose views extend not beyond this present mortal state; but in no view is it to be supported on the grounds of advancing the cause of truth and manly sentiment, and genuine, unadulterated Christianity.

April 30. Entered Col. and Mrs. Browne's name with my

own for admission some days hence at British Museum; list filled for two or three days.

May 4. Dined at Col. Browne's, there heard of Mrs. Sargent's death. Evening waited on Mrs. Browne to Covent Garden theatre, to see " *The Duenna.*"

May 7. To Mr. Maddocks' at Walworth, with Mr. Dalglish, to see his fine show of tulips, which unfavorable weather deforms greatly, preventing the beautiful, pleasing display that might otherwise be expected.

May 8. Passed forenoon at the public exhibition of paintings, sculpture, and drawings of the Royal Academy in Somerset House, Strand. A great concourse of well dressed, genteel people, as usual; large exhibition room crowded, but my good fortune secured an advantageous seat, almost central, which from arrangement and construction of room and pictures, yielded a fuller view and happier light; I kept in close connection with a gentleman of taste and judgment, disposed to communicate, and seeming happy to show off and please; by him I was entertained and instructed.

May 23. This day at eleven o'clock entered British Museum. Dr. Woide, the transcriber and publisher, complaisantly showed me the Alexandrian manuscript of the New Testament, favored me with many ingenious remarks, and read me several passages which I confess I should without his assistance have found it difficult to hobble through, from the peculiar manner of writing then used. It is said to be older than the Arian controversy, and is without the seventh verse of the fifth chapter 1st Epistle of St. John. It is written in Greek capitals, without distinction of points or words, letters following in equi-distant spaces. A fac simile copy is now preparing by my informant, who appears learned, and is very obliging. After having gone through part of our course in the rooms, my companions Col. and Mrs. Browne appeared and joined us. We were attended by Dr. Solander; some of our company were persons of distinction, Lady Dowager Wynne and her young son the baronet, and several others whose names I have forgotten. Among other curiosities were shown us King Edward VIth's journal, written with his own hand—volumes of royal letters, etc. It seems all letters from the princes of Europe to one another are preserved, and after death of writer sent back to their respective courts ; they are of one size—seal never broken, a ribbon through the wax is cut in order to open it. Dr. Solander showed us an oyster-shell of a roundish form, about four inches over, which he said was valued at a hundred guineas ; another larger beside it, of less brilliant water, of no more value than ten ; they both had a faint mother of pearl cast. On returning home found a letter from Arthur Savage, informing me of Mr. Thompson's compliments and wish to see me at eleven o'clock to-morrow, at his lodgings.

May 24. Went early in order to be at Mr. Benjamin Thompson's in time, and being a little before, heard he was not returned home from Lord George Germaine's, where he always breakfasts, dines and sups, so great a favorite is he. To kill half an hour, I loitered to the park through the palace, and on second return found him at his lodgings ; he received me in a friendly manner, taking me by the hand, talked with great freedom, and promised to remember and serve me in the way I proposed to him. Promises are easily made, and genteel delusive encouragement the staple article of trade belonging to the courtier's profession. I put no hopes on the fair appearances of outward behavior, though it is uncandid to suppose all mean to deceive. Some wish to do a service who have it not in their power ; all wish to be thought of importance and significancy, and this often leads to deceit. This young man, when a shop lad to my next neighbor, ever appeared active, good-natured and sensible ; by a strange concurrence of events, he is now under secretary to the American secretary of state, Lord George Germaine, a secretary to Georgia, inspector of all the clothing sent to America, and Lieut. Col. Commandant of horse dragoons at New-York ; his income arising from these sources is, I have been told, near seven thousand a year—a sum infinitely beyond his most sanguine expectations. He is besides a member of the Royal Society. It is said he is of an ingenious turn, an inventive imagination, and by being on one cruise in channel service with Sir Charles Hardy, has formed a more regular and better digested system for signals than that heretofore used. He seems to be of a happy, even temper in general deportment, and reported of an excellent heart ; peculiarly respectful to Americans that fall in his way.*

---

* Afterwards the celebrated Count Rumford.

Mem. A letter has been intercepted and published here, thought by some to be a genuine production and unintentionally fallen into British hands, signed Geo. Washington, showing his opinion of American inability to support this burdensome and expensive war, unless France and other allies bestir themselves and lend more essential aid than hirherto ; meeting Mr. Paxton and Treasurer Gray, they both agreed in sentiment that it is a genuine letter, and dictated by real judgment.

Drank tea at Mrs. Greene's by appointment ; met Mr. Wiswall, who was just going to his cure in Oxford. At his request I jumped into the carriage with him, and alighted at Crosskeys, Gracechurch-street ; thence to Boar's Head, Eastcheap, and in the identical spot where Nym, Pistol, Bardolph, Hal, and Sir John Falstaff were wont to assemble together to pass their jovial evenings three hundred years since ; after a regale of punch to the remembrance of these jovial blades, we returned to Crosskeys.

June 5. Visited Governor Browne and Mrs. Browne, both unwell ; promised to dine with them the last of the week.

June 8. Mr. Erving called.

June 11. Visited Mrs. Greene and Abel Willard ; drank tea with Mrs. Councel ; a Mr. Codner and Jones, both late from Boston, there ; no material intelligence obtained from them. They say provisions are double in price to usual in former happy times. Never did an infatuated people wanton away their felicity more foolishly.

June 13. Dined and passed the evening at Col. Browne's.

June 19. Paid farewell compliments to Elisha Hutchinson, going soon to his summer residence at Birmingham.

June 22. Through Moorfields came across a mountebank or stage doctor, on an elevated scaffold, covered with a ragged blanket, discoursing to the more dirty-faced ragged mob ; demonstrating to their satisfaction, no doubt, the superior excellence of his nostrums to those of the dispensary, and the more safe and secure state of patients under his management than hospitals and common receptacles of sick and wounded poor ; whose lives, health, and ease, he said truly, were as dear to them as those of the best gentry or highest nobility in the land ; and he further added, of as much use to the public, which for aught I know is equally true.

June 23.   Went to Col. Browne's to take the last farewell of him and Mrs. Browne, about to depart to his government at Bermuda ; never more expecting to see them again in this world.

June 25.   Young Gould, a Bostonian, bound to New-York, offered to take letters.

June 26.   Capt. Coombs from New England *via* New-York, whither he fled to escape persecution, as he said, (a Marblehead refugee,) called and breakfasted with me ; strolled together to Tyburn, and returned by the square lying north of the city.   Carried him home to dinner, thence to Chelsea ; returning by Brompton, met Treasurer Gray and Mr. Paxton ; the latter at first sight recollecting, accosted me, according to his usual custom, politely and with great openness.   The traces of his countenance have been lost in my memory, and I should have passed him.

June 28.   At New England Coffee-house ; saw more Bostonians than for some years past.

June 29.   Went to see the house in which the noted Jane Shore died ; found that it was demolished four years since, and a new one erected on the spot, in three small tenements, which stand in a lane directly facing Watergruel-row, so called.   Was informed that an underground communication had been discovered between that house and Bishop Bonner's palace in that neighborhood.

July 2.   Wm. Cabot and Capt. Coombs drank tea with me.

July 4.   Mr. A. Savage and Mr. T. Danforth called and took coffee with me.

July 9.   Meeting Mr. Deputy Ellis at a bookseller's in Cornhill, who resolved my doubt about the meaning of the word *molten*, as applied in Scripture to images or figures in brass on metal ; signifying melted.

July 10.   Left a note for Mr. A. Savage at Knightsbridge, to acquaint him that Mr. Erving had been to appoint to-morrow to call on him.

July 12.   Visited Mrs. Hay ; there met two Winthrops, one of whom, Thomas Lindall Winthrop,* had lately arrived from New England in Captain Timothy Folger's ship.

---

* The late Lieut. Governor of Massachusetts ; the other was his brother Benjamin Winthrop, now of this city, who then resided in London.

July 14.   Accompanied Mr. and Mrs. Snelson to Windsor ; passing by Hammersmith, stopped at Turnham-Green ; from hence to Staines, where we dined.   At seven o'clock arrived at " *Castle and Mermaid*," Windsor.   Evening, walked on terrace in the castle ; a pleasing prospect, filled with promiscuous company.

Windsor, July 15, *Sunday.*   At St. George's chapel, prayers at eight ; present, the King, Queen, Princesses Elizabeth and Sophia,—about a hundred hearers ; we joined the train to Queen's house, or rather to the gates.   The King was dressed in blue fly, cuffs small, open, and turned up with red velvet, cape of same, buttons white, breeches and waiscoat of white cotton, an ordinary white wig with a tail ribbon, a round black chip hat, small, as used in riding.   He is tall, square over the shoulders, large ugly mouth, talks a great deal, and shows his teeth too much ; his countenance heavy and lifeless, with white eyebrows.   Queen of the middle size and bulk, height five feet and a-half,—though far removed from beautiful, she has an open placid aspect, mouth large, foot splay :—at prayers their voices often heard, and they appeared devout.   They take no state upon them, walk freely about the town with only a lord in waiting.   At seven, every evening after tea, the King, Queen, Prince of Wales, Princess-royal, Princesses Sophia and Elizabeth, walk for an hour on terrace half a mile long, amidst two or three thousand people of all ranks.   The Prince of Wales appears a likely agreeable person, far more graceful than his father, who is ungainly.   The prince affects much the " *Jemmy* " dress and air ; age will doubtless soften down the juvenile taste and affectation.   The Queen's dress, a riding-habit, same color and facings as the King's—a small bonnet with a blue feather.   Conducted to picture gallery and state-rooms ; in one stands the Queen's bed, of a cream-color, worked in flowers with silk floss beautifully shaded, about seven feet long and six wide ; posts fluted, and gilt tester, having in the centre an oval compartment, thought to be the richest in England except Lady Clifford's at Wybrook, which was wrought and presented to her by the late Duchess of Norfolk,—twelve chairs and a screen, wrought by her present Majesty's own diligent hand.   In the evening on the terrace, the King was in full dress,—blue uniform, sword and cockade ; the Prince of Wales the same.   The

Queen in a faint greenish silk full dress, except her head, on which she had a bonnet with a feather of the same color as her dress.

July 16.   Crossed the river to Eton college or school, passing through cloisters and quadrangles.   I learnt from a lad that there were three hundred and thirty pupils belonging to the school ; the higher class had on gowns and caps of university fashion.   After breakfast, at castle, to hear the roll-call of Lord Falconberg's regiment, now on duty, and hear the music ; two bands of which were playing while the royal family were walking last evening.   Took our carriage and departed over Cranbrook bridge, and at two o'clock arrived at the *Eight*, so called, being a little island of two acres in the river Thames, opposite Kew, just above the bridge. We came hither expecting to have a fine dinner, but the boat had been robbed by some Londoners ; were disappointed.   Arrived at lodgings at seven o'clock.

July 17.   Took Captain Coombs to dine with me at the " *Thirteen Cantons;* "—called on A. Savage.   Spoke to Mr. Rowe of Treasury about Captain Coombs ; he encourages his application to Lord North.

July 23.   Met Mr. R. Clarke on horseback near Charing Cross ; walked in Charter-House square and gardens ; am told the number of men supported by the founder's munificence is fourscore, besides forty boys.

July 25.   Rode to Enfield to inquire respecting board ; result unsatisfactory.   I rambled to the borders of the *Chase*, now laid out in corn and grass, to the great advantage of the neighborhood. In this town is a large, and for the age it was built in, a lofty house of three floors, which had been the residence of Queen Elizabeth ; having on the walls within the court, the arms of England quartered with the fleur-de-lis of France, and Q. E. inscribed over in plaster of Paris, almost obliterated by time and weather.   Returned home on foot without much fatigue.

July 26.   Called for an interview with Mr. Benjamin Thompson ; he and Lord George Germaine not returned from the country.

July 27.   Called again on Mr. Thompson ; neither he nor Lord George returned.   Passed two hours in Mr. Waller's front dining-room, to have a sight of the French spy, De la Motte, who was dragged on a hurdle to place of execution, Tyburn, to be hanged; tall and well grown,—dress black, flapped hat.

July 28. Went with Mr. Arthur Savage on a curiosity walk, to gaze at Chiswick House and gardens; by a card (without which none are admitted) we found an entrance. It is a seat belonging to the Duke of Devonshire, but forsaken by him. It was left him by its former owner, the late Earl of Burlington. It is properly a miniature building, and in a peculiar taste; not a room I think twenty feet square, many smaller. The walls are covered with pictures, some fine originals, principally copies; grounds covered with sphinxes and urns. Walks in Chinese taste, long, straight, and gravelled; cut hedges. From a terrace is a beautiful view over a delightfully improved country, bounded by surrounding hills, interspersed with gentlemen's seats; farm houses, live hedges, corn grounds, pastures with trees in rows, clumps and wildernesses. In the grounds are a few temples and porticoes. Having satisfied curiosity, as far as time would admit, we entered the road and began our homeward course, and arrived at three o'clock.

July 29. Dined at Capt. Hay's, by invitation card of yesterday, with Mr. Danforth, and also Mrs. Geyer, just arrived from New-York.

July 30. Went to Westminster Abbey to meet Mr. Savage by agreement, to explain to him the meaning of mottoes under arms of the knights of the bath in Henry VIIth's chapel. Saw, for the first time, Lord Chatham's effigy in wax, having the wig, shoes, robes, etc., he had on when he expired in the House of Lords; said to be very like him, but very unlike every cut of him that had before come to my view.

July 31. Dined with Mr. Simpson and Mr. Higginson, and abode there till four o'clock; returned, and Mr. Smithson drank tea with me.

Aug. 1. Capt. Coombs breakfasted with me; accompanied him to the Treasury, in order to put his petition, with Sir William Pepperell's recommendation, into Mr. Rowe's hands; who returned it, advising to a further attestation of the alleged facts. Returning, we stepped into Lincoln's Inn Hall, where was sitting Lord Chancellor Thurlow in a case of lunacy, from whence I departed alone and dined at home.   Drank tea with Harrison Gray and wife at Brompton.

Aug. 3.   Called at Mr. Thompson's lodgings, in Pall Mall Court – disappointed—went to show Mr. Savage the grave of Judge Chambers Russell, in Bunhill Fields burying ground; which at sixty pounds expense has but a common grave stone.   Thence to the poor remains of a once royal palace, of which the outer gateway (St. John's Gate) is now standing, and only that; the site is now a cowyard and stable; so where once royalty was lodged, beasts inhabit.

Aug. 4.   Again disappointed in not finding Mr. Thompson at his house, nor at the Treasury.

Aug. 6.   Took tea at Mr. Copley's, with Mr. R. Clarke and the family.

Aug. 8.   In conversation with Mr. Peters, was informed that it is and has been all along the determination of the cabinet to set up the noblemen's claim against New England charters, annihilate all of them, and reduce the surviving inhabitants to a state of villenage, or expel them.   He says he has sufficient authority to assert this.   Cruel, barbarous determination!   May heaven disappoint their cursed device against innocence, justice, right, humanity, and every laudable principle and virtue.   May America and my countrymen, more dear to me than ever, be made acquainted with this more than brutal cruelty; may disappointment be the issue of their attempts, vexation and every evil the reward of such unexampled, oppressive, rapacious designs, for it is but yet in embryo, never, I hope, to see the light.   I doubt not heaven has in store ample revenge for this devoted country, whose rulers seem infatuated, and themselves on the verge of ruin thereby.

Aug. 9.   Mr. Jones, a Bostonian, drank tea with me.

Aug. 11.   After one hour's waiting, admitted to Mr. Thompson in the plantation office; he seemed inclined to shorten the interview, received me with a courtier's smile, rather uncommunicative and dry.   This reception has damped my ill grounded hopes, derived from former seeming friendly intentions to promote my views; this, my first, will be my last attempt to gain advantages from a courtier, of which I never entertained favorable impressions.

Aug. 18. Took tea and passed the evening at Mr. and Mrs. Hay's.

Aug. 21. Dined at Capt. Hay's, with four gentlemen.

Aug. 24. To the Gresham lecture room to see Copley's picture of Lord Chatham's death.

Sept. 4. Took tea with Dr. Jeffries, of Boston, a son of David Jeffries.

TO MR. THOMAS WYER, NEW-YORK.

London, Sept. 12, 1781.

Dear Sir :

Having the other day met Mr. Berry, who informed me you were settled in New-York with your wife, and that he would take charge of a letter and deliver it into your hands, I am encouraged to send this scrawl that serves to acknowledge the receipt of yours of a distant date, and thank you for it. I hope your situation is comfortable, though, at best, a man in the civil or commercial line has many reasons of complaint in a garrison of disorderly, licentious soldiers. I am glad to be informed that you are employed in business, and hope it will turn out to good account.

It has been my wish ever since I have been from my own home, that all who are in a state of exile, whether voluntary or not, except those immediately concerned in the revenue, who could not have remained in America, had been prudent enough to have kept their political opinions to themselves, especially after the frenzy had worked itself up so high in the minds of our zealous patriot neighbors, and remained at their own dwellings, and made the best shifts they could in these troubles. They might, I really think, have found themselves, for the most part, in less disagreeable circumstances than they now are ; at least I can truly say it respecting my own particular case. But the bad consequences of past errors are now only to be lessened by a prudent forbearance of harsh reproachful language against the present rulers in the American colonies that remain in subjection to Congress authority ; for whatever you warm transatlantic loyalists may think, it is probable, however the general war may terminate, there never will be established such a degree of British governmental authority in North America as will cause much matter of triumph to American refugees.   I wish America would dissolve the execrable French alliance, that they have sufficient reasons already to detest, and which will, if continued much longer, issue in greater ruin.

We are now hemmed in by the combined fleets of France and Spain, to the number of forty-nine capital ships, and eleven frigates, which have been cruising for some time in the chops of the English Channel.   Ours, under Admiral Derby, is at present in Torbay.   A large East and West India fleet is hourly expected under a slender convoy; but government has taken the precaution to send out some fast sailing cutters to apprise them of the danger.

Wishing you success and safety,

I am your friend,

S. Curwen.

Sept. 27.   Accompanied Messrs. Savage and Toulmin to Drury Lane, to see " School for Scandal," which was highly entertaining. On the appearance of Mrs. Cargill, appointed to one of the parts, a general hiss, followed by an unusual clap of approbation, for some minutes kept on to discountenance the hiss, occasioned by her whimsical caprices and rude disappointment of the public at Haymarket Theatre about two months since.   She is a pleasing performer and public favorite.

Oct. 2.   Took tea and passed the evening at Mr. John Savage's with Mr. A. Savage, except a walk to Chelsea Hospital.

Oct. 9.   Papers say Adam Woolridge is appointed American secretary's deputy, in lieu of Mr. Fisher, who now holds the office. Mr. A. Savage dined and passed the evening with me.

Oct. 15.   Went over to Chelsea; met Mr. Benjamin Hallowell there.   Another countryman, Commodore Loring, discharged from pension list by death, and another going same way; Brigadier Royall seized with small-pox, with hazardous symptoms.   Capt. Coombs dined with me.

Oct. 18.   Thirteen criminals executed at Tyburn—a melancholy consideration that robberies have of late greatly increased, as indeed has thieving of all kinds in the metropolis.

Oct. 20.   Mr. Arthur Savage, and Miss S., and Mr. John Savage, lady and son, drank tea with me.   By the papers I find some Salem privateers have fallen into the hands of the British.

Oct. 30.   Dined with Mr. and Mrs. Hay.

TO SAMUEL SEWALL, ESQ., SIDMOUTH.

London, Oct. 30, 1781.

DEAR SIR:

Inclosed is a bank post bill for £24 6s. 8d., the balance of your quarterly pension of £25 ; and while I reside in London will, with great readiness, serve you or any acquaintance in this or any way in my power.

You wish me to write you favorable news from America; would to God such was to be found written in the book of fate.

Respecting the state of the war in that quarter: the French, you know, are in possession of the Chesapeake, with a much superior fleet to that of Great Britain; for they reckon thirty-six capital ships to our twenty-four, even after Digby's junction. General Cornwallis's royal master is in the utmost distress for him, whom all the world here fears to hear will have been *Burgoyned,* and therefore an end to this cursed, ill-omened quarrel, though not in a way they wish; for which the instigators and continuers deserve execration. It is, however, reported that twenty thousand men are to be shipped off to America in February, part of whom are the five thousand before destined to the East Indies.

I am yours,

S. CURWEN.

Nov. 20. Letters from New-York inform us that New London, in Connecticut, is burnt, with all the shipping, by six hundred American Associators, so called, leagued in a band of destruction against their native country: together with the loss of lives and properties of the inhabitants, the assailants left of their number two hundred dead on the spot; their death the just punishment due to such parricides.

By the king's speech I find he intends, if parliament will furnish men and money, to continue his efforts to reduce his rebellious subjects in America to his royal will and pleasure, and his other enemies to his own terms, *if he can ;* and no doubt they will continue to furnish both as long as they last, and until they shall fairly and completely have dried up all the sources, which, perhaps, a few more expensive, unsuccessful campaigns will effectually accomplish. Would that this nation or its rulers were wise enough to sit down by its present losses, and make the best of what remains. Commerce and conquest are two things in nature very unlike, and require very different geniuses in carrying on ; and which is most congenial and natural to these islanders is obvious.

Nov. 22. The wind continues westerly, detaining Admiral Rodney's fleet of eight ships of the line in Torbay, bound for the West Indies. The court and all apprehend some great blow there, as they have reason from the great superiority of the French fleet gone from Charleston since Cornwallis's surrender on the 19th ult., of himself, officers, army, baggage, artillery, ammunition, *de guerre* and *de bouche*, to the American General George Washington, of whom some of the *wise men* of this country speak with undeserved contempt. This being the second instance that has happened to the *best forces* of this continent, and perhaps the first of the kind that ever befell this haughty America-despising people. And the flight of two English admirals, with a frequently declared superior fleet, Graves and Digby, (under the auspicious eye of one of the royal offspring, Prince William Henry, who is training up, and I hope will prove an ornament and a useful naval commander,) to New-York with Clinton and his garrison of cooped-up troops, who for a few weeks having breathed free air, are now chiefly returning back to their winter amusements and useful employment of dancing, card-playing, acting farces on mock stages, and decorating their pretty persons for the astonishment and delight of their female admirers.

Adieu to the character which once justly enough distinguished the army and navy of this little empire !

Nov. 23. Overtaken in the Park by a former travelling companion, named Aspdin, of Philadelphia, on horseback ; he recognised me after an interval of four years.

TO MR. ANDREW DALGLISH, GLASGOW.

London, Nov. 25, 1781.

DEAR SIR :

London, as you justly observe, to a pushing man and of abilities is the place to gain great advantages, if he knows the world and how to avail himself of lucky incidents, and is attentive to them ; but to one of a contrary character it is far otherwise.

Your request of my service need not be twice asked, if I know how to perform any thing essential for you, or any friend; but being placed by Providence out of the reach of rendering services, I am endeavoring to reason myself into the belief that I stand in need of none myself, though possessing very little more than the necessaries of life; 'tis a hard task, though if attended with success, shall not grudge my pains. Our townsman, Mr. Fisher, holds a quartered, precarious office, at I fancy less than half its real income, in, under, and returnable to Mr. Thompson, when he shall come back, which I doubt not will be in the spring or summer following.

Clerkships, as all offices under government, are at open market, and bought and sold as public stocks, the premium four, five, or six years' income. The Treasury Coffee-house, under the arches, is the place where the sellers or brokers are to be seen at business hours. If you have any connections that can recommend you to men of influence, and can really engage their interest, (for promises are the courtier's traffick, and mean nothing; people of breeding are too polite to disoblige in any other way but by neglect,) you may succeed; without, it will be vain to attempt. Merit is disregarded, implying a demand. Here it is not asked what you have done, but what you are capable of doing, is worth attending to. In whatever line you direct your views, I sincerely wish success; you might assuredly depend on my aid if it could or can be of any use to you.

> With real and hearty good will,
> > I am your friend,
> > > S. CURWEN.

Nov. 26. Going through the Park, I found great numbers there waiting for the king's passing to the parliament house, being first day of session, when it is opened by a speech from the throne; the king in his robes, crown on his head, which, if capable of feeling, must I think feel more distress than at any time since his brows bore this emblem of royalty. The total overthrow in Lord Cornwallis's defeat, of his long projected and self-promised subjugation of North America to an uncontrolled power, must have this effect. Man's designs are often overruled by a more powerful authority. Took tea at Mr. John Savage's, according to promise, with a room full of company.

Nov. 30.   Took my watch to London to be reformed, it proving a useless companion in its present state of false intelligence; borrowed one in the interim.

Dec. 5.   Mr. Thomas Hutchinson and Mr. A. Savage took tea with me.

TO REV. ISAAC SMITH, SIDMOUTH.

Brompton, Dec. 15, 1781.

DEAR SIR :

I delayed answering your last favor till I could send a satisfactory one to your question about your friend,Thomas Barnard, Esq., of Lincoln's Inn ; and now I have the pleasure to acquaint you that he and I were this day as usual fellow-worshippers at Essex House chapel, which seems to be his Sunday's resort, both for worship and the communion, at which he attends with becoming devotion. Our preacher to-day was Mr. Estin, of Lewinsmead, Bristol, for Mr. Lindsay himself always performs the liturgy service.

Since Lord Cornwallis's surrender, government, I am told, has laid aside all other thoughts than to maintain, if practicable, Carolina, Nova Scotia, New-York city, Charleston, and Georgia ; perhaps since the majority for carrying on the war in America, when the House of Commons consisted of more than four hundred, fell to forty-one only ; a proof, notwithstanding the irresistible influence of court, of the real sentiments of the landed interest.   For the aforesaid purpose immense quantities of army and navy ammunitions, *de guerre* and *de bouche*, will be sent over, and primarily furnish America, and ultimately, I fear, France, with the ability to dispossess Great Britain of every foot of ground on the continent of North America ; and it will be well if not the islands too.   But whoever is master of the ocean will doubtless command these; whether Great Britain is or is not at present, is a fact easily to be judged of ; whether she will be in time to come, must be read in a following page in the book of fate.   'Tis, I confess, foolish to anticipate evils ; a wise man said,

" If evils come not, then our fears are vain ;
And if they do, fear but augments the pain."

No mind is so fortified as not to feel concern for what may

happen, especially when smarting under the rod, nor insensible when oppressed.

Very truly yours,
S. CURWEN.

Dec. 20. Went to London in order to pass a day at Capt. Hay's ; he was departed to Portsmouth to meet his ship there.

Dec. 23. Sunday at Essex House chapel. Mr. Lindsay preached an admirable dissuasive against placing terms of acceptance with God on narrow party principles, as if he was engaged to support Calvin, Arminius, or the Council of Nice, or any body of patriarchs, archbishops or bishops whatever.

Dec. 31. Three days since was my birth-day, when I entered my sixty-sixth year. What reason have I to lament the loss of time and waste of powers that our indulgent Creator has bestowed upon us for wise and useful purposes.

Henry Laurens, Esq., late president of Congress, was admitted to bail and discharged from the Tower.

CHAPTER XVI.

Brompton, London, January 1, 1782.   Dined at Mr. John Savage's, in the Grove.

Jan. 3.   Called on Dr. Jeffries, a countryman of mine, at No. 28 South Moulton-street.   In my absence, Mr. Timmins and James Russell called.

TO SAMUEL SEWALL, ESQ., TAUNTON.

London, Jan. 8, 1782.

DEAR SIR :

Mr. Rowe names the 21st for delivering out his orders to the bank for payment of our quarterly stipends.   I shall be on the watch, and avail myself of the earliest day for myself and you.

I presume you have heard of the death of poor Abel Willard, your late friend, whose continuance on the London stage was of a few days only after his return from Oxford.   He is now gone to that retreat from suffering, where the wicked cease from troubling, and the weary are at rest.   I am told the surviving mate is a mourner in earnest.

I wish you the compliments of the season, and am glad to hear from you, that you are enjoying the pleasures of cheerful mirth and conviviality ; may they continue up to your desires, which I presume are ever confined within the bounds of temperance ; and hope a full restoration of your health and spirits.   Happy those who can amuse or gladden their hearts with anticipation of future good.   The present prospect is too gloomy for my weak mind to discover one gleam of hope.

Your faithful friend,

S. CURWEN.

Jan. 10.   Received a letter to convey to the widow Poynton, at Salem, from her late husband's kinsman of same name, in Orange-court, Leicester-fields, with a complaisant invitation to dine with him next Sunday.

TO SAMUEL SEWALL, ESQ., TAUNTON.

Yeoman's Row, Jan. 24, 1782.

DEAR SIR:

I have the pleasure to inclose you a bank post-bill for £24 6s. 8d., wishing it safe to your hands.

I am not happy enough to present you with any good news of our own selves or our public concerns, unless you will say none is such, at a time when bad only may reasonably be expected from almost all quarters of the globe. And though I would not raise imaginary ideal terrors in the breast of any of my acquaintance, I cannot forbear to mention a piece of intelligence received from an acquaintance here, communicated to him by a lady, who, he says, has intimate cabinet-council connections. He says, she has in times past more than once or twice informed him of secret deliberations and resolves done and acted there, that at the time surprised him, and were afterwards verified by the events. She told this in confidence, with great apparent concern of mind, etc., seeming firm in belief, and fear of its being put into execution within a few months. Hear then your doom:—it has been a subject of deliberation, and is thought to be determined in the cabinet, to withdraw from the American refugees in England all government support. So shameless and unexampled an act of barbarity, you probably may think, cannot be perpetrated in a civilized state; perhaps not. Politics and morals, however, are founded on very different grounds, and conducted by principles of a quite contrary complexion from each other. What is heterodoxy, base and unjustifiable in the one system, may be in the other sound state orthodoxy, and free from reproach; viewed in the single light of supposed good of the state. One cannot, therefore, tell what the administrators of public affairs may think it politically prudent to do in the paroxysms of public distress; and their ways and means are unhappily in one at this very time. I would fain disbelieve, but confess my fears step in between apprehensions on one side, and doubt on the other, and cast up the balance on the side of the latter. This day, I questioned Mr. Rowe at the Treasury on the subject; and he, with the apathy of a stoic, and the composed countenance of a ———, coldly replied, he had not heard of it. No, answered I, and I trust you never will. The nonchalance of his behavior rather increased my alarm than silenced my doubts. If you think it worth while to make inquiries about it, perhaps some friend who has connections with the court may convince you of its truth or falsity,—or, perhaps, you will prefer to postpone a knowledge of evils till they arrive, thinking that sufficient unto the day is the evil thereof.

Yours truly,

S. CURWEN.

TO JUDGE SEWALL, BRISTOL.

No. 1, *Yeoman's Row, Brompton, Feb.* 4, 1782.

DEAR SIR:

After so long a silence, I fancy you will wonder at this time to hear from me, and I confess I should hardly have thought of troubling you, but for a selfish purpose. I am directed by a son of Esculapius to heighten my diet by a moderate use of the most nutritive food, best dry wines, and spirits diluted in water, etc., excluding sweets, sours, and high seasonings,—in order to animate, warm, and invigorate, as far as possible, an old, cold and enfeebled body. Please inform me the proportions of spirits, milk, etc., of the mixture that was recommended to you by a London physician of note, to be taken by one in a decaying weak habit.

I durst not touch on the state of the nation, nor of our particular concerns as refugees, both of which, I presume, you suspect to be in a very unpromising condition.

I believe you will wonder how I came to the place from whence I date; my situation is, luckily, for the time I proposed to abide here, happy, from a coincidence of circumstances which could not be foreseen.   Your friend,

S. CURWEN.

Feb. 7. At the queen's house with Mr. Hopkins to see the plate, etc. ; the first object that struck me was three large maund baskets covered of table plate, as dishes, tureens, butter and sauce boats, all with covers, raised, embossed and engraved. The king's service was silver gilt; the prince's, silver. We also were conducted to the kitchen, where were eighteen male cooks busily employed in their several various lines; the men in white jackets and caps, and the women in white aprons and caps. By a late royal order, no one is to appear in the kitchen with their natural hair. When the king arrives from court at St. James's, (where he attends five days in the week, Tuesdays and Saturdays being the only ones he has in the week for his own private amusements, concerns, etc.,) dinner is called, on which a bustle ensues; the assistants of the silver scullery take such pieces as called for out of baskets, place them on a warm stove, whence they are taken by the cook and filled and taken to dining-room door, and delivered to the person appointed to place them on the royal table. Common dinner, five dishes of meat, four of garden stuffs, and one remove daily, and no more. He is exceedingly temperate, drinks generally water, and rarely partakes of more than one or two dishes. His supper is water-gruel, taken in a vessel peculiarly appropriated to his use, called the king's cup, and is of silver gilt,—shown me by the yeoman. The king's company at table is the queen, prince of Wales, (unless on his public dinner days,) the princess royal, princesses Sophia and Elizabeth: the rest of the children at another table in another apartment. The prince's dinner served up by his proper officers in the same manner as the king's. The queen, unless indisposed, always attends court and levee days; as soon as it is over she returns; immediately dinner is served up without waiting for her husband; a proof of good husbandship. It is said every king has a service of new table plate, the old being disposed of; the silver is kept in bags and put into presses. I took leave, and by advice returned by Buckingham Gate, Pimlico, Grosvenor-place, in preference to Constitution Hill, which sometimes is hazardous, and at eight o'clock got safe home.

FROM CHIEF JUSTICE OLIVER.

Birmingham, Feb. 9, 1782.

DEAR SIR:

Your favor of the 4th inst. informs me of two canisters of snuff which you have for me. I am much obliged to you for your care and trouble for an irritating powder for an American refugee, and doubt not that it will be of a more agreeable nature than the so many irritables we have all turned up our noses at for five or six years past. If you will be so kind as to send it to the Birmingham coach at the *Green Man and Still*, in Oxford-street, directed to me, I shall be glad; and if you will call upon Mr. Thos. Hutchinson,* he will pay you for me.

I am sincerely glad of the safe arrival of our friend Governor Browne;† I wish him an easy cushion for his chair, but I fear a barking crew of rebels will disrest him. Your friend Mr. Lakin inquires after you when I meet him.

Health and ease attend you; so wisheth

Your humble servant,

PETER OLIVER.

SAMUEL CURWEN, ESQ.

Feb. 15. Mr. Thomas Hutchinson called and passed an hour with me.

Feb. 17. The secret service list for the year 1781 is positively charged with the following sums :—

American departments exclusive of Refugees	£83,000 sterl'g.
Admiralty	46,000
War Office	10,500
Secretary of State	53,600
Treasury	72,000
	£265,100

The request long urged by General Burgoyne, of having a court martial appointed to decide upon his conduct in the affair of Saratoga, has at last been complied with, and orders transmitted from the war-office to the commander-in-chief in America for sending over such officers as mentioned by the General as necessary for his defence, by the first conveyance, to attend the trial. If no unexpected impediment takes place, it will be held in the spring. The administration seems loth to have an inquiry made; perhaps it will produce an exposure of orders, etc., judged not prudent at present for the public eye.

Feb. 20. Bishop Lowth of London, and Bishop Newton of Bristol, both died on the 14th inst.

Feb. 26. Walked to Chelsea with Mr. Dalglish, who returned and dined with me. Miss Savage and father joined us at tea.

---

* Governor Hutchinson's son.

† William Browne, of Salem, afterwards governor of Bermudas.

March 1. The Welsh procession from St. Andrew's church, Holborn, to the Crown and Anchor tavern in the Strand to dine ; the members, and all of that nation adorned with leeks and ornaments resembling them, stuck on the button-band of their hats, as is usual on this day, called in the Roman calendar St. David's Day ; still continued in his honor, who is the titular saint of the nation. This society is established for the support of the poor, for which they have a fund, schools, etc.

March 2. Wrote several letters to be sent home by a Mr. Sigourney.

TO DR. E. A. HOLYOKE.

London, · March 2, 1782.

DEAR SIR :

Since my tedious answer to your only favor, I have frequently thought of a mistaken notion asserted therein, which I naturally fell into for want of making proper inquiry and receiving information, arising from the vulgar prevailing notion in the province of Massachusetts Bay, that our soil was peculiarly unfavorable to the raising of wheat, which made me look upon the success of the Siberian as almost miraculous. A little while after I had sent off my answer, I happened to fall into a conversation with a curious sensible gentleman, who from repeated trials had proved the falsehood of our vulgar notions, and had raised frequent large harvests of excellent wheat from his own grounds, even from soils naturally weak and indifferent. I am therefore convinced he justly derived our people's pertinacious adherence to their own bad and wrong tillage from a mere obstinate and lazy attachment to old customs, handed down from father to son, and preferred in spite of yearly disappointments from generation to generation.

*　　*　　*　　*　　*　　*　　*

Your real friend and well wisher,

S. CURWEN.

March 2. Lord George Germaine, who was admitted into the administration on the idea of subjugating N. America to the unconditional authority of Parliament, having since Lord Cornwallis's surrender of himself and the whole army to the victorious arms of

France and Congress, abdicated his post of secretary in the American department, left the House of Commons, and gone up to the House of Lords by a patent of nobility. General Carleton, who is confessedly of superior ability in point of military knowledge and execution, is now appointed general-in-chief in America, when all manœuvres in his line are intentionally given up, and no opportunity is afforded for exertion, except in the way the former generals, his predecessors, have figured in amassing personal wealth out of this already cruelly oppressed people. Lord George Germaine's admission to the upper house was accompanied by many severe reflections and motions to address the king to prevent it; many lords thinking it disgraceful to suffer tamely one to be added to their number who stood disgraced by the sentence of a court martial, and was forbidden the society of any of the officers of the army. The Marquis of Caermarthen made the motion, and Lord Shelburne warmly seconded it. Many speeches on the occasion. Last Wednesday, General Conway concluded a long speech in the Commons with the following motion, viz.: Resolved, "That it is the opinion of this house, that a further continuance of an offensive war in America for the purpose of subduing by force the revolted colonies is totally impracticable, inasmuch as it weakens that force which we ought to employ against our European enemies, and is contrary to his majesty's declaration, who, in his gracious speech from the throne, expresses a wish to restore peace and tranquillity." This motion the ministerial party endeavored to dispose of by the attorney general's motion for an adjournment, when at half past one o'clock the house divided, and to the discomfiture of his majesty's ministers they were in a minority by nineteen. General Conway then moved that an address be presented to his majesty on the above resolution. This was seconded by Lord Althorpe, and carried without a division; the minister not daring to risk a second defeat. In consequence of this important decision, the nation is at last within the prospect of enjoying the blessings of a peace with America.

Lord Stormont wrote to the lord mayor and aldermen to prevent, if possible, illuminations in the city; none were exhibited but in the gallery on the top of the monument, which blazed with more than sixscore lamps. As soon as the joyful tidings of the minister's defeat and the nation's deliverance was announced in the lobby and avenues of the house to the numerous multitudes that waited in anxiety and perturbation to know the fate of their country, the most vehement and heartfelt shouts of acclamation pierced the ear, if it did not reach the heart of the minister, now tottering on the treasury bench. Those noble and distinguished characters, who by their steady perseverance and zeal had overcome the ruinous system of ministers, were hailed by the grave multitude as the saviours of their country. Expresses were despatched by the ambassadors to their several courts, announcing this important decision, which naturally changes the system by which the peace of Europe is disturbed. The king's answer to the address of the Commons in consequence of General Conway's motion for putting an end to the present war with America, contained the following : "There are no objects more near to my heart than the ease, happiness and welfare of my people ; and you may be assured, that in pursuance of your advice, I shall take such measures as shall appear to me most conducive to the restoration of harmony between Great Britain and the revolted colonies, so essential to the prosperity of both, and that my efforts shall be directed in the most effectual manner against our European enemies, until such peace can be obtained as shall consist with the interest and permanent welfare of my kingdom."

March 4. Advice of the surrender of Minorca to the combined armies of France and Spain, by Gen. Murray ; of the capture of St. Kitt's by the French, to which fate Nevis and Montserrat will probably soon submit. Essequibo and Demarara, taken by Rodney and Vaughan, are retaken by a French squadron, and it will be great good fortune if one single West India island be left to this wretched, devoted country.

March 7. The large banking house of Brown and Collinson, Lombard-street, was declared bankrupt to-day, and carries with it a train of ruin. They were of the society of Quakers, and therefore more unexpected, as people of that persuasion are generally prudent, and not engaged in expensive luxurious modes of life.

March 10. A gentleman lately from Brest acquaints Lord Sandwich that a piece of bad news had arrived there from the West Indies, which renders somewhat probable the report of a master just arrived, that St. Kitt's was retaken by Admiral Sir Samuel Hood, who hearing of de Grasse's departure, immediately sailed and obliged the French troops to the number of six thousand to surrender. They had not forced the English lines at Brimstone Hill, and were left exposed without a single ship to aid them. De Grasse, thinking himself sure of the conquest, after safely landing these, had left them to their chance, and went in quest of other adventures; probably to assist in retaking St. Lucia. May it prove true.

March 12. I find myself for some time laboring under distressing symptoms, which I have reason to believe my nature too feeble to withstand, and which must soon give way to and yield in the struggle. May I retire where undue passion, ungoverned appetite, and selfish regards shall have no rule or sway, and all shall be peace, harmony, mutual regards, and no intemperate gratifications.

March 18. This day advice is come from Ireland of the most serious nature; a large quantity of artillery is arrived there from France, under the pretext of securing the island from foreign invasion; but from the known general prevailing wish among the people, there is some reason to fear a general revolt from this government, and an independency thereon. Should it take place, wo betide this falling nation.

March 20. On the Earl of Surry's rising in the House of Commons to make his motion about removing ministers, Lord North arose, and after some altercation about the propriety of his standing up at the same time with the member, on his explaining his motives he was allowed to proceed, when he announced his (and the rest of the king's servants') quitting the administration, and moved for an adjournment till next Monday, by which time the business now in hand would be finished, and a new arrangement of ministers settled, not one of the old ones to remain in office. A greediness to share in the public plunder is, I fear, the *primum mobile*, nor shall we, it is greatly to be apprehended, gain much advantage by a new set, unless they shall totally change the system, form alliances, (for not one at present have we,) if that shall be practicable, put an end to the American dispute, and conciliate some of our victorious foes.

On this occasion Lord Surrey happened to espy Arnold, the

American seceding general, in the house, sent him a message to depart, threatening, in case of refusal, to move for breaking up the gallery; to which the general answered, that he was introduced there by a member; to which Lord Surrey replied, he might under that condition stay, *if he would promise never to enter it again,* with which General Arnold complied. This is the second instance of puplic disrespect he has met with: the king having been forced to engage his royal word not to employ or pension him; a just reward for treachery, which is ever odious.

March 26. The town full of talk about the new ministry; I doubt their success in settling with America: that poor continent is too much in the power of France to effect a reconciliation on any terms but such as the haughty court of Versailles shall approve of; and they, I dare say, will be humiliating enough to this infatuated country: which term, all the world will soon see, may with equal propriety be applied to English America.

March 27. Dined at Mrs. Snelson's on Ludgate-hill; passed an hour at the coffee-house before dinner, reading the newspapers containing the following list of the expected new ministry, which is a total change, there being, (as expressed,) " *not a hoof left of the old.*" Lord North and his compeers are obliged, from a minority in some questions, and a slender decreasing majority in others, to surrender their posts to the opposition; who come into play on principles professedly opposite to the late schemes of the cabinet respecting America, and the war consequent thereon :—

Marquis of Rockingham, First Lord of the Treasury.

Lord John Cavendish, Chancellor of the Exchequer.

Lord Camden, President of the Council.

Duke of Grafton, Lord Privy Seal.

Duke of Richmond, Master of Ordnance.

Secretary for Southern Department, Lord Shelburne.

   Do.   Northern   do.   Charles J. Fox.

Mr. Dunning, Attorney-General, with promise of being ennobled, seals first vacancy.

Mr. Lee, Solicitor-General.

Admiral Keppell, First Lord of the Admiralty.

General Conway, Commander in Chief of Forces.

Lord Howe,   do.   of Fleet.

Duke of Rutland, Master of the Horse.

Mr. Barré, or Mr. Thomas Townsend, Secretary at War.

Mr. Burke, Secretary to the First Lord of the Treasury, also Receiver and Paymaster-General.

Remaining Lords of the Treasury, Lord John Cavendish, Lord Althorp, John Spencer, James Greville, and Frederick Montague, Esqrs.

In order to keep in the present administration, the cabinet had come to a full determination to propose a dissolution of Parliament to the council; which being proposed, was at length agreed to as the only expedient to save their honor and support the present measures; the usual ministerial majority in the House of Commons being every day visibly lessened. But the chancellor, Lord Thurlow, with a fortitude and magnanimity peculiar to himself, and worthy of the highest praise, withdrew and refused to affix the seals, whereby this junto scheme is totally overset; nor dare the king nor his ministers discover any resentment at their disappointment. It is thought very serious consequences would have followed, and public royal disapprobation. Thank God that there yet remain any instances of virtue and regard to public safety amidst our deplorable situation, mercenary views, incredible dissipation, (wherein all ranks are involved,) profligacy and effeminacy of manners, and the open unrestrained practices of genteel vice and disregard of religion.

March 28. Visited Mr. Timmins for two hours; he returned with me. That the Prince of Wales is not content to take all upon trust, the following story perhaps will illustrate :—Returning lately from an airing on horseback, attended by a companion and one servant, on his arrival in St. James's Park, he alighted, and giving his horse to the servant, proceeded on foot with his friend to the gallery of the House of Commons, where he abode for some hours. Whilst there, having entered with his hat on, he was ordered to take it off, with which he complied, keeping his handkerchief up to his face to prevent the discovery of his person. Having heard many things before unknown to him, he departed, surprised and informed. This excursion continued so long as to delay the royal dinner for more than an hour, and occasioned an anxiety in his royal parents' breasts; his absence at meals being unusual. On his entering, being questioned, he frankly owned where he had been, not a little to the disapprobation of his father; who has since complied with his request to allow him a summer's progress through the kingdom, which he has often solicited, in case he would promise to make no more such elopements. It is a maxim of state for the present incumbent of the throne to keep the successor ignorant as possible, and totally unconcerned and unused to court measures and all public concerns, and this king seems inclined to put the maxim in practice to its extent.

March 29. Good Friday; attended worship at Whitehall chapel, Lord North present. Being disappointed in Westminster Abbey and St. Margaret's church, (at the former by the lowness of the reader's voice, at the latter by the service not having begun,) proceeding cityward, just as I came to the gate leading from Parliament-street to Scotland-yard, or Whitehall, who should cross me but a large clumsy gentleman with a blue ribbon across his breast, who, on inquiry, I found was Lord North. Following him into Whitehall chapel, I remained during the service. He is rather above the common height, and bulk greatly exceeding; large legs, walks heavily, manner clumsy; very large featured, thick lips, wide mouth, high forehead, large nose, eyes not lively; head well covered with hair, which he wears high before. The preacher was Dr. Noel, dean of Salisbury, the only Episcopal preacher that I ever saw or heard repeat the Lord's prayer by heart; not one of them daring to trust to their memory except this man. His manner and delivery very agreeable, and his discourse excellent and useful. Dined at Salisbury-court; met Mr. Dalglish, who accompanied me home to tea and passed evening.

March 30. Mr. Dalglish called, and we went together to the Bishop of London's terrace-walk on the banks of the Thames at Fulham, and returned by Little Chelsea.

March 31. Attended public worship at St. Paul's; Mr. Hyslop preached. Drank tea with Mr. Peters. He informed me administration would not consent to the independence of America; the ministerial plan is to govern America by a lord-lieutenant, and create nobility; and if she will not agree to Great Britain's proposal, to make a partition treaty of the colonies with France, to whom the northern colonies and Canada would be ceded, the southern colonies remaining to Great Britain,—a fine bargain, truly.

April 4.   Mr. Dalglish called at ten o'clock, and we departed on foot to Hampton Court, passing through Chelsea, part of Hammersmith to Fulham, crossed the river just above Putney bridge, passed through that town, and to Bornes Mortlake to back of Kew; from thence to Richmond, crossing the river at the bridge, proceeded through Twickenham to Hampton, passing Bushy Park, a tedious level of more than a mile in length, arrived at King's Arms inn at two o'clock, where we dined.   At four o'clock proceeded to the palace; entered with a large company of females, who arrived there at the same time with us, joining a master with a number of young persons, his pupils, and a governess with a score of young misses, rendering our company through the royal apartments very numerous.   The rooms almost all hung in rich tapestry of Brussels manufacture, wrought in gold and silver, which, being put up in King William's reign, time has somewhat tarnished. Pity that the room built for the reception of the Cartoons, and which they long adorned, is now by this king's whim robbed of them to cover the staircase walls of Buckingham House.   Returning we arrived at "King's Arms" inn, on the borders of Kew Green, and at the foot of the bridge leading to Brentford at eight o'clock, where we supped and lodged.

April 5.   We walked on Bankside terrace as far as Sion House, meaning opposite thereto.   Returning we passed the building, and taking the foot-path by the river, kept it through Chiswick and Hammersmith as far as it was continued, affording most agreeable views; then turning, crossed the country to Fulham and by little Chelsea, arriving at Don Saltero's café on the bank of the river, where we dined, and at four o'clock departed, arriving at my lodgings at five o'clock, having in two days walked thirty-two miles, (yesterday twenty-one, and eleven to-day,) and am at this present writing no more fatigued nor less able to take another walk to-morrow of the same length.

April 6.   Capt. Coombs and Mr. Dalglish drank tea with me.

April 7, *Sunday*.   Attended worship and communion at Essex House chapel; Mr. Lindsay read the service and officiated at the communion.   Dr. Priestley preached an excellent discourse.

TO SAMUEL SEWALL, ESQ., SIDMOUTH.

Brompton, April 8, 1782.

DEAR SIR:

I fancy you need not give yourself any concern about future supplies, which my last letter intimated. Government, it is probable, will not be guilty of such injustice as to withhold what the public faith has engaged. Some ill-founded grants will be stopped, and here the reform in this will end.

Truly your friend,

S. CURWEN.

April 8. Removed my lodgings from Yeoman's Row to Mrs. Smithson's, near the chapel, Brompton.

April 15. News from East Indies that our Admiral Hughes had taken three places from the Dutch on the coast of Malabar. Further accounts of the designed reform by new administration in national expenditures and abolition of all needless sinecure establishments—wish it may prove true and of lasting advantage.

April 18. The delegates of the associated counties held their first meeting in the new common council chamber at Guildhall. During the late administration they were refused it with some marks of contemptuous disapprobation. New men and new measures have effected a wonderful change in the common council of London.

April 19. This day seven years the fatal fight at Lexington, Mass., happened; productive of such baneful consequences to Great Britain and America; what will be its issue, is known only to Him who overrules the folly and wickedness of man, to serve his own wise purposes; may all of them who are so deeply interested therein be prepared for it.

April 20. It is affirmed that the cabinet, which consists of ten members, have been thrice equally divided; the lord president in that case makes report to the king, and he agrees with one opinion, which is then entered in the council books, with this addition, " by command of his majesty." The king refused to give his opinion, saying, " *Let it be done as they determine among themselves.*" " But, sire, they are divided." " *So let it remain then!*"—A strong ground of suspicion that neither measures nor men are to his liking.

> " The king in a pet, his affairs all deranged,
> Has at last his unmerciful ministers changed ;
> Brave news, quoth the Congress ; but better would be,
> Had the king when he changed them omitted the C."

April 24.   Admiral Barrington has sent into Portsmouth four French transports from Brest and a large ship armed *en flute*, and was left chasing four men-of-war near the harbor.

April 25.   Admiral Barrington arrived in harbor with ten ships of the line and nine transports—French prizes, intended for the East Indies, with another French ship of sixty-four guns armed *en flute*.

May 2.   To Westminster Hall ; sat an hour in chancery court, heard lord chancellor try three causes ; method summary.

May 9.   To Chelsea—took tea with Mrs. Timmins—Robert Hallowell first acquainted me with Clark Pickman's death.

TO RICHARD WARD, ESQ., SALEM.

London, May 11, 1782.

DEAR SIR :

Should your *great and good ally* obtain the two only very probable objects of her American alliance, the impoverishment of Great Britain and the consequent seizure of the late English colonies, which she seems at present in a fair way for, no man on this side the Atlantic in his wits would, I think, whatever regard he may feel for his native country, willingly forego a bare subsistence here for French domination and wooden shoes there.   I would just suggest to you, should America in this hour refuse the offers Great Britain may make of a separate peace ; or France refuse to suffer her, (for we well know here the power she has acquired over her,) and no partition treaty take place, (being in the present situation the best to be expected,) depend upon it, you fathers of the present age will have it in their power ere many revolutions of the sun, to tell their children the inestimable civil, religious and political privileges you of this generation have wantoned away, and with sad regret recount the happy condition of former days ; nor will the comparison with those you will then mournfully experience between English protection and French oppression, fail to enhance your misery. You will then find the little finger of French power heavier than the loin of the English government, with all its apprehended train of evils. As a proof of my needless fears or right judgment, convey my kind love to your wife and children.

Your friend,

S. CURWEN.

TO HON. JONATHAN SEWALL, BRISTOL.

London, May 12, 1782.

DEAR SIR:

Confined as I have been, for near two years, to a very narrow circle without variety, like monotony in music, every thing about me is become insipid. I am therefore going into a scene of new objects, and hey for Flanders for a month. Naturalists say change of air, even from bad to worse, is good for the health of the body; that of the Netherlands must, I think, be certainly salubrious and nutritive. How happy should I be to have so agreeable a companion as Judge Sewall. Who knows what effect a month's residence may produce? For my part I fancy my thin lathy body in that air, and by the use of rich generous Burgundy, etc., procurable there at a cheap rate, may increase to a manly bulk. My heart would dilate with pride and pleasure to receive a note of compliance with my request—nor should I be displeased if your kinsman Samuel Sewall should join and make a trio. Please remember me to your family and those of our countrymen with you with whom I am acquainted.

Very truly yours,

S. CURWEN.

May 12. It is suggested that the new administration mean to increase the power of the crown by their projected new militia. As they have, or one of them at least, deceived the people by frequently declaring he had a peace in his pocket, when the event showed the falsehood of those declarations; should their other pretensions prove as futile and groundless, they will deserve the execration of this and future generations, and will, I hope, meet a deserved fate. At best, however, I expect not much good, and

44

think ours an ill-compacted junto of very short duration: their principles are not uniform nor concurrent.

May 17. At New England Coffee-house heard the glorious news of Admiral Rodney's defeat and capture of the French Admiral de Grasse, with five capital ships, and one sunk. With Mr. Dalglish to Chelsea College Gardens—thence to Mr. Timmins's to tea.

May 18. Trinquemale, the strongest garrison belonging to the Dutch, and called the Gibraltar of the East Indies, being the principal fortress on the island of Ceylon, has been captured by Admiral Sir Edward Hughes, who was going against another fort, which he hoped to reduce.

May 23. Dined at New England Coffee-house with New England company.

May 24. With Mr. Dalglish went to Maddocks the florist's exhibition of tulips; he pointed out the bell king and bell queen stocks, a beautiful and singular plant, which he is unable to increase, having derived but one offset in twenty-two years; had been offered twenty-two guineas for it; the tints are exquisitely fine.

This day arrived further advice of Sir Samuel Hood's capture of two more French men-of-war, viz., L'Esprit of eighty guns, and Philo of seventy-four, and two frigates, the Amiable, thirty-two and Ceres eighteen, in the West Indies.

May 25. Loitering through St. James's Park, and seeing many people collected around the rails of Buckingham House, stopped to see the Prince of Wales, who soon appeared in a phaeton with Col. Tarleton, who, I was told, is frequently to be seen with him.

June 3. Crossed Westminster bridge to visit Mrs. Hay and Mr. Dalglish.

June 9. It is reported that the Russian ambassador announced that the czarina has declared, in case the Dutch refuse the offer Great Britain has made, which she pronounces liberal, that she will assist the English with her fleet—eighteen for channel service and twenty against the Dutch.

June 25. To Queen dock, Wapping, to see Capt. Coombs on board a ship he is appointed to keep guard in; stepped in at long room, custom-house.

June 28. To Mark-lane corn market, to inquire for Indian corn, and was told there had been none for two years. Afterwards met Mr. Flucker in the Park, and conversed with him half an hour. Met T. Goldthwait, and rode with him to Charing Cross ; invited me to dine at his house, Walthamstow.

June 29. Took a long walk with Mr. Hutchinson. Met a man with a mug in his hand, which he said was once the famous Shakspeare's, and that he inherited it from his wife's father, who was heir to all Shakspeare's effects, being a descendant from him in the female line ; and that Garrick had offered ten guineas for it when he celebrated the jubilee at Stratford upon Avon. The Public Advertiser to-day says, " Administration have very laudably determined on withdrawing their pensions from the American refugees ; so that next year," says the writer, " we may hope for some more haymakers than we are able to get for the present harvest." An ill-natured and I hope untrue declaration.

July 1. Visited Parson Peters ; meeting there Parson Wiswall, accompanied him to Battersea bridge, having stepped into Don Saltero's café, Chelsea, and drank tea.

TO REV. ISAAC SMITH, SIDMOUTH.

Near Brompton Chapel, July 2, 1782.

DEAR SIR :

You desire me to be communicative about myself—a poor subject, truly, to write about. I am, however, to thank you for your solicitude, and at present, as you see by the date, am very near the house of God, but never enter therein, keeping steady to our conventicle in Essex-street, Strand, which is my regular and constant Sunday's resort ; retaining still my old New England prejudice of observing the fourth commandment. My health is better than usual, having escaped the epidemic hitherto.

Three days since I received a letter from T. B., wherein he acquaints me that our friends are well. I presume you have heard of the death of Judge Lynde and Clark Pickman.

Your townsman Allen is dead, leaving Sir William Pepperell and George Erving his executors, directing that his remains shall be removed after the troubles to the vault under King's Chapel, Boston.

We have an American Thursday dinner club at the New England Coffee-house.

Very truly your friend,
S. Curwen.

July 3. Meeting Parson Wiswall, on whose recommendation I went to Battersea to engage lodgings for a fortnight; from thence to his church and attended prayers, where were present nine in the house exclusive of nine parish boys. From thence we set off by agreement on a walk to Kingston on the Thames, nine miles, arriving at the " *Sun,*" where took a cold repast, a pottle of strawberries; arrived at lodgings before nine o'clock. New arrangement of ministry; Lord Shelburne first commissioner of the treasury, Earl Temple secretary in lieu of Chs. Jas. Fox, and Mr. Pitt, a favorite patriotic speaker, in lieu of Lord Shelburne; Burke out, and Barré also, with a pension of £3,200 per annum; Duke of Manchester lord chamberlain.

July 4. Went to London to the Thursday dinner at New England Coffee-house.

July 5. Went to Westminster, and in the lobby of the House of Commons heard that Charles J. Fox, Lord John Cavendish, Edmund Burke, and General Conway, have been dismissed from the king's service; the former on account of his speech last Monday, declaring the independency of America to be agreed on, which Lord Shelburne denied, having steadily refused his consent thereto. Lord Rockingham's death, which happened last Monday, has very probably hastened the present event. Returned as far as Mr. Elisha Hutchinson's, Brompton, and drank tea with the family.

July 11. Dined as usual at New England fish-club dinner. The king prorogued Parliament, and made a speech from the throne in his robes and crown.

July 16. At Parson Peters's met young Parson Clarke, and observing him speak articulately, and with some degree of clearness, expressed my surprise; and inquiring the cause, he told me his speech came to him on a sudden, and on the very day seven years that he was first seized with the incapability of uttering sounds.

July 21. To Kensington Gardens; there met Thomas Danforth and Samuel Porter; the latter related an account of his voyage to Oporto.

July 22. Went to Clapham Common to dine with Mr. Gilbert Harrison; Mr. Toulmin and his lady's mother there. Returned through the fields; the hedges perfumed by sweet smelling blossoms.

July 25. Had a view of the Duke of Cumberland's sailing match on the river, from Mr. Hay's summer-house on the bank. River covered with barges and boats, oars, scullers and sails; the duke in his own barge, ensign red, having an anchor and a length of cable in gold-leaf depicted thereon. A great concourse attended; he was in going saluted by a discharge of small cannon; the boats departed from Blackfriars bridge, length of course to Putney bridge; premium a silver cup of £50 value.

July 27. Dined at New England Coffee-house on fish in company with Mr. Flucker, Francis Waldo, Mr. Hutchinson, Thomas Goldthwait, etc.

July 29. Through Hackney to Walthamstow, where dined with Mr. Goldthwait.

August 3. In passing Bird-cage Walk had a slight glimpse of Count de Grasse at Sir Peter Parker's window; he is a stout, very tall man.

August 4. At Battersea church; the vicar, Parson Gardner, preached.

August 21. Wrote Mr. Elisha Hutchinson at Birmingham. Afterwards went to Capt. Coombs' at a Mr. Birch's, beyond Folly Bridge, Dockhead; on the door of a meeting-house I passed observed the following words written in chalk, " *We have erred and strayed.*" Unless the supporters of the doctrine of necessity, or even expediency, of a universal conformity to a state establishment of the form of religious worship, can lay its foundation in reason or a command in holy writ, I defy the ablest disputant to prove me or any dissenter in England or elsewhere guilty of a fault in adhering to a different mode of external worship, or schism in a bad sense. On the contrary, all political establishments being tinctured with the reigning principles of the times when they were founded, and men's notions and opinions changing with fashions, usages, customs and language, a continued sameness is utterly impossible;

the endeavor therefore to compel men is offering a violence to the understanding, and denotes the character called in Scripture the *man of sin,* wherever found.

August 28. Over Westminster Bridge to Mrs. Chapman's, Kensington, to visit Mrs. Hay. Mr. Danforth called. Drank tea at Parson Peters's.

August 31. This day the papers announce Prince William Henry's* death, at New-York, being the second breach in the royal family, Prince Alfred, the youngest, having died last week. There remain a dozen, a heavy burden yet on the national finances. Called on Mr. Danforth, and there met Mr. Brewer, late governor of Bermuda; Mr. Danforth is assisting him in preparing his papers in answer to sixteen allegations or acts of complaint lodged in the king's council against him.

Sept. 1. Attended worship at St. Martin's; Mr. Harrison preached to a full assembly. After describing Christian poverty of spirit, and assigning some reasons why Christ began his first public discourse by recommending this virtue, he mentioned two sorts of men who were wholly destitute of it, viz., those Calvinistic professors who pretended to a certainty of their salvation, and those who claimed it as a merit due to their good works; both of whom he pronounced deficient in the distinguishing characteristic of Christ's religion.

Sept. 3. Capts. Peters and Walker called and took tea with me; the former a brother of Parson Samuel Peters, the latter from Worcester.

Sept. 5. In walking through Parliament-street and seeing crowds running through Scotland-yard, joined them, and on inquiry found they were accompanying Parson Lloyd, a clergyman, returned from Bow-street Justices' examination to Westminster Bridewell, from whence he was taken this morning on a complaint of highway robbery; and it is said he is identified. He seemed hardened, and of a rough, bold cast, and begged with a careless boldness money of every well dressed person that passed as he was being conducted to prison in irons; his right hand being also chained to an officer's, or one of the justice's men.

Sept. 6. Called at Mr. Wiswall's to accompany him to Holy-

* Premature—he became king at the decease of his brother George IV.

well-lane, as far as the gateway of King John's palace, which he never had seen before.

Sept. 7. Over Westminster Bridge to turnpike head of Kent-street, designing to go to Edmund's great gardens at Deptford; but the time being far spent, and they a mile and a half distant, I proceeded no further; and turning my steps homeward, passed through Kent-street, a long narrow one, of low ordinary houses, and inhabitants corresponding; scarcely one reputable person appearing in view.

Sept. 9. To Mr. Edmund's house, the great Deptford gardener, to see his asparagus lot of forty acres.

Sept. 11. Went with Mr. Peters to Mr. Hunter's seat at Hampstead, west end—arrived at one o'clock; kindly welcomed, dined, drank tea, and departed at six o'clock. Passing through the fields, arrived at the Edgeware road, where one of the queen's coaches returning to town received us in.

Sept. 13. Called on Parson Peters, from whom learned more of the convulsed state of Massachusetts and Connecticut than I had heard before. The people there are more impatient than elsewhere under public expenses, and retain more of the old republican leaven; but I know not whether they have not more political discernment and attend more closely to the steps of their rulers; and in truth the *Bible*, the *law-book*, and the *gun*, are more used there than in any part of the English dominions; therefore more than anywhere else on the face of the globe—no other country having had so great a share of political and civil liberty. By the packet from New-York, Sir William Pepperell here has received a letter from the Rev. William Walter there, informing him that the counties of Worcester and Hampshire, in the Massachusetts Bay, have declined sending members to the provincial assembly, and also the payment of the tax of eight shillings on each head through the United States, laid by Congress, amounting to four millions of hard dollars, and that it had only raised twenty thousand. That the said counties had sent to know of Sir Guy Carleton on what terms Great Britain would receive them. Also that courts of justice and all law proceedings were stopped in Berkshire as well as in Worcester and Hampshire, a general uneasiness having taken place by the Congress's requisition to pay the tax in hard money.

It is also reported that Dr. Saunders had received private letters, acquainting him that four of the colonies had protested against continuing any longer their French alliance.

Sept. 14.   Walked to Smithfield bars; saw for the first time since its demolition old Hicks's Hall, a few remains and rubbish only, leaving road to St. John's-street very commodious and wide.

Lord Howe sailed with thirty-four ships to the relief of Gibraltar.

Sept. 26.   It is announced that a commission was last Tuesday perfected under the great seal, empowering General Sir Guy Carleton and Admiral Digby at New-York to acknowledge American independence; and to treat with Congress, or either of the thirteen states, or any body of men.   A fine bargain, truly, has this once powerful wealthy state offered to their lately despised colonies.   But human policy sometimes overshoots its mark; human wisdom is narrow, and human designs are controlled by a wiser director than govern court-cabinet councils, and who acts on broader plans.

Sept. 30.   Went to the city to deliver a letter for conveyance to Rev. Mr. Peters; from Blackfriars Bridge had a sight of city barges with flags displayed, rowing down stream; having the sheriffs, lord mayor and aldermen returning from Westminster Hall, the former being this day sworn into office by one of the barons of the exchequer.

Oct. 4.   Advices received at Lord Shelburne's that the siege of Gibraltar is raised.

Oct. 7.   It is reported to-day, that the Spanish floating gun-batteries had been defeated before Gibraltar; eleven burnt, sunk, and destroyed, having one hundred and ninety-three brass cannon of twenty-four pound shot, besides one hundred and fifty iron, same calibre; between fifteen hundred and two thousand men; it having been a general assault, begun on St. Louis's day, September 9th, and completed 13th;—three hundred poor souls General Elliot picked up in the water after the batteries were sunk, and sent them in the same day to their friends and country: this by a letter from the Hague.

TO MR. ANDREW DALGLISH, GLASGOW.

London, Oct. 7, 1782.

DEAR SIR:

In Hampshire government the opposition has been so general and violent as to require a body of French soldiers to be sent against them, who, on attempting to reduce the insurgents, were attacked, and some lives on both sides lost, without accomplishing the purpose of their errand.* Yet for all this there is not the least disposition in general, as a state, to accept of the terms Great Britain has offered without the concurrence of their great and good ally. On General Carleton's proclamation, the Congress and continental governments declared it insidious, and despised the offer of independence, which they contemptuously said did not depend on the consent of Great Britain.

The letter you inquire about was written by Parson Walter, whom you know very well, and is of the same complexion with all advices received from that quarter, which, ever since the commencement of this quarrel, have been amusing the public with assurances of a speedy reduction of the rebellion, as they term it; florid descriptions of the desperate situation of the rebel army; the sufferings of the country, a growing dislike of Congressional authority, mutual heart-burnings and quarrels amongst its members, and an increasing affection towards the mother country; all which from the first I disbelieved, and it now proves in event, after a course of six years' delusion, to have been the phantoms of a heated party imagination.

I have seen at large a relation of the distresses and inability of the New-York government under the republican rulers, in a representation made by the House of Assembly to their government; the picture perhaps may serve for the rest of the colonies. It is the opinion of some refugees that New-York is by this time evacuated, and if one may judge from analogy, I think it is not improbable; for there never was a time when government had so fair a prospect of overturning that mighty colossus of independency as now:— their distresses never greater, their resources exhausted, loans not to be obtained, French troops few in number, and their own army

* Wholly incorrect.

dwindled to a pitiful size; but the die is cast, and as the same ill
star which has had the ascendant ever since this baneful quarrel
commenced still continues to shed its malignant influence, government has formally offered America unconditional independency
under the royal sign manual.   Gen. Carleton writes that the colonies are so determined against all governmental connections with
Great Britain, that if they cannot maintain their independency, they
will declare themselves colonies of France, and if they must be
slaves they will take a new yoke, however galling, rather than put
on the old one; this, by the way, is carrying political resentment
to the highest pitch of folly and frenzy.

Very truly your friend,

S. Curwen.

Oct. 9.   This day, for sundry reasons, ought to be inserted in
the very short list of *dies albi*, (white days,) which I note, that on
inspection I may refresh my memory with a pleasing recollection
amidst the gloom, that from a constrained absence from my native
country but too generally overspreads my grief-laden mind.

Oct. 11.   Attended Mayne the banker's sale of goods, and also
Beranger's, late gentleman of the horse to his majesty; bought
nothing; things well sold. Mr. William Clarke drank tea with me.

Oct. 15.   I am told by Mr. Rose no orders are to be delivered
till the commissioners, consisting of two members of parliament,
Mr. Coke and Mr. Wilmot, have examined the refugee claimers
and their claims; that it may require more than a month's time.
Proceeded to Oxford-street to pay Mr. Danforth a visit; whilst
there Mr. Hale entered.   Met in streets many returning from an
execution of ten felons at Tyburn.

Oct. 16.   In conversation with a gentleman at an ordinary, I
observed in him the prevailing characteristic infirmity of this
nation, rendering them both envied and hated by Europe, viz., an
overweening conceit of English bravery, accompanied with a contempt for other nations; which in this day of their distress they
now feel the sad effects of, in the cool indifference the other states
view her embarrassments, though without producing a reformation
as far as I can perceive.   It is generally believed the French and
Spaniards will retire from before Gibraltar on the approach of the

fleet under Lord Howe; in case of reverse, I know not what rage, disappointment, and despair might be the natural effects; the political evils are too obvious not to be seen and dreaded.

Oct. 17. It is reported the Bavarian resident minister has received the following important advices, viz., that Lord Howe has had an engagement with the combined fleets; taken twelve and destroyed seven, with the loss of four or five of his own ships; all taken are Spanish, not a French one among them; they retreated into Cadiz harbor, and he pursued his course to Gibraltar, which is thereby relieved, being the great object of his voyage.

A few hours after, the above was followed by another, viz.,— that Lord Howe in defence of Gibraltar had surrendered to the successful arms of the combined fleet.

By Captain Afflick from New-York, is arrived a confirmation of the loss of the French seventy-four, the Magnifique, with the Triumphante of eighty guns from the West Indies under Vaudreuil, bound to Boston; the one foundered, the other ran ashore at Point Alderton; also the loss of the British ship Lion of sixty-four guns on her passage to New-York. 'Tis said also transports are gone from New-York to take off the troops, etc., from Charleston, and that they are also abandoning New-York; government being in that case determined to take away every difficulty respecting American independence, to bring on a treaty for a general peace.

Oct. 18. Passing through Tooley-street in the Borough, observed the name of Southernwood on a door; having knowledge of one of that name in my first voyage to London in 1738, I am determined to call and make inquiry about the family of Cottenbilt, with whom I then lived.

Oct. 19. Went on a visit to Mr. Danforth; acquainted him with Mr. and Mrs. Hay's compliments and invitation to dinner tomorrow with me at their house No. 4 Golden-square; staid till eight.

Oct. 23. To Treasury; gave a card with my name and address to a Mr. Allen, clerk to Mr. Townshend, one of the secretaries of state, agreeably to an order, to be questioned as to my claims as a refugee for support; the value of my estate and effects left behind, losses sustained, etc. etc.

Oct. 25. Went at eleven o'clock, in compliance with a summons from Messrs. Wilmot and Cooke, (members of Parliament, chosen by the lords of the treasury to examine the claims of the American sufferers, state their claims and produce vouchers,) to attend them at the American secretary's office, Treasury-house, Whitehall. Was examined and dismissed, after being directed to bring a certificate of my being a person of property, and of steady uniform attachment to principles of loyalty, which I propose to bring from the late provincial secretary, Mr. Flucker.

Oct. 26. Drank tea at Samuel H. Sparhawk's, Bedford-court, Red-Lion square, and remained till nine o'clock.

Oct. 28. Passed afternoon and evening at Mr. Danforth's, who assisted me in drawing up my certificate to present to the commissioners. In the evening Dr. Jeffries, a brother exile, called in and announced the arrival of an express with advice that Lord Howe is relieving Gibraltar; the French and Spanish looking on him from Algeziras bay without even attempting to loose ground and meet him; an apparent proof that with fifty-one capital ships they thought themselves unequal to his fleet of thirty-four. It is likewise added, that the Spaniards by the late high wind have lost three ships.

Oct. 29. Went to Mr. Flucker's with the following certificate for his signature, viz. :—" General Gage and Governor Oliver being absent from London, we, the subscribers, do certify that Samuel Curwen, Esq., late of Salem, in the province of Massa-chusetts Bay, is descended from an ancient and respectable family in said province. That he has been a deputy Judge of Admiralty and Provincial Impost Officer, and for near thirty years in the commission of the peace for the county of Essex; had always maintained a most respectable character, and was early distinguished for his attachment to the established constitution of the province, and its dependence on and subordination to the authority of the king of Great Britain, and was esteemed a gentleman of considerable property and fortune."

Called in the afternoon and received my certificate, signed, " Thomas Flucker, secretary of the province of Massachusetts Bay." While there, joined by Col. Morrow, just arrived from Cowbridge, in Wales, on a like errand.

Oct. 31. Called at Mr. Timmins's; he was engaged in packing up his goods in order to remove to Wolverhampton, where he is about commencing business.

Nov. 1. To Pimlico, where took tea with Parson Peters.

Nov. 2. Reported that Lord Howe has had an engagement with the combined fleet, and has defeated and dispersed it.

Nov. 8. Saw in my landlord's parlor the poorest nobleman I believe in the three kingdoms, a *Lord Kirkcudbright,* brought up a glover, and who for years worked at this trade in Glasgow ; he is now a captain in the king's guards. Passing a coach, I observed its number 1000, the highest number licensed.

Nov. 11. Received my order for quarter's pension of £25 ; the first given to any refugee on the new establishment of no deduction to the officer of commissions.

Nov. 25. Cold air; St. James's canal frozen hard enough to bear skating on.

Nov. 26. The meeting of Parliament summoned for to-day is postponed to Thursday 5th proximo, in expectation that the commissioners at Paris may by that time come to their ultimate determination about peace or war ; or on the preliminaries whereon a peace is to be founded. France and Holland fancy they see too well the probable consequences of prolonging the war, to accept the terms proposed ; presuming in the issue Great Britain must accede to what they shall demand, and who does not ? None, I dare say, but those who will not, and only such are blind.

Nov. 27. Newspapers filled with contradictory reports about peace ; all dread a continuance of this nefarious, ill-omened, ill-judged, distracted quarrel.

Nov. 30. Dined and passed the day at Capt. Hay's. Mrs. Chapman, with whom these my friends board at Kensington Common, near Vauxhall Gardens, says that the famous Sterne, author of " *Tristram Shandy,*" " *Sentimental Journey,*" etc., was totally void of the fine feelings of humanity, which he so beautifully paints, and are characteristics of his writings, which in respect thereto show him to be an original genius ; and but ill discharged the various relative duties of life ; one instance only excepted, which was an immoderate fondness of an only daughter. As a proof among others, he suffered an aged mother, which but for the proof of it is hardly to be credited, to die in a jail for want of money to discharge a debt of twenty pounds. The public ought to know the character of a writer who so ill in practice exemplified what his pen so justly and beautifully describes. This was told her by a very intimate acquaintance of Sterne, who was personally informed of his whole history.

Dec. 3. Yesterday Vergennes' secretary brought notice that the commissioners appointed by Great Britain and the thirteen United States, had signed a provisional treaty, whereupon stocks rose five per cent. The following letter was published:

Whitehall, Dec. 3, 1782.

THE RIGHT HONORABLE THE LORD MAYOR:

In consequence of my letter to your lordship of the 22d ult., I take the earliest opportunity of acquainting you that a messenger is this moment arrived from Paris with an account of provisional articles having been signed on the 30th ult., by his majesty's commissioners and the commissioners of the United States of America, to be inserted in and constitute a treaty of peace, which is to be concluded when terms of a peace shall be agreed upon between Great Britain and France.

I am, etc.,

I. TOWNSHEND.

Dec. 4. Called on Mr. Heard at Herald's office; there learned, in a conversation with a Mr. Webb, of seeming great political knowledge, that at the time the House of Commons left the late administration in a minority, or in other words, refused to support Lord North's measures, the king took it to heart, and resented it so far as to declare he would leave them (as he expressed it) to themselves, and go over to Hanover, from whence his family came, and proceeded so far as to order the administration to provide two yachts to transport himself there; whereupon the queen interfered, and remonstrated against such a desperate measure, so fatal to her and his family, as well as his own personal interest. Others, too, represented the distressful condition to which the nation would be reduced by the absence and want of royal authority, though it seemed to little effect, so sadly chagrined and provoked was he.

Lord Rockingham also joined the remonstrants, and showed the necessity of a change of men and measures, with no better success;—so naturally obstinate and pertinaciously bent was he on his favorite plan of subjugating his (here called) rebellious subjects in America, and bringing them to his feet, till he was told that as sure as he set his foot out of the kingdom, the parliament would declare the crown abdicated and the throne vacant, nor would he ever be permitted to re-enter the kingdom again,—which argument, it seems, brought him to a more cool and juster sight of the folly of such a step, and the absolute necessity of stooping to a compliance with the requisitions of the public. I do not pretend to indicate the measures of opposition, but a more unsuccessful administration, from whatever cause it proceeded, which time will satisfactorily perhaps explain, was never before engaged to promote royal designs. What may be the condition of Great Britain and America at the period of the present distressful war, God knows; for my own part, I tremble at the event, as desirable as it may be, for I can view neither country without the most fearful apprehensions of dreadful distresses; whoever began and voluntarily continued this unreasonable, pernicious dispute, does and will deserve the execration of this and future ages, and in the language of * * * *, " The child will rue, that is yet unborn, the fatal measures of Lord North's administration."

Dec. 5. The king delivered his speech from the throne. I went to see him robe and sit on the throne at the House of Lords; he was clothed in green laced with gold when he came, and when he went, in red laced; it being the custom to change his garments. The tail of his wig was in a broad, flowing, loose manner; called the coronation tail. His abode in the lords' chamber scarce exceeded half an hour, in which he read his speech of eleven pages.

As one proof among many that might be given of the restraint and disguise of real sentiments on the part of courtiers, from the highest character in the presence chamber to the lowest lounger and attendant at ministerial levees, take the following :—When the king found himself obliged to take new ministers, and give up Lord North and his associates, it is notorious that it was abhorrent to the royal mind, and being naturally of a pertinacious, obstinate temper, was with the utmost difficulty brought to yield a reluctant consent. On the first court day after the appointment, when he was in a manner forced out of his closet into the room of audience, he re-

ceived his new servants with a smile, and transacted business with
them afterwards with as much seeming cordiality and openness, as
if they had been in his favor, and in his most intimate conceits; so
seemingly satisfied and so serene was the royal countenance, that
all the newspapers sounded forth the gracious monarch's obliging,
condescending goodness to the public wishes, though nothing was
farther from his heart, had not the necessity of his affairs impelled
him thereto.   At the same time coming up to Mr. Wilkes, he said
he was glad of the opportunity to thank him for his very proper
and laudable behavior in the late riot; took notice of his looks,
which indicated a want of health, advised him to a country air and
exercise, which, said his majesty, I find by experience an excellent
expedient to procure and preserve health; all this with the same
apparent sincerity, as if they had been in a continued course of
paying and receiving compliments, congratulations, and acknowledgments for mutual kindnesses and good offices, though all the
world knows there was not a man in the three kingdoms more
thoroughly hated, nor whom he had taken a more foolish and un-
necessary pains to ruin.· The above-mentioned interview being
told of in company, Mr. Wilkes took occasion to remark in the
following words :—" To have heard the king, one would have
thought I was consulting a quack on the score of my health."

   Dec. 6.   Read the king's speech, declaring his offer of independency to America, and his hopes soon of a general peace.

   Dec. 16.   Received from a Cumberlander a note informing me
of Miss Curwen, an heiress of said county, having married with a
Mr. Christian, possessing a small estate adjoining her large one.

   Dec. 17.   Dined at Capt. Hay's, with Mr. Danforth and a Mr.
Burges, a warm opposer of American independence, who asserted
that a great majority of his countrymen (English) abhor the idea,
(which Mr. Danforth silently controverts,) declaring they will forcibly oppose the plan ; thinks the minister who attempts it deserves
the gallows, and will join in bringing him to it; with this reserve
only, should Lord North and a great majority of the parliament co-
incide, then it would be proper for the nation to acquiesce; he
also declared his abhorrence of the successors of Lord North and
his associates.

   Dec. 20.   Went to general court martial at the Horse Guards,

on General Murray, and abode in the crowd two hours, till adjournment at three o'clock; in the course of the trial, a witness in favor
of the impeached had been several times called for on account of
some privateers he was accused of being concerned in, particularly
the Hannah, afterwards bought for government service.   Sir William Draper proposed that the witness should be asked whether
Gen. Murray had received any profits on the sale of prize goods;
the demand threw Gen. Murray into an apparent embarrassment,
and cast a concern on his face, to me very plainly to be seen; but
his witness, Neal, with an unblushing, unembarrassed, brazen
countenance, relieved his friend by giving a direct negative.   Sir
William, expressing great astonishment, turning to him asked,
" Do you, upon your oath, say that you do not know that General
Murray had any profits arising from the sale of prize goods?"
The witness repeatedly said he did not know he had, which seemed
to put Sir William into an agitation.   This thorough-paced witness
appeared determined not to do his work by halves.   I know not
what effect a true answer to the question would have had, but it
seems it might have led to an inquiry which the general would,
perhaps, be glad to prevent.

Dec. 21.   At court-martial, and in the course of this day's evidence, it appears that Sir Wm. Draper catches hold of every circumstance that can possibly admit of the least complaints; and what
man's conduct, who is possessed of discretionary powers, does not;
at least, it appears General Murray has not acted a base, rapacious
part, nor tyrannical; at least, not seemingly beyond the limits of
his written commissions as governor and vice-admiral of the island
and its dependencies — prudently saving appearances.   In the issue,
by the complexion of facts at this stage, not to anticipate, I fancy
he may acquit himself, if not with great honor, at least without
blame : nor perhaps may Sir William incur the disgraceful blame
of Admiral Keppel's accuser, Sir Hugh Palliser.   Though the
prosecution of both really proceeded from the same cause, a real
dislike; the accusers of each, in other respects, stand under very
different predicaments.

Dec. 23.   Two hours at the Horse Guards at General Murray's
trial; letters between the parties were read that manifested sufficiently mutual heart-burnings and antipathies.

Dec. 28.   The papers announce the refugees forsaken or neglected by Lord Shelburne and his compeers; the gratitude of courts ought to be reckoned among the nonentities of Lord Rochester's list.   For my own part, I am too far down the hill of life to be much distressed at the events of a peace with America on any terms, or continued war—let the younger look to it.   This day completes my sixty-seventh year; with more propriety than Jacob, I may truly say, " *Few and evil have been the days of the years of my life.*"   God best knows when a period will be put to them; its suddenness I deprecate not—may I not be unprepared for the event.

Dec. 31.   Walked in the Park with Robert Lechmere.   Capt. Coombs took tea with me, and Mr. Wiswall called.

CHAPTER XVII.

London, Jan. 6, 1783. Walked for two hours in the Park; saw Lord Shelburne for the first time to my knowledge. He is of a middling size and well set; walks strong and springy; his dress a brown frock and boots, with a whip in his hand.

Jan. 7. On an inquiry concerning Mr. Cottenbilt, I find he died about six years since, and his wife about twenty: two daughters, six and seven years old when I lodged with them in Whalebone-court, in 1738, are now living and widows, one at Enfield, and the other in Holland.

Jan. 9. Walked to Brompton; visited Mr. Hutchinson; drank tea and passed the evening with Mr. Danforth in philosophical conversation.

Jan. 17. Met my former townsman and neighbor, George Deblois, in Cheapside, whom I have not seen for more than seven years; gave him my address.

Jan. 21. In passing along Parliament-street, saw a long funeral procession, say fifty carriages; on inquiry, found it was an officer named Townshend, who had served in America.

Jan. 23. Advices have arrived that the British troops have left Charleston and arrived at New-York; and yesterday the Commons completely liberated Ireland from its oppressive thraldom, to which it has been subject to the king and his ministers for many years.

Jan. 24. This day strong reports that preliminaries of peace are signed. It is said great sacrifices are to be made by the British in the east; if that be all, it will be well. Lord Grantham, one of the secretaries of state, acquainted the lord mayor that the preliminaries were signed; this is a matter of joy to all well disposed to the true interest of their country. It is said to be a much more favorable peace than, all things considered, could be expected.

Jan. 25. George Deblois and Capt. Coombs took tea with me and passed the evening.

Jan. 28. Mr. Danforth told me of a meeting of Massachusetts refugees at Sir William Pepperell's, to deliberate on what may be proper to be done respecting an application. Meeting adjourned till Saturday next at same place.

Jan. 29. At king's bench, Westminster Hall; heard a judgment on a point of law respecting the license of a dissenting meeting-house, given against the justices, who endeavored to avail themselves of a subterfuge to avoid granting it; wherein Lord Mansfield spoke sharply to the counsel for the justices. Afternoon at New England Coffee-house, reading the preliminaries of peace, which I confess astonish me:—a tract equal to half of Europe is surrendered.

Jan. 30. *King Charles's Day.* Attended service at Westminster Abbey; a considerable throng of fellow-worshippers in the great aisle of the choir; my station or seat was in the prebend's stall. Dr. Bagot, the lately elected bishop of Bristol, of a most diminutive size, preached a loyal court sermon, giving the Church of England's styled loyal martyr a most exalted character; which if just, that unhappy prince has been sadly misrepresented. He did not, however, descend to scurrillities or abuse; thorough-paced in hierarchical principles, but not intolerant.

Feb. 1. Attended a meeting of refugees at Sir William Pepperell's house, Wimpole-street, to consider of somewhat to be done respecting an application to Parliament, if agreeable to administration. Chose Sir William Pepperell agent to inquire of Mr. Secretary Townshend and Lord Shelburne, first lord of the treasury, if this course is acceptable to them.

Lord North approves of it, and advises all the colonies to unite together. Broke up at three o'clock; number present thirty-three —being all or nearly all in town that had received treasury allowances.

Feb. 3. Met my countryman Mr. John Powell, from Ludlow; also met Mr. De Berdt, whom I had not seen for seven years; he having resided in the country since his marriage, six years ago. Agreed to dine with him to-morrow. My townsman, Samuel Porter, also came to see me; neither time, climate, change of place or circumstances will ever alter this man's character; I never knew one whose characteristic qualities are so deeply impressed as his.

Feb. 5. Attended the adjournment of the Massachusetts refugees at Turk's Head, Gerard-street, Soho; when Sir William Pepperell reported that Lord Shelburne, by Mr. Secretary Townshend, thought the present an improper time to present a petition to Parliament. We enlarged his powers, etc., and after much conversation on sundry particulars adjourned to next Saturday week at same place. Thirty present.

Feb. 7. By the papers of this day it appears that the ratification of the preliminaries was signed by the French king on the 3d instant, and are arrived here as soon as completed. The part of France received by Mr. Fitzherbert and forwarded. The Dutch have not yet acceded. An armistice or cessation of hostility by sea agreed on between us.

Feb. 11. Informed that Sir William Pepperell has summoned a part of the Massachusetts refugees to meet at " Turk's-Head" for a special occasion:—called at the Treasury, was informed that a board would be held this week, and the commissioners' report acted on, and orders respecting the Americans given out.

Feb. 13. Notified to attend a meeting of refugees—voted to empower Sir Wm. Pepperell to join in a petition to Parliament *malgré au ministre d'état,* (in spite of the minister of state.)

TO REV. ISAAC SMITH, SIDMOUTH.

London, Feb. 11, 1783.

Dear Sir:

Perhaps it may not be unpleasing to you to be made acquainted that the refugees from the province of Massachusetts Bay, under the denomination of loyalists, to the number of thirty· three, met at Sir William Pepperell's to consult about the choice of an agent to confer with the agents of the other provinces, in order to form a plan for addressing, remonstrating, or petitioning Parliament; but whether of the three I am ignorant, though present at the choice, which by an unanimous vote fell on Sir William;—and also to receive a report from him of Mr. Secretary Townshend's answer respecting Lord Shelburne's approbation or disapprobation, without the former it being judged improper to proceed. Mr. Townshend excused himself to Sir William for not having applied to Lord Shelburne, by pleading business, but promised to call on him the next day, etc., if practicable, and thus the affair stood till the 5th inst., to which time the meeting was adjourned, when Sir William reported that Lord Shelburne thought the present an improper time to present a petition to Parliament. Since the meeting I find there are those averse to all measures at present, and amongst others I confess myself a dissentient for the following reason : the king having taken the refugees under his care by recommending their case to the consideration of Parliament.

Expectation is on tiptoe respecting the result of the commissioners, Wilmot and Coke, chosen by the lords of the treasury to examine, settle, adjust and proportion the claims and allowances of the refugees, who have been and are on the list of grantees— before whom we in that class have been. Some are apprehensive of a retrenchment ; some have too much reason to fear a total excision ; very few, indeed, have hopes of an addition. It is reported and expected that the petitioners who hitherto have had no allowances, will be soon called before them to show the grounds of their pretences to governmental charity, when probably some pittance will be granted. The salaries of all the officers under the crown in the thirteen United States have been for some time past struck off; and part to some will be given under the same denomination with us, who have held none before. Judge Auchmuty of Boston has for these several months been annihilated, and reduced to the condition of a humble petitioner for a hundred pounds.

Sir William finding his powers too limited, they were enlarged, and he is now empowered to consult and act in all cases in conjunction with the agents from the other provinces, giving his private word not to take any important step without consulting his constituents ; which precaution was universally thought necessary, as Joseph Galloway is suspected of sinister designs.

It is said that they are making great retrenchments in offices and officers' salaries and fees. Think you while this spirit lasts, we useless, burdensome aliens shall escape untouched ? that we dogs shall be longer suffered to take the bread out of their own children's mouths ? I trow not.

I fancy you wonder at the terms granted America, as all the world does ; but perhaps it may abate when you shall be told the agent Mr. Oswald is eighty-two years old, has been a correspondent of Congress, and is a very particular friend of Mr. Laurens.

As Americans will have a right by treaty to navigate the lakes to and from the ocean, and almost the whole of the country where furs are taken lies within the territories, it will be well if Great Britain gets any supply of that commodity but from the high mightinesses of America.   Whether our rulers had any, and what concealed purpose in this American treaty, I have not penetration enough to discover ; that it proceeded from ignorance is hardly supposable, if from inattention, unpardonable ; and I confess the last most likely ; for had the wish of administration been ever so violent to compromise at all events matters with America, it is not supposable she would ultimately have insisted on such immeasurable tracts, which far exceed all Europe in extent.   But it is now irrecoverable ; the die is cast—the ratification completed here and sent to France, and on the 3d was ratified there and exchanged. That a peace was necessary, all moderate men allow, and most, that in all other respects saving America it is as favorable as could have been expected ; in my mind better.   I think our enemies have shown laudable moderation.

With great regard,
S. Curwen.

TO REV. ISAAC SMITH, SIDMOUTH.

London, Feb. 14, 1783.

Dear Sir :

In a letter I received yesterday from my friend William Pynchon, Esq. of Salem, is the following :—" Capt. John Derby will most willingly accommodate any of his countrymen who may wish to return with him."   Capt. Derby, in a large ship of his brother's, is now at Nantz, to return in a month ; which is encouraging to all not under the ban of the states, and I am told their prejudices are surprisingly abated, and there seems a disposition to forget past animosities and kindly receive all the fugitives.

*   *   *   *   *   *   *

This day I went to the Treasury to inquire about my allowance, and to my comfort found it stood as at first.   A few are raised, some struck off, more lessened.   Of those that have come to my knowledge, Gov. Oliver's is lessened £100, out of £300 ; Mr. Williams, who has married a fortune here, is struck off ; Harrison

Gray, with a wife and two children, struck off; his brother Lewis lessened to £50; D. Ingersoll reduced from £200 to £100; Samuel H. Sparhawk from £150 to £80; Benjamin Gridley from £150 to £100; Thomas Danforth's, Samuel Sewall's, Samuel Porter's, Peter Johonnot's, G. Brinley's, Edward Oxnard's and mine, continue as at first; Chandler's raised £50; Samuel Fitch's £20; Col. Morrow's £50; one whose name I forget is sunk from £100 to £30; and many names and sums totally forgotten. On the whole, it is said the sum paid last year to refugees, amounting to near £80,000, is now shrunk by the late reform to £38,000; and if the commissioners act on the same frugal plan respecting the petitioners whose cases will probably soon be considered, I very much doubt whether the sum of last year's expenditure under this head, including all their additional allowances, will not exceed this year's.

This is the great, the important day on which the preliminaries are to undergo a most critical and severe discussion, and will determine the fate of Lord Shelburne's administration; news unluckily for it has arrived, that the government of Virginia has declared they will pay no regard to any remonstrance, or request, or requisition respecting refugees, which manifests the fatality of the preliminary article recommending the same.

Your faithful friend,   S. Curwen.

Feb. 17.   Mr. Flucker died suddenly in his bed yesterday morning, and is the forty-fifth of the refugees from Massachusetts within my knowledge, that have died in England.   He was secretary of state for Massachusetts.

Feb. 18.   Mr. Deblois told me that Virginia had expressly declared they would not regard any remonstrance, requisition, or request of Congress respecting the loyalists of their province, as the fifth preliminary article between Great Britain and America stipulates: the fatality of which was visible enough before this proof. It is likely the rest of the states will copy so laudable an example, and exhibit thereby to the world a specimen of their power, want of virtue, moderation, and disregard to the principles of humanity. Shame to Great Britain that these unhappy persons stand in need of a recommendation promising such small efficacy—a striking lesson to future generations never to support the reins of government against the determined resolution of a very numerous people. The House of Commons did not rise till seven o'clock this morning; being engaged in debate on preliminary articles of peace, and provisional articles between Great Britain and America. The magnitude and importance of the subject deeply employs the attention not only of the managers, but the public universally, who are all ears for the result. Lord Shelburne and administration are left in a minority by sixteen in the Commons. In the House of Lords strong opposition to the terms of peace. English pride cannot brook to receive the dictates of a conqueror.

Feb. 19. Evening at Dr. Graham's lecture on health, in his " *Temple of Health,*" in Pall Mall, near St. James's. The first room entered was properly a vestibule, from whence through folding doors one passes into the apartment holding the electric bed, about seven feet square, raised three feet from the floor; over the frame at the head are fixed two balls gilded of four inches diameter and one inch apart, to receive the electric spark from the machine above, continued down in a glass tube through the floor. Passing this, you enter the room of Apollo, through a narrow entry, having on each hand two or three niches containing statues gilded, about half the natural size. The first object that meets the eye is the temple of Apollo, being a round cupola five feet in diameter, supported by six fluted pillars of the Corinthian order and eight feet high, in imitation of scagliola; in the centre stands a tripodal frame with concave sides, on which rests in each angle a lion *couchant*, supporting a long frame for the branch of six or eight lamps, adorned (or rather overcharged) with crystals, whose tremulous motion by the company's walking adds great brilliancy to the appearance, the walls all around having many branches with three candles each, besides two more large central branches, suspended by gilt chains from the ceiling. The decorations in the frippery kind are in great profusion in this as well as in the other room, consisting of glass in various forms and sizes, inlaid and hanging—many gilt statues of Apollo, Venus, Hercules, Esculapius, etc., besides a few pictures. The master discovered a ready elocution, great medical knowledge, and appeared well qualified to support the character he assumes.

47

March 4.   Called at G. Deblois's lodgings, and found that he
sailed for Halifax on the 1st.   Met Capt. Coombs, who informed
me that Mr. Rowe at Treasury was drawing our pensions; hastened and received my order.

March 7.   Government unsettled.   Old administration out, no
successors agreed on.   Lord Gower has been solicited by the king
to accept the premiership, or to be first lord of the treasury—the
lord chancellor and Charles Jenkinson are of the interior cabinet.
It is said the king has scarce eaten these two days, and is violently
reluctant to take Charles J. Fox into his counsels; and the party
wherein he is engaged is by far the most powerful, to which Lord
North has lately allied himself; to separate which has been the
king's endeavor, but it seems without success.   It is generally
thought the king must at length yield.   He will have to adopt the
whole Rockingham party, or suffer the wheels of government to
stop till Parliament remonstrate, which it soon must if the arrangement is not immediately made, all national business being at a
stand.

March 15.   Administration not fully settled; the king claim-
.ing the right of filling up .vacancies in the cabinet in case of death
or removal, and the new administration demanding to have none
added but by their consent, that there may be no jarring among
themselves; and they will not act till this be settled.

March 17.   Visited Mr. Richard Clarke—thence to the Treasury to inquire when the commissioners were to meet again, and
meeting Mr. Alleyn, a clerk, was informed about Mrs. Gen. Winslow's* allowance; finding a mistake had been made by Mr. Rowe
to her prejudice, I proceeded to inform her brother Clark of it, and
from thence to her own lodgings; she being absent I returned, and
stopping at her sister Deblois's, found her there, and rejoiced her
heart by acquainting her that her allowance stood as at first granted, and received her thanks.

March 19.   Walked to Park.   Meeting Mr. Thomas Hutchinson, joined and accompanied him to Hyde Park corner; he acquainted me that Col. Phips, who is just arrived, relates that,
during his captivity at Boston he was civilly treated by all ranks,

---

* Lady of Gen. John Winslow of Marshfield, a refugee.

and although obliged to reside at Cambridge, the state forbidding strangers a residence at Boston, he could easily obtain leave to visit there in the daytime.

TO ANDREW DALGLISH, ESQ., GLASGOW.

London, March 17, 1783.

DEAR SIR :

My design herein is to give you my crude, and ask in return your better digested thoughts, on the present critical situation of Great Britain and the States of North America.   However exulting they may feel in this first hour of their deliverance from British governmental authority, they have in my poor opinion an immeasurable distance of road to travel over, intercepted with bogs, precipices, cloud-topped, scraggy mountains and deep valleys, before they will be able to arrive at an improvable champaign country, where ease, plenty and content are to be found :—in other words, that country abounds in lawless, ungovernable subjects, disposed, however, to imitate the vices, follies and luxurious fashions of wealthy states, with comparatively little running cash, immense debts, no funds established, and permanent and powerful creditors to account with.   I was yesterday told by Mr. R. Clarke that Massachusetts was answerable for a yearly interest of twenty thousand sterling due for a loan.   We are at this period in this country in a kind of anarchy ; no settled administration, the most important national concerns neglected or delayed.

The Rockingham party is, evidently, the most numerous, and therefore most powerful, and since the coalition between the man of prerogative and the man of the people, the latter, very justly so styled, can carry all before him.   The great obstacle, however, to a full establishment of the cabinet is, it seems, whether the present lord chancellor and Lord Stormont shall be of it ; which the king insists upon, designing them, if he can prevail to bring them in, as checks on the rest, these two being professed abhorrers of the present designs of the embryo administration.   The other point is the king's right to fill up vacancies that may happen by death or removal, which is refused him, saying they will have none but those in whom they can confide.   If the king gains his point, affairs will go on in the old channel, and there will be no reform ; if he yields, he will scarcely be more than a doge of Venice, and the cabinet will rule and possess the whole power of the state.

Respecting the public, it seems to be of no importance who is in or who is out; all are in pursuit of one plan invariably to the neglect of the general welfare, or more properly at the expense of it. In this inter-reign Lord Shelburne sits and acts in the treasury, and Mr. Pitt as chancellor of the exchequer:—as to the character of the former, though I profess no veneration for him, yet, as an active minister at the head of affairs, whether the public could, in this crisis, have been better served, is a doubt in my mind, notwithstanding the clamor raised by the newspaper writers. I fancy if you will read his speech of the 14th February, and that published in the Advertiser of this day, you will see more reasons for the minister's justification than disappointed pride, private interest, personal dislike and party rage will allow; but when one reflects on the almost universal cry of the nation for peace; the act of the legislature last session, wherein the independence, the only bone of contention, was as good as given up, and the king almost commanded to put an end to the war in America; the insupportable load of the national debt, and without some capital reform, which in a time of war is utterly impracticable, will in the event prove so; the ruinous prospects from a decided superiority in the East and West Indies, which would have enabled our proud, revengeful enemies to require much more humiliating demands than the present terms; one would think the nation should rather rejoice to have escaped so dreadful a catastrophe as a continuance most probably might have brought on, and be thankful our enemies were inspired with such a moderate spirit. It is not to be conceived that proud, stubborn, successful enemies, just on the eve of obtaining the long wished object of their ambition, would be persuaded to relinquish all the advantages gained in war without any compensation. The great moderation of the French court under such advantageous circumstances as they now confessedly are, was shown before parties appeared so prominent; but Britons, unused to receive the law, cannot without hard struggles submit—time and cool reflection will clearly manifest the wisdom of the act of last session, and if that be acknowledged, the conduct of the late administration, meaning Lord Shelburne and his associates, must of consequence be approved.

Before the preliminaries are ratified or hostilities ceased in the channel, an American ship laden with oil, with her thirteen stripes flying, came into the river from Nantucket by way of Ostend, and our London traders were but little less in a hurry; for within a few days after the preliminaries were published, ten or twelve vessels were posted up in the coffee-houses, advertising for freights to New-York and Boston.   Nor, indeed, does government seem much less precipitate, for a commercial treaty act is now under consideration of a committee of the whole house, and will probably in a few days be ready for the royal signature. The loyalists have been for these two months very deeply engaged in forming plans to counterbalance the dreadful evils consequent on ministerial neglect in the late treaty.   I can foresee no good to arise from their industry; on the contrary, apprehend mischief, and therefore decline attending.

What think you of returning to your late abode, Salem? Should it be my lot, I shall wish for a few old acquaintances, without which the great revolutions in public and private, will, I apprehend, render my return not desirable.   Please favor me with your undisguised sentiments freely on the foregoing, and whatever intelligence you may think proper.

Very truly your friend,

S. CURWEN.

March 20.   Attended the Royal Society's weekly meeting at Somerset House; going into the antechamber common to the Antiquarian Society and Royal Society, one waits until an acquaintance or friend appears to procure your name to be set down in the list, which is read aloud by an attendant at the president's order; when the society, who are already met, are about to begin, each person regularly enters and takes his seat, (long slips being placed on either side a middle aisle.)   At the head of the room sits the president, now Sir Joseph Banks, with his hat on his head, all others uncovered; he in a chair of state elevated three or four steps; just below it and on the same level with the floor is a half round mahogany table, having only two assessors, viz., the two secretaries, Dr. Matty, a person of profound knowledge and learning, but of a

most diminutive, unpromising person, and a Mr. Grey, who read
the communications to the society respecting experiments and any
acquisitions of knowledge in astronomy, etc. Among others on
this occasion was read a letter from the famous Herschel, lately invited from Bath to Windsor by the king, and for his use the round
tower there is assigned : by his discoveries in astronomy it seems
our solar system is travelling through the immensity of space in a
progressive motion, which he deduces from an apparent change of
relative situation of some fixed stars most visible or of largest diameter, and therefore nearest to us. The election of members is
by ballot, each member putting in his vote into the box, presented
to each separately, which being delivered into the president's
hands, he empties out on the desk before him, and after counting,
declares the candidate elected (or otherwise) a fellow of this society ; an instance I saw this night, and it is not a common sight.
A candidate stands four months after proposed before balloted for.
Dr. Cope, Bishop of Clonfert, being this night proposed, the president out of regard to his dignity as a peer of Ireland, dispensed
with the usual forms and proceeded to a ballot, which was not objected to. The assembly was in number to appearance scarce
short of two hundred—the room a noble one, eighty feet by
thirty, and twenty high ; the walls covered on all sides with half
length and quarter portraits, arranged one above the other—Sir
Isaac Newton's being at the head of the room in the centre of the
middle space, and opposite the door. A person of modest assurance may push himself in amongst the company, few of the visitors being known, and no inquiry made on whose account one
appears there. A friend engaged Dr. Fothergill to insert my name,
which he entered by speaking to Dr. Matty, without entering his
name. Every one who appears is presumed to have some relish
for and acquaintance with some one or more of the branches of
literature, etc., for that reason the society is not strict in examining
their pretences to attend. The meeting begins at eight, and commonly ends at ten—none spoke but the president, nor read but the
secretaries.

March 21. Met the king in a sedan chair, accompanied by ten
or twelve yeomen and footmen, going to St. James's. New min-

istry is said to have been settled; Lord North, 'tis said, to return to public life as a secretary of state. If so, probably at the king's earnest entreaty, otherwise it is hard to account for.

March 24. To the reproach of the king and the nation, government is without a ministry, notwithstanding the daily reports of an arrangement; selfishness, venality, rapacity and dissipation are the characteristics of this age and nation; to which must be added, in order to finish the picture, a total disregard of the idea of public welfare, which all men speculatively consider as a necessary, but as a crazy phantom, and therefore practically neglected.

March 28. At the lobby of the House of Commons, which soon after meeting adjourned to Monday. Favored for the first time with a sight of young *Pitt*, that forward political plant; may he imitate his father as well in integrity and *amor patriæ*, as in oratorical ability and natural powers. Some think appearances promise a more abundant harvest; should he continue in the national councils the public will be highly favored of heaven.

March 29. At Treasury, informed by Mr. Rowe that Lord Shelburne had surrendered his seat as first lord. No ministry settled, nor to appearance is like to be soon; the king unyielding, and the candidates as stiff and uncomplying. The old story of Lord Bute's pernicious influence prevails again; there is some advice unseen that supports the king's obstinacy, for I know not what else to call his non-compliance.

March 30. At St. James's, in the gallery; the king and queen passed through from the chapel to the green-room; on leaving the antechamber I luckily, being small, crowded myself under the elbow of a good-natured yeoman, and in the front rank had a full view of the king, queen, prince of Wales, and the court train. On the other side of the yeoman stood a boy, who on the king's approach, bending one knee, presented a petition; the king took it without any further notice, and after walking a few steps, put it into the hand of the lord in waiting. Soon after I departed, leaving the gallery filling, and the passage under the piazzas in the court middle lined double on both sides, to have a sight of the company going up.

March 31. Samuel Porter, Peter Frye and myself, visited Mr. Hughes at dinner and tea.

April 2. Read a Boston newspaper, where I saw poor Coombs' estate in Marblehead advertised for sale. I really pity my poor fellow refugee, and think him cruelly treated by his savage townsmen. This day's paper announces administration settled :—

Duke of Portland, First Lord of the Treasury.
Lord John Cavendish, Chancellor of the Exchequer.
Lord North and Charles J. Fox, Secretaries of State.
Lord Stormont, President of the Council.
Earl of Carlisle, Lord Privy Seal.
Lord Keppel, first Lord of the Admiralty.
Mr. Burke, Paymaster of the Forces.
Colonel North, Treasurer of the Navy.

April 5. Called at Mr. Tassey's to have a sight of the curious cabinet of satin wood, inlaid and decorated with many devices, figurative, etc., on front and sides : its contents, rows of drawers containing impressions of intaglios, cameos, seals, etc., to the number of more than six thousand, duplicated, to be sent to the Empress of Russia by her express order,—value, several thousands; she is a great encourager of ingenious artists, particularly English ones.

April 7. Passed a crowd attending procession in Parliament-street, going to take the Westminster candidate, Charles J. Fox, from his lodgings to the hustings under St. Paul's, Covent Garden portico. First marched musicians two and two, then four men supporting two red painted poles having on top the cap of liberty of a dark blue color; to each was fastened a light blue silk standard about nine feet long and five wide, having inscribed thereon in golden letters these words, " The Man of the People ;" followed by the butchers with marrow-bones and cleavers; then the committee two and two, holding in their hands white wands; in the rear the carriages. They stopped at his house in St. James's-street, where taking him up, he accompanied them in Mr. Byng's carriage through Pall Mall and the Strand to the hustings, when the election proceeded ; made without opposition, no competitor appearing against him.

April 13. Called on Mr. Jonathan Williams and Captain Johnson, and conducted them to Essex House chapel; Mr. Lindsay preached ;—subject, the address of the gospel to the poorer and middling ranks, which shows both the wisdom and goodness of God.

April 19. Met two numerous companies of sailors parading through the streets with an ancient; told they were going to demand of the king their wages, having been discharged without payment; but in returning through the Park could get no intelligence of their having made any demand at the Palace or Admiralty, and conclude they had been persuaded to separate on a promise of speedy payment; a number yesterday having obtained the king's promise that the sailors should be relieved by the first instalment of the present loan to be made in a few days.

May 13. Captain Coombs called early by agreement with me, and then departed to take coach for Kew Bridge at nine o'clock; arrived at eleven; from thence on foot through Kew and the terrace to Richmond, and through Twickenham to Hampton Court; dined at King's Arms; proceeded through the gardens to the palace, and passing through observed the paintings in better order than before; was informed they were lately cleaned by the king's order, and some new ones brought from the queen's house and Kensington; returned back through Bushy Park by a returned chaise. Was told that Kensington Palace may be seen as well as the others; and also, that Hyde Park came to the crown by the Duchess of York, Lord Clarendon's daughter, the mother of queens Mary and Anne, and would in eight years revert back, unless the the king should obtain a new lease thereof.

May 14. Went to Shoreditch work-house to see a Mr. Best, who is remarkable as a most perfect textuarian, and without looking in the Bible refers to particular texts, repeating the very words and all of them, to the number of many verses, often sometimes apposite to the circumstances of the applier;—seems not at a loss for any word or order in the text, and repeats slowly. He first looks into the right hand, pretending to a great knowledge of palmistry; among other parts, he applied the 3d, 4th, and 5th verses of 30th Deuteronomy to me, being then a refugee from America in London. His language is only in Scripture phrases; his room, large in extent, is filled almost with work of his own, in straw, of Scripture stories—as the creation, flood, passage of the Israelites over the Red Sea, etc.;—New Testament—the nativity, baptism in Jordan, miracle of loaves and fishes, broad and narrow way, crucifixion, lying in the tomb, rising from the dead—called ascension—day of judgment, last trumpet sounding, etc. These are separate compartments made of straw, with divisions in the same style and materials; he is continually, when not interrrupted by company, at work in making small works of flowers, rings in imitation of large seal rings, one of which he put on my finger. By his ready application and repeating the very words of Scripture, and the places where they are to be found, he seems to have got the whole Bible by heart; after looking into my hand, he referred me to sundry texts, some of which I confess struck me with astonishment and confusion. Though not more than fifty-five years of age, he is so totally void of care respecting himself, that he must be put to bed and taken out, fed with meat and drink like an infant; he will not bear to be called Mr. nor thanked for his presents,—loves fruit, and will accept of it, but not money. The posture he receives his visitors in is sitting within his little straw cell; looks on one only when he takes a hand to examine, and if he likes his visitor, on his departure seizes the hand in both his and kisses it warmly, bidding God speed in Scripture phrase.

May 19. Went out accompanied by Mr. Pickman to Drury Lane play-house to see Mrs. Siddons, the favorite tragic actress of the public, in the character of Jane Shore, which she well supported.

May 22. Informed that the refugees', or as they affect to denominate themselves, loyalists', petition to Parliament is presented, and supported by Lord North and all in administration, that all who have pensions may receive them by their agents, go where they will, even if they shall return to either of the United States.

June 15. Joseph Hooper called and drank tea; gave him a certificate as he desired, though I fancy it will be of no effect, respecting his property, business, and manner of living; of which, as I know, I can say but little.

June 19. Walked to White Conduit House, to see a great cricket match played; Lords Winchelsea, Easton, and Strathaven, and Sir Peter Burrill, etc.; a very severe headache drove me off the field.

June 30. Visited the artificial flower-garden at Spring Gardens; a beautiful imitation, laid out in walks, containing in its borders a great variety of the most curious flowers and many species of wall fruit, with birds of the season and climate placed in natural attitudes on the boughs in good preservation; having also a small piece of water, with a *jet d'eau* in the centre, and a swan floating on its surface, besides a stream of water falling down a rugged precipice into a basin: the upper part of the sides covered with perspective views, which enliven the room, being of faint green ground, and eighty feet by fifty and twenty-five high, the top almost an entire skylight.

July 9. At the gallery of the House of Lords; Mr. Cooper, a counsellor at law, pleading at the bar in a case wherein the distillers were concerned; on the third reading of bill, Lord Effingham rose and objected to various clauses, all of which were overruled, and the bill passed. A message from the Commòns was received and read. In the former case, Lord Effingham called the first lord of the treasury, the Duke of Portland, who rose, and to my seeming acquitted himself very indifferently; in his person he is unpleasing in figure and countenance. Lord Effingham had the appearance both in person and dress of a common country farmer; a green frock coat, with brass buttons, his hair short, straight, and to appearance uncombed; his face rough, vulgar and brown, as also his hand; in short he had the look of a laboring farmer or grazier. There were three bishops and twenty-three lay lords present: remained there two hours.

July 11. At the bottom of Buckingham-street, on the bank of the river, is a very convenient stone alcove, where I met a foreigner, who proving communicatively inclined, I attended for near an hour to his relations; the subject being the small degree of liberty this country enjoys compared with the states of Germany, particularly the king of Prussia's dominions, which he endeavored to exemplify from that monarch's readily redressing all acts of injustice from his courts, or from the oppressions of one subject to another. Another proof was the burdensome taxes of this country, to which the German states are not liable; the demesnes of the princes, and other sources, furnishing them with an income independent of taxes. A third was the exorbitant fees and delays of justice in our courts, which are just causes enough for complaint, crying aloud for redress; which, alas! there is but little reason to hope for.

July 12. By appointment, dined at Mr. De Berdt's, a brother of the late Mrs. Joseph Reed of Philadelphia; about six o'clock, departed with Mrs. De Berdt in her chaise for their country house, in Wormly parish, on Sir Abraham Hume's land and manor, Herts; passing through Shoreditch parish, Kingsland, Stoke Newington, Tottenham, High Cross, Edmonton, Pender's End, Enfield, Waltham Cross, Theobalds, and Cheshunt.   Mr. De Berdt arrived soon after on horseback.

July 13, *Sunday*.   Attended worship at a meeting-house in Turnford in the morning; in the afternoon at the parish church, standing on Sir Abraham's ground, who is the presentee thereof; a miserable, dark, old, forsaken temple, seemingly in a state of dereliction, though its revenues are far from contemptible, amounting to £200 and more; its present incumbent is a D. D.   Accompanied my friends to the christening of a daughter and churching of the mother; after service partook of tea and christening cake.

July 14.   Set off through Lord Monson's grounds for Mr. Hughes' at Hoddesdon; arrived in an hour, and passed another hour with him; then returned and rode with Mr. and Mrs. De Berdt over the Lea and New rivers into Essex, along the meadows; leaving there, we entered a rough, lonesome road that continued to the top of a very long hill of quick ascent.   On the summit stands Roydon, from whence forward both lands and road had a very different appearance; passed Stansteadbury church, standing on the edge of the eminence, and half a mile distant from the town or any house, except one gentleman's seat in its neighborhood, overlooking the extensive field called the Ryehouse field, perhaps from the grain of that kind for which it is noted.   Descending into the plain, stretching for a mile or two on either hand, we passed the house well known in the history of Charles II., for the real or imaginary plot against government laid there; and also the two rivers, New and Lea, running scarce more than ten rods asunder, through the whole length of the plain, and parallel to each other; at ten o'clock arrived home.

July 21.   Wrote to Thomas Russell, Esq., Boston, and introduced Mr. Coap.

TO WILLIAM PYNCHON, ESQ., SALEM, N. E.

London, July 26, 1783.

DEAR SIR :

The raging fever of the times will doubtless abate, for no violent fermentations are lasting, but not perhaps till the purposes of raising it are answered. The political frenzy of your country, and the peculiarly critical situation of American refugees here, put it out of my power to be decided respecting my future destination. However, as I wrote Mr. Ward, age and infirmities have made such inroads on me, as render of little importance the public decisions here or there. I ardently wish and pray for the welfare of both countries; but to whisper a truth in your ear, I should not entertain a single thought of crossing the Atlantic at my advanced time of life, even under the pleasing prospect of a friendly and kind reception, was it not for the short enjoyment of my friends and acquaintance; much less is the thought pleasing with such prospects as must present themselves to those misguided, unfortunate persons, who retired from America to Europe and elsewhere in the beginning and during the late troubles. I strongly suspect America will not find such a cordial and unrestricted liberty from the European powers respecting commerce and the creation of a powerful navy, as she fondly and delusively imagined. Now the hurry of war is over, men's minds are more at leisure to view the importance of keeping within proper bounds the new rising states, of such vast extent of sea coast, such variety of soils, such capability of improving its native materials, and which, if suffered, will grow to a dangerous height.

Please present my kind respects to friends and acquaintance, and believe me

Your friend,

S. CURWEN.

July 27. To the Tower, and encompassing it once round on the ramparts, left it, and passing over Little Tower-hill, joined a company attending a field speaker; one in the outer ring proved boisterous and severe, but the preacher was too much engaged to attend to the noise that disturbed most in that quarter.

July 29.   Called on Mr. and Mrs. Mather; afterwards William Vans called; I took a stroll with him and tea at Bagnigge Wells; thence home by way of Peerless-pool and Moorfields.

TO GEORGE RUSSELL, ESQ., BIRMINGHAM.

London, July 20, 1783.

DEAR SIR:

Your kind wishes I read with heartfelt satisfaction, for I meet with very few who profess the slightest regard; on this subject I could enlarge, but my feelings would urge to a style prudence forbids me to use. You express yourself as one not callous to impressions of humanity, as interest and passion render too many; " that when the horrors of war cease, there should end all animosities." I wished and hoped it too, but with what success the world too evidently sees; not a single expectation of mine through the progress of this baneful war but has ended in disappointment. To keep myself from all future mortifications, I am determined to take no further part or concern in public measures, than what arises from unavoidable constraint by personal interest; and considering the sour aspect of American politics respecting absentees, I cannot but think my plan an obvious dictate of wisdom. Local attachment having lost its force in me, and so averse as I am to a tedious voyage, that could I persuade a few friends that it was not for want of a due regard, I know not whether, at this advanced time of life, I should not retire to some quiet village, and there pass in undisturbed ease, unknowing and unknown, the short portion of my remaining days. Perhaps, at your time of life it is hard to conceive the propriety of the foregoing intimation; but you will remember old age blunts the passions as well as the reason, and renders rigid and stiff the finer fibres of the brain, those vehicles of animal spirit, by means of which impressions of all kinds are less frequent and strong.

You very justly observe, that the true state of the case is not always to be known from newspaper representation, and I can add, scarce ever even when public instruments are pretendedly copied. However, in the present case, I fancy you may, without injury to truth, believe the resolves from the town of Worcester to be genuine; nor less those very curious ones from the New Jerseys, in the Morning Chronicle of the 26th inst., (if I have not mistaken a day or two,) wherein you will see the predicament of us poor refugees in the opinion of our late fellow-subjects; but party zeal is blindness as well as madness. Both the foregoing as well as others of like import, I have seen in my own town newspaper, called the Salem Gazette, nor does it want confirmation from verbal testimony, and a multitude of letters from friends and foes corroborate the same. Your wish and expectation that the present delirium, as I call it, will not be lasting, is common; it is in all men's mouths; its continuance will, I dare say, be of fatal length to me, as well as in its operation.

To show on what footing I stood before the news of peace had intoxicated them, take the following extracts. In one letter, dated 2d January last, from a worthy friend and correspondent, he says: —" It is the general desire that you be urged to return, with assurances that you will be joyfully and respectfully received, and may reside here in peace and safety." Another writes :—" Your friends and acquaintance ardently wish for your return, and continuance among us in peace and security all your days."

The ship Captain, (Holton Johnson of Lynn,) with whom I came from America, was, by a revolution common at such periods, translated into a legislator in our Massachusetts Assembly ; being about two months since in London, told me that had not his interest and efforts prevailed, my name would have been inserted in the banishment list, and my estate confiscated. The reality of this fact depends on the relator's veracity ; the reasons, if any, must be private pique and malice ; no public crime was ever alleged, but merely leaving the country in her distress. If success is justification, I confess guilt.

A subsequent letter of 12th May, says :—" It seems clear to your best friends that your caution was not groundless." In one of June 5th :—" Since plundering and privateering have declined, the *reverend* Dr. Whitaker exerts himself on the wharves as well as in the desk against the return of Americans; let your patience and fortitude continue a month or two longer, and I believe that you may safely leave faction and party rage to spend their utmost spite without harm." In one of 14th June, from the same :— " Mrs. P. hath been at Providence, etc., and finds that Rhode

Island and Connecticut are surprised at the conduct of Massachusetts, as to the return of absentees who have not been inimical to America. That Mr. Sparhawk and others, who went thither from New-York and other places, were treated with great humanity and respect; that they encourage the return of Americans. These and other occurrences considered, I doubt not of seeing an alteration of measures before the end of the present session of the Assembly; I trust we shall not long continue to drive our own people into other states."

The Dr. Whitaker before mentioned, of Salem, is a notorious character in America, and not unknown here, whose employment some years ago was that of an itinerant preacher, leading about a tawny native of America for people to look at, and hear his preachment; he was also at the same time engaged in the more profitable pursuit of soliciting charity for the establishment of an Indian college in the frontier wilderness of my country. He is usually called Dr. Meroz in America, from his constantly applying the 23d verse of the 5th chapter of Judges to the poor refugees.

I am far from wishing ill to the cause of liberty, much less to that of my native country, to which on the contrary, as a citizen of the world and a friend to the inalienable rights of mankind, I wish every kind of good, but am equally far from thinking America has gained its delusively fancied prize by independence. By some congressional manœuvres of late, a train I fear is laid for the establishment of a power much more fatal to liberty than Great Britain durst have aimed at, whilst she could have retained any governmental authority there. Their liberation is a doubtful proof of the divine approbation of their cause. Many there thirsted after it, and so did the Israelites for a king, which God at length gave them, in his anger : and he has, I fear, given them their heart's desire by way of punishment for wantoning away those singularly great advantages of a civil, religious and political nature, with which he had favored them above all people upon the face of the whole earth. They often were used to compare themselves to God's highly favored people, and I truly think their case is not unlike ; mercies and preservations as numerous, nor does their folly and ingratitude fail to finish the comparison. If any expressions here are not altogether of the complexion of your own notions, I know your candor will make allowances for the difference of our situation, though I am not aware of an unfriendly bias in my mind.

Your faithful friend,
S. Curwen.

August 6.   At New England Coffee-house to read the papers, filled with relations of the rising spirit of Americans against the refugees, in their towns and assemblies.   Intoxicated by success, under no fear of punishment, they give an unrestrained loose to their angry, malevolent passions, attribute to the worst of causes the opposition to their licentious, mobbish violation of all laws, human and divine; and even some of the best of the republican party seem to think, at least their practice squints that way, that the supposed goodness of their cause will justify murder, rapine, and the worst of crimes.   But cool impartial posterity will pass a better judgment, and account for the violences of the times from party rage, which knows no bounds.

TO MR. JOHN TIMMINS, WOLVERHAMPTON.

London, August 9, 1783.

Dear Sir:

By the newspapers from America, particularly our quarter, I find there remain but slender grounds of hope for success in attempting the recovery of debts or estates; a general shipwreck is seemingly intended of all absentees' property—the towns in their instructions to the representatives making it a point to prevent the return of them, and consequent confiscation of all their property, notwithstanding the provision in the fifth preliminary article.   These lawless people regard not any obstacle when the gratification of their angry passions or the object of gain is in view;—some of their resolves perhaps you may have seen.   I yesterday read in a Boston Gazette, published (in June) by Edes, the well known sedition-trumpeter, the following copied out for your view from the resolves of the town of Lexington, of the same complexion with the rest of their town meeting measures: "Common sense and the laws of nature and nations concur to pronounce them one and all aliens from the commonwealth.   As to the idea of admitting some and rejecting others, it is easy to see that the wisdom of angels would be puzzled to

49

draw a line—to determine when or where to stop.   Upon the whole
we cannot but think it indispensably necessary for the peace and
welfare of this state, and the freedom and happiness of the United
States, that a decided part be taken to prevent the return and the
recovery of their estates, and property that was formerly theirs."—
Though in this you see the temper is unfriendly and adverse, the
language is decent.   From a paragraph of to-day's paper is the following :   " Letters by an American vessel yesterday from Boston
brought certain information of a very unfavorable nature to the
loyalists, whose situation is extremely precarious, and no step is
likely to be taken for their relief."   The same letters add, that
" several parts of the country are in a state of convulsion, in a struggle to get repossessed of estates seized by individuals during the
troubles."   Sitting by Frederick Geyer in the N. E. Coffee-house, he
said that John Amory had written him that he was made to hope by
his friends for a readmission into Boston, having already been permitted to have a sight of his children, &c.   He had received letters
by Callahan from Boston, by whom thirteen passengers have just
arrived; among them are Leonard Jarvis, Samuel Eliot, and a Mr.
Seaver.

I suppose you have heard of Capt. Smith's treatment at Philadelphia.   Such, however, is the course of human affairs, and it may
be, for aught I know of, consummate wisdom and a just retribution
of rewards and punishments; for I am far from thinking there is
such a very great disproportion of happiness here below among
individuals, as is the common opinion, or that external circumstances are of any weight in the question of the quantity of human
happiness of each one individual compared to another.   In a little
space of time I shall be dead to a sense of all these puzzling
events ; it may be, shall see the reasonableness and equity of the
providential government in a clear and satisfactory light.

Heartily wishing you health, success, competency and contentment, I am, with cordial esteem,

                                         Your friend,
                                            S. CURWEN.

Aug. 12.   *P. S.*—The London Evening Chronicle of this day
contains a sensible and excellent circular letter from General
Washington to the several state governors; the forementioned di-

rected to Governor Greene, of Rhode Island.   If you have not seen it, the liberality of that government absolves this from all imputations on the score of tolerating the Roman Catholics in Canada—they having far outgone these by admitting persons of all faiths as well as none to a full participation, not only of the liberty of living and exercising their religion among them, but to all the immunities, rights, privileges, emoluments, and honors of the state.   This is, I confess, carrying toleration to the very largest extent.   S. C.

TO RICHARD WARD, ESQ., SALEM.

London, August 11, 1783.

DEAR SIR :

I refer you to my letter by Mr. Conant for an explicit answer to your question, " Do you propose to spend the remainder of your days abroad ?" though I do not think my expression, " The wished for period of my return is not arrived," carried any doubts of what were my intentions.   With regard to that event, you best can tell whether I or any exile from America, whatever our wishes may be, shall ever be suffered to make an attempt ; a subject I consider with some indifference, age and infirmities having made such inroads on my constitution as leave me but little to hope or fear from the result of public councils or the imprudence of private conduct. So far, however, am I from indifference to the real welfare of America, that I ardently wish moderate counsels may prevail, for it is the universal opinion that her credit and interest will be essentially hurt, should an illiberal, impolitic exclusion of all absentees take place.   I am free to declare my apprehension that the lower, illiterate classes, narrow-minded and illiberal all over the world, have too much influence, and that political and civil events bear some proportion to the wisdom of public councils ; not always, as instances of a contrary kind may be adduced through a succession of many ages in the history of mankind.

Please to acquaint the " *Social Library*" company, whatever occasions they may have for a supply from hence, they shall be freely welcome to my services.   With best love to my niece and your children,

I am your friend,

S. CURWEN.

Aug. 17.   Attended public worship at St. Giles's, Cripplegate. The number of youthful voices accompanying the organ rendered that part of the service pleasing and devout.   After service walked to the altar to see the funeral monument of a woman rising out of a coffin ; the inscription too high for me to read, but said to perpetuate the extraordinary event of a woman of this parish being brought to life after interment, by the sexton's descending into the vault to cut off from her fingers some rings, which by swelling could not otherwise be recovered.   Report adds, that raising herself in the coffin, she quitted it and followed the sexton out of the church, and proceeded homewards, and arriving there at midnight and knocking hard at the door, awakened the maid, who went trembling to her master, saying she was sure the knock was that of her mistress ; on going down and opening the door, to their astonishment found it to be her mistress indeed. Report further adds, that this same woman lived to have seven or eight children.   On asking the female pew-opener, she replied : " That is the report, but having been but a late parishioner, she could not say, but some thought it meant to denote the resurrection of the body."   Below is the bust of the famous martyrologist " *Johannes Foxus*," put up by his son Samuel about 1590.

Aug. 31.   Attended worship at the church of St. Austin and St. Faith the Virgin, united parishes close under St. Paul's, and the latter so called as I was informed on inquiry at St. Paul's of the verger ; he further said that it was in the gift of the dean and chapter.   A Mr. Ryder, author of a history of England, preached an ingenious and entertaining discourse.   Afternoon at the Magdalen, where heard an excellent, pathetic, and finely adapted address to the tenants by Mr. Sellon, minister of Clerkenwell, one of the justly celebrated preachers of the day.

Sept. 3.   Mr. Foster, the late appointed clerk to commissioners for examining loyalists, advertises to-day for them to bring in an estimate of their estates, effects, losses, etc., to him at his chambers, Middle Temple, before the 29th inst.

Sept. 19.   Yesterday evening received a note from Mr. De Berdt, inviting me to accompany Mrs. D. to his country house at Broxburn Herts to pass a few days during his absence in Wiltshire, where, after three hours, we arrived in Mrs. D.'s chaise before tea.

Sept. 23. At twelve o'clock set off with Mrs. D. for Ware, through Hoddesdon, Ryefields, Stansfield, Mardock Mill, the late residence of Mr. De Berdt.

Sept. 25. To Hoddesdon; meeting Mr. James Inman and another gentleman, accompanied the former home.

Sept. 26. Proceeded with Mrs. De Berdt Londonwards, meeting and overtaking multitudes in carriages and on foot, bound to the Waltham Abbey-statute for servants—a day established by act of Parliament, following the last day of Fairs, for hiring servants. The males appear with the tools or insignia of their respective employments; the females of the domestic kind are distinguished by their aprons, viz., cooks in colored, nursery-maids in white linen, and the chamber and waiting-maids in lawn or cambric. Here resort all who want to go into, or are out of service, as well as those families who stand in need of servants. After a few delays and the interval of three hours, arrived in London, passing through Clapton and Hackney, deviating from the usual road for variety sake.

Sept. 29. Visited Mrs. Hay; first time since her return from Scotland. At New England Coffee-house, saw a number of young Massachusetts men bound home in Callahan, gone down the river. In Oxford-street, called at Mr. Danforth's and S. Porter's; both absent.

Oct. 4. At ten o'clock, set off with Mr. D. in a post-chaise for Lord Tylney's seat, Epping Forest; conducted through the rooms and from them to the grotto, which, in my opinion, is the most pleasing and elegant I ever saw; though Goldney's at Clevedon is by some esteemed before this; and which, perhaps, in the richness of some of its spars may exceed.

Oct. 6. This day was proclaimed peace with France, Spain, and Holland, with the usual formalities, at Palace, Charing Cross, Cheapside Conduit, and the Royal Exchange; had a sight of the procession in Pall Mall, but the crowds disappointed me from hearing the proclamation, or seeing the ceremony of admission through Temple-bar into the city.

Oct. 8. At New England Coffee-house in company with Mr. Nathaniel Gorham, lately arrived from Boston, whom I had well known. He is a native of Charlestown, late a member of Congress, and of the Massachusetts Assembly, and who is now here on the score of obtaining a benevolence for the sufferers at the destruction of that town, June 17, 1775, by the king's troops; which, all things considered, carries with it such a face of effrontery as is not to be matched. Invited him to tea; received a letter from my wife's brother, James Russell.

TO HON. JAMES RUSSELL, LINCOLN, MASS.

London, Oct. 8, 1783.

My Dear Sir :

I thank you for your favor of the 21st August, the first from you since my unhappy abandoning my former home in April, '75. You write, " I give you joy on the return of peace ;" as far as it shall be productive of real good to the parties concerned, it has my approbation ; respecting myself it is an event of the smallest moment, were the appearances in your quarter ever so bright and pleasing ; how much less when the thirteen late peaceable happy colonies are reduced to the licentious and gloomy condition wherein they now are, if general report may be depended on. In truth, were your sister* no more, there would need no act of Massachusetts or any other assembly, or senate, to prohibit my return. So far as to America and myself; now to another point, that of interest. After I had written to your son Thomas of Boston on the subject, I had heard of the sale of your late son Charles's estate at Lincoln to your son Chambers ; I will presume you did not forget my demand of £300 sterling, and somewhat more for his bond to me, though your silence respecting it has since raised my apprehension. Mr. Thomas Russell will address you on this subject, and I trust sufficient will be received to remunerate him for monies obtained on his credit by me for my support soon after my arrival here. Wishing you and your family every good,

I remain, my dear sir,
Your affectionate brother,

S. Curwen.

Oct. 9. Received a note from Mr. De Berdt, inviting me to dinner on Friday with Mr. Gorham and Mr. Barrett of Boston.

* Mrs. Curwen.

Oct. 25.   Accompanied Mr. Gorham to House of Commons and Westminster Abbey.

Oct. 28.   Saw Captain Nathaniel West and Captain Smith for the first time; received information from the former that his brother Eben was living, (whom I feared was dead,) and about to return to Salem.

Oct. 29.   Mr. J. Fletcher drank tea with me, and related in detail his misfortunes, present condition and views.

TO MRS. ABIGAIL CURWEN, SALEM.

London, Oct. 30, 1783.

My Dear Wife :

The peace, or rather acknowledged dismemberment of the late English colonies from their mother country, has, it seems, been so far from affording a prospect to such of the American absentees who might be willing to return back, that, on the contrary, from what appears, the present governing party are determined to pass bills of final exclusion of all such as left their country after the troubles commenced. If their government is in the hands of what their *great and good allies* call the " *mesne peuple,*" which two short words you have Anglo-Gallic friends enough among you to translate, no liberal public measures are to be expected. If it was not for your sake, or that you would follow my fortune or accompany my fate, I should not hesitate for a moment taking up my future abode, which cannot possibly be but of short continuance, somewhere out of the limits of the republican government. " The world," as Adam said on his expulsion from paradise, " is all before me, where to choose my place of rest, and Providence my guide." By this you see, I have not fixed my views; nor can I, prudently, till your government shall have come to a final determination respecting your *runaways,* or, as they affect to call themselves by the pompous character of *loyalists ;* which, however, does them no more credit here than with you. Wishes for the welfare of my friends still warm my heart ; as to the rest, I read with cold indifference the insurrections in Pennsylvania, and the carryings-on in the late English colonies, having lost local attachment.

If your fortitude has increased in the proportion that your health and spirits have improved, perhaps you will not find it an insurmountable difficulty to resolve on a land tour to Canada, or a voyage to some other English settlement. Whatever shall be the result of your thoughts, let me be made acquainted therewith as soon as convenient. Should a final expulsion be concluded on, you will no longer hesitate.

Mr. Jay and John Adams are here, and if administration was kindly affected towards American sufferers, perhaps some good might arise; though for my own particular case, I have no favorable opinion of the gratitude, or even justice, of kings or courts; nor of the friendly regards of the two forementioned Americans towards us in the unhappy predicament of petitioners for the bounty, not to say justice, of the court; from the latter, [Adams,] it is currently said and believed, harsh declarations have fallen here as well as in Holland and France respecting us, nor has he probably changed his mind. The ancients say, *"Qui trans mare currunt, cœlum non animum mutant."**

Of a different complexion and temper is Mr. Nathaniel Gorham, with whom I have had several interviews; he is moderate, reasonable, and conciliatory; would that his views prevailed among his countrymen. He has just informed me that on the 4th proximo, agreeably to Charles J. Fox's appointment, he was going to wait upon Lord Keppel; if a member of the American Continental Congress can lower himself to use the derogatory term of *waiting* on the first lord of the English admiralty.

Yours, in all affection,
S. CURWEN.

Nov. 5. Last night a very destructive fire consumed many houses, upwards of forty, between Aldersgate, Bartholomew Close, and Cloth Fair, supposed the most extensive in London for many years; the fire yet unextinguished; no account yet given of the damage, loss, etc.

Nov. 24. At the American commissioner's office, late Duke of Newcastle's house, Lincoln's-Inn-Fields, for directions respecting a memorial.

Nov. 25. Attended among the rest of expectants to have a

---

* Those who cross the seas, change their abode but not their minds."

sight of the air-balloon discharged from the Artillery-ground, at one o'clock; it rose moderately, and in a southerly direction; was in sight ten or twelve minutes; its appearance to my eye, after it diminished to four or five inches in diameter, was like three round balls in contact, in shape of a triangular body with obtuse angles. I should think the numbers in Moorfields exceeded fourscore thousand. The sight was amusing; perhaps posterity may improve on this newly investigated subject, and make what is now only a pleasing show, a commodious, perhaps pernicious, aerial conveyance.

Nov. 28. Capt. Carpenter, of Salem, called; he is just from Lisbon.

TO WILLIAM PYNCHON, ESQ.

London, Nov. 28, 1783.

DEAR SIR:

However unfavorable to my wishes the result of the American Assemblies may be, I shall be gratified by receiving the earliest advices. Capt. Nathaniel West brings me a message from the principal merchants and citizens of Salem, proposing and encouraging my return; which instance of moderation I view as an honor to the town and respectful to myself, and I wish to return my thanks through you. It affords me pleasure, and I would cheerfully accept the offer; but should the popular dislike rise against me, especially if co-operating with governmental resolves, to what a plight should I be reduced, being at present (but for how long is a painful uncertainty) on the British government list for £100 a year, (a competency for a single person exercising strict economy,) to surrender this precarious allowance without public assurances of personal security.

It would be little short of madness, should the popular rage combine with the public decisions to prevent our future residence; deprived of all assistance, and even the last refuge of the wretched, hope here, expelled there. Imagine to yourself the distress of an old man, without health, under such adverse circumstances, and you will advise me to wait with resignation till the several Assemblies shall have taken decisive measures on congressional recommendation, agreeably to the provisional treaty, if that body shall

50

deem it prudent to conform to what their commissioners have agreed to. But enough of this. One of your Massachusetts public ministers, Mr. John Adams, is here in all the pride of American independence; by Mr. Gorham I am told he uttered to him the following speech, that *"together with the war he had buried all animosity against the absentees."* Though he is of a rigid temper, and a thorough-paced republican, candor obliges me to give him credit for the humanity of the sentiment, being spoken in private, and to one of his own party, and probably without an intention to be published abroad. In a conversation with my informant, he further replied, that he chose to consider himself as a plain American republican; his garb plain, without a sword, which is carrying his transatlantic ideas, I fear, a little too far. Should he have the curiosity, or his public character render it expedient, to attend at a royal levee, or at a drawing-room at St. James's on a court day, I hope he will not deserve and meet with as mortifying a repulse as our late chancellor, Lord Thurlow, at the court of Versailles; whose surly pertinacity in wearing a bob-wig occasioned his being refused admittance into the king's presence. However frivolous a part of dress soever a sword may appear to one of Mr. Adams's scholar-like turn, he is by this time, I fancy, too well acquainted with the etiquette of courts to neglect so necessary an appendage, without which no one can find admittance out of the clerical line.

I have nothing further to add but my ardent wishes for an increase of the health and happiness of yourself and family; for I am very truly,

Your friend,

S. CURWEN.

Nov. 30. Attended worship at the chapel in Margaret-street, Cavendish-square, where Mr. Ford, from Liverpool, officiated, using the liturgy appointed for the dissenters on the plan of preconceived forms in that place; it being the first use of it in London.

Dec. 2. Mr. Gorham passed three hours with me.

Dec. 5. Evening at Covent Garden Theatre, to see old Macklin in the characters of Shylock in the Merchant of Venice, and in Sir Archy McSarcasm in Marriage à la Mode, a farce of his own writing; in both he excels, and although more than fourscore years of age manifests an exertion that would credit even youth. The house crowded; the character of Portia, in the former, performed by a Miss Roscoe, her first appearance.

Dec. 18. Yesterday Charles J. Fox's famous East India bill was on a second reading thrown out of the House of Lords, by a majority of nineteen, the vote being seventy-eight in favor, and ninety-seven against it. The Prince of Wales in the minority, being his first vote as one of that house.

Dec. 20. House of Commons in an uproar, occasioned by a supposed design to dissolve them and form a new arrangement of administration; the members of which, one of the papers has, as usual in extraordinary cases, presented the public with.

Dec. 28. Attended public worship at Essex House chapel. Mr. Lindsay preached from—" For we know that if the earthly house of this our tabernacle were dissolved, we have a building of God, a house not made with hands, eternal in the heavens; for in this we groan earnestly, desiring to be clothed upon with our house which is in heaven. If so be that being clothed, we shall not be found naked." A text and discourse not unsuited to my particular situation, this day completing my sixty-eighth year, and in a disconsolate condition, laboring under bodily infirmities, dreadful uncertainties respecting my temporal supplies, and but too conscious of many more imperfections and follies, moral and natural; however doubtful what may be the consequence of a separation of soul and body, I most ardently long for a deliverance from personal evils, and a retreat to that state of quietude where the weary are at rest.

Dec. 31. Visited Mr. De Berdt by invitation; from thence to Capt. Hay's, and engaged to dine there next Friday.

This concludes a most unpleasing, unprofitable year, meaning in such a sense as dignifies the rational nature of mortal men. May the following year be productive of better moral effects than the last.

CHAPTER XVIII.

London, Jan. 17, 1784.   At New England Coffee-house, recognised by Col. Tonge, whom at first sight I knew not, till he made himself known.

Jan. 24.   Last night Mr. Pitt's East India bill lost by a majority of eight; probably a dissolution of Parliament will follow. A wretched plight is this distracted nation in, from an obstinate, despotically inclined king, and a set of profligate, unprincipled men of influence and politicians.   I fear there is not sense enough left of the importance of public interest and liberty among the people, to oppose the pernicious designs and measures of court and Parliament, and that the people, from whose efforts alone good may be expected, however unaided by nobles or gentry, will soon, oppressed and overloaded by taxes, submit to any measures their haughty imperious masters shall impose.   Thus the government, once the boast of Great Britain and the envy of the world, will soon find itself on a level with the most contemptible of those nations on whom it justly looked with pity, and imprudently with contempt. I think its ruin near enough for my old age to have the cruel mortification of seeing, brought about by the most impolitic and foolish of all attempts, the late American war ; and in the short space of nine years fallen, when at the highest pinnacle of power, glory, and wealth it had ever attained, to its present state of despair.

Feb. 2.   Disturbed by disagreeable dreams from whatever cause, which, however, I pretend not satisfactorily to account for to myself; I find my imagination much more busily employed now than in my youth.

Feb. 3.   Joseph Hooper called on me to accompany him to the American Commissioner's office in Lincoln's-Inn-Fields, which I did, and gave a relation on oath, which proved my unacquaintedness with his affairs of no advantage to his cause.   Afterwards at New England Coffee-house, reading the papers, filled with melancholy accounts of the party squabbles in the House of Commons between Foxites and Pittites, the former of whom have got a majority to address the king to turn out the latter and his associates, which has produced such a chagrin in the king's mind, it is said, as has determined him to retire to Hanover, and leave this distracted country under the government of guardians of the realm, of which his son, the Prince of Wales will be first in the commission.

Feb. 9.   The extreme severity of the weather seems to ill-influence the tempers of the state managers, whose pertinacious obstinacy forebodes, by their struggles in the House of Commons and their opposition in the House of Lords, to bring on a state convulsion.   Should healing measures not soon be adopted, and the meeting bill run out, the army will of course be left without restraint, and the dogs of war be let loose; the consequence all have reason to dread, none fully foresee.

Feb. 13.   The two political game-cocks, Pitt and Fox, are at length to compromise, and the public business, for a while at least, be suffered to go on, which during the contests between the House of Commons on the one side, and the king supported by the House of Lords on the other, has stagnated, to the great reproach of the contenders, and injury of the public interest, which, however, in this period of venality and selfishness, seems to be a consideration of the smallest importance, if any at all.

Feb. 17.   Received several letters from Salem, encouraging me to hope I may be permitted to return to my native country.

FROM WILLIAM PYNCHON, ESQ.

Salem, Jan. 2, 1784.

DEAR SIR:

I have made inquiry amongst your friends, and all agree that although there seems to be no prospect of a repeal of the laws against absentees, yet the inhabitants of this town, the committees, and all orders, seem very desirous of your returning in the spring. As Mr. Cabot, by whom I shall send this, is urgent for it, and can inform you of the present temper and disposition of the people towards you, it will be needless for me to give you particulars. Assurances from hence as to security, etc., while the laws remain unrepealed, we cannot give you, other than private opinion only. Mr. Cabot will acquaint you, and, by what Mr. Vans says, you will have it in letters from several, that there is little or no danger of

any prosecutions on the laws but from the respective towns, committees, etc., where the absentee belonged ; and all seem to agree
there can be, from present appearances, no danger from any of this
town. Mr. Cabot will acquaint you as to the successes of all who
have returned hither, and as to such as have returned to other
states. At Providence, and in some parts of Connecticut, those who
returned have been more cordially received and treated, and we
hope a like temper will take place in Massachusetts in the spring
and summer. Alcock *evasit et abdicavit* with bag and baggage,
and Whitaker seems to be hastening after him. These two politicians seem to have been the authors and promoters of more mischief than it is possible that any two who are left behind them
either should or would effect, or even attempt. They resembled
Swift's committee of ways and means for continuing the war and
promoting malevolence and contention as long as possible ; but at
length they became contemned and deserted by all, and I cannot
recollect any better proof or assurance you can have than the fate
of these two persons as to the temper of the people of this town,
and as to their disposition for peace and benevolence. However,
you will doubtless attend to what you see in the public prints, as
the resolves of assemblies in this and the other states, and judge for
yourself. Mr. Dana has returned from Russia, and if you return
here, during his continuance among us, it may prove a fortunate
circumstance to you, as I have heard him repeatedly say much in
favor of your attachments, connections, etc.

I remain, dear sir, most respectfully, your friend,

WILLIAM PYNCHON.

Feb. 28. Mr. Pitt by invitation in the city, at Grocer's Hall,
Cheapside; great throngs attended ; he was drawn in his carriage
by men. Returning late in the night, he was assaulted, and his
and other carriages broken to pieces by men armed with bludgeons ;
supposed, not without reason, by Fox's party, and his party's encouragement—a peevish, ill-judged resentment.

March 7. Met Mr. William Walter, late from Nova Scotia,
who at first sight recollected me and spoke; my eye and memory
weakened by age, and his features somewhat hardened, I could not
suddenly recognize him.

March 16.   Met my friend and countryman Mr. Isaac Smith, on the eve of his departure for Boston ; took him home to tea, but could not persuade him to pass the evening, being before engaged with the " *Dr. Franklin Club*" at London Tavern.

March 20.   Mr. Pitt, the great popular minister, because Charles J. Fox's antagonist, who is become *the man of the people*, (as Fox and his supporters arrogantly assumed to be, now the *popular odium*, on account of his East India bill,) dined this day at the London Tavern, being the third public dinner of late in the city ; and who in his turn will probably, before the expiration of many months, be as much condemned and hissed as he is now caressed and applauded—popular breath rarely if ever long keeps one direction.

March 26.   Proclamation issued for dissolving Parliament, this being the third session, the House of Commons proving refractory and unyielding to the king's measures and servants, young Pitt, Thurlow, Gower, etc.   The great seal was stolen last night from Lord Thurlow's, Great Ormond-street, with two swords and thirty guineas.

April 3.   Accompanied my friend Mr. Isaac Smith and his brother in a post-chaise to Gravesend, the former being bound to Boston in the ship United States.   Lodged at the Falcon inn.

April 4.   Took a long stroll to Milton Abbey ; saw the small remains of its ruins.

April 6.   The poll finished at Guildhall, the four former city members rechosen.   A Mr. Cooper, owner of a wine vault, stated at my lodgings that contested elections generally consumed six thousand hogsheads of port wine extra, and that twenty-four thousand was the average yearly consumption of Great Britain and Ireland.

April 8.   Mr. Alleyn, at Treasury, stated that no payment would be made these two months at soonest, for the public embarrassments will greatly delay our quarterly payments.

April 10.   Drank tea at Mr. De Berdt's, where met General Reed, late from Philadelphia.

April 14.   Visited Col. Willard at No. 81 Charlotte-street, Portland-place, to inquire about government's offer to convey refugees inclined to reside in Nova Scotia, with allowance to be continued as if in England.

April 30.   Walked to Limehouse church ; returned by Stepney church-yard, and saw therein a tomb inclosed within iron rails, in form of a coffin, said to contain the remains of a wife buried above ground in compliance with the will of a testator, who gave the husband an estate on that condition : he is depicted on a glass window fronting the burial-ground as looking out at her tomb.   Afterwards, at New England Coffee-house, met Mr. Cox, who asked me to tea with young Smith ; which I accepted, meeting there his father-in-law and Mr. Jackson of Newburyport.

May 2.   Attended service at Limehouse church ; Dr. Watson, bishop of Llandaff, preached a most excellent charity sermon to a crowded assembly.   Bidding prayer was long, catholic, and charmingly delivered ; concluding sentence was, " *Now to the King eternal*," etc., instead of the usual one, " *Now to God the Father, God the Son*," etc.   His enunciation is loud, sonorous and manly, his person robust and tall.

May 3.   Attended the scrutiny in aldermen's room, Guildhall, between Sawbridge and Atkinson, a case decided in favor of an act of Parliament against city right of aldermen's consent to the removal of a livery man from one company to another, without which it was asserted he was disqualified to vote for a member of Parliament, although of the livery and free.

May 4.   Mr. Danforth met me, and together we visited Mrs. Hay and staid till eight o'clock.

FROM WILLIAM PYNCHON, ESQ.

Salem, March 2, 1784.

DEAR SIR :

As Messrs. Sparhawk, Bartlett and others are going in the Pilgrim, it will be needless to attempt giving you a particular account of occurrences here.   You will doubtless hear from them of the alteration in the temper of the people towards absentees, particularly of our town.   Alcock's going off, (or absconding,) with Dr. Whitaker's sinking in the esteem of the people, even at the fish-market and brandy-shops, has produced a good effect ; many show their disapprobation, and some their utter detestation of certain intolerant dispositions and persecuting measures.

I said nothing about our Social Library, because of the present state of our finances and the want of regular meetings of the society. Mr. E. Hasket Derby has lately imported a considerable library of modern books, which proved to be very dear, as many think, and might have been purchased much cheaper by you; therefore the proprietors wish to avail themselves of your advice and assistance, whether you shall continue in England or return hither. I find Mr. D. Oliver, third son of your good friend Andrew Oliver, Esq., goes also in the Pilgrim. All who can cross the Atlantic seem determined to go and procure their goods from England; not one discovers a disposition to receive them from France, notwithstanding their generosity towards us. Going to England is now as formerly called *going home.*

Many of our politicians seem desirous of seeing an English ambassador in America to balance the increasing interest and influence of France, whose intrigues perplex and alarm us. You doubtless have heard of Mr. Dana's return from the court of Russia without concluding a commercial treaty there: he is now chosen a member of Congress, and is soon to set out, warmly engaged in opposition to French politics.

I have advised Mr. Oliver to seek you out and inform you about us all, who wish and expect your return in the summer; as he is young, and a stranger, I doubt not you will notice him and render him all the kind offices which you may observe him to need. I have desired Mr. Bartlet to advise with you as to some of the latest and best plays, farces, etc., which we wish much to see.

March 4. The Pilgrim not sailing this morning, I find time to recollect an omission I made last night. Some Americans have lately returned *via* Philadelphia to Boston, among them William McNeal, who went off with the troops from thence, and E. Williams, who was an officer in the British service at New-York, and now receives half pay. McNeal, by means of the Committee of Safety, was taken up and used roughly on account of his conduct, as it is said, during the blockade at Boston; but Williams met with no insult or obstruction there or at Salem, but is gone into the country to settle his affairs and then return to Nova Scotia. It is true he did not choose needlessly to go to the parade, or insurance offices, etc., but went about Salem visiting his particular friends, and met with no indecency in the streets or elsewhere. Many have urged me heretofore to write, that you might return and reside here without the least danger or insult; but while such as Alcock and Whitaker had the lead, I could not think nor say so. Now I may safely tell you what I have heard heretofore in the market-place, from some that are most desirous now for your return :—" Oh, let them return, by all means; but they must remember, that they are to down on their knees to the General Court in the first place, to the committee in the next, and to their townsmen too, and ask pardon, and then we may even let them stay among us, provided they behave as they ought; even your Col. Browne himself must submit to this."

Your own and your friends' feelings require no observation on such insolence. This cannot now tend in the least to discourage your return; lest it should heretofore, I thought best not to mention it. Farewell.

Yours truly,
WILLIAM PYNCHON.

TO WILLIAM PYNCHON, ESQ., SALEM.

London, May 9, 1784.

MY DEAR SIR :

Your favor of the 2d and 4th March was delivered into my hands by Mr. Bartlet, the sight of whom was as unexpected as agreeable. He acquaints me with an event foretold to the late Mr. Barnard and myself at Hartford, some thirteen years ago, by a clergyman of that town, concerning the mischievous incendiary (Dr. Whitaker) lately dismissed from the remnant of God's heritage over which he had for too long a time lorded, viz., that his proud, restless, turbulent spirit would not suffer him to continue long without attempting to disturb the peace of all within reach of his pernicious influence, and must force the neighborhood sooner or later to banish him. I confess, though at this great distance of time and place, I cannot resist the most pleasurable sensations on hearing this event. Whatever is the cause of an alteration in the people's notions, the effects probably will prove advantageous to their characters and interest.

My design being to continue in England till autumn, if the proprietors of the Social Library shall think me likely to serve their interest in the purchase of books, no exertions shall be wanting in my power to do them justice. There is one circumstance relating to books with which you may be unacquainted : the first edition of a book of character and quick sale bears a high price till the run has abated ; besides, the modish outside dress, emblematic of the taste of the age, enhances the price not a little. Second hand books, and those out of the tonish line, may generally be bought reasonably ; books of amusement and the beauties of modern writers are in common estimation, and sell dear.

Respecting Mr. Hasket Derby's library, if it was sent through a merchant, probably an addition was put to the bookseller's price of at least 25 per cent., not an uncommon practice here.

Your mention of young Mr. Daniel Oliver is sufficient to recommend him to my respect and notice, if he shall see fit to desire it ; without which it is not likely I may see him, being rarely in the way of Americans, having forsaken the New England Coffee-house, grown old, the transatlantics young and unknown to me, and their manners and language unpleasing.

The easy credit obtained here is astonishing, and characterizes truly this nation, who are credulous, generous, unsuspecting, and wealthy beyond belief ; if great mutual complaints and sufferings do not follow the immense indiscriminate exports to America, I shall be much out of my reckoning.

It will not be surprising to me if French politics will be as much execrated among you as they were admired and praised during the war ; it is morally impossible, that despotic as the court of Versailles is, she can relish the republican principles and maxims of the United States longer than she can make them subservient to her own ambitious purposes. All the world knows the ruin of Great Britain was the only object of her assisting America to throw off her dependence, and the folly of her statesmen has aided the views of that intriguing power. Never had this country a fairer opportunity of disappointing the pernicious views of her rival neighbors than the present, were there a public spirit in this infatuated nation ; but, alas ! a regard to the public welfare is no more to be found among its rulers. However indignantly I behold the conduct of her neighbors, I confess France should be considered only as a rival power, striving to give the law to a state that has for more than a century made it a professed principle to thwart all her political views. I hope your people will have more wisdom than to permit an aristocratic spirit to take place among you; for of all civil oppressions that is most intolerable.

I sincerely thank you for all your favors, particularly the last; the contents of your letters might have been published at the market-cross without injury to your character in the height of the war, unless with such persons as Alcock and Whitaker, whose mad party zeal construed into guilt every innocent word and act of those they were disposed to slander and vilify.

I am, with great truth,

Your faithful and grateful friend,

S. Curwen.

May 9. After service proceeded to Mr. Danforth's lodgings to take him by agreement to Kensington Gardens, where after a few turns adjourned to " Adam and Eve" ordinary. Mr. Samuel Porter and young Farnham afterwards joined us in the gardens, which we found excessively crowded; among others the Duke of Chartres, brother of the French king, and two other French noblemen.

May 11. Saw John Sparhawk from (near) Portsmouth for the first time.

May 13. Saw Captain Ingersoll from Salem.

May 15. With Mr. Bartlet purchased plays for Mr. Pynchon, and law-books for Mr. Ward. Mr. Bartlet presented me with a medal struck in Philadelphia;—in a round compartment stands, " U. S. . . . . . 5 . . . . 1783 ;"—round, " *Libertas et Justitia ;*" on the other side, in the centre, an eye surrounded by a glory; the whole encompassed by *thirteen stars,*—with the legend, " *Nova Constellatio.*"

May 17. To Covent Garden; abode an hour amidst very numerous throngs, this being the last day of polling, and Fox to be chaired, it is feared; great riots and destruction will be the consequence. The foot-guards and a squadron of horse are ordered to hold themselves in readiness, and approach within a callable distance. In the afternoon went to Covent Garden, now emptied; the company gone to attend Mr. Fox's procession,—the hustings removed, and all the stands taken down. Proceeded thence to Charing Cross, which, to my surprise, I found crowded; the procession then just beginning to march by from Westminster Hall, in the following order :—the officers of each parish distinct, with their peculiar standards, attending two and two, with wands in their hands; bands of music; next gentlemen on horseback; then others on foot; in the rear was Mr. Byng, whose appearance was announced by " *Byng and Fox for ever!*" Then followed a few horsemen; then *Mr. Fox*, mounted on a lofty chair, on and around interwoven with a laurel bower almost encompassing him; soon after appeared a lofty white silk banner, with this inscription,— " *Sacred to female patriotism ;*" and was immediately followed by the Duchesses of Portland and Devonshire in their coaches, around which were laurel festoons, each drawn by six horses; the whole concluded with about thirty private carriages. An innumerable crowd attended, and with vociferous acclamations, but no riot nor mobbing; government having wisely provided the horse and foot-guards, which probably discouraged the ill-disposed.

May 20. Parson Walter and Mr. Danforth visited me and took tea.

May 21. Visited by Captain Ingersoll from Salem, from whom I have heard more particulars relative to the present state of the town and its inhabitants than for several years.

TO WILLIAM VANS, ESQ., SALEM.

London, May 21, 1784.

DEAR SIR:

Your favor of 2d January, was, I acknowledge, unexpected; but did not surprise me, though at this late day. *The difference of your sentiments from mine and those of my mistaken friends,* needed not to have caused the destruction of your former letter; for how wide soever our political notions have been, or perhaps now are, that letter, I dare say, conceived in purity of intention, and brought forth in decency of expression, could not have failed to prove informative and amusing; and on that score a welcome present. Besides, I sit in judgment on no man; wishing for candor towards myself, I think it my duty to practise it in my turn to all; referring it to God alone to approve or condemn, who alone has the right; and to knaves and fools who have none, to usurp that right.

The doubts that have hitherto discouraged my attempting to trust the faithless waves again, are derived from more than one source. However wanting in respect the appellation, I had rather be accounted a timid friend, a light you say I am viewed in, than an enemy; a reproach I am not conscious to have deserved.

Your report of the returned penitents to their former habitations, strengthens my belief of lenity towards myself, should I ever be in a condition to stand in need of such *lenity*. However, if I rightly understand the meaning of your caution to address to the care of a friend, you yourself, sanguine and positive as you are of the safety of my person and property, think it a proper precaution to slip behind the curtain for a while after entering on the territories of the United States; a part, Mr. Vans, I shall on no account stoop to act, dissimulation being no part of my character, and I am too late in life to assume new habits.

I am well pleased to hear of the singular moderation of the town of Salem; if other towns have been violent in words only, as your letter intimates, their character is greatly injured and the public abused.

Having answered your letter, I now take leave, after subscribing myself with due regards,   Your friend,

S. Curwen.

June 8.   William Browne, lately arrived from Gibraltar, where he served as an officer during the siege, son of Colonel Browne, now governor of Bermudas, called on me after an interval of six years; he appears intelligent, and his manners much refined.

June 11.   To my townsman, S. Porter's lodgings, Kensington, through the gardens. There seems no inclination in him or any refugees to return back; fed, I presume, with delusive hopes of a compensation, or rather deluding themselves with ungrounded expectations founded only in their vain wishes and desires of court compassion, which may be justly added to Lord Rochester's list of ideal nothings.

June 19.   At one o'clock the funeral procession of Sir Barnard

Turner, sheriff, passed through Bishopgate-street amidst great crowds, though much lessened by the delay which the populace mistook for its being laid aside ; the body had been arrested after it was put into the hearse, in the street, for a considerable debt, which was afterwards compromised, on whose or what account is variously stated. The hearse was preceded by two lines of the artillery association, headed by an officer and five privates abreast, their firelocks reversed, marching in slow pace, muffled drums beating, trumpets sounding, and other instruments playing the 104th psalm tune ; the hearse was adorned with large flowing plumes of ostrich feathers, just before which was led the horse of the deceased, dressed in black ; on the saddle were laid the hat, sword, and boots crossed. A small detachment of the artillery company followed the carriage of the deceased and those of his brother sheriffs ; after which the whole closed by fourteen carriages, each drawn by two pair of horses ; the whole was to proceed nine miles, to Tottenham ; solemn and pompous in the extreme.

June 22. At New England Coffee-house read Mr. Pitt's speech and motion to stop the smuggling of tea, by a repeal of the heavy duty on that article, and substituting a lighter one ; and to prevent any injury to the revenue, by laying an additional house and window tax, whereby the poor and middling classes will be eased; and the burden, as it ought, will lay on the wealthy. Polling in the Borough for the election of a member in the room of the late Sir Barnard Turner ; candidates, Sir Richard Hotham, and Mr. Paul Mesurier.

FROM HON. JONATHAN SEWALL.

Bristol, June 28, 1784.

DEAR SIR :

Accept my thanks for your kind communication of your intentions to revisit America, and for your obliging offer of accepting any services I may wish to trouble you with. I am clear in my judgment that you are perfectly right in your present determination ; you have taken no active part,—your family has remained unmolested, and Mr. F. Cabot assures me, that whenever you choose to return you will be received with the warmest cordiality by all your old friends, and will receive no insult from any ; in short, that you may go as safely as he can. This was his closing expression. You have not told me when you intend to embark; if you think proper to give me seasonable notice of the time, perhaps I may trouble you with the care of one or two letters, provided you dare be the bearer of them from an *alien—traitor* by law, *vide Act of* 1779. If you have any qualms, as I don't know but you may, upon good grounds, give me but a hint of your fears or wishes, and I shall conform to either, as my letters will be of no importance to myself or my correspondents—no treason, no politics, I assure you. If you go, as I with twenty-eight others still remain exiles, it is not probable we shall ever see each other again, in this world· God only knows what kind of one the next will be, whether more or less dirty—be it what it may, if we meet I shall most joyfully take you by the hand.   Indeed I don't absolutely despair of seeing you again in this strange world, for upon my soul, though I was born and bred yet I am a stranger in it ; but my design is to go out to N. Scotia this autumn or early in the spring—there, if you wish, you may see me, but while the unjust, illiberal, lying act of 1779 remains unrepealed, never will I set foot on the territories of the thirteen United Independent States. I feel no resentment against them.   I wish them more happiness in their unnatural independence than my judgment allows me to hope for them—but I have been mistaken throughout the whole voyage; yet, however I may have been out in my former opinions, I wish my judgment may still be erroneous—I wish, most sincerely, my native country may meet all the happiness she has sought, *per fas et nefas*—she thinks she has obtained it—I wish she may not be mistaken ; but I have my doubts.

Mrs. Sewall accepts with thanks your compliments, and returns them most cordially ; my sister, whom you kindly remember, died, poor girl, on the 17th of May last, after a paralytic stroke about three months before ; I think I may say, she has gone with as few faults on her head as any of us can expect to go with. I miss her greatly,—but why should we complain ?

I am your humble servant and sincere friend,

JONA. SEWALL.

TO HON. JUDGE SEWALL, BRISTOL.

London, June 29, 1784.

DEAR SIR:

On some accounts I shall return to America with reluctance, having many doubts on my mind of meeting such a reception as will encourage my continued abode in that land of purity, sanctity and liberty. I feel too independent a spirit within to apprehend or regard any danger from republican licentiousness, which ever has been my contempt and abhorrence.

The following *inter nos.* The success of my application to the commissioners, now sitting in the Treasury, I am as yet ignorant of; my memorial or petition was this day delivered in, and is to be considered to-morrow. Whatever shall be the event I shall endeavor to support the same spirit, though a success equal to my supposed just expectations would serve as pillars or buttresses in an old tottering edifice, to add strength and support thereto.

Please make my compliments to your family, and to Mr. Samuel Sewall if in your neighborhood.

Dear sir, your affectionate friend, etc.,

S. CURWEN.

June 29. After composing the following petition, I proceeded with it to the Treasury—dubious of its fate or fortune.

" To the Commissioners appointed by act of Parliament to consider the sufferings and service of the American loyalists:

" The petition of Samuel Curwen humbly showeth : That your petitioner was forced to abandon his home and dwelling by the repeated menaces of the people within a few days after the unhappy rencounter at Lexington, who reproached all persons with the invidious appellation of *tories,* as they chose to call such as did not openly accuse the king's troops as aggressors, were for supporting law and order, and for forbearing future violences ; among which number your petitioner was one. Taking refuge aboard a vessel bound to Philadephia, he arrived there, hoping to find an asylum from outrage and indignity; but in this he was mistaken, for though that city had during all former wars shown a manifest dislike to military levies and arrangements, and when in the late dis-

pute, a singular moderation; at this period the political frenzy
had risen to an equal height as in New England, and your petitioner was soon informed that that city could prove no refuge to him,
even by those friends under whose protection he sought for safety;
the only condition of his continuing there was a public renunciation
of his principles, acknowledging his errors, and promising future
obedience to the new assumed powers. Loth to be held up to the
public in so disgraceful and mortifying a view, and to confess a
falsehood, he took the only alternative in his power. All communication with the northward by sea being forbidden by the city
committee of safety and inspection, lest General Gage's troops at
Boston should be supplied with flour, etc., and by land no letters
could be sent but under the inspection of the state inquisitors—the
regular post-office established by act of Parliament being shut up,
and travelling by land dangerous to any but those called *sons of
liberty*—he therefore took shipping again, and after a series of
dangers in a very tedious passage, arrived in London, where and
in the country, he has resided to the present time, subsisting whilst
his own stock lasted on that, and since on the public bounty.
Having received some overtures since the peace took place from
some of his townsmen of Salem, which, together with the sad derangement of his affairs there, makes him wish to revisit his native
country of New England, but the advices from his friends rendering
it still doubtful whether he can with safety and comfort pass the
remainder of his days there—being near the verge of threescore
years and ten—he proposes therefore to retreat to Nova Scotia
or one of the royal colonies, in case he cannot obtain a resettlement
on the forementioned conditions, and therefore humbly requests
liberty to appoint an agent here to receive the usual allowance
hitherto indulged him, and for so long a time as may be judged
proper to continue it.

And your petitioner as in duty bound, etc.,

SAMUEL CURWEN."

July 2. Went to Treasury; returned *re infecta*, not a little
deranged but not much disappointed; my expectations from court
not being high, I can suffer but rarely any inconvenience, taking
care not to put myself in the way of frequent mortification. The

present application is of a kind I should have thought not liable to a repulse, many such favors having been already granted, if the request deserves not rather the appellation of a just demand.

July 5. Went to the Treasury, and there received the agreeable information that the commissioners had granted my petition to appoint an agent to receive my quarterly allowance after my departure from England, on making satisfactory proof of my being alive at the successive periods of payment. From this I date an end to my doubts respecting my embarkation ; its issue time must reveal.

July 7. Made an early visit to Mr. Gorham, to talk on the subject of our passage with Capt. Ingersoll.

July 8. On 'change met Capt. Folger and John Sparhawk, both of whom I wish to embark with Mr. Gorham and myself with Capt. Ingersoll. Mr. Jonathan Jackson called on me for a letter of introduction to Mr. George Russell of Birmingham, which I cheerfully gave, acquainting Mr. Russell that he possessed an unblemished reputation and extensive property, in case he may form any commercial arrangement there.

TO REV. JOSEPH BRETLAND, EXETER.

London, July 9, 1784.

DEAR SIR :

I could not, with my strong sense of obligation to Mr. Bretland for the many instances of respectful attention received from him during my residence in the west, leave England without acknowledging them. My departure from London will be within a fortnight—a voyage at this late hour of my life is an undertaking, even were the prospects bright, I would gladly dispense with ; but duty and interest call too loudly to be resisted. I presume your acquaintance on the western continent lies in a very narrow compass ; however, if it shall be in my power to serve or amuse you in respect to the concerns in that distant quarter, I shall feel myself obliged by gratifying your wish.

I know not in what employment I am to pass the small remnant of my days, should Providence permit my safe return home ; but I shall not think part of it ill-bestowed in directing and assisting the studies and pursuits of my niece's children, who are just of an age to receive useful ideas—with regard to the English, Latin and Greek tongues, I shall esteem it a peculiar favor if you will be pleased to forward me a list of books and the order in which they should be used.

Very truly your friend,

S. Curwen.

July 10.   To the Treasury ; found the American door besieged by a score of mendicants like myself, waiting their turns—though I thought my early attendance would have entitled me to No. 1, I was glad to stand No. 21 ; so great was the crowd that I was more than once about to depart and leave them.

July 11.   With Capt. Coombs took an airing to the tower, having encompassed it on the ramparts, and taken a view of the American thirteen stripes flying on eight vessels lying in one tier ; the first view I ever distinctly had of their independent naval glory. Arranged about going with Capt. Ingersoll.

July 16.   Gave a power of attorney to George Bainbridge of Bread-street, to receive my pension quarterly.

July 18.   Mr. Cassini, the French mathematician, having presented through his ambassador in London a memorial, praying that some person would undertake to carry triangles from Greenwich to Dover to meet the French at Calais, in order to determine the exact distance between the observatories of Paris and Greenwich ; his majesty, who is ever ready to patronize useful schemes, immediately granted one thousand pounds for the carrying it on, and General Roy was, by his own consent, fixed upon for the undertaking.

TO REV. JOSEPH BRETLAND, EXETER, DEVON.

London, July 19, 1784.

Dear Sir :

Your obliging favor of the 17th is just received.   For a long time I was flattered with the expectation that my philosophical acquaintance would comply with his promise to answer your favor, till I had in truth forgotten I had not written you, and my delay arose from his, which at last ended in a refusal.   He seems to value himself on a freedom from the shackles of fear, and thinks that an advantage which no believer in the existence of a Deity can boast of, and to that principle refers all those labored treatises to prove one; and though fully convinced of the truth of his system, is satisfied a universal belief of them in the present state of things would not be productive of beneficial effects in society, which to me is instead of a thousand arguments to manifest their falsity.

I would with unfeigned pleasure travel further than the distance between us to meet my worthy friend, but unless the weather prevent, or some unforeseen accident intervene, to which human affairs are liable, I shall take shipping within four days. It repents me much that I had not availed myself of leisure to have visited you; but past neglects may be, like this, lamented, not repaired.

Your kind information in respect to method of teaching, I thank you for; your friendly caution I take in good part, and shall not fail to attend to it; and your request, you may depend on my compliance with.

Be pleased to make my respectful compliments to all friends.

I remain, with real regard,

Yours,

S. CURWEN.

July 20. Went to Mr. Copley's, George-street, Hanover-square, to take my leave of him, and pay my last compliments to his father-in-law, Mr. R. Clarke, and the family. Mr. Copley absent at Tunbridge.

July 22. Accompanied by Mr. Nathaniel Gorham, breakfasted on board ship Union, Capt. Jonathan Ingersoll, wherein I have engaged my passage to Boston; met Benjamin Pickman the elder and younger. Dined at Mr. De Berdt's, in company with General Joseph Reed of Philadelphia, and Mr. Gorham; also drank tea and passed the evening there.

July 25, *Sunday.* Attended worship at Mr. Lindsay's chapel, Essex-street, Strand; took my final leave of Mr. Lindsay and Dr. Disney at the chapel door.

July 28. Took leave at lodgings 107 Bishopgate-street within, and proceeded to the ship Union, lying at Irongate, where I purpose to abide till my arrival at Gravesend. Paid twenty guineas in part for my passage money. From henceforth I bid an ever-lasting farewell to London. At ten o'clock the Tower guns, to the number of eighty, were discharged; this being the day appointed by royal proclamation to be observed as a thanksgiving for the general peace. Despatched a boat to bring Capt. Coombs from his brig Minerva; Capt. Patterson and Cleves also drank tea with us.

Aug. 1. Proceeded down the river with a fair wind.

Aug. 2. Anchored off Deal.

Aug. 3. Capt. Ingersoll with two passengers arrived on board; immediately after the ship broke ground, and in an hour entered the Channel; and now hey for the ocean.

Aug. 4. This morning all our passengers breakfasted together for the first time; their names, Nathaniel Gorham, William Smith, Lewis and Francis Deblois, of Boston, a Mr. Isle, and myself.

Aug. 6. Stood in for St. Helen's road; thence proceeded to Cowes harbor, Isle of Wight, where we anchored; went ashore, took tea and supped at the Vine inn.

Aug. 7. With four fellow-passengers took coach for Newport, the only borough town on the island, consisting of four hundred houses; it lies at the head of water beyond Cowes five miles; remarkable for no manufactures or productions, natural or artificial: thence trudged it on foot to Carisbrook Castle, on an eminence a mile or more distant, now in ruins, and inhabited by a family named Poney, consisting of two or three maidens and their servants. The church is a living of £120 per annum. After dinner we all set off for our ship.

Aug. 8. Got under weigh, and at six o'clock are now in the bay, steering for Lymington road, where we arrived at nine o'clock and anchored, waiting for the ebb to carry us through the Needles at a league's distance. These rocks lie on the island side of the entrance, and on the opposite shore of the main land of England. On a point, of a mile or so in length, stands *Hurst Castle*, remarkable in history for being the prison of King Charles, not long before his execution.

Aug. 10. Supposed off Berryhead, at five leagues distant. Afternoon changed our course and entered Dartmouth harbor.

Aug. 11. At six o'clock A. M. in the offing, *Start* bearing N. by E., four leagues distant; dead calm; ten vessels in sight.

Aug. 13. Spoke brig Paragon, twenty-eight days out from Alexandria, with Mr. and Mrs. Hughes on board.

Sept. 25. Arrived at Boston, and at half past three o'clock landed at the end of Long-wharf, after an absence of nine years and five months, occasioned by a lamented civil war, excited by ambitious, selfish men here and in England, to the disgrace, dishonor, distress, and disparagement of these extensive territories. By plunder and rapine some few have accumulated wealth, but many more are greatly injured in their circumstances; some have to lament over the wreck of their departed wealth and estates, of which pitiable number I am; my affairs having sunk into irretrievable ruin.

TO CAPT. MICHAEL COOMBS, LONDON.

Salem, Mass., Oct. 9, 1784.

DEAR SIR :

This day fortnight, at half past three P. M., I landed on the head of the Long-wharf, in Boston, being the first American ground I had touched since May 12, 1775, when I departed from Philadelphia. It is no less strange than unaccountable, how low, mean and diminutive every thing on shore appeared to me. On Sunday, being the day following, I left for this place, where I alighted at the house of my former residence, and not a man, woman, or child, but expressed a satisfaction at seeing me, and welcomed me back. Thus much for myself.

The few things for your *widow* I have delivered into her hands, and I find her a woman of uncommon vigor and equanimity, nor do I think one to be met with who has better acquitted herself in the late trying times. By her resolution she has preserved the household furniture from confiscation and waste, and your accountbooks from inspection, though menaced and flattered by the state agents. The melancholy derangement of my own affairs has so entirely unsettled me, that I can scarce attend to any thing. I think it very unlikely my house can be saved.* It shall be among my first engagements to attend to your affairs.

With real regard, your friend,

S. CURWEN.

---

* It was saved from confiscation.

TO JONATHAN SMITH, ESQ., PHILADELPHIA

Salem, Oct. 9, 1784.

DEAR SIR :

A few days since I returned to the place of my nativity, after an absence of more than nine years, in which interval I find great revolutions to have taken place, not only with regard to the civil and political state of America in general, but also with respect to the property of individuals. Whilst some from the narrowest and baset condition have arisen to high honors and great wealth, others from comfortable, reputable, and even respectable and affluent, have fallen into indigent and distressed circumstances; and although the latter is not exactly my case, I confess myself verging to that point; my affairs are sadly deranged, but I hope time and application will cure the disorder. For that purpose, I beg you will forward to me a box containing my account-books left in your father's hands for security during my absence.

Your most obedient servant,

S. CURWEN.

TO CAPT. MICHAEL COOMBS, LONDON.

Salem, Nov. 15, 1784.

DEAR SIR :

I have waited on Mr. Sewall,* a lawyer of your town ; from him I learn he has undertaken to procure the necessary papers, and will, at my pressing instance, set about it immediately ; my argument being constantly, *delay is almost as fatal to my friend as total neglect.*

I am now to congratulate you on the salvation of your wharf and warehouse from the villainous hands of the rapacious harpies, the commissioners ; that part of your real estate, by great luck was neglected in the libel by which your other was seized and confiscated, and therefore it still remains your property. What debts are claimed and proved, must, by the law that confiscates, be levied on and taken out of the estate sold, the remainder escheats to the

---

* Mr. Samuel Sewall, of Marblehead, afterwards chief justice of Massachusetts.

public treasury. But so infamously knavish has been the conduct of the commissioners, that though frequent attempts have been made to bring them to justice, and respond for the produce of the funds resting in their hands, so numerous are the defaulters in *that august body,* the General Court, that all efforts have hitherto proved vain. Not twopence in the pound have arrived to the public treasury of all the confiscations!

Mr. Sewall says, were you disposed, he would advise you not to come here, until the act respecting refugees or absentees be passed, which will be, it is thought, this session.

The triumphant here look down with contempt on the vanquished; their little minds are not equal to the astonishing success of their feeble arms. God bless the worthy and blast the villainous of every party.*

Very truly yours,
S. CURWEN.

TO HON. JUDGE SEWALL, BRISTOL, ENGLAND.

Salem, Nov. 22, 1784.

DEAR SIR:

I find myself completely ruined. I confess I cannot bear to stay and perish under the ruins of my late ample property, and shall, therefore, as soon as I can recover my account-books, left in Philadelphia on my departure from America, and settle my deranged affairs, retreat to Nova Scotia, unless my allowance shall be taken from me. I am ignorant whether it may be prudent to make application to the commissioners on American refugees' affairs; but being here by their indulgence, I wish my allowance may continue. And if in this representation you can afford me any assistance by yourself, or in concert with Mr. Danforth, to whom I have also written, I shall thankfully acknowledge your counsel and aid, as a kind endeavor to rescue from want your old and faithful friend,

S. CURWEN.

---

* Capt. Coombs, to whom the foregoing letter was addressed, and who is often mentioned in Judge Curwen's Journal, was a respectable merchant of Marblehead, Mass., to which place he returned some years after the peace, and died there at an advanced age.

1795. [The following letters were written ten years after Judge Curwen's return, when in his eightieth year. He survived several years longer, having died at Salem April, 1802.]

TO SAMUEL CURWEN, ESQ.

Dorchester, Feb. 6, 1795.

DEAR SIR :

Many years are elapsed since I saw you. Hearing lately that you were returned to Salem, I have taken this opportunity to write to you. In the year 1741 I was taken ill, and continued poorly several years, but as Providence ordered it, got better and have kept school here fourteen years ; I was treasurer for the town thirty-seven years, and one of the selectmen and assessors thereof forty years. Although the most of our class that are dead seemed more likely to live long than I, yet to a wonder I am spared. It pleased God in his holy providence a few years since to deprive me of my habitation by fire ; by the help of friends I have got up a house, and have so far finished it that I and my family live in it.

Be pleased to let me hear from you, if you can send a letter to Mr. Hopestill Capens, a kinsman of mine living in Boston, near the market ; I hope I shall receive it. If you come to Boston, be pleased to come over and see me ; I live within four miles of the state-house.

From your classmate,

NOAH CLAP.

TO NOAH CLAP.

Salem, February 18, 1795.

MY FRIEND CLAP :

Your unexpected but agreeable letter of the 6th inst. was received about a week since, wherein you say you are among the very few of our fellow-students and classmates that are still in the land of the living. This has been a subject of my frequent thoughts and inquiry ; the result follows : Willis, Clap, Cook, Curwen, Parsons, Smith, Pierce, Snell ; Hovey uncertain.* You observe, " *although*

---

* Judge Curwen was of the class (thirty-eight in number) graduated at Harvard College in 1735 ; of whom it seems eight, and perhaps nine, were living in 1795.

most of our classmates that are dead and gone seemed more likely to live than I," etc.; on which I remark, it is a subject of constant observation among persons of thought and reflection, to which by experience I subscribe, that most of those whose health-promising countenances, lively spirits, and great bodily strength promise long life, are most commonly cut off in the midst of life, while the more feeble, complaining, and those frequently confined by illness, are continued to a comparatively long life, and rendered capable of more enjoyment than in the days of youth and middle age, of which number I profess myself to be one. Thanks to the gracious Being who has, in mercy I hope, lengthened my life to one of the longest periods in these days, being entered, more than two months, in my eightieth year; which I presume is your length of years.

Agreeably to your invitation, I shall, when the roads and weather prove favorable for travelling, continue my next journey as far as your dwelling, and in the mean time I remain, with due regards,

Your friend and well wisher,

S. Curwen.

Samuel Curwen
past 70 y^{rs} old
Apl 7: 1786.

SUPPLEMENT;

CONTAINING

ILLUSTRATIVE DOCUMENTS,

AND

BIOGRAPHICAL NOTICES OF INDIVIDUALS

MENTIONED IN THE FOREGOING WORK.

SUPPLEMENT.

ILLUSTRATIVE DOCUMENTS.

ADDRESS OF THE MERCHANTS AND OTHERS OF BOSTON,
TO GOV. HUTCHINSON.

Boston, May 30, 1774.

We, merchants and traders of the town of Boston, and others, do now wait on you, in the most respectful manner, before your departure for England, to testify, for ourselves, the entire satisfaction we feel at your wise, zealous, and faithful administration, during the few years that you have presided at the head of this province. Had your success been equal to your endeavors, and to the warmest wishes of your heart, we cannot doubt that many of the evils under which we now suffer, would have been averted, and that tranquillity would have been restored to this long divided province; but we assure ourselves that the want of success in those endeavors will not abate your good wishes when removed from us, or your earnest exertions still on every occasion to serve the true interest of this your native country.

While we lament the loss of so good a governor, we are greatly relieved that his Majesty, in his gracious favor, hath appointed as your successor a gentleman who, having distinguished himself in the long command he hath held in another department, gives us the most favorable prepossessions of his future administration.

We greatly deplore the calamities that are impending and will soon fall on this metropolis, by the operation of a late act of Parliament for shutting up the port on the first of next month. You cannot but be sensible, sir, of the numberless evils that will ensue to the province in general, and the miseries and distresses into which it will particularly involve this town, in the course of a few months. Without meaning to arraign the justice of the British Parliament, we could humbly wish that this act had been couched with less rigor, and that the execution of it had been delayed to a more distant time, that the people might have had the alternative either to have complied with the conditions therein set forth, or to have submitted to the consequent evils on refusal; but as it now stands, all choice is precluded, and however disposed to compliance or concession the people may be, they must unavoidably suffer very great calamities before they can receive relief. Making restitution for damage done to the property of the East India Company, or to the property of any individual, by the outrage of the people, we acknowledge to be just; and though we have ever disavowed, and do now solemnly bear our testimony against such lawless proceedings, yet, considering ourselves as members of the same community, we are fully disposed to bear our proportions of those damages, whenever the sum and the manner of laying it can be ascertained. We earnestly request that you, sir, who know our condition, and have at all times displayed the most benevolent disposition towards us, will, on your arrival in England, interest yourself in our behalf, and make such favorable representations of our case, as that we may hope to obtain speedy and effectual relief.

May you enjoy a pleasant passage to England; and under all the mortifications you have patiently endured, may you possess the inward and consolatory testimonies of having discharged your trust with fidelity and honor, and receive those distinguishing marks of his Majesty's royal approbation and favor, as may enable you to pass the remainder of your life in quietness and ease, and preserve your name with honor to posterity.

William Blair,	John Greenlaw,
James Selkrig,	Benjamin Clark,
Archibald Wilson,	William McAlpine,
Jeremiah Green,	Jonathan Snelling,
Samuel H. Sparhawk,	James Hall,
Joseph Turill,	William Dickson.
Roberts & Co.,	John Winslow, jr.,

Theophilus Lillie,
Miles Whitworth,
James McEwen,
William Codner,
James Perkins,
John White,
Robert Jarvis,
William Perry,
James & Patrick McMasters,
William Coffin,
Simeon Stoddard, jr.
John Powell,
Henry Laughton,
Eliphalet Pond,
M. B. Goldthwait,
Peter Hughes,
Samuel Hughes,
John Semple,
Hopestill Capen,
Edward King,
Byfield Lynde,
George Lynde,
A. F. Phipps,
Rufus Green,
David Phips,
Richard Smith,
George Spooner,
Daniel Silsby,
William Cazneau,
James Forrest,
Edward Cox,
John Berry,
Richard Hirons,
Ziphion Thayer.
John Joy,
Joseph Goldthwait,
Samuel Prince,
Jonathan Simpson,
James Boutineau,
Nathaniel Hatch,

Martin Gay,
Joseph Scott,
Samuel Minot,
Benjamin M. Holmes,
Archibald McNiel,
George Leonard,
John Borland,
Joshua Loring, jr.,
William Jackson,
James Anderson,
David Mitchelson,
Abraham Savage,
James Asby,
John Inman,
John Coffin,
Thomas Knight,
Benjamin Green, jr.
David Green,
Benjamin Green,
Henry H. Williams,
James Warden,
Nathaniel Coffin, jr.,
Silvester Gardiner,
John S. Copley,
Edward Foster,
Colbourn Burrell,
Nathaniel Greenwood,
William Burton,
John Winslow,
Isaac Winslow, jr.,
Thomas Oliver,
Henry Bloye,
Benjamin Davis,
Isaac Winslow,
Lewis Deblois,
Thomas Aylwin,
William Bowes,
Gregory Townsend,
Francis Green,
Philip Dumaresq,

Harrison Gray,

Peter Johonnot,

George Erving,

Joseph Green,

John Vassall,

Nathaniel Coffin,

John Timmins,

William Tailor,

Thomas Brinley,

Harrison Gray, jr.,

John Taylor,

Gilbert Deblois,

Joshua Winslow,

Daniel Hubbard,

Hugh Turbett,

Henry Lyddell,

Nathaniel Cary,

George Brinley,

Richard Lechmere,

John Erving, jr.,

Thomas Gray,

George Bethune,

Thomas Apthorp,

Ezekial Goldthwaite,

Benjamin Gridley,

John Atkinson,

Ebenezer Bridgham,

John Gore,

Adino Paddock.

ADDRESS OF THE INHABITANTS OF MARBLEHEAD TO GOV.
HUTCHINSON.

Marblehead, May 25, 1774.

His Majesty having been pleased to appoint his Excellency the
Hon. Thomas Gage, Esq., to be governor and commander-in-chief
over this province, and you, (as we are informed,) being speedily
to embark for Great Britain: We, the subscribers, merchants,
traders, and others, inhabitants of Marblehead, beg leave to present
you our valedictory address on this occasion; and as this is the
only way we now have of expressing to you our entire approbation
of your public conduct during the time you have presided in this
province, and of making you a return of our most sincere and
hearty thanks for the ready assistance which you have at all times
afforded us, when applied to in matters which affected our navigation and commerce, we are induced from former experience of
your goodness, to believe that you will freely indulge us in the
pleasure of giving you this testimony of our sincere esteem and
gratitude.

In your public administration, we are fully convinced that the
general good was the mark which you have ever aimed at, and we
can, sir, with pleasure assure you, that it is likewise the opinion of
all dispassionate thinking men within the circle of our observation,
notwithstanding many publications would have taught the world to

think the contrary; and we beg leave to entreat you, that when you arrive at the court of Great Britain, you would there embrace every opportunity of moderating the resentment of the government against us, and use your best endeavors to have the unhappy dispute between Great Britain and this country brought to a just and equitable determination.

We cannot omit the opportunity of returning you in a particular manner our most sincere thanks for your patronizing our cause in the matter of entering and clearing the fishing vessels at the custom-house, and making the fishermen pay hospital money; we believe it is owing to your representation of the matter, that we are hitherto free from that burden.

We heartily wish you, sir, a safe and prosperous passage to Great Britain, and when you arrive there may you find such a reception as shall fully compensate for all the insults and indignities which have been offered you.

Henry Saunders,	Nathan Bowen,
Richard Hinkly,	Thomas Robie,
Samuel Reed,	John Stimson,
John Lee,	John Webb,
Robert Ambrose,	Joseph Lee,
Jonathan Glover,	Thomas Lewis,
Richard Phillips,	Sweet Hooper,
Isaac Mansfield,	Robert Hooper,
Joseph Bubler,	Jacob Fowle,
Richard Stacy,	John Pedrick,
Thomas Procter,	Richard Reed,
John Fowle,	Benjamin Marston,
Robert Hooper, 3d,	Samuel White,
John Gallison,	Joseph Hooper,
John Prince,	John Prentice,
George McCall,	Robert Hooper, jr.
Joseph Swasey,	

ADDRESS OF THE BARRISTERS AND ATTORNEYS OF MASSACHUSETTS TO GOV. HUTCHINSON, MAY 30, 1774.

A firm persuasion of your inviolable attachment to the real interests of this your native country, and of your constant readiness, by every service in your power, to promote its true welfare and prosperity, will, we flatter ourselves, render it not improper in us, barristers and attorneys at law in the province of Massachusetts Bay, to address your Excellency upon your removal from us, with this testimonial of our sincere respect and esteem.

The various important characters of Legislator, Judge and first Magistrate over this province, in which, by the suffrages of your fellow-subjects, and by the royal favor of the best of kings, your great abilities, adorned with a uniform purity of principle, and integrity of conduct, have been eminently distinguished, must excite the esteem and demand the grateful acknowledgments of every true lover of his country, and friend to virtue.

The present perplexed state of our public affairs, we are sensible, must render your departure far less disagreeable to you than it is to us,—we assure you, sir, we feel the loss; but when, in the amiable character of your successor, we view a fresh instance of the paternal goodness of our most gracious sovereign; when we reflect on the probability that your presence at the court of Great Britain, will afford you an opportunity of employing your interests more successfully for the relief of this province, and particularly of the town of Boston, under their present distresses, we find a consolation which no other human source could afford. Permit us, sir, most earnestly to solicit the exertion of all your distinguished abilities in favor of your native town and country, upon this truly unhappy and distressing occasion.

We sincerely wish you a prosperous voyage, a long continuation of health and felicity, and the highest rewards of the good and faithful.

We are, sir, with the most cordial affection, esteem and respect,

Your Excellency's most obedient and very humble servants,

Robert Achmuty,	Andrew Cazneau,
Jonathan Sewall,	Daniel Leonard,
Samuel Fitch,	John Lowell,
Samuel Quincy,	Daniel Oliver,
William Pynchon,	Sampson S. Blowers,
James Putnam,	Shearjashub Brown,
Benjamin Gridley,	Daniel Bliss,
Abel Willard,	Samuel Porter,

David Ingersoll,	John Sprague,
Jeremiah D. Rogers,	Rufus Chandler,
David Gorham,	Thomas Danforth,
Samuel Sewall,	Ebenezer Bradish.

From the Essex Gazette of June 14, 1774.

MESSRS. HALL :

As it is generally known that an Address from the Merchants, Traders and others, in the town of Salem, to the late Governor Hutchinson, was signed by numbers of gentlemen belonging to the town ; and it being as well known that his Excellency gave his answer to the same, it remains now a matter of great speculation, especially amongst those of the town of Boston who were foremost in promoting a plan so apparently beneficial in the present exigency of affairs in this province, what sufficient reason can be assigned by the subscribers, (contrary to the very design of such an address,) for then not making it public. Many conjectures might be admitted upon this matter, not to the honor of the concerned, which we shall omit for the present.   Yours,

Z. Y.

From the Essex Gazette of June 1, 1775.

Salem, May 30, 1775.

Whereas we the subscribers did some time since sign an address to Governor Hutchinson, which, though prompted to by the best intentions, has, nevertheless, given great offence to our country : We do now declare, that we were so far from designing by that action, to show our acquiescence in those acts of Parliament so universally and justly odious to all America, that on the contrary, we hoped we might in that way contribute to their repeal ; though now to our sorrow we find ourselves mistaken. And we do now further declare, that we never intended the offence which this address has occasioned ; that if we had foreseen such an event we should never have signed it ; as it always has been and now is our wish to live in harmony with our neighbors, and our serious determination is to promote to the utmost of our power the liberty, the welfare, and happiness of our country, which is inseparably connected with our own.

John Nutting,	E. A. Holyoke,
N. Goodale,	William Pynchon,
Ebenezer Putnam,	Thomas Barnard,
Francis Cabot,	Nathaniel Dabney,
N. Sparhawk,	William Pickman,
Andrew Dalglish,	C. Gayton Pickman.

In Committee of Safety, Salem, May 30, 1775.—The declaration, of which the above is a copy, being presented and read, it was voted unanimously that the same was satisfactory ; and that the said gentlemen ought to be received and treated as real friends to this country.

By order of the Committee,

RICHARD DERBY, JR., Chairman.

In the same paper of June 1, 1775, immediately following the above, is a communication to the Committee of Safety, from the late Rev. Thomas Barnard, dated May 25, 1775 :—

GENTLEMEN :

A suspicion of being inimical to those with whom we are connected in society, and whom we esteem and love, cannot but give severe pain to a generous mind. Unhappily, I have been viewed by my countrymen in a light so disagreeable. The address which I signed to Governor Hutchinson upon his leaving this province, I signed with no party views, with no design whatever of injuring that country with the prosperity of which my dearest human interests are closely connected, but with strong hopes of promoting the lasting peace and welfare of my native land. But I own, my fond expectations arising therefrom have been disappointed. The cause of America I look upon capable of full defence by the voice of justice and the British constitution; and shall be ever ready to support it in that way which the united wisdom of the continent shall dictate.

Such are my sentiments, and upon the strength of them I would request of my countrymen to throw the veil of charity and forgiveness over any incautious action of mine, which may have led them to think unfavorably of me, and to grant me a place in their esteem, which I shall ever think myself happy in deserving.

THOMAS BARNARD, JR.

In Committee of Safety, Salem, May 25, 1775.—The declaration, of which the above is a copy, being presented and read, it was voted unanimously that the same was satisfactory ; and that the said gentleman ought to be received and treated as a real friend to his country.

By order of the Committee,

RICHARD DERBY, JR., Chairman.

From the Essex Gazette, June 14, 1774.

Last Saturday, (June 11th, 1774,) the following address was presented to his Excellency the Governor :—

To his Excellency Thomas Gage, Esq., Captain-General, Governor and Commander-in-Chief of the Province of Massachusetts Bay in New England, and Lieutenant-General of his Majesty's Forces.

May it please your Excellency :

We, merchants and others, inhabitants of the ancient town of Salem, beg leave to approach your Excellency with our most respectful congratulations on your arrival in this place.

We are deeply sensible of his Majesty's paternal care and affection to this province, in the appointment of a person of your Excellency's experience, wisdom and moderation, in these troublesome and difficult times.

We rejoice that this town is graciously distinguished for that spirit, loyalty, and reverence for the laws, which is equally our glory and happiness.

From that public spirit and warm zeal to promote the general happiness of men, which mark the great and good, we are led to hope under your Excellency's administration for every thing that may promote the peace, prosperity, and real welfare of this province.

We beg leave to commend to your Excellency's patronage the trade and commerce of this place, which, from a full protection of the liberties, persons and properties of individuals, cannot but flourish.

And we assure your Excellency we will make it our constant endeavors by peace, good order, and a regard for the laws, as far as in us lies, to render your station and residence easy and happy.

John Sargent,
Jacob Ashton,
William Wetmore,
James Grant,
Henry Higginson,
David Britton,
P. G. Kast,
Weld Gardner,
Nathaniel Daubney,
Richard Nicholls,
William Cabot,
Cabot Gerrish,
William Gerrish,
Rowland Savage,
William Lilly,
Jonathan Goodhue,
Nathan Goodale,
William Pickman,
C. Gayton Pickman,
Nathaniel Sparhawk,
William Vans,
Timothy Orne,
Richard Routh,
Stephen Higginson,

John Prince,
George Deblois,
Andrew Dalglish,
Joseph Blaney,
Archelaus Putnam,
Samuel Porter,
Thomas Poynton,
Samuel Flagg,
Benjamin Lynde,
William Browne,
John Turner,
P. Frye,
Francis Cabot,
William Pynchon,
John Fisher,
John Mascarene,
E. A. Holyoke,
Jos. Bowditch,
Ebenezer Putnam,
S. Curwen,
John Nutting,
Jos. Dowse,
Benjamin Pickman,
Henry Gardner.

THT " LOYAL ADDRESS FROM THE GENTLEMEN AND PRINCIPAL INHAB-
ITANTS OF BOSTON TO GOVERNOR GAGE ON HIS DEPARTURE FOR
ENGLAND, OCTOBER 6, 1775," WAS SIGNED AS FOLLOWS:

John Erving,
Thomas Hutchinson, jr.,
Silvester Gardiner,
Wm. Bowes,
John Timmins,
Nathaniel Coffin,
John Winslow, jr.,
Alexander Bymer,
Robert Hallowell,
Robert Jarvis,
David Phips,

John Tayler,
Archibald McNeal,
Francis Green,
Benjamin Davis,
John Sampson,
William Tayler,
John Inman,
Wm. Perry,
John Gore,
Isaac Winslow, jr.,
Thomas Courtney,

John Love,
Hugh Tarbett,
Nathaniel Perkins,
John Powell,
James Selkrig,
Archibald Cunningham,
William Cazneau,
David Barton,
John Semple,
Henry Lawton,
William Brattle,
John Troutbeck,
Stephen Greenleaf,
William Walter,
James Perkins,
Phillip Dumaresque,
Joshua Loring, jr.,
Henry Lloyd,
William Lee Perkins,
George Leonard,
Thomas Brinley,
Daniel Hubbard,
Samuel Fitch,
John Atkinson,
Joseph Turill,
Samuel Hirst Sparhawk,
Ebenezer Brigham,
William Codner,
Jonathan Snelling,
Benjamin Gridley,
Gilbert Deblois, .
Edward Hutchinson,
Miles Whitworth,
Daniel McMasters,
John Hunt, 3d,
James Lloyd,
William McAlpine,
John Greecart,

William Dickerson,
William Hunter,
Robert Semple,
John Joy,
Gregory Townsend,
Isaac Winslow,
Byfield Lyde,
Richard Clarke,
Benjamin Fanieul, jr.,
Thomas Amory,
George Brindley,
Ralph Inman,
Edward Winslow,
Benjamin M. Holmes,
William Jackson,
Richard Green,
James Murray,
Joseph Scott,
Peter Johonnot,
Nathaniel Cary,
Martin Gay,
Samuel Hughes,
William Coffin, jr.,
Adino Paddock,
Andrew Cazneau,
Henry Lindall,
Theophilus Lillie,
Henry Barnes,
M. B. Goldthwait,
Lewis Gray,
Nathaniel Brinley,
John Jeffries, jr.,
Archibald Bowman,
Jonathan Simpson,
Nathaniel Tayler,
James Anderson,
Lewis Deblois.

THE LOYAL ADDRESS TO GOVERNOR GAGE ON HIS DEPARTUTE, OCTOBER 14, 1775, OF THOSE GENTLEMEN WHO WERE DRIVEN FROM THEIR HABITATIONS IN THE COUNTRY TO THE TOWN OF BOSTON, WAS SIGNED BY THE FOLLOWING PERSONS:

John Chandler,	Jonathan Stearns,
James Putnam,	Ward Chipman,
Peter Oliver, sen.,	William Chandler,
Seth Williams, jr.,	Thomas Foster,
Charles Curtis,	Pelham Winslow,
Samuel Pine,	Daniel Oliver,
David Phips,	Edward Winslow, jr.,
Richard Saltonstall,	Nathaniel Chandler,
Peter Oliver, jr.,	James Putnam, jr.

CONSPIRACY ACT.

An Act to confiscate the estates of certain notorious conspirators against the government and liberties of the inhabitants of the late province, now state, of Massachusetts Bay.

Whereas the several persons hereinafter mentioned, have wickedly conspired to overthrow and destroy the constitution and government of the late province of Massachusetts Bay, as established by the charter agreed upon by and between their late majesties William and Mary, late King and Queen of England, etc., and the inhabitants of said province, now state, of Massachusetts Bay; and also to reduce the said inhabitants under the absolute power and domination of the present king, and of the parliament of Great Britain, and, as far as in them lay, have aided and assisted the same king and parliament in their endeavors to establish a despotic government over the said inhabitants:

Sect. 1. Be it enacted by the Council and House of Representatives, in General Court assembled, and by the authority of the same, that Francis Bernard, baronet, Thomas Hutchinson, Esq., late governor of the late province, now state, of Massachusetts Bay, Thomas Oliver, Esq., late lieutenant governor, Harrison Grey, Esq., late treasurer, Thomas Flucker, Esq., late secretary, Peter Oliver, Esq., late chief justice, Foster Hutchinson, John Erving, jr., George Erving, William Pepperell, baronet, James

Boutineau, Joshua Loring, Nathaniel Hatch, William Browne, Richard Lechmere, Josiah Edson, Nathaniel Rea Thomas, Timothy Ruggles, John Murray, Abijah Willard, and Daniel Leonard, Esqs., late mandamus counsellors of said late province, William Burch, Henry Hulton, Charles Paxon, and Benjamin Hallowell, Esqs., late commissioners of the customs, Robert Auchmuty, Esq., late judge of the vice-admiralty court, Jonathan Sewall, Esq., late attorney general, Samuel Quincy, Esq., late solicitor general, Samuel Fitch, Esq., solicitor or counsellor at law to the board of commissioners, have justly incurred the forfeiture of all their property, rights and liberties, holden under and derived from the government and laws of this state; and that each and every of the persons aforenamed and described, shall be held, taken, deemed and adjudged to have renounced and lost all civil and political relation to this and the other United States of America, and be considered as aliens.

Sect. 2. Be it enacted by the authority aforesaid, that all the goods and chattels, rights and credits, lands, tenements, and hereditaments of every kind, of which any of the persons herein before named and described, were seized or possessed, or were entitled to possess, hold, enjoy, or demand, in their own right, or which any other person stood or doth stand seized or possessed of, or are or were entitled to have or demand to and for their use, benefit and behoof, shall escheat, enure and accrue to the sole use and benefit of the government and people of this state, and are accordingly hereby declared so to escheat, enure and accrue, and the said government and people shall be taken, deemed and adjudged, and are accordingly hereby declared to be in the real and actual possession of all such goods, chattels, rights and credits, lands, tenements and hereditaments, without further inquiry, adjudication or determination hereafter to be had; any thing in the act, entitled, "An act for confiscating the effects of certain persons commonly called absentees," or any other law, usage, or custom to the contrary notwithstanding; provided always, that the escheat shall not be construed to extend to or operate upon, any goods, chattels, rights, credits, lands, tenements or hereditaments, of which the persons afore named and described, or some other, in their right and to their use, have not been seized or possessed, or entitled to be seized or possessed, or to have or demand as aforesaid, since the nineteenth day of April, in the year of our Lord one thousand seven hundred and seventy-five.—[*Passed April* 30, 1779.   *Not revised.*]

STATE OF MASSACHUSETTS.

An Act for confiscating the estates of certain persons commonly called absentees.

Whereas every government hath a right to command the personal services of all its members, whenever the exigencies of the state shall require it, especially in times of an impending or actual invasion, no member thereof can then withdraw himself from the jurisdiction of the government, and thereby deprive it of the benefit of his personal services, without justly incurring the forfeiture of all his property, rights and liberties, holden under and derived from that constitution of government, to the support of which he hath refused to afford his aid and assistance : and whereas the king of Great Britain did cause the parliament thereof to pass divers acts in direct violation of the fundamental rights of the people of this and of the other United States of America; particularly one certain act to vacate and annul the charter of this government, the great compact made and agreed upon between his royal predecessors and our ancestors; and one other act, declaring the people of said states to be out of his protection; and did also levy war against them, for the purpose of erecting and establishing an arbitrary and despotic government over them ; whereupon it became the indispensable duty of all the people of said states forthwith to unite in defence of their common freedom, and by arms to oppose the fleets and armies of the said king; yet nevertheless, divers of the members of this and of the other United States of America, evilly disposed, or regardless of their duty towards their country, did withdraw themselves from this, and other of the said United States, into parts and places under the acknowledged authority and dominion of the said king of Great Britain, or into parts and places within the limits of the said states, but in the actual possession and under the power of the fleets or armies of the said king; thereby abandoning the liberties of their country, seeking the protection of the said king, and of his fleets or armies, and aiding or giving encouragement and countenance to their operations against the United States aforesaid:

Sect. 1. Be it enacted by the Council and House of Representatives, in General Court assembled, and by the authority of the same, that every inhabitant and member of the late province, now state, of Massachusetts Bay, or of any other of the late provinces or colonies, now United States of America, who, since the nineteenth day of April, Anno Domini one thousand seven hundred and seventy-five, hath levied war or conspired to levy war against the government and people of any of the said provinces or colonies, or United States; or who hath adhered to the said king of Great Britain, his fleets or armies, enemies of the said provinces or colonies or United States, or hath given to them aid or comfort; or who, since the said nineteenth day of April, Anno Domini one thousand seven hundred and seventy-five, hath withdrawn, without the permission of the legislative or executive authority of this or some other of the said United States, from any of the said provinces or colonies, or United States, into parts and places under the acknowledged authority and dominion of the said king of Great Britain, or into any parts or places within the limits of any of the said provinces, colonies, or United States, being in the actual possession and under the power of the fleets or armies of the said king; or who, before the said nineteenth day of April, Anno Domini one thousand seven hundred and seventy-five, and after the arrival of Thomas Gage, Esq., (late commander-in-chief of all his Britannic Majesty's forces in North America,) at Boston, the metropolis of this state, did withdraw from their usual places of habitation within this state, into the said town of Boston, with an intention to seek and obtain the protection of the said Thomas Gage and of the said forces, then and there being under his command; and who hath died in any of the said parts or places, or hath not returned into some one of the said United States, and been received as a subject thereof, and (if required) taken an oath of allegiance to such states, shall be held, taken, deemed and adjudged to have freely renounced all civil and political relation to each and every of the said United States, and be considered as an alien.

Sect. 2. And be it further enacted by the authority aforesaid, that all the goods and chattels, rights and credits, lands, tenements, hereditaments of every kind, of which any of the persons herein before described were seized or possessed, or were entitled to possess, hold, enjoy or demand, in their own right, or which any other person stood or doth stand seized or possessed of, or are or were entitled to have or demand to and for their use, benefit and behoof, shall escheat, enure and accrue to the sole use and benefit of the government and people of this state, and are accordingly hereby declared so to escheat, enure and accrue.—[*Passed April* 30, 1779. *Not revised.*]

MANDAMUS COUNSELLORS.

Salem, Aug. 9, 1774. The following were appointed by his majesty, counsellors of this province by writ of mandamus,* viz :—

Col. Thomas Oliver, Lieut. Governor, President ; Peter Oliver, *Thomas Flucker, Foster Hutchinson,* Thomas Hutchinson, Jr. *Harrison Gray,* Judge Samuel Danforth, Col. John Erving, Jr. James Russell, Timothy Ruggles, *Joseph Lee, Isaac Winslow,* Israel Williams, Col. George Watson, Nathaniel Ray Thomas, Timothy Woodbridge, William Vassall, *William Browne,* Joseph Greene, *James Boutineau,* Andrew Oliver, Col. Josiah Edson, Richard Lechmere, *Commodore Joshua Loring,* John Worthington, Timothy Paine, *William Pepperell,* Jeremiah Powell, Jonathan Simpson, Col. John Murray, Daniel Leonard, Thomas Palmer, Col. Isaac Royall, Robert Hooper, Abijah Willard, *Capt. John Erving, jr.*

STATE OF MASSACHUSETTS.

An Act to prevent the return to this state of certain persons therein named, and others who have left this state or either of the United States, and joined the enemies thereof.

Whereas Thomas Hutchinson, Esq., late governor of this state, Francis Bernard, Esq., formerly governor of this state, Thomas Oliver, Esq., late lieutenant governor of this state, Timothy Ruggles, Esq., of Hardwick, in the county of Worcester, William Apthorp, merchant, Gibbs Atkins, cabinet maker, John Atkinson, John Amory, James Anderson, Thomas Apthorp, David Black, William Burton, William Bowes, George Brindley, Robert Blair, Thomas Brindley, James Barrick, merchant, Thomas Brattle, Esq., Samp-

---

* Those whose names are in italics alone took the oath of office.

son Salter Blowers, Esq., James Bruce, Ebenezer Bridgham, Alexander Brymer, Edward Berry, merchants, William Burch, Esq., late commissioner of the customs, Mather Byles, Jun., clerk, William Codner, book-keeper, Edward Cox, merchant, Andrew Cazneau, Esq., barrister at law, Henry Canner, clerk, Thomas Courtney, tailor, Richard, Clark, Esq., Isaac Clark, physician, Benjamin Church, physician, John Coffin, distiller, John Clark, physician, William Coffin, Esq., Nathaniel Coffin, Esq., Jonathan Clark, merchant, Archibald Cunningham, shop-keeper, Gilbert Deblois, merchant, Lewis Deblois, merchant, Philip Dumaresque, merchant, Benjamin Davis, merchant, John Erving, Jun., Esq., George Erving, Esq., Edward Foster and Edward Foster, Jun., blacksmiths, Benjamin Faneuil, Jun., merchant, Thomas Flucker, Esq., late secretary for Massachusetts Bay, Samuel Fitch, Esq., Wilfret Fisher, carter, James Forrest, merchant, Lewis Gray, merchant, Francis Green, merchant, Joseph Green, Esq., Sylvester Gardiner, Esq., Harrison Gray, Esq., late treasurer of Massachusetts Bay, Harrison Gray, Jun., clerk to the treasurer, Joseph Goldthwait, Esq., Martin Gay, founder, John Gore, Esq., Benjamin Hallowell, Esq., Robert Hallowell, Esq., Thomas Hutchinson, Jun., Esq., Benjamin Gridley, Esq., Frederick William Geyer, merchant, John Greenlaw, shop-keeper, David Green, merchant, Elisha Hutchinson, Esq., James Hall, mariner, Foster Hutchinson, Esq., Benjamin Mulbury Holmes, distiller, Samuel Hodges, book-keeper, Henry Halson, Esq., Hawes Hatch, wharfinger, John Joy, housewright, Peter Johonnot, distiller, William Jackson, merchant, John Jeffries, physician, Henry Laughton, merchant, James Henderson, trader, John Hinston, yeoman, Christopher Hatch, mariner, Robert Jarvis, mariner, Richard Lechmere, Esq., Edward Lyde, merchant, Henry Lloyd, Esq., George Leonard, miller, Henry Leddle, book-keeper, Archibald McNeil, baker, Christopher Minot, tide-waiter, James Murray, Esq., William McAlpine, bookbinder, Thomas Mitchell, mariner, William Martin, Esq., John Knutton, tallow-chandler, Thomas Knight, shop-keeper, Samuel Prince, merchant, Adino Paddock, Esq., Charles Paxon, Esq., Sir William Pepperell, baronet, John Powell, Esq., William Lee Perkins, physician, Nathaniel Perkins, Esq., Samuel Quincy, Esq., Owen Richards, tide-waiter, Samuel Rogers, merchant, Jonathan Simpson, Esq., George

Spooner, merchant, Edward Stowe, mariner, Richard Smith, merchant, Jonathan Snelling, Esq., David Silsby, trader, Samuel Sewall, Esq., Abraham Savage, tax-gatherer, Joseph Scott, Esq., Francis Skinner, clerk to the late council, William Simpson, merchant, Richard Sherwin, saddler, Henry Smith, merchant, John Semple, merchant, Robert Semple, merchant, Thomas Selkrig, merchant, James Selkrig, merchant, Robert Service, trader, Simon Tufts, trader, Arodi Thayer, late marshal to the admiralty court, Nathaniel Taylor, deputy naval officer, John Troutbeck, clerk, Gregory Townsend, Esq., William Taylor, merchant, William Vassal, Esq., Joseph Taylor, merchant, Joshua Upham, Esq., William Walter, clerk, Samuel Waterhouse, merchant, Isaac Winslow, merchant, John Winslow, jr., merchant, David Willis, mariner, Obadiah Whiston, blacksmith, Archibald Wilson, trader, John White, mariner, William Warden, peruke-maker, Nathaniel Mills, John Hicks, John Howe, and John Fleming, printers, all of Boston, in the county of Suffolk, Robert Auchmuty, Esq., Joshua Loring, Esq., both of Roxbury, in the same county, Samuel Goldsbury, yeoman, of Wrentham, in the county of Suffolk, Joshua Loring, jr., merchant, Nathaniel Hatch, Esq., both of Dorchester, in the same county, William Brown, Esq., Benjamin Pickman, Esq., Samuel Porter, Esq., John Sargeant, trader, all of Salem, in the county of Essex, Richard Saltonstall, Esq., of Haverhill, in the same county, Thomas Robie, trader, Benjamin Marston, merchant, both of Marblehead, in said county of Essex, Moses Badger, clerk, of Haverhill, aforesaid, Jonathan Sewall, Esq., John Vassal, Esq., David Phipps, Esq., John Nutting, carpenter, all of Cambridge, in the county of Middlesex, Isaac Royall, Esq., of Medford, in the same county, Henry Barnes, of Marlborough, in said county of Middlesex, merchant, Jeremiah Dummer Rogers, of Littleton in the same county, Esq., Daniel Bliss, of Concord, in the said county of Middlesex, Esq., Charles Russell, of Lincoln, in the same county, physician, Joseph Adams, of Townsend, in said county of Middlesex, Thomas Danforth, of Charlestown, in said county, Esq., Joshua Smith, trader, of Townsend, in said county, Joseph Ashley, jr., gentleman, of Sunderland, Nathaniel Dickenson, gentleman, of Deerfield, Samuel Bliss, shopkeeper, of Greenfield, Roger Dickenson, yeoman, Joshah Pomroy, physician, and Thomas Cutler, gentleman, of Hatfield, Jonathan Bliss, Esq., of Springfield, William Galway, yeoman, of Conway, Elijah Williams, attorney at law, of Deerfield, James Oliver, gentleman, of Conway, all in the county of Hampshire, Pelham Winslow, Esq., Cornelius White, mariner, Edward Winslow, jr., Esq., all of Plymouth, in the county of Plymouth, Peter Oliver, Esq., Peter Oliver, jr., physician, both of Middleborough, in the same county, Josiah Edson, Esq., of Bridgewater, in the said county of Plymouth, Lieutenant Daniel Dunbar, of Halifax, in the same county, Charles Curtis, of Scituate, in the said county of Plymouth, gentleman, Nathaniel Ray Thomas, Esq., Israel Tilden, Caleb Carver, Seth Bryant, Benjamin Walker, Gideon Walker, Zera Walker, Adam Hall, tertius, Isaac Joice, Joseph Phillips, Daniel White, jr., Cornelius White, tertius, Melzar Carver, Luke Hall, Thomas Decrow, John Baker, jr., all of Marshfield, in the said county of Plymouth, Gideon White, jr., Daniel Leonard, Esq., Seth Williams, jr., gentleman, Solomon Smith, boatman, all of Taunton, in the county of Bristol, Thomas Gilbert, Esq., Perez Gilbert, Ebenezer Hathaway, jr., Lot Strange, the third, Zebedee Terree, Bradford Gilbert, all of Freetown, in the same county, Joshua Broomer, Shadrach Hathaway, Calvin Hathaway, Luther Hathaway, Henry Tisdel, William Burden, Levi Chace, Shadrach Chase, Richard Holland, Ebenezer Phillips, Samuel Gilbert, gentleman, Thomas Gilbert, jr., yeoman, both of Berkley, in the said county of Bristol, Ammi Chace, Caleb Wheaton, Joshua Wilbore, Lemuel Bourn, gentleman, Thomas Perry, yeoman, David Atkins, laborer, Samuel Perry, mariner, Stephen Perry, laborer, John Blackwell, jr., laborer, Francis Finney, laborer, and Nehemiah Webb, mariner, all of Sandwich, in the county of Barnstable, Eldad Tupper, of Dartmouth, in the county of Bristol, laborer, Silas Perry, laborer, Seth Perry, mariner, Elisha Bourn, gentleman, Thomas Bumpus, yeoman, Ephraim Ellis, jr., yeoman, Edward Bourn, gentleman, Nicholas Cobb, laborer, William Bourn, cordwainer, all of Sandwich, in the county of Barnstable, and Seth Bangs, of Harwich, in the county of Barnstable, mariner, John Chandler, Esq., James Putnam, Esq., Rufus Chandler, gentleman, William Paine, physician, Adam Walker, blacksmith, William Chandler, gentleman, all of Worcester, in the county of Worcester, John Walker, gentleman, David Bush, yeo-

56

man, both of Shrewsbury, in the same county, Abijah Willard, Esq., Abel Willard, Esq., Joseph House, yeoman, all of Lancaster, in the said county of Worcester, Ebenezer Cutler, trader, James Edgar, yeoman, both of Northbury, in the same county, Daniel Oliver, Esq., Richard Ruggles, yeoman, Gardner Chandler, trader, Joseph Ruggles, gentleman, Nathaniel Ruggles, yeoman, all of Hardwick, in the said county of Worcester, John Ruggles, yeoman, of said Hardwick, John Eager, yeoman, Ebenezer Whipple, Israel Conkay, John Murray, Esq., of Rutland, in said county of Worcester, Daniel Murray, gentleman, Samuel Murray, gentleman, Michael Martin, trader, of Brookfield, in the said county of Worcester, Thomas Beaman, gentleman, of Petersham, in the same county, Nathaniel Chandler, gentleman, John Bowen, gentleman, of Princeton, in the said county of Worcester, James Crage, gentleman, of Oakham, in the same county, Thomas Mullins, blacksmith, of Leominster, in the said county of Worcester, Francis Waldo, Esq., Arthur Savage, Esq., Jeremiah Pote, mariner, Thomas Ross, mariner, James Wildridge, mariner, George Lyde, custom house officer, Robert Pagan, merchant, Thomas Wyer, mariner, Thomas Coulson, merchant, John Wiswall, clerk, Joshua Eldridge, mariner, Thomas Oxnard, merchant, Edward Oxnard, merchant, William Tyng, Esq., John Wright, merchant, Samuel Longfellow, mariner, all of Falmouth, in the county of Cumberland, Charles Callahan, of Pownalborough, in the county of Lincoln, mariner, Jonas Jones of East Hoosuck, in the county of Berkshire, David Ingersoll, of Great Barrington, Esq., in the same county, Jonathan Prindall, Benjamin Noble, Francis Noble, Elisha Jones, of Pittsfield, in the said county of Berkshire, John Graves, yeoman, Daniel Brewer, yeoman, both of Pittsfield, aforesaid, Richard Square, of Lanesborough, in the said county of Berkshire, Ephraim Jones, of East Hoosuck, in the same county, Lewis Hubbel, and many other persons have left this state, or some other of the United States of America, and joined the enemies thereof and of the United States of America, thereby not only depriving these states of their personal services at a time when they ought to have afforded their utmost aid in defending the said states, against the invasions of a cruel enemy, but manifesting an inimical disposition to the said states, and a design to aid and abet the enemies thereof in their wicked purposes, and whereas many dangers may accrue to this state and the United States, if such persons should be again admitted to reside in this state:

SECT. 1. Be it therefore enacted by the Council and House of Representatives, in general court assembled, and by the authority of the same, that if either of the said persons, or any other person, though not specially named in this act, who have left this state, or either of said states, and joined the enemies thereof as aforesaid, shall, after the passing this act, voluntarily return to this state, it shall be the duty of the sheriff of the county, and of the selectmen, committees of correspondence, safety, and inspection, grand jurors, constables, and tythingmen, and other inhabitants of the town wherein such person or persons may presume to come, and they are hereby respectively empowered and directed forthwith to apprehend and carry such person or persons before some justice of the peace within the county, who is hereby required to commit him or them to the common gaol within the county, there in close custody to remain until he shall be sent out of the state, as is hereinafter directed; and such justice is hereby directed to give immediate information thereof to the board of war of this state: and the said board of war are hereby empowered and directed to cause such person or persons so committed, to be transported to some part or place within the dominions, or in the possession of the forces of the king of Great Britain, as soon as may be after receiving such information; those who are able, at their own expense, and others at the expense of this state, and for this purpose to hire a vessel or vessels, if need be.

SECT. 2. And be it further enacted by the authority aforesaid, that if any person or persons, who shall be transported as aforesaid, shall voluntarily return into this state, without liberty first had and obtained from the general court, he shall, on conviction thereof before the superior court of judicature, court of assize and general gaol delivery, suffer the pains of death without benefit of clergy.— [*Passed, September*, 1778.]

WORCESTER RESOLUTIONS RELATING TO THE ABSENTEES AND REFUGEES.

The following votes were passed by the citizens of Worcester,

May 19, 1783, and contain the substance of their doings relative to the refugees :

Voted,—That in the opinion of this town, it would be extremely dangerous to the peace, happiness, liberty and safety of these states, to suffer those, who, the moment the bloody banners were displayed, abandoned their native land, turned parricides, and conspired to involve their country in tumult, ruin and blood, to become the subjects of and reside in this government; that it would be not only dangerous, but inconsistent with justice, policy, our past laws, the public faith, and the principles of a free and independent state, to admit them ourselves, or have them forced upon us without our consent.

Voted,—That in the opinion of this town, this commonwealth ought, with the utmost caution, to naturalize or in any other way admit as subjects a common enemy, a set of people who have been by the united voice of the continent, declared outlaws, exiles, aliens and enemies, dangerous to its political being and happiness.

Voted,—That while there are thousands of the innocent, peaceable and defenceless inhabitants of these states, whose property has been destroyed and taken from them in the course of the war, for whom no provision is made, to whom there is no restoration of estates, no compensation for losses; that it would be unreasonable, cruel and unjust, to suffer those who were the wicked occasion of those losses, to obtain a restitution of the estates they refused to protect, and which they have abandoned and forfeited to their country.

Voted,—That it is the expectation of this town, and the earnest request of their committees of correspondence, inspection and safety, that they, with care and diligence, will observe the movements of our only remaining enemies; that until the further order of government, they will, with decision, spirit and firmness, endeavor to enforce and carry into execution the several laws of this commonwealth, respecting these enemies to our rights, and the rights of mankind; give information should they know of any obtruding themselves into any part of this state, suffer none to remain in this town, but cause to be confined immediately, for the purpose of transportation according to law, any that may presume to enter it.

CURWEN HOUSE, SALEM.

NOTICES OF THE CURWENS.

GEORGE CURWIN, the first of the name in New England, came, as stated in the introduction, from Workington, Cumberland, England, where he was born December 10, 1610, and where, says Camden, " *is the stately, castle-like seat of this ancient, knightly family.*" He settled at Salem, and in company with the celebrated Hugh Peters laid the foundation of the mercantile enterprise of Salem, and first commenced building vessels in that port ; he was afterwards extensively engaged in commerce during the whole of his long life. His books of account, and his mercantile correspondence with Sir William Peake, (lord mayor of London in 1666,) show that he had embarked in the London trade previous to the year 1658. The late Rev. Dr. Bentley thus notices him in his Sketch of Salem, published in the Collections of the Massachusetts Historical Society, in 1800 :—" This year (1685) Salem lost another eminent man, Capt. George Curwin, who came here in 1638 with his family, and was rich. He was often engaged in town affairs, and commanded a troop of horse. He was also a representative in the general court. There is a three-quarter portrait of him in the hands of Samuel Curwen, Esq.,* son of the Rev. George Curwin, and his great-grandson. He had a fine round forehead, large nostrils, high cheek bones, and gray eyes. His dress a wrought-flowing neckcloth, a sash covered with lace, a coat with short cuffs and reaching half way between the wrist and elbow, the shirt in plaits below ; an octagon ring and cane, which still remain."

He died on the 3d of January, 1685, leaving no debts, and one of the largest estates that had been administered upon in the colony, which was inventoried at only £5,964 19*s.* 7*d.*, but comprised besides the homestead, four dwelling-houses, four warehouses, and two wharves in Salem ; three farms in the vicinity, containing fifteen hundred acres; a warehouse and wharf in Boston; the ketches

* Author of the foregoing journal.—ED.

George, Swallow, John, and William, valued at £1050; in merchandise £2,232; in gold and silver coin £93 7s. 0d., in English
and New England money, and 621 ounces of plate. Among the
wearing apparel inventoried, are a silver-laced cloth coat, a velvet
ditto, a satin waistcoat, embroidered with gold, a troping scarf and
hat band, golden topped and embroidered gloves, and a silver-
headed cane, which still remains.

In the settlement of the estate, Capt. Curwin's widow Elizabeth, who was a daughter of Hon. Herbert Pelham, one of the
council of assistants, and also sister-in-law of Governor Josiah
Winslow, of Plymouth colony, claimed some plate given her by
the lord mayor, by her father, and by the governor; together with
*eight pounds in gold which her husband had received from Mr. Pope,
being the "produce" of an Indian boy sent her by the governor and
council from Plymouth.*

His five daughters married Hon. James Russell and Edward
Lynde, Esq., of Boston, William Browne, jr., Esq., and Josiah
Wolcott, Esq., of Salem, and President Wadsworth of Harvard
College.

Annexed is a view of the house erected by Capt. Curwin, in
1642, still standing at the corner of Essex and North streets. It
was altered by the late Richard Ward, Esq., about seventy years
ago, and his daughter (the present occupant, to whom it has
descended) is the last survivor of the fifth generation from the original owner; her granddaughter, who resides with her, is of the
seventh generation of the family born in it. The unfortunate persons arrested during the witchcraft delusion were examined in this
house by Justices Corwin and Hathorne, before being committed.

Capt. JOHN CORWIN, the eldest son, was born in Salem, July 28,
1638. He became a merchant, and was elected deputy to the
general court, from Salem, where he resided. He married Margaret, third daughter of John Winthrop, jr., governor of Connecticut, in May, 1665; her mother was the only child of the famous
Hugh Peters, who suffered with the regicides at the restoration of
the monarchy, in London, in 1660. Capt. Corwin died in 1683,
leaving an only son, George, born February, 1666. The latter, who
married Susannah, and afterwards Lydia, daughters of the Hon.
Bartholomew Gedney, of the provincial council, is the Captain

Corwin mentioned in Hutchinson's History of Massachusetts, in the expedition against Canada, under Sir William Phips, in 1690. He was unfortunately sheriff of the county of Essex in 1692, and for officiating during the witchcraft delusion, was severely persecuted by the friends of the sufferers, till his death, which took place in 1696.

BARTHOLOMEW CORWIN, the only son of the last mentioned George, removed to Amwell, Hunterdon county, New Jersey, and married Esther Burt; he had four sons, viz., George, John, Joseph, and Samuel, and died May 9, 1747. Samuel Corwin, of Amwell, a grandson of Bartholomew, informed the editor in 1822, that the books and papers left by his grandfather were destroyed, with other movables, during the revolutionary war, when his uncle Joseph removed to Canada, and the family of his uncle George, who died in 1780, removed to Kentucky. Probably Governor Corwin of Ohio is a descendant of this branch. He also informed the editor that John Corwin, a great grandson of Bartholomew, was living at Baltimore.

HON. JONATHAN CORWIN, second son of the first mentioned George, was born at Salem, Nov. 14, 1640. He commenced his public career as a deputy to the general court, and the following extract from the records of Salem, shows much confidence in him; and at the same time the action of that town towards re-establishing a government under the venerable Bradstreet, in opposition to the tyranny of Sir Edmund Andros :—" May 7, 1689. Captain John Prince and Mr. Jonathan Corwin were chosen to assist in the council at Boston, to be held on the 9th inst.; and we desire that the honorable the governor, the magistrates, and deputies chosen in the year 1686, would (having always due respect to our dependence on the crown of England, and the obligation we are under by the late declaration before the surrender of the last government) reassume our charter government, by taking their places and forming a general court as soon as possible; unto which, we shall readily and cheerfully subject ourselves, and be always assisting to the utmost of our power with our lives and estates as formerly."

Mr. Corwin was named a provincial counsellor in the charter of 1691, and served until he was appointed a judge of the supreme court in 1702 ; the latter office he resigned in consequence of ill health, in 1715. He died in July, 1718, leaving a widow; the daughter of Sir Henry Gibbs of Dorsetshire, whose estate was sequestrated in 1648, during the revolution. Of their children, Anne died in youth; Elizabeth married James Lindall, Esq., of Salem; and George, born in 1682, who was graduated at Harvard college in 1701. He prepared himself for the church, and was ordained and settled in that of his ancestors in Salem; the first founded in the colony of Massachusetts Bay. He is thus noticed in the historical collections of Massachusetts, as copied from the records of the church :—

" Died, at Salem, Nov. 23, 1717, the Rev. George Curwin, in the thirty-fifth year of his age, and the fourth of his ordained ministry. He was highly esteemed in his life, and very deservedly lamented at his death; having been very eminent for his early improvement in learning and piety, his singular abilities and great labors, his remarkable zeal and faithfulness. He was a great benefactor to our poor."

There is a good half-length portrait of him in the gallery of the Essex Historical Society. He married Mehitable Parkman; and their sons were Samuel, author of the foregoing Journal, born in 1715; and George, born in 1717. The latter graduated at Harvard college in 1735, and engaged in commercial pursuits with success, until interrupted by hostilities with France; which induced him to join in the expedition against Louisburg. His commission as commissary, bears the signature of Governor Shirley, and is dated February 1, 1745. He married Sarah, daughter of Benjamin Pickman, Esq., of Salem; and died in the prosecution of a mercantile enterprise at St. Eustatia, in 1746. His children were, George, born in 1739, who early embarked in commerce, and was drowned while on a voyage to the West Indies in 1761; Sarah, who died unmarried; and Mehitable, who married the late Richard Ward, Esq., of Salem, and died in 1813, at the age of seventy-two.

The late Samuel Curwen Ward, Jr., a grandson of the last mentioned, at the request of Judge Curwen, took his name, by an act of the legislature of Massachusetts; and the three sons of the former are all that now bear that name in New England.

BIOGRAPHICAL NOTICES.

GEN. PEPPERELL.

GENERAL SIR WILLIAM PEPPERELL, Baronet, was born at Kittery Point, Maine, in 1696. His father, Col. William Pepperell, a native of Cornwall, England, settled in 1676 at the Isles of Shoals, where he was for many years extensively engaged in the fishing business. After acquiring considerable property, he removed to Kittery Point, and erected there a large mansion house, now standing, where he died on the 15th February, 1734, opulent and well esteemed. One of his daughters married the Hon. John Newmarch; the other died in 1766, having successively married Hon. John Frost, Rev. Dr. Colman, and Rev. Benjamin Prescott, all of whom she survived. Sir William was his only son, and about the year 1727 was chosen a member of his majesty's council for the province of Massachusetts, to which he was annually re-elected until his death, a period of thirty-two years. With a vigorous frame, firm mind, and great coolness when in danger, he was well fitted for his residence in a country exposed to a ferocious enemy, and soon attained the rank of colonel.

When the expedition against Louisburg was contemplated, all eyes were turned to him, then president of the council, and he was commissioned by the governors of New England to that all-important command, on the 31st January, 1745. He furnished this motto for the flag, which gave the enterprise the air of a crusade: " *Nil desperandum Christo duce.*" He invested the city in the beginning of May, and articles of capitulation were signed in July. After this important and brilliant achievement, by command of his majesty he repaired to England and received a colonelcy in the army, from which he was raised to be a major-general in 1755, and a lieutenant-general in 1759. Besides the dignity of a baronet, which was conferred upon him, he obtained the thanks of the ministry, and peculiar tokens of respect from several of the royal family. His affability gained him friends among all classes, and his manners were not affected by his exaltation. The welfare of his country alone could have taken him from his domestic enjoyments and the head of the provincial council, to the fatigues of the camp and to doubtful victory. He married Mary, daughter of Grove Hirst, a granddaughter of Chief Justice Sewall. Their only son Andrew, graduated at Harvard College in 1743, and died March 1, 1751, aged twenty-five ; and their only daughter Elizabeth married Col. Nathaniel Sparhawk, member of the council of Massachusetts. Sir William's dress was in the expensive style of his day, scarlet cloth trimmed with gold lace ; portraits of him and Lady Mary are preserved at Portsmouth, N. H., and there is a full length of him in the gallery of the Essex Historical Society, at Salem, Mass. Sir William died at his seat in Kittery, (near Portsmouth,) June 6, 1759, aged sixty-three ; and Lady Mary on the 25th November, 1789. Her natural and acquired powers were highly respectable, and she was admired for her wit and suavity of manner.

Sir William was succeeded by his grandson, William P. Sparhawk, who assumed his name, and was created a baronet ; he was a loyalist in the revolution, and died in London, December, 17, 1816, when the title became extinct.

GOV. SHIRLEY.

WILLIAM SHIRLEY, governor of Massachusetts, was a native of England, and was bred to the law. After his arrival at Boston, about the year 1733, he practised in his profession, till he received his commission as governor, in 1741, in the place of Mr. Belcher. He planned the successful expedition against Cape Breton, in 1745; but, while his enterprising spirit deserves commendation, some of his schemes did not indicate much skill in the arts of navigation and war. He went to England in 1745, leaving Spencer Phips, the lieutenant-governor, commander-in-chief, but returned in 1753. In 1754, he held a treaty with the eastern Indians, and explored the Kennebec, erecting two or three forts. In 1755, being commander-in-chief of the British forces in America, he planned an expedition against Niagara, and proceeded himself as far as Oswego. In June, 1756, he was superseded in the command of the army by Abercrombie. He embarked for England in September, and was succeeded by Mr. Pownall. After having been for a number of years governor of one of the Bahama islands, he returned to Massachusetts, and died at his seat in Roxbury, March 24, 1771. Though he held several of the most lucrative offices within the gift of the crown in America, yet he left no property to his children. The abolition of the paper currency was owing in a great degree to his firmness and perseverance. His penetration and unremitting industry gained him a high reputation. But it was thought that, as a military officer, he was not sufficiently active in seizing the moment for success. During his administration, England became acquainted with the importance of this country, and the colonists learned to fight. Governor Shirley published Electra, a tragedy, and Birth of Hercules, a mask, 1765.

COL. MOULTON.

Colonel Jeremiah Moulton was born in York, Maine, in 1688, and was taken prisoner by the Indians, January 22, 1692, old style, when York was destroyed by the Indians. He was released, with other children, in gratitude for the humanity of Colonel Church, who in one of his expeditions had released several Indian prisoners, old women and children. The savages were not ungrateful for acts of kindness. In August, 1724, he and Captain Harmon with two hundred and eight men, and three Mohawk Indians, marched against the Indian settlement at Norridgewock, in consequence of attacks upon the frontiers. There being four companies, the other commanders were Captain Bourne and Lieut. Bean. They left Richmond fort August 8, old style, or August 19; the next day arrived at Taconic Falls on the Kennebec, where they left their boats and a guard of forty men. August 21, they marched by land, and in the evening fired upon two Indians, who proved to be the daughter and wife of Bomaseen; the former was killed, the latter taken prisoner. August 23, they approached the village; Harmon with eighty men marching circuitously by the fields, and Moulton with eighty men directly upon Norridgewock, which he surprised. The Indians, consisting of about sixty warriors, were defeated, and the chapel and village destroyed. Father Ralle was killed in a wigwam, and twenty-six Indians, among whom were Bomaseen, and his son-in-law Mog, also Job, Canabesett, and Wissememet, all noted warriors. One of the Mohawks was killed, but none of the whites. Harmon carried the scalps to Boston, and having been chief in command, was made a lieutenant-colonel for the exploit of Moulton, who obtained no reward. At the reduction of Louisburg in 1745, he commanded a regiment, and was afterwards sheriff of the county, councillor, and judge of the common pleas and of probate. He died at York, July 20, 1765, aged 77. His son and grandson were sheriffs of York county.

COL. VAUGHAN.

LIEUT. COL. WILLIAM VAUGHAN served under General Pepperell, in the expedition against Louisburg, in 1745; although he refused any regular command, he made himself highly useful during the whole siege by his advice in councils, vigilance in reconnoitering the enemy, and promptitude while in command of perilous enterprises.

He died in London, December, 1746, in the prime of life, where he went to press his claim for the above service. The immediate paternal ancestor of Col. Vaughan, was Major William Vaughan, who came from England about the middle of the seventeenth century, and settled at Portsmouth, where he became a wealthy merchant. He died in 1720. His son George was lieutenant-governor of New Hampshire; born in 1668, graduated at Harvard College in 1696. Afterwards agent for the province, and on the accession of George I. was appointed lieutenant-governor in 1715; he died December, 1725. His son William, the subject of the above, was born at Portsmouth, Sept. 12, 1703. He had settled at Damariscotta, thirteen miles below fort Pemaquid, and his men were employed in fishing. Here he conceived the idea of the capture of Louisburg, repaired to Boston, and conferred with Governor Shirley upon the subject; proposing that it should be taken by surprise by going over the walls in winter upon drifts of snow.

COL. GRIDLEY.

COL. RICHARD GRIDLEY was born in Boston, 1711. After serving as an engineer at the reduction of Louisburg, in 1745, he entered the army as colonel of infantry and chief-engineer, in 1755. Under Winslow he was concerned in the expedition to Crown Point, 1756, and constructed the fortifications on Lake George. He served under Amherst in 1758, and was with Wolfe on the plains of Abraham, the following year. At the commencement of the revolution, he was appointed chief-engineer, and skilfully laid out the works in fortification of Breed's Hill, the day before the battle of June 17, 1775, in which he was wounded. He died at Stoughton, June 20, 1796.

GOV. BERNARD.

SIR FRANCIS BERNARD, Bart., governor of Massachusetts, arrived in the province from New Jersey, as successor to Governor Pownall, August 2, 1760, and continued at the head of the government nine years. His administration was during one of the most interesting periods in American history. He had governed New Jersey two years, in a manner very acceptable to that province; and the first part of his administration in Massachusetts was very agreeable to the general court. Soon after his arrival, Canada was surrendered to Amherst. Much harmony prevailed for two or three years, but this prosperous and happy commencement did not continue; there had long been two parties in the province,—the advocates for the crown, and the defenders of the rights of the people. Governor Bernard was soon classed with those who were desirious of strengthening the royal authority in America; the sons of liberty, therefore, stood forth uniformly in opposition to him. His indiscretion in appointing Mr. Hutchinson chief-justice, instead of giving that office to Colonel Otis of Barnstable, to whom it had been promised by Shirley, proved very injurious to his cause. In consequence of this appointment he lost the influence of Colonel Otis; and by yielding himself to Mr. Hutchinson, he drew upon him the hostility of James Otis, the son, a man of great talents; who soon became the leader on the popular side. The laws for the regulation of trade, and the exactions of the officers of customs, were the first things which greatly agitated the public mind; and afterwards the stamp act increased the energy of resistance to the schemes of tyranny. Governor Bernard possessed no talent for conciliating; he was for accomplishing ministerial purposes by force; and the spirit of freedom gathered strength from the open manner in which he attempted to crush it. His speech to the general court after the repeal of the stamp act, was by no means calculated to assuage the angry passions that had lately been excited. He was the principal means of bringing the troops to Boston, that he might overawe the people; and it was owing to him that they were continued in the town. This measure had been proposed by him and Mr. Hutchinson, long before it was executed. While he professed himself a friend to the province, he was endeavoring to undermine its constitution, and to obtain an essential alteration in the charter, by transferring from the general court to the crown the right of electing the council. His conduct, though it drew upon him the indignation of the province, was so pleasing to the ministry, that he was created a baronet, March 20, 1769. Sir Francis had too little command of his temper; he could not conceal his resentments, nor could he restrain his censures. One of his last public measures was to prorogue the general court in July, in consequence of their refusing to make provision for the support of the troops. The general court, however, before they were prorogued, embraced the opportunity of drawing up a petition to his majesty for the removal of the governor. It was found necessary to recall him; and he embarked, August 1, 1769, leaving Mr. Hutchinson, the lieutenant-governor, commander-in-chief. There were few who lamented his departure; he died in England, June, 1779.

If a man of greater address and wisdom had occupied the place of Sir Francis, it is very probable our revolution would not have taken place so soon. But his arbitrary principles, and his zeal for the authority of the crown, enkindled the spirit of the people; while his representations to the ministry excited them to those measures, which hastened the separation of the colonies from the mother country. From the letters of Governor Bernard, which were obtained and transmitted to this country by some secret friend, it appears he had very little regard to the interests of liberty. His select letters on the trade and government of America, written in Boston, from 1763 to 1768, were published in London in 1774; his other letters, written home in confidence, were published in 1768 and 1769.*

GOV. HUTCHINSON.

THOMAS, (son of Colonel Thomas Hutchinson, an eminent merchant and member of the council, who seized the famous pirate, Kidd, when he resisted the officers sent to arrest him,) was graduated at Harvard College, in 1727. He at first embarked in commercial pursuits, but did not succeed. He then studied the common law of England, and the principles of her constitution. He was elected for ten consecutive years to the assembly, and for

* See Allen's Biography.

three years was speaker. He succeeded his uncle, Edward Hutchinson, as judge of probate, in 1752. He was a member of the council from 1749 to 1766; lieut. governor from 1758 to 1771. On the death of Judge Sewall, in 1760, he was appointed chief-justice; all which he filled with distinguished ability. " His oratory charmed beyond that of any man; there was equal fluency and pathos in his manner; he could be argumentative and smooth; he was active, diligent and plausible; and, upon all occasions seemed to be influenced by public spirit more than selfish considerations. His respect to religious institutions, his sympathy with the distressed, his affability, integrity, industry and talents, procured in a very high degree the public confidence." In 1767, he was appointed one of the commissioners for settling the boundary with New-York; and, amidst all the vituperations against him, Massachusetts has cause to remember with gratitude that his advice only prevented the other commissioners, Hancock, Hanly and Brattle, from abandoning the claim to the western territory of New-York, which was retained and sold for a large sum.

On the departure of Governor Bernard in 1769, the administration devolved on Lieut. Governor Hutchinson; and in March, 1771, he received his commission as governor just as he had concluded to advise the government that it would be desirable for him to remain chief-justice, and pass his days in peace. Unhappily for himself he accepted the appointment, and from this time till his departure in 1774, he was constantly in dispute with the council and assembly. Among the subjects of controversy, was the provision made for his support by the crown. By his speech of Jan. 6, 1773, asserting the supreme authority of parliament, he provoked a discussion by the council and house which had better never been uttered; and the minister recommended him not to renew the discussion. His views he at all times candidly and manfully explained to the legislature; in many speeches and messages which display his learning, temper and abilities.

The confidential letters written by him, and others to Mr. Whately, a former member of parliament, in opposition to the ministry, which caused so much excitement in 1772, were procured by Dr. Franklin through Mr. Temple, (afterwards consul general to United States,) from Mr. Whately's executor, and caused a duel between the two latter. Dr. Franklin sent them to Mr. Cooper, with an injunction that they should not be copied or published; of which restriction the Doctor remarked, that " *as distant objects seen only through a mist appear larger, the same may happen from the mystery in this case.*" In this state they remained six or eight months, and finally were communicated to the legislature in secret session. In the letters was no sentiment the governor had not avowed in his public addresses. All that was objected to, and for which the council reproached him, was the following :—" I never think of the measures necessary for the peace and good order of the colonies without pain ; there must be an abridgment of what are called English liberties. I doubt whether it is possible to project a system of government, in which a colony three thousand miles distant shall enjoy all the liberty of the parent state." For this, the council and assembly voted an address for his removal; and at a hearing before the privy council of his friends, Mr. Manduit and Mr. Wedderburne, on his behalf, the decision was in favor of " the honor, integrity, and conduct of the governor."

In an unpublished letter of John Adams to Colonel Joseph Ward, dated Quincy, Oct. 24, 1809, he says :—" If I was the witch of Endor, I would wake the ghost of Hutchinson, and give him absolute power over the currency of the United States and every part of it ; provided always, that he should meddle with nothing but currency. As little as I revere his memory, I will acknowledge that he understood the subject of coin and commerce better than any man I ever knew in this country. He was a merchant, and there can be no scientific merchant without a perfect knowledge of the theory of a medium of trade. It will be in vain to talk of public credit, until we return to a pure, unmixed circulation of standard gold and silver. There can never be a government of laws in money matters, without a fixed philosophical and mathematical standard. Contracts can never be inviolable without a stable standard."

Governor Hutchinson deserves great honor for his labors in regard to the History of Massachusetts, which he published from its first settlement to the year 1760. In so high estimation was it held, that at the expiration of more than half a century after its publication, successful efforts were made by the most influential persons there to obtain the unpublished part of this history, which they pronounced, " *a work of inestimable value, resting on the solid basis of utility and truth ; the accuracy and fidelity of which was universally felt and acknowledged.*" These efforts of the government of Harvard College, the Historical Society, of Judge Davis, Governor Gore, Dr. Kirkland, Dr. Lowell, and James Savage, Esq., who secured the private circulation of five hundred copies before publication, and whose sentiments on the leading subject are at variance with those of its author ; are proud testimonials of the character of Governor Hutchinson in the field of his labors and sacrifices, and amidst the descendants of his persecutors.

Governor Hutchinson died at Brompton, near London, June 3, 1780, aged sixty-nine, and was buried at Croydon.

JOHN HANCOCK.

In the posthumous volume of Governor Hutchinson's History of Massachusetts,* he says:—" Mr. HANCOCK's name has been sounded through the world as a principal actor in this tragedy. He was a young man, whose father and grandfather were ministers in country parishes, of irreproachable characters, but, like country ministers in New England in general, of small estates. His father's brother, from a bookseller became one of the most opulent merchants in the province; he had raised a great estate with such rapidity, that it was commonly believed among the vulgar, that he had purchased a valuable diamond for a small sum and sold it at its full price. But the secret lay in his importing from St. Eustatia great quantities of tea in molasses hogsheads, which sold at a very great advance; and by importing, at the same time, a few chests from England, he freed the rest from suspicion, and always had the reputation of a fair trader. He was also concerned in supplying the officers of the army, ordnance and navy, and made easy and advantageous remittances; when he died, he left to his nephew more than fifty thousand pounds sterling, besides the reversion after the death of his widow, of twenty thousand more. The uncle was always on the side of government; the nephew's ruling passion was a fondness for popular applause. He changed the course of his uncle's business, and built and employed in trade, a great

* Published in 1828.

number of ships; and in this way, and by building at the same
time several houses, he found work for a great number of tradesmen; made himself popular—was chosen selectman—representative—moderator of town meetings, etc. He associated with those
who were called friends of liberty. His natural powers were
moderate, and had been very little improved by study, or application to any kind of science. His ruling passion kept him from
ever losing sight of its object, but he was fickle and inconstant in
the means of pursuing it; and though, for the most part, he was
closely attached to Mr. Samuel Adams, he has repeatedly broken
off from all connection with him for several months together.
Partly by inattention to his private affairs, and partly from want of
judgment, he became greatly involved and distressed; and the estate
was lost with much greater rapidity than it had been acquired."

President Quincy, in his invaluable History of Harvard University, has devoted a chapter to the wrongs which that institution
suffered at the hands of Mr. Hancock as its treasurer; and closes
the detail as follows:—" From respect to the high rank which
John Hancock attained among the patriots of the American Revolution, it would have been grateful to have passed over in silence
his long denial of the rights of the college, and withholding its
property, had truth and fidelity of history permitted. But justice
to a public institution which he essentially embarrassed during a
period of nearly twenty years, and also to the memory of those
whom he made to feel and to suffer, requires that these records of
unquestionable facts, which at the time when they occurred
were the cause of calumny and censure to honorable men, actuated
in their measures solely by a sense of official fidelity, should not
be omitted. In republics, popularity is the form of power most
apt to corrupt its possessor, and to tempt him, for party ends or
personal interest, to trample on right or set principle at defiance.
History has no higher or more imperative duty to perform, than
by an unyielding fidelity to impress this class of men with the
apprehension that, although through fear or favor they may escape
the animadversions of contemporaries, there awaits them in her
impartial record the retribution of truth."

President Quincy also says of him:—" His manners were full
of suavity and attraction; his love of place and popularity intense.

He early joined the patriotic party, whose leaders perceived the advantage of placing him at their head; and giving him every distinction they could command. By the continued influence of these possessions, manners and circumstances, he acquired a popular power, which in this country has scarcely been exceeded."

" The style of living he adopted, and the openness of his hand to every object coinciding with his views or his interests, kept his ample resources in a perpetual state of exhaustion. It suited both his interest and policy to postpone debts, and gratify friends."

SAMUEL ADAMS.

Of this distinguished patriot of the Revolution, Gov. Hutchinson, in the posthumous volume already quoted, says : " Mr. SAMUEL ADAMS's father had been one of the directors of the Land Bank in 1741, which was dissolved by act of parliament. After his decease his estate was put up for sale by public auction under authority of an act of the general assembly. The son first made himself conspicuous on this occasion. He attended the sale, threatened the sheriff to bring an action against him and all who should attempt to enter upon the estate under pretence of a purchase ; and by intimidating both the sheriff and those who intended to purchase, he prevented the sale, kept the estate in his possession, and the debt to the land company remains unsatisfied. He was afterwards collector of taxes for the town of Boston, and made a defalcation, which caused an additional tax upon the inhabitants. These things were unfavorable to his character, but the determined spirit he showed in the cause of liberty would have covered a multitude of such faults. He was for near twenty years a writer against government in the public newspapers ; at first but an indifferent one ; long practice caused him to arrive at great perfection, and to acquire a talent of artfully and fallaciously insinuating into the minds of his readers a prejudice against the characters of all whom he attacked, beyond any other man I ever knew. This talent he employed in the messages, remonstrances, and resolves of the House of Representatives, most of which were of his composition, and he made more converts to his cause by calumniating governors and other servants of the crown, than by strength of reasoning. The benefit to the town from his defence of their liberties, he supposed an equivalent to his arrears as their collector; and the prevailing principle of his party, that the end justified the means, probably quieted the remorse he must have felt from robbing men of their characters, and injuring them more than if he had robbed them of their estates."

JOHN ADAMS.

The same writer has the following notice of another eminent leader of the revolution : " Mr. JOHN ADAMS was a distant relation and intimate acquaintance of Mr. Samuel Adams. After his education at the college he applied to the study of the law, a short time before the troubles began. He is said to have been at a loss which side to take. Mr. Sewall, who was with the government, would have persuaded him to be on the same side, and promised him to desire Governor Bernard to make him a justice of the peace. The governor took time to consider of it, and having, as Mr. Adams conceived, not taken proper notice of him, or given him offence on some former occasion, he no longer deliberated, and ever after joined in opposition. As the troubles increased he increased in knowledge, and made a figure, not only in his own profession, but as a patriot, and was generally esteemed as a person endowed with more knowledge than his kinsman, and equally zealous in the cause of liberty; but neither his business nor his health would admit of that constant application to it which distinguished the other from all the rest of the province. In general he may be said to be of stronger resentment upon any real or supposed personal neglect or injury than the other, but in their resentment against such as opposed them in the cause in which they were engaged, it is difficult to say which exceeded. His ambition was without bounds, and he has acknowledged to his acquaintance that he could not look with complacency upon any man who was in possession of more wealth, more honors, or more knowledge than himself."

LIEUT. GOV. CUSHING.

THOMAS CUSHING, LL. D. was the son of a very popular speaker of the Assembly of Massachusetts; graduated at Harvard College in 1744; was fond of public life, and paid too little attention to pecuniary considerations; was many years a representative, and in

1763, when Governor Bernard negatived Mr. Otis as speaker, he was elected in his place, and continued in that office till chosen a member of the first Congress, to meet in Philadelphia in 1774. He was elected lieut. governor in 1779, which office he held till his death in 1788. His name as speaker having been signed to all the public papers, made it known abroad, where he was considered the leader of the whigs. Dr. Johnson, in his pamphlet called " *Taxation no Tyranny,*" says, " one object of the Americans is to adorn the brows of Mr. Cushing with a diadem." And he was at other times the object of the sarcasm of ministerial writers. He was a member of the corporation of Harvard College, and attentive to its affairs, from which he received a diploma of doctor of laws.

JUDGE PAINE.

ROBERT TREAT PAINE, L.L. D., one of the signers of the declaration of independence, was born in Boston, 1731; graduated at Harvard College in 1749; studied law; and conducted the prosecution on the part of the crown with great reputation, in the absence of the attorney general, in the trial of Capt. Preston and his men of " *Boston massacre*" memory in 1770. In 1773 he was elected a member of the General Assembly, and afterwards was chosen a member of the continental Congress, which met at Philadelphia in 1774. The following four years he was re-elected and rendered important services in introducing the manufacture of saltpetre, then imperfectly understood, while the colonies were suffering for the want of gunpowder. He was also of the committee for the encouragement of the manufacture of cannon, and other implements of war. In a letter to the Hon. Joseph Palmer, as president of the Massachusetts provincial Congress at Watertown, he complains of an intrigue to supplant him in the good opinion of his constituents, and says he " *has just discovered a malicious and slanderous correspondence between John Adams and Thomas Cushing.*" On the organization of the Supreme Court in Massachusetts in 1776, he was named for one of the judges, which he declined at first, as John Adams, many years his junior, had obtained the appointment of chief justice; but upon the resignation of the latter, Mr. Paine took his seat on that bench. His son, who afterwards bore his name, was a distinguished writer of national and patriotic poetry.

GOV. HARRISON.

Col. Benjamin Harrison, one of the signers of the declaration of independence, was a native of Virginia, and graduated at the college of William and Mary. He commenced his political career as early as 1764, in the legislature of his native colony. The royal government offered him a seat at the council board, a tempting bait for young ambition, which he had the resolution to refuse, as the measures of the ministry were already unfriendly to the liberty of the provinces; and when the time came for active resistance to arbitrary power, he was ready for service. He was in the first general Congress of 1774, and the three succeeding ones, and was particularly useful as chairman of the board of war. After his resignation in 1777, he was elected speaker of the House of Burgesses of Virginia, and filled the chair till 1782, when he was elected governor, to which office he was twice re-elected. He retired in 1785 to private life, but in 1788 became a member of the convention which ratified the Constitution of the United States. He died in 1791. Gov. Harrison was father of General William H. Harrison, late President of the United States.

LIEUT. GOV. A. OLIVER.

Of Lieut. Governor Andrew Oliver, Gov. Hutchinson says, " A very small portion of mankind have so well deserved to be characterized, " *Integer vitæ seclerisque purus.*" Scarce any man ever had a more scrupulous and sacred regard to truth, and yet, to such a degree did the malignant spirit of party prevail as to cause a writer[*] in the public papers in England to bring against him a charge of perjury. The Council of Massachusetts Bay, from whose votes and resolves this writer attempted to support the charge, by a vote which they caused to be printed, repaired the injury as well as they could; but a consciousness of his innocency and integrity was his best support. This abuse, however, together with the reproaches most injuriously cast upon him by the resolves of the council and house, in which he was treated as the determined enemy to the liberties of his country, the interest whereof,

---

[*] Arthur Lee, under the signature of Junius Americanus.

according to the best of his judgment, (which was much superior to that of his most virulent persecutors,) he always had at heart, affected his spirits and evidently accelerated his death."

Lieut. Gov. Oliver was a son of Hon. Daniel Oliver, of Boston, and graduated at Harvard College in 1724. He was a representative from Boston, member of the council, and secretary of the province, before his last troublesome dignity as lieut. governor, which office he filled from 1770 to 1774; until death closed his career on the 3d March in that year. His removal had been clamorously called for by the people through the provincial assembly. Lieut. Gov. Oliver was a liberal benefactor to his *alma mater* in books, ancient manuscripts and anatomical preparations.

HON. S. QUINCY.

Samuel Quincy, brother of Josiah and Edmund, of Boston, graduated at Harvard College in 1754, was a poet and an elegant prose writer. As solicitor for the crown, he was engaged with Robert Treat Paine in the memorable trial of Capt. Preston and the British soldiers in 1770; his brother was opposed to him on that occasion, and both reversed their party sympathies in their professional position. He was an addressor of Gov. Hutchinson, and went to England early in 1775. He was included in the banishment act of September, 1778. In April, 1779, he was appointed comptroller at Parkin Bay, Antigua, and died on his passage from Tortola to England for his health, August 9, 1789, aged 55. Mr. Quincy married a sister of the late Henry Hill, Esq., of Boston. His son, of the same name, who graduated at Harvard College in 1782, was an attorney at law in Lenox, Massachusetts, where he died, Jan. 1816, leaving a son Samuel, now an alderman of Boston. His other son, Josiah, is an eminent counsellor at law of Romney, New Hampshire, and president of the senate of that state.

HON. JON. SEWALL.

Jonathan Sewall, LL. D., was born at Boston, August, 1728. His father, Jonathan Sewall, merchant, was a nephew of Chief Justice Stephen Sewall, and grandson of Major Stephen Sewall, of Salem. He graduated at Harvard College in 1748, and was a teacher at

Salem till 1756. He married Esther, daughter of Edmund Quincy, Esq., of Braintree, afterwards of Boston, and sister of Dorothy Quincy, wife of Governor Hancock, and of Elizabeth Quincy, wife of Samuel Sewall, Esq., of Boston, the father of the late Hon. Samuel Sewall, chief justice of Massachusetts. Mr. Sewall studied law with Judge Chambers Russell, of Lincoln; commenced practice in his profession at Charlestown, and at the death of Jeremy Gridley, Esq., he was appointed attorney-general of Massachusetts, September, 1767. He was an able and successful lawyer. The elder President Adams was his intimate friend, though opposite in politics, and has done justice to his memory. He was solicitor-general before he succeeeded Gridley in the office of attorney-general. His eloquence is represented as having been soft, smooth, and insinuating, which gave him as much power over a jury as a lawyer ought ever to possess. It is proper here to take notice of one fact relative to Sewall. He commenced the suit in May, 1769, in favor of a negro against his master for his freedom, viz., James *vs.* Richard Lechmere, of Cambridge. The late Chief Justice Dana was counsel for the defendant. The suit terminated the following year in favor of the negro; and I believe it was the first case where the grand question was settled abolishing slavery in that state. The case of the negro Somerset, which Blackstone commends so highly, and which has been a matter of self-gratulation in England, was not settled till 1772; two years after the decision in favor of James. In 1768, he was appointed judge of admiralty for Nova Scotia, and although he went there once or twice in that capacity, he remained but a short period. At the commencement of the revolution, he was residing at Cambridge, in the Vassall house, afterwards Washington's head quarters, and since occupied by Andrew Cragie. He left this country for England early in 1775. He had before ably vindicated the characters of Governors Bernard, Hutchinson, and Oliver, and was esteemed an able writer. He was proscribed in the Conspirator's Act of April 30, 1779. He resided chiefly in Bristol till 1788, (for the education of his children,) when he removed to St. John's, New Brunswick, having been appointed judge of the vice-admiralty court there, where he resided till his death, which occurred September 26, 1796, at the age of sixty-eight. His widow survived him, and removed to Montreal, where she died at an advanced age. His son Jonathan, was at school at Hackney in 1777, and afterwards resided at Quebec, where he sustained the offices of solicitor and attorney-general, and judge of the vice-admiralty court, until 1808, when he was appointed chief justice of the province, which he resigned in 1838, and died November 12, 1839, aged seventy-four. In 1832, he received the degree of doctor of laws, from Harvard College. His son Stephen was appointed solicitor-general in 1810, and resided in Montreal, but lost that office in 1814, in consequence of political differences with the governor; he died there of Asiatic cholera in the summer of 1832.

ISAAC SMITH.

REV. ISAAC SMITH graduated at Harvard College in 1767, where he was a tutor 1774–5, when he left for England, having a brother settled there. He was a loyalist, and a dissenting minister, much esteemed for the catholic tenor of his discourses. He was ordained June 24, 1778, over a society of dissenters at Sidmouth, Devonshire, but returned to New England after the peace, and became librarian in Harvard College, from 1789 to 1791, and subsequently preceptor of Dummer academy, at Byfield, near Newburyport, Massachusetts. He was a brother of William Smith, Esq. of Boston.

JOSEPH GREEN.

JOSEPH GREEN, Esq., a wit and poet, born at Boston, 1706, received the rudiments of learning at the South Grammar School from Mr. Williams, and graduated at Harvard College, 1726. He was the author of many fugitive pieces, chiefly satirical, against the governor or assembly, as chance might direct. He was a fine classical scholar. He turned his attention to commerce, of which he obtained a comprehensive knowledge, and acquired a handsome property. To integrity and generosity were added in him politeness and elegance. His humor, learning and taste might have connected him with the influential, and procured for him almost any distinction; but he would never accept public office. He signed an address to Governor Hutchinson on his leaving the government. In 1774, when an act passed Parliament depriving Massachusetts of her charter, a number of counsellors were appointed by mandamus;

59

among them was Mr. Green, who declined the honor as soon as summoned, giving in his resignation to Governor Gage. Of his poetical pieces, " the Elegy on Mr. Old Tenor," and the satire on the processions of Free-masons, have passed through many editions. During the Whitfieldian controversy, there was a club of sentimentalists who wrote what they pleased, and, as the pamphlets were emitted from the press, it was easy to conjecture the parts he wrote, especially if a line of poetry was introduced. They also took a part in politics, and began by attacking the administration of Governor Belcher, putting his speeches into rhyme. In the controversy with Great Britain, previous to the Revolution, most of these gentlemen joined the party of loyalists. Mr. Green was included in the act of banishment of 1778, and having left Boston early in 1775, passed the remainder of his days in England, where he died at London, December 11, 1780, aged seventy-four.

JASPER MAUDUIT.

JASPER MAUDUIT, Esq., of London, the friend of Governor Hutchinson and Lieutenant Governor Oliver, successfully vindicated their characters respecting their letters to the privy council, assisted by Mr. Wedderburne. He was for a long time treasurer of the Society for propagating the Gospel among the Indians of New England, and agent for the Assembly of Massachusetts Bay in London. His zeal was greater for the conversion of Indians, than for the important concerns of the province.

ISRAEL MAUDUIT.

ISRAEL MAUDUIT, Esq., secretary of Lord George Germaine, was distinguished as the writer of several pamphlets, in which the character of General Howe was severely attacked.

WARD NICHOLAS BOYLSTON.

WARD NICHOLAS BOYLSTON, Esq., the son of Benjamin and Mary Hallowell, (his mother being the sister of Nicholas Boylston,) was born at Boston in 1749 ; by the desire of his maternal uncle, his name was changed in 1770. In 1773, he embarked for Newfoundland ; from thence he sailed to Italy ; travelled through Turkey, Syria, Palestine, and Egypt, and along the Barbary coast ; and returned through France and Flanders to England, in 1775. He entered into business as a merchant, and remained in London till 1800, when he returned to Boston, and continued to reside in Massachusetts till his death, which occurred in January, 1828, at the age of seventy-eight.

He possessed a mind emulative of the spirit of his maternal ancestry, which he acknowledged in a letter dated May 20, 1800, when he founded at Cambridge the " Boylston Medical Library." In this he expressed the pride he felt in being nearly allied to his maternal great-uncle, Dr. Zabdiel Boylston, " who first introduced the inoculation for the small-pox into America, from whence it was carried to England, and has ever since been extending its beneficial influence through the world ;" and also to his uncle, Nicholas Boylston, " whose memory is known and honored for his liberal donations to Harvard University." In 1840, Mr. Boylston's fund for a college and anatomical museum amounted to nine thousand dollars ; which was in addition to the medical library of eleven hundred volumes, and the fund for prize dissertations, established by him in 1800.

JOHN PRINCE.

DR. JOHN PRINCE, of Salem, Mass., a refugee, who removed to Halifax, in 1775. He married a daughter of Hon. Richard Derby, of Salem, and was proscribed in the banishment act of Massachusetts, Sept. 1778. John Prince, Esq., of Boston, who married a daughter of E. H. Derby, Esq., is a son.

JOSEPH HOOPER.

JOSEPH HOOPER, Esq., of Marblehead, was a graduate of Harvard College in 1763, and a refugee in 1775. He was a son of Peter Hooper, Esq., a " mandamus" counsellor, who rose from abject poverty to apparently inexhaustible wealth ; engrossing for years a large part of the foreign fishing business at Marblehead, which was very extensive about the year 1760. For a while he purchased all the fish brought into that quarter, sent it to Bilboa and other ports in Spain, and received gold and silver in return, with which he purchased goods in England, etc. He built splendid houses in town and country, rode in a chariot like a prince, and was ever after known as " King Hooper." For years he knew not the state of his affairs, and died insolvent in 1790. At his elegant house in Danvers, (since Collins's,) he entertained Governor Gage for some time in 1774. The mansion late Chief Justice Sewall's, in Marblehead, was built by his son Joseph Hooper. He became a paper manufacturer at Bungay, Suffolk, England ; where he died in August, 1812. Although his name does not appear in the proscribing act, a rope walk of his and some lots of land were sold by the commissioners, with other confiscated property, in 1781.

GENERAL CARLETON.

Sir Guy Carleton, (afterwards Lord Dorchester,) a distinguished British officer in America ; was appointed a brigadier-general in this country in 1766 ; he was made major-general in 1772. At the close of the year 1774, a commission passed the seals, constituting him captain-general and governor of Quebec. When Canada was invaded by Montgomery in 1775, Carleton was in the most imminent danger of being taken prisoner upon the St. Lawrence after the capture of Montreal ; but he escaped in a boat with muffled paddles, and arrived safely at Quebec, which he found threatened by an unexpected enemy. Arnold, though he had been repulsed by Colonel McLean, was yet in the neighborhood of the city, waiting for the arrival of Montgomery, previously to another attack. General Carleton, with the skill of an experienced officer, took the necessary measures for the security of the city ; his first act was to oblige all to leave Quebec who would not take up arms in its defence. When Montgomery approached, his summons was treated with contempt by the governor, whose intrepidity was not to be shaken ; by his industry and bravery, Carleton saved the city. After the unsuccessful assault of the last of December, in which Montgomery was killed, he had nothing more immediately to apprehend. In May, 1776, he obliged the Americans to raise the siege ; and it was not long before he compelled them to withdraw entirely from Canada. In October, he recaptured Crown Point ; but as the winter was advancing, he did not attempt the reduction of Ticonderoga, but returned to St. John's. In the beginning of the next year he was superseded in his command by Burgoyne, who was intrusted with the northern British army. Carleton's experience, abilities, and services were such as rendered him worthy of the command, which was given to another. Though he immediately asked leave to resign his government, he yet contributed all in his power to secure the success of the campaign. In the year 1782, he was appointed, as successor of Sir Henry Clinton, commander-in-chief of all his majesty's forces in America; he arrived at New-York with his commission in the beginning of May. After the treaty was signed, he delayed for some time the evacuation of the city, from regard to the safety of the loyalists; but November 25, 1783, he embarked, and withdrew the British ships from the shores of America. He died in England at the close of the year 1808, aged eighty-three; he was a brave and an able officer, and he rendered important services to his country. Though he was not conciliating in his manners, and possessed the severity of a soldier, yet his humanity to the American prisoners, whom he took in Canada, has been much praised. In excuse for the little attention which he paid to the honorable burial of Montgomery, it can only be said that he regarded him as a rebel.*

GENERAL BURGOYNE.

It is curious that a man of such celebrity as a writer, a senator, and an officer, as 'the late Lieutenant General John Burgoyne, should be found among the number of those of whose youthful days no memorial has been preserved. Neither the time, place, nor circumstances of his birth are known. Even his parentage is doubtful. He is said, but upon what authority it does not appear, to have been a natural son of that Lord Bingley who died at an advanced age, in 1774. That he had the advantage of a liberal education and early intercourse with polished society, is sufficiently evident from his writings; and it is probable that he was early devoted to the profession of arms, for on the 10th of May, 1759, he was raised to the rank of Lieut. Colonel, and in the August of the ensuing year, he was appointed Lieut. Col. Commandant of the 16th Light Dragoons. His after services at different periods, in Spain, Portugal and America, are all well known, especially the unfortunate termination of his military career at Saratoga, which, though it tarnished not his honor, cast a shade

* See Allen's Biography.

over his brow, ever afterwards conspicuous to the physiogno-
mical eye. He arrived in England on parole in May, 1778, and
published a letter to his constituents, throwing the blame of the
failure of the expedition on Lord Sackville, (George Germaine,)
the secretary of the American department; and a reply to it,
doubtless written by Lord Sackville, exhibits some of the peculiarities of the style of Junius. He made on certain occasions no ordinary figure in parliament, and towards the close of the year 1781,
when a majority of parliament seemed resolved to persist in the
war, he joined the opposition, and advocated a motion for the dis-
continuance of the fruitless contest. He knew that it was impossible to conquer America. "Passion, prejudice and interest," said
he, " may operate suddenly and partially; but when we see one
principle pervading the whole continent, the Americans resolutely
encountering difficulty and death for a course of years, it must be
a strong vanity and presumption in our own minds, which can only
lead us to imagine that they are not in the right." He moved in the
first circles, and married Lady Charlotte Stanley, a daughter of the
Earl of Derby; and yet we know not who and what originally he
was. He was the author of four successful dramas: The Maid of
the Oaks, the Lord of the Manor, Richard Cœur de Lion, and the
Comedy of the Heiress; and yet the curiosity of his biographer,
even in this anecdote-dealing and memoir-sifting age, cannot trace
his origin, or the scenes of his education. The fable of the Lord of
the Manor seems, in some degree, to have been suggested (though
sufficiently disguised in the modification of character and circumstances) by the incident of his own matrimonial connection; for
his was a clandestine and unauthorized marriage, at a time when
he held only a subaltern's commission in the army, and is said to
have excited at first the resentment of the lady's father to such a
degree, that he declared his resolution never to admit the offenders
into his presence, though in process of time the anger of the earl
subsided, a reconciliation was effected, and was succeeded by a
warm and lasting attachment. It is probable, also, that the memory of his lady, who died in the year 1776, at Kensington Palace,
during his absence in America, is embalmed by the affectionate
regrets of the General in that beautiful air in the first act of that
opera :

'' Encompassed in an angel's frame,
  An angel's virtues lay ;
Too soon did heaven assert the claim,
  And call its own away.

My Anna's worth, my Anna's charms,
  Must never more return !
What now shall fill these widow'd arms ?
  Ah, me ! my Anna's urn !''

It is some confirmation of this conjecture, that General Burgoyne contracted no second marriage. Taste and sentiment, rather than vigor and originality, and familiarity with local manners and the superficies of character, rather than the comprehensive views of the sources of human action and penetration into the deepest recesses of the human heart, characterize the genius of this writer; and his satire, though well pointed, will accordingly lose its interest when the memory of the fleeting follies and temporary politics at which it is levelled shall have died away. Of his dramatic works, incomparably the most valuable is the comedy of "The Heiress," which may, indeed, be called the last comedy produced on the English stage.

From the peace till his death, which took place in August, 1792, he lived as a private gentleman, devoted to pleasure and the muses. The following letter, addressed by him to Garrick, is characteristic :

TO DAVID GARRICK, ESQ.

Wednesday, Nov. 9, 1774.

My dear Sir:

Your obliging and most friendly letter was delivered to me yesterday, at the moment I was sitting down to dinner with company, or I should have endeavored on the moment to return my acknowledgments, with a warmth of expression due to that with which you have honored me. In regard to the very signal distinction you propose to me of the freedom of the house, and the manner of presenting it, I hope you will permit me to decline the parade, and at the same time believe me truly sensible of the honor of it. I should feel myself as proud to be seated in Drury Lane by your deliberate judgment of my talents, as ever an old Roman did in acquiring the freedom of *his* theatre by public services ; but you are at present too partial towards me ; and, till I appear in my own eyes more worthy, I must request you to bound your kind intentions to an order for admittance occasionally to your green-room, where I promise neither to criticise your men ill-naturedly, nor lead astray yourself. The having contributed the songs and music, and other reasons alleged for my introduction to your re-hearsals, will, I conclude, equally pass with the company for this additional favor, without the necessity of any farther discovery. But as you kindly insist upon my directions, I desire it to be done by a simple order to Johnson, and no gold box, nor silver box—not even a mulberry one : you must give me a reception *Hamlet-like*—I will have no *appurtenances of welcome*. I think I may, without vanity, congratulate you upon the piece having laid hold of the audience last night. A general relish was very discernible. I could not help agreeing with a critic who sat near me, and who expressed himself delighted with the genteel scenes, that the intro-duction of the lamplighters was too coarse to assort with the rest. Suppose three or four of your girls were introduced in the act of weaving cords of flowers, such as the dancers use in the second act. They might fix one end of the cord to the scene, and keep slipping back as they weave the flowers, in the manner the rope-makers do, which would be picturesque. In that case, O'Daub's part might begin with his conversation with the architect ; and he might present himself to the girls in some nonsense like the follow-ing : " *O'Daub.*—If these pretty maids would pay me with a kiss a-piece, 'faith, I'd paint them all round for nothing at all. Surely they look as bright as a May morning already, and a touch of my brush will make them remembered by those who never saw 'em." If after this the two additional verses of the song were added, the words would apply, and Moody's action might have effect. Should you approve this idea, or any one like it, the alteration is so short it might be studied and acted in half an hour ; but I submit it to you on the sudden, like many crudities with which I have troubled you. Lord Stanley is come to town, and very earnest to see " The Maid of the Oaks." I send to Johnson's for a box for Lady Betty to-morrow, that she may do him the honors, and I hope I shall succeed. If you could send me the copy this afternoon, I would

return it in time for you to put it into the printer's hands to-morrow afternoon. Believe me, with the truest sense of the value of
your friendship, dear sir, your faithful and obedient, etc., etc.

J. BURGOYNE.

GENERAL CLINTON.

SIR HENRY CLINTON, an English general, son of the colonial
Governor Clinton, was the grandson of the Earl of Lincoln. After
distinguishing himself in the battle of Bunker Hill in 1775, he was
sent unsuccessfully against New-York and Charleston. He afterwards, in September, 1776, occupied the city of New-York.
October 6, 1777, he assaulted and took forts Clinton and Montgomery. In 1778, he succeeded Howe in the command at Philadelphia, whence Washington compelled him to retire. In May,
1780, he took Charleston. It was he who negotiated with Arnold
in his treason. He returned to England in 1782, and died Dec.
22, 1795; a few months before, he had been appointed governor
of Gibraltar. He published a narrative of his conduct in America,
1782; Observations on Cornwallis's Answer, 1783; Observations
on Stedman, 1784.

LORD CORNWALLIS.

CHARLES CORNWALLIS, Marquis, commander of the British army
in America, surrendered at Yorktown, October 19, 1781; an event
which brought the war to a close. In 1790, he was governor-
general of India, and by his victories in the war with Tippoo Saib
acquired high reputation. Again was he appointed, in 1805,
governor of India; where he died, at Ghazepore, October 5. He
married in 1768, Miss Jones, a lady of large fortune; who is said to
have died of a broken heart, in consequence of his engaging in the
American war. He published an answer to the Narrative of Sir
Henry Clinton, 1783.

LORD HOWE.

ADMIRAL EARL HOWE was born in 1725, and on the death of his
brother the general, succeeded to his title and estate. He commanded the British fleet which arrived at Staten Island July 12,
1776; and was named in the commission to offer proposals of

peace. In July, 1777, he convoyed the two hundred and seventy transports in which the army sailed from New-York to the Chesapeake. He repaired to Newport in the winter as a safe harbor; which place he relieved on the 30th Aug., 1778, when threatened by the Americans and French, by arriving from New-York with a hundred sail of ships. In September, he resigned the command to Admiral Gambier. On the 1st of June, 1794, he obtained a victory over the French, and died August 5, 1799. Lord Howe was the brother and successor in his title of the General Lord Howe who fell in the attack on Ticonderoga in 1758, in whom, said Mante, " *the soul of the army seemed to expire ;*" and to commemorate whom the province of Massachusetts Bay caused a monument to be erected in Westminster Abbey.

GENERAL HOWE.

GENERAL SIR WILLIAM HOWE, brother of Richard, Earl Howe, was the successor of General Gage in command of the British forces in America. He first arrived at Boston in May, 1775, with General Burgoyne, and commanded in the battle of Bunker Hill; he took possession of New-York in September, 1776; and was one of the commissioners to offer terms of peace. In July, 1777, Sir William sailed for the Chesapeake, and entered Philadelphia, Sept. 27; he defeated the Americans on the 4th of October, same year, at Germantown. In May, 1778, he was succeeded by General Clinton. In the House of Commons, in December same year, when assigning his reasons for quitting his command in America, he particularly blamed Lord Sackville, (formerly Lord George Germaine,) the minister, for not sending reinforcements, nor co-operating in his plans; and in the January following, Lord Sackville, if he was the author of the letter to Admiral Howe, returned the invective. He published a second edition of his narrative relative to his command in 1780; he died in 1814. General Charles Lee said, " Howe was the most indolent of mortals, and never took pains to examine the merits or demerits of the cause in which he was engaged. That the king and parliament formed the supreme power; that supreme power is absolute and uncontrollable; and consequently all resistance *rebellion ;* that he was a soldier and bound to obey in all cases whatever: these were his notions, and this his logic. He was naturally good-natured, and as an executive soldier all fire and activity; brave as Cæsar. His understanding good, but confounded by the immensity of the task imposed upon him."

GENERAL GATES.

Horatio Gates, a major-general in the army of the United States, was a native of England; is said to have been a natural son of Horace Walpole, Lord Orford. In early life he entered the British army, and laid the foundation of his future military fame; he was aid to General Monckton at the capture of Martinico; and after the peace of Aix-la-Chapelle, he was among the first troops which landed at Halifax under General Cornwallis. He was with Braddock at the time of his defeat in 1755, and was shot through the body. When peace was concluded, he purchased an estate in Virginia, where he resided until the commencement of the American war in 1775; when he was appointed by Congress adjutant-general, with the rank of brigadier-general, and accompanied Washington to Cambridge. In August, 1777, he took command of the northern department, and succeeded in capturing Burgoyne in October. Congress passed a vote of thanks, and ordered a medal of gold to be presented to him by the president. His conduct towards his conquered enemy was marked by a delicacy, which does him the highest honor; he did not permit his own troops to witness the mortification of the British in depositing their arms. After Gen. Lincoln was taken prisoner, he was appointed, June 13, 1780, to the command of the southern department; August 16, he was defeated by Cornwallis at Camden. After the peace he retired to his farm in Berkley county, Virginia, where he remained until the year 1790, when he came to reside in New-York; having first emancipated his slaves, and made a pecuniary provision for such as were not able to provide for themselves. Some of them would not leave him, but continued in his family. On his arrival at New-York, the freedom of the city was presented to him. In 1800, he accepted a seat in the legislature; his political opinions did not separate him from many respectable citizens, whose views differed widely from his own; he died April 10, 1806, aged 77. A few weeks before his death, he wrote to his friend Dr.

Mitchell, then at Washington, on some business, and closed his letter, dated Feb. 27, 1806, with the following words :—" I am very weak, and have evident signs of an approaching dissolution. But I have lived long enough, since I have lived to see a mighty people animated with a spirit to be free, and governed by transcendant abilities and honor." He retained his faculties to the last; he directed that his body should be privately buried, which was accordingly done. General Gates was a whig in England, and a republican in America; he was a scholar, well versed in history and the Latin classics. While he was just, hospitable and generous, his manners and deportment yet indicated his military character.

JUDGE DANA.

FRANCIS DANA, LL.D., chief justice of Massachusetts, was a descendant of Richard Dana, who died at Cambridge about 1695. His father was Richard Dana, an eminent magistrate; he was born at Charlestown in August, 1742, and after graduating at Harvard College in 1762, studied law with Judge Trowbridge; he passed the year 1775 in England, where he had a brother, Edmund, a minister at Worcester, who died in 1823. In 1776, he was appointed a delegate to Congress, and taking his seat in November, 1777, continued in that body until in November, 1779, he accompanied Mr. Adams to Paris, as a secretary of legation. He was elected December, 19, 1780, as minister to Russia; where he remained, though not publicly received, from August, 1781, till the close of the war, returning in December, 1783. He was chosen a delegate to Congress in 1784; and a member of the Massachusetts Convention, where he advocated the constitution. The office of envoy extraordinary to France in 1799, he declined; and Mr. Gerry was deputed in his stead, with Messrs. Marshall and Pinckney. Appointed chief justice of Massachusetts in 1792, he discharged very impartially and ably the duties of that office until his resignation in 1806; he died at his seat in Cambridge, April 25, 1811, aged sixty-eight. Judge Dana was a learned lawyer, and presided in court with great dignity; his opinions on the bench were remarkable for their clearness and perspicuity. In his politics during the days of violent excitements, he was strongly attached to the federalists. His correspondence while in Europe, is contained in Sparks's Diplomatic Correspondence, vol. 8th.

COLONEL PICKERING.

Hon. Timothy Pickering, LL. D., the son of a prominent citizen of Salem of the same name, was born there on the 17th July, 1746, and graduated at Harvard College in 1763. The memorable distinction of conducting the first resistance in arms to the power of the mother country fell to his lot, at his native place, on Sunday the 26th of February, 1775, when the march of Col. Leslie's regiment of royal troops was resolutely intercepted, and his further progress arrested by him at the head of the militia, at the bridge over the North River. The draw of the bridge was hoisted, and Col. Pickering presented himself on the opposite side. He informed Col. Leslie that the military stores he came to seize were the property of the people, and that they would not be surrendered without a struggle. Col. Leslie ordered his men into a large gondola at the wharf, to secure a passage over the river. In a moment Major Sprague, the owner of the gondola, sprang on board and beat a hole through the bottom, by which it was sunk. While effecting this he was wounded by the soldiers with their bayonets, and thus was here shed the first blood of the Revolution. The Rev. Mr. Barnard now interposed, and by judicious persuasions prevented the impending catastrophe ; and Leslie, pledging his honor, that if Col. Pickering would let him pass the bridge, so that it might appear a voluntary act on his part, he would abandon the attempt to seize the stores ; and this being acceded to on the part of Col. Pickering, the former returned immediately to his transports at Marblehead, and re-embarked his regiment from the harbor that night.

Col. Pickering marched at the head of the Essex regiment as soon as he heard of the Lexington affair, on the 19th of April of the same year, to Medford, in order to intercept the enemy, but was not in season. He also took up the line of march with his regiment for the heights of Charlestown on the 17th June, but arrived too late to participate in the affair of Bunker Hill. Col. Pickering compiled a manual for the drill and exercise of the troops, which was in general use until the Baron Steuben published his more extensive work. He was appointed the same year a judge of the com-

mon pleas, and succeeded Mr. Curwen as admiralty judge for the
district including Boston and Salem.   In the autumn of 1776, he
commanded the Essex regiment under General Washington in
New Jersey.

The following is an extract of a letter from General Washington to Congress, dated at Morristown, May 24, 1777 :

" I beg leave to inform Congress, that, immediately after the
receipt of their resolve of the 26th of March, recommending the
office of adjutant general to be filled by a person of ability and
unsuspected attachment to our cause, I wrote to Colonel Timothy
Pickering, of *Salem*, offering him the post, in the first instance, and
transmitting at the same time a letter to Colonel William R. Lee,
whom Congress had been pleased to mention, to be delivered to
him in case my offer could not be accepted.   This conduct in preference of Col. Pickering, I was induced to adopt from the high
character I had of him, both as a great military genius, cultivated
by an industrious attention to the study of war, and as a gentleman
of liberal education, distinguished zeal, and great method and activity in business.   This character of him I had from gentlemen of
distinction and merit, and on whose judgment I could rely.

" When my letter reached Col. Pickering, at first view, he
thought his situation in respect to public affairs would not permit
him to accept the post.   That for Col. Lee he sent immediately to
him, who, in consequence, repaired to head quarters.   By Col.
Lee I received a letter from Col. Pickering, stating more particularly the causes which prevented him accepting the office when it
was offered, assuring me that he would, in a little time, accommodate his affairs in such a manner as to come into any military post
in which he might be serviceable and thought equal to.

" Here I am to mark with peculiar satisfaction, in justice to
Col. Lee, who has deservedly acquired the reputation of a good
officer, that he has expressed a distrust of his abilities to fill the appointment intended for him ; and hearing that Col. Pickering would
accept it, he not only offered, but wished to relinquish his claim to
it in favor of him, whom he declared he considered, from a very intimate and friendly acquaintance, as a first-rate military character ;
and that he knew no gentleman better or so well qualified for the
post among us. Matters being thus circumstanced, and Colonel Lee

pleased with the command he was in, I wrote to Col. Pickering on his return, who accepted the office, and is daily expected."

He immediately marched with the army to Pennsylvania, and was by the side of Washington at the battle of Brandywine, on the 14th September; he was also present at that of Germantown, October 4. He was soon after elected by Congress a member of the Board of War, with Generals Gates and Mifflin. The arrangement of the staff department was also intrusted to him and General Mifflin. In August, 1780, he succeeded Gen. Greene as quartermaster-general, and discharged the arduous and complicated duties of that department with promptness and fidelity.

Col. Pickering was employed in various negotiations with the Indian tribes, and in 1791 was appointed postmaster-general, which office he held till 1794, when he succeeded Gen. Knox as secretary of war. In August, 1795, he temporarily had charge of the state department, and upon the resignation of Mr. Edmund Randolph, in December, received the appointment of secretary of state. This was the last office he held under Washington; from which he was removed by President Adams, in May, 1800. It was this circumstance to which the eloquent and eccentric John Randolph alludes when Col. Pickering's political course was attacked in the House of Representatives some years after; on that occasion Randolph declared that he would gladly surrender all his own riches and honors to be able to say, what that patriot (Pickering) could say, viz., " that he ever enjoyed the unbounded confidence of Washington while living—and the enmity of his successor."

On Col. Pickering's removal from office, he commenced the settlement of new lands in the back woods of Pennsylvania; but soon after disposing of them, he returned to Massachusetts, and at Wenham, near his native town, he, like Cincinnatus, cultivated with his own hands a farm which he purchased. He could not long be spared from public life, and from 1803 to 1811 he was a senator of the United States, and from 1814 to 1817 he represented his district in Congress, to the delight and satisfaction of his constituents. He died at Salem on the 29th June, 1829, aged 84. His active life afforded but little leisure for literary pursuits, yet his writings were vigorous and elegant. From early life he was a professor of Christianity. In the service of his country he was faithful, disinterested, and energetic. His feelings were strong, and in his political controversies he was ardent and sometimes vehement; but his exemplary morals, strict integrity, and pure principles satisfied all of his sincerity. Col. Pickering has left a number of descendants; the most distinguished is the great philologist, the Hon. John Pickering, LL. D., his eldest son, now president of the American Academy of Arts and Sciences.

JUDGE BLOWERS.

Hon. Sampson Salter Blowers, a native of Boston, and grandson of the Rev. Thomas B. Blowers, second minister of Beverly, Massachusetts, graduated at Harvard College 1763, of which institution he is now *senior alumnus*, or the oldest living graduate. He was born in March, 1742, and is consequently *one hundred years* of age. He studied law with Governor Hutchinson, and married the daughter of Benjamin Kent, a lawyer celebrated for his eccentricity and wit. Mr. Blowers was, with John Adams and Josiah Quincy, jr., engaged to defend Capt. Preston and the British soldiers, on their trial at Boston, November, 1770, for what was termed " the Boston massacre." On the eve of the Revolution, in 1774, he sailed for England, and returned in the autumn of 1778, just in time to find his name in the proscribing act of the Massachusetts Provincial Assembly. He was forthwith imprisoned, but soon liberated and sent in a cartel to Halifax. From this time he pursued his profession there; was raised to the supreme bench in 1795; became the chief justice in 1801, and resigned all his honors in 1803. Judge Blowers has never revisited his native place. His sister died at Boston in March, 1842, at the age of ninety-eight; she was the widow of an officer of marines, who fell on board the Alliance frigate, in an action with two British sloops of war, May, 1781.

The following notice of Judge Blowers appeared in the Boston Daily Advertiser, in March last :—

" The old man of whom ye spake ; is he yet alive ?"

The Hon. Sampson Salter Blowers, of Halifax, [Harvard University, 1763,] this day completes his *century of years ;* the elder patriarch of Harvard's LIVING ALUMNI. He was a native of Boston, his father living (as we some time ago learned from an authority

near in blood) at the time in Quaker-lane, now Congress-street : a
nephew of Pyam B., merchant, [H. U. 1721,] and grandson of Rev.
Thomas B., second minister of Beverly, [H. U. 1695.] Young
Blowers entered upon the study of law with Hutchinson, then simply
judge of probate and lieutenant-governor ; and married the daughter
of Benj. Kent, Esq.,* [H. U. 1727,] an attorney at law in Boston,
" celebrated for his eccentricity and wit," who, like himself, became a refugee, and died in Halifax, at an advanced age, in 1788.
In November, 1770, then in his noviciate at the bar, he was employed as junior counsel to Messrs. Adams and Quincy (the latter
his classmate) in behalf of the eight British soldiers of the 29th
regiment on their trial for what was long and most absurdly called
" the Boston massacre." The victims of that night (March 5th,
1770) though magnified by the effervescence of the time into *mar-
tyrs of liberty*, did but poor credit indeed to the name, and as to
most of them, abundantly provoked the death they found. Gordon,
with strange looseness for one who was writing in the midst of the
scene, says, (Vol. I. 194,) " The soldiers had the same counsel as
their commander." But Robert Auchmuty, who according to Eliot
made, in defence of Capt. Preston, a plea so memorable and persuasive, as " almost to bear down the tide of prejudice against him,
though it never swelled to a higher flood," had no concern in the
succeeding trial ; while the subject of this notice was certainly not
retained in the earlier one. On the eve of the Revolution (1774)
S. S. B., for some reason or object sailed for England, and returned
in the fall of 1778, just in time to find his name in the proscribing
act of the provincial assembly of Massachusetts, (October,) which

* Kent was a minister of Marlborough, a very brief period [1733-'35] ;
though so unclerical was his deportment, and his humor, that we might rather
have wondered had his stay been longer. He removed to Boston ; and so late
as 1769, his name is found, in somewhat odd association, with those of the
most prominent and strenuous Whigs of the place, as a committee of safety
in a communication to Dr. Franklin. To him it is, we suppose, that the doctor, in a letter written from Philadelphia, within the last year and a half of
his own life refers :—" You tell me our poor friend Ben Kent is gone ; I hope
to the regions of the blessed : or at least to some place where souls are prepared for those regions. I found my hope on this, that though not so orthodox
as you and I, he was an honest man and had his virtues. If he had any hy-
pocrisy, it was of that inverted kind, with which a man is not so bad as he
seems to be." (See Sparks's Franklin, VII. 366, X. 460.)

could not then have been passed many weeks. He was imprisoned forthwith; but within the next fortnight was despatched in a cartel to Halifax. From this time, as we are told, he steadfastly pursued his profession there; being raised to the supreme bench in 1795, becoming its presiding head in 1801, and resigning all his honors in 1833.

Though his lot was cast with the obnoxious side, Judge B. stood by no means alone among his companions. The class of 1763 was fruitful in loyalists, generally also refugees:—*Bliss* of Springfield, and *Upham* of Brookfield, (the last, father of the present minister of Salem,) were constituted a few years after judges of the highest court of New Brunswick;* *Dr. John Jeffries* of Boston, (after signalizing himself in a then novel sphere,) returned a few years in the rear of the peace, to resume practice in his native town; *Hooper* of Marblehead, second son of "old King Robert," and *Porter*, for a time an eminent attorney in Salem, both died in England.

Judge B. has left behind him in the race the longest-lived of his classmates by more than TEN years. *Col. Pickering*, of Salem, one of the *three* latest survivors, died Jan. 29, 1829. The last of the trio, *Samuel Perley*, settled successively at three several places in New Hampshire, and finally in Gray, Maine, finished his course at the latter, November 28, 1831. Of the *thirty-six hundred* departed sons of Harvard, our living Methuselah (with the exception of the venerated Dr. Holyoke) has alone fairly rounded his century; Mr. Porter, of Ashfield, on Connecticut river [H. U. 1745] who died February, 1820, having failed only one month of that honorable mark.†

* No other class perhaps can show so many instances of the highest judicial elevation. Three refugee judges of the supreme court! to which must be added the *Hon. Nathan Cushing*, of Scituate—a zealous Whig—who deeply ingratiated himself with the popular party by the spirit of his decisions, as first judge of admiralty in 1776, against captured British vessels; and who at a later period [1789–1801] was one of the highest bench of Massachusetts. There is yet one other distinction to which the class of 1763 appropriates. The *first English Oration*, ever heard upon the Commencement boards was pronounced by *Jed. Huntington* of Norwich, Conn., (afterwards well known as a general officer in our revolutionary contest, and father of the late Rev. Josh. Huntington, of the Old South Church.)

† In such a connection as this, and for the sake of the narrow circle who

That the usual concomitants of such longevity should be here also found in its train, few will probably be surprised to read. It has been well known for four or five years past that decay had been coming over the mind of this centennial patriarch; and on the recent progress (autumn of 1840) of the Hon. J. Q. Adams through the provinces of Nova Scotia, by whom Judge B. also was visited, this fact was anew confirmed.

This notice must not be closed without adding, what all readers (it need hardly be qualified) will be surprised to be told :—There yet lives in this city, long sequestered from the world, a sister of the distinguished graduate, before us, a widow of more than sixty years' date, "whose days have almost even run with his," (ninety-eight,) a coincidence alike extraordinary and interesting. The husband

are curious in such matters, it may not be amiss to specify the twelve alumni who have reached the highest point of longevity. Those unasterized, it will be observed, we presume not to number their days, but give their age at the moment we are writing.

* 1746. Dr. E. A. Holyoke, of Salem, died March 31, 1829, 100 years 7 months.

1763. Hon. S. S. Blowers, Halifax, Nova Scotia, 100 years.

* 1745. Rev. N. Porter, minister of Chebacco parish (Ipswich) and of Ashfield, died February 29, 1820, 99 years 11 months.

* 1759. Hon. Paine Wingate, minister a few years at Hampton Falls, N. H., and afterwards in high civil trusts, died at Stratham, N. H., March 7, 1838, 98 years and 10 months.

* 1744. Col. Peter Frye, formerly of Salem, and in various public trusts, died (as a refugee) at Camberwell, Surrey, near London, February 1, 1820, (his birthday,) 97 years.

* 1712. Mr. John Nutting, Salem, successively grammar schoolmaster, register of deeds, and collector of the port, at different times, died May 20, 1790, 96 years 4 months.

* 1753. Rev. Peter Thacher Smith, minister of Windham, Me. [1762-'90] d. as P. T. S. "Esq.," October, 1826, 95 years 3 months.

1765. Dr. Ezra Green, surgeon in the continental navy, under John Paul Jones, and since physician in Dover, N. H., 95 years ten months.

* 1728. Thaddeus Mason, Esq., register of deeds for Middlesex, died at Cambridge, May 1, 1802, 95 years 4 months.

1767. Hon. Timothy Farrar, New Ipswich, N. H., formerly a judge of the S. J. C. of N. H., 94 years 8 months.

* 1741. Mr. Joseph Waldo, merchant in Boston, died (as a refugee) in Bristol, England, April, 1816, 94 years.

* 1710. Rev. Joseph Adams, minister of Newington, N. H., 37½ years, died May 26, 1783, 94 years.

April 2, 1842.

of the latter, a lieutenant of marines in the celebrated and ever-fortunate Alliance frigate, fell in an engagement of that ship on her passage from France, with two sloops of war, May, 1781. Though not wanting in inducements to the contrary therefore, it is worthy of record that Judge B. has never, as we are told, revisited his native place, since he went forth from it an exile with the flaming sword behind him, interdicting his return.

T. BRINLEY.

THOMAS BRINLEY, a merchant of Boston, graduated at Harvard College, 1744. He was an " *addresser*" of Gov. Gage and Gov. Hutchinson. A refugee in England in 1775. Proscribed in the act of banishment of the assembly of Massachusetts, Sept., 1788. Probably died abroad.

N. COFFIN.

NATHANIEL COFFIN, Esq., of Boston, the father of Sir Isaac Coffin, Bart., who was his fourth and youngest son. Mr. Coffin graduated at Harvard College in 1744 ; was cashier of the customs at Boston ; an " *addresser*" of Gov. Gage ; a refugee in 1775 ; was proscribed in the banishment act of 1778, and died in England before November, 1783.

GOV. CASWELL.

HON. RICHARD CASWELL, of North Carolina, at the head of a regiment Feb. 1776 ; he defeated General McDonald with a party of fifteen hundred Scottish emigrants and ignorant and disorderly frontier inhabitants, styling themselves " *loyalist regulators*," at Morris Creek bridge, about sixteen miles from Wilmington, with the loss of seventy killed and wounded, and fifteen hundred excellent rifles. His force was but one thousand strong, and the victory of essential service to the American cause.

Besides being a member of the first congress, he was president of the convention which formed the constitution of North Carolina, under which he was governor from 1777 to 1780, and from 1785 to 1787. He died at Fayetteville, Nov. 20, 1789. His equanimity of temper endeared him to his friends and commanded the respect of his opponents ; for his constant watchfulness of the welfare of the people and his private virtues prevented his having *enemies*.

JOSEPH HEWES.

Hon. Joseph Hewes, of North Carolina, as a member of congress early patronized the celebrated John Paul Jones, and was ever his confidential correspondent. It is to Mr. Hewes's discriminating judgment of character, in no small degree, that we owe the train of unsurpassed naval victories achieved by that hero; for there was great opposition to his preferment on the score of foreign birth and want of influential connections, which latter consideration had great weight at that period. Jones relied inplicitly on Mr. Hewes, and in a letter says, " I will cheerfully abide by whatever you think right," and to him he referred the Hon. Robert Morris, respecting his claim for rank, who ever after was his friend.

DR. SHIPPEN.

William Shippen, M. D. of Philadelphia, graduated at Nassau Hall, New Jersey, in 1754, and completed a medical education at Edinburgh. He delivered in 1764, at Philadelphia, the first course of anatomical lectures ever pronounced in America. He was the founder of the medical school, which finally rivalled that of Edinburgh. He was early opposed to " *the supremacy of parliament over the colonies in all cases whatsoever*," and, in 1777, was appointed director general of the medical department in the army of the United States. Dr. Shippen died at Germantown, July 11, 1808, in the seventy-fifth year of his age.

GOV. MIFFLIN.

Thos. Mifflin, of Pennsylvania, was actively engaged in opposition to the measures of the British parliament. He was a member of the first congress in 1774, and was among the first commissioned at the organization of the continental army, having been appointed quarter-master-general. In October, 1788, he succeeded Dr. Franklin as president of the supreme executive council. In September, 1790, the constitution for Pennsylvania was formed by a convention, over which he was chosen the first governor. He possessed extraordinary powers of elocution, which he exercised with success during the insurrection in Pennsylvania in 1794. He retired from the gubernatorial chair at the close of the year 1799, and on the 20th Jan. 1800, died at Lancaster in the fifty-seventh year of his age.

JUDGE ALLEN.

WILLIAM ALLEN, chief justice of Pennsylvania, was the son of William Allen, an eminent merchant of Philadelphia, who died in 1725. On the approach of the Revolution he retired to England, where he died, September, 1780. His wife was a daughter of Andrew Hamilton, whom he succeeded as recorder of Philadelphia in 1741. He was much distinguished as a friend to literature. He patronized Benjamin West, the historical painter. By his counsels and exertions Dr. Franklin was much assisted in establishing the college in Philadelphia. He published " the American Crisis," London, 1774, in which he suggests a plan " for restoring the dependence of America to a state of perfection." His principles seem to have been not a little arbitrary. On his resignation of the office of chief justice, to which he had been appointed in 1750, he was succeeded till the Revolution by Mr. Chew, attorney-general, and Mr. Chew by his son Andrew Allen. This son died in London, March 7, 1825, aged eighty-five. At the close of 1776 he put himself under the protection of Gen. Howe, at Trenton, with his brothers John and William. He had been a member of congress and of the committee of safety; and William a lieutenant-colonel in the continental service.

GEN. REED.

JOSEPH REED graduated at Nassau Hall, New Jersey, in 1757. He engaged with zeal in opposition to parliament, was of the committee of correspondence, and afterwards president of the convention of New Jersey. On the organization of the army, he became first aid to ;General Washington; the next year adjutant-general. While he was a member of congress, in 1778, the commissioners from England arrived, and one of them, Gov. Johnstone, addressed private letters to him, Francis Dana, and Robert Morris, to secure their influence towards the restoration of harmony, with intimations of honors and emoluments. Mr. Reed's former despondence being known, a lady, supposed to be the wife of Dr. Adam Ferguson, (the secretary of the commissioners,) assured him as from Gov. Johnstone, that ten thousand pounds sterling and the best office in America should be at his disposal, if he would effect a reunion. He replied that " he was not worth purchasing, but such as he was, the king of Great Britain was not rich enough to do it."

In October, 1778, he was chosen president of Pennsylvania, which office he held till the autumn of 1781. He died March 5, 1785, aged forty-three, having visited England for his health the year before without good effect.

Mr. Reed published remarks on Gov. Johnstone's speech in parliament, with authentic papers relative to his propositions in 1779, and an address to the people of Pennsylvania in 1783.

WILLIAM PYNCHON.

WILLIAM PYNCHON, Esq., an eminent counsellor at law, of Salem, Massachusetts, was a loyalist, but did not leave the country. The windows of his house in Summer-street were broken by the mob on demanding his recantation as a Hutchinsonian addresser, previous to the Revolution; and he left them long in ruins, except that they were boarded up, in testimony of the licentiousness and lawlessness of the times. Mr. Pynchon was a native of Springfield, and graduated at Harvard College in 1743; he died, March 14, 1789, aged sixty-eight.

JOSEPH LEE.

HON. JOSEPH LEE, of Cambridge, Mass., was the son of a Salem merchant. Having remained in Boston during the siege, he subjected himself to unpopularity with the patriots, although his lukewarmness in the loyalist principles prevented his becoming an object of public notice. He was judge of the common pleas for Middlesex; and died at his seat in Cambridge, December, 1802, at the advanced age of ninety-three years. His brother, Thomas Lee, Esq., a merchant of Salem, graduated at Harvard College in 1722; and during the revolutionary war resided at Newark, New Jersey. He had been appointed mandamus counsellor, but was compelled by the people to resign, Sept. 2, 1775.

JUDGE OLIVER.

HON. ANDREW OLIVER, of Salem, son of Lieut. Gov. Andrew

Oliver, and nephew of Chief Justice Peter Oliver, graduated at Harvard College in 1749; studied law; was often a representative to the assembly, and a judge of the common pleas for Essex previous to the Revolution. He was one of the founders of the American Academy of Arts and Sciences, and a member of the American Philosophical Society at Philadelphia; he was reckoned among the best scholars of his day, and possessed fine talents. Judge Oliver was never fond of public life, but ardently attached to his books and his friends. Besides an Essay on Comets, which was published in 1772, several valuable communications of his are contained in the first volume of the Transactions of the American Academy. He was honored with a commission of mandamus counsellor, which he declined; he married Mary, daughter of Chief Justice Lynde, and several descendants remain of the second and third generations; he died in December, 1799, aged sixty-eight. Judge Oliver was a loyalist, and the only member of his family who did not renounce his country in consequence of the Revolution.

BENJAMIN GOODHUE.

Hon. Benjamin Goodhue, was born at Salem, Massachusetts, October 1, 1748, and graduated at Harvard College in 1766. He early embarked in commerce, with credit and success; he was a whig of the Revolution; represented the county of Essex in the senate of his native state, from 1784 to 1789, when he was elected a representative to the first United States Congress under the new constitution; and with Mr. Fitzsimmons of Philadelphia, formed our code of revenue laws, a majority of which have remained in force to this day. In 1796, Mr. Goodhue was elected a senator in congress for Massachusetts, where he was distinguished as chairman of the committee of commerce, but resigned and retired from public life in 1800; his colleague in the senate was Caleb Strong, for many successive years the popular governor of Massachusetts. Mr. Goodhue's politics were of the Washington school; and that party is now generally admitted to have been the purest ever known in our country. He died July 28, 1814, leaving an irreproachable name to his only surviving son, Jonathan Goodhue, Esq., of New-York; a merchant, who in character and credit has stood second to none in this commercial emporium, during a residence of thirty-six years.

DR. HOLYOKE.

EDWARD AUGUSTUS HOLYOKE, M.D., L.L.D., son of President Holyoke of Harvard College, was born August 13, 1728, and graduated in 1746. In 1755, he married Judith, daughter of Col. Benjamin Pickman of Salem ; and after her death, which occurred within the year, Mary, daughter of Nathaniel Viall, Esq., of Boston. " The period of the Revolution was a trying one to him, and he never loved to dwell upon the recollection of it ; his feelings in the spring and summer of 1775 were intensely painful. In referring to that period, he said he thought he should have died with the sense of weight and oppression at his heart; he had sent his family to Nantucket, and the loneliness of his home increased the feeling of desolation. Most of his intimate friends and near connections favored the royal cause ; and his own education had attached him to the established order of things, while his peaceful temper shrunk from the turmoil of a revolution. Although most distinguished men who had adopted the royal cause, found it expedient to leave the country, it does not appear that he was ever impeded in the prosecution of his professional business or studies for a single day. Once only he committed himself, by signing a complimentary address to Governor Hutchinson, in common with a number of the most distinguished citizens of the town of Salem, when the governor was about leaving the country. He afterwards felt himself obliged, as well as a number of his associates, to publish a sort of apology for this act ; which " *recantation*," as it was called, contained nothing that was servile or disgraceful. He died March 31, 1829, at the great age of *one hundred years.*

" In deeds of piety and benevolence he was ever active, and his gifts were bestowed with the most scrupulous secrecy ; and from his intimacy in the families of all classes, seldom misapplied."

He had been a practising physician in Salem for seventy-nine years. On some days he made a hundred visits ; and at one period, there was not a dwelling-house in Salem which he had not visited professionally. About fifty medical gentlemen of Boston and Salem gave him a public dinner on his centennial anniversary.

JUDGE LYNDE.

HON. BENJAMIN LYNDE, of Salem, chief justice of the supreme

62

court, (as was his father of the same name,) was born at Salem,
and graduated in 1718, at Harvard College. He was judge of
probate from 1745 to 1771; he presided in November, 1770, at
the trial of Captain Preston and his soldiers, for the part they took
in what was called "the Boston massacre." He resigned his seat
on the bench of the supreme court in 1771, and died October 3,
1781, aged eighty-one. It was a remarkable coincidence, that
father and son should have been chief justices of the supreme
court, and occupied a seat on that bench between them for nearly
sixty years. Judge Lynde's daughter, Mary, was the wife of the
Hon. Andrew Oliver of Salem, author of the Essay on Comets.

JUDGE ROPES.

HON. NATHANIEL ROPES, of Salem, born in 1727, was graduated
at Harvard College in 1745, and applied himself to the study of
the law. The violent measures in opposition to government were
obnoxious to him; and when he found he could no longer be useful there, he retired from the council in 1769, and from the bench
of the superior court just before his death, in the spring of 1774; he
was firm in loyalist principles.

After ineffectual negotiations with Gov. Hutchinson, the inflexible assertor of royal prerogative, at the termination of the first
session of 1773, it was resolved, "that any of the judges who while
they hold their offices during pleasure shall accept support from the
crown, independent of the grants of the general court, will discover
that he is an enemy to the constitution, and has it in his heart to
promote the establishment of arbitrary government." In February,
1774, four of the judges, Trowbridge, Hutchinson, Ropes and
Cushing, on the appeal being made by the assembly, replied that
they had received no part of the allowance from the king; which
was deemed satisfactory. Judge Ropes' house was assailed, notwithstanding, by a mob, and the furniture and windows throughout
broken the night before his death, (by small-pox,) which event it
doubtless accelerated.

With the exception of the reports of his decisions in the supreme court, the following obituary notice from his political opponents is all that is on record respecting him:

From the Essex Gazette, March 22, 1774.

"Died, on the 18th inst., in the forty-eighth year of his age, the

Hon. Nathaniel Ropes, some years since representative of this town in the general assembly, afterwards a member of the council, chief justice of the common pleas, and judge of probate of wills for the county of Essex, and also a justice of the superior court for this province."

Judge Ropes married a daughter of the Rev. John Sparhawk of Salem, and their deceased sons were merchants of that place. Nathaniel married a daughter of Dr. Putnam, and John a daughter of Jonathan Haraden, Esq., a distinguished naval commander in the Revolution against Great Britain. Their daughters married William Orne, Jonathan Hodges, and Samuel Curwen Ward, also merchants of Salem, all deceased; of their descendants many are now living.

THOMAS ROBIE.

THOMAS ROBIE, Esq., of Marblehead, a son of Dr. Thomas Robie, who was graduated at Harvard College, in 1708, and after being a resident fellow or tutor there, established himself in the practice of physic at Salem, and married a daughter of Major Stephen Sewall. The subject of this notice became a merchant, and married a daughter of the Rev. Simon Bradstreet, who was the great-grandson of Gov. Bradstreet, called the "Nestor of New England." Mr. Robie being strongly on the side of the royal government, was an addresser of Gov. Hutchinson, and quitted the country about the commencement of the war; he first went to Halifax, but afterwards to London, February 5, 1776. He passed his time of exile mostly in Halifax, where one of his daughters married Jonathan Stearns, Esq., another refugee, who graduated at Harvard College in 1770, became attorney-general of Nova Scotia, and died 1798; another was married to Joseph Sewall, Esq., late treasurer of Massachusetts. His son, Simon Bradstreet Robie, Esq., of Halifax, solicitor of the province of Nova Scotia, is a gentleman of great wealth and respectability. Mr. Thomas Robie returned after the peace, and re-embarked in commercial pursuits in Salem, to a limited extent. He was amiable, intelligent and exemplary, and died at Salem about thirty years since, well esteemed.

JOHN SARGENT.

JOHN SARGENT, Esq., a merchant of Salem, who became a refugee and was banished by the act of 1778.

JUDGE CHIPMAN.

HON. WARD CHIPMAN graduated at Harvard College, 1770, grandson of Rev. John Chipman of Beverly, and son of John C., Esq., of Marblehead. Mr. Chipman studied law in company with Jonathan Sewall and Thomas Aston Coffin, (a cousin of Sir Isaac Coffin,) afterward secretary of Sir Guy Carleton, and in 1784 commissary-general at Quebec. Mr. Chipman became judge of the supreme judicial court of New Brunswick, and died at Fredericton, February 9, 1824. He was brother-in-law of the late Hon. William Gray, and retained an affection for New England, though an exile. His son, of the same name, and successor to his station and honors, was the most conspicuous member of the class which graduated at Harvard College, in 1805.

COL. MURRAY.

COL. JOHN MURRAY was a representative of influence in the assembly of Massachusetts for many years from Rutland. Daniel Bliss, Esq. married one of his daughters, the other the Hon. Joshua Upham, aid to Sir Guy Carleton, afterward judge of supreme court, Brunswick. His son Daniel graduated at Harvard College 1771; a mandamus counsellor, was a major of dragoons, proscribed in 1778; lived on half-pay 1830. His son Samuel graduated at Harvard College 1772, acccompanied the British troops to Lexington in 1775, and died before 1785; he was proscribed in 1778.

BENJAMIN FANEUIL.

BENJAMIN FANEUIL, Esq., a merchant of Boston, and with Joshua Winslow, consignee of one-third of the East India Company's tea destroyed in 1773; was a refugee to Halifax, afterwards in England.

JAMES BOUTINEAU.

JAMES BOUTINEAU, Esq., attorney of Boston, father-in-law of John Robinson, commissioner of customs, who made the personal attack on James Otis, Esq., which produced so great a derangement of mind in the latter, as to lead to his withdrawal from the public service.

CAPT. FENTON.

CAPT. JOHN FENTON, expelled, being a loyalist, from the assembly of New Hampshire, July, 1775, on which account he expressed himself freely as to public measures. This enraged the populace, and he fled to the governor for protection; they placed a mounted field-piece before the door, threatening to discharge it, when he was delivered up and sent to Exeter for trial. Gov. Wentworth upon this took refuge in the fort.

Capt. Fenton had been a captain in the navy, but sold out his commission; he was permitted to retreat to England.

JOHN ERVING, JUN.

COL. JOHN ERVING, son of Hon. John E., of Boston, graduated at Harvard College, 1747, was colonel of the Boston regiment of militia, a warden of Trinity church, a mandamus counsellor in 1774, a refugee, proscribed in 1778, died at Bath, England, June 17, 1816, aged eighty-nine. He married a daughter of Gov. Shirley; his son, Dr. Shirley Erving, entered Harvard College in 1773, but his education was cut short by the Revolution; he became a respectable physician at Portland, Me., and died at Boston, July 7, 1813, aged fifty.five. The widow of Dr. Erving is still living at Boston, aged eighty-two. She has two sons and one daughter; the latter the wife of Rev. B. C. C. Parker, of the Episcopal church.

JONATHAN SIMPSON.

JONATHAN SIMPSON graduated at Harvard College, 1772, son-in-law to John Borland, Cambridge; was a refugee, proscribed in 1778; was a commissary of provisions in the British army, at Charleston, S. C.; closed his days at Boston, December 7, 1804, aged eighty-two.

RICHARD ROUTH.

HON. RICHARD ROUTH was collector of the customs at Salem; married Abigail, a daughter of Wm. Eppes, Esq., Virginia, (a granddaughter of Col. Benjamin Pickman, of Salem.)   At the death of Mr. Eppes, which soon after occurred, his widow married Dr. Sylvester Gardner of Boston.   Mr. Routh became a refugee, and was collector of the customs for the island of Newfoundland, and subsequently its chief justice ; he died in 1801.   His son, Sir Randolph Isham Routh, is commissary-general to the British army in Canada ; another son, H. L. Routh, Esq., is a merchant of high character in New-York ; others are engaged in commerce in different parts of Europe.

DR. BYLES.

REV. MATHER BYLES, son of the Rev. Mather Byles, D. D., graduated at Harvard College, 1751, was minister at New London, Conn., the desk of which was closed to him in 1768 ; he was then an Episcopal minister of Boston till the Revolution, when he was a refugee, and proscribed in the act of 1788.   He died a rector at St. John's, New Brunswick, in March, 1814.

The father of the Rev. Dr. Byles was a distinguished minister and loyalist of Boston ; and for his political principles was, during the violent times of 1777, separated from his people, to whom he was never afterwards united.   In 1776, he was denounced in town meeting as inimical to his country, and obliged to enter into bonds for his appearance at a public trial before a special court, at which he was pronounced guilty, and sentenced to confinement on board a guard ship, and in forty days to be sent to England with his family.   When brought before the board of war, by whom he was treated respectfully, his sentence seems to have been altered, and it was directed that he should be confined to his own house, and there guarded.   After a few weeks the guard was removed ; a short time after, a guard was again placed over him, and again dismissed. Upon this occasion he observed, in his own manner, that " *he was guarded, reguarded, and disregarded.*"   The substance of the charges against him was, that he continued in Boston with his family during the siege ; that he prayed for the king, and the safety of the town.   He died July 5, 1788, aged eighty-two.   Dr. Byles's first wife was a niece of Gov. Belcher, and his second, the daughter of Lieutenant Governor Tailer.   His literary mer t introduced him to the acquaintance of many men of genius in England ;

the names of Pope, Lansdown, and Watts are found among his correspondents. Pope sent him a copy of his Odyssey in quarto, and from Dr. Watts he received copies of his works as he published them.

Mr. Mather Brown, afterwards artist to the king, a grandson of Dr. Byles, embarked for Europe in 1780, with a letter of introduction from his grandfather to Harrison Gray, Esq., London, a firm friend of the family.

Mr. Copley had likewise been intimate with Dr. Byles before he left Boston. An amusing little circumstance took place the morning after the birth of Mather Brown. Mr. Copley entered the house full of gaiety and animation, and after congratulating the family, requested to see the infant. The nurse brought it; he caught it from her arms and ran down stairs with it; the nurse, not understanding the matter, followed him in great consternation, entreating for the child. When he reached the street door he laid it carefully on the mat, and left the house. It is to this circumstance that the following letter of introduction alludes.

" A certain ancient gentleman in New England dictates the following words :

" *Boston, December* 5, 1780.

" MY DEAR COPLEY :

" Do you forget your old connections ? I am always rejoicing to hear of your reputation and felicities, on your side of the water. You will, I am very certain, be pleased to see the gray-eyed little boy (as you always called him, though his eyes were very black) that you left upon the entry-floor, at New Boston. See how times have turned them ! I may not write, and need not say more to one [on whose friendship I have so firm a reliance." Here the old patriarch leaves off.

" To Mr. Copley, in the solar system."

His intention was first to go to France; and Dr. Byles desired him immediately to call on Dr. Franklin, with whom he was well acquainted. In a letter, dated Paris, 23, 1781, he writes :

" Dr. Franklin has given me a pass, and recommendatory letters to the famous Mr. West. He treats me with the utmost politeness; has given me an invitation to his house, and shown me many new electrical machines and experiments ; one of which, contrived for perpetual motion, greatly pleased me. I delivered him my grandfather's message; he expressed himself with the greatest esteem and affection for him, and has since introduced me at Versailles, as being grandson to one of his most particular friends in America."

In his first letter from London, 1781, he writes:

" In consequence of the recommendation of Dr. Franklin, at Paris, who gave me letters to his fellow-townsman, the famous Mr. West, of Philadelphia, I practise gratis with this gentleman, who affords me every encouragement, as well as Mr. Copley, who is particularly kind to me, welcomed me to his house and lent me his pictures, etc. At my arrival, Mr. Treasurer Gray carried me and introduced me to Lord George Germaine, who promised me his protection during my stay."

In a letter, 1783, he thus wrote: " I have exhibited four pictures in the exhibition ; the king and queen were yesterday there." In 1784: " I have painted several Americans. Yesterday I had two pictures shown to his royal highness the Prince of Wales; they were carried to his palace by his page. He criticised them, and thought them strong likenesses. I believe I never told you that the king knew a picture of mine, in the last exhibition, of the keeper of Windsor Castle, and took particular notice of Mr. Gray's picture; asked who it was, and who did it, and what book he had in his hand. Mr. West told him it was the treasurer of Boston painted by his pupil, a young man, Mr. Brown of America. The king asked what part. He told him Massachusetts."

In 1785, he writes: " Among other great people, I have painted Sir William Pepperell and family, and the Hon. John Adams, ambassador to his Britannic Majesty. On the 20th of June, I had the honor to be introduced to the Duke of Northumberland at his palace ; his grace received me with the utmost politeness."

In a letter, 1786, he writes: " I have near a hundred pictures of my countrymen in my rooms, which are universally known; Messrs. Adams and Jefferson on one side of the room, and on the other, Treasurer Gray and Sir William Pepperell."

It may well be supposed that this intelligence rejoiced the hearts of his relatives in Boston. Dr. Byles added a postscript to one of his daughter Catharine's letters, in these words : " *You will*

*be glad to see your grandfather's hand—my God, bless the lad!—
There you see his heart."*

ROBERT TEMPLE.

ROBERT TEMPLE, ESQ., of Tenhills, near Boston, was an elder brother of Sir John Temple, baronet, the first consul general from England to the United States. Mr. Robert Temple's eldest daughter married the Hon. Hans Blackwood, afterwards Lord Duffrin; the second Temple Emmet, Esq., and youngest died single. Mr. Temple died in England before 1783, and his death is noticed in the "list of exiles who died during the Revolution," published in the American Quarterly Review, 1841.

SAMUEL H. SPARHAWK.

SAMUEL HIRST SPARHAWK, graduated at Harvard College 1771, an addresser of Gov. Gage, and a refugee to England with his brothers Nathaniel and William, was the third son of Col. Nathaniel Sparhawk of Kittery, who married the only child of Sir William Pepperell, baronet, the hero of Louisburg in 1745. Mr. Sparhawk's brother William became heir to the estate and honors of his grandfather, having been created a baronet in 1774. The former died in Kittery, August 29, 1789, aged 38.

STEPHEN GREENLEAF.

STEPHEN GREENLEAF, of Boston, an addresser of Gov. Hutchinson, May, 1774, and of Gov. Gage, in October, 1775. Was sheriff of Suffolk county. He died Jan. 26, 1795.

COUNT RUMFORD.

SIR BENJAMIN THOMPSON (Count Rumford) was born in Woburn, Massachusetts, in 1752, and while a clerk in the employment of Mr. John Appleton, merchant of Salem, first displayed his fondness for experimental philosophy, (when accidentally his face was somewhat marked by a pyrotechnical explosion,) in which he was afterwards a proficient under the professor of natural philosophy at Cambridge, and became a teacher. He made an advantageous marriage, and became a major of militia; was instrumental in preserving the library and philosophical apparatus when the colleges were converted into barracks; as a loyalist he rendered important services to the British generals, and was received by Lord George Germaine as under secretary in the office for colonial affairs. Towards the close of the war he was sent to New-York, and raised a regiment of dragoons, of which he was the colonel. He commanded at Huntington, Long Island, in 1782–3, where he caused a fort to be erected in the church-yard, contrary to the wishes of the inhabitants. He returned to England in 1784, and received the honors of knighthood and became under-secretary of state. Subsequently, recommended by the prince of Deux Ponts (afterwards king of Bavaria), he entered the service of the reigning elector palatine and duke of Bavaria, where he effected many useful reforms, civil and military; among them a scheme for the suppression of mendicity, which he carried into execution at Munich and other places, providing labor for able-bodied paupers, and exciting a spirit of industry among the poorer classes of people, for which he was rewarded by the sovereign of Bavaria with the commission of a lieut. general, several orders of knighthood, and created Count Rumford. He returned to England in 1799, and employed himself in making experiments on the nature and application of heat and other subjects of economical and philosophical research. He suggested the plan and assisted in the foundation of the Royal Institution. In 1802 he removed to Paris, and his wife being dead, he married the widow of the celebrated Lavoisier. He purchased a country house at Auteuil, about four miles from Paris, and embellished the grounds. He died there in August, 1814, leaving only a daughter, the offspring of his first marriage in the United States. Besides a great number of communications in scientific journals, he published four volumes of essays, political, economical, experimental, and philosophical. In 1796 he remitted five thousand dollars in three per cent. stocks, to the American Academy of Arts and Sciences; the income to be appropriated as a premium to the author of the most important discovery on light and heat. By his last will he laid the foundation of that professorship to Harvard University, which has rendered his name justly esteemed with its friends. His useful and eventful life has been the subject of faithful history. He bequeathed an annuity of one thousand dollars, and the reversion of another of four hundred dollars, also the reversion of his whole estate, which amounted to upwards of twenty-six thousand dollars, "for the purpose of founding a new institution and professorship, in order to teach by regular courses of academical and public lectures, accompanied with proper experiments, the utility of the physical and mathematical sciences for the improvement of the useful arts, and for the extension of the industry, prosperity, happiness and well-being of society."

THOMAS HUTCHINSON, JUN.

THOMAS HUTCHINSON, Esq., eldest son of Gov. Hutchinson, a merchant of Boston, and, with his brother Elisha, a consignee of a third of the East India Company's tea which was destroyed. He was a refugee, and proscribed in the act of 1778. He had been denounced in 1769, as a foreign importer, contrary to the agreement of the Boston merchants. He had been a judge of the common pleas for Suffolk, from 1772 to the commencement of the Revolution. He died at Heavitree, near Exeter, England, in 1811, aged 81.

WILLIAM CLARK.

REV. WILLIAM CLARK, son of Rev. Peter Clark, of Salem village (Danvers,) graduated at Harvard College 1759; was the Episcopal minister of Quincy, from 1768 to 1777, when, in consequence of aiding two distressed loyalists to an asylum, he was prosecuted as unpatriotic. Being forcibly taken before the revolutionary tribunal at Boston, and refusing to swear allegiance to the commonwealth, he was condemned to be transported to foreign parts, and was immediately confined to a prison ship in the harbor. By the efforts of Dr. Ames, a zealous whig, in his behalf, he was liberated, after losing his health and speech. He went to England, obtained a pension, and died Nov. 4, 1815.

FRANCIS GREENE.

FRANCIS GREENE, Esq. of Boston, a merchant; graduated at Harvard College 1760; a refugee, proscribed in the act of 1777; married a widow lady, by which he became step-father to two deaf and dumb children, and his interest in them made him an author; ("Essay on imparting Speech to the Deaf and Dumb," London, 1783.) Some changes in the funds reduced his property, and in his last days he was dependent on his half pay as a British officer, having been at the capture of Havana in 1762. He died at his residence, Medford, April 21, 1809, aged 67.

For the share he had in the farewell address to Gov. Hutchinson, he was beset when travelling in July, 1774, through Norwich and Windham, Connecticut.

COL. BORLAND.

JOHN LINDALL BORLAND, eldest son of John Borland, of Cambridge, took to the profession of arms, after having graduated at Harvard College, 1772; and at his death in England, Nov. 16, 1825, he is styled a lieut. colonel of his majesty's forces. Dr. Francis Borland, second son of J. Borland, Esq., of Cambridge, graduated at Harvard College, 1774, was a physician in Portsmouth, N. H., a few years; died at Somerset, Bristol Co., Mass., 1826.

COL. BROWNE.

HON. WILLIAM BROWNE, governor of Bermuda, son of Samuel Browne, Esq., of Salem, and a grandson of Gov. Burnet, graduated at Harvard College in 1755. He was colonel of the Essex regiment, and succeeded Judge Ropes on the bench of the supreme court in 1774, for a short time. The provincial assembly urging their title to nominate to judicial and civil trusts, he was requested to resign that office, held under the royal seal, as also the honor of mandamus counsellor, to which he had been called by a county committee, which he contrived to evade. He was one of the seventeen " *rescinders*" in 1768. In the several capacities of representative, colonel, counsellor and judge, he rendered himself obnoxious by adhering to government; which was thus incidentally noticed in a newspaper, when he found it expedient to take refuge in Boston in the autumn of 1774 :

" Agreeable to the advice of the respectable provincial congress, the training band company of Lynn, being part of the first regiment in the county of Essex, formerly commanded by William Browne, Esq., (*politically deceased of a pestilent and mortal disorder, and now buried in the ignominious ruins of Boston,*) met on Monday, the 15th inst., for the purpose of choosing, etc. etc."

Col. Browne was esteemed among the most opulent and benevolent individuals of that province prior to the Revolution; and so great was his popularity, that the gubernatorial chair was offered him by the " *Committee of Safety*" as an inducement for him to remain and join the " *sons of liberty*." But he felt it a duty to adhere to government, even at the expense of his great landed estate, both in Massachusetts and Connecticut, the latter comprising fourteen valuable farms, all which were afterwards confiscated. He went to England viâ Halifax, in April, 1776, and was governor of Bermuda from 1781 to 1790, when he returned to England, where he died in Percy-street, Westminster, Feb. 13, 1802, aged 65. Col. Browne married his cousin, a daughter of Gov. Wanton, of Rhode Island, and was doubly connected with the Winthrop family; the wives of the elder Browne and Gov. Wanton being daughters of John Winthrop, F. R. S. great-grandson of the first governor of Massachusetts, who graduated at Harvard College in 1700. Col. Browne's son William was an officer in the British service at the siege of Gibraltar in 1784.

JUDGE SMITH.

Hon. William Smith, chief justice of the province of New-York, (his father of the same name, was an eminent lawyer and judge of New-York supreme court, died 22d Nov. 1769, aged 73,) was graduated at Yale College, 1745; was a loyalist in the Revolution, and subsequently became chief justice of Canada. In 1757, he published a history of the province of New-York to 1732, to which the New-York Historical Society published a posthumous continuation to 1762. Governeur Morris studied law with him, as did also many other distinguished men.

GOV. WENTWORTH.

Sir John Wentworth, Baronet, governor of New Hampshire, was born in 1736; graduated at Harvard College in 1755; was a son of Mark Hunking Wentworth, and nephew of Benning Wentworth, who was his immediate predecessor in the gubernatorial chair. He was appointed to that office in 1767, and filled it to the satisfaction of all parties, till the commencement of the Revolution in 1775, when, being a loyalist, he took refuge on board a man-of-war in July, for Nova Scotia, and was appointed lieut.

governor in 1792.   Soon after he went to England and was created a baronet, and was succeeded by Prevost of New Brunswick in 1808.   He possessed a sound judgment, liberal views, and a highly cultivated taste.   He was the friend of learning and learned men.   Dartmouth College was established during his administration, and flourished under his patronage.   He always endeavored to promote the interest of the province, and through his influence its settlements rapidly increased.   He exerted himself to preserve the union between this country and Great Britain, but was obliged to yield to the spirit of the times, and submit to a separation.   He greatly promoted agricultural improvements.   He erected a splendid mansion on his farm at Wolfsborough, on the border of Lake Winnipiseogee.   He died at Halifax, April 8, 1820, aged 83.   He married the widow of Theodore Atkinson, jr., whose maiden name was Frances Deering, in 1769.   Portraits of Sir John and Lady Frances are preserved at Portsmouth, New Hampshire.

JUDGE INGERSOLL.

Hon. Jared Ingersoll, a judge of admiralty, was born in Milford, Connecticut, in 1722, and graduated at Yale College in 1742; settled as a lawyer in New Haven, and in 1757 was agent for the colony in England.   He was appointed a distributor of stamps for Connecticut under the famous stamp act, and thereby lost his popularity; the people compelled him to resign, August 24, 1765, which was soon after his return from England, but not deeming his resignation sufficiently explicit, a large number from the eastern part of Connecticut set off for New Haven, and meeting Mr. Ingersol at Weathersfield, compelled him to renounce the office and cry out "*Liberty and property.*"   The next day five hundred men escorted him to Hartford.

On being appointed admiralty judge for the middle district, about the year 1770, he removed to Philadelphia.   In consequence of the Revolution he returned to New Haven, and died in August, 1781, in his 60th year.

ELISHA HUTCHINSON.

Elisha Hutchinson, Esq., second son of Gov. Hutchinson, graduated at Harvard College 1762.   He was in company with his eldest brother Thomas consignee of one third of the East India Company's tea, destroyed at Boston in 1773. He went to England a refugee, in 1775; was proscribed in the banishment act of 1778, and resided in England till his death, which took place at the house of his son, Rev. John Hutchinson, Blurton parsonage, Trentham, Suffolk, in 1824, at the age of 81.

His brother William Sanford Hutchinson, died of consumption in England, Feb. 20, 1780, aged 28.

WILLIAM HUTCHINSON.

WILLIAM HUTCHINSON, Esq., nephew of Gov. Hutchinson, graduated at Harvard College in 1762; was a refugee in 1775; and died Feb. 6, 1791, in Europe, aged 57. He was a king's counsellor at the Bahamas.

JOHN S. COPLEY.

JOHN SINGLETON COPLEY, Esq., a distinguished historical painter, was born at Boston. His mother was a daughter of Gen. Winslow, and his sister the wife of Col. Henry Bromfield, who resided in London, 1775. He married a daughter of Richard Clarke, Esq., one of the consignees of the East India Company's tea; and being an addresser of Gov. Hutchinson, was early a refugee loyalist. Mr. Copley visited Italy in 1774, and joined his wife and children in England in 1776. He resumed his profession in the metropolis with unsurpassed success. His "Death of Chatham," " Defence of Gibraltar," and " Charles I. in the House of Commons," placed him among the first artists of the age. He died in the full exercise of his talent, suddenly, in 1815. Many of his superb portraits adorn the mansions and galleries of Massachusetts. His only surviving son, Lord Lyndhurst, as distinguished in the legal profession as his father was as an artist, was born in Boston in 1772, and graduated at Trinity College, Cambridge, where he distinguished himself, winning many prizes. In 1816 he was elected to parliament. In 1819 became solicitor-general; in 1826, on the death of Lord Gifford, master of the rolls, and in 1827 lord high chancellor of England, which honorable post he at present holds for the third time; all of which offices he has filled with distinguished ability. He was raised to the peerage in 1827, and his armorial motto, "*ultra pergere*," may well apply to his former career. A sister of Lord Lyndhurst married Gardner Greene, Esq. of Boston.

REV. S. A. PETERS.

Samuel A. Peters, D. D., an Episcopal clergyman, of Hebron, Connecticut, where he was born, December 12, 1735. He graduated at Yale College 1757. In consequence of loyal principles he was dismissed in 1774 from his charge of the churches at Hebron and Hartford, and went a refugee to England. He remained abroad until 1805, when he returned to New-York. In 1817 and 1818, he made a journey to the west as far as the falls of St. Anthony, claiming a large territory under an Indian grant to Capt. Jonathan Carver. He is the reputed author of a History of Connecticut, published at London, in 1781. It is of a similar stamp with Knickerbocker's History of New-York, and does but little credit to its author. Dr. Peters would never acknowledge the paternity of this work, but the fact is now well established. He died at New-York, April 19, 1826, aged ninety. His remains were entombed at Hebron. Dr. Peters was chosen bishop of Vermont, while in England, but did not accept the charge.

He left one daughter, who accompanied him in exile, and married Mr. Jarvis, afterwards secretary of the province of Upper Canada; she is now living at Queenstown. Dr. Peters also left a son, who died of yellow fever at New Orleans, where the eldest son of the latter now resides.

TIMOTHY ORNE.

Timothy Orne, Esq., of Salem, graduated at Harvard College in 1768; became a merchant, and married a daughter of William Pynchon, Esq. He died before 1791.

MAJOR HAWLEY.

Joseph Hawley, of Northampton, Massachusetts, was born in 1724, was graduated at Yale College, and possessed strong natural powers, improved by the study and practice of the law. He early embarked in political life, and retired from the assembly in 1776, with an influence seldom equalled, obtained not less by his great talents than his unsullied and unimpeachable integrity. His opinions were followed almost implicitly, and the leaders in the assembly despaired of carrying any measure to which he was opposed. At a time when the distresses of the war had produced disaffection, and a faction was organized in the western part of Massachusetts, in almost open resistance to the constituted authorities, he induced nearly all to sign a humble petition to government, praying for an act of indemnity for the past, and promising future obedience.

Major Hawley declined all honors and employment when his popularity was at the highest, and thus formed an example of those public spirited, generous citizens, (ready to share the peril and decline the reward,) who illustrate the idea of a commonwealth, and who, through the obstruction of human passions and infirmities, being of rare occurrence, will always be the most admired and noble ornaments of a free government.

He was certainly a great man, and a thoroughly upright one; a disinterested patriot whose feelings and convictions were in behalf of freedom. He closed his earthly career at Northampton, in 1788, at the age of sixty-four.

R. CLARK.

RICHARD CLARK, Esq., of Boston, graduated at Harvard College in 1729, became an eminent merchant, and, with his sons, was consignee of a third of the East India Company's tea destroyed in Boston in 1773, on which account his house in School-street was assaulted. Went to London, where he arrived December 24, 1775. Was proscribed in the banishment act of the assembly of Massachusetts, October, 1778. He was one of the addressers of Gov. Gage on his departure from Massachusetts. He resided in London till his death, at the house of his son-in-law, John Singleton Copley, February 27, 1795. Mr. Clark was a pall-bearer at Gov. Hutchinson's funeral in 1780. Jonathan, his son and partner, who accompanied his father, returned to America after the peace, and resided in Canada.

T. FLUCKER.

THOMAS FLUCKER, Esq., secretary of Massachusetts 1771, on the promotion of Mr. Oliver to be lieutenant governor; was a refugee, and passed his remaining days in London, where he died, February 16, 1783. His son Thomas graduated at Harvard College, 1773, was a lieutenant in the 60th British regiment. His daughter was the wife of Maj. Gen. Henry Knox, of the revolutionary army, and afterwards secretary at war.

S. SEWALL.

SAMUEL SEWALL, Esq., the friend of Attorney General Jonathan Sewall, in exile, was a great-grandson of Ch. Justice Samuel Sewall, and grandson of Samuel Sewall, Esq., of Brookline, who married Rebecca Dudley, a daughter of the governor. His father was Henry Sewall, Esq., of Brookline; a gentleman much respected, who died there in 1771, aged fifty-two years. This son Samuel, born December 31, 1745, graduated at Harvard College 1761, lived unmarried a counsellor at law in Boston; was an " addresser" of Gov. Hutchinson and Gov. Gage; left for England in 1775, was proscribed in the banishment act of September, 1778 ; passed the remainder of his life in England, and died at Bristol, May 6, 1811, aged sixty-six years. His large estate in Brookline, inherited in right of his mother, was forfeited.

HARRISON GRAY.

HARRISON GRAY, Esq., receiver-general of Massachusetts, was born at Boston, and bred a merchant. His patrimonial inheritance, aided by industry, enabled him to acquire a handsome fortune. In June, 1753, he was chosen treasurer of the province by the general court, and continued in that office till October, 1774. He adhered to government from the beginning of the controversy, but the moderation of his conduct, his superior fitness for the office, and the confidence in his integrity, secured him public favor through the stormy period which commenced soon after his first election, and continued until his appointment to and acceptance of the office of mandamus counsellor in 1774. But this was an unpardonable offence in the eyes of the sons of liberty. It was, however, unsolicited, unexpected, and accepted with great reluctance, being strenuously pressed upon him by the leaders of the loyalist party ; and as most of those who had been appointed his colleagues, living in the country, were compelled by popular excitement to decline the office, he was led to believe that residing in Boston, then garrisoned by an army, he had no such apology for shrinking from the service, aad accordingly sacrificed inclination to 'a conscientious sense of duty.   In October, 1774, the royal government being ended in fact, the provincial congress resolved, " *that no more taxes be paid to him,*" and soon after made choice of Henry Gardner for his successor.   This authority he could not be expected to recognise ; he therefore retained the books and files at his office, till the evacuation by the British troops, and then left them in exemplary order ; they are still in the public archives of Massachusetts, and show the model of a faithful state treasurer.   He might perhaps have been justified in retaining a lien upon these as a security against loss and damage to a very valuable real and personal estate which he left, and which was soon after confiscated ; but his high sense of official duty forbade his recourse to any such precaution, and he withdrew from a country which he loved not less than did those who stayed at home, taking nothing which belonged to the public ; but being himself a creditor to many of the principal persons among the sons of liberty, at the head of whom was *John Hancock,* who owed him a large sum for borrowed money, no part of which would he pay in his lifetime, and of which a small part only was received from his executors.   When the British fleet retired from Boston, Mr. Gray, urged by a sense of duty, with the male members of his family tore himself away from his adored and only daughter, Mrs. S. A. Otis, and went to England, where he lived to a great age upon a small pension from the British government.

Perhaps no man among the many excellent persons who went into exile at that time, was more beloved and regretted by his political enemies; for a more genuine model of *nature's* nobleman never lived.

J. FISHER.

JOHN FISHER, Esq,, collector of Salem in 1768, a brother-in-law of Gov. Wentworth, of New Hampshire ; a refugee, he was employed as secretary to Lord George Germaine, the American secretary, on the departure of Mr. Thompson (Count Rumford) to America, in which office he was succeeded by Mr. Adam Woolridge in 1781.

E. OXNARD.

EDWARD OXNARD, Esq., graduated at Harvard College in 1767; afterwards a merchant at Falmouth, (Portland,) Maine, and a temporary reader at the Episcopal church at that place, from the departure of Mr. Wiswall in May, 1775, to the burning of the town. He was a refugee during the contest; was proscribed in the banishment act in 1778, and returned at the close of the Revolution, and again embarked in commercial pursuits. He died July 2, 1803.

JUDGE BLISS.

HON. JONATHAN BLISS was born at Springfield, which he represented in the assembly of Massachusetts. He graduated at Harvard College in 1763, and attended Lord Percy to Concord on the 19th April, 1775; was a proscribed refugee by the banishment act of 1778 ; he had been one of the "*rescinders*" in Gov. Bernard's administration. He married a daughter of Col. John Worthington, of Springfield, a loyalist; another daughter married the Hon. Fisher Ames. He became chief justice of New Brunswick, his associates, being Ward Chipman, and Edward Winslow, refugees, and sons of Harvard. He died at Fredericton, N. B., 1822, aged eighty years.

GENERAL RUGGLES.

TIMOTHY RUGGLES, born in Rochester, Massachusetts, Oct. 1711, eldest son of Rev. Timothy Ruggles, of that place, graduated at Harvard College, 1732, and soon after commenced the study of the law. He represented his native town in the provincial assembly at the age of twenty-five, and procured the passage of an act still in force, prohibiting sheriffs from filling writs. He practised some years in Rochester, when he removed to Sandwich. His reputation was so great that he was early and frequently employed in the adjoining counties of Barnstable and Bristol, and was the principal antagonist of Col. Otis in causes of importance. He occasionally attended the courts in Worcester early in his professional career. He removed to Hardwick as early as 1763. In 1757 he was appointed judge, and in 1762 chief justice of the common pleas, which he held till the Revolution. He was also surveyor-general of the king's forests, an office of profit, attended with but little labor. Besides professional employment, he was engaged in military and political occupations. In 1756, he was a colonel in the army under Sir William Johnson, in the expedition against Crown Point. In September of the same year, he was next in command to Johnson at the battle of Lake Geerge, where the French army, under Baron Dieskau, met a signal defeat. He was actively engaged in the campaigns of 1756–'57, and in the following year, with the commission of brigadier-general, was under Lord Amherst, and served with him in his expedition against Canada in 1759–'60.

Gen. Ruggles was speaker of the provincial assembly in 1762–'63. In consequence of the grievous exaction of the British government, delegates were chosen by the legislature to meet the delegates from the other colonies at New-York, to seek out some public relief from immediate and threatened evils, by a representation of their sufferings to the king and parliament. Gen. Ruggles was chosen as one of the delegates on the part of Massachusetts, and was president of that celebrated congress of distinguished men from nine of the colonies. At this meeting, October 19, 1765, an address to the king was voted, and certain resolves framed, setting forth the rights of the colonies, and claiming an entire exemption from all taxes, excepting those imposed by the local assemblies. Gen. Ruggles refused his concurrence in the proceedings, for which he was censured by the house of representatives, and was reprimanded by the speaker in his place. Hutchinson says, when he consented to be a delegate, he expected nothing more would be required of him than was expressed in the vote of the assembly, and left the house in order to prepare for his journey; that afterwards, on learning that the house had voted to instruct the delegates to insist upon the exclusive right of the colonies to tax themselves, he determined not to serve, but was finally prevailed with by his friends. In 1774, he was made mandamus counsellor, accepted and was qualified. Continuing firm in his adherence to the loyalist party, with whom were all his predilections, he was compelled to leave the country, and all his large estates were confiscated. He remained in Boston during the siege; afterwards spent a few months on Long Island, and then went to Nova Scotia, where he died in 1798, aged 87. Few in the province were more distinguished, and few more severely dealt with in the bitter controversies preceding the Revolution ; as a military officer he was distinguished for cool bravery and excellent judgment and science in the art of war, and no provincial officer was held in higher esteem for those qualities. His appearance was commanding and dignified, being much above the common size ; his wit ready and brilliant; his mind clear, comprehensive and penetrating; his judgment was profound, and his knowledge extensive. His abilities as a public speaker placed him among the first of his day ; and had he been so fortunate as to embrace the popular sentiments of the times, there is no doubt he would have been ranked among the leading characters of the Revolution.

D. OLIVER.

DANIEL OLIVER, Esq., son of Chief Justice Peter Oliver, a learned and accomplished lawyer of Worcester county, graduated at Harvard College ih 1762. A refugee loyalist of the Revolution, he died at Ashted, Warwickshire, May 6, 1826, aged 82. His father was an antiquarian, and copied with his own hand Hubbard's manuscript History of New England, which the son refused the loan of to the Massachusetts Historical Society for publication in their Collections.

MAJOR BRATTLE.

THOMAS BRATTLE, graduated at Harvard College in 1760 ; an absentee, proscribed in the act of 1778 ; long after his return from England, he remained at Newport, R. I., his fate being in suspense. He finally recovered his confiscated house and grounds at Cambridge ; he died Feb. 7, 1801, aged 59.

SAMUEL PORTER.

SAMUEL PORTER, Esq., an eminent attorney at law, of Salem, Massachusetts; graduated at Harvard College in 1763; an addresser of Gov. Hutchinson in 1774, and a refugee to England ; was proscribed in the banishment act of 1778, and died in London, June, 1798.

DR. AUCHMUTY.

Rev. Samuel Auchmuty, D. D., brother of Robert Auchmuty, Esq., of Boston, graduated at Harvard College in 1742 ; was rector of Trinity church, New-York. The degree of D. D. was conferred on him by Oxford University ; he died March 3, 1777. His son, Sir Samuel Auchmuty, G. C. B., a lieut. general in the British army, died in 1822.

JUDGE AUCHMUTY.

Hon. Robert Auchmuty, of Boston, judge of the admiralty court in 1768 ; was a brother of the Rev. Dr. Samuel Auchmuty, rector of Trinity church, New-York, who died in 1777. Their father was also a judge of the admiralty court. The son appeared once after his appointment, says Eliot, in defence of Captain Preston and his soldiers, and his argument was described as so memorable and persuasive, " as almost to bear down the tide of prejudice against him, though it never swelled to a higher flood." He was a zealous loyalist, and died in England ; he wrote some of the obnoxious letters to Mr. Whately, surreptitiously obtained with those of the governor and others.

REV. J. TROUTBECK.

John Troutbeck was assistant minister at King's chapel, Boston ; a refugee, he died in exile some time before November, 1783.

DR. OLIVER.

Peter Oliver, of Salem, third son of Lieut. Governor Andrew Oliver, a refugee, was driven into Boston in 1775 ; signed the address to Gov. Gage ; died in London, April 4, 1795 ; surgeon in the British army. His widow, (daughter of Col. Peter Frye), was afterwards married to Admiral Sir John Knight, and died at her seat at Camberwell near London.

REV. J. WISWALL.

John Wiswall, son of the grammar school master of Boston of the same name, graduated at Harvard College in 1749, and was the first minister of the first Episcopal church at Portland, Maine, in 1764. When Capt. Mowatt's little squadron lay in the harbor, April, 1775, to which the town (then called Falmouth) shortly after owed its destruction, Mr. Wiswall's intimacy as well as that of some other citizens with its officers, procured his arrest and close examination by the committee of safety. In May he left his people and the place, and never returned. He was proscribed in the banishment act of 1778. Mr. Wiswall was a curate at Oxford, in 1781. After the peace he came to Nova Scotia, and was induced at their urgent request to take charge of a portion of his former flock, with other emigrants from the United States gathered at Cornwallis in that province.

COLONEL PICKMAN.

BENJAMIN PICKMAN, Esq. was born at Salem in 1740; graduated at Harvard College in 1759. He was a merchant in early life, a representative of the provincial assembly, and commandant of the first regiment of Essex county. He did not take a popular view of the subject of revolution, but left the country at the commencement of it, and consequently was proscribed, and his estate included in the confiscation act; but after his return from England a portion of it was recovered, not however without much difficulty. Col. Pickman married a daughter of Dr. Toppan of Boston, and died at his native place in April, 1819, aged 79. He was a son of the Col. Pickman who died at Salem, in 1773, aged 66; a member of the provincial council and judge of the common pleas, whose sisters married Curwen, Ward, and Ropes, the father of Judge Ropes, and whose brother Samuel was governor of Tortola. The first mentioned Col. Pickman left a number of children. The late Dr. Thomas Pickman, who graduated at Harvard College in 1791, was one, whose first wife was a daughter of Jonathan Haraden, Esq., a distinguished naval commander during the Revolution, on the side of America; and after her death, Miss Palmer, granddaughter of Hon. Joseph Palmer, president of the Massachusetts provincial congress of 1776. William Pickman, Esq., another son, resides in Salem; and Col. Benjamin Pickman, who graduated at Harvard College in 1784, and immediately commenced his travels by the way of England. He married a daughter of Elias Hasket Derby, Esq.; was extensively and successfully engaged in commerce; represented Essex south district in congress; and for several years the county, in the senate of the state. His philanthropy was unbounded, and Salem has sustained a great loss by his removal to Boston, to reside with the widow of his son Col. Benjamin T. Pickman, late president of the senate of Massachusetts;—she is a niece of the Rev. Isaac Smith, so often referred to in the body of this work.

It is a remarkable coincidence, that of four successive generations, the eldest sons bearing the same name have been colonels, and three of them in command of the same regiment. The last mentioned was for several years at Exeter academy, and completed a commercial education in the counting-house of Messrs. P. and H. Le Mesurier and Co., of London, preparatory to establishing himself in mercantile business at Boston. He was an aid-de-camp of Gov. Brooks; and like all his above-mentioned ancestors, possessed a great share of public spirit, and a dignity and elegance of manner rarely attained; his many virtues array themselves before the writer on every recollection of the friend of his youth.

COL. FRYE.

PETER FRYE, Esq., of Salem, was born in Andover, and graduated at Harvard College in 1744. He was a judge of the common pleas and register of probate for Essex county, and colonel of the first regiment. He was for several successive years a representative in the provincial assembly, and was one of the seventeen noted "rescinders" in February, 1768; a term of reproach applied to the minority, whose votes sustained Gov. Bernard in his demand that an obnoxious vote be rescinded, at the Earl of Hillsborough's request. In the event of refusal he was directed to dissolve the assembly. The vote repelling the demand was 92 to 17. Col. Frye adhered to government, and was a refugee in 1775. He married a daughter of Col. Pickman, of Salem. His daughter Love married Dr. Peter Oliver, and afterwards Admiral Sir John Knight, K. C. B., and died at her seat at Camberwell, near London, in 1839. Col. Frye died also at the residence of his daughter, on the 1st of February, 1820, aged 97. He was included among the banished by law in September, 1778.

SAMUEL WATERHOUSE.

SAMUEL WATERHOUSE, Esq., was appointed collector of the customs for Boston, in 1772; a loyalist in 1775; he retreated to Philadelphia soon after the battle of Lexington ; was an absentee, and included in the proscription act of September, 1778.

JUDGE PUTNAM.

HON. JAMES PUTNAM, born in 1725, in the part of Salem now called Danvers, was a relative of the distinguished patriot General Israel Putnam ; he graduated at Harvard College in 1746 ; studied law with Judge Trowbridge, who was ever his friend and associate. He commenced practice at Worcester, where his office was soon thronged with clients, whose confidence he ever retained. He became eminent as a well-read lawyer, skilful in pleading and safe in counsel. He was appointed attorney-general of the province when Jonathan Sewall was raised to the bench of the court of admiralty, and was the last under the provincial government. Putnam was a firm and zealous loyalist, and took refuge in Boston, accompanied the British army to New-York, thence to Halifax, where he embarked for England in 1776.

On the organization of the government of the province of New Brunswick in 1783, he was appointed a member of his majesty's counsel, and a judge of the superior court. He resided in the city of St. John's, and continued in office till his death, which occurred 23d Oct., 1789.

He was stern as a judge, but patient and inflexibly just. Reserved in private life, his wit and humor were irresistible. It was said (to Charles S. Putnam, Esq., of Fredericton, a descendant) by a successor on the bench, that he was " *an unerring lawyer, never astray, and I am inclined to think, the best lawyer in North America.*"

DR. RUSSELL.

DR. CHARLES RUSSELL, son of Hon. James Russell, of Charlestown, succeeded to his uncle Judge Chambers Russell's estate at Lincoln ; graduated at Harvard College, 1757 ; married Elizabeth, only child of Col. Henry Vassall, of Cambridge ; sailed for Martinique in April, 1775 ; was proscribed in the Massachusetts banishment act of 1778 ; was a physician at Antigua, where he died in 1780.

JOHN VASSALL.

John Vassall, Esq., Cambridge, graduated at Harvard College 1757 [son of Col. John Vassall, who graduated in 1732]; the noble mansion he built became Washington's head-quarters in 1775–6. He lived in princely style there, but, having taken a very active part to uphold the royal cause in vain, he resigned all to the ravagers; and large estates being still left to him in Jamaica, went with his family to England. His loyalty went so far that he would not use on his arms the family motto, " *sæpe pro rege, semper pro republica.*" Of his four sons, Spencer, the eldest, rose to be a lieut. colonel in his majesty's service, and his gallantry at the assault on Monte Video, where he fell, Feb., 1807, won for him abundant praise.

He was proscribed by the Massachusetts assembly in the banishment act, Sept., 1778; and died at Clifton, England, October 2d, 1797, aged 60, immediately after rising from a hearty dinner. His widow died there, March 31, 1807.

LIEUT. GOV. T. OLIVER.

Hon. Thomas Oliver, the last colonial lieut. governor of Massachusetts, a native of Dorchester, graduated at Harvard College 1753. In 1774 he was made lieut. governor, as well as mandamus counsellor, but his life had been previously so retired, and his habits and tastes so much in unison, as to give some color to the rumor of the day, that *Thomas* had been mistaken for *Peter* (the chief justice) in making out the commission. He is spoken of by the few who remember him, as a model of affability and courtesy. He married a daughter of Col. John Vassall; built and occupied the elegant mansion in Cambridge, long the residence since of Gov. Gerry. Col. Oliver was a refugee, and included in the proscription act of September, 1778. He died at Bristol, England, Nov. 29, 1815, aged 82. He was a man of letters, and lived in the shades of retirement while he was in Europe.

CAPT. POYNTON.

Thomas Poynton, of Salem, Massachusetts. His windows were broken by the mob, because he refused to recant for addressing Gov. Hutchinson; retreated to England in 1775, where he died.

T. DANFORTH.

Thomas Danforth, Esq., son of Judge Danforth, of Cambridge,

where he graduated in 1762; pursued the profession of the law at Charlestown till the Revolution, when he became a refugee. He ended his course in London, April, 1820, where he practised many years in his profession. He was proscribed in the act of Massachusetts, Sept., 1778.

CHIEF JUSTICE OLIVER.

HON. PETER OLIVER, LL. D., chief justice of Massachusetts, and brother of Lieut. Governor Andrew Oliver. Their father was the Hon. Daniel Oliver, of Boston, a member of the council, distinguished alike for his piety, public spirit and philanthropy. Judge Oliver was born in 1713, and graduated at Harvard College in 1730. He was appointed to the supreme bench of the province September 15, 1756. His residence was at Middleborough. On the appeal made to the judges by the general assembly in February, 1774, whether they had received any part of their allowance from the king, he alone of all the judges dared to brave popular sentiment, and answered that he " had accepted the king's bounty, and could not refuse it in future without royal permission." This caused the concentrated weight of indignation to fall upon him. The assembly voted that he had rendered himself obnoxious to the people as an enemy, and immediately presented a petition for his removal. Articles of impeachment for high crimes and misdemeanors were exhibited, which Gov. Hutchinson refused to countenance. The grand jury at Worcester, on the 19th of April following, presented to the court a written refusal to serve under the chief justice, considering it illegal for him to preside until brought to answer to the above-mentioned charges. He became a refugee in 1775, and died at Birmingham, England, in October, 1791, aged 79. His son Peter died at Shrewsbury, England, in 1822, aged 81.

JUDGE RUSSELL.

HON. CHAMBERS RUSSELL, son of Hon. Daniel Russell, of Charlestown, Massachusetts, graduated at Harvard College in 1731. Was a representative from Lincoln in the legislature ; afterwards a judge of the supreme court of Massachusetts, from 1752 to 1761; also a judge of admiralty. He died Nov. 24, 1767, aged 54, in London, whither he went in pursuit of health.

DR. LLOYD.

JAMES LLOYD, M. D., was born at Lloyd's Neck, Long Island, (New-York,) in 1728 ; a son of Henry and grandson of James Lloyd of Boston, who died there in 1693.   At the age of seventeen he removed to Boston, where his two elder brothers were settled; one of them was agent of purchases for the British government, and held the office at the commencement of the Revolution. Here he commenced the study of medicine under Dr. Clarke, and after completing his studies in Paris, he commenced practice in 1752. He was soon after surgeon of the garrison in Castle William in Boston harbor, and was in extensive practice in the town and vicinity, before the arrival of the troops in 1775, under command of Sir William Howe, who sought out and renewed his acquaintance with Dr. Lloyd, his former physician.   Sir William and Earl Percy became his tenants, having rented an adjoining estate (late Gardner Green, Esq.'s) then under his care, belonging to his relative Mr. Vassall.

Immersed in the labors of his profession, and interfering no further in politics than an expression of his sentiments ; not theorizing as to the future, and seeing the country at large generally happy and increasing, it is not surprising that with many other patriotic men, Dr. Lloyd should have thought that the time for final separation from the mother country had not arrived, and that a course less decisive might have procured a redress of grievances without passing through the hazards of a revolution.   Events may have proved the errors of these opinions, but as the results of an honest independence of judgment, they were never disguised by Dr. Lloyd. He was an addresser of Gov. Gage in 1775, and consequently a loyalist, though never molested.   In 1785 he protested against the alteration of the liturgy at King's Chapel, Boston.   He died at Boston in March, 1810, "full of years and full of honors ; an ornament to his profession, an example to his survivors, with the esteem of all who knew him, and the blessing of those ready to perish." He left a daughter, Mrs. Sarah Borland, relict of Leonard Vassall Borland, and a son worthy of such a father, the late Hon. James Lloyd, LL. D., who for many years represented Massachusetts in the senate of the United States.

F. WALDO.

Francis Waldo, second son of General Waldo of Portland, Maine; he was a representative of Falmouth, now Portland, in 1761–2, and the first collector of that port. He graduated at Harvard College in 1747 ; was a refugee in 1775, and died in Kent, England, May 9, 1784.

B. HALLOWELL.

Benjamin Hallowell, Esq., a comptroller of the customs, Boston, but resided at Medford; went to England a refugee ; at the peace returned to America and resided in Canada, where his daughter married Chief Justice Elmsly, and now resides at Toronto, a widow, with her son and daughter.

D. BLISS.

Daniel Bliss, Esq., eldest son of Rev. Samuel Bliss, of Concord, born in 1740; graduated at Harvard College in 1760; studied law with Abel Willard, Esq., and was admitted to the bar May, 1765. He married a daughter of Col. John Murray, of Rutland. He had a high standing at the bar, being well versed in his profession, and enjoying a good reputation as a general scholar, and as a man of high moral and religious principle. He was early imbued with principles favorable to the prerogative; but was never a bitter, nor even a warm partisan. He was urged to join the popular party, but his oath of allegiance awakened scruples of conscience, and his family ties, friendship, and society, gave force to his objections. He repaired to Boston with his family a few days before the commencement of hostilities, and thence with the British troops to Quebec. He was appointed commissary of the army, and for not making use of the facilities and opportunities which the office afforded for speculation, all he got for his honesty was, as he told a friend, to be laughed at by the British officers.

At the close of the war, he settled at Fredericton, New Brunswick, where he sustained the office of chief justice of the inferior court, and resided till the time of his death in 1806. He revisited his native state, and would gladly have spent his days there in the midst of his early associations, but the decree of government was an effectual barrier to it.

He possessed an active and sprightly mind, with great fluency and fascination in conversation. Of his sons, the elder, in the British army, resides in Ireland; the younger, John Murray Bliss, is a distinguished judge in New Brunswick.

COL. UPHAM.

JOSHUA UPHAM, Esq., the son of Dr. Upham, of Brookfield, was born in that town in 1741. He was graduated at Harvard University in 1763,* in a class with several who afterwards acted important parts on the general stage. One of the first woollen factories ever attempted in this country he established in 1768, at Brookfield. On finishing his professional studies, he was admitted to the bar in Worcester, August, 1765. He commenced practice in his native town, and pursued his business with successful assiduity in the courts, till 1776, or the following year. He removed from Brookfield to Boston, where he resided till 1778, and thence to New-York, where he continued during the remainder of the war. While in New-York he was aid-de-camp to Sir Guy Carleton, and before he left the British army, became a colonel of dragoons.

On the organization of the government of the province of New Brunswick, in 1784, Upham, who had been one of the first settlers there, returned to his favorite science, the law. He was appointed judge of the highest court in the province, and sustained the important and responsible duties of his office with industry and ability.

In 1807, he was selected by his brethren on the bench to visit England, for the purpose of obtaining from the government a more perfect organization and arrangement of the judiciary in the British American provinces. He fully succeeded in the object of his appointment, but did not live to return to his country. He died in London in the year 1808.† While in London, he enjoyed the

---

* The late Timothy Pickering was his class-mate and room-mate. Their early friendship survived the bitter and hostile spirit that grew up *inter partes* iu the revolutionary war. On the return of peace, they renewed their correspondence, which is said to have been of an affectionate and delightful character.

† He was buried in the church of Mary-le-bone. Judge Upham was twice married. His first wife was a daughter of Col. Murray of Rutland ; and the second a daughter of Hon. Joshua Chandler, of New-Haven.

friendship of Mr. Palmer, who afterwards bequeathed his valuable library to our university, of Sir John Wentworth, Sir William Pepperell, Lord Dorchester, and Mr. Percival.*

Judge Upham held a high rank as counsellor and advocate; he had a great command of language; not a mere flow of words, but the music and harmony of arrangement and style; the well of English undefiled, and adorned with classical elegance. He possessed, in a remarkable degree, that rare talent, fine powers of conversation, of which Lord Bacon laid down the true rule, and indulged occasionally in a happy vein of satire. With brilliancy and wit,† he united many virtues, and a sound judgment. "The prevailing excellence of his character," to use the words of one who fondly cherishes his memory, "was a benignity of spirit, which seemed to affect the exercises of his intellect, as well as of his affections."

Judge Upham was pleasing in his person and address, while he was imbued with all that grace which comes before education, and which education can hardly bestow. Like Bliss, he was of that peculiar class of the old school of manners, of which, probably, even the youngest among us have seen some surviving specimens.

COL. WILLARD.

Abijah Willard, of that part of Lancaster now called Harvard, Worcester county, Massachusetts, where he was born in 1722; was appointed one of the mandamus counsellors, took refuge at Brooklyn, Long Island, and at the close of the war settled at Lancaster in New Brunswick, where he died, in May, 1789, aged 67. His family returned to Lancaster, Massachusetts, after

* Mr. Percival, then prime minister, a few days before he was assassinated, sent to the son of Judge Upham £100 sterling to assist him in his education. This son is the Rev. Charles W. Upham, now of Salem, Massachusetts, well known by his historical writings.

† Major Garden, in his interesting volume of anecdotes of the war in the southern department, relates an anecdote of Upham that may well be introduced here. The British troops, it will be recollected, were in red, and the American in blue uniforms. "About the period of the final departure of the British from New-York, an excellent repartee made by Major Upham, aid-de-camp to Sir Guy Carleton, to Miss Susan Livingston, has been much cele-

his death. A son and daughter are now living at the homestead; the daughter was the second wife, and is now the widow of the Hon. Benjamin Goodhue, late senator in Congress from Massachusetts. Mr. Willard was in the army in different grades, from the taking of Louisburg to the peace of 1763. He was at the taking of Quebec, where he commanded a regiment, and what is somewhat remarkable, he raised his regiment in thirty days, and was ready to march for the reduction of Canada under Lord Amherst. There were few in his station that did more for his country than he, in civil or military capacity, until 1775, when the troubles with the mother country commenced. He was the first person persecuted for his loyalty in America, which induced him to reside under the British government the remainder of his life. He never bore arms against America; though offered a colonel's commission by Gen. Howe, he refused, saying, " *he would never fight against his country.*" He was commissary to the British troops at New-York, and much ridiculed by the officers for accounting to the government for various items that loose commissaries had habitually appropriated to their own use as perquisites.

ABEL WILLARD.

ABEL WILLARD, Esq., the earliest lawyer in the north part of Worcester county, was the son of Col. Samuel Willard, of Lancaster, who for some years was one of the judges of the court of common pleas. The son was born at Lancaster, Jan. 12, 1732, graduated at Harvard University in 1752, and studied law in Boston, with Benjamin Pratt, the distinguished scholar and jurist, well known at that period. He was admitted to the bar in Worcester, November term, 1755; he at once went into extensive business in his native town, and devoted his time and opportunities to the profession till the period of the Revolution. His talents were quite respectable; he was regarded as a sound jurist, and much reliance

brated. 'In mercy, major,' said Miss Livingston, "use your influence with the commander-in-chief to accelerate the evacuation of the city ; for, among your incarcerated belles, your meschianza princesses, the *scarlet fever* must continue to rage till your departure.' 'I should studiously second your wishes,' replied the major, 'were I not apprehensive that, freed from the prevailing malady, a worse would follow, and that they would be immediately tormented with the *blue devils.*' "

was placed upon his opinion. No one was ever a greater benefactor in the neighborhood in which he lived; instead of fomenting
quarrels, and lending himself to the complaint of every one who
might come to him with a list of grievances, he did all in his power
to check the angry passions of clients, and promote peace. He
would frequently accompany a client to the party complained of,
and succeed in reconciling their differences. Indeed, so far did he
overcome the prejudices of the many, then entertained against the
profession, that he was emphatically termed *the honest lawyer.*
Willard possessed that true modesty that ever marks the ingenuous
mind; and, although of a cast of character approaching somewhat
to timidity, he was full of moral courage, of stern integrity, and
unyielding purity of principle. In his person he was tall and of
good figure. In his disposition he was mild and conciliating, and
his good qualities were marked in his benignant expression.

In September, 1770, he formed a partnership in his profession
with the late Judge Sprague, of Lancaster, which is believed to
have been the earliest connection of the kind in the county of
Worcester. He might have remained in that town in peace and
respect, and indeed with high personal consideration, during the
invading bitterness and the easily adopted suspicions and prejudices of our revolutionary struggle; but, alarmed at the approaching tempest, and with many others believing that it would
overwhelm every thing in its course, he resorted to Boston during
the impending danger, when the character of the contest became
at once fixed, and it was impossible again to pass the dividing line.
He left the country during the war, and died in England, Nov.
1781. His widow* survived him, and died in Boston but a few
years since. Col. Abijah Willard, before noticed, was his brother.

RUFUS CHANDLER.

Rufus Chandler, Esq., the son of Col. John Chandler, was
born at Worcester, May 18, 1747. He was fitted for college by
the Rev. Mr. Harrington, of Lancaster, and graduated at the uni-

---

* A daughter of the late Rev. Daniel Rogers of Littleton; another daughter
was the wife of Samuel Parkman, Esq., of Boston, and Rev. Jonathan New.
hall of Stow.—*Address of J. Willard at Worcester,* 1829.

versity in Cambridge in 1766; he commenced the study of the law with James Putnam, and was admitted to the bar Nov. term, 1768. From that time till the closing of the courts in 1774, he continued in the profession at Worcester. Like most of the influential family of his name, who had had extensive and almost unbounded sway in that county *ab primo origine,* he adhered to the royal party, and left the country during the war. He ever afterwards resided in London as a private gentleman, till his death, October 11th, 1823; he was proscribed by the act of 1778. He was not distinguished for eloquence, nor for great intellectual power, but he held a respectable rank in his profession, and gained much praise in the practical parts of his business; and for his neatness, accuracy, and punctuality as an office lawyer. His fidelity to his clients insured him their esteem, and a very considerable amount of business. Through life he observed the strictest rules of economy, the rather from a regard for such as had a right to his aid, than from any love of money for its own sake. In his personal habits he was remarkably precise; he was *the* nice man; he possessed great moral worth and purity, and a conciliating disposition.*

COMMODORE LORING.

Joshua Loring, of Dorchester, Mass., was one of the five commissioners of the revenue, and proscribed in the act of 1778; his son Benjamin, who graduated at Harvard College in 1772, was an absentee, but not proscribed; his eldest son, Joshua Loring, jr., was an addresser of Gov. Gage, and proscribed in 1778.—Commodore Loring died an exile, in 1781.

ISAAC ROYALL.

Hon. Isaac Royall, of Medford, was remarked by every one for his timidity; he halted between two opinions respecting the Revolution, until the cannonading at Lexington drove him to Newburyport, where he embarked for Europe. He was a proscribed refugee, and his estate, since that of Jacob Tidd, Esq., was confiscated. He died of small pox in England, Oct. 1781. His bounty laid the first professorship of law at Cambridge, and a legacy of plate to the first

* See Mr. Willard's Worcester Address.

church at Medford shows that his regard for his country was not weakened by distance, nor seared by proscription. He bequeathed more than two thousand acres of land in Granby and Royalton, in Worcester county, for the establishment of the aforesaid professorship. He was for twenty-two years a member of the council. His virtues and popularity at first saved his estate, as his name was not included with those of his sons-in-law, Sir William Pepperell and George Erving, in the " conspirators' act,"—but on the representation of the selectmen of Medford, " *that he went voluntarily to our enemies*," his property was forfeited and taken under the confiscation act. He made bequests to Medford and Worcester, and legacies to the clergymen. While a member of the house of representatives, he presented the chandelier which adorns its hall.

SIR T. BERNARD.

SIR THOMAS BERNARD, Bart., D. C. L., third son of Sir Francis, governor of Massachusetts, graduated at Harvard College 1767 ; entered early at Lincoln's Inn, and was called to the bar in 1780 ; made treasurer of the Foundling Hospital 1795. The death of his brother (Sir John) in the West Indies, 1809, devolved a baronetcy upon him. Oxford created him soon after a doctor of the civil law. He was the active and liberal patron of various charities, and author of divers small tracts, the best known of which " *The Comforts of Old Age*," saw a fifth edition (12mo) in 1820. Sir Thomas died at Leamington Spa, Warwickshire, July 1st, 1818.— His sister, Mrs. King, was authoress of a volume entitled " *Scripture Characters of Females.*"

GEORGE ERVING.

GEORGE ERVING, Esq., merchant of Boston, was a refugee included in the conspirators' act ; married previously a daughter of Isaac Royall, Esq., of Medford. He died in London, January 16th, 1806, aged 70.

LORD G. GERMAINE.

LORD GEORGE GERMAINE, afterwards Lord Sackville, was tried by court martial on account of his conduct at the battle of Minden in 1759, and disgraced. To him has been attributed the authorship of

Junius's Letters; but it is hardly possible that an officer who had been publicly pointed at and formally convicted by a court martial as a coward, would pen the following remark of Junius respecting himself: " His character is known and respected in Ireland as much as it is here; and *I know he loves to be stationed in the rear as well as myself.*"

He was secretary of state for the American department during the war of the Revolution, and it is generally admitted that his administration was bad.

In a letter to Lord Howe, on his naval conduct, attributed to Lord Sackville, he says, " Had your lordship and your brother saved the northern army, which you had abundant power to do, the rebellion, then in its infant state, must have been suppressed; the war with France and Spain had not happened; and what is yet of more moment to the peace and safety of the empire, that faction, which is daily distracting the councils of state and wrenching asunder the union of power which is necessary to its safety, would now hide its monstrous head in the dark cells of its own folly and treason."

Gen. Howe had friends in parliament, and Lord George Germaine's orders and instructions were the subject of their philippics; and they were powerful enough to make that minister retire.

SIR W. DRAPER.

SIR WILLIAM DRAPER rendered himself famous by his correspondence with " Junius," in vindication of the character of the Marquis of Granby as commander-in-chief; for although as a writer he was second only to Junius, he was foiled by him, and withdrew from the contest extremely mortified. He soon after left England, arrived at Charleston, S. C., in January, 1769, and travelled towards the north as far as New-York, receiving every attention on his way. At New-York he married Miss De Lancey,* " *a lady of great connections there and agreeable endowments,*" says the London Magazine for 1766. She died in 1778. In 1778 he was appointed Governor of Minorca. He built at Clifton near Bristol a monument of taste, and called it " Manilla House;" and he also erected in College

* Daughter of James De Lancey, chief justice and lieut. governor of New York, who died in 1760.

Green, Bristol, a mausoleum over the remains of his parents, whom he delighted to honor.

SIR WM. PEPPERELL.

SIR WILLIAM PEPPERELL, Bart., son of Col. Nathaniel Sparhawk, of Kittery, and grandson of Sir William Pepperell, Baronet, the hero of Louisburg, whose only daughter was mother of the subject of this notice. He graduated at Harvard College in 1766, and was for many years a member of the council of Massachusetts. After the decease of his grandfather, (who adopted him on the death of his only son Andrew,) he was created successor to his title in October, 1774. He married Elizabeth, daughter of Hon. Isaac Royall, of Medford. He was a refugee, and proscribed in the act of 1778. He died in Dorset-street, Portman-square, Dec. 2, 1816, aged 70, having previously lost lady Pepperell and his only son William. His daughters were married as follows :—Elizabeth to the Rev. Henry Hutton, A. M., of London ; Mary to Sir William Congreve, and Harriet to Sir Charles Thomas Palmer, Bart.—Lady Palmer and Lady Congreve were living in 1832.

On the 16th Nov. 1774, in a county congress, held at Wells, York county, Maine, he was denounced as follows in the fourth resolution passed that day :

" Resolved—Whereas the late Sir Wm. Pepperell, honored and respected in Great Britain and America for his eminent services, did honestly acquire a large and extensive real estate in this county, and gave the highest evidence not only of his being a sincere friend to the rights of man in general, but of having a paternal love to this county in particular ; and whereas the said Sir William, by his last will and testament made his grandson residuary legatee and possessor of the greatest part of said estate, who hath, with purpose to carry into force acts of the British parliament made with apparent design to enslave the free and loyal people of this continent, accepted and now holds a seat in the pretended board of counsellors in this province, as well in direct repeal of the charter thereof as against the solemn compact of kings and the inherent rights of the people. It is therefore resolved, that he hath therefore forfeited the confidence and friendship of all true friends of American liberty, and, with other pretended counsellors now holding their seats in like manner, ought to be detested by all good men : and it is hereby recommended to the good people of this county, that as soon as the present leases made to any of them by him are expired, they immediately withdraw all connection, commerce and dealings from him—and that they take no further lease or conveyance of his farms and mills until he shall resign his seat pretendedly occupied by mandamus. And if any persons shall remain or become his tenants after the expiration of their present leases, we recommend to the good people of this county not only to withdraw all connection and commercial intercourse with them, but to treat them in the manner provided by the third resolve of this congress."

COL. DAVID PHIPS.

COL. DAVID PHIPS, son of Lieutenant Governor Spencer Phips, of Massachusetts, was graduated at Harvard College in 1741; was colonel of the troop of guards in Boston, 1773 ; an addresser of Gov. Hutchinson in 1774, and of Gage in '75; high sheriff of Middlesex county in 1775. Driven into Boston, he went to England, which country he left in April, 1777, for America, with Admiral Montague, and afterwards served under General Knyphausen. His house at Cambridge, afterwards Wm. Winthrop's, was confiscated. He died in England, July 7, 1811, aged eighty-seven, styled in the Gentleman's Magazine " Capt. David Phips, R. N."

His sisters married Andrew Bordman, Judge Joseph Lee, Col. John Vassall, and Richard Lechmere, all magnates of Cambridge.

Several books of the British peerage represent the family of the Marquis of Normanby (Lord Mulgrave) as descended from Sir William Phips, governor of Massachusetts in 1691. This is a manifest error ; Sir William having no children adopted his nephew Spencer Phips, (afterwards lieut. governor of Massachusetts,) father of Col. Phips, the subject of this article. The ancestor of Lord Mulgrave was Sir Constantine Phipps, an eminent London lawyer in the reign of Queen Anne.

JOSEPH GALLOWAY.

JOSEPH GALLOWAY, an eminent lawyer and speaker of the assembly of Pennsylvania ; a member of the first congress, 1774 ; changed sides, and joined the British in New-York in December, 1776;

went to England, and with Gen. Robertson, in 1778, misrepresented the state of the public mind and resources of the provinces.   Col. Trumbull, in a letter to Gov. Trumbull, dated Sept. 12, 1780, says : " Mr. John Temple (afterwards Sir John, consul-general) has been indefatigable in his endeavors to defeat the misrepresentations of Gen. Robertson and Mr. Galloway at the bar of the house of commons, and to convince this country of the impracticability of coercing America.   His acquaintances among the friends of America are the Dukes of Richmond and Rutland, Mr. D. Hartley, Dr. Price, Mr. Burke, etc., who pay great attention to his information." He died in England, 1803, aged seventy-three years, after publishing several works.   Mr. Galloway appeared as an evidence against Gen. Howe, in the house of commons, at the instance of Lord George Germaine ; and Eliot says of Galloway : " Nothing can exceed the perfidy of that satellite of the minister of war, whose own ignorance and gross absurdities were more glaring than Gen. Howe's."

BENJAMIN GRIDLEY.

BENJAMIN GRIDLEY, Esq., graduated at Harvard College, 1751, and practised law at Boston.   He was an addresser of Gov. Gage; proscribed in the act of September, 1778.

E. WILLIAMS.

ELIJAH WILLIAMS, Esq., attorney at law, of Deerfield, Massachusetts, graduated at Harvard College, 1764 ; became an officer in the British army, soon after the affair at Lexington, in April, 1775; returned in the spring of 1784, and received half pay during life.   Died in 1793, aged forty-seven.

J. JACKSON.

HON. JONATHAN JACKSON was treasurer of Harvard College from 1807 to 1810, when he died.   He was much esteemed as a man of talents, integrity, and of amiable and courteous manners.

ADMIRAL WINTHROP.

ROBERT WINTHROP, vice-admiral in the British navy, was the youngest son of John S. Winthrop, Esq., of New-London, Connecticut, where he was born, Sept. 7, 1764. On his father's side, he was a lineal descendant of the early governors of Massachusetts and Connecticut, of the same name ;* his mother was Elizabeth, daughter of William Sherriffe, Esq., of London, whose first husband was Capt. John Hay, of the British army. After the death of his father, young Winthrop, when fourteen years of age, left New-London for New-York under a flag of truce, consigned to the care of a maternal uncle attached to the British force stationed here, by whom a midshipman's warrant was obtained for him in the royal navy. Of his subsequent career the following notice, taken from an English publication,† furnishes an interesting though concise account.

"May 10th, 1832, died at Dover, of paralysis, aged seventy, ROBERT WINTHROP, Esq., vice-admiral of the blue. Mr. Winthrop was a midshipman on board the Formidable, bearing the flag of Sir George B. Rodney, in the memorable battle of April 12, 1782. He was a lieutenant in 1790, and at the conquest of Martinique, in 1794, he commanded a battalion of seamen, attached to Prince Edward's brigade. In the spring of 1796, he commanded the Albicore sloop at the capture of St. Lucia ; and about the same time, he captured near Barbadoes, l'Athenienne, French corvette, of fourteen guns. He was afterwards appointed to the Undaunted frigate, and in that ship had the misfortune to be wrecked, on the Morant Keys, during a heavy gale of wind, August 27, 1796. His post commission bore date Dec. 16, following.

" Captain Winthrop's next appointment was to the Circe, of twenty-eight guns, stationed in the North Sea ; and in June, 1798, he served in the expedition sent against Ostend. Major General Coote, who commanded the army employed on that occasion, has recorded in his despatches, ' the indefatigable exertions and good conduct' of Captain Winthrop, who superintended the landing of the troops. In the summer of 1799, Capt. Winthrop was intrusted

---

* The line of descent was as follows :—1. John Winthrop, first governor of Massachusetts, died in 1649. 2. John Winthrop, jr. governor of Connecticut, d. 1676. 3. Wait S. Winthrop, chief justice of the superior court of Massachusetts, d. 1717. 4. John Winthrop, F. R. S., d. 1747. 5. John S. Winthrop, father of the admiral, d. 1776.

† Gentleman's Magazine. London, 1832.

with the command of a small squadron, employed on the coast of Holland, the boats of which, in the night of the 27th of June, very gallantly cut out twelve sail of merchantmen from the Wadde, without having a man hurt, notwithstanding they were much annoyed by the fire from the enemy's batteries and gun-boats. On the 10th of July, the boats also cut out three more valuable vessels, and burnt another laden with stores.

" In the following month the Circe assisted at the capture of the Helder ; on which occasion all the Dutch ships lying in the Nieuwe Diep, together with the naval magazine at the Nieuwe Werk, containing a large quantity of stores, were taken possession of by Captain Winthrop. This event led to the surrender of the enemy's fleet in the Texel. In October of the same year, Capt. Winthrop's boats, under his own immediate direction, carried off from the port of Delfzel a sloop of war and schooner ; the Lynx of twelve guns, and the Perseus of eight guns.

" In the autumn of 1800, in the expedition against Ferrol, Captain Winthrop commanded the Stag frigate, but which was unfortunately stranded in Vigo bay, on the 6th of September, and was obliged to be destroyed by fire, after the stores had been removed.

" On the renewal of war, after the peace of Amiens, Captain Winthrop obtained the command of the Ardent, a sixty-four gun ship, stationed on the coast of Spain ; where he drove on shore La Bayonnaise, French frigate, of thirty-two guns and two hundred men, from the Havana bound to Ferrol. The crew, to prevent her being taken possession of, set her on fire, by which she was totally destroyed. The Ardent was subsequently employed off Boulogne, under the orders of Lord Keith. From that ship he was removed into the Sybille frigate, about July, 1805, and on the 3d of May, 1807, he captured l'Oiseau, French letter-of-marque. In the ensuing summer, he was appointed to the command of the Dover district of sea-fencibles. He attained the rank of rear-admiral in 1809, and of vice-admiral in 1830.

" Admiral Winthrop married, December 23, 1804, Miss Far-brace, of Dover, by whom he has left a family of two sons and four unmarried daughters."

THOMAS LINDALL WINTHROP.

THOMAS L. WINTHROP, LL. D., half-brother of the preceding, was born at New-London, Conn., March 6, 1760. His mother was the only daughter of Francis Borland, Esq., a merchant of Boston, and granddaughter of Timothy Lindall, Esq., of Salem. Mr. Winthrop began his collegiate course at Yale College, but finished it at Harvard, where he graduated in 1780. Soon after taking his bachelor's degree, he embarked at Nantucket for Amsterdam, in a merchant ship, which was captured on the passage and carried into an English port ; by permission of Admiral Duckworth, however, he was allowed to visit London on his parole, and afterwards travelled in the interior of the country, and on the continent. At the close of the war, he returned to the United States with Commodore Truxton, and engaged in commercial pursuits at Boston, where he continued to reside during the remainder of a long, useful, and not unhonored life.

In 1786, Mr. Winthrop was married to Elizabeth, daughter of Sir John Temple, and granddaughter of Governor Bowdoin. The only son of the latter having no issue to perpetuate the family name, Mr. Winthrop's second son, the late James Bowdoin, of Boston, a gentleman of great personal worth and literary distinction, assumed it by the desire of his uncle, taking with the name a large estate.* Another son of Mr. Winthrop, Hon. Robert C. Winthrop, has recently represented the city of Boston in congress, with distinguished reputation.

In politics Mr. Winthrop belonged to the old republican party ; he was several times elected to the Massachusetts senate, and in 1826, was chosen lieut. governor of the state, by the votes of both political parties, which office he continued to fill by successive annual elections, until his retirement in 1832. He was an active and liberal patron of literary and benevolent institutions, over several of which he presided during the latter part of his life. He was for a long period an officer of the American Academy of Arts and Sciences. At the time of his decease he was president of the American Antiquarian Society, the Massachusetts Historical Society, and the State Agricul-

* Mr. Bowdoin contributed many valuable papers to the Collections of the Mass. Hist. Society, being deeply conversant with the early history of New England.

tural Society ; and the libraries of the two former institutions were greatly indebted to his liberality for many important additions to their historical treasures. Governor Winthrop was also a member of various other learned and economical institutions both in this country and Europe, with some of which he maintained a constant correspondence. Indeed, the greater part of his time for several years before his death was devoted to these objects, and to the promotion of the religious and benevolent enterprises of the day. He died universally beloved for his many virtues, and respected for his public services, at his residence in Boston, on the 22d of Feb., 1841, having nearly completed the eighty-first year of his age.

Governor Winthrop was in his person tall and commanding, and remarkable for the elegance and suavity of his manners ; enjoying an ample fortune, he lived in a style of generous hospitality, and for many years was in the habit of receiving at his table most strangers of consideration who visited the New England metropolis. The members of the state legislature, and of the numerous associations with which he was connected, have reason to remember the liberal character of his hospitable attentions ; and the latter lost in him a munificent patron and benefactor. In his religious opinions he was firm, but catholic and tolerant ; attached to the communion of the Episcopal church, he died as he had lived, a humble and sincere Christian.

N. GORHAM.

Hon. Nathaniel Gorham, born at Charlestown, Mass., 1738, was often a member of the legislature, and in 1784 was elected to congress, of which body he was afterwards president. He was also a judge of the common pleas for several years, and assisted in forming the constitution of the United States, as a member of the convention. His early advantages were only those of a common school, but possessing talents of a high order, he appeared to advantage in company with literary men. He at one time engaged in mercantile pursuits, but left them for public life. In debate he had independence enough to dissent from measures he disapproved, and therefore he did not escape the obloquy of the ignorant, who confounded all moderate men with those who were unfriendly to the cause of liberty. He died in 1796.

DR. APTHORP.

REV. EAST APTHORP, D. D., born in Boston, 1733, educated at Cambridge, England; took orders, returned, and was settled over the church erected under his care at Cambridge, Massachusetts. Here he published a pamphlet in defence of the conduct of the " Society for Propagating the Gospel," which was attacked by Dr. Mayhew, who was answered by Dr. Secker, Archbishop of Canterbury. This controversy rendered his situation irksome, and he left for England. It was thought by many, that the establishment of the Episcopal church at Cambridge was for the purpose of converting the students, who were generally dissenters, and with ulterior views, which excited the most acrimonious jealousy. Dr. Apthorp was afterwards successively vicar of Croydon, and rector of Bow church, London, which he exchanged for the prebendary of Finsbury; he had many friends among the dignitaries of the church, and was generally beloved and respected. He married a daughter of Foster Hutchinson, Esq., brother of Gov. Hutchinson. His only son was a clergyman. His daughters married Dr. Cary and Dr. Butler, heads of colleges, and a son of Dr. Paley.— His sisters were married to Dr. Thomas Bulfinch, of Boston, and Robert Bayard, Esq., of New-York. He published two volumes of Discourses on the Prophecies, delivered at the Warburton lecture, Lincoln's Inn, and a volume in answer to Gibbon. The last twenty-six years of his life he passed at Cambridge, England, with almost total loss of sight; he died April, 1816.

R. WARD.

RICHARD WARD, Esq., of Salem, son of Joshua Ward, one of the justices for Essex county, first appointed on the establishment of republican government in Massachusetts, was born in Salem, April 5, 1741. He ardently espoused the popular cause with his father, and opposed the arbitrary measures of parliament. He was a member of the committee of safety and protection during the entire period of the Revolution, and under direction of Gen. Charles Lee constructed at the neck the fort bearing his name, for the defence of the harbor and town of Salem. He accompanied Col. Pickering with the regiment in which he was a subaltern officer as soon as the Lexington affair was known, to Medford, in order to intercept the enemy, but they were not in season. They also took up the line of march for the heights of Charlestown, on 17th June, but arrived too late to participate in the affair of Bunker Hill.

His commission, dated at Watertown, June 6, 1776, as " *captain of the third company of the first regiment of Essex county, whereof Timothy Pickering, jr., is colonel,*" was granted " *by the major part of the council of the Massachusetts Bay, in New England,*" and by them signed during the interval between colonial and republican government, on paper bearing the impress of the crown and the sign manual of the king, with the colonial seal appended. The following are the signatures attached to it, and of those who signed it, one was afterwards president of the continental congress, and six were governors and lieutenant-governors of Massachusetts :—viz., J. Bowdoin, J. Winthrop, Caleb Cushing, R. Derby, Jr., T. Cushing, B. Lincoln, S. Holten, Jabez Fisher, Moses Gill, B. White, William Phillips, Benjamin Austin, John Whetcomb, Henry Gardner, Daniel Davis, and D. Hopkins. Mr. Ward had married the daughter of George Curwen, in 1762, and owing to her feeble health, the cares of his numerous family devolved upon him ; and its imperative claims, as well as that of their uncle's family, (the author of the foregoing Journal), pressed so heavily that he was obliged, after having served with his regiment commanded by Col. Pickering in New-Jersey, under Washington, in 1777, to retire from the military service of his country. He was for a long period at the head of the town government, and a member of the state legislature, as well as an acting justice of the quorum for Essex county many years. He was from the beginning prominent in the ranks of the anti-federal or old republican party, but never a heated partisan.

Mr. Ward possessed great firmness and equanimity of temper, and his suavity of manners and obliging disposition endeared him to all. He died in November, 1824, in the eighty-fourth year of his age, and a widowed daughter only survives of his large family. Children of his sons, George C., Samuel C., and Richard, are living in different parts of the union.

S. A. OTIS.

Hon. Samuel Allyne Otis, a brother of the Hon. James Otis and General Joseph Otis, was born in 1741, and graduated at Harvard College in 1759. He soon after became a merchant of Boston. In 1776 he was first elected a representative to the general court, and he was also a member of the convention which framed the constitution of Massachusetts. During the Revolution he was a member of the board of war. In 1787, he was one of the commissioners to negotiate with the insurgents of " *Shay's Rebellion.*" He was elected a member of congress in 1788, and after the adoption of the new constitution was secretary to the senate of the United States, which office he filled with scrupulous fidelity and suavity of manner, without being absent from his post a single day during a period of thirty years, and till his death, amidst the collision of party strife, to the entire satisfaction of all. He died at Washington, April 22, 1814, aged seventy-three. Mr. Otis was first married to the only daughter of the Hon. Harrison Gray, receiver-general of Massachusetts, and afterwards to the widow of Edward Gray, Esq. His son, Samuel A. Otis, Esq., died at Newburyport the same year with his father. His other son is the Hon. Harrison Gray Otis, of Boston, long the able and eloquent representative of Massachusetts in the national senate.

S. GARDINER.

Sylvester Gardiner, M. D., was born at Narragansett, Rhode Island, in 1717; commenced the practice of medicine in Boston, by which, and the importation of drugs, he accumulated great wealth; he also inherited an extensive landed estate in Maine. · He married the widow of William Eppes, Esq., of Virginia, who was a daughter of Col. Benjamin Pickman, of Salem, Massachusetts, and died at Poole, England, leaving a son William Eppes, who married a Miss Randolph, of Bristol, England, and whose son is an assistant commissary-general of the British army; a daughter, Love Eppes, who married Sir John Lester, of Poole, and Abigail Eppes, who married Richard Routh, Esq., also a loyalist.

From his high standing and extensive acquaintance, Dr. Gardiner selected his associates from such as were congenial to his taste, and his house was the resort of the literary and scientific

from both sides the Atlantic.   Among his guests were Sir William
Pepperell, Gov. Hutchinson, Earl Percy, Admiral Graves, Majors
Pitcairn and Small, and General Gage.   The Revolution broke up
these associations, and after the siege of Boston he sought shelter
at Halifax, and afterwards in England, where he passed with
heavy heart ten years of exile.   For being a refugee, his large
estate and stores of drugs were confiscated, but owing to some error, his lands in Maine were recovered after his return, at the close
of the war.   He closed his eventful life at Newport, Rhode Island,
August 8, 1786, in his 69th year.   The following tribute is inscribed
on a monument erected to his memory at Gardiner, Maine :

Sacrum Memoriæ

SYLVESTRIS GARDINER,

Qui natus, haud obscuro genere, in insulâ Rhodi,
Studuit Parisiis, et Bostoniæ diù medicinam felicitèr
Exercuit. Postquam satis opum paravisset,
Navavit operam ad domandam ornandamque
Hanc orientalem regionem, tunc incultam.
Hìc sylvas latè patentes evertit, molas omnigenas
Ædificavit, omnia rura permultis tuguriis ornavit,
Templum Deo erexit,
Atque hæc loca habitantibus pater-patriæ dici
Profectò meruit.
Vir acerrimo ingenio, medicus sciens,
Maritus fidelis, pius in liberos,
In obeundis negotiis vigilans, sagax, indefessus,
Integer vitæ, in sacris literis doctus,
Christianæ fidei omnino addictus,
Ecclesiæque Anglicanæ observantissimus,
Mortuus est in insulâ Rhodi,
Anno Domini MDCCLXXXVI, ætatis LXXIX.

Ut viri de ecclesiâ deque Republicâ optimè meriti
Memoriam commendaret posteris, suæque insuper
Erga avum venerandum pietatis monumentum extaret,
Honorarium hoc marmor erexit,
Nepos hæresque,
Robertus Hallowell Gardiner.

DR. JEFFRIES.

Dr. John Jeffries, of Boston, son of David Jeffries, Esq., born Feb. 5, 1744; graduated at Harvard College in 1763; studied in London, and was honored with the degree of M. D. at Aberdeen in 1769. He was a physician in Boston till the Revolution; afterwards surgeon of a ship in the British squadron in Boston harbor, and attended the wounded at Bunker Hill; went to Halifax in 1776 as surgeon-general, and to England in 1779, and had in both places professional employment under the crown. He recommenced his regular medical life in London in 1780, and on the 7th January, 1785, he acquired a sort of eclat by crossing the English channel with Blanchard in a balloon, when he landed in the forest of Guines in France, which procured for him the attention of the most distinguished personages of the day, and an introduction to all the learned and scientific societies of Paris. He returned to Boston in 1789, to an extensive practice; and delivered the first public lecture on anatomy, a branch of his profession of which he was very fond. After a successful practice of fifty-three years, he died at Boston on the 16th of September, 1819, aged seventy-six years.

C. PAXTON.

Charles Paxton, Esq., one of the commissioners of the customs, and the writer of one of the obnoxious letters to Mr. Whately, took refuge in England during the war. He was a pall-bearer at Gov. Hutchinson's funeral in 1780. Of his subsequent career we have no information.

LIEUT. GOV. COLDEN.

Cadwallader Colden was born at Dunse, Scotland, 17th Feb., 1688; he was educated at the University of Edinburgh, and devoted himself to medicine and mathematics, in both of which he made great proficiency.

He emigrated to Pennsylvania in 1708, where he practised physic for several years, and then returned to Great Britain, and acquired reputation as a medical writer. He came a second time to America in 1716, and after passing two years in Pennsylvania, he settled at New-York, and the next year was appointed the first surveyor-general of the lands of the colony, and a master in chancery. In 1720 he was a king's counsellor under Gov. Burnet. He had resided on a tract of land, for which he received a patent, near Newburgh on the Hudson, then on the frontier, where he was exposed to attacks from the Indians. He was appointed lieut. governor of New-York in 1761, and occupied this station during the remainder of his life, being repeatedly at the head of affairs by the absence or death of several governors. While acting governor, the stamps arrived and were placed under his care in Fort George. The people assembled in great numbers, determined to destroy them; but although the fort was pronounced untenable by engineers, and the people threatened to kill him, he defended his trust, and succeeded in securing it on board of a British man-of-war. He was burnt in effigy by the populace, who destroyed his carriage. After Gov. Tryon's return in 1775, he retired to his seat at Flushing on Long Island, where he died Sept. 28, 1776, in his 89th year.* Mr. Colden wrote, besides numerous medical and botanical essays, a valuable history of the Five Indian Nations, and an essay on the " Principles of Action in Matter," to which is annexed a Treatise on Fluxions.

Among his correspondents were Linnæus, Gronovius, the Earl of Macclesfield, Dr. Franklin, and many other of the most scientific men of his time.

DR. COOPER.

MYLES COOPER, D. D., president of King's, now Columbia College, New-York, was born in 1734, and educated at the university of Oxford, where he graduated as master of arts in 1760. Arriving in New-York, and recommended by the archbishop of Canterbury as well qualified to assist in a college, he was received by President Johnson in the most affectionate manner, and appointed professor of moral philosophy. After the resignation of Dr. Johnson, he was chosen to the presidency in February, 1763. Soon after, Dr. Clossey, a graduate of Trinity College, Dublin, where he had

---

* The seat of Gov. Colden at Flushing was called Spring Hill ; it was confiscated, and is now the property and residence of Hon. Benjamin W. Strong.

also taken the degree of doctor of physic, was appointed professor of natural philosophy.

A grammar school was also established and connected with the college, under the charge of Mr. Cushing, from Boston. The classes were now taught by Dr. Cooper, Dr. Clossey, and Mr. Harper, with great advantage.

In 1775 Dr. Cooper was a stanch loyalist, and on being discovered as a public writer on the side of the crown, a large mob assailed him in the night at the college, with threats against him, but Alexander Hamilton kept them at bay by his unsurpassed eloquence, while Dr. Cooper escaped to a friend's in the upper part of the city, from whence he was put on board a vessel bound to England. This was in the month of May, 1775.

On the 10th of the same month, prior to his departure, Dr. Cooper wrote to his friend and fellow-sufferer, Isaac Wilkins, Esq., who had preceded him to London, as follows : " All things yet in *statu quo.* On Sunday I went to Morrisania to visit Mrs. Wilkins ; she was as well as could be reasonably expected, after parting with *you,* and returned that evening to Castle Hill, where I hope she will enjoy your return in safety. I had not time, you know, to write by you, save to Mr. Blackburn and Mr. Vardill, but they will sufficiently introduce you to all whom you would wish to see for for the present. If I think of any thing I can do for you, I will write by Mr. Cooke, for Bristol next week, and I will let no opportunity escape that I hear of, without giving you a line, whilst I continue in this country of confusion, which for the sake of the college I am minded to do as long as I can with any degree of prudence. Should this congress be as hot as the last, we are undone; should cooler measures be adopted, we may yet be preserved; for Britain, though stout, is exorable."

From Oxford, Feb. 4, 1777, where he had resided for three months, he thus writes to the same friend then at Long Island: " Mr. Wetherhead wrote me about Mr. Seabury's pay; I have applied to the bishop of London to interfere with the admiralty, and hope all will be settled to his satisfaction. I wish much to hear from him ; in the mean time, my best respects to him, Wetherhead, Samuel Bayard, etc. I will write to as many as I can by this packet, but, like an improvident man, I have deferred the business to the last, and now am called upon by the provost to attend some affairs of the college, which are agitating before the house of commons; so that it is out of my power to say whether or not I shall be able to write another line. Dr. Clossey shall hear from me presently."

From Edinburgh, 26th Feb., 1779, he wrote to the same friend at Long Island, as follows: "I received your obliging letter of 2d October, in London; I had not been there for a year before, and was only there then for a few days, having gone from this remote region into the south to take possession of a very small living presented me by the present chancellor, from which business I returned as quickly as possible to this city, which has been my residence for fourteen months past, and where I am too agreeably situated to think of moving unless for the better; or unless I should be obliged to reside on the little living aforesaid; or unless, which would be best of all, a happy termination of American disputes should enable me to resume my old situation; and till such an event takes place, I do not expect to be completely satisfied.

"You gave me spirits by representing matters in your quarter in a better light than I had viewed them. Indeed, Drs. Inglis and Seabury had been uniform in their information, so much of it as came to my knowledge, of the same purport; but the corroborative evidence even of a layman to two priests still had its effect. I wish to heaven you may not be wrong in your opinions. My most affectionate regards to Mr. Cutting, Mr. Colden, the Ludlows, Dr. Ogden, etc., whom I suppose you frequently see."

To the same friend, care of Rev. Dr. Inglis at New-York, he wrote from Edinburgh, May 30, 1783, as follows: "O, my dear friend! I shed tears most copiously when I first opened your letter, and upon the perusal of it *now* in order to answer it, I am more affected than before. Heavens! what confusion must you all be witnesses of in your unhappy situation. And yet I cannot help forming some hopes, that now the contest is ended the governing powers will relax their severity, and endeavor to bring over to them the minds of those whose persons and properties they have possession of. I long for accounts from New-York that I can depend upon; for I have not received a line from any of my correspondents there since their independency; a circumstance that must occasion such changes in the American system as cannot be conceived, I trust, by the wisest at this distance.

" 'Tis true I have taken a living ; it is in Berkshire, half-way between London and Bath, and twenty-six miles from Oxford ; a spot as delightful as can well be imagined, yet I don't know if ever I shall go thither to reside. I am as pleasantly situated here as I could wish to be."

He had been for some time one of the ministers of the Episcopal chapel of Edinburgh, where he died May 1, 1785, at the age of 51. Dr. Cooper possessed wit and humor to a great degree ; and pleasing manners, united to agreeable conversational powers. Although he had long expected death, he died suddenly, soon after writing the following epitaph of himself :

> " Here lies a priest of English blood,
> Who, living, liked whate'er was good ;
> Good company, good wine, good name ;
> Yet never hunted after fame.
> But, as the first he still preferred,
> So here he chose to be interred ;
> And, unobserved, from crowds withdrew,
> To rest among a chosen few ;
> In humble hope that Sovereign Love
> Will raise him to the blest above."

SIR F. BARING.

SIR FRANCIS BARING, Bart., born April 18th, 1750, was a son of John Baring, of Larkbeer, near Exeter, England, from which city the former was first elected to parliament on the 9th Nov. 1776, an interesting account of which is contained in the third chapter of this work. He early distinguished himself by his accurate knowledge and dexterity in financial calculations at the eventful period in which his public career commenced, and the reputation thus early acquired continued throughout his life. He exhibited a just knowledge of the interest of his country, and an anxiety to extend her commerce. In negotiating the various loans required from time to time, his affluence and talents enabled him to assist the minister, and he finally became the leading member of the monied interest ; and even the prosperity of England, at certain periods, may be said to have revolved around him as its *primum mobile.* He was designated by

Mr. Erskine as " the first merchant of the world," and his services on all occasions of great national interest, particularly as a director of the East India Company and as a member of parliament, were too important to escape the notice of administration, and entitle his memory to grateful recollection. The honor of baronetcy was conferred upon him on 29th May, 1793.

Sir Francis possessed such influence in the commercial world, that his death, which occurred on the 12th September, 1810, occasioned a sensible depression in the public stocks. He married a daughter of William Herring, Esq., a cousin and coheiress of Dr. Herring, archbishop of Canterbury.

The sister of Sir Francis married the celebrated lawyer John Dunning, afterwards Lord Ashburton, which title became extinct at the decease of their only son.

Sir Thomas Baring, born in 1772, succeeded his father in the baronetcy. Another son, Alexander Baring, now Lord Ashburton, became the head of the great commercial house, and did not retire from it until 1830. He was born in 1774, visited this continent in 1794, and travelled through the greater portion of the then United States on horseback, before 1797. He met the present king of France at the Falls of Niagara when there was but one house in Buffalo, and that a very indifferent one. Mr. Baring married a daughter of the Hon. William Bingham, one of the most opulent and public spirited citizens of Philadelphia, then a senator in congress from Pennsylvania. The house of Baring, Brothers & Co. have with scrupulous fidelity attended to the interests of the United States as government agent for nearly half a century, which entitles every member of it to our gratitude ; and we can never too highly appreciate the services and sacrifices of Lord Ashburton in his recent embassy, which has secured to Great Britain and the United States a treaty satisfactory to all the right minded of both countries.

Mr. Baring, having served as a member of the house of commons for many years, and held with honor, for a short period, the chancellorship of the exchequer, was elevated to the peerage in 1835, a proud testimonial of his distinguished abilities, and a just reward for a life devoted to the honor and best interests of his country.

B. MARSTON.

BENJAMIN MARSTON, Esq., son of Col. Benjamin Marston, of Salem, Massachusetts, graduated at Harvard College in 1749. Became a merchant at Marblehead, and was a refugee, proscribed in 1778. He closed his career as a commissary in the service of the African Company at Baalam's Isle, on the coast of Africa, in 1793.

E. WINSLOW, JUN.

HON. EDWARD WINSLOW, jr., of Plymouth, Massachusetts, was graduated at Harvard College in 1765; he was compelled to take refuge in Boston in 1775, and became a colonel in the British service.

He was afterwards a counsellor and judge of the superior court of New Brunswick, where he died, at Fredericton, in 1815, aged 70. He and his cousin, Pelham Winslow, were among the founders of the " Old Colony Club" in 1769, now the "Pilgrims' Society."

S. ROGERS.

SAMUEL ROGERS, merchant of Boston, who graduated at Harvard College in 1765, was proscribed as an absentee, Sept. 1778, and returned to Boston, where he died June 1, 1804, aged 57.

S. WILLIAMS.

SETH WILLIAMS, Esq., of Taunton, graduated at Harvard College in 1755—pursued the study of the law, and was in practice at the commencement of the Revolution. He was a refugee, and died in London previous to 1791.

COUNT DE GRASSE.

FRANCOIS JOSEPH PAUL, Count de Grasse Tilly, born in 1723, made his first appearance in the war between England and France as the ally of the North American colonies, in command of the frigate Robuste, in the battle of Ouessant, July, 1778; the first serious act of hostility between the two powers, and the first step of the Count de Grasse in defence of American liberty. Under Count d'Estaing, in command of a squadron, he aided in taking the island of Grenada, in 1779, when the British fleet was saved from total defeat by a calm at the close of the action. After three years of distinguished services he left Brest in 1781, in command of a fleet of a hundred and fifty sail, (twenty of the line,) and in thirty-six days fell in with Admiral Hood, then blockading Martinique, whose superiority of sailing alone enabled him to escape, with severe damage to four of his ships.

After a short stay at Port Royal de la Martinique, he concerted with the Marquis de Bouillé the attack of Tobago, the success of which, and its rapidity of execution, are well known.

His distinguished talents and zeal in the cause of America gained her entire confidence; and measures of co-operation were concerted between Generals Washington and Rochambeau and the French admiral, which resulted in the defeat of Cornwallis at Yorktown, and virtually closed the war between Great Britain and America. Count de Grasse was solicited for protection against the British fleet daily expected upon the coast, for a reinforcement of troops, for provisions " *de guerre and de bouche*," and for 1,200,000 francs for the more pressing necessities of the French troops. To all of these demands he lent most zealous and efficient aid, and in the short space of twelve days he collected all his disposable naval force, (without endangering St. Domingo,) embarked three thousand four hundred troops, and by his personal influence, and the actual pledge of his estates in St. Domingo and France, raised the funds desired. The expedition (necessarily a secret one) arrived at the capes of the Chesapeake on the 28th August, the same day that Admiral Hood appeared off New-York with fourteen vessels of the line. He succeeded in landing the troops, and on the 5th September was prepared and engaged the British fleet until nightfall, when they separated. After four days' vain search for his opponents, he returned to the capes in time to intercept two frigates, the " Iris" and " Richmond," which were leaving the bay with despatches they had been unable to deliver to Cornwallis. The allied armies (informed of the approach of the French fleet, by the frigate " La Concorde," on 15th August) arrived at the mouth of the Elk on 6th September, one hour only after the bearer of despatches from Count de Grasse. Count Rochambeau spoke of this coincidence as most remarkable, that a combined expedition of land and naval forces, the one from the north of America and the other from the West Indies, should both arrive in the same bay only one hour apart. On the 19th October, Lord Cornwallis capitulated to the united forces of France and America; six thousand five hundred men were made prisoners of war, one hundred and sixty cannon, twenty-two flags, and forty transports fell into the hands of the allies.

This expedition originated with Count de Grasse; the plan was matured by Washington, Rochambeau and himself in concert.

To the activity of all the commanders is mainly due this transcendant success, as only eight days after the capitulation was signed an increased British naval force arrived off the capes with seven thousand troops on board; enough, in all probability, to have sustained the royal authority in the south.

Congress passed a resolution on the 28th October, to erect a monument at Yorktown in commemoration of this great event, and also the following : "That the thanks of the United States, in Congress assembled, be presented to his excellency the Count de Grasse, for the skill and valor he has shown in attacking and beating the British fleet, in Chesapeake Bay, and for the zeal and ardor by which he gave, by the naval force under his command, the most effective and distinguished succor and protection to the allied army in Virginia." Congress also presented him four pieces of cannon, inscribed as follows : "Taken from the English army, by the combined forces of France and America, at Yorktown, Virginia, August 19, 1781. Presented to his Excellency Count de Grasse, in testimony of the inestimable services rendered by him on that day."

The cannon remained at the château of Tilly, fourteen leagues from Paris, until during the French Revolution the property and all its dependencies were lost to the family.

On the 13th February, 1782, the island of St. Christopher surrendered to Count de Grasse and the Marquis de Bouillé.

In command of the united forces of France and Spain, in the West Indies, the count sustained his high naval reputation, and defended himself successfully against the English fleet, until the 12th April, when (his vessels having been injured by contact with each other, his own ship, the "Ville de Paris," being run afoul of by the "Zélée") he was attacked by eleven of the enemy. His sails torn and ships ungovernable, his crews fasting and worn down with the

69

exertions of the previous nights, and without chance of success, he hauled down his flag, after combatting from eight A. M. till six P. M.   History offers no example of a longer or more spirited naval engagement, or a more obstinate resistance.   It was proved at a court of inquiry, that the most important manœuvres, as well as nine signals from the admiral, were neglected.   Count de Grasse (which is worthy of notice) never left the quarter-deck during the action, nor received a wound ; he had a hundred and twenty-one killed on board the Ville de Lyons, and a very large number wounded.

Carried a prisoner to England, the hero became negotiator, and exerted himself with that government to incline it to peace.   He had the gratification of taking to France, in August following, verbal propositions of peace to the French government, from Lord Shelburne, first lord of the treasury.   France insisted upon the acknowledgment of the independence of the United States as a condition of the treaty, and the preliminaries were signed at Paris on the 30th November, 1782.

History shows that the United States are as much indebted to the unceasing efforts of the Count de Grasse in her favor after his return to Europe, as for his brilliant achievements in the Chesapeake and West Indies.   It may be said that his life was consecrated to securing independence to the North American colonies ; for its accomplishment he employed all his valor, all his talents, all his zeal, and finding his task completed, and object gained, he died on the 14th January, 1788, in the sixty-fifth year of his age.

Count de Grasse left an only son, who served with honor in the several grades of the French army, and was decorated by Count Rochambeau at St. Domingo with the cross of St. Louis in behalf of Louis XVI.   At the massacre of Cape Francois, he saved himself and family on board an American vessel, which landed them in complete destitution at Charleston, where, with other exiles, they experienced the hospitality and sympathy of the inhabitants. Count de Grasse became a citizen of the United States, and subsequently returned to the service of his country, his attachment to which was manifested in the campaigns of Italy and Spain.

The French Revolution deprived him of his estates, and he has in vain awaited from government, to the age of seventy-eight, a recompense of his services. Should we do more than justice to the memory of one of the bravest and most devoted defenders of our liberties, in sharing with him the inheritance acquired by the united valor of our fathers?

The only surviving daughter of the first Count de Grasse, is the widow of the late Francis Depau, Esq., of this city, one of our most enterprising, opulent, and public spirited merchants, to whom all praise and credit is due for greatly extending our commerce with France, by establishing the first line of packets between New-York and Havre.

COL. EDSON.

JOSIAH EDSON, Esq., of Bridgewater, graduated at Harvard College in 1730, was a representative in the general assembly of Massachusetts, from that town. He was a refugee, and banished by the act of September, 1778; he had been commissioned a mandamus counsellor in August, 1778, but declined serving; he died previous to 1782.

W. VASSALL.

WILLIAM VASSALL, Esq., of Boston, was appointed a counsellor in 1774, by writ of mandamus, but did not serve; he was a refugee, and banished by the act of September, 1778. He died in Surrey, England, in 1800, aged eighty-five; he graduated at Harvard College in 1733.

JUDGE HUTCHINSON.

HON. FOSTER HUTCHINSON, a brother of Governor Hutchinson, and one of the last judges in the supreme court of Massachusetts under the charter, to which he was appointed in 1771. He graduated at Harvard College in 1743; he accepted the appointment of mandamus counsellor in 1774, and soon after was compelled to take refuge in Boston, and became an absentee. He was proscribed in 1778, and charged by the act of 1779, as a conspirator against the liberties of his country; he died at Halifax, in May, 1799.

N. R. THOMAS.

NATHANIEL RAY THOMAS, Esq., of Taunton, Bristol county, Mass., was graduated at Harvard College in 1751; appointed by writ of mandamus a counsellor in 1774, but declined serving. He was proscribed in the act of 1778, and died in Nova Scotia, 1791.

PELHAM WINSLOW.

PELHAM WINSLOW, Esq., an attorney of Plymouth, Massachusetts, was a son of General John Winslow, of Marshfield; and graduated at Harvard College in 1753. He was driven into Boston, and was a major in the British service; proscribed by the act of 1778; and died at Flushing, Long Island, in 1783.

JUDGE LEONARD.

HON. DANIEL LEONARD, of Norton, Massachusetts, graduated at Harvard College in 1760; a member of assembly. He was a distinguished political writer, and a member of the legal profession. In 1774, he was the antagonist of John Adams, in relation to " *the rights and prospects of the colonies,*" under the respective signatures of Novanglus and Massachusettensis. He was a refugee in 1775, and was proscribed in 1778; he was afterwards chief justice of Bermuda, and died in London, June 27, 1829, aged eighty-nine.

COL. SALTONSTALL.

COL. RICHARD SALTONSTALL, was the eldest son of Richard Saltonstall, of Haverhill, Mass., a judge of the superior court of that province. He was born, April 5, 1732, and graduated at Harvard College with distinguished honor, in 1751. Colonel Saltonsall entered into the military service of the province in the *French war*, in 1756, and was at Fort William Henry, Lake George, at the time of the memorable capitulation and massacre, August 9, 1757. When the Indians fell upon the unarmed prisoners, he escaped, and arrived a few days afterwards at Fort Edward, on the Hudson, nearly exhausted by hunger and fatigue. He commanded a regiment from 1760 to the close of the war. On his return to Haverhill, he was appointed sheriff of the county of Essex, which office he held until he left the country.

When the difficulties between the colonies and the mother country came on, Colonel Saltonstall was opposed to forcible resistance; he believed that it must be ineffectual, and that the colonies would fall before the power of Great Britain. He was greatly beloved and respected ; he often represented the town in the general court. It was long before he lost his popularity, notwithstanding his opinions ; but in the autumn of 1774, a great number of persons collected before his house, armed with clubs, etc., and with threats of violence, contrary to the advice of some friends who were with him, and who had gone for the purpose of aiding in his escape, he came to the door and addressed the excited assembly with great calmness, firmness and dignity ; reminding them of his services for his country, that he had exposed his life in its defence, etc. Seldom has a speech been more effectual ; it quelled the excited passions of the multitude, and they dispersed. He was soon after compelled to take refuge in Boston, and embarked for England, in 1775.

Col. Saltonstall refused to accept a commission in the British army, saying, that if he could not conscientiously engage on the side of his country, he would not take up arms against her. His reputation as an officer was high, and it is supposed that he might have had an important command in the American army, if he had embraced the popular cause.

Col. Saltonstall was proscribed by the law of 1778, and passed the remainder of his days in England. In one of his letters, written soon after the peace, he expressed great affection for *the delightful place of his nativity ;* but he added,—" I have no remorse of conscience for my past conduct. I have had more satisfaction in a private life here, than I should have had in being next in command to General Washington, where I must have acted in conformity to the dictates of others, regardless of my own feelings." Colonel Saltonstall resided on the beautiful family estate in Haverhill, known as " the Saltonstall place," where he lived in a style of liberal hospitality, sustaining the character of a truly upright and honorable man, and an accomplished gentleman ; he was never married.

He was kindly received by his remote family connections in England ; and his friends erected a monument to his memory at Kensington, with the following inscription :

" Near this place are interred the remains of RICHARD SALTON-STALL, Esq., who died October 1, 1785, aged fifty-two. He was an *American loyalist*, from Haverhill in the Massachusetts ; where he was descended from a first family, both for the principal share it had in the early erecting, as well as in rank and authority in governing that province. And wherein he himself sustained, with unshaken loyalty and universal applause, various important trusts and commands under the crown, both civil and military, from his youth till its revolt ; and throughout life maintained such an amiable private character, as engaged him the esteem and regard of many friends.

"As a memorial of his merits, this stone is erected."

Col. Saltonstall was a descendant in the sixth generation from Sir Richard Saltonstall, one of the patentees of the colony of Massachusetts Bay, and who arrived at Salem, in the Arabella, (or Arbella,) June 12, 1630, with Governor Winthrop and their associates, " bringing out the charter with them." He was also a patentee of Connecticut, and may be considered as one of the principal founders of both colonies. A memoir of this family may be found in the publications of the Mass. Historical Society.

Dr. Nathaniel Saltonstall, brother of Colonel Saltonstall, was a decided whig of the Revolution. The Hon. Leverett Saltonstall, of Salem, an able and eloquent representative, now in congress from Massachusetts, is his son.

N. CHANDLER.

NATHANIEL CHANDLER, son of Col. John Chandler of Worcester, graduated at Harvard College, in 1768, was a practising attorney at Petersham, when the troubles commenced, and was compelled on account of his principles to take refuge in Boston. He was proscribed in 1778. Had for a while led a corps of volunteers in the British service at New-York. He afterwards went to England, returned, and died at Worcester, 1801, aged fifty-one.

DR. B. S. OLIVER.

BRINLEY SYLVESTER OLIVER, M. D., fourth son of Lieut. Governor Andrew Oliver, graduated at Harvard College in 1774, studied medicine and surgery, and was afterwards a surgeon in the British service.

DR. PAINE.

WILLIAM PAINE, M. D., son of Timothy Paine, Esq., of Worcester, Mass., graduated at Harvard College in 1768. He was practising professionally at Worcester at the commencement of the Revolution; was a refugee, and proscribed in 1778. Became an apothecary to the British forces in Rhode Island and New-York. At the peace he settled at New Brunswick, and was a representative for Charlotte county. He removed to Salem, Mass., where he practised from 1787 to 1793, with success in his profession. The death of his father caused him to return to Worcester, where he closed his checkered life, on the 18th April, 1833, at the age of eighty-three.

WM. CHANDLER.

WILLIAM CHANDLER, Esq., youngest son of Col. John Chandler, of Worcester, Mass., was compelled to take refuge in Boston, and was proscribed in 1778. He returned after peace was restored, and died in his native place, July, 1793, aged forty. Mr. Chandler graduated at Harvard College, in 1772.

CHARLES CURTIS.

CHARLES CURTIS, of Scituate, Mass., graduated at Harvard College, 1765. Driven into Boston, he was proscribed in 1778, and died in New-York, previous to 1832.

DR. P. OLIVER.

PETER OLIVER, Jr., second son of the chief justice of the same name, both of Middleborough, Plymouth county, Mass.; the former graduated at Harvard College in 1761. He had practised in Scituate in early life; was driven into Boston, and in consequence became a refugee in England, where he died, at Shrewsbury, in Sept. 1822, aged eighty-one.

REV. M. BADGER.

REV. MOSES BADGER, of Haverhill, graduated at Harvard College, 1761; was a refugee, proscribed by the act of Sept. 1778. After the peace he returned, and was rector of King's Chapel, Providence, Rhode Island, where he died, Sept. 19, 1792.

J. D. ROGERS.

JEREMIAH DUMMER ROGERS, Esq., an attorney at law of Little-ton, graduated at Harvard College, 1762. He was a refugee, pro-scribed in 1778, and died at Halifax, 1784.

T. A. COFFIN.

THOMAS ASTON COFFIN, Esq., son of William Coffin, of Boston, and cousin of Sir Isaac Coffin, remained in Boston after the siege, and was proscribed in 1778. He was private secretary to Gen. Carleton, and in 1784 was appointed commissary-general to the British troops at Quebec. He died in London, May 3d, 1810, aged fifty-six. Mr. Coffin graduated at Harvard College in 1772.

REV. B. LOVELL.

REV. BENJAMIN LOVELL, youngest son of the grammar school master at Boston, was graduated at Harvard College in 1774. He became a refugee, first to Halifax, where he married, and after-wards to England. Mr. Lovell took orders, and was settled at Ashe, Surrey, where he died, March 14, 1828, aged seventy-three.

J. PUTNAM, JR.

JAMES PUTNAM, Jr., Esq., son of Hon. James Putnam of Wor-cester, graduated at Harvard College in 1774; was a refugee in 1775; became barrack-master, and subsequently one of the house-hold of the late Duke of Kent; of whose will he was executor. He died in London, March, 1838.

GOV. FRANKLIN.

HON. WILLIAM FRANKLIN, born in 1731, a natural son of the celebrated Dr. Franklin, was the last of the royal governors of New Jersey, and one of the most conspicuous persons in opposition to the principles of the Revolution. Although born upon the American soil, he was from feeling and principle a loyalist; and his firm adherence to government, under the most adverse circum-stances, and with all the influence of his father's example to con-tend against, as well as his disapprobation of the course he took, showed a self-sacrifice seldom equalled, and renders him well worthy of notice, while his sufferings entitle him to our sympathy.

Of his early history very little is known; he was a captain in the army during the French war, and served with credit at Ticonderoga. He afterwards accompanied his father to England, where he appears to have been received with distinction. He was honored by the university of Cambridge with the degree of Master of Arts, and we find him enjoying the intimacy and confidence of the Earl of Bute, on whose recommendation Lord Halifax appointed him, in 1763, the governor of New-Jersey.

Governor Franklin seems to have studied the best interests of his province, and for some time enjoyed considerable popularity, but he did not possess the good fortune to retain it. In the first dispute which occurred between him and the assembly, in relation to the removal of a defaulting treasurer, he manifested a useless obstinacy, in opposition to their wishes, which served to deprive him of their confidence, and to prevent any influence which he might otherwise have exerted in opposition to the Revolution. He also gave offence by showing, in all contests between the mother country and her colonies, that he remained faithful to his principles; for he steadily advocated the claims of government, and in answer to the strong remonstrances of the assembly he invariably aimed to show them that their situation was much to be preferred to the uncertain results of a revolution. At length the current of opinion became strong against him, and he found that his exertions served only to excite a more determined opposition. He labored assiduously to prevent the formation of an independent provincial government and the union of the colonies, and afforded encouragement and protection to the most violent opponents of the Revolution. But what gave the greatest offence was his proclamation calling together the royal assembly, in order to oppose their action to that of the provincial congress. This measure alarmed the latter body, and they at once resolved that his proclamation ought not to be obeyed, that he had acted in violation of their resolves, and had proved himself an enemy to the liberties of his country; that measures should be taken to secure his person, and that all payments of salary to him should cease. He was then arrested by order of the convention, and on his refusal to sign a parole, detained in close custody. In the mean time an application had been made to the continental congress for advice as to the course to be pursued, suggesting that it would be more safe to confine him in some other state than New-Jersey; and that body recommended that, after an examination, he should be transferred to the custody of the governor of Connecticut. He was accordingly brought before the convention for examination, but his firmness did not desert him, and he steadily refused to answer any questions, denying the authority of that body, which he asserted had usurped the government. He was then sent to Connecticut, and after a confinement at Middletown of nearly two years, was liberated in exchange for an American general officer, when he retired to England, on a pension, which was continued during life. He died on the 17th November, 1813, at the age of eighty-two.

Gov. Franklin, though wanting the genius of his father, was a man of talents, firmness, and integrity. That his conduct was the result of sincere convictions cannot be doubted. He had been raised to his dignified station without any solicitation on his part, or on the part of his father, and it is probable that a feeling of gratitude may have held him more steadily in his course. It is evident that he sacrificed much in acting as he did, if it were only the friendly intercourse with his parent, who had previously bestowed upon him much of his confidence and affection. The letters between them had been frequent, but when the course of the governor became manifest, their intercourse entirely ceased. The last of the doctor's letters was in January, 1774, and he had no further communication with his son till after the peace, when the latter, in 1784, wrote to his father, proposing a reconciliation. The doctor remarks in his answer, that nothing had ever caused him so much pain as " to find himself deserted, in his old age, by his only son :" he finds for him, however, an excuse in his situation, but remarks that " there are natural duties which precede political ones, and cannot be extinguished by them." The intercourse thus recommenced continued, probably, till the death of the illustrious philosopher and statesman.

Gov. Franklin was twice married, and left, at his death, one son, William Temple Franklin, editor of the works of his grandfather, who died in Paris, May 25, 1823.

Gov. Franklin caused a monumental tablet to be placed in the chancel of St. Paul's church, New-York, with the following inscription:

"Beneath the altar of this church are deposited the remains of Mrs. Elizabeth Franklin, wife of his Excellency William Franklin, late governor, under his Britannic Majesty, of the province of New-Jersey. Compelled to part from the husband she loved, and at length despairing of the soothing hope of his speedy return, she sunk under accumulated distresses, and departed this life 28th July, 1778, in the forty-ninth year of her age.

Sincerity and sensibility,
Politeness and affability,
Godliness and charity,

were, with sense refined and person elegant, in her united. From a grateful remembrance of her affectionate tenderness and

constant performance of all the duties of a good wife,
this monument is erected, in the year 1787,
by one who knows her worth,
and still laments her loss."

I. WILKINS, D. D.

ISAAC WILKINS, of Westchester, New-York, son of Martin Wilkins, Esq., who in infancy, at the decease of his father, an opulent planter, and an eminent man of the island of Jamaica, was brought to the province, and received the best education the country afforded. The former married Isabella Morris, a sister of that eloquent patriot and statesman, Gouverneur Morris.[*] Mr. Wilkins first prepared himself for the church, but did not take orders. As a member of the provincial assembly, he was subsequently distinguished for loyalist principles, and his eloquence and integrity acquired for him an influence rarely attained, and which for a considerable time prevented the prostration of the colonial government.

The following extract from his speech on the resolutions for adopting the measures recommended by congress, shows the interest he felt in the subject:

"We have before us the choice of peace or war, of happiness or misery, of freedom or slavery; and can we hesitate which to choose? By proceeding in a firm, but loyal and constitutional

---

[*] Another brother, Sir Staats Morris, K. C. B., who entered the British army in early life, attained the rank of lieut. general, and married the duchess of Gordon.

manner, in the settlement of this unhappy difference with our mother country, we cannot fail, I am convinced, of meeting with success, of securing to ourselves a free constitution, and of a restoration to the favor and protection of the parent state, which, next to the favor of heaven, will be our best and strongest safeguard and security. This is the critical moment of our fate; we have it now in our power to do the most essential good or mischief to ourselves and our posterity. If we neglect this opportunity of promoting our common felicity, and of establishing our liberties on a firm and lasting basis, we may perhaps never have another, and shall repent of our fatal infatuation and folly when too late to retrieve the mistake; when the horrors of civil war shall be increased by the curses of our wretched and deluded constituents, who, in the bitterness of their hearts, shall point us out as the authors of their ruin, and when we shall be obliged to submit to the laws of conquest, or the penalties of rebellion. I have shown that the rise of this dispute with Great Britain has been an unreasonable jealousy on our part, originating from an impolitic exertion of authority on hers; and that it is our interest, as well as duty, to cultivate the closest union with her. I have shown that by a peaceful conduct we may procure for ourselves, and perhaps for our sister colonies, a more perfect system of government than that we have hitherto enjoyed, which was indeed better calculated for our infant state than for the present period of our maturity; a period that requires, however paradoxical it may seem, more liberty and a stricter government. I will only add, that if contrary to my most ardent wishes, contrary to the dignity of this house, to the dictates of humanity, and our duty to our constituents and country, you adopt the measures of congress, and by that means involve our country in a civil war, that most dreadful of calamities, I declare my honest indignation against your course, and call heaven to witness I am guiltless of the blood of my fellow subjects that will be shed on the occasion—I am guiltless of the ruin of my country."

About the 1st of May, 1775, Mr. Wilkins was compelled to abandon his family and country, and embarked for England, after taking the following leave of his countrymen, which appeared in Rivington's Gazette, of May 3, 1775:

" My Countrymen :

" Before I leave America, the land I love, and in which is contained every thing that is valuable and dear to me, my wife, children, friends, and property, permit me to make a short and faithful declaration, which I am induced to do, neither through fear, nor a consciousness of having acted wrong. An honest man and a Christian hath nothing to apprehend from this world. . God is my judge and witness, that all I have done, written, or said, in relation to the present unnatural dispute between Great Britain and her colonies, proceeded from the honest intention of serving my country. Her welfare and prosperity were the objects towards which all my endeavors have been directed. They still are the sacred objects which I shall ever steadily and invariably keep in view, and when in England, all the influence that so inconsiderable a man as I am can have, shall be exerted in her behalf.

" It has been my constant maxim through life to do my duty conscientiously, and to trust the issue of my actions to the Almighty. May He, in whose hands are all events, speedily restore peace and liberty to my unhappy country ; may Great Britain and America be soon united in the bands of everlasting amity, and when united, may they continue a free, virtuous, and happy nation, to the end of time.

" I leave America and every endearing connection, because I will not raise my hand in opposition to my sovereign, nor will I draw my sword against my country ; when I can conscientiously draw it in her favor, my life shall be cheerfully devoted to her service.   " Isaac Wilkins."

Bishop Seabury wrote Mr. Wilkins on the 30th of May, 1775, that Drs. Cooper and Chandler had sailed from New-York the previous week for England.

Mr. Samuel Bayard, jr., wrote Mr. Wilkins in London, dated New-York, 6th June, 1775, " that the few soldiers who were here embarked on board the Asia yesterday ; their baggage was stopped by some of our inhabitants, and one or two soldiers deserted. Stopping the baggage is said to have been contrary to the sentiments of most people here. We are, however, very quiet. The military made no resistance, as the officers were afraid of greater desertions if the soldiers remained in the streets." On the 5th July he writes as follows : " Wooster's camp I suppose you know is within two miles of us—it is in a field adjoining the sand-hill, and on the left hand side of the new road which runs through N. Bayard's land, so that this road is on the east side, and the road over the sand-hill on the north side of the camp. The number is said to be fourteen hundred. These are a part of the five thousand which the continental congress have directed to be kept in this province. We have for ten days past received contradictory accounts of an action between Gen. Gage and the provincials, which happened on the 17th June. No account from Gen. Gage yet. Surely, if those who now direct affairs had a real love of the country at heart, they would use every means to obtain their desires before they involved us in the horrors of war. If influenced by laudable motives, their measures appear to be the effect of infatuation ; the uncertainty of what this may urge them to is such, that when I go to bed I know not whether I may not be waked by the noise of cannon battering the town, as there is the Asia of sixty guns lying just opposite my bed."

On the 13th of July he further writes as follows : " Yesterday some of our Connecticut troops seized the cutter of the Asia, with eight or ten men, who came on shore to bring a sick man. They hauled the boat into the street, (the men belonging to her sitting in, huzzaing and calling them their horses ;) some time after they put the boat in the water and set fire to her. I hear Gen. Wooster has wrote a polite letter to Capt. Vandeput, assuring him that this outrage was without his knowledge, and contrary to his wishes. It is said the boat will be paid for." August 2, he also writes thus : " Although we are but looked upon as enemies to the liberty of our country, yet I can answer for you, as I believe you can for me, that we as sincerely wish her every blessing and the enjoyment of every liberty which the nature of civil government can admit, as the loudest of those who at this time are in opposition to government ; and I am convinced you will use all your influence and abilities to promote the good of your country ; which I hope our infatuated countrymen will one day be convinced of and acknowledge."

Mr. Wilkins returned to Long Island in 1776, then under control of the British, where he remained until the close of the war.

While in England, Mr. Wilkins recommended to Lord North terms on which the breach could be healed, but they were not heeded.

On the 4th of Feb., 1777, from Oxford, Dr. Cooper, formerly president of King's College, New-York, wrote to Mr. Wilkins, at Long Island, as follows: "I have heard of your sufferings with much pain, though I own without surprise ; you may remember I tried to dissuade you from going so soon on that very account. But that * * *   * * * should have been the very instrument of this wickedness, is far more than I could have supposed, and I heartily pray, (with a safe conscience, too,) that he may have an ample and speedy reward. The same good wishes attend all the laborers in the vineyard of Satan, wheresoever dispersed."

At the close of the war, Mr. Wilkins was, by the terms of the banishment act, compelled to leave the republic, and he repaired to Shelburne, Nova Scotia, where he remained several years, and subsequently removed to Lunenburgh, in the same province. He obtained leave to return to his native land previous to 1803, and having taken orders, was settled over the parish of West Chester, where he continued highly esteemed for lofty principle, ever exhibited through a protracted and checkered life, which closed soon after penning the following epitaph :

Sacred
To the memory of
THE REV. ISAAC WILKINS, D. D.
who for 31 years was the
diligent and faithful minister of
this parish,
placed here, as he believed, by his Redeemer.
He remained satisfied with the
pittance allowed him, rejoicing that even in that
he was no burden to his
parishioners :
nor ever wished nor ever went forth
to seek a better living.

Mr. Wilkins died 5th February, 1830, aged eighty-nine years.

REV. IVORY HOVEY.*

Rev. Ivory Hovey was born at Topsfield, near Salem, Mass., on the 3d of July, O. S. 1714. He graduated at Harvard College in 1735, in the class of Mr. Curwen. He studied theology, and was settled at Matapoiset, a parish of Rochester, Massachusetts, in 1740. He left that place in 1765, and was soon after resettled in a parish of Plymouth, where he passed the remainder of an unusually long and useful life. He married in 1739, Olive, daughter of Capt. Samuel Jordan, of Biddeford, Maine, who survived him a few months. Mr. Hovey was able to continue his ministerial labors till a few days before his death, which took place on the 4th of November, 1803, in the ninetieth year of his age. It is remarked by Dr. Alden, (from whose Collection these particulars are obtained,) that for some time before his decease, Mr. Hovey " was but the *third* among the *living* of his alma mater." He probably outlived all of his classmates, although he survived Mr. Curwen by only eighteen months.

For sixty-five years before his death, says Alden, Mr. Hovey kept a journal, in which those things designed for his own particular use were penned in a short hand, as is said, of his own invention. This journal, closely written, amounts to the astonishing number of seven thousand octavo pages. The same author publishes an excellent letter of great length, addressed by Mr. Hovey to a young candidate for the ministry, written twelve days only before his death.

---

* See above, page 418, where it is mentioned as uncertain whether this classmate of Mr. Curwen was living in 1795. The present notice of Mr. Hovey has been prepared since that part of the work was printed.

SAMUEL QUINCY.

[The following additional particulars and documents relating to this unfortunate gentleman are derived from original papers, of which copies have been made and forwarded to us since the preceding notice of him was in type. Aside from the fact that they have been communicated by a lady, (Miss ELIZA S. QUINCY, jr., of Cambridge, Massachusetts,) these documents possess too deep an interest to be withheld from the public, although their publication renders the article more voluminous than is strictly consistent with the plan of this work.]

MR. QUINCY was born in that part of Braintree now Quincy, Massachusetts, April 13, 1735. He was the second son of Josiah Quincy, who at that time resided on the estate of his ancestor in that town, and who afterwards removed to Boston, and became an eminent merchant of that place. His mother's name was Hannah Sturgis, daughter of John Sturgis, Esq. of Yarmouth, Massachusetts. She died in Boston, August, 1755, aged 43, leaving three sons and one daughter. She was an excellent and religious woman, and had received the best education the country at that time afforded. Her children honored her memory, and the eminence and usefulness of their lives and characters bore testimony to the virtuous principles she had early instilled.

Endowed with fine talents, Mr. Quincy became eminent in the profession of the law, and succeeded Jonathan Sewall as solicitor-general of Massachusetts. He was also distinguished for his knowledge and attainments in general literature, and as the author of numerous fugitive essays in prose and verse, that appeared in the journals of the day. He was the intimate friend of many of the most distinguished men of that period, and an early correspondent of John Adams.

In early life he appears to have coincided in his political course and opinions with his brothers. During the movements preceding the Revolution, his name appears on the records of the town of Boston, associated with that of Josiah Quincy, jr. From the letter written by him to his brother, so ardent a patriot, on receiving a copy of his "Observations on the Boston Port Bill,"

71

it appears that their affection for each other remained unaltered.*

The feelings of his father and family, who were all devoted to the cause of freedom and independence, were undoubtedly deeply wounded by the course Samuel Quincy pursued, as a letter of his sister, Mrs. Lincoln, evinces. But they always continued to take an affectionate interest in his fate and fortunes; and the want of letters from his father and friends, to which he alludes in his letters from London, undoubtedly arose from the difficulties of transmitting letters to London at that troubled period. His father was then advanced in life, and lived in retirement at Braintree on his paternal estate.

The following impassioned letter was written to Mr. Quincy by his sister, Mrs. Lincoln, when on the eve of his departure for England:

TO SAMUEL QUINCY.

Braintree, May 11, 1775.

My dear Brother:

I write this in hopes to put it into the letter my father has just written. If it should reach you, it may serve to convince you that I have not forgotten that you are my *only* brother. He must judge what I feel, when I tell him that I fear I shall never see him again.

Our two departed brothers died upon the seas. You perhaps will say your body is sound; it may be so, but the sick in mind call for more than Esculapian aid.

If any thing could surprise me *now*, the hearing of your going *home* would; but of late every thing that is marvellous and strange is to be expected. I have not time to enlarge upon the complicated distresses of our country, of families, or of individuals, but shall briefly say that our connections have experienced such a series of melancholy events as are not to be paralleled. We, my brother, I hope, can sympathize in sorrowing for the loss of a brother, whose character was, as far as any man's of his age ever was, unimpeachable.

In his labors for the salvation of his country, he was indefati-

* See Memoir of J. Quincy, jr., by his son President Quincy, p. 160.

gable. His death, I hope, will prove a warning to others—not to pursue too eagerly *any point*. Nature kept upon the stretch will give way. He did not sufficiently consider the tenderness of his frame, and it may truly be said he fell a martyr in the cause of liberty.

In the monody on our eldest brother I find the following lines; they may with equal propriety be applied to the younger:

> " That heart which late, inflamed with patriot zeal,
> Braved the bold insults of its country's foe,
> No more its pious frenzy can reveal,
> Nor e'er in Freedom's cause again shall glow."

Let it not be told in America, and let it not be published in Great Britain, that a brother of such brothers fled from his country—the wife of his youth—the children of his affection—and from his aged sire, already bowed down with the loss of two sons, and by that of many more dear, though not so near connections, to secure himself from the reproaches of his injured countrymen, and to cover such a retreat, obliged to enlist as a sycophant under an obnoxious Hutchinson, who is a tool under a cruel North, and by them to be veered about, and at last to be blown aside with a cool " to-morrow, sir."

> "Refusal, canst thou wear a smoother form ?"

My blood chills at the thought of the meanness of a seeker, and flames with indignation at such treatment from those in power. Arouse from your lethargy—let reason take the helm—disregard all greatness but greatness of soul;—then the little trappings that royalty can confer will lose their lustre, that false lustre which I fear inclines you to the *prerogative* side. Spare me, and do not call what I have written impertinent, but ascribe it to the anxiety of a sister, really distressed for thee. I behold you leaving your country, " a land flowing with milk and honey," and in which, as yet, iniquity of all kinds is punished, and its religion as yet free from idolatry, (how long it will continue so God only knows—we have reason to fear a depredation on our religious system next,) for a country where evil works are committed with impunity. Can you expect there to walk uprightly ? Can you take fire into your bosom and not be burned ?

I take a long farewell, and wish you success in every laudable undertaking.

Your affectionate sister,

H. LINCOLN.

TO HENRY HILL, ESQ., CAMBRIDGE.

Boston, May 13, 1775.

DEAR BROTHER :

There never was a time when sincerity and affectionate unity of heart could be more necessary than at present. But in the midst of the confusions that darken our native land, we may still, by a rectitude of conduct, entertain a rational hope that the Almighty Governor of the universe will in his own time remember mercy.

I am going, my dear friend, to quit the habitation where I have been so long encircled with the dearest connections.

I am going to hazard the unstable element, and for a while to change the scene—whether it will be prosperous or adverse, is not for me to determine. I pray God to sustain my integrity, and preserve me from temptation.

My political character with you may be suspicious ; but be assured, if I cannot *serve* my country, which I shall endeavor to the utmost of my power, I will never *betray* it.

The unhappy event which took place yesterday, was as unexpected as it was distressful ; my concern for your safety, as well as my anxiety for the agitation of my dear partner, wounded me to the heart. Oh, cruel separation. I had many things to say ; I could have talked with you for ever ; but the will of Heaven forbade it.

The kind care of my family you have so generously offered, penetrates me with the deepest gratitude. If it should not be in my power to reward you, you will have that recompense greater than I can give you, the approbation of your own heart. Would to God we may again enjoy that harmonious intercourse I have been favored with since my union with your family. I will not despair of this great blessing in some future and not very distant period. * * God preserve you in health and every earthly enjoyment, until you again receive the salutation of

Your friend and brother,   SAMUEL QUINCY.

EXTRACTS FROM MR. QUINCY'S LETTERS.

London, July 25, 1775.

* * I have now been here a month. I have not yet seen Lord North or Lord Dartmouth, not because I could not, but because I have not been sent for, and choose my own time if I do it at all. I mention this to show you how mistaken you are when you suppose I shall be strictly examined. I have just returned from a visit to one of the first law officers, by whom I was very politely received. As to politics I say nothing ; suffice it that my opinion of men and things remains the same, and is confirmed every hour. * * We have just received the news of the battle of the 17th of June, by the Cerberus; but this is a subject on which I dare not venture. Every thing is peace here ; I wish it may soon return to my dear, dear country.

TO HENRY HILL, ESQ.

London, August 18, 1775.

You conjure me by the love of my country, to use my best endeavors to bring about a reconciliation, suggesting that the Americans are still as determined as ever to die free, rather than live slaves ; I have no reason to doubt the zeal of my fellow-countrymen in the cause of freedom, and their firmness in its defence, and were it in my power, my faithful endeavors should not be wanting (nay, I have a right to say they are not) to effect an accommodation. But, my good friend, I am unhappy to find that the opinion I formed in America, and which in a great measure governed my conduct, was but too justly founded. Every proposal of those who are friendly to the colonies, to alter the measures of government and redress the grievances of which they complain, is spurned at, unless attended with previous concessions on their part. This there is less reason every day to expect, and thus the prospect of an accommodation is thrown at a distance ; nor is there yet the least reason to suppose that a formidable if any opposition will be framed against administration in favor of America. The people of this country are united in their attachment to the reigning prince and his family. The king's ministers are their own ; and though a clamor against those who are in power, which is ever the case in popular governments, in some measure divides the metropolis, the city politics never were on a lower ebb. Their petitions and remonstrances are received with indignation, as they are conceived to originate from an *anti-ministerial* spirit, and not as the offspring of true patriotism or friendship to America. The political subordination of the colonies is in this island a sacred tenet. It is not, therefore, very surprising, that the late alarming strides of colony opposition have taught them to suspect a determination to emancipate the continent from every civil connection with this country, and a dangerous design of independency, notwithstanding the denial of it in words. Under this apprehension, the yeomen, merchants, and manufacturers, in the inland parts of the country, who were wont to be advocates for America, as far as I am able to form a judgment both from information and observation, are beginning to murmur against them. Their common answer is, Whilst you were reasonable in your demands and complained of real burdens, we were willing to support you, but we cannot venture to assist American *independence*, lest we lay a foundation for the destruction of both countries. Their produce and manufactures are in quick demand, and likely to continue so, owing principally to the equipment of the Spanish flota, and the late Russian war. They are therefore at peace and contented, immersed in wealth and commerce, and caring little what passes beyond them. Some of the principal American merchants here with whom I have conversed, are projecting an association promising their aid to government, and publicly to convince America that they are not to expect the assistance of the trade here in support of what they call her extravagant claims. We look, say they, upon your attempts to distress us by stopping your commerce, as a mark of your want of honesty, and your pretended flame for liberty as only a desire for domination and empire. When the lord mayor carried up to St. James's the late city remonstrance and petition for the removal of the troops from Boston, his procession, with the usual parade, attended by the sheriffs, aldermen and common-council, excited little attention, and was honored at the palace gate with but a dumb peal even from the tattered rabble.

The effect of the battle of Bunker Hill is a resolution to send more ships and troops, every species of ammunition and warlike implements, and all kinds of supply for the support of Boston; many of them are already embarked. Admiral Shuldam supersedes Admiral Graves, and Sir Jeffery Amherst, it is said, has consented to accept the command, and General Gage will have leave to return. What number of troops will be sent I am not able to say, but I understand much greater in the spring, if a negotiation does not take place. I mention these things minutely, to show you of how small importance are those flattering articles of intelligence which sound well upon paper, and appear highly spirited and influential. These are facts, not of conjecture only, but visible and operative. Your reflection will perhaps be, we must then work out our own salvation by the strength of our own arm, trusting in the Lord. Really, my friend, if the colonies, according to their late declaration, have made a resistance by force their choice, the contest is in short reduced to that narrow compass. I view the dangerous and doubtful struggle with fear and trembling; I lament it with the most cordial affection for my native country, and feel sensibly for my friends. But I am aware it is my duty patiently to submit the event as it may be governed by the all-wise counsels of that Being ' who ruleth in the heavens, and is the God of armies. '

TO MRS. QUINCY.

London, Jan. 1, 1777.

* * The continuance of our unhappy separation has something in it so unexpected, so unprecedented, so complicated with evil and misfortune, it has become almost too burdensome for my spirits, nor have I words that can reach its description. There are passing before me a thousand varying objects, some of them affording amusement, and others admiration. I see many faces I have been used to. America seems to be transplanted to London. St. James's Park wears an appearance not unlike the Exchange in Boston. * * I long much to see my father. It is now more than eighteen months since I parted with him in a manner I regret. Neither of you say any thing of the family at Braintree. They ought not to think me regardless of them though I am silent; for, however

lightly they may look upon me, I yet remember them with pleasure. * * * Mr. David Greene is gone to Antigua. Mr. Bergwin, of North Carolina, is now with me. * *

London, March 12, 1777.

You inquire whether I cannot bear contempt and reproach, rather than remain any longer separated from my family? As I always wished, and I think always endeavored, not to deserve the one, so will I ever be careful to avoid the other. You urge as an inducement to my return, that my countrymen will not deprive me of life. I have never once harbored such an idea. Sure I am I have never merited from them such a punishment. Difference of opinion I have never known to be a capital offence, and were the truth and motives of my conduct justly scrutinized, I am persuaded they would not regard me as an enemy plotting their ruin. That I might yet be able to recover in some respects the esteem of my friends, I will not doubt while I am conscious of the purity of my intentions. When I determined on a voyage to England, I resolved upon deliberation, and I still think, with judgment. I did not, indeed, expect so hurried a succession of events, though you must remember, I long had them in contemplation. Had an accommodation taken place, my tour would have been greatly advantageous, especially on the score of business; what it will be now, time must tell.

I am sorry you say nothing of my father, or the family at Braintree; I have not received a line nor heard from them since I left America. * * God bless you all; live happy, and think I am as much so as my long absence from you will permit.

March 20, 1777.

I am not surprised much that, to the loss of property, I have already sustained, I am to suffer further depredations, and that those to whom I am under contract should avail themselves of this opportunity and endeavor to make what is left their own. All I ask is that my brother and my other friends (if I have any) would think of me as they ought, and to be assured, that as far as they interpose their assistance to save me from suffering, they will not hereafter find me deficient in return.

October 15, 1777.

If things should not wear a more promising aspect at the opening of the next year, by all means summon resolution to cross the ocean. But if there is an appearance of accommodating this truly unnatural contest, it would be advisable for you to bear farther promise ; as I mean to return to my native country whenever I may be permitted, and there is a chance for my procuring a livelihood. But I do not say that I will not accept of an opening here, if any one should offer that I may think eligible.

London, April 18, 1778.

The late unexpected change of the state of public affairs in this kingdom has occasioned a variety of speculation among men of moderate principles in both parties. While some construe the concessions of parliament as the effect of fear and pusillanimity, others regard them as the offspring of humanity, a desire to put an end to war and the fruitless effusion of kindred blood. The prospect of a foreign rupture has doubtless its weight ; but a wish to restore the confidence of America by generous overtures, and its dependence by a mild administration of government, I believe is really a principal foundation of the present terms. Would to God they may be such as will meet the voice and wish of the colonies, and the result be a reunion of two countries whose interests, in my opinion, can never be divided. I have lived to see the beginning, and thus far the progress of this cruel convulsion ; my prayer is that I may live to see the end of it. It has produced effects wonderful and illustrious ; in some of which we may discern and admire the great hand of Providence, in others the havoc of corrupt passions and ambition. Devastation and death are inseparable attendants in the train of war. I regret my once happy conntry has, in so short a time, experienced so large a share of them. They are events I have long ago trembled at as a picture of imagination only ; my heart is, however, now disburdened in some degree by a prospect that the wrath of man will no longer prevail to the destruction of life and property.

By the favor of Lord Willoughby (of Parham) with whom, by the kindness of my friend Mr. Fraser, I have the honor of an intimate acquaintance, my curiosity has been several times gratified

72

by an access to the house of lords, during the most important in-quiries; particularly about ten days since, when the great Lord Chatham came down to the house tottering upon his feeble limbs, to give his voice and advice on the present critical and dangerous exigence of the state. The business of the day being introduced by the Duke of Richmond, Lord Chatham rose, and in a faltering tone of voice, manifestly enfeebled since I heard him before, began his remarks by recurring to former periods of national alarm, compared them to the evils now complained of, pointing out the causes and their remedy, and then delivered his opinion on the two great questions of a war with France, and the independence of America. His speech was short to what I expected, and I believe much shorter than he intended. The Duke of Richmond rose in reply, and with some asperity objected to what had fallen from the noble earl. Whether this or mere bodily weakness was the cause I know not, but just as the duke had finished, his lordship suddenly fainted. The house was immediately ordered to be cleared, and the doors and windows set open ; but eager to see so celebrated a senator, as I thought in his last moments, I ventured to press in again, and saw him borne off on the shoulders of the Duke of Cumberland and other noblemen of the first distinction, pale and speechless.

> " Silent that tongue,
> On which, enrapt, admiring senates hung."

It was a grand though an affecting sight ! Supposing him to be near his exit, I almost wished to see him die within those walls, where for so many years he has figured to his own honor and the glory of his country. * * *

If there is an accommodation, I shall certainly turn my views to some part of the continent, unless something very promising should offer elsewhere. It would grieve me very much to think of never again seeing my father ; God bless him, and many other worthy friends and relations in New England ; but a return to my native country I cannot be reconciled to until I am convinced that I am as well thought of as I know I deserve to be. I shall ever rejoice in its prosperity, but am too proud to live despised where I was once respected—an object of insult instead of the child of favor. * *

You suggest, that had I remained, I might still have been with you in honor and employment. It may be so, but when I left America I had no expectation of being absent more than a few months, little thinking operations of such magnitude would have followed in so quick a succession; I left it from principle, and with a view of emolument. If I have been mistaken it is my misfortune, not my fault. My first letters from my friends congratulated me on being out of the way; and I was pleased to find my undertaking met with their approbation as well as my own. The hearts of men were not within my reach, nor the fortuitous event of things within my control. " I am indeed a poor man ;" but even a poor man has resources of comfort that cannot be torn from him, nor are any so miserable as to be always under the influence of inauspicious stars. I will therefore still endeavor to bear my calamities with firmness, and to feel for others.

* * Those who have befriended my family are entitled to my warmest gratitude, and I hope you will never fail to express it for me. Whether it ever will be in my power to recompense them I know not, but no endeavor of mine shall be wanting to effect it.

* * * I conjecture, though you do not mention from what quarter, you have received unkindness. There are in this world many things we are obliged and enabled to encounter, which at a distance appear insupportable. You must have experienced this as well as I ; and it ought to teach us that best doctrine of philosophy and religion—resignation. Bear up, therefore, with fortitude, and wait patiently in expectation of a calmer and brighter day.

London, May 31, 1778.

By the public prints we are made acquainted with an act of the state of Massachusetts Bay, that precludes those among others from returning, who left it since the 19th of April, 1775, and "joined the enemy." You do not mention this act, nor have I any information by which I am to construe what is meant by " joining the enemy." The love of one's country, and solicitude for its welfare, are natural and laudable affections ; to lose its good opinion is at once unhappy, and attended with many ill consequences ; how much more unfortunate to be for ever excluded from it without offence ! It is said also that there is a resolve of congress, " that no absentee shall be permitted to take up his residence in any other colony without having been first received and admitted as a citizen of his own." This may have some effect on a movement I had in contemplation of going southward, where I have a very advantageous offer of countenance and favor.

London, March 15, 1779.

"You may remember in some of my former letters I hinted my wish to establish a residence in some other part of the continent, or in the West Indies, and particularly mentioned to you Antigua—where my kinsman Mr. Wendell, my friend Mr. David Greene, Dr. Russell and his family, Mr. Lavicourt, Mr. Vassall, and others of my acquaintance, will give the island less of the appearance of a strange place. By the passing of the act of proscription the door was shut against me in my own country, where I own it would have been my wish to have ended my days. This confirmed my resolution. I have since unremittedly pursued various objects, endeavoring to drive the nail that would go.

My first intention was that of transplanting myself somewhere to the southward. On this subject I thought long, and consulted others. I considered climate, friends, business, prospects in every view, and at last formed my opinion. The provinces in the south part of America in point of health were not more favorable than the islands—in point of friends they might be preferable, but with respect to business or the means of acquiring it, uncertain; public commotion yet continued, violent prejudices are not easily removed. I had neither property nor natural connections in either of them. I could have no official influence to sustain me. What kind of government or laws would finally prevail it was difficult to tell. These and other reasons determined me against the attempt. But to stay longer in England, absent from my friends and family, with a bare subsistence, inactive, without prospects, and useless to myself and the world, was death to me! What was the alternative? As I saw no chance of procuring either appointment or employ here, the old object of the West Indies recurred, where in my younger days I wished to have remained; and by the influence of some particular gentlemen I have 'at last obtained the place of " Comptroller of the Customs at the port of Parham in Antigua;"

for which island I mean to embark with the next convoy. My view is to join the profits of business in the line of my profession to the emoluments of office. This I flatter myself will afford me a handsome maintenance. I grow old too fast to think of waiting longer for the moving of the waters, and have therefore cast my bread upon them, thus in hopes that at last, after many days, I may find it.

Transmit to my father every expression of duty and affection. If he retains the same friendship and parental fondness for me I have always experienced from him, he will patronize my children, and in doing this he will do it unto me. It was my intention to have written to him, but the subjects on which I want to treat are too personally interesting for the casualties of the present day. He may rest assured it is my greatest unhappiness to be thus denied the pleasing task of lightening his misfortunes and soothing the evening of his days. Whatever may be the future events of his life, I shall always retain for him the warmest filial respect, and if it is my lot to survive him, shall ever think it a pleasure as well as my duty to promote to my utmost the welfare of his posterity. My mother will also accept of my duty and good wishes; the prosperity of the whole household lies near my heart, and they will do me injustice if they think me otherwise than their affectionate friend. * * *

Col. Scott yesterday received a letter from his wife, by the Marquis de la Fayette, by which I learn you were all well the 4th January last. * *

With respect to my property in America, my wish and desire is, if I have any control over it, that my friends there collectively, or some one singly under your direction, would take it into their hands, and consolidating the debts I owe into one sum, apply it to their discharge. I can think of no better way than this. If eventually I am deprived of it, I will endeavor to bear it with that fortitude which becomes a Christian and philosopher.

P. S. I could wish above all things to preserve my law books.

TO HENRY HILL, ESQ.

London, May 25, 1779.

" * * I have obtained an appointment at Parham, in Antigua,

as comptroller of the customs, and am to embark soon for St. Kitts.
* *   It is this day four years since I left Boston, and though I
have been racked by my own misfortunes and my feelings for the
distresses of my family and friends, I have still by a good Providence been blessed with health and comforted by the kindness of
many friends. If I have not been in affluence, I have been above
want, and happy in the esteem of numbers in this kingdom to whom
I was altogether a stranger. * *   The education of my children
is uppermost in my heart. The giving my son the benefit of classical learning by a course of college studies, is a step I much approve.
The sequestration of my books is more mortifying to me than any
other stroke. If they are not yet out of your power save them for
me at all events.

TO THE REV. DR. WIGGLESWORTH, HOLLIS PROFESSOR OF DIVINITY,
CAMBRIDGE.

                                        Antigua, June 28, 1782.
    * *   Nothing has laid so near my heart during my absence
and misfortunes as the advancement of the education of my children. The honor my son is about to receive at the approaching
solemnities I hope will be well earned. * * *   It was always my
desire, and more than once have I intimated to you my inclination,
to turn my thoughts and influence towards the prosperity of the
college; how that object has been defeated needs no explanation.
I was ever their well wisher—they would have found me their
benefactor.

    In a copy of a letter to a friend, apparently in the West Indies,
but whose name does not appear, Mr. Quincy thus expresses
himself:

                                        Antigua, Feb. 1, 1782.
    You ask of me an account of my coming to the West Indies,
the manner of my existence, and destination, &c. The story is
long, and would require many anecdotes to give the true history,
but you will excuse me if at present I say only, that in the year
1775, just after the battle of Lexington, I quitted America for London on motives of business, intending to return in a few months;
but my absence was construed by our good patriots as the effect of

my political principles, and improved first to my proscription, afterwards to the very flattering title of traitorous conspirator, and
the confiscation of my estate. I remained in England several
years, but, tired of waiting for the moving of the waters, and unwil-
ling to waste the flower of my age in a state of indolence, neither
profitable to myself nor my family, I resolved to seek my fortune in
this part of the world, where I had been in my younger days,—
obtained a berth in the customs, which, together with the emoluments of my profession, afford me a comfortable subsistence, and
the prospect of something beyond.

Your friend, &c.,
SAMUEL QUINCY.

TO HENRY HILL, ESQ., EOSTON.

St. Christopher, July 26, 1783.

MY DEAR BROTHER :

I am sorry to find that the letters you wrote me after the tidings
you received of my loss of your dear sister,* never reached me, as
by that means I was deprived of the consolations, which the sympathy of our friends affords in the hour of grief. * * For strange
as it may seem, however painful the idea that we are *for ever*
separated from our friends, there is something pleasing to me in
calling to memory the conversations, the attitudes, which present
them in the strongest point of view, the occasions upon which, and
the places where they have most administered to our felicity and
comfort. If this is not the case, how great a part of the small pittance of enjoyment allotted to us in this life is broken off. How
many of our former friendships and sweetest intercourse would be
for ever obliterated, and dead to recollection ; our fund of gratification would be confined to the narrow limits of the objects immediately around us.

There is in some persons a strange kind of reluctance to
conversing about their dead friends ; as if those passages in their
character which render their memory dear, could not be thought
upon without recalling the circumstances of their departure.

To die is the lot of humanity ; if the sentiments and conduct
of those who have been separated from us, are such as have

* The wife of Mr. Quincy, who died Nov. 1782.

afforded us either amusement or instruction, and their example worthy of imitation, the more we meditate or confer upon their native and ornamental graces, the more we pay them honor; the more likely are we (at the same time that we receive a sensible gratification) to imbibe the amiable qualities in which they excelled, and to adopt their virtues. * * * *

If the events of life were under our control, it is probable we should endeavor to govern them to the purpose of our views. In that case I should soon be in the society of my nearest friends; it would be immaterial to me in what part of the world, for I have long since learned that happiness is not confined to any particular spot: diffused equally through the immense space of air and earth, the animal part of creation, whether rational or brute, possess it in every region; and most likely were we permitted to carve for ourselves, our fortunes would be still more chequered than they are. This reflection, at the same time it expands our idea of the Deity, has a tendency to teach us acquiescence in the state to which we are destined. Change seems to be as necessary to sustain the present link of being as air and food, for though the accidental ties of birth, kindred, and friendship, have a powerful influence on our affections, if the latter is met with where least expected, it has there its most peculiar energy, and the former gradually lessen as the probability of restoring them is removed in a greater or less degree.

TO SAMUEL QUINCY, JR., CAMBRIDGE.

June 10, 1785.

How anxious soever I may feel to see my friends and relations once more, I cannot think of doing it at the expense of my liberty; nor will I ever visit that country where I first drew my breath, but upon such terms as I have always lived in it; and such as I have still a right to claim from those who possess it,— the character of a gentleman. * * * The proposal Judge Sumner has hinted to me of keeping his old berth for you at Roxbury, is a good one, at least better than Boston. Cultivate his good opinion, and deserve his patronage; he will bestow the latter for my sake, I trust, as well as his personal esteem for you. It will also stand you in stead at court, where I hope you will one day figure as a legislator as well as an advocate. All depends upon setting out right. You are at the edge of a precipice, or ought to consider yourself so ; from whence, if you fall, the *" revocare gradum,"* is a task indeed. Resolve, then, to think right, and act well; keeping up to that resolution will procure you daily the attention of all ranks, and command for you their respect. Keep alive the cause of truth, of reason, of virtue, and of liberty, if I may be permitted to use that name, who have by some injuriously been thought in a conspiracy against it. This is the path of duty, and will be the source of blessing.

July 24, 1789.

I am exceedingly sorry to hear of the distracted political situation of Massachusetts. * * * A constitution founded on mere republican principles has always appeared to me a many-headed monster, and, however applauded by a Franklin, a Price, and a Priestley, that in the end it must become a suicide. Mankind do not in experience appear formed for that finer system, which, in theory, by the nice adjustment of its parts promises permanency and repose. The passions, prejudices, and interests of some will always be in opposition to others, especially if they are in place. This, it may be said, is the case in all governments, but I think less so in a monarchy than under a republican code. The people at large feel an overbalance of power in their own favor; they will naturally endeavor to ease themselves of all expenses which are not lucrative to them, and retrench the gains of others, whether the reward of merit or genius, or the wages of a hireling.

Tortola, June 1, 1789.

MY DEAR SON :

Your short letter of the 14th February gave me pleasure, as it informed me of your health and that of your family, and other friends in the neighborhood of Roxbury. * * *

It would be my wish to make you a visit once more in my life, could it be ascertained I might walk free of insult, and unmolested in person. Two things must concur to satisfy me of this,—the repeal of the act passed 1779, against certain crown officers, as traitors, conspirators, &c.; and accommodation with those who have against me pecuniary demands. The first I have never yet learned to be repealed, either in whole or in part, and therefore I consider it as a stumbling-block at the threshold; the second, no steps I suppose have been taken to effect, although I think it might be done by inquiry and proposition—with some by a total release from demand, and with others by a reasonable compromise. If you ever wish your father to repose under your roof, you will take some pains to examine the list, and make the trial. I shall shortly, I hope, be in a situation to leave this country, if I choose it; but whether Europe, of the two objects I have in view, will take the preference, may depend on the answer I may receive from you, upon the hints I have now thrown out for your consideration and filial exertions. *   *   *

I have been, as I informed you in my last, a good deal indisposed for some time past. I find myself, however, better on the whole at present, though I feel the want of a bracing air. Adieu.

Your affectionate parent,

SAMUEL QUINCY.

Soon after the date of this last letter, Mr. Quincy embarked for England, accompanied by his wife.* The restoration of his health was the object of the voyage, but the effort was unsuccessful; he died at sea, within sight of the English coast. His remains were carried to England, and interred on Bristol hill. His widow immediately re-embarked for the West Indies, but her voyage was tempestuous. Grief for the loss of her husband, to whom she was strongly attached, and suffering from the storm her vessel encountered, terminated her life on her homeward passage.

* Mr. Quincy was married to a second wife at Antigua.

LINES BY DR. COOPER, PRESIDENT OF KING'S, NOW COLUMBIA, COLLEGE.

The following lines were written by Dr. Cooper, in England, on the 10th of May, 1776, the anniversary of his departure from New-York. As it is descriptive of his precipitate flight from the college, to avoid the outrages of a mob, this effusion may be regarded as a document of historical interest, aside from the beauty of the poetry.

To thee, O God! by whom I live,
The tribute of my soul I give,
  On this revolving day :
To thee, O God! my voice I raise,
To thee address my grateful praise,
  And swell the duteous lay.
Nor has this orb unceasing run
Its annual circle, round the sun,
  Since when the heirs of strife,
Led by the pale moon's midnight ray,
And bent on mischief, urged their way
  To seize my guiltless life.
At ease my weary limbs were laid,
And slumbers sweet around me shed
  The blessings of repose :
Unconscious of the dark design,
I knew no base intent was mine,
  And therefore fear'd no foes.
When straight a heaven-directed youth,*
Whom oft my lessons led to truth,
  And honor's sacred shrine,
Advancing quick, before the rest,
With trembling tongue my ear addrest,
  Yet sure in voice divine :
"Awake! awake! the storm is nigh—
This instant rouse—this instant fly—
  The next may be too late :
Four hundred men, a hostile band,
Access importunate demand,
  And shake the groaning gate."
I wake—I fly—whilst loud and near
Dread execrations wound my ear,
  And sore my soul dismay ;
One avenue alone remain'd,
A speedy passage there I gain'd
  And wing'd my rapid way.
That moment all the furious throng,
An entrance forcing, pour'd along,
  And fill'd my peaceful cell ;†
Where harmless jest, and modest mirth,
And cheerful laughter oft had birth,
  And joy was wont to dwell.
Not ev'n the Muses' hallow'd fane,
Their lawless fury can restrain,
  Or check their headlong haste ;
They push them from their solemn seat,
Profane their long rever'd retreat,
  And lay their Pindus waste.

Nor yet content—but hoping still,
Their impious purpose to fulfil,
  They force each yielding door ;
And whilst their curses load my head,
With piercing steel they probe the bed,
  And thirst for human gore.
Meanwhile along the sounding shore,
Where Hudson's waves incessant roar,
  I work my weary way ;
And skirt the windings of the tide,
My faithful pupil by my side,
  Nor wish the approach of day.
At length ascending from the beach,
With hopes reviv'd by morn, I reach
  The good Palemon's‡ cot ;
Where free from terror and affright,
I calmly wait the coming night,
  My every fear forgot.
'Twas then I scal'd the vessel's § side,
Where all the amities abide
  That mortal worth can boast ;
Whence, with a longing, lingering view,
I bid my much-lov'd York adieu,
  And sought my native coast.
Now all compos'd, from danger far,
I hear no more the din of war,
  Nor shudder at alarms ;
But safely sink each night to rest,
No malice rankling through my breast,
  In freedom's fostering arms.
Though stripp'd of most the world admires,
Yet torn by few untain'd desires,
  I rest in calm content ;
And humbly hope a gracious Lord
Again those blessings will afford,
  Which once his bounty lent.
Yet still for many a faithful cause,
Shall day by day my vows ascend
  Thy dwelling, O my God !
Who smiling still in virtue's cause,
Despising faction's mimic laws,
  The paths of peace have trod.
Nor yet for friend alone—for all
Too prone to heed sedition's call,
  Hear me, indulgent Heaven !
O! may they cast their arms away,
To Thee, and George, submission pay,
  Repent and be forgiven !

* Mr. Nicholas Ogden.
‡ Mr. Stuyvesant's seat in the Bowery.

† King's, now Columbia College.
§ Kingfisher, sloop of war, bound to England.

NEW-YORK CONFISCATION ACT.

An Act for the Forfeiture and Sale of the estates of Persons who have
adhered to the Enemies of this State, and for declaring the Sove-
reignty of the People of this State in respect to all property within
the same.—Passed, October 22, 1789.

Therefore be it enacted by the People of the State of New-York, etc.,
That John Murray, Earl of Dunmore, formerly governor of the colony of
New-York, William Tryon, Esq., late governor of the said colony, John
Watts, Oliver De Lancey, Hugh Wallace, Henry White, John Harris
Cruger, William Axtell, and Roger Morris, Esq., late members of the
council of the said county; George Duncan Ludlow and Thomas Jones,
late justices of the supreme court of the said colony; John Tabor Kempe,
late attorney-general of the said colony; William Bayard, Robert
Bayard, and James De Lancey, now or late of the city of New-York,
Esqs.; David Matthews, late mayor of said city; James Jauncey, George
Folliot, Thomas White, William McAdam, Isaac Low, Miles Sherbrook,
Alexander Wallace, and John Wetherhead, now or late of the said city,
merchants; Charles Inglis, of the said city, clerk, and Margaret his wife;
Sir John Johnson, late of the county of Tryon, knight and baronet; Guy
Johnson, Daniel Claus, and John Butler, now or late of the said county,
Esq.; and John Joost Herkemer, now or late of the said county,
yeoman; Frederick Philipse and James De Lancey, now or late of the
county of Westchester, Esqs.; Frederick Philipse, (son of Frederick,)
now or late of the said county, gentleman; David Colden, Daniel Kis-
sam the elder, and Gabriel Ludlow, now or late of Queen's county, Esqs.;
Philip Skeene, now or late of the county of Charlotte, Esq., and Andrew
P. Skeene, son of Philip Skeene, late of Charlotte county; Benjamin
Seaman and Christopher Billop, now or late of the county of Richmond,
Esqs.; Beverly Robinson, Beverly Robinson the younger, and Mal-
com Morrison, now or late of the county of Dutchess, Esqs.; John Kane,
now or late of the said county, gentleman; Abraham C. Cuyler, now or
laie of the county of Albany, Esq.; Robert Leake, Edward Jessup, and
Ebenezer Jessup, now or late of the said county, gentlemen; and Peter
Du Bois and Thomas H. Barclay, now or late of the county of Ulster,
Esqs.; Susannah Robinson, wife to the said Beverly Robinson, and
Mary Morris, wife to the said Roger Morris; John Rapelje, of Kings
county, Esq.; George Morrison, Richard Floyd, and Parker Wickham,
of Suffolk county, Esqs.; Henry Lloyd the elder, late of the state of
Massachusetts Bay, merchant; and Sir Henry Clinton, knight, be and
each of them are hereby severally declared to be, ipso facto, convicted
and attainted of the offence aforesaid; and that all and singular the
estate, both real and personal, held or claimed by them the said persons
severally and respectively, whether in possession, reversion or remainder,
within this state, on the day of the passing of this act, shall be, and hereby is declared to be forfeited to, and vested in the People of this State.

ERRATA.

Page 71—for "*Barack*" read "*Barrick.*"
328—10th line from top, for "*Barnard*" read "*Bernard.*"
365—20th line from top, for "*au*" read "*le.*"
467—9th line from bottom, for "*Peter Hooper,*" read "*Robert Hooper.*"
591—2d line from bottom, for "*his*" read "*this.*"